CREATING
POWERFUL THINKING
IN TEACHERS
AND STUDENTS

CREATING POWERFUL THINKING IN TEACHERS AND STUDENTS

DIVERSE PERSPECTIVES

EDITED BY

JOHN N. MANGIERI-ARKANSAS STATE UNIVERSITY

AND

CATHY COLLINS BLOCK-TEXAS CHRISTIAN UNIVERSITY

HARCOURT BRACE COLLEGE PUBLISHERS

FORT WORTH   SAN DIEGO   PHILADELPHIA   NEW YORK   ORLANDO   AUSTIN   SAN ANTONIO
MONTREAL   TORONTO   LONDON   SYDNEY   TOYKO

Publisher	**Ted Buchholz**
Acquisitions Editor	**Jo-Anne Weaver**
Developmental Editor	**Helen Triller**
Project Editor	**John Haakenson**
Production Manager	**Tad Gaither**
Art Director	**Don Fujimoto**
Text and Cover Design	**Bill Maize, Duo Design Group**

Reprinted by permission of the publisher from Newmann, Fred M., STUDENT ENGAGEMENT AND ACHIEVEMENT IN AMERICAN SECONDARY SCHOOLS. (New York: Teachers College Press, © 1992 by Teachers College, Columbia University. All rights reserved.) Excerpts from throughout the book.

Duckworth, Eleanor, "Understanding Children's Understanding" in BUILDING ON THE STRENGTHS OF CHILDREN, Windley, V., Dorn, M.S., and Weber, L., editors. Department of Elementary Education, The City College of New York. Pages 275–277.

Permission to reprint Figure 6.1 (page 154) granted by Lawrence Erlbaum Associates, Inc. The figure originally appeared in "Thinking Development Through Intervention: Middle School Students Come of Age," in Cathy Collins and John N. Mangieri, editors, TEACHING THINKING: AN AGENDA FOR THE TWENTY-FIRST CENTURY.

Requests for permission to make copies of any part of the work should be mailed to: Permission Department, Harcourt Brace & Company, 8th Floor, Orlando, Florida 32887.

Address for Editorial Correspondence:
Harcourt Brace College Publishers, 301 Commerce Street, Suite 3700, Fort Worth, TX 76102.

Address for Orders:
Harcourt Brace & Company, 6277 Sea Harbor Drive, Orlando, FL 32887, 1-800-782-4479, or 1-800-433-0001 (in Florida).

Printed in the United States of America

3 4 5 6 7 8 9 0 1 2   039   9 8 7 6 5 4 3 2 1

ISBN: 0-15-500984-2

Library of Congress Catalog Card Number: 93-77631

DEDICATION

To Ernest L. Boyer, a friend of all teachers and of quality
education, who has made the lives of countless
individuals better for having known him and for following
his wise words

AND

To William H. Koehler, a friend and a colleague, who daily
shows us what being a professional truly means.

PREFACE

Creating Powerful Thinking in Teachers and Students: Diverse Perspectives is designed as a textbook or supplemental book of readings for special seminars in educational psychology, curriculum and instruction, and psychology. The book can also be used in graduate teacher education seminars and internship programs, in courses with a thinking development emphasis, in advanced learning theory classes, in advanced educational psychology seminars, and in courses that are cross-listed in education and psychology departments. It is also being distributed by IBM to school superintendents, the National Association of State School Boards of Education, and the Council of Chief State School Officers.

The aim of this book is to help teachers, students, and other educational professionals improve thinking and professional competencies and to report methods of developing cognitive abilities. It documents recent research in the fields of educational psychology, cognitive science, and educational administration. It is the first text to combine the works of so many contemporary leaders in educational research that are engaged in ongoing studies concerning the advancement of learning and thinking. This book includes strategies for restructuring school environments to provide for more effective education. It is among the first to include methods for developing the higher level thinking of at-risk and young students in both restructured and traditional school settings; to contrast and compare the philosophies of Vygotsky and Piaget, in light of contemporary psychologists like Feurstein and Bruner; and to describe specific strategies for advancing thinking development in teacher education programs.

We were motivated to write this book by the results of two surveys one of us conducted. A survey of 125 educators demonstrated that whereas 82% recognized the importance of teaching thinking and indeed were willing to teach it, 75% could not identify even a single activity in their instructional program being used to do so. Equally distressing were data obtained from more than 100 national business leaders. While all of these individuals ranked themselves as "excellent" or "above average" in thinking ability, 22% did not believe that people can be taught to think better. Of the 78% who felt schools and corporate training programs could enhance cognitive development, only 3% indicated that thinking development was a part of their corporate training programs. Unfortunately, this 3% was designed only as "basic thinking skill" instruction for new employees, primarily in clerical positions.

FORMAT OF THE TEXT

This textbook contains 14 chapters, along with a final discussion, and is organized into four sections: (1) Instructional Environments: An Assessment; (2) Strategies for Improving Learning and Thinking in Our Schools; (3) Strategies for Improving Instruction for At-Risk Children; and (4) Strategies for Improving Instruction in Early Childhood. This organization provides students with a general understanding of the issues and then proceeds to descriptions of specific actions that they can take to create powerful thinking for themselves, other teachers, and students.

In Section 1, users of the book will assess themselves, their learning environments, their students, and specific content areas, looking for opportunities to improve their own and their students' thinking and learning. Specific strategies for improving learning and thinking are introduced in Section 2. Sections 3 and 4 contain discussions of improving thinking development in at-risk and early childhood programs. An overview of each chapter follows.

In Chapter 1, Gerald Duffy explains how students using this book can advance schooling through "how they think of themselves as educators." He encourages teachers to think rather than to be passive recipients of others' ideas.

Chapter 2 will provide readers with a genuine sense of excitement about what classrooms and schools *can be* if the ideas advocated by Joe Onosko and Fred Newmann are implemented. Drs. Onosko and Newmann explain new dimensions that educators, practitioners, and prospective teachers should consider in their quest to enhance the thinking processes and cognitive development of students at all levels.

In Chapter 3, Penelope Peterson demonstrates how "what students know and need to know in schools [should not] continue to be narrowly defined by and confined to the reading, writing, and 'rithmetic curriculum that has been taught in elementary schools for years." Her illustrations vividly portray how teachers and students can switch roles in the dynamic instructor/learner interactions that occur in classrooms today.

In Chapter 4, Judith Langer examines the language and instruction in classrooms where teachers provide an environment that fosters critical reasoning. Dr. Langer compares the higher level thinking elicited by eight high-school teachers who teach American literature, American history, biology, and physics.

In Chapter 5, Michael Pressley discusses specific strategies to enhance reading comprehension. In this chapter, he not only provides an overview for subsequent chapters in this section but delineates specific methods for improving learning and thinking in elementary and secondary schools. His suggestions are based on empirical and field-based tests that can be implemented by teachers/administrators working collaboratively or individually.

In Chapter 6, Cathy Collins Block presents several instructional interventions that increase elementary and middle-school students' problem-solving abilities. As one reviewer stated: "This is the most thorough and insightful presentation of strategies to improve decision making and problem solving in our body of literature to date."

In Chapter 7, David Berliner presents nine propositions that develop expertise, a cognitive process that is more complex than those described in Chapters 5 and 6. Dr. Berliner specifically focuses on the development of expert teachers.

In Chapter 8, Ernest Boyer suggests several feasible and thought-provoking ideas as to what types of thinking and education can foster increased and enhanced scholarly thought. And in Chapter 9, Mary Kennedy and Henrietta Barnes suggest methods for implementing teacher and educational administration programs presented by all previous chapters in this text.

In Chapter 10, Shirley Brice Heath introduces ways that after-school programs, such as youth organizations, advance the thinking abilities of at-risk students. She describes the strategies used in these organizations and how they can be adapted for public and private school use.

In Chapter 11, Barbara Presseisen, Barbara Smey-Richman, and Francine Beyer extend the discussion of cognitive development for at-risk students. They describe the characteristics of teachers and of classroom environments that exist in restructured classrooms for expanding the thinking of at-risk students. They also discuss curriculum changes, instructional approaches, and nontraditional assessment systems that educators can implement to advance the cognitive development of *all students*.

In Chapter 12, Alex Kozulin presents explicit and distinctive explanations of Piagetian and Vygotskian views on the cognitive development of young children. Dr. Kozulin is the first Vygotskian scholar to compare and contrast these two views as they relate to the development of higher level thinking.

Chapters 13 and 14 extend Dr. Kozulin's discussion. Joseph Walters, Steve Seidel, and Howard Gardner describe ways student reflection can be increased and self-assessment can be used in early childhood programs. Their chapter includes many samples of such instructional and evaluative methods. In Chapter 14, Elizabeth Sulzby identifies ways that thinking originates through preschool instructional experiences.

The text concludes with a discussion by David Berliner. Berliner adds his understanding and vision of schools in which the data in this text have been implemented, and in which teachers and students have become more powerful thinkers.

Each chapter in this book is organized in a similar way. The authors trace the history of their ideas and research so that students are introduced to major names and literature in the field. Then, the authors describe important research that can improve our educational system and help ensure students' cognitive development.

We wanted to develop a text that went beyond mere regurgitating of facts to foster students' ability to think in an original manner. We hope that your students take the information in each chapter and "run with it" in their own lives. Tolstoy once said: "Everyone thinks of changing humanity, but no one thinks of changing himself." We hope that your students are also stimulated to investigate problems that are important to them. We hope that this book will add to their knowledge of ways *they* can make innovations at their elementary or secondary schools. We hope this book will change how many people think about thinking, education, and schooling.

In closing, we would like to express our gratitude to our contributing authors who gave so much of their time to this book. We also thank the following reviewers, whose helpful suggestions added to the development of the book: P.J. Karr-Kidwell, Texas Woman's University; Joy J. Rogers, Loyola University, Chicago; Atilano A. Valencia, California State University, Fresno.

John N. Mangieri
Cathy Collins Block

CONTENTS

▼

ABOUT THE EDITORS

Dr. John N. Mangieri is president of Arkansas State University. He has authored or coauthored numerous articles and authored and edited seven books, including *Excellence in Education* and *Teaching Thinking: An Agenda for the Twenty-First Century*. He served as a Fulbright Scholar and leader for the Danforth Foundation Program for Leadership for School Administrators. He is a counselor for Oak Ridge Associated Universities, a delegate of the National Association of State Universities and Land-Grant Colleges, an editorial consultant and reviewer for *The International Journal of Educational Reform*, and a member of the Board of Directors of the American Association of University Administrators.

Dr. Cathy Collins Block is professor of education at Texas Christian University. She coedited the book titled *Teaching Thinking: An Agenda for the Twenty-First Century*, serves on the editorial boards for *The Reading Teacher* and the *National Reading Conference Yearbook*, and is Editor for Thinking Development for *America Tomorrow*. She was the Chairperson of the National Commission to Infuse Critical Thinking into Curriculum and Instruction and is active and holds offices in numerous professional associations, including the American Educational Research Association, International Reading Association, National Council for Excellence in Thinking Instruction, and the National Reading Conference. She has published numerous articles in professional journals and several textbooks, including *Teaching the Language Arts: Expanding Thinking Through Student Centered Instruction*. This past summer she served as a United States Citizen Ambassador to Russia and Hungary to develop critical thinking curriculum in these countries.

1

INSTRUCTIONAL ENVIRONMENTS: AN ASSESSMENT

CHAPTER ONE

HOW TEACHERS THINK OF THEMSELVES

A KEY TO CREATING POWERFUL THINKERS

GERALD G. DUFFY

▼

WHITWORTH COLLEGE

Dr. Gerald G. Duffy is a visiting professor at Whitworth College and a professor emeritus at Michigan State University. During his twenty-five year tenure at MSU, he was involved in numerous innovative teacher education programs as a reading educator and was a senior researcher in the Institute for Research on Teaching. His teaching and research have resulted in numerous publications in professional journals and scholarly volumes, with a prevailing focus on classroom instruction, teacher development, and teacher education, particularly as these relate to literacy. He is a past president of the National Reading Conference and a participant in a variety of other professional organizations. Since joining the faculty at Whitworth College in 1992, he has directed an innovative masters degree program and continues his research and writing on teacher development and literacy instruction.

I have been a teacher educator in one form or another since 1960. During that time, I have probably promoted more technical behavior than teacher mindfulness because I was one of those well-intended people who supported mastery learning and early process-product research (see, for example, Duffy & Sherman, 1971; Duffy, 1981). I wanted to help teachers; I wanted to simplify their lives for them. To do so, I gave teachers "answers." Because I had been a successful classroom teacher myself, I told them what I had done. That's what I thought teacher education was—telling teachers what I, and other successful teachers, had done.

And teachers loved me for it. My classes always received high ratings. Teachers said I was "practical."

But as the years went by, I began to suspect

that something was terribly wrong. I continued to visit schools and the classrooms of teachers I had taught—teachers who as students had been my champions. Unfortunately, however, while they still "talked a good game," what I saw them doing during reading and writing instruction was more often than not an example of disjointed, inert, fragmented, and artificial forms of literacy rather than the principled, generative form of critical and interpretive literacy I thought I had taught them to teach. More often than not, they seemed to implement new ideas and new research findings as superficial "add-ons" without altering the conceptual basis of their instruction.

These experiences caused me in 1975 to focus my research on teachers' beliefs and practices. Working with volunteer teachers from a variety of urban and rural school districts in Michigan over the course of several long-term programs of research, I have found little evidence of teachers making substantive judgments regarding what to teach or how to teach it (see, for example, Duffy & Anderson, 1984; Duffy, Roehler & Putnam, 1987). To the contrary, I have been struck by the uniformity of elementary school literacy instruction, by an apparently widespread compliance with prescriptions, and by a persistent emphasis on low-level skills and on instructional practices that promote such learning.

This does not mean that I have found teachers to be lazy or indifferent or otherwise unprofessional. To the contrary, I have found them to be almost universally caring, dedicated, hardworking, and conscientious. This has made the problem all the more intriguing. Why would good people like teachers engage in such uninspiring instructional practices?

This happens because many of today's teachers are followers. They follow a curriculum that tells them what to teach, and they follow directions for how to teach content. To develop problem solving, for example, many teachers follow prescriptions embedded in commercially produced instructional materials, such as the following workbook exercise teachers are encouraged to use with students (Greenberg, 1990):

In front of you is a doodah made of three pennies, a piece of wood and washer, tied together with a piece of string. You also have another penny, a second washer, and another piece of string. How long is the piece of string holding the doodah together?

But instructional materials are *not* the problem in the limited thinking development that occurs in our schools today. The problem is that teachers follow these instructional materials. They do so because of a pervasive psychology of teacher education, and the mental model it causes teachers to build for themselves. This psychology—similar to a technical, bureaucratically controlled, and authoritative model which has permeated business and government since the 1960s—assumes that ordinary teachers cannot manage the complexity of school teaching and that, instead, they must be directed.

This has had two effects. First, it has spawned a variety of "directors" who make decisions for teachers—"master developers" who write instructional materials, policy makers at the state and local level who mandate practices, researchers who provide lists of "what works," school administrators who use evaluation practices that force compliance with specified procedures, and staff developers and teacher educators who promote preferred theories, techniques, and programs rather than professional thinking. Second, it has created a generation of teachers who view themselves as technicians carrying out the prescriptions of others. The result is a caste system—the "directors" lead and the teachers follow.

Such a corps of teachers—directed by their "directors"—educate children to be what McCaslin and Good (1992) call "compliantly cognitive." Today, however, compliant cognition is not enough. Instead, today's goal must be interpretive and proactive problem solving—what this book calls "powerful thinkers." Like the second graders in a class I observed recently who refused to select *any* answer on a multiple choice test because "none really fit," our citizens must be critically analytical and must act on their analysis.

This goal cannot be reached when students are taught by compliant teachers who submit to the judgment of paternal authorities. Instead, we need a new psychology of teacher development which authorizes independent teacher thought. We need to have teachers who themselves understand, analyze, and problem solve if we hope to develop students who understand, analyze, and problem solve.

Consequently, this chapter proposes an alternative psychology of teacher development. Based on the assumption that the current model produces teacher technicians who in turn produce student technicians, the new psychology strives for teacher mindfulness as a means for achieving student mindfulness.

BACKGROUND

The following sections describe the rationale for this chapter—how we currently develop teachers, forces that make a change essential, and the fieldwork that undergirds my premise.

THE CURRENT PROPENSITY FOR TRAINING TEACHERS

It is uncomfortable to think of our teachers as compliant followers. As teacher educators, we don't like it, and we often get defensive as a result, arguing that *our* particular courses do not encourage following. But, like scholars who invent a concept and then go out and find it, we often *think* we are creating thoughtful teachers and, when we visit schools, convince ourselves that what we see there is what we intended to create. However, our intentions may be more accurately reflected in the propensity of staff developers and teacher educators to refer to their work as teacher "training."

This is not to suggest that we intentionally set out to "train" technicians. To the contrary, conscientious educators of the past 30 years used various forms of mastery learning (Bloom, 1968;

Gusky, 1985) and early results of research on teaching (Brophy & Good, 1986; Rosenshine & Stevens, 1986) in well-intended efforts to improve teaching. The goal was to simplify teaching by prescribing teacher behaviors and actions that "worked," thereby bringing a science to the art of teaching (Gage, 1978).

This well-intended drive toward simplicity was reinforced by descriptive research revealing how difficult classroom teaching is and can be (Duffy, 1983). In response to such findings, educational leaders reasoned that teachers' lives would be easier if they could follow directives created by experts. We rationalized these directives as temporary "scaffolding" to be removed at some undefined later time when teachers became "experts."

But in trying to simplify teachers' lives, we *taught* them to be compliant. We did so by creating ever more prescriptive textbooks, ever more restrictive policy mandates, ever more specific teacher evaluation practices, and ever more persuasive arguments from teacher educators and staff developers regarding their favored theories, philosophies, packages, and programs (conveyed together with an implicit, if not explicit, expectation that teachers should follow *their* words of wisdom and not anybody else's).

The result was that teachers learned to do what authority said to do and to avoid decisions—at least, decisions which might modify the authority's message. A good example is Hunter's (1967) TIP (Theory Into Practice), which teachers implement by adhering to certain narrow technical specifications, although Hunter insists that TIP is a decision-making model (Berg & Clough, 1992; Hunter, 1991).

Teachers' reliance on prescriptive programs, and their tendency to emphasize low levels of learning, has been documented in Durkin's (1978–79) classic study, as well as in a steady stream of other research on classroom practice in a variety of school settings (Duffy & McIntyre, 1982; Herrmann, 1986). Echoing from most such reports is teachers' beliefs that "the people who wrote these materials know more than I do."

While pockets of exceptions are sometimes

cited, especially by whole language advocates (Goodman, 1989), there is no evidence that these exceptions represent a groundswell of change. To the contrary, much of the research of the last 10 years indicates that classroom practice has *not* changed appreciably for decades (Elmore & McLaughlin, 1988; Cuban, 1984).

We have not seen change because the current psychology of teacher development, in which authorities prescribe for teachers, is designed to constrain teachers, not emancipate them. Even whole language is subject to this psychology, especially when principles of whole language are presented with an intolerance for alternative perspectives (Edelsky, 1990). Instead of freeing teachers to engage in inspired teaching based on creative response to the needs and interests of students, such authoritarian insistence on one philosophy or approach constrains teachers. It convinces them that they must follow "approved" policy instead of using their own professional judgment.

This propensity for basing teacher education on authority is evident in many settings. For example, at a recent planning session for a school district's summer staff development program, which involved several veteran staff developers and university professors, a consultant who was to teach teachers about cooperative learning insisted that *all* teachers would have to do it *her* way; adaptation, modification, or integration with other ideas was not to be tolerated. In short, teachers were to be *trained* in this person's version of the "answer." Such experiences convince teachers that they can only make narrow, safe change; change which does not alter in any substantial way what the authority prescribed.

Sometimes this mind-set is subtly insidious. One colleague reports that a major professional literacy journal selected one article over another for publication because it provided "more structure" for teachers. That is, it was more directive. In doing so, of course, the journal implicitly communicates to teachers the message that teachers are *supposed* to follow directives.

Others, however, are less subtle. For example,

no one embraces the technical view of teaching with less apology than Englemann (1991). The original developer of DISTAR (Englemann & Bruner, 1974), a reading program in which teachers are trained to follow an instructional script verbatim, he insists on limiting teachers to low-level pedagogical tasks:

> Teachers should have a special kind of knowledge about teaching. That knowledge derives from the ability to execute the details of effective instruction. The teacher should know how to present tasks to students and should demonstrate appropriate pacing, appropriate inflections and stress, appropriate responses to students who perform well and appropriate responses to students who make mistakes. (p. 218)

However, the world of teaching has changed. And as it has, it has become clear that Englemann's "details of effective instruction" are no longer enough.

WHY WE NEED THOUGHTFUL TEACHERS RATHER THAN "TRAINED" TEACHERS

Our psychology of teacher development must change because new insights about learning make thoughtful teachers a necessity. Perhaps teacher technicians were acceptable when we thought teaching was a matter of students passively receiving input from teachers, or when we defined learning as memory for a narrow set of factual knowledge. Now, however, learning is " . . . the development of understanding, or the ability to perform complex cognitive tasks that require active management of different types of knowledge around concrete problems" (Elmore, 1992). This kind of learning requires that teachers do much more than Englemann's "details of effective instruction."

What follows are four characteristics of this

new learning and the way each calls for thoughtful, adaptive teachers.

Authentic Experience

Teacher thoughtfulness is especially necessary when providing students with authentic tasks. Students cannot become analytical, critical solvers of problems encountered in the real world when all they are required to do in school is solve artificial problems created by a "master developer." Unfortunately, that is what happens when instructional improvement is based on a technical model—a program of prepackaged tasks which are developed and which teachers are expected to deliver to students intact. For example, one publisher of a "curriculum for global problem solving" (McKisson & MacRae-Campbell, 1990) asks teachers to assign a workbook page in which students complete sentences such as, "What if the polar ice cap melts? Then . . . " From this students are expected to learn how to problem solve. It is an artificial, unsituated experience and, as such, does not result in understanding about polar ice caps or strategies for framing and solving problems. What is needed is an authentic task.

Teachers can create authentic tasks. For example, in classes I have visited recently, I observed second graders learning strategies for reading about the weather because a TV meteorologist was going to visit the class, special education students learning strategies for reading about birdhouses because they were going to build and sell birdhouses to raise money, and fifth graders learning strategies for reading about how to make water run up hill because they were making a fountain to beautify a neglected part of the school grounds. These authentic tasks did not happen by accident. They were orchestrated by thoughtful teachers who are responsive to students and who create activity that capitalizes on the students and conditions in a specific classroom.

Teacher thoughtfulness does not stop once authentic tasks have been selected. The teacher must then decide how, within pursuit of that task, to integrate content from various subject matter areas, to guide students to more mature understandings of content, and to develop higher order thinking and the skills, strategies, techniques, and procedures associated with thoughtfulness. In providing that guidance, teachers cannot rely on a single method or instructional technique. Rather, teachers select from among a wide array of techniques such as language experience, reciprocal teaching, direct explanation, and cooperative learning, and then vary and modify those to fit the needs of their particular situation. What instructional technique to use—or what adaptation of an instructional technique to use—cannot be determined in advance. It depends on the outcome being sought and on the specifics of the particular situation. And only a thoughtful teacher on-the-spot can make the necessary judgments.

Conceptual Change as the Goal

From authentic tasks comes a different kind of learning—conceptual understandings comprised of networks of integrated knowledge that can be applied in principled and generative ways. However, such a goal poses serious problems for a teacher. As Prawat (1992a) has said, "On the one hand, the teacher must honor students' 'inventions' or they will not share them. On the other hand, the teacher needs to guide students toward a more mature understanding, which frequently means challenging student constructions" (p. 11).

Such dilemmas and distinctions cannot be handled by giving teachers technical directions to follow. Instead, teachers must analyze such situations themselves and decide what sense students are making of it. Are students constructing networks of associations resulting in intended conceptual understandings? Or do they understand the task to be something less than that? When assignments are given, for example, do students understand that they are to construct a conception or do they think they are simply to get the task done? And if it is the latter, what teacher decision will move students to the desired understanding? Judgment is demanded—judgment based on an analysis of the contextual situation. Only the teacher is in a position to do this.

Personal, Social, and Cultural Aspects of Learning

Additionally, we now understand that learning is expedited by personal awareness of how we are learning (metacognition) and by the social and cultural conditions in which we learn it (collective construction of knowledge). Learning is enhanced when people are aware of what they are learning, why they are learning it, and how to do it. This awareness occurs more easily when people talk together, engage in public reasoning, share problem-solving responsibilities, and otherwise jointly construct knowledge.

This, too, calls for teacher thoughtfulness. Rather than being a font and dispenser of knowledge, teachers must orchestrate things so that students not only know, but know *how* they know; they must listen to students, interpret their statements, and decide what to do next; it means teachers must be what Leinhardt (1992) calls "a highly knowledgeable member of the community." It is not possible for master developers to prescribe in advance the teacher-student interactions that will result in personal understanding of how one knows or to prescribe in advance the interactive exchanges in a genuine learning community. These decisions demand on-the-spot judgment. Only thoughtful teachers can provide this.

The Generative Aspects of Learning

Traditionally, schools have been places where students passively receive knowledge; but today's schools must be places where students generate knowledge, create understandings, construct new interpretations, and make judgments based on values and appreciation as well as on rationality.

However, generative learning requires changes in how teachers do things. Consider assessment as just one example. Fill-in-the-blank items and multiple choice tests call for passive rather than generative student thinking, and the use of publisher-provided answer keys calls for passive rather than generative *teacher* thinking. Such assessment

is pervasive, but it does not promote generative thinking. To promote generative thinking, teachers must cultivate student thinking, which means that teachers themselves must think and make judgments. They cannot refer to an answer key.

Perhaps even more important, however, is the fact that generative learning also includes what Prawat (1992b) calls "idea-based constructivism," which inspires children to wonder and appreciate, and what Purpel (1989) calls "personal development," in which moral and spiritual elements receive more emphasis than the traditionally trivial curricular elements. Developing these outcomes also requires thoughtful teachers; they cannot be developed by technicians.

Summary

In sum, we are at the point in educational history where mindfulness—developing powerful thinkers who are interpretive, analytical synthesizers of various types of knowledge, solvers of complex cognitive problems, and creators of principled, generative, affective, and even ethical ideas—is replacing the mechanistic, fragile, inert, disconnected kinds of learning that have traditionally dominated American education. Developing such student mindfulness, however, requires teachers who make judgments in the context of their particular situations—judgments about when to honor inventions and when not to, judgments about orchestrating interactions, judgments about how to make learning tasks authentic, judgments about how to integrate into those tasks "the basics" that must be learned in order to be an efficient thinker, judgments about how students are interpreting instructional activities and how to modify those activities so students will interpret them in an intended way, and judgments about how to hook students on the beauty of ideas as well as on the practicality of being "mindful."

If we want learning for understanding, we must abandon the notion that "answers" can be put in teachers' hands ahead of time. Instead, substantive reform demands a psychology of teacher development in which teachers see themselves as thinkers. Rather than Englemann's (1991) "details of effective instruction," we must view teaching, as Hargreaves and Dawe (1990) do, as "a profoundly moral craft involving difficult and innumerable professional judgments about what and how things are to be taught" (p. 234). And as Herrmann and Sarracino (1990) point out when describing some of their prospective teachers, this may call for a major change in how teacher educators think about their work:

> While we don't necessarily agree with how some of them are thinking about literacy teaching, we no longer think that is what is important. What is important is that they learned to think for themselves; that they learned what it means to develop their own theoretical perspectives about literacy teaching through on-going critical reflection about their own instruction, rather than adopting verbatim the theoretical perspectives of others they consider to be "more expert."

To which I would only add that prospective teachers also document that the children in their charge will indeed become thoughtfully literate.

THE FIELD WORK WHICH GROUNDS MY PREMISE

In study after study, teachers report that they do what they do because they *must* follow prescriptions of one kind or another. At first I thought this was a "cop-out." Eventually, however, it became clear that we have taught teachers to think this way. The following teacher's explanation for why she followed prescriptions is typical (Duffy, 1992): "It's because I was never, ever encouraged or taught that I could possibly have enough knowledge, enough ability, to make my students effective readers unless I followed these [the basal's] words of wisdom."

I have been forced to conclude that most teachers believe that their work is controlled by a "great textbook author in the sky"—an absentee master developer—and that they must comply with mandates prescribed by this (and other) authoritative "experts" who are more qualified to make instructional decisions for individual classrooms than are teachers. And teachers feel powerless as a result.

So, I began studying ways to change teachers' feelings of powerlessness (Duffy, 1991). A particularly fruitful occasion for this study began in 1987 when several small rural school districts in the northwestern lower peninsula of Michigan heard there was going to be a revision of the state's mandated reading assessment test. Those school districts asked the Traverse Bay Area Intermediate School District for help in preparing for the test. (In Michigan, an intermediate school district is a service agency for school districts in a particular geographical region.) The intermediate school district, in turn, contacted me. Together, we designed a five-year staff development plan to help area schools upgrade literacy instruction.

However, our goal was not simply to prepare students for the test. It was to develop students who are genuinely literate—that is, who possess attitudinal and conceptual understandings about reading as reasoning and meaning-getting, who understand that being a reader means being a thinker, and who epitomize Brown's (1991) "literacy of thoughtfulness."

To accomplish this, we employed a nonstandard approach to staff development. Instead of "training" teachers in the use of a program or package, we employed a reasoning that goes like this:

1. Students in school are doing artificial literacy tasks because teachers are trained to use prepared materials and prescriptions as academic work (Doyle, 1983);

2. In order for students to become good readers and thinkers, they must *experience* what good readers and thinkers do—that is, their academic work must represent *authentic* literacy and, within those situations, they must experience being literate;

3. Therefore, we need to focus teachers on the limitations of prepackaged academic work and on the possibilities inherent in

"turning into" students; we need to help teachers use what they learn from students to create academic work which represents authentic literacy, adapting materials to those authentic experiences and then teaching specific elements of reading and writing within those experiences.

For example, we showed teachers currently popular commercial programs that claim to develop student thinking, such as a workbook page in which students are given answers regarding things having to do with fairy tales (e.g., "the wicked witch") and are directed to fill in the blank with the correct question (Vydra, 1986) or a section of another workbook in which students are asked to read three pages about castles and are then directed to do activities such as "construct a sand castle model" or to answer questions such as "How important were castles?" (Patton & Maxson, 1989). We analyzed these materials in light of the thinking that students would usually develop if teachers simply followed directions and assigned the materials as the programs suggested. We also sought to determine what kind of thinking students might develop if teachers altered the directions to involve students in creating a unit on fairy tales or castles. Further, we discussed what thinking students would develop if teachers themselves were metacognitive about the thinking they *wanted* to develop, if they involved students in authentic activity that required such thinking as the opportunities arose, and so on.

In short, we promoted teacher mindfulness. We did so believing that thoughtful teachers tend to provide broad, meaningful experiences with literacy which, in turn, encourage students to construct attitudes and concepts consistent with "real reading," as opposed to the "school reading" students typically do in association with academic work, such as the fairy tale and castle activities cited above. This position is not unlike that taken by Saranson (1990), who argues that teacher learning and vitality in the intellectual aspects of their careers are essential preconditions for productive *student* learning. With that in mind, our objectives were to have teachers (a) learn to think of teaching as intellectual (and moral) work, not technical work, and to have them construct mental models of themselves accordingly; (b) to understand that they can control their own professional destinies and construct their own professional knowledge; and (c) to understand that they should not view themselves as workers to be supervised and directed or as technicians who follow prescriptions.

To achieve these objectives, we employed two major instructional activities. First, each month for the past four years I met with all the teachers in a large group for a three-hour session during which we discussed literacy content generally and the state's reading test specifically. Operating on the assumption that teachers could not become thoughtful unless they possess professional knowledge to think with, I presented background information about specific programs and models, including sample curriculum lists and instructional techniques. In doing so, however, I emphasized that I expected teachers to deviate from the content and adapt it—that I did *not* want them to adopt it and follow it unquestioningly.

Second, my colleagues and I worked with teachers in their classrooms twice monthly as they put to work with their five lowest achieving students the understandings they had constructed during the monthly staff development sessions. We had pre-lesson conferences with teachers regarding their intentions, observed lessons, interviewed the five targeted students following lessons to determine *their* understandings, and had post-lesson conferences with the teachers. When appropriate, we also did demonstration lessons for teachers, worked with teachers as they planned units, consulted with them about special problems, and supported their inquiry about their own work.

The ultimate goal was to develop student thoughtfulness. Results indicate that this goal has been achieved. The five targeted students in each classroom achieved greater reading level gains than is normally expected for at-risk students (see Table 1-1 and Table 1-2).

More importantly, targeted students demonstrate a more interpretive, metacognitive, and

TABLE 1-1   STUDENT GAINS IN INSTRUCTIONAL READING LEVEL, 1990–91

Of 37 first graders:
   3 grew two grade levels
  24 grew one grade level
  10 did not increase in reading level

Of 10 second graders:
   9 grew one grade level
   1 did not increase in reading level

Of 45 third graders:
   1 grew three grade levels
  18 grew two grade levels
  26 grew one grade level
   0 did not increase in reading level

Of 6 fourth graders:
   1 grew three grade levels
   4 grew two grade levels
   1 grew one grade level
   0 did not increase in reading level

Of 11 fifth graders:
   1 grew three grade levels
   4 grew two grade levels
   5 grew one grade level
   1 did not increase in reading level

Of 7 sixth graders:
   2 grew two grade levels
   5 grew one grade level
   0 did not increase in reading level

Of 5 special education/Chapter 1 students:
   2 grew three grade levels
   3 grew two grade levels
   0 did not increase in reading level

Total number of at-risk kids: 121

Average growth in reading level: 1.26 years

NOTE: Gains in instructional reading levels were determined by administering the *Qualitative Reading Inventory* (Leslie & Caldwell, 1990) to each target student in early September 1990 and again in May 1991. All tests were administered by the author and his staff development colleagues.

---

mindful understanding of what they are doing when reading and writing. For example, in end-of-year interviews our at-risk project students often describe their reading as this second grader did: "Before I read, I think about the story and predict, and if I get stuck, I stop, go back, read it over again and try to make sense out of it." Similarly, another second grader reasoned as follows when he encountered the word "current" in the sentence, "They were careful to avoid the strong current which might carry them away":

> He substituted the word 'curtain,' read on and, two lines later, returned to 'current' and corrected it, saying, "There wasn't anything to carry them away—a curtain couldn't do it and they were in a lake so I went back and I knew it was 'current' because it said 'cur-' and it said it had to be strong enough to carry them away."

When non-project students describe how they read, in contrast, they mention only "sounding out" and "ask the teacher" as useful strategies.

Such student thoughtfulness does not occur unless teachers are thoughtfully responsive during instruction. And many of our teachers have learned to do that. They have broken the tyranny of the master developer and taken charge of their own work. This does not mean that they do not use the resources offered in commercially produced instructional materials; it means that they

TABLE 1-2   STUDENT GAINS IN INSTRUCTIONAL READING LEVEL, 1991–92

Of 49 first graders:
 2 grew two grade levels
 23 grew one grade level
 24 did not increase in reading level

Of 35 second graders:
 1 grew three grade levels
 10 grew two grade levels
 24 grew one grade level
 0 did not increase in reading level

Of 39 third graders:
 2 grew three grade levels
 9 grew two grade levels
 20 grew one grade level
 8 did not increase in reading level

Of 24 fourth graders:
 4 grew two grade levels
 10 grew one grade level
 10 did not increase in reading level

Of 34 fifth graders:
 1 grew three grade levels
 3 grew two grade levels
 13 grew one grade level
 17 did not increase in reading level

Of 24 sixth graders:
 7 grew two grade levels
 9 grew one grade level
 8 did not increase in reading level

Of 27 special education/Chapter 1 students:
 3 grew two grade levels
 18 grew one grade level
 6 did not increase in reading level

Total number of at-risk kids: 232

Average growth in reading level: 1.17 years

NOTE: Gains in instructional reading levels were determined by administering the *Qualitative Reading Inventory* (Leslie & Caldwell, 1990) to each target student in early September 1991 and again in May 1992. All tests were administered by the author and his staff development colleagues.

---

use these materials adaptively, that they listen to students first and then figure out how to adjust the materials. The following examples from the northern Michigan project are illustrative:

- A kindergarten teacher wanted to teach her students the five standard elements of a story structure to help them be strategic when comprehending stories read to them, but, when her students were unable to handle the complexity of this, she revised her plan and developed a simplified story structure.

- A first-grade teacher had been conducting a unit on a particular children's author with the intent of culminating the unit with a particular activity, but when, on the day of the activity, a student came to school with a new book by that author, she abandoned her planned activity and created a new activity that featured the author's new book.

- A second-grade teacher used students' desire to give their mothers flowers on Mother's Day to initiate a flower-growing project in the classroom and an accompanying science unit on plants.

- Another second-grade teacher was listening to her students as they explained what they do with words they do not know; she noticed that even though the students said they would skip the word and use context, they still felt they had to get the word "right" and as a result were not attending to comprehension. So this teacher invented for her students a technique in which they "held the unknown word in their minds" until they understood the meanings of the passage.

- A third-grade teacher was having difficulty explaining to her students that different readers use different strategies to solve the same reading problem, so she put her students in partners and then went from group to group using the students' own difficulties when reading to illustrate her point that thoughtful readers employ a variety of strategies when solving any particular problem.

- A fourth-grade teacher had no plan to teach context clues on a particular day, but when several of her students substituted words that did not make sense in the text, she immediately initiated a lesson on context clues.

- A fifth-grade teacher was using a poem about death with her students and wanted them to use prior knowledge to infer the poem's meaning, but when approximately half the class "didn't get it," she provided spontaneous examples to illustrate.

This kind of "taking charge" is not limited to individual teachers. In some cases, it permeates the entire school. Consider, for example, the note one of our project teachers sent to her colleagues regarding what they needed to do in order to prepare for a new principal who had just been hired:

We need to do one BIG thing before the end of the year—make plans for next year. With a new principal in the wings, it's important that we work out what our program is,

what we want to do in terms of intellectual community, how often we want coaching sessions, who will coach whom, school restructuring, external coaches, visitations and *every* aspect you find pertinent—and *get it in writing* to present to the principal. To do this, we have five or six substitute teachers lined up for May 26 so people can rotate in and out of an all-day meeting to develop our plans.

As a result of the May 26 meeting, a note (reproduced in part here) was sent to the new principal:

Dear Mike,

The staff and I put together a little light reading to get you acquainted with out literacy project. Packet #1 should explain much of it.
We are aware that it is not easy to step into a program that is already up and running. Here is what we need:

1. We would like you to attend our meetings and gradually become involved at your pace.

2. At times, we might need some creative financing.

3. We'd like you to be open to restructuring time for planning.

4. In dealing with our work, we need positive support. Some of our teachers are very sensitive to criticism; it can be very crippling. Please show that you recognize the huge effort we put into our work. One reason our school has achieved much more than some of the other schools in this literacy project is that our principal strongly supports teacher empowerment. We have the freedom to take risks. This causes constant self-evaluation, adjustments, new attempts. Our reading programs are continually evolving, improving. Reading is alive for us, it encompasses more and more of our entire curriculum, and we enjoy the knowledge that, however good it is now, it will be different and better next year and the year after that.

5. If you choose, you are welcome to try coaching once you become comfortable with it.

A NEW PSYCHOLOGY AS A KEY FACTOR

No doubt many factors contributed to this project's success. It was important, for example, that teachers' learning was situated in the authentic task of improving instruction for five targeted students and that improving those students' literacy (as opposed to completing academic tasks I might assign) was what counted; that conceptual understandings (as opposed to technical procedures) were valued as the grist of professional thinking; that teachers' learning emphasized both metacognition and socially constructed learning; and that generative teacher thinking was promoted.

The crucial thing, however, was that teachers created different mental models of themselves. We believe that the key to this was that teacher development occurred in "intellectual communities" in which all participants collaborated in a spirit of professional egalitarianism. This is quite different than traditional teacher education. It incorporates a new psychology of teacher development that puts teachers in position to take charge of their own work.

An intellectual community is an occasion for professionals to collectively inquire about fundamental conceptual and philosophical issues relating to their work (as opposed to managerial, organizational, procedural, and technical problems, which are left to be discussed at staff meetings). Huberman (1990) describes it as "conceptually informed discussion." Teachers, principals, staff developers, and professors, working as equals, discuss dilemmas, hypotheses, and alternatives to explore and test. Teachers are expected to be thoughtful professionals who control their own work; to *interpret* curriculum mandates, teachers' guides, and other directives; and to be analytical, creative, flexible, and adaptive problem solvers themselves. In doing so, they are in a better position to model thoughtfulness for their students and to particularly model that there are few definitive and final answers but, rather,

that mindfulness is a perpetual search for greater understanding.

In sum, the thrust of this new psychology is to make on-going inquiry about one's own work and the work of colleagues a central feature of school teaching. In reversing the mind-set that teachers do what superiors tell them to do or what programs prescribe for them to do, teachers learn to deal with the uncertainties and ambiguities of teaching by asking questions about these uncertainties and ambiguities, studying their own practice as a means for "getting smarter," discussing emerging ideas with colleagues to build "collectively rational" hypotheses, testing those ideas, asking new questions and so on in a continuous cycle of change.

Consequently, intellectual communities are places where teachers discuss and debate and test issues in the context of classroom life. In intellectual communities, teachers do not *talk* about being professionals, they experience it.

This is not a new idea. For example, Holt (1964) argued:

> Once we understand that some of the things we teachers do may be helpful, some merely useless, and some downright harmful, we can begin to ask which is which. But only teachers can ask such questions and use their daily work with students to test the answers. All other kinds of research into ways of improving teaching lead mostly to expensive fads and nonsense. (p. 54)

Recently, more and more staff development efforts operate on some variation of "intellectual community." Johnston and Wilder (1992), for example, describe their staff development efforts in this way:

> Previously, teachers had attended workshops that were primarily a lecture format in which someone else planned the agenda. In the new model, study groups are formed in which every member is responsible for teaching and learning, for choosing topics that

interest and challenge them, and for making curriculum decisions based on the results of their study. (p. 627)

Regrettably, this movement is by no means universal. As Hargreaves and Dawe (1990) point out:

> There are forms of instructional and professional intervention which withhold from teachers opportunities for wider reflection about the context of their work; which deprofessionalize and disempower teachers in denying them opportunity to discuss and debate what and how they teach; which smuggle bureaucratically-determined ends into ostensibly neutral procedures for improving technical skills. (p. 239)

Such non-examples sometimes show up even in places where one would least expect them. For example, some efforts to create Professional Development Schools in association with Holmes Group (1990) reform have inadvertently ended up making teachers feel disempowered (Duffy, in press).

EXAMPLES OF INTELLECTUAL COMMUNITIES

Intellectual communities can occur in a great variety of situations. I describe here four which I recently observed in the northern Michigan project.

University/Staff Development Settings

Intellectual communities can occur in university classes and staff development sessions. In the northern Michigan project, for example, the monthly whole group staff development sessions are often suspended to allow groups of teachers of like grade levels to debate and discuss information I present. One recent example followed my presentation of a particular way to organize reading curriculum into attitude, process, and content

outcomes (Duffy & Roehler, 1989). A group of third-grade teachers, meeting as an intellectual community during the large group session, took exception to certain aspects of my structure and created an adaptation that was more appropriate for them.

At another monthly session, teachers met in grade level "intellectual communities" to share the various ways they were using portfolios as alternative assessment tools. In the course of the discussion, the teachers changed the focus from what would be put in a portfolio to how portfolios can be used to encourage students to construct more accurate concepts about reading and writing.

Such examples illustrate central features of intellectual communities: that while it is essential that I present professional content, co-construction of knowledge is also crucial; that teachers and professors are partners; that professional knowledge is tentative and situational; and that teachers can modify professional content to fit their own situations.

School Settings

Intellectual communities also occur in school contexts. For example, I have recently observed gatherings of teachers, staff developers, and professors in different schools and on different days who (a) used a particular student comment as a springboard to discuss classroom interaction patterns generally and the higher level thinking that would result if alternative patterns were encouraged; (b) discussed what their students should know following a television program about Hirsh's (1989) cultural literacy; (c) discussed whether a reading curriculum should be influenced by what the community wants, with one group arguing that teachers are professionals who make decisions that ordinary citizens are not prepared to make and another arguing that teachers are hired to teach what the community wants; and (d) discussed the relative importance of developing esthetic literary outcomes in rural northern Michigan schools where there is little community support or practical application for such outcomes.

None of these discussions resulted in definitive solutions, but the inquiry itself was substantive, the discussion was generative, the uncertainty and dilemma-ridden nature of teaching was highlighted, and teachers were stimulated to refine their own ideas, concepts, and attitudes. Most important, however, these teachers gained direct experience in how questions emerging from their own practice relate to more general and abstract theories, and how their thoughtfulness in testing and applying such theories enhances their work.

Teacher-Teacher Pairs

Another form of intellectual community occurs in teacher pairs. In the northern Michigan project, such pairing is common, and I frequently observe the benefits. For example, following a fifth-grade teacher's lesson using expository text, which was observed by another fifth-grade teacher, I watched as the teacher and his colleague engaged in a post-lesson conference. They discussed together whether the way I had organized metacognitive strategies into three categories (i.e., before reading, during reading, and after reading) is really appropriate for expository text. They ended up agreeing (at least tentatively) that, because expository text is topic-governed and not plot-governed, it might be better when teaching comprehension of expository text to focus exclusively on schema reorganization "after reading" since the goal is to alter one's schema about the topic.

Whether these teachers were "right" about expository text in some final sense is not important per se. What is important is the process of professional inquiry that results in a cycle of principled change. Intellectual analysis and the testing of new ideas give teachers opportunity to experience the relationship between action and principled thought about teaching. Their subsequent actions in similar circumstances are guided by such discussion and by the results of their testing; those results, in turn, will be reexamined critically and reconstituted.

Coaching

Intellectual communities are not limited to teachers. Professors and staff developers are also part of the community and, as such, are part of the dialogue. In the northern Michigan project, the dialogue is frequently associated with coaching, because professors and staff developers work so often with teachers in their classrooms.

The concept of intellectual communities alters the usual meaning of coaching. Traditionally, coaching has had a technical emphasis, focusing on getting teachers to implement particular and preferred models of teaching in particular ways while ignoring questions about ends, goals, and values. As Hargreaves and Dawe (1990) point out, technical coaching is another way to shackle teachers to authoritative decisions about what and how to teach: "Technical coaching fits excellently into an educational system which is becoming ever more inclined to bureaucratic forms of control over its employees. . . ."

Note, however, the tenor of a coaching session I observed in which one of my colleagues coached two first-grade teachers who wanted to build their own teaching plan but did not understand how to do so:

> **Staff Developer:** So what do you think needs to be taught to these first graders at this time?
>
> **Teacher 1:** Well, we used to drill in vocabulary but we've learned that we don't have to spend so much time on that.
>
> **SD:** So what do you want them to be able to do?
>
> **Teacher 2:** Well, I guess first of all we want them to use context to put in a word that fits the meaning.
>
> **SD:** So let's think about how we do that.
>
> **T2:** Well, the problem is that they really don't want to stop and use a strategy. They have learned to monitor predictions and stuff but even though they monitor and discover that they don't know the word, they don't want to stop.

SD: Well, let's talk about that. What should we do?

T1: Well, I tried modeling it, but I don't know . . . Do you think they need more modeling?

SD: What do you do after modeling?

T1: What do you mean?

SD: I mean, do the students do it after you model it?

T2: Yeah.

SD: Well, maybe this concept of scaffolding that we've talked about would be useful here. Remember how we talked about providing gradually reduced amounts of scaffolding? Could we apply that here?

T2: How would you do that?

SD: Well, you could do a couple together.

T1: And we could talk to the students about what they are already doing right. They do a lot of this right. It's just that they need. . . .

SD: Okay, good. Now, where do we go from here in planning the unit?

This coach encourages teachers themselves to articulate important outcomes and attempts to put teachers in positions where they can take the lead, express their desires and needs, and make their own decisions. The coach suggests, expedites, encourages, and reminds, but does not direct. It is a discussion among colleagues, not technical coaching.

THE VALUE OF INTELLECTUAL COMMUNITIES

As the above examples illustrate, intellectual communities not only give teachers voice, but they also give teachers power to decide. They respect what Hargreaves and Dawe (1990) call "the dignity, quality and sophistication of teachers' practical knowledge and judgment" and put teachers in position to argue disputable educational purpose, to tailor new knowledge to partic-

ular kinds of personality and beliefs, and to adapt actions to the particular characteristics of the school and classroom. They validate distinctive and sophisticated forms of reasoning embedded in teachers' professional actions.

As such, intellectual communities convey a new psychology of teacher development—one that helps teachers build mental models of themselves as empowered professionals. In the process, professors, staff developers, and teachers are put on an equal footing, and teachers are emancipated from the expectation that they must be compliant followers. As Cochran-Smith and Lytle (1990) point out:

> Teachers take control over their classrooms and professional lives in ways that confound the traditional definition of teachers and offer proof that education can reform itself from within. (p. 9)

This is the most import value of intellectual communities.

Conversely, on another level, intellectual communities are valuable because they promote change. Hargreaves and Dawe (1990) say that such activity is "an essential prerequisite to securing educational change in any enduring sense," while Ellis (1990) says that collaborative interaction among teachers "improves the ability of teachers to implement a complex innovation in classrooms." Similarly, both the Holmes Group (1990) and the Carnegie Task Force (1986) argue that successful reform depends on a workable professional environment in which teachers have time to reflect, plan, and discuss teaching innovations and problems.

Intellectual communities promote change by viewing it differently. In the past, change has been viewed as a temporary matter. That is, when new research or a new idea or technique (or, in the northern Michigan project, a new state assessment test based on reading comprehension research) becomes available, we convene staff development sessions and communicate the change to teachers. Once teachers have been informed, staff development terminates.

Intellectual communities, however, are rooted in a much more complex view of teacher change. First, teaching is seen as a human endeavor and changing it is replete with all the uncertainties that accompany any mind-to-mind activity. Second, teaching occurs in a complex ecosystem in which everything is interdependent, so changing one thing often means changing (ultimately) lots of other things. Consequently, change cannot be a one-dimensional, temporary phenomenon associated with a particular innovation or research finding. Instead, change is permanent and ongoing. No one change fits all, but any one change is the beginning of a chain reaction of change. It never ends.

Intellectual communities work, therefore, because they promote a teacher autonomy and informed self-reliance that accounts more effectively for the realities of educational change. The idea is to change schooling from the inside out And from the bottom up through changes in teachers themselves.

BLUEPRINT FOR THE FUTURE

Intellectual communities appeal to the romantic in idealistic educators. But to achieve a new psychology of teacher development, we must be hard-headed rather than romantic because intellectual communities are full of problems. And when these problems prevail, mindfulness is impeded.

Most of the problems are rooted in values. For example, intellectual communities cannot work unless professors and school administrators value teachers as equal participants, rather than as persons to be directed; unless educators value teaching's problematic, changeable, and uncertain characteristics, rather than yearning for a predictable set of behaviors; unless researchers value teachers' personal, practical knowledge just as much as they value academic knowledge; and unless administrators and teacher educators value teacher judgment and the practitioner's process of combining thought and action in ways which may seem messy to those not actually working in the classroom situation. In a word, many of those

currently in power *like* the current psychology of teacher development because it keeps them in power, and they are reluctant to participate in intellectual communities because doing so means that power must be shared.

I provide here two sets of illustrations—both encountered in the northern Michigan project—of how value conflicts often make it difficult to alter the prevailing psychology of teacher development. One set is university related; the other is school related.

University-Related Problems

Intellectual communities are sites for collaboration, not mere cooperation. But for collaboration to occur, participants must be equal. Intellectual communities, and a new psychology of teacher development, cannot be achieved if a belief prevails that professors are somehow "better" than teachers. This belief is debilitating in two ways.

First, it promotes differences in the two communities. On the one hand, it encourages professors to see the world in terms of academic research, formal rationality, and intellectual coherence uncontaminated by messy reality; on the other, it encourages teachers to see the world in terms of the daily demands and multiple variables of uncertain classroom environments while ignoring principles and theories. As long as professors and teachers "see the world through a different prism" (Goodson, 1991), intellectual communities of teachers and professors are not likely to endure.

Second, it promotes an endemic form of elitism that is fatal to collaboration. The professor, as the knowledge producer, is valued more than the teacher, who merely uses knowledge. Consequently, professors see themselves as working *on* teachers rather than working *with* teachers. The clash makes it virtually impossible for the two groups to engage in anything more than superficial cooperation.

Second, and closely related to the first, is the debilitating effect of researchers' current view of "research dissemination." For decades researchers have looked at research dissemination as what Huberman (1990) calls "replicable technology."

That is, researchers produce research findings which are then delivered to teachers as discrete entities. Research on "wait time" (Rowe, 1974), for example, is often presented to teachers as a technical fact—that it has been "proven" that you should count to 10 in your head before moving on to another student. McCaslin and Good's (1992) description of the way classroom management findings have been disseminated is another good example of how, in "delivering" research findings, major issues relating to mindfulness can be obscured.

Viewing research findings as something to be handed down as technical information ignores the reality that teachers must make strategic decisions about when to apply findings, how to adapt them to certain situations, and even when it might be appropriate to ignore a research finding altogether. Research dissemination, therefore, is not just a matter of passing on information; it is also a matter of adapting research findings to the complexities of teachers' lives. And this, in turn, requires an intellectual community of teachers and researchers.

School-Based Problems

In the northern Michigan project, we have observed that it is more difficult to change the psychology of teacher development in some schools than in others. The problem is often the superintendent's (and, therefore, the principal's) perception of organizational or political realities. While superintendents are often facile users of the rhetoric of teacher empowerment and talk effusively about the importance of putting teachers in charge of their own work, they also understand that actually giving teachers power may disrupt and challenge what Elmore (1992) calls "the regularities of schooling." As a result, some superintendents still communicate to principals (often implicitly rather than explicitly) organizational and political agendas that sabotage teacher empowerment. The one we see most frequently makes the raising of test scores the priority; teacher empowerment is a distant second to this powerful political agenda (even when test scores are not measures of mindfulness). When superin-

tendents and principals use their authority to impose control over teachers' professional actions this way, teachers feel like technicians rather than like professional thinkers. Teachers then, in turn, use *their* authority to impose control over students, making them into technicians rather than thoughtful readers. As a result, neither teachers nor students are free to be mindful; both teachers and students feel "controlled."

Unfortunately, it is not only schools' organizational and political agendas that impede intellectual communities, it is also the tone and atmosphere of a school and what it says regarding what education is all about. In one school, for example, students—and the quality of students' experiences with literacy—come first. In this school, the principal, teachers, aides, custodian, secretary, and kitchen workers all share in the goal, all act like educators, all assume responsibility for students, all feel they make valued contributions to the educational enterprise, and all contribute to a focus on genuine literacy despite lack of resources, crowded conditions, and a preponderance of at-risk students. In another school, one with more resources and fewer at-risk students, the tone is debilitating. It puts students in the background and puts adult agendas in the foreground. For example, the teachers will not allow the librarian to read to children because she does not have a degree in library science; one teacher is not speaking to another because she supported the principal in some dispute; the school secretary has a feud going with the principal about where to put the copy machine; the kitchen help complain about their grievances in front of students; and the teachers' discussions about literacy instruction reflect guilt and worry and finger-pointing about low achievement test scores.

Does all this make a difference in teachers' professional lives? It certainly does. In the first school, teachers routinely discuss and test various adaptations for improving instruction and collaborate on school-wide literacy projects, which bring to the whole school an aura of excitement and unity about literacy. In the second school, however, teachers spend virtually all their time arguing over which "program" to adopt as a way to bring "structure" to their curriculum; and while the teachers in the second school claim to be a "close-knit staff," there is virtually no evidence of school-wide collaboration or of willingness by teachers to examine difficult issues or to risk substantive change. And the superintendent denies it all.

So does this make a difference for students? It seems to. Forty-two targeted at-risk students in the first school, for example, made an average gain in reading level of 1.45 years; the 27 targeted students in the second school, however, gained only .89 in average reading level. Additionally, target students in the first school are willing to take risks while reading, and are confident in their ability to state a hypothesis while reading and to test out its validity; targeted at-risk students in the second school, however, are tentative in their reading and typically will, when encountering an unknown word, wait indefinitely for an adult to provide the word rather than risking a hypothesis of their own. This is not because teachers do not teach strategies (we have observed teachers in both schools teaching strategies). Rather, it is a perspective they bring to strategies. In the second school, control is the goal; teachers control students' strategy use and the thinking associated with strategy use in ways which deny students the opportunity to exercise their own judgment. Consequently, students in the second school have inaccurate conceptions of what it means to be thoughtful readers.

While university- and school-based problems certainly influence the mental model teachers construct for themselves, teachers themselves are most important. And teachers have difficulty taking charge of their work because their past experiences have convinced them that they are to follow, not question. In the northern Michigan project, we have found very few teachers who have experienced what it means to translate technical questions into intellectual questions. Instead, they have been so well schooled in the technical tradition—during their "apprenticeship of observation" (Lortie, 1975) when they were students themselves, during their preservice

teacher education, and during their induction into teaching—that they simply do not know how to engage in an intellectual discussion about their work and, furthermore, see no value in it. Unless they are blessed with enlightened leadership or a previously established tradition of professional inquiry, veteran teachers often seem content to be technicians. It is familiar to them. And, as such, it is comfortable.

WHERE TO FROM HERE?

Experience in the northern Michigan project has convinced me of two things. First, teachers *are* capable of taking charge of their professional work. When they do so, benefits accrue to both them and to their students, benefits which are particularly relevant to mindfulness.

Second, teachers do *not* embrace this new psychology easily. Veteran teachers are convinced that they must be compliant followers, and they find it terribly difficult to reconceptualize themselves as thinkers who control their own instruction. Many just are not comfortable with it.

Consequently, we cannot start with veterans if we are to develop a corps of thoughtful teachers. We must start with preservice teachers, and make thoughtfulness a fundamental element of teaching from the beginning.

As a result, I am now focusing my work on preservice teacher education and on the study of my own practice as I attempt to develop mindfulness in teachers from the beginning of their teacher education experience. This work is based on four major premises.

First, teacher mindfulness cannot be delayed until after prospective teachers develop the "basics" of teaching. There is an analogy here between teaching reading and teaching teachers. In teaching young children to read, we have rejected our earlier assumption that children must first learn basic phonetic and morphological principles before engaging in "real reading"; instead, they must be engaged in genuinely literate activity from the start (and learn the "basics" in the process). The same thing is true when educating teachers. When we begin by emphasizing technical basics of teaching—classroom survival skills—teachers conceptualize teaching as a technical act. Then they must "unlearn" this conception later when we try to teach them to be thoughtful. But, as the northern Michigan experience demonstrates, this "unlearning process" is difficult for teachers to do. A more reasonable way to create thoughtful teachers is to engage preservice teachers in professional mindfulness from the very start. Then the chances are greater that they will conceptualize teaching as an intellectual and moral pursuit characterized by creative and idiosyncratic responses to students, and stick with this conception when they become practicing teachers.

Second, inquiry should be a central focus of learning to teach. That is, preservice teachers should learn from the beginning how to do analytical and creative thinking, how to collect, process, and apply evidence, and how to imagine new possibilities. The focus should be on development of a "habit of mind" in which, from the very beginning of their professional education prospective, teachers understand that the key to effective teaching is not the purchase of a commercial program but the thoughtful application of professional knowledge; that while ethical and moral aspects of teaching tend to be stable, content and pedagogical knowledge is often situational; that one never "masters" teaching but, instead, spends a career in continuous learning; and that intellectual inquiry about one's own work is the key to professional growth and vitality.

Third, learning to teach must be situated in classrooms, not at the university. Again, an analogy between teaching reading and teaching teachers applies. We know that teaching children to read requires immersing them in the act of being literate (see, for example, Prawat, 1991); similarly, prospective teachers must be immersed in the act of teaching. Teacher education is not primarily a matter of learning *about* teaching as an abstract entity isolated in the warm nest of the ivory tower; it is primarily a matter of *doing* teaching in the messiness of classrooms and then reflecting on what happened, why it happened,

and how we can bring professional knowledge to bear in principled ways to increase effectiveness.

Fourth, teacher education should be a collaborative venture involving partnerships among university professors and school personnel. Rather than the current practice of the university being the "brains" of the teacher education operation and schools being passively cooperative agencies providing practice sites, both sets of participants must be equally involved. Both must actively inquire about the processes of teaching and teacher education, both must construct knowledge about the work of educating students and teachers, both must teach each other and work in each other's classrooms, both must propose modifications, and both must be jointly accountable for teacher education and for students' education. A structure such as the Holmes Group's (1990) Professional Development School (PDS) can be a model for making this a reality. However, establishing a PDS to carry out a university-dominated agenda alone will not work (Duffy, in press). The PDS must be a site which exemplifies a genuine partnership, which means that the PDS must meet the school's agenda as well as the university's agenda.

Incorporated into these four premises, of course, is the spirit of an intellectual community. The entire endeavor should be characterized by a move away from the image of teachers as uncritical adopters of procedures "proven" effective by research and by a move toward communities of professional colleagues inquiring together about the practical realities of classroom teaching.

Consequently, what I envision is a preservice teacher education program characterized by the following:

1. Preservice teachers, like children in school, are mediators of experiences who come to understand teaching by making sense of experiences with teaching. Given that most preservice teachers' "apprenticeship of observation" have been in schools featuring a technical model of teaching, they must be put in a learning situation that is a "break with

experience" (Buchmann, 1989; Buchmann & Schwille, 1983)—which provides teaching experiences that are innovative, creative, and thoughtful ventures, not technical ventures.

2. The place where this break with experience occurs is a public school, modeled on the Holmes Group's (1990) Professional Development School. In this school, teachers, administrators, and teacher educators commit themselves to an egalitarian partnership dedicated to creating an environment in which learning for understanding (for *both* students and prospective teachers) is the criterion.

3. Both professors and teachers participate in helping preservice teachers learn to inquire about professional work: how to think about dilemmas of teaching, how to analyze innovative ideas, how to frame problems of teaching as problems for study, how to determine what would be useful evidence, how to collect evidence as a part of everyday teaching, how to use evidence to think about instruction, and how to generate improvements from the evidence gathered.

4. The bulk of teacher education courses are taught in the public school, where preservice teachers assume teaching responsibilities and are taught by both teachers and teacher educators (in groups and individually).

5. The spirit of an intellectual community dominates, with all participants engaging in conceptually informed discussions about how to be analytical, creative, flexible, and adaptive in creating mindfulness in students.

6. Preservice teachers receive a "passing grade" and, ultimately, teaching certification not by receiving an "A" on a professor's midterm examination or by completing a term paper or academic project but, rather, by establishing their suc-

cess in developing mindfulness in students and, in the process, demonstrating professional inquiry.

CONCLUSION

This book is dedicated to positive interventions that advance thinking. This particular chapter argues that we cannot advance thinking unless we put teachers in the position to be thinkers themselves.

Doing so will not be easy. Although Kincaid (1992) was writing about Native Americans and not about teachers, he may have captured the essence of the difficulty:

> To get to that new language, that new vision and way of being that might (maybe, who knows?) heal us and our world, we need to set aside what we will not be able to set aside, we need to give up habits of mind so deep and prolonged they very nearly constitute what we *are*. To see differently, we must be and do differently; and to be and do better we must see better. (p. 29)

To create a new psychology of teacher development—one which promotes teacher mindfulness—we must set aside habits of mind about teachers and teacher education that are so deeply embedded they very nearly constitute what we are. And to do that, we must see better.

What we must see particularly is that power must be distributed differently in education. Traditionally, professors and school administrators held the power. Change was assumed to occur through lectures and bureaucratic mandates. Those in power led; teachers followed.

For change to occur, teachers must be emancipated. They cannot continue to be subservient followers. They must be free to be creative in responding to the conditional, tentative, contextually constrained character of schooling. In Elmore's (1992) words, we must allow teaching practice to drive organizational structures rather than having organizational structures drive practice.

For this to happen, we need a new psychology of teacher development, one in which teachers are given a legitimate voice in their professional work. Anything less dooms to failure the goal of mindfulness.

REFERENCES

Berg, C., & Clough, M. (1991). Hunter lesson design: The wrong one for science teaching. *Educational Leadership, 48,* 79–81.

Bloom, B. (1968). Learning for mastery. *Evaluation Comment, 2*(1), 1–12.

Brophy, J., & Good, T. (1986). Teacher behaviors and student achievement. In M. C. Wittrock (Ed.), *Handbook of research on teaching* (3rd ed., pp. 328–375). NY: Macmillan.

Brown, R. (1991). *Schools of thought.* San Francisco: Jossey-Bass.

Buchmann, M. (1989). Breaking from experience in teacher education: When is it necessary? How is it possible? *Oxford Review of Education, 15*(2), 181–195.

Buchmann, M., & Schwille, J. (1983). Education: The overcoming of experience. *American Journal of Education, 92,* 30–51.

Carnegie Task Force on Teaching as a Profession. (1986). *A nation prepared: Teachers for the 21st century.* Washington, DC: Carnegie Forum on Education and the Economy.

Cochran-Smith, M., & Lytle, S. (1990). Research on teaching and teacher research: The issues that divide. *Educational Researcher, 19*(2), 2–11.

Cuban, L. (1984). *How teachers taught: Consistency and change in American classrooms, 1890–1980.* NY: Longman.

Doyle, W. (1983). Academic work. *Review of Educational Research, 53*(2), 159–199.

Duffy, G. (1983). Context variables in reading teacher effectiveness. In J. Niles & L. Harris (Eds.), *Searches for meanings in reading: Language processing and instruction* (pp. 289–291). 32nd National Reading Conference Yearbook. Rochester, NY: National Reading Conference.

Duffy, G. (1981). Teacher effectiveness research: Implications for the reading profession. In M. Kamil (Ed.), *Directions in reading: Research and instruction* (pp. 113–136). 30th National Reading Conference Yearbook. Washington DC: National Reading Conference.

Duffy, G. (1991). What counts in teacher education? Dilemmas in educating empowered teachers. In J. Zutell & S. McCormick (Eds.), *Learner factors/teacher factors: Issues in literacy research and instruction* (pp. 1–18). 40th National Reading Conference Yearbook. Chicago: National Reading Conference.

Duffy, G. (1992, April). Learning from the study of practice: Where we must go with strategy instruction. Paper presented at the annual conference of the American Educational Research Association, San Francisco.

Duffy, G. (in press). Professional development schools and the (dis)empowerment of teachers and professors: A search for the elusive egalitarianism. *Phi Delta Kappan.*

Duffy, G., & Anderson, L. (1984). Teachers' theoretical orientations and the real classroom. *Reading Psychology, 5*(2), 97–104.

Duffy, G., & McIntyre, L. (1982). A naturalistic study of instructional assistance in primary grade reading. *Elementary School Journal, 83,* 15–23.

Duffy, G., & Roehler, L. (1989). *Improving classroom reading instruction: A decision making approach* (2nd ed.). NY: McGraw-Hill.

Duffy, G., Roehler, L., & Putnam, J. (1987). Putting the teacher in control: Instructional decision-making and basal text books. *Elementary School Journal, 87*(3), 357–366.

Duffy, G., & Sherman, G. (1971). *Systematic reading instruction.* NY: Harper & Row.

Durkin, D. (1978–79). What classroom observation reveals about reading comprehension instruction. *Reading Research Quarterly, 14,* 481–533.

Edelsky, C. (1990). Whose agenda is this anyway? A response to McKenna, Robinson and Miller. *Educational Researcher, 19*(8), 7–11.

Ellis, N. (1990). Collaborative interaction for improvement of teaching. *Teaching and Teacher Education, 6*(3), 267–277.

Elmore, R. (1992). Why restructuring alone won't

improve teaching. *Educational Leadership, 49*(7), 44–48.

Elmore, R., & McLaughlin, M. (1988). *Steady work: Policy, practice and reform of American education.* Santa Monica: Rand.

Englemann, S. (1991). Teachers, schemata, and instruction. In M. Kennedy (Ed.), *Teaching academic content to diverse learners.* NY: Teachers College Press.

Englemann, S., & Bruner, E. (1974). *DISTAR reading level I.* Chicago: Science Research Associates.

Gage, N. (1978). *The scientific basis of the art of teaching.* NY: Teachers College Press.

Goodman, K. (1989). Whole language research: Foundations and development. *Elementary School Journal, 90*(2), 207–221.

Goodson, I. (1991). Sponsoring the teacher's voice: Teachers' lives and teacher development. *Cambridge Journal of Education, 21*(1), 35–45.

Greenberg, J. (1990). *Problem solving situations: A teacher's resource book.* Brattleboro, VT: Teachers' Laboratory, Inc.

Gusky, T. (1985). *Implementing mastery learning.* Belmont, CA: Wadsworth.

Hargreaves, A., & Dawe, R. (1990). Paths of professional development: Contrived collegiality, collaborative culture and the case of peer coaching. *Teaching and Teacher Education, 6*(3), 227–241.

Herrmann, B. (1986). Reading instruction: Dealing with classroom realities. *Community College Review, 1*(1), 28–34.

Herrmann, B. A., & Sarracino, J. (1991, December). *Effects of an alternative approach for teaching preservice teachers how to teach strategic reasoning: Three illustrative cases.* Paper presented at the annual meeting of the National Reading Conference, Palm Springs, CA.

Hirsh, G. (1987). *Cultural literacy: What every American needs to know.* Boston: Houghton Mifflin.

Holt, J. (1964). *How children fail.* NY: Dell.

Holmes Group, Inc. (1990). *Tomorrow's schools.* East Lansing: Michigan State University.

Huberman, M. (1990). Linkage between researchers and practitioners: A qualitative study. *American Educational Research Journal, 27*(2), 363–391.

Hunter, M. (1967). *Teach more—faster!* El Segundo, CA: TIP Publications.

Hunter, M. (1991). Hunter lesson design helps achieve the goals of science instruction. *Educational Leadership, 48*, 79–81.

Johnston, J. S., & Wilder, S. L. (1992). Changing reading and writing programs through staff development. *The Reading Teacher, 45*(8), 626–631.

Kincaid, J. R. (1992, May 3). Who gets to tell their stories? *New York Times Book Review*, pp. 11–29.

Leinhardt, G. (1992). What research on learning tells us about teaching. *Educational Leadership, 49*(7), 20–25.

Lortie, D. (1975). *Schoolteacher.* Chicago: University of Chicago Press.

McCaslin, M., & Good, T. (1992). Compliant cognition: The misalliance of management and instructional goals in current school reform. *Educational Researcher, 21*(3), 4–17.

McKisson, M., & MacRae-Campbell, L. (1990). *Endangered species: Their struggle to survive.* Tucson: Zephyr.

Patton, S., & Maxson, D. (1989). *Architexture: A shelter word.* Tucson: Zephyr.

Prawat, R. (1992). From individual differences to learning communities—Our changing focus. *Educational Leadership, 49*(7), 9–13.

Prawat, R. (1991). The value of ideas: The immersion approach to the development of thinking. *Educational Researcher, 20*(2), 3–10.

Prawat, R. (1992). *The value of ideas II: Problems versus possibilities in learning.* Unpublished paper, Michigan State University.

Purpel, D. (1989). *The moral and spiritual crisis in education.* NY: Bergin & Garvey.

Rosenshine, B., & Stevens, R. (1984). Classroom instruction in reading. In P. D. Pearson (Ed.), *Handbook of reading research* (pp. 745–798). NY: Longman.

Rowe, M. (1974). Wait time and rewards as instructional variables. *Journal of Research in Science Teaching, 11*, 84–94.

Saranson, S. (1990). *The predictable failure of educational reform.* San Francisco: Jossey-Bass.

Vydra, J. (1986). *The magic carpet ride.* San Luis Obispo, CA: Dandy Lion Publications.

SUPPLEMENTARY READINGS ABOUT TEACHERS, TEACHER THINKING, AND TEACHER DEVELOPMENT

Brown, R. (1991). *Schools of thought.* San Francisco: Jossey-Bass.

Elmore, R. (Eds.). (1991). *Restructuring schools: The next generation of educational reform.* San Francisco: Jossey-Bass.

Goodson, I. (1992). *Studying teachers' lives.* New York: Teachers College Press.

Grossman, P. (1990). *The making of a teacher: Teacher knowledge and teacher education.* New York: Teachers College Press.

Hargreaves, A., & Fullan, M. (Eds.). (1992). *Understanding teacher development.* New York: Teachers College Press.

Johnson, S. (1990). *Teachers at work.* New York: Basic Books.

Joyce, B. (1990). Changing school culture through staff development. *1990 Yearbook of the Association for Supervision and Curriculum Development* (pp. 169–183). Alexandria, VA: ASCD.

Lieberman, A. (Ed.). (1989). *Building professional cultures in schools.* New York: Teachers College Press.

Lieberman, A., & Miller, L. (Eds.). (1991). *Staff development for education in the '90s: New demands, new realities, new perspectives..* New York: Teachers College Press.

Lieberman, A., & Miller, L. (1992). *Teachers: Their world and their work.* New York: Teacher College Press.

McDonald, J. (1984). *Teaching: Making sense of an uncertain craft.* New York: Teachers College Press.

Purpel, D. (1989). *The moral and spiritual crisis in education.* New York: Bergin & Garvey.

Schon, D. (1983). *The reflective practitioner.* New York: Basic Books.

Wasley, P. (1991). *Teachers who lead: The rhetoric of reform and the realities of practice.* New York: Teachers College Press.

The following chapter was supported in part by a grant from the Office of Educational Research and Improvement (Grant No. G-008690007) and by grants from the Center for the Humanities and the Graduate School of the University of New Hampshire. Any opinions, findings, and conclusions or recommendations expressed in this publication are those of the authors and do not reflect the views of the supporting agencies. Major contributions to this work have been made by Dae-Dong Hahn, Bruce King, James Ladwig, Cameron McCarthy, Francis Schrag, Robert Stevenson, and the cooperative staff and students in sixteen high schools. Some material here is taken from previous reports such as Newmann (1990a, 1991a, 1991b, 1992) and Onosko (1991).

CHAPTER TWO

CREATING MORE THOUGHTFUL LEARNING ENVIRONMENTS

JOSEPH J. ONOSKO

DEPARTMENT OF EDUCATION, UNIVERSITY OF NEW HAMPSHIRE

FRED M. NEWMANN

CENTER ON ORGANIZATION AND RESTRUCTURING OF SCHOOLS AND DEPARTMENT OF CURRICULUM & INSTRUCTION, UNIVERSITY OF WISCONSIN

Dr. Joseph J. Onosko is an assistant professor of education at the University of New Hampshire, teaching courses and serving as advisor to students in the education department's master's and doctoral programs. His research has focused on teachers' thinking, teachers' instructional practices and staff development activities related to promoting classroom thoughtfulness, and students' higher order thinking. He has conducted system-wide school evaluations for the Casey Foundation, analyzed social studies departments nationwide for the National Center on Effective Secondary Schools, and has led staff development activities to enhance classroom thoughtfulness in numerous schools. Professor Onosko presently serves as vice-chairman of the Adolescent/Young Adult Social Studies Committee of the National Board of Professional Teaching Standards.

Dr. Fred M. Newmann, professor of curriculum and instruction, University of Wisconsin, Madison, directed the National Center on Effective Secondary Schools and now directs the Center on Organization and Restructuring of Schools. He has 30 years experience in research, teacher education, and curriculum development in secondary social studies, including projects in the analysis of public controversy, community service, and citizen participation. His publications deal with curriculum for citizenship, higher order thinking in social studies, education and the building of community, alternatives to standardized testing, and student engagement.

Developing the higher-order thinking of America's youth is a persistent theme of educational reform in the United States (Cuban, 1984a; Mann, 1979). Unlike many educational goals, the past decade has witnessed a number of sincere and productive efforts in this area, both in theory (e.g., Glaser, 1984; McPeck, 1981; Newmann, 1991a; Schrag, 1988; Seigel, 1988) and in practice (e.g., Alter & Salmon, 1987; Chance, 1986; Costa, 1985; Pressiesen, 1986; Sizer, 1984, 1992). Nonetheless, research continues to document that low-level cognitive work dominates classroom life (Brown, 1991; McNeil, 1986; Powell, Farrar & Cohen, 1985).

Why is it so difficult for reform efforts to make instructional activities more intellectually challenging? The primary purpose of this chapter is to identify the dominant barriers to higher-order thinking and the ways in which these barriers can be overcome to create greater levels of thoughtfulness in secondary classrooms and schools. We begin by offering a conception of higher-order thinking that can guide teaching and a framework for observing the extent to which it is promoted in classrooms. We then briefly summarize a four-year study conducted at the National Center on Effective Secondary Schools that analyzed the extent to which individual high-school teachers and departments challenged students to use their minds well. Next, we identify the kinds of changes that need to occur if higher-order thinking is to be supported more frequently in classrooms of the future. This involves identifying persistent and deeply rooted barriers that inhibit the promotion of higher-order thinking and recommending measures that need to be considered if significant and lasting change is to occur. Finally, we suggest needed areas of future research.

DEFINING HIGHER-ORDER THINKING

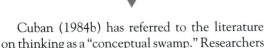

Cuban (1984b) has referred to the literature on thinking as a "conceptual swamp." Researchers and educators have advocated many conceptions: critical thinking, divergent or creative thinking, reasoning (moral, inductive, deductive, formal, informal), problem solving, decision making. These conceptions can all be subsumed under the larger construct of higher-order thinking and made distinct from lower-order thinking. Defined broadly, higher-order thinking is expanded use of the mind to meet new challenges; lower-order thinking represents routine, mechanistic application and limited use of the mind. Expanded use of the mind occurs when a person must interpret, analyze, or manipulate information, because a question to be answered or a problem to be solved cannot be resolved through the routine application of previously learned knowledge. In contrast, lower-order thinking generally involves repetitive operations such as listing information previously learned or memorized, using previously learned formulae (e.g., computing Fahrenheit to Celsius), applying procedural rules (e.g., footnotes to a research paper), and other routinized or algorithmic mental activities.

Challenging problems can appear in many forms and in all curriculum subjects. They may lead to single, correct, and well-defined answers or to multiple, ambiguous, conflicting solutions. The challenges may involve different kinds of inquiry (logical, empirical, esthetic, ethical), different forms of expression (oral, written, nonverbal), and different types of intelligence (verbal, mathematical, kinesthetic, interpersonal).

No particular question or problem, however, necessarily leads to higher-order thinking for all students. For one person, trying to understand and follow a bus schedule may require higher-order thought, but for another the same task will be routine. In this sense, higher-order thinking is relative: To determine the extent to which a task will involve an individual in higher-order thinking, one presumably needs to know much about that person's history with the task. In addition, one would need to "get inside" the person's head or experience his or her subjective state of thought to assess the extent to which an individual is participating in the analysis, interpretation, and manipulation of information (Schrag, 1989).

This definition poses an operational problem. It is difficult to determine reliably the extent to which a person is involved in higher-order thinking. Teachers who interact with several students at once have little opportunity to diagnose students' individual mental states. Instead, they must make assumptions about the prior knowledge of groups of students and about the kinds of mental work that particular tasks are likely to stimulate. The teaching of thinking, therefore, is a rather imprecise enterprise. The best we can do is to engage in what we predict will be challenging problems, guide student manipulation of information to solve problems, and support students' efforts.

This conception has several positive features. First, it assumes that any person, young or old, regardless of experience or prior knowledge, can participate in higher-order thought. Students will differ in the kinds of challenges they are able to undertake and master, but all can confront challenges in the interpretation, analysis, and manipulation of knowledge. Second, the conception encompasses cognitive activity in a wide range of school subjects as well as in nonacademic areas. Third, it does not require acceptance of any particular theory of cognitive processing or rely on a particular pedagogy. This is an advantage, because persuasive evidence on the best techniques for the promotion of thinking does not exist. Finally, this conception is hospitable to providing students with three important resources for thinking that are recognized widely in the literature: content knowledge, intellectual skills, and dispositions of thoughtfulness. We now turn to a discussion of these resources.

THE NEED FOR KNOWLEDGE, SKILLS, AND DISPOSITIONS

Research on the nature of thinking (summarized by Walsh & Paul, 1987, and by Nickerson, Perkins & Smith, 1985) indicates that for students to successfully meet higher-order challenges, they need a combination of in-depth knowledge, intellectual skills, and attitudes or dispositions of thoughtfulness. These three components are the

core of a curriculum focused on higher-order thinking, but how much emphasis to give to each is widely disputed. We summarize below key arguments that can be made for each of these critical resources.

The Knowledge Argument

One cannot think in a content vacuum. Sophisticated understanding and mastery of higher-order challenges occur only through the use of knowledge in a subject or topic, whether it be consumer decision making, the design of a bridge, or critique of a theater performance. Of course, subjects can be taught in ways that fail to promote thinking, but thinking cannot be taught apart from knowledge. Some would argue that the proper teaching of a subject is equivalent to, or sufficient for, promoting higher-order thinking (Glaser, 1984; McPeck, 1981; Nickerson, 1988; Prawat, 1991), because it demands that students interpret, analyze, and manipulate knowledge to face new challenges within the subject and because it draws the student closer to the thinking of experts in the field. Beyond substantive knowledge of the topic, students need analytic knowledge (e.g., the structure of well-reasoned arguments, distinctions between empirical, conceptual and normative claims, criteria to judge reliability of evidence) and metacognitive knowledge (i.e., awareness and self-monitoring of one's thought processes).

The Skills Argument

While knowledge is undoubtedly important, for purposes of teaching thinking, skills are critical because they are the tools that permit knowledge to be used or applied to the solution of new problems. For example, good thinkers can identify a problem, state alternative solutions, detect bias, judge logical consistency, hypothesize, synthesize, infer, and so on. Some of these skills may be specific to a domain under study, while others may be more generic. Skills themselves may be construed or labeled in a variety of ways, but the main point is to recognize their role as cognitive processes that put knowledge to work. In practice, knowledge is usually transmitted from teacher to students without an expectation that the student will manipulate the knowledge to solve higher-order challenges. Unless the essential processes of using knowledge (i.e., skills) are stressed as central goals of education, higher-order thinking is likely to be neglected and the knowledge transmitted to remain inert. Perhaps for this reason many educational reformers past and present prefer to advocate not the teaching of thinking, but instead the teaching of thinking skills (Beyer, 1987; de Bono, 1983; Ennis, 1962; Marzano, et al. 1988).

The Dispositions Argument

Without dispositions of thoughtfulness, neither knowledge nor the skills for applying knowledge are likely to be used intelligently. Those who emphasize the importance of dispositions suggest several traits, including: a persistent desire that claims be supported by reasons (and that the reasons themselves be scrutinized); a tendency to be reflective—to take time to think problems through for oneself, rather than acting impulsively or automatically accepting the views of others; a curiosity to explore new questions; a flexibility to entertain alternative and original solutions to problems; and a habit of examining one's own thinking processes (Dewey, 1933; Hare, 1985; Passmore, 1967; Perkins, Jay & Tishman, in press; Schrag, 1988; Siegel, 1988). Thoughtfulness thereby involves attitudes, personality or character traits, habits of mind, general values, and beliefs or epistemologies about the nature of knowledge (e.g., that rationality is desirable; that knowledge itself is socially constructed, subject to revision, and often indeterminate; and that thinking can lead to the understanding of and solution to problems). Without these dispositions, knowledge and skills are likely to be taught and applied mechanistically, or worse, nonsensically. Of the three main resources, dispositions have attracted the least attention in the professional literature, but a good argument can be made that dispositions are central in generating both the will to think and qualities of judgment that steer knowledge and skills in productive directions.

It is important that teachers design instruction explicitly to help students acquire and use in-depth knowledge, skills, and dispositions; but there appears to be no clear ordering of priorities among the three resources. The classroom observation scheme presented next attempts to capture teachers' efforts to develop these resources without giving center stage to any one resource.

ASSESSING CLASSROOM THOUGHTFULNESS: A FRAMEWORK

To conduct our research on higher-order thinking in social studies classrooms at the secondary level, we needed to identify indicators that would provide information on the extent to which it was being promoted in the classes we observed. Since it is logistically impossible to examine the actual thinking of individual students during class lessons, we needed a tool for describing thoughtfulness in the lessons as a whole. But how specific should the criteria be?

Interviews with history and social studies teachers indicated that highly specific lists of knowledge, skills, and dispositions would be unlikely to facilitate widespread consensus (and we believe this would be true in other disciplines as well). Instead, social studies teachers are likely to support a plurality of types of thinking, but even these will be grounded primarily in the teaching of different topics and issues. Thus, a broad conception of thinking, adaptable to a variety of content and skill objectives, is more likely to interest a diverse population of teachers. Langer describes these differences in Chapter 4.

We therefore moved from a consideration of the nature of thinking in individual students to consideration of qualities that promote thoughtfulness in classrooms; that is, we tried to identify observable qualities of classroom activity most likely to help students achieve depth of understanding, intellectual skills, and dispositions of thoughtfulness. Emphasizing general qualities of classroom talk and activity, rather than highly differentiated skills and behaviors, helps avoid the danger of teaching a host of isolated thinking skills that can actually eliminate purposeful higher-order thinking through step-by-step serialization.[1] A general framework may also hold more promise both for students to solve new problems and for teachers to promote thinking across diverse lessons and subject areas.

Equally important, a broad set of criteria can strike at the heart of an underlying malady identified by many studies: Much classroom activity fails to challenge students to use their minds in any valuable way. The more serious problem, therefore, is not the failure to teach some specific aspect of thinking, but rather the profound absence of thoughtfulness in classrooms. Our general framework addresses this basic issue. Ultimately, of course, teachers must focus on the content-specific activities that enhance student understanding of subjects, but the point here is to arrive at a general framework through which classes studying diverse subjects can be identified as promoting or undermining higher-order thinking.

In devising indicators of classroom thoughtfulness responsive to the above points, we initially rated lessons on 15 possible dimensions, summarized in Table 2-1. Each dimension was used to make an overall rating of an observed lesson on a 5-point scale from 1 = "a very inaccurate" to 5 = "a very accurate" description of this lesson. After observing these qualities for a year in five "select" schools and examining them further from a theoretical point of view, we chose the six dimensions below as the most fundamental indicators of classroom thoughtfulness.[2]

1. **There was sustained examination of a few topics rather than superficial coverage of many.**

   Mastery of higher-order challenges requires in-depth study and sustained concentration on a limited number of topics or questions. Lessons that cover many topics give students only vague familiarity or awareness and thereby reduce the possibilities for building the complex knowledge, skills, and dispositions needed to understand a topic.

2. **The lesson displayed substantive coherence and continuity.**

   Progress on higher-order challenges demands systematic inquiry that builds on relevant and accurate substantive knowledge in the field and that works toward the logical development and integration of ideas. In contrast, lessons that teach material as unrelated fragments of knowledge undermine such inquiry.

3. **Students were given an appropriate amount of time to think, that is, to prepare responses to questions.**

   Thinking takes time, but often recitation, discussion, and written assignments pressure students to make responses before they have had enough time to reflect. Promoting thoughtfulness, therefore, requires periods of silence when students can ponder the validity of alternative responses, develop more elaborate reasoning, and experience patient reflection.

4. **The teacher asked challenging questions and/or structured challenging tasks (given the ability level and preparation of the students).**

   By our definition, higher-order thinking occurs only when students are faced with questions or tasks that demand analysis, interpretation, or manipulation of information. In short, students must be faced with the challenge of how to use prior knowledge to gain new knowledge rather than the task of merely retrieving prior knowledge or conducting other routinized operations.

5. **The teacher was a model of thoughtfulness.**

   Teachers themselves must model thoughtful dispositions if students are to succeed with higher-order challenges. Key indicators include showing interest in students' ideas and in alternative approaches to problems; showing how he or she thought through a problem (rather than only the final answer); and acknowledging the difficulty of gaining a definitive understanding to questions and problems.

TABLE 2-1	INITIAL CRITERIA FOR CLASSROOM THOUGHTFULNESS

Classes were rated from 1–5: 1 = "very inaccurate" description of class; 5 = "very accurate."

*1.   In this class, there was sustained examination of a few topics rather than a superficial coverage of many.

*2.   In this class, the lesson displayed substantive coherence and continuity.

*3.   In this class, students were given an appropriate amount of time to think, that is, to prepare responses to questions.

4.   In this class, the teacher carefully considered explanations and reasons for conclusions.

*5.   In this class, the teacher asked challenging questions and/or structured challenging tasks (given the ability level and preparation of the students).

6.   In this class, the teacher pressed individual students to justify or to clarify their assertions in a Socratic manner.

7.   In this class, the teacher tried to get students to generate original and unconventional ideas, explanations, or solutions to problems.

*8.   In this classroom, the teacher was a model of thoughtfulness. (Principal indications are: the teacher showed appreciation for students' ideas and appreciation for alternate approaches or answers if based on sound reasoning; the teacher explained how he or she thought through a problem; the teacher acknowledged the difficulty of gaining a definitive understanding of the topic.)

9.   In this class, students assumed the roles of questioner and critic.

*10.   In this class, students offered explanations and reasons for their conclusions.

11.   In this class, students generated original and unconventional ideas, explanations, hypotheses, or solutions to problems.

12.   In this class, student contributions were articulate, germane to the topic, and connected to prior discussion.

13.   What proportion of students were active participants?

14.   What proportion of time did students spend engaged in thoughtful discourse with each other?

15.   What proportion of students showed genuine involvement in the topics discussed? (Cues include raising hands, attentiveness manifested by facial expression and body language, interruptions motivated by involvement, length of student responses.)

*These variables are considered minimal requirements for a thoughtful lesson.

---

6. Students offered explanations and reasons for their conclusions.

The answers or solutions to higher-order challenges are rarely self-evident. Their validity often rests on the quality of explanations or reasons given to support them. Therefore, beyond offering answers, students must also be able to produce explanations and reasons to support their conclusions.

Teachers' lessons were scored on each of the six dimensions and were then combined into a single measure (Comprehensive Higher Order Thinking, or CHOT) that served as the indicator of classroom thoughtfulness for an observed lesson.[3] Each teacher's set of observed lessons was then combined to create an overall CHOT score. How often do classrooms reflect the above criteria of thoughtfulness? How much do teachers differ? How much do departments differ? What can schools do to infuse more thoughtfulness into their classrooms? To answer these and other questions we conducted a study of high-school social studies departments according to the design described below.

PROJECT DESIGN AND METHODOLOGY

The study was conducted from Fall 1986 to Spring 1990. In-depth interviews were conducted and questionnaire responses were gathered in 16 social studies departments nationwide from 56 teachers and from each department chair and principal. In addition, nearly 500 classroom observations of teachers' lessons were gathered by a six-member research team. The main goal of the study was to determine how some social studies departments may be able to overcome barriers to higher-order thinking that others have not. Rather than concentrating primarily upon differences between individual teachers, this study explored the problem of institutionalization: What is required for department-wide promotion of higher-order thinking? The strategy was to identify exemplary social studies departments and then, by contrasting these departments with others, to draw inferences about barriers and opportunities for success.

Through a national search that involved nominations, phone interviews, and site visits, three different sets or types of departments were identified: (a) those that place special emphasis on higher-order thinking, but that organize instruction according to familiar patterns in the comprehensive high school (hereafter called the five "select" departments); (b) those that make no special department-wide efforts toward higher-order thinking and are also conventionally organized (hereafter called the seven "representative" departments); and, (c) those that involve a departmental emphasis on higher-order thinking and, in addition, have made significant changes

in the organization of instruction (hereafter called the four "restructured" departments).

Teachers, department chairs, and principals were each interviewed for at least two hours. Researchers probed their written responses to questionnaires that explored their conceptions of and commitment to higher-order thinking as an educational goal, the factors they perceived as necessary to accomplish it, the barriers that stand in the way, and the kind of leadership devoted to it within their school. In addition, students were interviewed and/or surveyed about the kind of instruction they found challenging and engaging. A more complete summary of the study's design and methodology can be found in Newmann (1990b, 1991b, 1992).

STUDY FINDINGS

A detailed presentation of results is beyond the scope of this chapter. Instead, we will highlight major conclusions.

- The level of classroom thoughtfulness (i.e., CHOT) varied considerably between teachers within and across departments, though teachers themselves were consistent in the extent to which they promote thoughtfulness (Newmann, 1992);

- Departments committed to higher-order thinking as a fundamental instructional goal exhibited more classroom thoughtfulness than departments not committed to this goal (Newmann, 1991b);

- The ability level of the class, but not race or age, had a sizable correlation with lesson thoughtfulness. However, in the most thoughtful departments (i.e., highest overall CHOT) ability level had no effect, indicating that some departments are able to equitably distribute classroom thoughtfulness across all classes regardless of students' background characteristics (Newmann, 1992);

- Based on classroom observations, open-ended interviews with students, and survey questionnaire items, data indicate that students are more likely to try, to concentrate, and to be interested in academic study when they are challenged to think (Newmann, 1992);

- Teachers who scored highest on CHOT think differently about their work than the lowest scoring teachers. In contrast to low scorers, high scorers were more likely to (a) identify student thinking as a primary instructional goal, (b) identify breadth of content coverage as detrimental to the promotion of thinking and make efforts to reduce content coverage, (c) possess elaborate conceptions of higher-order thinking, and (d) view students as capable of doing higher-order thinking (Onosko, 1989, 1992);

- Departments that scored highest on CHOT differed from the lowest scoring departments with respect to goals, curriculum, pedagogy, leadership, and school culture. Top scoring departments led by strong department chairs and principals aimed toward a common vision for promoting students' thinking and worked to construct curriculum to that end, whereas in the bottom scoring departments leadership, vision, and curriculum change to promote thinking was lacking. In addition, department heads at the top schools made special efforts to comment on their colleagues' teaching, to support peer observation and discussion of specific pedagogy that promotes thinking, and to foster a collegial faculty culture. Heads of low scoring departments did not engage in these efforts (King, 1991; Newmann, 1992);

- The highest scoring departments did not differ substantially in structural features from the lowest scoring departments. Stated another way, three of the five "select" departments (i.e., departments that emphasize thinking but are traditionally

organized) were among the group of four highest scoring schools overall, whereas none of the four "restructured" schools achieved this status. It appears that innovative structural features alone offer no advantages; strong program design appears to be more important. This does not preclude the possibility that strong program design *and* organizational restructuring, if combined, would produce the highest levels of thoughtfulness (Ladwig, 1991; Newmann, 1992).

Perhaps the most important finding to emerge from this study is that even among the most successful teachers and departments there is considerable room for improvement; that is, only 12 of 48 teachers on a 5-point scale averaged above 4.0 on CHOT, and the mean on CHOT for the four highest scoring departments was only 3.92 (Newmann, 1992). Clearly, some of the finest social studies teachers and departments in the country continue to face serious difficulties in their quest to promote students' thinking.

What stands in the way and what needs to be done to help secondary teachers and schools become more effective in this area? In the next section we discuss dominant and persistent barriers that inhibit teachers' efforts and suggest various in-service and other reform measures that should be considered if teachers and schools are to create more thoughtful learning environments that promote students' thinking.

PROMOTING THOUGHTFULNESS: BARRIERS AND REFORM RECOMMENDATIONS

The barriers to and recommendations for reform suggested in this section draw heavily, but not completely, upon the research described above. We also borrow from the practical wisdom of staff developers as described in Newmann,

Onosko, and Stevenson (1990), more recent research in restructured schools, and other relevant literature that focuses on the promotion of higher-order thinking. In addition to the problem of teachers' self-perceptions that Gerry Duffy addressed in the previous chapter, we found five barriers that inhibit higher-order thinking in schools.

THE BARRIERS

School reform activities and measures designed to increase classroom emphasis on higher-order thinking should begin with awareness of the persistent barriers or obstacles to its promotion. Little progress will be made unless reform strategies within and out of school attack these problems directly. The barriers are rooted in five main sources: a view of teaching as knowledge transmission, a bloated curriculum, teachers' low expectations of students, an intellectually oppressive organizational structure, and a culture of teacher isolation (Onosko, 1991). An elaboration of these barriers can help to identify directions for leadership, in-service, and restructuring to improve the quality of thinking in schools.

Teaching as Knowledge Transmission

The dominant forms of classroom "discourse" past and present are teacher lecture and teacher-led recitations (Cuban, 1984b). The overriding agenda is to transmit to students information and ideas, and then request that students reproduce them either orally or in writing. The focus is on the products of others' (i.e., authorities') thoughts, deemed important by society. Acquiring the products of others' inquiries tends to displace from the school agenda students' own participation in inquiry and other forms of higher-order thinking.

In the activity of knowledge transmission, the assemblage of evidence and inferential thinking that undergirds the knowledge delivered is often ignored. Much like crossing a bridge, students see the road surface but not the pilings and support

beams. Students are less likely to give reasons and explanations because the goal is to demonstrate acquisition of facts and concepts (i.e., products or "truths"), not the reasoning that validates them. Questions and solutions are not presented as problematic, nor are students required to interpret, analyze, or manipulate information in ways that go beyond the teacher's or text's presentation of it. As Duckworth (1987) stated, "In most classrooms it is the quick right answer that is appreciated." Our research supports Duckworth's assessment, as do the observations of many others (Brown, 1991; Sarason, 1982; Sizer, 1984).

A Bloated Curriculum

School curricula are typically designed to expose students to an ocean of information and ideas organized around broad surveys and presented as fragmented bits of knowledge (Newmann, 1988; Wiggins, 1989). Students race (or are dragged) through an endless stream of textbook chapters and lecture notes that superficially cover numerous facts, concepts, theories, events, issues, and problems. The press for coverage emanates from a number of sources, including: (a) professional, political, economic, and other interest groups that influence curriculum guidelines, textbooks, and texts, (b) the dominance of survey courses, lecture formats, and memorized "learning" in teachers' own high-school and college experiences which, in turn, leads future teachers to do the same, and (c) the society's deeply entrenched belief that the core or nucleus of education and intelligence is possession of numerous, discrete, bits of knowledge.

The bloated curriculum allows little time for students to explore information, to reflect upon it, to recast it, to draw connections, to ask questions about it—in short, to think about rather than mindlessly absorb information. Teachers resort to questions that require only simple recall (you have it or you do not) and fast-paced question-and-answer sequences to ensure that all of the content gets delivered. What is there to probe or explore in a curriculum that is a mile wide and an inch deep? The vast number and variety of facts and ideas make it virtually impossible to construct lessons and units that exhibit substantive coherence, promote dispositions of thoughtfulness, and allow students to hone skills related to inquiry and problem solving.

Teachers' Low Expectations of Students

Low expectations of students on the part of many teachers take diverse forms, though they have the common effect of suppressing classroom thoughtfulness. Students perceived to be incapable of succeeding with or unwilling to attempt higher-order challenges are relegated to a steady diet of factual information, fill-in-the-blank worksheet activities, and tedious teacher-centered recitations that test their acquisition of knowledge bits.

What is the basis for many teachers' low expectations of students? Some teachers in our study assumed that students lacked the inherent mental capacity, the raw "brain power," to engage in higher-order thinking, especially those students labeled low achievers or low ability.[4] For other teachers the problem was not inherently low cognitive capacity, but rather students' underdeveloped cognitive skills due to deficiencies in students' prior learning. When students are perceived to lack thinking skills, many teachers are less likely to craft lessons that require higher-order challenges. Another group of teachers noted deficits in students' knowledge as the reason for their poor performance on thinking tasks. This often leads to extensive and tedious attempts to teach "the facts" before students are allowed to think about the material. Finally, a number of teachers in our study expressed frustration with students' low motivation (if not outright resistance) to entertain higher-order challenges.

An Intellectually Oppressive Organizational Structure

Students facing higher-order challenges need constructive and reasonably detailed oral and/or written feedback on their approaches to problem solving, both as they proceed and after they have developed solutions. Students also need to be nurtured and encouraged, as tasks involving high-

er-order thinking place students at greater risk of failure and at higher levels of frustration (Doyle, 1983). Teachers have few opportunities to provide individualized critique or nurturance when their average class size is 25–35 students (Cuban, 1984b; Shaver et al., 1979). Written expression is particularly hampered when teachers are responsible for 125–175 students each semester. For example, assigning a two-page essay to 125 students once a week, and allocating 15 minutes for reading and reacting to each essay, buries a teacher under more than 31 hours of additional work per week.

Large class size also raises real and imagined concerns for classroom management, especially when leading whole-group discussions. Students display frustration while waiting their turn to speak. For fear of losing the attention of much of the class, teachers refrain from probing a student's ideas or from offering students time to reflect before responding to a difficult question. Large class size reduces the quality of discussions and frequency with which teachers are willing to hold discussions, and reinforces a pedagogy of transmission, because classroom control seems more easily maintained through a one-way flow of information.

Structuring thoughtful learning experiences on five different days for 45–50 minutes each limits the kinds of problems that can be studied and the types of inquiry available to solve them. Certainly deadlines and time constraints exist when solving problems outside of school, whether it be on the job or during one's leisure time, but these constraints are rarely so rigid as the scheduling of thinking in schools. In addition, this structure asks students to think seriously about five to six different topics or subjects per day, an unreasonable if not impossible task.

Another organizational barrier that needs to be highlighted is the minimal planning time allotted teachers. In traditionally organized schools, one 45–50 minute time block is typically allocated for teacher planning. In that single period teachers must review or acquire initial understanding of the ideas and problems to be addressed in class, find appropriate reading materials for students, craft lessons that will challenge students to think, begin to map out the direction of upcoming units, complete administrative chores (e.g., record attendance, administer make-up tests, complete progress reports), and meet with students individually.

Finally, some problems require resources beyond the classroom to which the student needs access (computers, libraries, experts in the community, nature itself). To the extent that schools confine students to classrooms, they also limit the potential for higher-order thinking. In each of the above ways (class size, total student load, time schedule, student course load, lack of teacher planning time, and class confinement), the organization of learning in secondary schools thwarts teachers' efforts to improve the quality of students' thinking.

A Culture of Teacher Isolation

A culture of teacher isolation is common to many departments and schools (Brown, 1991; Bullough, 1987; Little, 1990; Lortie, 1975; McLaughlin, Pfeifer, Swanson-Owens & Yee, 1986; Sarason, 1982). Teachers spend their day almost exclusively with students, operating in isolation from one another, much like separate galaxies in a vast universe of instruction. This isolation severely limits teachers' access to the curricular and instructional ideas of colleagues and shields them from both constructive criticism and positive recognition of their instructional practices. Opportunities are rarely available to discuss teaching techniques related to thinking, or specific ideas and issues regarding subject matter (and strategies to address this content with students). Staff development activities are limited to a few half-day sessions per year and are usually unrelated to any long-term agenda such as the promotion of higher-order thinking. All too often outstanding teaching techniques and superb lesson and unit ideas, while only a classroom away, are not shared among colleagues.

Such a culture discourages collective action even though teachers frequently face very similar instructional concerns. The culture of isolation, in fact, leads some teachers to withhold from colleagues their "hard earned" instructional ideas. In addition, individualism, noncommunication and, at times, competition contribute to the development of indiscriminate, uncritical attitudes toward instruction; that is, teachers "agree" to respect the practices of their colleagues regardless of their colleagues' effectiveness. The implicit rule is, "you don't bother me, I won't bother you."

Though presented as separate, these barriers are interconnected. For example, large total student load and large class size limit opportunities for thoughtful interaction between teachers and students, a situation which, in turn, contributes to teachers' low expectations of students. Instruction by transmission tends to foster a curriculum of coverage, and, in reciprocal fashion, the demands of content coverage necessitate instruction by lecture (transmission) to ensure that everything gets covered (if not learned). Limited planning time for teachers to exchange ideas with colleagues contributes to the continuation of a culture of isolation and traditional methods of instruction. Many additional linkages between the barriers could be identified.

The interconnection among barriers suggests that high-school reform efforts need to consider all of the barrier when mapping a plan of action. Ignored barriers are likely to reduce the effectiveness of any reform effort. For example, through in-service activities teachers may come to hold high expectations of students and reject transmission models of teaching, yet changes in the level of classroom thoughtfulness will be modest if teachers remain addicted to coverage or are given little planning time to discuss and change curriculum and instructional practices. Likewise, breaking down teacher isolation and reducing student load will have limited impact on instruction for higher-order thinking if teachers maintain low expectations of students or continue to regard teaching as the transmission of information and ideas.

If, indeed, the barriers are interconnected and all need to be addressed to achieve significant and sustained improvement in the promotion of students' thinking, then there may be no single logical starting point or necessary sequence with which to attack the barriers. The recommendations that follow, therefore, are not proposed as a specific "game plan," but rather as a summary of the kinds of activities and measures that are likely to help secondary schools overcome the various barriers to achieve greater levels of classroom thoughtfulness.

REFORM RECOMMENDATIONS

Because our study focused at the department rather than school-wide level, the recommendations are directed to departmental change. The recommendations are appropriate for a large audience because departmentalized structures dominate secondary schools and because outstanding examples of teacher collaboration and innovative teaching occur within a departmental context (McLaughlin, in press). Secondary schools considering or already exhibiting alternative organizational units (e.g., interdisciplinary teams, self-contained classes, house concepts, or "humanities departments" that combine English and social studies) could also benefit from these suggestions.

Five areas of reform are identified and specific suggestions are made with respect to each. For a variety of reasons, it will be difficult for any school, department, house, or interdisciplinary team interested in promoting classroom thoughtfulness to implement all of our recommendations. Ultimately, however, successful reform would seem to require substantial work in each of the five areas.

Make Higher-Order Thinking a Central Instructional Goal

The promotion of students' higher-order thinking needs to become a central if not the primary instructional goal in secondary schools. Other goals diffuse instruction for thinking and enable content coverage and instruction by transmission to maintain their dominant influence. Teacher enthusiasm for and commitment to the goal of thinking can be fostered by providing teachers with opportunities to engage in higher-order thinking with their peers about the subjects they teach, whether it be in department meetings, workshops, or in-service sessions (Newmann, Onosko & Stevenson, 1990). We especially recommend critical inquiry and discussion about a question or issue within teachers' disciplines of instruction. Having two colleagues offer opposing interpretations of a short story or poem during an English department meeting (followed by a full department discussion), or bringing in a scholar during a half-day in-service to help social studies staff critically analyze competing interpretations of an historical event can serve this purpose. Teachers struggling with higher-order challenges within their subject can prove exciting enough to enhance their own thinking, foster a commitment to thinking as a goal for their own intellectual growth as well as their students', and can call into question instructional practices that present "packaged" or unproblematic "answers" to questions, issues, and events. Hill (in press) believes these experiences move teachers away from the role of "teller" (or transmitter) to that of "learner," and help create a faculty culture that mirrors a classroom culture devoted to "active student learning."

Faculty discussion of the fundamental purposes of education and schooling also serves to instill commitment to thinking. Analysis of alternative rationales for promoting higher-order thinking in schools provides teachers with the intellectual "armor" and personal conviction necessary to risk new instructional approaches, limit content coverage, and justify this behavior to an, at times, questioning public. The process of rationale building opens lines of communication and creates the opportunity for the development of a common vision focused on thinking among a previously fractionated group of teachers.

Considering rationales for thinking should lead faculty to build more explicit conceptualizations of thinking itself—another activity that can develop teacher commitment to this goal. Reading and discussing models of thinking in the professional literature can provide teachers with a new and shared language to discuss their teaching efforts with colleagues. Our research indicates that the particular conception that emerges is of less importance than whether or not this discussion occurs. The most thoughtful schools in our study held different conceptions, but they all spent considerable time reflecting on the nature of thinking (King, 1991). Interestingly, of the three resources needed for thinking (knowledge, skills, and dispositions), the most thoughtful schools emphasized the knowledge component; that is, exploring with students difficult concepts, problems, and questions within the discipline. In light of secondary teachers' primary identification with their subject area of instruction, and research findings that skills do not readily transfer (Glaser, 1984; Larkin, 1989; Resnick, 1987), conceptions of thinking that emphasize subject matter understanding (i.e., knowledge) may prove most beneficial.[5]

Conceptualizing thinking can also play an important role in overcoming the barrier of teachers' low expectations of students, as teachers come to realize that higher-order thinking is a relative construct and therefore an intellectual adventure open to all students. The most thoughtful departments in our study were the only ones that provided in equal measure thoughtful learning experiences regardless of students' prior achievement. Reflecting upon the nature of higher-order thinking can also reveal to teachers how the press for coverage limits students' access to the in-depth knowledge, skills, and dispositions needed to carry out higher-order challenges. The most thoughtful teachers in our sample were comfortable with their decisions to reduce the breadth of their curricula, in part, we believe, because they not only were more committed to the goal of thinking, but possessed more elaborate conceptions of thinking relative to their less successful peers (Onosko, 1989).

Having teachers engage in higher-order thinking, build rationales for it, and develop conceptualizations of it will not guarantee a prominent place for thinking in teachers' instructional agendas, particularly in school districts where the principal indicators of teaching success is student performance on standardized norm-referenced exams. In districts such as these there is little incentive for teachers to emphasize higher-order thinking, and, in fact, such tests often prove

counterproductive to thinking (Fredericksen, 1984; Shepard, 1991). School leaders must shift public attention away from assessment practices that highlight knowledge retention to practices that demonstrate students' skilled use of knowledge[6] and, at the same time, reward teachers for instructional practices that reflect these new priorities. With school administration and public support, teacher commitment to higher-order thinking will increase through collaborative discussion and design of assessment practices that demonstrate students' abilities to interpret, analyze, and manipulate information and ideas. Issues surrounding assessment are addressed in much greater detail by Joe Walters, Steve Seidel, and Howard Gardner in Chapter 13.

Change Curriculum to Promote Thinking

The dilemma of breadth vs. depth of coverage cannot be resolved by choosing one over the other, in large part because a legitimate goal of education, indeed, definition of education itself, is to gain familiarity with a myriad of words, ideas, procedures, events, conventions, and so on. However, because research consistently indicates that in-depth inquiry is rare, curriculum designers need to balance the coverage dilemma by reducing breadth and significantly increasing opportunities for in-depth learning that involve students in higher-order challenges.[7] How is this to be achieved?

Designing in-depth lessons and units that challenge students' thinking is a novel undertaking for most secondary school teachers. Curriculum units need to be designed around one or a few focused questions and problems, rather than around a broad topic that typically serves as a "blackhole" or "magnet" for large quantities of expository information. Without a question or problem, there is little motivation or need to think. Question-based curricula encourage teachers to abandon the role of "knowledge transmitter" and instead assume the role of "inquiry facilitator." Students actively gather information and pursue ideas with a purpose (i.e., to address the problem or issue), rather than entertain "inert ideas" (Whitehead, 1929). In short, problem-based curricula can limit coverage, check teacher transmission of knowledge, consistently place students in the role of problem solver, and integrate instructional activities into a substantively coherent learning experience.[8]

To design effective problem-based units, teachers may need workshops, weekend or summer institutes, and other enrichment programs to gain deeper understanding of concepts, issues, and problems that can constitute the substance of curriculum aimed at higher-order thinking. This enrichment activity can begin in department meetings and in-service sessions. Eventually, teachers will need less formal assistance to explore substantive issues in their subjects with colleagues and their students. In the humanities and social sciences, these topics may include the nature of informal reasoning, inductive argument, normative inquiry, statistical proof, and, most importantly, conceptual understanding of the issues at hand (e.g., justifications for and challenges to the use of violence during the Civil Rights movement, or alternative strategies to recovery from economic depression). Facility with such concepts is needed to effectively probe student understanding through Socratic questioning during teacher-led discussions. This facility is also critical to the design of challenging classroom activities that place teachers in less dominant instructional roles, such as student-led debates or mock trials (Wineburg & Wilson, 1988).

To build their own "deep" understanding of subject matter, especially when few curriculum resources emphasize higher-order thinking in the subject, teachers will need to spend much more time discussing with colleagues broad course goals, ways to think about the subject matter itself, ways to organize and deliver it in units and lessons, and resource materials that will appropriately challenge students to think. We saw examples of curriculum design teams that taught the same course and worked effectively to create challenging lessons and units. Initially, teams of teachers might meet simply to share ways in which they construct lessons and units to address the same course content. Eventually the goal is

to encourage teams to meet regularly (daily or at least a few times per week) to plan lessons and units collectively, and to critique and revise those that have been recently taught. Exciting discussions can occur over which question or problem should frame the study of a particular topic, how best to introduce the issue, and which resource materials best provide competing perspectives or offer data without giving students the conclusive analysis.

To identify the central content (i.e., critical issues, problems, questions, and challenging concepts that will frame courses), experts in the field can be helpful in discussing various possibilities. At one of the outstanding departments, a history professor met with staff on a few occasions to discuss major themes, issues, movements, concepts, and ideologies important to the study of United States history. Teachers can also benefit from visits to other schools to observe alternative courses designed to challenge students' thinking. Teams will need opportunities to design curriculum during the summer as well as during the academic year.

An outstanding department in our sample recruited its best teachers to rebuild a required course disliked by all faculty, Freshman Social Studies (a combined study of world history, world cultures, and the social sciences). The team met regularly to design and critique lessons and units, and kept a detailed record of the course curriculum, including lesson summaries, handouts, readings, and homework assignments. The team created an exciting course that is now one of the most popular to teach among staff.

To build curriculum oriented more toward thinking, staff will need to discuss two important issues. One is how to acquire useful instructional materials; the other is how to reduce the breadth or vast range of course offerings. Limited monies necessitate careful selection of instructional materials. At present the bulk of curriculum dollars is allocated to coverage-oriented texts. Instead, trade books and other source materials that pursue problems and issues in-depth need to be purchased, and more resources are needed for photocopying (to facilitate the distribution of non-textbook readings and materials). Most of the thoughtful teachers we observed used textbooks sparingly, creating instead their own lessons and units by pulling from a wide variety of sources.[9]

With respect to the issue of course offerings, school and community must agree to reduce the range of courses currently available to students. The vast number of electives prevents common inquiry among teachers about how to teach, because teachers are less likely to find themselves teaching the same course. In this way the curriculum itself creates an organizational isolation that inhibits dialogue among teachers. It is also unreasonable to expect teachers to plan high-level study of three or more different sets of issues and problems, a situation confronting those teachers assigned more than two course preparations at once.

Revise Pedagogy to Promote Thinking

Accepting the goal of higher-order thinking, developing teachers' facility with issues and problems in their subject areas, and providing opportunities to collaboratively design curriculum is not enough to ensure thoughtful instruction. We observed some planning teams that focus almost exclusively on the substance of courses and units, with no collective attention as to how to teach it. Some team members taught didactically, others used Socratic dialogue and inquiry. Even when teams did discuss both lesson content and specific instructional moves, the actual level of classroom thoughtfulness experienced by students often varied considerably among team members. Interestingly, in both situations, teachers assumed that colleagues were providing similar learning experiences to students. Since secondary teachers rarely observe, discuss, and critique one another's classroom instruction, they have scant awareness of the details of how instruction varies within a team or department.

The sharing of actual teaching behavior with one or more colleagues can enhance classroom thoughtfulness. Discussion of instruction without observation can be useful, but verbal reconstruc-

tions of teaching cannot convey the important nuances and contextual cues required to understand why something may or may not "work." In large part this is probably due, as Bloom has coined it, to the "automaticity" of expert performance and their inability to articulate many of the specifics of how they do what they do (Bloom, 1986). Of the reform activities we have suggested, sharing instructional performances will prove most threatening to teachers, as many of their deeply held assumptions and beliefs about the nature of "good" teaching will, at times, be called into question. To support this new form of exchange, specific steps must be taken.

Chairs and outstanding department teachers at the most thoughtful schools in our sample demonstrated innovative teaching at department or in-service meetings, either live or with videotapes of their lessons. Both successful and "failed" efforts were discussed and critiqued. Teachers gained new ideas for teaching, were surprised to witness sophisticated thinking by some of their former students, found that critique of a colleague's lesson was appreciated and productive (rather than taboo), and valued the risk taking of the presenters. Demonstration lessons by outsiders in teachers' own classes are especially powerful, because teachers immediately see the effectiveness of an approach. Teachers with low expectations of their students have their assumptions called into question, if not fundamentally changed, when they witness their students performing at a high level of discourse previously dismissed as impossible. Such demonstrations can also help to break down a commonly held assumption that extensive didactic presentation of information needs to occur before students can be asked to think about material. Demonstration lessons can also illustrate the emphasis upon depth of focus in instructional activities. Staff developers typically design similar activities with teachers and cite similar benefits (Newmann, Onosko & Stevenson, 1990).

The type of communication advocated here involves much scrutiny and personal risk and, therefore, should be introduced gradually. It may be helpful to begin dialogue about instruction at a general level (e.g., broad course goals or curriculum frameworks), then move toward discussing and planning lesson activities (but without classroom visits), and, eventually, to participate in peer observation and follow-up analysis. Sharing instructional ideas both verbally and in written form with or without direct observation can be very beneficial. This can illustrate motivating introductory activities to begin a unit or learning sequence; questioning sequences that move a class of dispassionate students to animated and rigorous exchange of ideas; small group activities that stimulate student inquiry; or, specific analogies that stretch, refute, or fortify student understanding of difficult concepts, issues, or problems. As this type of sharing increases and teachers begin to trust and feel that they know the work of their colleagues, direct observation will become less threatening.

It is unclear whether observation only by the department chair (or lead teacher) will prove sufficient to significantly improve teachers' instruction for thinking at most schools, though this arrangement existed at one of the outstanding departments in our sample. More cross-fertilization of instructional ideas will take place (not to mention more intimate and diverse collegial relations) when the chair promotes reflection on pedagogy among all department members.

Also open to question is whether team teaching is needed to significantly increase classroom thoughtfulness, or whether peer observation is sufficient for the task. Team teaching creates additional challenges of coordination and curriculum planning. Minimally, it would seem, teachers need opportunities to regularly share and discuss their instructional performances with at least one or more colleagues. Nothing less than ongoing clinical observation must become an accepted and built-in part of teachers' jobs.

Finally, our discussions with teachers indicated that many have greatly benefitted from enrichment activities away from their home schools that involve working with and learning from teachers from other institutions. Participating in networks that allow sharing among like-minded "strangers"

is apparently less threatening and engenders greater confidence and risk taking upon return to one's school. These experiences validate teachers' work and thereby enhance teachers' commitment to promoting students' thinking by revealing to them that they are part of a much larger educational movement.

Alter Organizational Features

To effectively pursue the reform measures suggested above (i.e., to gain teacher commitment to the goal of higher-order thinking and to revise curriculum and pedagogy to promote students' thinking), many organizational features of today's schools require modification.

Collaboration and planning time for teachers needs to be increased. Teachers should have at least two hours of preparation time per day to work with colleagues in ways already identified, to assemble materials, to work individually with students, to call parents, and to complete other administrative duties.[10] At one of the most thoughtful schools in our study, the department chair juggled schedules to ensure that each day all teachers of at least one of the required courses could meet as a group to plan lessons and units. Usually teachers interested in collaboration have to meet before and after school, or during lunch. Reducing elective course offerings, as mentioned in a previous section, is one way to increase the likelihood that teachers teaching the same course will be able to find a planning partner during one of their preparation periods. However, creating an extra period for teachers at the beginning or end of each day may be the best and least complicated way to ensure that teachers within and across departments are allocated structured time to collaboratively discuss curriculum and instruction issues related to higher-order thinking.[11]

Another important change is to extend class meeting time beyond the customary 45–50 minute period and to reduce the number of different subjects students confront each day. Teachers cannot expect high quality work from students if they are given less than an hour to produce it, and students cannot be expected to seriously think about five to six different topics per day. Creating larger time blocks and reducing students' daily course load will generate controversy. The school community will need to debate the merits of more concentrated in-depth inquiry vs. broader coverage.[12]

The issue of reduced course loads also applies to reform leaders, be they department chairs, lead teachers, or heads of interdisciplinary teams. Fewer teaching assignments per day (only one or two) will enable reform leaders to work more closely with staff to improve classroom thoughtfulness. This work may include team teaching with a colleague, modeling instruction for a colleague or observing their instruction, covering a class so a colleague can attend an afternoon workshop, peer planning a lesson or unit, identifying and purchasing resource materials for staff, and so on. Chairs at two of the three outstanding departments in our sample had reduced teaching loads (one to two classes per semester) and were conducting just these sorts of activities with staff (King, 1991). The third chair operated without a reduced load, yet engaged in many of the same activities at great personal sacrifice. He used his own planning periods to work with staff, or would meet with colleagues before and after school and in the evenings.

To significantly improve the quantity and quality of oral and written dialogue between teachers and students, it also seems necessary to reduce teachers' average class size to 20 or fewer and their total student load to about 80. As discussed earlier in the section on barriers, classroom discourse and teacher nurturance of students' thinking is undermined when classes are large, and teachers refrain from assigning written tasks and reacting to students' thinking on paper when large total student load creates too much additional work. Without a reduction in the number of students per class and all day, higher-order thinking will continue to be found only in the classrooms of the exceptionally committed and talented teachers. It is unreasonable to expect the vast majority of teachers to make, year after year, the kinds of personal and family sacrifices that are necessary to promote higher-order thinking in schools as currently organized. Teachers need to be aware of these structural, school-wide impediments to their efforts, both to limit self-castigation for achieving modest success at promoting students' thinking and to heighten their awareness of the need to work politically to improve the working and learning conditions of teachers and students.

Finally, reformers may want to consider providing common work areas for teachers, rather than assigning separate rooms that serve as buffers and private offices, to further structure opportunities for faculty dialogue and to create a culture of collaboration. At two of the three outstanding departments in our sample, teachers' work stations were next to each other, creating an atmosphere and expectation of frequent and informal exchange of classroom ideas and experiences. Structuring this space enhanced not only faculty dialogue of education-related matters, but enriched teachers' understanding of colleagues as individuals.

Develop Strong and Shared Leadership

Strong leadership directed to the promotion of classroom thoughtfulness is needed to generate changes in teachers' beliefs, curriculum, pedagogy, and school organization. Strong leadership is particularly critical at the department level (or teaching team level). Department leaders and teachers will require, and may have to help generate, strong support for higher-order thinking from the community, central administration, and the principal. In addition, strong leadership needs to be found and cultivated within the ranks of the teaching staff by the chair or other reform leader. The histories of the three outstanding departments in our study each reveal strong department chair leadership that, over time, became shared leadership among many in the department.[13] In what ways can this shared leadership be fostered?

Department chair reformers need to encourage the efforts of teachers who are interested in developing better ways to promote students' thinking and learning. Chairs (with financial support and encouragement from the principal and central administration) create opportunities to enable these teachers to learn more about higher-order thinking. They may:

- provide release time to attend or present at a workshop on higher-order thinking;

- bring in an outside expert to share instructional strategies designed to promote thinking, or to discuss how one's resolution of the coverage dilemma is intimately connected to one's overriding educational goals;

- provide release time to visit innovative schools to learn of their approaches to teaching and curriculum design;

- secure summer monies for members to collaboratively write curriculum that places a premium on cognitive challenge;

- encourage teachers to experiment with new approaches in their classrooms;

- share successes with fellow staff members informally and during department meetings.[14]

If members of the public, school administrators, or others express reservations about the new attention to thinking in the curriculum, the chair offers support through both explanation and the organization of political influence.

Reform-minded chairs use department meetings and in-service days to promote reflective, substantive discussions whether the topic is about prospective candidates in a local election, students limitations in writing a persuasive essay, the merits and demerits of ability grouping, or deciding upon the main instructional goals of the department for the year. Such discussions help to foster a serious intellectual climate and prepare the groundwork for a faculty learning community focused on the promotion of students' thinking (Hill, 1992). Department meetings can include other valuable activities such as sharing and critique of videotaped lessons, small group competitions to create the best lesson plan using only the specified pages of a textbook or a published article, or brainstorming provocative questions to frame a unit and debating the merits of each.

Department chair reformers need not only to coordinate opportunities for staff, they must model many of the practices and attitudes associated with teaching for higher-order thinking. For example, chairs must be able to model instructional activities new to staff that promote students' thinking (e.g., generating hypotheses with students on why there is an increased incidence of suicide among youth). They should be comfortable asking colleagues for help in the design of lessons and units. They should encourage staff to visit their classes and to offer feedback and suggestions. They should express commitment to low achievers and demonstrate it by teaching classes comprised in part or completely of low achievers.

Finally, department reformers need to be exempted from the process of formally evaluating staff. The risk-filled world of instruction for thinking necessitates that teachers know it is safe to try and fail at new instructional approaches and to openly share their concerns and vulnerabilities with the chair and staff. Formal evaluation must be left to other administrative personnel if the chair is to help create and participate fully in a collaborative, collegial department culture.

It is through these leadership efforts that teachers come to reevaluate their teaching goals, revise curriculum to challenge students' thinking, show interest in instructional practices that promote higher-order thinking, and request changes in organizational structure that are more conducive to thoughtfulness. Because teachers' (and students') efforts to become more thoughtful can be thwarted by staff who continue traditional practice, significant and sustained improvement in the promotion of students' higher-order thinking requires the involvement of most if not all of the school's teaching staff. The skill, understanding, and compassion of department chairs (or other reform leaders) is essential for this faculty transition to occur.

NEEDED AREAS OF FUTURE RESEARCH

Much work needs to be done to better understand the process of creating more thoughtful learning environments in schools, including empirical tests of the recommendations we have proposed. A few of the many questions that need exploration include:

- How do thoughtful teachers go about constructing and delivering lessons and units that emphasize higher-order thinking? Ideally, we need to uncover general principles and strategies of design and teaching, assuming they exist, and, if Shulman (in Brandt, 1992) is correct, we also need detailed case studies across the entire range of topics and issues contained in the school curriculum.

- We know that higher-order thinking involves not only knowledge and skills, but also curiosity, motivation, and risk taking (i.e., dispositions). How do teachers create challenging yet exciting and safe learning environments that encourage students to take intellectual risks, ask questions, challenge one anothers' ideas, and persist at difficult tasks? What behaviors and attitudes on the part of teachers help to foster and then sustain these environments? Relatedly, how do teachers cultivate dispositions of thoughtfulness? Compared to skill instruction and teaching for understanding, we know very little about how to develop thoughtful habits of mind.

- How do school reformers change department and faculty dialogue from "administrivia" and other procedural concerns to substantive discussion of curricular and instructional issues related to promoting students' higher-order thinking? How do they nurture dialogue and risk taking among staff? What are some of the more effective strategies/activities to facilitate this transition? What attributes and interpersonal skills do successful reform leaders (department chairs, team leaders, lead teachers) bring to this process?

- What are the advantages and disadvantages to school-wide vs. department-based reform efforts to promote thinking? Do school-wide reform efforts present generic skills conceptions of thinking rather than in-depth knowledge conceptions due to the diversity of the audience? Compared to school-wide efforts, is productive, open communication more likely to occur among department members since some degree of collegiality and personal relationship has already been established? In short, to what extent should reform efforts be structured around departmental change, rather than attempting to work with the school staff as a single unit?

CONCLUSION

We have offered a conception of thinking and a framework with which to assess classroom thoughtfulness. We have also described dominant barriers to the promotion of students' thinking and suggested reform activities and measures that are likely to help schools overcome these barriers and achieve greater levels of classroom thoughtfulness.

We would like to claim that if schools followed many or most of our recommendations, success would be virtually guaranteed. Unfortunately, this is not the case. Most students, parents, teachers, civic leaders, and other citizens have consistently made the cultivation of thoughtfulness a low priority among educational aims, in spite of paying lip service to the ideal for years. Why? It appears that powerful forces of human personality, social structure, and cultural values may stand in the way of committed implementation of these otherwise reasonable suggestions. Higher-order thinking often calls for the resolution of conflicting views, tolerance for uncertainty and ambiguity, self-criticism, independence of judgment, and serious consideration of ideas that may challenge or undermine conventional wisdom. In this sense, thinking involves difficult mental work that can be personally unsettling, because it disrupts cognitive stability, order, and predictability. For many, it is psychologically more comfortable not to think too deeply about anything.

Critical thinking also increases the probability of youth challenging adult authority and of citizens challenging economic and political centers of power. Thus, thinking can be considered subversive and socially dangerous by dominant interests whose legitimacy is questioned. Some would argue that the very survival of certain social institutions (e.g., advertising, hierarchies of labor

within corporations) depends on limiting the opportunity to think to a small segment of the population.

Finally, cultural orientations that prescribe certain forms of interpersonal relations, play, recreation, and religious and artistic expression can minimize the importance of the kind of mental activity promoted here as higher-order thinking.

All is not doom and gloom—our findings indicate that it is possible for high-school departments to promote higher-order thinking, and that students find thoughtful classes more engaging and interesting. However in light of the issues just raised, those interested in the promotion of thinking will need to view this process as more than the sum total of analyses and reform recommendations presented here. Instead, it must be seen more broadly as a complex, long-term, and risky adventure in social change.

FOOTNOTES

1. The high degree of specificity that can occur in the naming of thinking skills is illustrated in Marzano et al. (1988), which notes 21 different core thinking skills, including such items as defining problems, setting goals, observing, ordering, inferring, summarizing, and establishing criteria.

2. The development of these indicators and selection of the six most critical are described more fully in Newmann (1990a, 1990b). See also Schrag (1987, 1989).

3. To estimate inter-rater reliability, 87 lessons were observed independently by different pairs of raters drawn from a team of six researchers. Considering the six dimensions in the CHOT scale, each scored from "1" to "5," the two observers agreed precisely in 64% of the ratings, they differed by one point or less on 96% of the ratings, and the overall average correlation between two raters was .76.

4. Keating's (1988) review of the research on adolescent thinking uncovered no support for the argument that students lack the cognitive capacity to successfully engage in higher-order thinking. Because higher-order thinking is a relative rather than an absolute concept, all students

regardless of cognitive capacity can, in theory, be given a problem or task that involves them in higher-order thinking.

5. See Prawat (1991) for a detailed discussion of this view.

6. Wiggins (1989a, 1989b, 1991) and Sizer (1992) have discussed assessment practices and standards that demonstrate students' higher-order thinking and understanding.

7. Curriculum and instructional practices in postsecondary schools must also reduce emphasis on survey curriculum and transmission forms of pedagogy if the next generation of teachers is to acquire concrete models of, appreciation for, and skill at conducting lessons that challenge students to think.

8. A more detailed summary of student-active, indepth, problem-based unit design can be found in Onosko (1992), along with a sample unit plan by Ms. Elizabeth Wood.

9. State or national projects could help by creating better banks of resource materials designed to challenge students' thinking. At present, teach-

ers must often create their own curricula, which drains time and energy away from other important tasks such as reflection on pedagogy or responding to students' individual work.

10. Stigler and Stevenson (1991) document how American teachers relative to their more successful Asian counterparts have much less planning time per day and structured opportunities to work with colleagues. According to the authors, these organizational obstacles prevent teachers from "preparing lessons that require the discovery of knowledge and the construction of understanding."

11. An extra period would require that teachers formally extend their school day in the morning or afternoon. Teacher resistance would be greatly reduced if the other organizational changes suggested here were also implemented. Sizer (1992) has proposed an alternative school schedule designed for departmentalized teams that ensures daily collective planning time for team members and time to meet with other school staff at the beginning and end of each day.

12. This change could take at least one of two forms. The less drastic move would be to have students continue to take four to six different courses each semester (or quarter, or year) but schedule the courses for every other day. In this way, students would pursue two to three subjects on one day, the remaining two to three the next day, back to the original two to three on the third, and so on. The more radical move would be to have students pursue the same two to three subjects each day, cutting in half the total number of subjects studied in a given quarter, semester, or year.

13. Chairs at the three outstanding departments in our sample all said that one of their goals was to make themselves obsolete.

14. See Hill (in press) for a discussion of the ways in which department chairs can facilitate the development of a culture of teacher collaboration directed toward the promotion of students' thinking.

REFERENCES

Alter, J., & Salmon, J. (1987). *Assessing higher order thinking skills.* Northwest Regional Educational Laboratory.

Beyer, B. (1987). *Practical strategies for the teaching of thinking.* Boston: Allyn & Bacon.

Bloom, B. S. (1986). Automaticity: The hands and feet of genius. *Educational Leadership, 43*(5), 70–77.

Brandt, R. (1992). On research on teaching: A conversation with Lee Shulman. *Educational Leadership, 49*(7), 14–19.

Brown, R. (1991). *Schools of thought: How the politics of literacy shape thinking in the classroom.* San Francisco: Jossey-Bass.

Bullough, R. (1987). Accommodation and tension: Teachers, teacher role, and the culture of teaching. In J. Smyth (Ed.), *Educating teachers: Changing the nature of pedagogical knowledge.* London: Falmer Press.

Chance, P. (1986). *Thinking in the classroom: A survey of programs.* New York: Teachers College Press.

Costa, Arthur L. (1985). *Developing minds: A resource book for teaching thinking.* Alexandria, VA: A.S.C.D.

Cuban, L. (1984a). *How teachers taught: Constancy and change in American classrooms; 1890–1980.* New York: Longman.

Cuban, L. (1984b). Policy and research dilemmas in

the teaching of reasoning: Unplanned designs. *Review of Educational Research, 54*(4), 655–681.

DeBono, E. (1983). The direct teaching of thinking as a skill. *Phi Delta Kappan, 64*(10), 703–708.

Dewey, J. (1933). *How we think.* Boston: D.C. Heath.

Doyle, W., Sandford, J., Clements, B., Schmidt-French, B., and Emmer, E. (1983). *Managing academic tasks: An interim report of the junior school study* (R & D Report 6186). Austin: University of Texas, Research and Development Center for Teacher Education.

Duckworth, E. (1987). *The having of wonderful ideas.* New York: Teachers College Press.

Ennis, R. (1962). The concept of critical thinking. *Harvard Educational Review, 32*(1), 81–111.

Fredericksen, N. (1984). The real test bias: Influences of testing on teaching and learning. *American Psychologist, 39*(3), 193–202.

Glaser, R. (1984). Education and thinking: The role of knowledge. *American Psychologist, 18*(3), 93–105.

Hare, W. (1985). Open-mindedness in the classroom. *Journal of Philosophy of Education, 19*(2), 251–259.

Hill, D. (1992). *Building a learning community: The challenge of department leadership.* Stanford University, Palo Alto, CA: Center for Research on the Context of Secondary School Teaching.

Keating, D. (1988). *Adolescents' ability to engage in critical thinking.* Madison, WI: National Center on Effective Secondary Schools.

King, M. B. (1991). Leadership efforts that facilitate classroom thoughtfulness in social studies. *Theory and Research in Social Education, 19*(4), 366–389.

Ladwig, J. G. (1991). Organizational features and classroom thoughtfulness in secondary social studies departments. *Theory and Research in Social Education, 19*(4), 390–408.

Larkin, J. (1989). What kind of knowledge transfers? In L. Resnick (Ed.), *Knowing, learning, and instruction* (pp. 283–306). Hillsdale, NJ: Erlbaum.

Little, J. (1990). The persistence of privacy: Autonomy and initiative in teachers' professional relations. *Teachers College Record, 91*(4), 509–536.

Lortie, D. (1975). *Schoolteacher.* Chicago: University of Chicago Press.

Mann, L. (1979). *On the trail of process: A historical perspective on cognitive processes and their training.* New York: Grune & Stratton.

Marzano, et al. (1988). *Dimensions of thinking.* Alexandria, VA: Association for Supervision and Curriculum Development.

McLaughlin, M. (in press). What matters most in teachers' workplace context. In J. Little & M. McLaughlin (Eds.), *Cultures and contexts of teaching.* New York: Teachers College Press.

McLaughlin, M., Pfeifer, R., Swanson-Owens, D., & Yee, S. (1986). Why teachers won't teach. *Phi Delta Kappan, 67*(6), 420–426.

McNeil, L. M. (1986). *Contradictions of control: School structure and school knowledge.* New York: Routledge & Kegan Paul.

McPeck, J. (1981). *Critical thinking and education.* New York: St. Martin's Press.

Newmann, F. (1988). Can depth replace coverage in the high school curriculum? *Phi Delta Kappan, 68*(5), 345–348.

Newmann, F. (1990a). Higher order thinking in social studies: A rationale for the assessment of classroom thoughtfulness. *Journal of Curriculum Studies, 22*(1), 41–56.

Newmann, F. (1990b). Qualities of thoughtful social studies classes: An empirical profile. *Journal of Curriculum Studies, 22*(3), 253–275.

Newmann, F. (1991a). Higher order thinking in the teaching of social studies: Connections between theory and practice. In D. Perkins, J. Segal, and J. Voss (Eds.), *Informal reasoning and education,* (pp. 381–400). Hillsdale, NJ: Lawrence Erlbaum.

Newmann, F. (1991b). The prospects for classroom thoughtfulness in high school social studies. In C. Collins, J. Mangieri (Eds.), *Teaching thinking: An agenda for the twenty-first century.* Hillsdale, NJ: Lawrence Erlbaum.

Newmann, F. (1992). Higher order thinking and prospects for classroom thoughtfulness. In F. Newmann (Ed.), *Student engagement and achievement in American secondary schools.* New York: Teachers College Press.

Newmann, F., Onosko, J., & Stevenson, R. (1990). Staff development for higher order thinking: A synthesis of practical wisdom. *Journal of Staff Development, 11*(3), 48–55.

Nickerson, R. S. (1988). On improving thinking through instruction. In E. Z. Rothkopf (Ed.), *Review of Research in Education, 15,* 3–57.

Nickerson, R. S., Perkins, D., & Smith, E. (1985). *The teaching of thinking.* Hillsdale, NJ: Erlbaum.

Onosko, J. (1989). Comparing teachers' thinking about promoting students thinking. *Theory and Research in Social Education, 17*(3), 174–195.

Onosko, J. (1991). Barriers to the promotion of higher order thinking in social studies. *Theory and Research in Social Education, 19*(4), 340–365.

Onosko, J. (1992a). Exploring the thinking of thoughtful teachers. *Educational Leadership, 49*(7), 40–43.

Onosko, J. (1992b). An approach to designing thoughtful units. *The Social Studies, 83*(5), 193–196.

Passmore, J. (1967). On teaching to be critical. In R. S. Peters (ed.), *The concept of education.* London: Routledge & Kegan Paul.

Perkins, D., Jay, E., & Tishman, S. (in press). Beyond abilities: A dispositional theory of thinking. *The Merrill-Palmer Quarterly.*

Powell, A., Farrar, E., & Cohen, D. (1985). *The shopping mall high school: Winners and losers in the educational marketplace.* Boston: Houghton Mifflin.

Prawat, R. (1991). The value of ideas: The immersion approach to the development of thinking. *Educational Researcher, 20*(2), 3–10.

Pressiesen, B. (1986). *Critical thinking and thinking skills: State of the art definitions and practice in public schools.* Philadelphia, PA: Research for Better Schools.

Resnick, L. B. (1987). *Education and learning to think.* Washington, DC: National Academy Press.

Sarason, S. (1982). *The culture of the school and the problem of change.* Boston: Allyn & Bacon.

Schrag, F. (1987). *Evaluating thinking in school.* Madison, WI: National Center on Effective Secondary Schools.

Schrag, F. (1988). *Thinking in school and society.* New York: Rutledge.

Schrag, F. (1989). Are there levels of thinking? *Teachers College Record, 90*(4), 529–533.

Shaver, J., Davis, O., & Helburn, S. (1979, February). The status of social studies education: Impressions from three NSF studies. *Social Education, 43,* 150–153.

Shepard, L. (1991). Interview on assessment issues with Lorrie Shepard. *Educational Researcher, 20*(2), 21–23.

Siegel, H. (1988). *Educating reason.* New York: Routledge & Kegan Paul.

Sizer, T. (1984). *Horace's compromise: The dilemma of the American high school.* Boston: Houghton Mifflin.

Sizer, T. (1992). *Horace's school: Redesigning the American high school.* Boston: Houghton Mifflin.

Stigler, J., & Stevenson, H. (1991). How Asian teachers polish each lesson to perfection. *American Educator, 15*(1), 12–20.

Walsh, D., & Paul, R. (1987). *The goal of critical thinking: From educational ideal to educational reality.* Washington, DC: American Federation of Teachers.

Whitehead, A. (1929). *The aims of education.* New York: Free Press.

Wiggins, G. (1989). The futility of trying to teach everything of importance. *Educational Leadership, 47*(3), 44–59.

Wiggins, G. (1989a). Teaching to the (authentic) test. *Educational Leadership, 47*(4), 41–47.

Wiggins, G. (1989b). A true test: Toward more authentic and equitable assessment. *Phi Delta Kappan, 71*(5), 703–713.

Wiggins, G. (1991). Standards, not standardization: Evoking quality student work. *Educational Leadership, 49*(2), 18–25.

Wineburg, S., & Wilson, S. (1988). Models of wisdom in the teaching of history. *Phi Delta Kappan, 70*(1), 50–58.

CHAPTER THREE

KNOWLEDGE TRANSFORMING

TEACHERS, STUDENTS, AND RESEARCHERS AS LEARNERS IN A COMMUNITY

PENELOPE L. PETERSON

MICHIGAN STATE UNIVERSITY

Dr. Penelope L. Peterson is University Distinguished Professor of Education at Michigan State University. Dr. Peterson has conducted numerous studies concerning children's learning. She also serves as codirector of the Institute for Research on Teaching at Michigan State University. She has published extensively in the fields of learning and teaching mathematics, and teachers' knowledge of students' knowledge and cognitions in mathematics.

Within current education reform contexts, teachers are being asked to change. Not only are they being asked to change what they teach and how they teach, but they are also being asked to change their fundamental beliefs and knowledge and to reconsider what they have known and thought all their lives. They are being asked to teach children who are growing up and learning in diverse social and cultural contexts in a global community—contexts that differ from those in which the teachers themselves grew up and learned. Having grown up and learned in a world their students never knew, teachers are being asked to prepare students to live in a global community they do not now know and to live in a world they themselves will not live to see. To prepare students for such an unknown world, teachers are being told, they need to teach their students to think for themselves and to learn their whole lives long after they leave school.

Not only are these changes that teachers are being asked to make nontrivial in themselves, but they are nontrivial because they require fundamental changes in views of knowledge. Teachers and students are living in a world at a time when knowledge is swiftly changing, access to knowledge is widening and growing, and the availability and sophistication of tools to access, use, and share knowledge are increasing rapidly. But in classrooms in schools, most teachers and students see knowledge as static and unchanged, access to knowledge as narrowly confined by the textbook and the teacher, and the use of tools as limited in scope and purpose. And what students know and need to know in schools continues to be narrowly defined by and confined to the reading, writing, and 'rithmetic curriculum that has been taught in elementary schools for years.

Why have teachers' practices and students' learning in school remained so little changed over the years while the world has changed and knowledge has grown all around them? Three years ago while reading aloud to my three-year-old daughter the story of her favorite literary character, Pippi Longstocking, I came across a passage that helped me see more clearly the problem. I came to understand at last what sociolinguists have been pointing out for a long time—how students' knowledge and learning has been framed within the task structures and discourse patterns of elementary school. These task structures, discourse patterns, and frames for analyzing students' knowledge in school have remained static and unchanged across time and space. In the following passage written in 1950, children's author Astrid Lindgren portrays what happens when a world-wise nine-year-old girl, Pippi Longstocking, goes to school for the first time. Pippi lives by herself with her horse and her monkey in a small town in Sweden and knows, understands, and does wondrous things all by herself, and occasionally with the help of her two friends, Tommy and Annika, but always without the aid of grownups. In Lindgren's story the grownups in the town where Pippi lives decide that it is scandalous for a nine-year-old girl to live all by herself in Villa Villekulla because "all children must have someone to advise them, and all children must go to school to learn the multiplication tables." So Pippi goes to school, and after introducing herself, she has the following conversation with her teacher:

"Indeed?" said the teacher. "Well, then we shall call you Pippi too. But now,"

she continued, "suppose we test you a little and see what you know. You are a big girl and no doubt know a great deal already. Let us begin with arithmetic. Pippi, can you tell me what seven and five are?"

Pippi astonished and dismayed, looked at her and said, "Well, if you don't know that yourself, you needn't think I'm going to tell you."

All the children stared in horror at Pippi, and the teacher explained that one couldn't answer that way in school.

"I beg your pardon," said Pippi contritely, "I didn't know that. I won't do it again."

"No, let us hope not," said the teacher. "And now I will tell you that seven and five are twelve."

"See that!" said Pippi. "You knew it yourself. Why are you asking then?"

The teacher decided to act as if nothing unusual were happening and went on with her examination.

"Well, now, Pippi, how much do you think eight and four are?"

"Oh, about sixty-seven," hazarded Pippi.

"Of course not," said the teacher. "Eight and four are twelve."

"Well now, really, my dear little woman," said Pippi, "that is carrying things too far. You just said that seven and five are twelve. There should be some rhyme and reason to things even in school . . . "

The teacher decided there was no point in trying to teach Pippi any more arithmetic. She began to ask the other children the arithmetic questions.

"Can Tommy answer this one?" she asked. "If Lisa has seven apples and Axel has nine apples, how many apples do they have altogether?"

"Yes, you tell, Tommy," Pippi interrupted, "and tell me too, if Lisa gets a stomach-ache and Axel gets more stomach-ache, whose fault is it and where did they get hold of the apples in the first place?"

The teacher tried to pretend that she hadn't heard, and she turned to Annika . . . .[1]

What Astrid Lindgren has captured so poignantly in this passage is a failure to understand, but it is not just a failure to understand by the student, but also a failure to understand by the teacher.[2] While Pippi sees the task as trying to make sense, the teacher sees the task as assessing what Pippi "knows" against a body of mathematical knowledge that is "fixed" and defined and known by the teacher who is the authority for knowing. The teacher is operating within a standard discourse frame typically used in school— question, answer, teacher response. In this frame the discourse is convergent—the teacher expects only one answer, and only one answer is appropriate. But Pippi is operating with a discourse frame typically used in life—one of conversation where both parties are trying to understand and communicate with each other. In a conversation the discourse is open and the two participants jointly construct where the conversation goes and ends up. Pippi makes several attempts to open up the discourse and engage in an authentic exchange of ideas with her teacher. But each time her teacher does not respond because she doesn't see or understand Pippi's perspective. From the teacher's perspective, she is the "teacher" and this is the way you teach. The teacher decides that there is no point in trying to "teach" Pippi, and she turns to quiz the other children. She poses a word problem to Tommy. Unwilling to be silenced and still considering herself to be part of the conversation, Pippi tries to turn the word problem into an authentic one. Finally the teacher uses the ultimate weapon that any participant has in a conversation—she withdraws from the conversation. While the teacher appears to be unchanged and not to have learned from the interchange, it is less clear whether or not Pippi has changed or learned. Perhaps Pippi learned what reformers argue many students have learned in our nation's schools: tasks and talk in school

needn't make sense, school tasks shouldn't be seen as authentic activity but rather seen as only part of school, and the ultimate weapon that any person has is to withdraw from the conversation and to cease to participate.

In our nation's classrooms today, most discourse, mathematical tasks, and frames for analyzing student learning are still of the type that Lindgren so aptly characterized nearly half a century ago. Most discourse is teacher question, student reply, and teacher evaluative response.[3] Most mathematics tasks on which students work in classrooms are computational or routine problems. Most often the authority for knowing resides with the teacher, and the teacher attempts to analyze what a student "knows" by looking and listening for convergent thinking and "right" answers.[4]

But reformers today are arguing for a different kind of mathematics teaching that encourages the kind of mathematical knowledge and mathematical power that children of today are going to need in the changing world of tomorrow. What will such "visionary" mathematics teaching look like? How will teachers learn what they will need to know to teach this way? What kind of changes and learning by others will be needed to transform teachers and teaching in these ways? How might research and researchers contribute to these transformations? We consider these questions through case analysis of the knowledge, learning, and teaching of one teacher, Annie Keith, who has transformed her mathematics teaching practice; and we consider her changes in relation to her learning and the learning of researchers and other teachers with whom she has been involved.

RELATING RESEARCH TO LEARNING AND TEACHING: ANNIE KEITH AND "CGI"

Annie Keith, had just completed her first year of teaching in the summer of 1986 when she began participating in the development of Cognitively Guided Instruction (CGI)—a research-based approach to elementary mathematics learning and teaching. I first met Annie Keith as one of the three researchers who was involved in developing CGI.

THE RESEARCHERS' PERSPECTIVE

In 1985 three of us at the Wisconsin Research and Development Center—Thomas Carpenter, Elizabeth Fennema, and I—began to develop a research-based intervention aimed at changing first-grade teachers' mathematics practices in ways that might follow from neo-constructivist learning theory and research conducted in the late '70s and early '80s on the development of children's problem-solving knowledge in addition and subtraction (Carpenter, Moser, & Romberg 1982; Riley, Greeno, & Heller 1983). In our approach, which we call CGI, we made explicit the actual evidence for our own constructivist views of mathematics learning by sharing with teachers what Tom Carpenter had learned from his research about children's extensive knowledge and abilities to solve addition and subtraction problems before they even enter school. Rather than presenting this research-based knowledge to teachers as decontextualized principles or conclusions, we presented the teachers with the actual data from Carpenter's study in the form of videotaped cases of five-year-old children solving various types of addition and subtraction word problems, including those types that most adults have believed young children incapable of solving. We also presented teachers with two frameworks or sets of ideas constructed by Carpenter (1985) from these data. One framework described the 11 addition/subtraction word problem types as children think about them; the other presented the several kinds of strategies that children tend to develop to solve these problems as they progress from using concrete modeling and counting strategies toward using their knowledge of remembered addition and subtraction number facts. Also, rather than presenting the teachers with either a curriculum program or a preconceived and prepackaged set of instructional procedures

that we had developed based on this knowledge, we worked with teachers to figure out how this new research-based knowledge of children's mathematics learning and problem solving in addition and subtraction might be useful in their classroom practices.

At the beginning of our National Science Foundation–supported project, we recruited 40 first-grade teachers from the Madison, WI, area. With the understanding and agreement of the teachers, we assigned the teachers randomly to either an experimental group that experienced the monthlong CGI workshop the first summer in 1986 or a control group that experienced the same workshop the second summer in 1987. During the workshop (for which the teachers received university credit), the teachers were given access to two frameworks—one for problem types and a second for children's solution strategies—through a set of readings written by Fennema and Carpenter, through presentations by Carpenter, and through class discussion. Teachers viewed videotapes of children solving addition/subtraction word problems until the teachers could identify both the problem types and strategies with relative ease. Teachers also interviewed five- and six-year-old children to see for themselves whether children actually used the solution strategies that had been discussed. We designed the workshop in the following way:

> We did not tell teachers what to do with the knowledge they had gained. We discussed the importance of a teacher's knowledge of how each child solves problems; the place of drill on number facts; and the necessity for children to think and talk about their own problem solutions to each other and to the teacher. We talked about adapting the problems (by type of problem or size of number in the problem) given to a child depending on what the child understands and can do. We discussed writing problems around themes related to children's lives and classroom activities. We gave the teachers time to plan how they would use their new knowl-

edge in their classrooms during the following year. Teachers talked extensively with us and with other teachers about possible implications of the knowledge about addition and subtraction. Most teachers wrote examples of all of the problem types to use in their classrooms, and tentatively planned one unit that they would teach sometime during the school year. (Peterson, Fennema, & Carpenter, 1991, pp. 75–76)

Since the initial workshop, we have written extensively about our findings related to teachers' use of CGI and the influence of CGI on teachers' knowledge, beliefs, practices, and on their children's problem solving in addition and subtraction and children's knowledge of number facts (Carpenter, Fennema, Peterson, Chiang, & Loef, 1989; Peterson, Fennema, Carpenter, & Loef, 1989; Peterson, Fennema, and Carpenter, 1991). After the first year, we concluded that teachers who experienced the CGI workshop during summer, 1986, and used CGI in their teaching the following year, changed their assumptions about learning to be more in line with CGI ideas. More specifically, when compared with the control teachers, CGI teachers agreed more strongly on a written survey with the following ideas:

> children construct rather than receive mathematical knowledge;
>
> mathematics instruction should facilitate children's construction of knowledge rather than teachers' presentation of knowledge;
>
> mathematics instruction should build on children's knowledge and understanding and the development of mathematical ideas in children should provide the basis for sequencing topics for instruction;
>
> number facts should be learned within the context of problem solving and as interrelated with understanding.

When compared with control teachers, CGI teachers spent significantly more time on word problem solving, and they spent significantly less time drilling on addition and subtraction number facts. CGI teachers encouraged their students to solve problems in many different ways, listened more to their students' verbalizations of ways they solved problems, and knew more about their individual student's mathematical thinking. At the end of the 1986–87 school year, students in CGI teachers' classes did better than students in control teachers' classes on written and interview measures of problem solving and number fact knowledge.

A Teacher's Perspective After the Initial Year

Annie Keith was among the teachers assigned randomly to the "experimental" (CGI) group, so she participated in the monthlong CGI workshop in summer, 1986. As she had just completed her first year of teaching, Annie was the most novice teacher in a group of experienced first-grade teachers. Up until the workshop that year and throughout her own schooling, Annie hated mathematics, and she thought of herself as math "phobic." In her preservice teacher education at the University of Wisconsin–Madison, Annie took two courses in mathematics for elementary teachers. When she began teaching in 1985, she still did not feel comfortable with mathematics. According to her, the turning point was when she became involved with the CGI project. One of the things that she learned during her first year of involvement with the CGI project was that in mathematics it was OK to ask "Why?" and "How come?" A second thing that she learned was that a teacher needs to become a better listener to the thoughts children express. As Annie put it:

> I think I was always a good listener to kids. I think a teacher needs to know some things to listen for. I found that CGI set up a kind of framework or grid in my mind so I started to think of things to listen for. When I would hear things being said by the kids, it would

fit in somewhere, and it would make sense to me.

At the end of the first year, Annie was asked whether she had changed her mathematics teaching and if so, how. She reported that she "put more stress and more time on oral story problems and talking—a lot more time on talking about how you are doing something and talking about, 'How are you getting the answer?' "

Annie Keith became more involved with the CGI project with each passing year. After the initial year, Annie became one of six teachers who were case study teachers and were the focus of continued study by Fennema and Carpenter. As part of this research, Annie Keith got to know well and met together frequently with the five other case study teachers including Sue Gehn and Mazie Jenkins. Annie also began giving workshops on CGI to other teachers in the Madison school district.

A RESEARCHER'S PERSPECTIVE FOUR YEARS LATER

Although I moved to Michigan State University after the original yearlong study, I continued to be involved with the CGI project and to work collaboratively with Carpenter and Fennema on writing up results of our research. In 1990, I initiated on my own a follow-up study of 20 of the original teachers, either three or four years after they had completed the initial CGI workshop. (The "control" teachers participated in the CGI workshop the summer following the experimental group workshop.) Because most research-based interventions have not had substantial long-term influences on teaching practice (Clark & Peterson, 1986), I was curious to learn what teachers thought of CGI four years later and whether or not they were still using CGI.

Nancy Knapp, a graduate student working with me, conducted telephone interviews with the 20 teachers who, three or four years earlier, had participated in the in-service workshops on CGI. All interviews were recorded and transcribed verbatim for later analysis. We then conducted qualita-

tive content analyses of the interview transcripts, using as our main tool the *Hyperqual* program developed by Dr. Raymond Padilla of Arizona State University. This program facilitates sorting, group, regrouping, and analysis of qualitative data such as the text data from our interviews.

Knapp and I found that all 20 teachers except one reported still using CGI to teach mathematics. But teachers varied mostly in their use of CGI—some using it occasionally or supplementally; others using it mainly or solely. (See Knapp & Peterson, 1991, for a complete description of this study and the results.) We found teachers' use to be significantly related to their ideas about what it means to "know" mathematics, how students learn mathematics, and what responsibilities and roles teachers and students have in learning mathematics. Three patterns of change in teachers' CGI use emerged: Group 1 teachers (eight teachers) reported steady, gradual increase to reach their current main or sole use of CGI; Group 2 (four teachers) reported having never used CGI more than supplementally or occasionally and were settled in that use; Group 3 reported using CGI in earlier years, but now only supplementally or occasionally.[5] These patterns of use were related to the meanings that teachers had constructed for CGI. In their espoused beliefs and practices, Group 1 described CGI conceptually, and Group 2 described CGI procedurally, as using manipulatives or word problems.

From our perspectives as researchers, Group 1 and Group 2 teachers' beliefs and practices seem internally consistent, while Group 3 teachers showed a marked incongruity between their espoused belief and espoused practices. For three of the Group 3 teachers, this gap was apparent to us but not to them. For three of the teachers we studied, though, this incongruity between what they believe about mathematics and mathematics teaching and what they actually do in their classrooms was keenly felt. Kathy Pirelli, who taught 24 first graders in a Madison school last year, was unusually honest in sharing her feelings of conflict with us. First, Kathy described a typical mathematics lesson in her classroom—one which somewhat resembled a lesson described by a Group 2 teacher:

> A typical lesson might be where I would start out and review what we had done the day before, and talk about what we're going to do that day. Then lots of times in our book (Addison-Wesley), they'll have little story problems that you can do, like the problem of the day. I've done those once in a while. I really haven't been real good about doing those . . . then I might say to them, "This is what we're going to do for the math period; we're going to learn this today," . . . and they might do some independent work, you know . . . and then, before the math lesson ends, we would have a story problem time where I would recite some story problems that would relate to whatever concept I was trying to get across. . . . I have them sit; their counters are out, and they're doing it, and I'm walking around and monitoring. [After they discuss the problems] I'll ask, you know, "What was your answer?" and then somebody has a chance to explain how they got the answer, what they did, and then I'll say, "Well, did anybody else do it a different way?" and then somebody else might raise their hand and say, "Well, I did it this way." And during the time that they're saying that, you know, a new strategy might be brought up.

Yet, Kathy was not very satisfied with what she does:

> I always get very excited at the end of the year when I'm going through my files and I think "Why didn't I do that? The year's slipped away . . . I know that I don't do [story problems] as much as I did the first year . . . the kids love it . . . and [I] usually make a point of doing it, but I don't do it as much as I would like to. I think because, again, it's time. It's knowing what I want to get across to them that day, and also knowing that I want to do some story problems for enrichment, but it's finding the time to fit it all in . . . [Time] really

locks you into what you like to do versus what you really can do.

And, Kathy Pirelli described, almost wistfully, how she would like CGI to affect all her teaching:

> I guess I get into this thing where I'm asking questions and they're simply reciting, and I sometimes stop, and I think, "I know that answer: I know that student knows that answer. I want something more. I want to ask a deeper type of a question" . . . I'm trying to ask more questions that don't have a right answer, "Explain that to me. Why do you feel that way?" or whatever, instead of always just going to the easy one. I think I do that many times during the day, as far as just [going for] the right answer. But somewhere in the back of my head, [I know] that it's so important to ask them, "How did you get that?" I saw those videotapes of students doing things, and it was always "How did you get that?" That relates to everything.

Teachers as Learners: Comparing CGI Teachers Across Groups.

In contrast to Kathy Pirelli and the other teachers in Group 3, Group 1 teachers reported that CGI had begun to affect all their teaching. For these teachers who used CGI as their main or only program, the relationship between their substantive knowledge and beliefs about these ideas and their mathematics practice seemed to have been conceptual and interactive. Gradually over three or four years, teachers' knowledge, beliefs, mathematics practice had been transformed. These teachers constructed their mathematics practice from several key CGI ideas—the major one being that children have a lot of mathematical knowledge and understandings from which the teacher should build and develop mathematics instruction. These teachers' mathematics practices were dynamic, changing, and growing as they learned from their children and as they learned by using CGI. Annie Keith was among the eight teachers in Group 1.

We came to realize that these teachers—for

whom CGI involves substantive ideas and assumptions from which they develop their mathematics practice—formed one important group of teachers using CGI. These eight teachers (Group 1) showed a continuous, developing pattern of use in their mathematics teaching, as well as some use of CGI ideas in their teaching of other subjects (e.g., asking students more "Why?" and "How do you know?" questions; finding out what students know and understand about a subject and then building on that in practice).

From Group 2 teachers we heard a different story. Knapp and I found it particularly interesting that Group 2 teachers talked about CGI as a set of strategies or procedures even though we—the researchers involved (Carpenter, Fennema, & Peterson)—did not see CGI as a set of procedures but rather as a set of ideas developed from research on young children's mathematics problem solving. Further, we, the researchers, thought we had made a special attempt to present CGI to teachers *not* as a problem or set of procedures but rather as research-based knowledge from which teachers might draw their own implications for their practice and construct their own ways of using CGI in their mathematics teaching. Florio-Ruane and Lensmire (1990) reported similar findings of proceduralization of substantive ideas from research on literacy and the teaching of writing.

The story told by Group 3 teachers was discouraging. Group 3 teachers' use of CGI had peaked and diminished. Although earlier in their use of CGI, these teachers might have been learning—growing and developing in their knowledge and use of CGI—this seemed no longer to be the case. Although these teachers reported using CGI extensively in earlier years, they now used it only supplementarily or occasionally. While CGI ideas still seemed to figure prominently in the views and thinking, Group 3 teachers' self-described practice seemed markedly more traditional than CGI-like, and most of these teachers seemed to be on a downward trajectory toward the vanishing point of CGI ideas from their mathematics practice completely.

Although the gloom and doom story of the Group 3 teachers is not a new one in the field

of mathematics education, where reforms have waxed and waned over time, and where innovations of one decade all but disappear from classrooms the next, it is particularly distressing. Whereas we, the researchers, had thought to empower first-grade teachers by giving them access to research-based knowledge of first-grade children's mathematics learning and encouraging them to use, develop, and transform the knowledge in ways that fit with their own beliefs, values, and context, the Group 3 teachers felt either disempowered or disinclined to do so. Indeed, Group 3 teachers frequently mentioned "barriers" that constrained them from teaching the way they would like. Barriers most frequently mentioned by Group 3 teachers included lack of planning time and class time, the type of students they had, the expectations that the next teacher would have for these students, standardized tests that their students would take to assess computational skills in mathematics, and the fact that there was no "packaged" curriculum for CGI. One Group 3 teacher who was teaching second and third grade felt particularly powerless and frustrated because "they" (the researchers) had not made a framework for CGI in second and third grade, and she felt insecure about trying CGI on her own without such a framework. What CGI meant for her was defined rather narrowly in terms of the children's strategies for solving addition/subtraction word problems and the addition/subtraction problem types. She did not seem to have a broader conceptual understanding of CGI as related to ideas of children's construction of mathematical knowledge, students as sources of mathematical knowledge, or children as responsible for their own learning. Further, this teacher did not see herself as having the authority, responsibility, and knowledge to develop her own ideas and use CGI on her own. She was still waiting for her researchers to do it.

This teacher's dilemma raised an interesting question for me as a researcher. What role can or should research-based knowledge play in transforming learning and teaching? In what ways might research-based knowledge (such as the addition/subtraction problem types and children's strategies) be illuminating? In what ways might research-based knowledge such as this become constraining?

TRANSFORMING RESEARCH-BASED KNOWLEDGE WITHIN THE CONTEXTS OF LEARNING

Two years ago Cathy Brown and I were asked by Tom Carpenter, Elizabeth Fennema, and Megan Loef Franke to conduct a study of the teachers at John Muir Elementary School in Madison, in which the researchers and teachers were working to "extend the principles of CGI to the primary mathematics curriculum" (kindergarten through third grade) (Carpenter, Fennema, & Franke, 1992). Annie Keith was then serving as the mentor teacher on the CGI project in that school, teaching full-time in the school and working with the other teachers there.

Although each CGI teacher creates her own unique practice, CGI classrooms have been characterized typically by a focus on problem solving, particularly the solving of word problems; students' sharing of their diverse strategies for solving the problems; and teachers and students listening hard to students' solutions and ideas for solving problems (see, for example, Peterson, Fennema, & Carpenter, 1991). When I observed Annie Keith's first-grade classroom in May 1991, I observed that these were important aspects of her mathematics teaching. Annie's first graders wrote their own word problems and posed them to each other. Children solved word problems and shared their solution strategies with one another. These characteristics of CGI classrooms were typical not only of Annie Keith's classroom, but also of the classrooms of all the other six first- and second-grade teachers at Muir School. But I began to notice some differences in the discourse, in the mathematics, and in the way in which knowledge was represented and conceived in Annie's classroom compared with other CGI teachers. These new "wrinkles" or transformations in CGI became more apparent in Annie's

teaching when I observed her classroom during the following year, in March 1992.

ANNIE KEITH'S CLASSROOM: A RESEARCHER'S PERSPECTIVE

In Annie Keith's spacious first-grade classroom every nook, cranny, wall, and floor space is filled. Yet the room seems cheerful, airy, and brimming with richness rather than crammed, cluttered or closed. Colorful posters, student work, and class work (such as "webbings") adorn the bulletin board and walls. Arranged in areas with bookshelves between, the room has large spaces for science, mathematics, and reading. The reading area also serves as the meeting area for the whole class. When not sitting on the rug in the meeting area, the children sit at one of five tables arranged around the room.

Every day, Annie Keith teaches mathematics to her first-grade class from about 8:30 to 10:30 in the morning. The class starts the day with a meeting or whole-class conversation with students sitting on the rug. On this particular day, a Thursday morning in March 1992, the children gathered on the rug in the meeting area. Twenty students were present: thirteen were Caucasian, five were African-American, one was Hispanic, and one was Egyptian. Twelve were boys, and eight were girls. After taking attendance and the lunch count, Annie asked one of the students to count the sticks representing students who were going to eat hot lunch. One of the boys counted the hot lunch sticks and concluded that there were seven. Annie asked, "How do you know it's seven?" The boy then counted the sticks one at a time, counting aloud as he did so. Turning to the class, Annie asked the children if they thought it was seven, and the class counted aloud together as the boy put the sticks down on the rug one at a time. At that point, Peter piped up and said that they would need one more to make eight, "Cuz after the seven comes eight. You have to have two fours to make eight."

In reply, Annie queried: "Does it help sometimes to know some of these facts—some of these doubles about some numbers to help you solve other things?" The class responded, "Yes." And when Annie asked, "What do you mean, Erica?" Erica suggested that, "Two is an even number, and this is an even number (she showed two fingers on her right hand) so if you put two together (she showed two more fingers on her right hand) that would make four, so this would be an even number. And eight would be an even number if you put another four again (she showed four fingers on each hand)."

Erica's remark opened up the door for a conversation that lasted nearly 40 minutes and in which the students and their teacher traversed territory that included odd and even numbers, positive and negative numbers, zero and negative zero, and "touchpoints" on numbers.[6] The following selection came midway through the conversation when Erica returned the conversation to the question of whether there was a negative zero or not by piping up, "On the number chart there's not a zero negative." (Here Erica was referring to the number line on the wall that extended from −20 to 100.)

Following up on Erica's remark and realizing that she was responding to an idea that Daniel and Alex put forth earlier—the idea of a "negative zero"—Annie queried, "Daniel, did you hear what Erica's first comment was because I think that is kinda aimed at you?" Annie asked Erica to tell Daniel what she meant, and Erica did this. Then Annie asked, "Daniel, what are you thinking about that?

CONVERSING ABOUT ZERO—IS THERE A NEGATIVE ZERO?[7]

Annie: Hmmm. What about that idea of zero? She doesn't agree. She says there is just zero, not zero and negative zero. What do you think about her comment?

Daniel: I think I agree with Alex—because it's if zero is odd, then one would be even. There has to be a starting for negatives too.

Annie: So you're thinking that zero is

an even number? So you're thinking there's a zero and a negative zero?

Daniel: Yeh, I would say that.

Annie: Do you think there's a zero and a negative zero?

Peter: Yeh. Before we didn't know about the negatives, zero was really like a starting. But now that we know about them there has to be a starting point for negatives too.

Alex: But then we'd have to keep on counting zeros and negative zeros.

Peter: No, there is only going to be one of each.

Annie: Erica. I think you need to come and listen to this 'cuz I think we need you in on this conversation.

Annie: Let me recap this: Peter you think there is a zero and a negative zero. Erica, you don't think there is a negative zero. Why not?

Erica: Because there's not.

Annie (to another girl who shook her head "no"): You don't think there's a negative zero.

Other students: Me either.

Annie: Let's listen to some of what you guys are thinking about it.

Erica: Because it doesn't go "negative zero, zero, one, two three."

Annie: What does it do?

Erica: It just goes "one, two, three, four, five, six, seven, eight, nine."

Annie: So going up on the positive side it goes like this. Then what happens on the negative side?

Erica: It goes negative one, negative two, negative three. Maybe the number chart on the negative side isn't right, but I still don't think there is a negative zero.

Annie drew the following number line on the board as Erica explained it:

<----------->
−3 −2 −1 0 1 2 3

Annie: So you don't think it goes zero,

negative zero, negative one? Hmmm. Some-body else, what do you think about this idea right here about zero or negative zero?

Hannah: I don't think there is a nega-tive zero because if it went zero negative zero, there would be just like two zeros in a row.

Alex: And the ones there would have to be two rows, the two would have to be two rows . . .

Annie: So you're thinking if it went like this (drew a new number line on board) and like this (drew on board) and this would be a negative one and a posi-tive one, two. So you're thinking that wouldn't . . .?

Annie drew the number line on the board as she thought Alex saw it:

$$<\text{-----------------------}>$$
$$-3 \quad -2 \quad -1 \quad -0 \quad 0 \quad 1 \quad 2 \quad 3 \quad 4$$

Alex: Yeh, that might be it because there would be one zero for each set. One zero for that set (pointed to negative numbers) and one zero for that set (pointed to positive numbers).

Annie: Erica, you made a comment, you thought that zero was a _____ (pause)?

Erica: A divider.

Annie. A divider. Can you elaborate on that a little more? What do you mean?

Erica: If you had 10 numbers, then you put a zero, then you would need one more in order to make 10. And then if you need another one, you would need two more to make 10. If you count the zeros in it, you would have to count the other ones to get the other zeros. (While Erica spoke, Annie interjected "OK" and "Hmmm.")

Annie: So how does this zero act as a divider. What does it divide?

Erica: It divides the negatives right here and the positive numbers. (Erica went to the board and pointed to show this.)

Annie: Oh, you're thinking zero is kinda like a . . .

Heather: Which are the positives?

Annie: Which are the positive num-bers?

Erica (pointed as she said this): This is a positive number because it doesn't have this (pointed to a negative sign of one of the numbers on the number line) or else it would be not really a positive number, a negative number. Then if you had a neg-ative zero, then this wouldn't be a divider, and this would be a positive and this would be a negative.

Annie: Hmmm.

ASSUMPTIONS ABOUT KNOWING AND MATHEMATICS IN MS. KEITH'S CLASS

In the above episode, Annie's children come up with several provocative ideas. One is the idea of "zero as a divider." Although this idea is not completely unpacked during the course of the discussion, it seems that at least one of the chil-dren, Erica, might be wrestling with ideas of place value in her thinking about the use of zero. Another idea is Daniel's conjecture that there is a "negative zero" because zero is the starting point for positive numbers, and "there has to be a start-ing point for negatives too." The children pursue this idea vigorously bringing up arguments and justifications for their assertions on either side of the question—there is a negative zero or there is not a negative zero. The class period ends with no clear resolution, but the implication is that the students will continue to think about negative zero and pursue the question in further conversa-tions and debates.[8]

What is mathematics? In the field of mathe-matics, knowledge is changing and growing, and in Annie's classroom it is as well.

The mathematics discussed in Annie Keith's class is not finite or fixed, the mathematical ideas are certainly not typical of first grade, and some would say they are unusual, if not exceptional. Annie herself acknowledges that the mathematical ideas that her first graders are considering are different from those she used to teach and from those in a typical scope and sequence chart for first grade. These new ideas include odd and even numbers, negative numbers, and infinity. She says that in a traditional first-grade class, "Numbering starts at zero." But Annie herself remembers being confused as a child when she was taught later that there were "other numbers besides zero because for so long you were just taught that numbers start actually with one and go on and then you have this zero appearing and now there's something else!" In contrast, in her class she said that from day one of the first week of school her students were talking about infinity and about the idea that numbers go "either way" or in "both directions." And they are talking about these mathematical ideas because the children brought them up and because they were interested in them and puzzled by them.

Interestingly, in Annie's interview two years ago in May 1990, she talked about her first-grade children bringing up negative numbers even during that year. Apparently, Annie's students talked about and discussed negative numbers two years ago as well. But this year negative numbers, infinity, and odd and even numbers seemed to have become even more a part of the discussion in Annie's classroom, and they seemed to represent more than just a change in the mathematics discussed, but also a change in Annie's thinking of where the mathematics comes from that she teaches. This year all these kinds of numbers came up at the beginning of the year when the students were doing a "webbing" for mathematics. (A webbing is a technique that the Muir teachers use to diagram the network of knowledge that the class has at the beginning. The concept is placed in the center of the web. The class reconsiders and modifies its web for mathematics over the year. For example, in the web the class constructed for mathematics at the beginning of the year, they had a line for numbers and a line for counting extending out from mathematics in the center. Then they placed infinity on a line connecting counting and numbers.)

Annie recounted a story of how negative numbers continued to be a focus of conversation in her classroom. One day T. J. came up to Annie, and he had constructed the following problem and written it in his mathematics notebook: "There were 12 dogs and 25 of them ran away. How many dogs are there?" T. J.'s answer was "–13 dogs."

> Greg Thoyre, a graduate student with the CGI project, came up to T. J. and said, "You know, T. J., I'm having a really hard time visualizing this problem. You know if there are this many dogs and this many run away, I don't know. What would negative 13 dogs look like?" T. J. goes, "Oh, you, there wouldn't be any 'cuz below 0, you wouldn't see any. You just have to 'magine. It would be negative 13."

Annie and T. J. continued to talk, and they came up with a mathematical representation that helped them think about negative numbers—using thermometers. They talked about using things where you do see negative numbers and how they could write story problems that would reflect things in the environment around them.

Annie's story about T. J. shows how mathematics and worthwhile mathematical tasks are created in her first-grade class. They come from the children, and the mathematical knowledge, representations, problems, and tasks the children construct are very much theirs as well as hers. Annie credits her first-grade students for the positive influences on her mathematics understanding and in her confidence and interest in mathematics.

LEARNERS AS KNOWLEDGEABLE "SENSE MAKERS"

In discussing her six- and seven-year-old students, Annie says that "her kids know so much." By this she means not only that her children know much of the domain of elementary mathematical knowledge as she construes it, but also that the children have knowledge, understandings, and insights that she doesn't have. From their perspectives as children in a multicultural school in a diverse society in an information age, the children bring to the classroom and create within the classroom important understandings about mathematics, about learning and teaching, about relationships, and about living and working together. Because Annie believes that children have a lot of knowledge, she believes that she learns much from them, and indeed, credits much of her change to learning from her students.

Annie makes visible through her words and actions that she learns from her children. Because learning is by all parties—teacher and students—Annie is not the authority for knowledge in the classroom. There are multiple authorities and multiple ways of knowing. In mathematics, students "prove" their mathematical solutions to themselves and to others, explain why they think something is true, and give reasons and justify their thinking. Even Annie has to justify her reasons and her actions to her students. She says that some teachers might consider CGI students to be a little bit "obnoxious," because they expect their teacher to listen to them and take them seriously. She talks about her students coming in already empowered because they had CGI in kindergarten. The students expect to be able to share all their ways of solving mathematical problems, and if she stops discussion before they have been heard, the students want to know why.

Annie creates a learning environment where students bring up mathematical ideas and choose and create problems and mathematical tasks that interest and challenge them and where they justify their mathematical thinking to themselves and within their community. Authority for knowing and learning rests with the students and the community rather than with the teacher. Such a learning environment seems designed to foster mathematical power in the ways suggested by the National Council of Teachers of Mathematics' (NCTM) (1989) *Curriculum Standards* and NCTM's (1991) *Professional Teaching Standards*.

LEARNING IN A COMMUNITY: LEARNING AS SOCIAL AS WELL AS INDIVIDUAL

The learning context in Annie's classroom is one of community. Drawing on her work in creating a classroom "community of readers and writers" in language arts, in her mathematics teaching Annie attempts to help her students see themselves as a community of mathematicians. At the beginning of the year, the class jointly defined the following qualities of mathematicians:

> Mathematicians listen to each other. Mathematicians never say "can't." They will always do their best and try their hardest. Mathematicians help each other. Mathematicians can solve a problem in many ways. Mathematicians use different kinds of math tools.[9]

When in her classroom, Annie and her students are often heard to repeat aloud these ideas about mathematicians. These words serve to make explicit not only assumptions about how mathematical knowledge is created, but also norms for discourse and learning in the classroom.

In Annie's classroom as in a community of real mathematicians, worthwhile mathematics problems and tasks are constructed jointly by the participants. In the whole-class meeting each day, the mathematics emerges as part of the flow of the ongoing conversation. In her mathematics learning centers, Annie herself still often decides what the mathematics tasks will be. But, increasingly, she has moved to having the students themselves plan what will happen in the mathematics learning center for the week. On an ongoing basis in her classroom, students decide what problems are challenging and interesting for them. They think about mathematics, converse about, and wrestle with mathematical ideas. In the process, they are involved in inventing new mathematics in that they are expanding previously conceived notions of what kinds of mathematical ideas first-grade students are interested in and capable of thinking hard about.

Conversing: Listening, Querying, Justifying, Making Thinking Visible

Listening is an important part of mathematics learning and teaching in Annie's classroom. Listening serves the same purpose that it does in authentic conversation—for the participants to come to understand each other's perspectives.

In Annie's class, students talk and listen to one another rather than, or in addition to, the teacher. The students and the teacher take students' responses seriously and treat them with respect. Annie listens carefully and seriously to students' responses, and students listen to each other. Why? Annie provided one rationale when she told me about how they actually talk about listening:

> I always go through this thing where I say to them, "Yeh, but I've done first grade. I don't even have to listen to you guys anymore." And they just get appalled, and they think that's just horrendous to say that. And they'll give me all the reasons why I need to listen to them. They know so much, and they'll say, "You really need to listen to us today so you know what we're doing and how we're solving the problems. You need to listen to us because you can learn some new things from us. You need to listen to us because you have to fill out report cards and tell our parents what we're doing. You have to listen to us so you know if we've learned new things. You have to listen to us so you know what kind of problems to give to us."

Questioning as well as listening is encouraged. The teacher asks many questions, but these are different sorts of questions than in most classrooms. The forms of Annie's queries in the episode above most frequently are, "Why?" or "What are you thinking?" These questions elicit descriptions of students' thinking and students' justification of their ideas, answers, and thinking. The questions also focus discussion around the ebb and flow of students' thinking, and indeed the words "think" or "thinking" are used more than 40 times by Annie or the students during the class conversation. As in most mathematics classrooms, the teacher questions the students, but unlike most classrooms, in Annie's class, the students also query one another and they query their teacher.

In contrast to most classrooms, Annie's response to students' responses in this episode seems nonevaluative. In the videotape of the session, Annie's nonverbal behavior expresses sincere listening. For example, her body posture is such that she often crouches down to be nearer to the position of her small students so that she can really hear and listen. Her verbal responses are nonevaluative as well. She withholds judgment, often saying, "Hmmm," in response to students' comments. The only time that Annie "told" the students something during this episode was when she said that positive numbers and "regular" numbers were the same, and this idea was actually introduced by Peter, not Annie. Annie's stance is related to her desire to transfer the authority for knowing to the community of mathematicians in her classroom.

HOW AND WHY HAS ANNIE KEITH LEARNED AND CHANGED?

When I asked Annie if this kind of conversation about negative zero would have happened in her class last year, she said "no," and she had several responses for why things are different this year. These were connected with what Annie saw as opportunities for her learning as well as for the learning of her students. These opportunities are situated within the multiple embedded contexts or communities in which Annie teaches and learns.

The Sea Change of Ideas as a Context for Teacher Learning

The national context for education and the public discourse about education is one that is emphasizing change and reform. This wave of reform has swept in a "sea change of ideas" which includes ideas about revising educational practices toward greater encouragement of student thinking, collaboration, and ability to use and apply knowledge outside of school. The wave includes new ideas about assessment and empowerment of learners and teachers. These new ideas are reflected in multiple documents that call for reform including NCTM's *Curriculum Standards* and *Professional Teaching Standards* (1989; 1991), which present new visions of mathematics curriculum, assessment, and teaching, as well as in reports of the Carnegie Foundation (1986) and the Holmes Group (1986), which called for the need for teachers to learn to think for themselves if their students are to learn to think for themselves. As ideas for these and many other reform documents are reported in the media, and enhanced as they are by the advancements in information technology, they make their way quickly into the public discourse about education. This living, swirling sea of ideas offers a potentially rich environment for learning and growth of knowledge.

THE CGI PROJECT AS A CONTEXT FOR LEARNING

The CGI project fits neatly within the reform culture of the school and within this sea change of ideas. The principal, who is new to the school, the district, and the state, sees what they're doing with CGI mathematics in the school as a "result of what we're finding out about teaching and learning from the university." On a day-to-day basis, the CGI project has a "presence" in Muir School because one or two graduate students are often in the school to collect data. In addition, the resident CGI mentor teacher, Annie Keith, teaches first grade in the school; and another CGI mentor teacher, Mazie Jenkins, frequently comes to the school to work with CGI teachers and students.

STUDENT DIVERSITY AS A CONTEXT FOR LEARNING

Located in a middle-class neighborhood in Madison, Muir School is an elementary school with a population of 470 children in grades kindergarten through sixth. For the past 20 years or so, the school has served a neighborhood population of white, middle-class families, as well as an additional population of students from a nearby low-rent housing area. Over the years the latter population has changed to include a substantial Indo-Chinese immigrant population as well as Hispanics and African-Americans. During the 1991–92 school year, the ethnic breakdown of the school included 73% white, 12% African-American, 7% Asian and Indo-Chinese, and 8% Hispanic. In the school, 27% of the students receive free or reduced lunch, and 9% received Chapter 1 assistance. Two-thirds of these Chapter 1 students are both academically and economically at risk; one-third of these are academically at risk, and 12% are English as a Second Language (ESL).

From the principal's perspective, some parents of Muir students fear that the staff will "pay too much attention to the minority population and . . . forget about the kids in the middle and at the other end." The principal understands these parents' concerns, because he is a parent too; but as a principal, he is "sensitive to the fact that we need to meet the needs of all children." He sees CGI math as an opportunity because he can say that "CGI is a math program that caters to the needs of all kids." It fits within a diverse school like Muir because it promotes a "positive dialogue" between white children and black children and Asian children and Hispanic children where "they're learning that things aren't always black and white, but there are different ways, different approaches . . . that there are lots of different ways to solve a problem—that really brings dignity to kids."

THE SCHOOL AS A LEARNING CONTEXT

The staff at Muir School share a vision of themselves as an innovative and progressive school, and they see themselves as constructing and implementing curriculum in line with current reform efforts. For example, the principal describes the school as having an "integrated curriculum" so that "students are seeing content areas in their whole and are able to generalize the skills they learn into different circumstances and different situations." He sees CGI and whole language as going together, because they "fall nicely" under the "primary education model" umbrella of developmentally appropriate curriculum, and they "emphasize process as opposed to product."

One idea that all the first- and second-grade teachers see that the two approaches have in common is the assumption that teachers should build on children's knowledge and understanding in their teaching. Thus, in literacy this means having students write a lot and encouraging children to use their own words and "invented" spelling. In mathematics, this means building on children's developing strategies for solving problems including direct modeling, counting, and derived facts. Many teachers construe both the whole-language approach to literacy and the CGI approach to mathematics as teaching children to be strategic in their thinking. They encourage children to use explicit strategies such as predicting, comparing, and using prior knowledge in their reading and to use the research-based CGI strategies of direct modeling with manipulatives, counting all, counting on, and deriving facts from memorized ones. Other teachers make connections through using stories as a context for then having students write story problems about characters or themes in the stories. Some first- and second-grade teachers at Muir then have the children write, revise, and "publish" their mathematics word problems in the same way that they write and publish stories that they have written.

THE FIRST-GRADE TEAM AS A COMMUNITY OF LEARNERS

The first-grade team consists of four teachers, each of whom teaches a class of about 20 students. While teaching at Crestwood, another elementary school in Madison, Annie met two members of her current first-grade team at Muir—Sue Berthoux and Barbara Wiesner. She "teamed" with each of these teachers in different years while she was at Crestwood. Annie moved to Muir

School two years ago, and Barb came to Muir and joined the team last year. The first-grade teachers themselves, as well as the other teachers in the school, view the first-grade team as being the farthest ahead in implementing innovations such as CGI and the whole-language approach, as being most advanced in integrating their instruction across subjects through the use of themes, and most together both in their approach and in their thinking because they "team" together, which means planning together and constructing their curriculum.

The first-grade teachers plan jointly, and they feel that it is a "support" mechanism and more fun, because they can "leap off of each other's ideas." They feel free to take what they want to use in their classrooms. Each teacher decides what to use from the joint planning and how to teach it based on her analyses of her own children's knowledge.

While each first-grade teacher teaches in her own classroom and has her own class of students, the teachers' classrooms are all located next to each other in their own wing of the building. The first-grade teachers walk freely into one another's classrooms during the day and after school, and they share a one-hour planning period each week when they meet.

ANNIE'S CLASSROOM AS CONTEXT FOR LEARNING

This year Annie seems to use her classroom as the primary situation for her own learning as well as for the learning of her students. In fact, she herself admits somewhat guiltily that she hasn't wanted to be out of her classroom this year so she has not done much "mentoring" that takes her into other teachers' classrooms. In her classroom Annie seems most willing and able to take risks in trying new things, and there she encourages and makes it safe for her students to take risks. There she engages in the co-construction of meaningful learning tasks with her students. There she asks her students hard questions while she is asking herself hard questions. There she and her students create a learning community where everyone has a voice; diverse opinions, knowledge, and understandings are valued, but also questioned and probed; and students and the teacher have choice, not only over the tasks but over their participation in the tasks and in the community of discourse. The personal, affective, cultural, and social are important aspects of creation of the learning community in Annie's classroom along with the individual, cognitive, and academic aspects of learning.

THE DEVELOPMENT OF SHARED UNDERSTANDINGS: RECIPROCITY IN LEARNING AMONG TEACHERS, STUDENTS, RESEARCHERS

Annie described several situations that she saw as providing opportunities for learning and that she viewed as influential in the major changes in her thinking and teaching. She described learning from her students, learning from her teacher colleagues, and learning from CGI researchers and workshops. Interestingly, the researchers and teachers from whom Annie learned, also described situations in which their thinking had been changed profoundly by conversations with Annie or by experiences in the classroom with Annie and her students.

ANNIE'S LEARNING FROM HER STUDENTS

Annie thinks that much of her changed teaching practice came about because of differences in her children's knowledge when they entered her class:

> These kids seem to be a little more advanced in their thinking; no, "advanced" isn't the right word. But it seems like this class this year has gone further than last year's class in their thinking and in their really pushing to understand. I guess I attribute it to that they came in being all set—in that frame of mind. Because last year they had it [CGI] in the

kindergarten, and I think that really has made a difference.

When I asked, "In what way?" Annie continued:

> In their belief system—they believe that problems are solved in many ways, and that it's important to listen to each other. We get into big dialogues about why it's important to listen . . . why it's important for adults to listen, and why it's important for me to listen.

I laughed and asked Annie, "Do they [the students] tell you that?"

> Yeh, they'll tell me for different reasons . . . because I can learn something from them. Perhaps they'll teach me something I didn't know—which is true. I mean I tell them all the time I've learned so much in the last five years, or six years. 'Cuz six years ago I hated math. Now I love it.

So I queried, "What have you learned?"

> What have I learned? I've learned how much fun math really is, and how exciting it is. I think I probably learned even this whole idea of place value with understanding through watching these kids. You know just really getting at their thinking and understanding . . . I just find them so incredible.

ANNIE'S LEARNING FROM THE CGI PROJECT AND RESEARCHERS

As she sees it, Annie began the reform of her mathematics teaching six years ago when she was a first-year teacher at Crestwood Elementary School in Madison and when she enrolled in the summer workshop that began the original CGI study. In the original workshop she learned how much intuitive knowledge children really have about addition and subtraction. She learned about addition/subtraction problem types and children's solution strategies for these types of problems. Annie says that her changes and learning were gradual, and it is just this year—six years later—that she feels really comfortable with the CGI mathematics. She also feels comfortable asking questions of Tom Carpenter and Elizabeth Fennema. She feels comfortable calling up and talking with them or "just going down and sitting in the CGI office" at the university. Annie says that it never fails that if she takes off a half day, she will go down and sit in the office, and she will always have a conversation with Elizabeth or Tom or both of them. She "knows that they're really interested because of the questions that they'll ask" or their responses to her questions. Annie says she always walks away thinking new thoughts about things or questioning her beliefs and practice.

A Research Project Director's Learning from a Teacher and Her Students

Tom Carpenter recalls vividly when he was in Annie's classroom this year and the children discussed "a million." Annie had written the number 10,000 on the board. The students all agreed that it could be ten thousand. The question was, "Could it also be called a million?" One child said, "That's ten thousand so it can't be a million." Another child argued that the same number can have different names. The example was that 1,200 might be called twelve hundred or one thousand, two hundred. From Tom's perspective, Annie had been "very open and tried to let the kids resolve it." Annie had made the point to Tom that a good discussion would ensue. Tom realized that Annie wanted her children to engage in "authentic discourse," and she wanted to avoid having her children see her as the arbiter of information.

But how do you discover social convention? Tom thought there was no way to discover a social convention. Tom explained to me that by social convention he meant, "a million is a name for a particular number." As Tom explained it: For the British, 1,000,000,000,000 is a billion (1 followed by 12 zeroes), and for us in the United States, 1 followed by 9 zeroes is a billion. Tom thought that the children were seeing it like

this—ones, tens, hundreds, thousands—every digit was getting a new name. Tom said the children thought that a million should be the next named digit. "That's what Daniel seemed to be saying because we didn't say ten hundred, which we could." But Tom admitted that Annie had been right—a wonderful discussion ensued.

After observing Annie Keith, Tom thought about the relationship between knowledge and CGI teachers' practice. Tom has been comparing the practices of the two CGI teachers they are doing case studies of this year—Annie Keith and Sue Gehn. For example, he noted that in CGI classrooms a lot of common things occur. Students solve problems, and teachers and students listen to children's solution strategies. But then he noted that there are many differences. For example, in her mathematics teaching Annie Keith seems to him to be more like Deborah Ball, another CGI teacher, than like Sue Gehn.[10] Moreover, Tom thinks that he could never teach like Annie. He thinks that, for a lot of people, Gehn's teaching will be the easier model to follow—her routines look pretty well established. For a beginning teacher, there is so much going on in Annie's class, it is so hard to figure out how she got it that way. Sue Gehn's class on any given day looks pretty much the same at a surface level. Sue poses a variety of challenging problems for the whole class; she has set routines for organizing her classroom and for how the problems get discussed in the classroom. In Annie's class there are more different things happening—a lot more open-ended discourse and discussion of affect. Although both teachers have established warm, accepting relationships with their students. Annie has more explicit discussion and demonstration of affect in her class.

Tom says that Sue and Annie provide contrasting styles in the way they have used the information they have been given in the CGI workshops. But ultimately for Tom, implementing CGI means "building on students' knowledge and extending that," and by students' knowledge he means the problems students can solve, the formal and informal knowledge they have.

The question with which Tom is wrestling

most seriously is: To what degree does CGI reflect the extension of very particular research-based knowledge? And a related question then is: Is Deborah Ball a CGI teacher?

Tom's perspective is that there is a broad conception of teaching that encompasses the basic principles of CGI: the idea of attending to children's thinking and knowledge and attempting to build upon that. Deborah Ball would be a teacher that falls under this conception. CGI is embedded within this larger conception as a way of instantiating this principle. The analysis of children's thinking is at the core, but as you get away from the core, it gets "fuzzy." People interpret this core knowledge in different ways—they construct their own meanings and interpretations. The fundamental dilemma is this: On the one hand, you want to provide the latitude for teachers to take the broader conception, but on the other hand, as researchers and developers, Elizabeth Fennema and Tom Carpenter have taken a particular analysis of children's thinking. Where do you draw the line when someone has adopted this broader perspective on teaching?

THE TEACHER'S PERSPECTIVE ON LEARNING FROM A RESEARCHER IN HER CLASSROOM

In addition to conversing with Tom Carpenter, Elizabeth Fennema, and Megan Loef Franke, Annie also has had ongoing conversations this year with CGI researcher, Ellen Ansell. These conversations have been facilitated this year by Ellen's presence in Annie's classroom doing a case study. Annie credits Ellen's presence in her classroom this year with really having helped her change. One of the ways that Annie feels that Ellen has helped her has been through the *kinds of questions* that Ellen has asked as well *as the way Ellen has asked questions and the stance that Ellen has taken* in her questioning.

Annie describes the kinds of questions that Ellen asks as "making her think about different things." Some of the kinds of questions that Annie recalls are, "What did you think about how Justin solved this problem today? What were

you thinking about when 'so and so' said this? Has that influenced what you think in terms of? Why do you think that? Annie is sure that Ellen's questions have really made her "think about the kids" because she finds that when Ellen isn't there in her classroom, Annie will call her up and say, "Wow, you really have to hear what Heather said today ... " and then Annie will just, "tell her everything that happened."

When I asked what Ellen might say, Annie commented that Ellen would just smile and write it all down. Annie is amazed at how good Ellen is at not putting in a "whole lot of opinions about things."

Annie is also amazed at how Ellen is able to keep to her reflective stance as a researcher, and in this, Annie sees Ellen as playing a useful and important role as a researcher. Annie talked about how different Ellen is from a parent or student teacher who really "gets actively involved." In contrast, Ellen will walk around the classroom and ask the children, "So why'd you do this or tell me about this?" Ellen can figure out what the students are doing, too. But as Annie put it: "She doesn't take on a role like where she's helping them. She just keeps asking them the questions and they just explain to her." Annie is intrigued by how Ellen can keep her role separate—she's not doing a lot of persuading or teaching. But then when I asked Annie to compare her stance as a teacher to that of Ellen as a researcher, Annie replied:

> Well, that's a good question! That's really interesting because I guess I do the same kinds of things (pause) where I'm really listening to the kids. Though I guess my role is a little bit different because I'll set up situations, or I'll pose the situations and she's recording these situations.

Annie noted that there have been some times when she has asked Ellen, "What about this?" Annie gave the example of Peter who solved a problem in a way that she couldn't figure out so Annie told Peter to show it to Ellen because she (Annie) didn't "get it." Peter told Ellen about it and afterwards Annie asked Ellen, "Now will you tell me what I don't understand? What do you think he's doing here?" Annie commented that she and Ellen still haven't figured out how Peter had been thinking about it.[11]

At other times when Annie asked Ellen a question, Annie noted that Ellen would also question her. Alternatively, Ellen might say, "Well, think about where you were before" and where you are now. In both of these ways, Annie thought Ellen helped her thinking: "It's kind of like what I do—you know in a way I guess in a way she's modeling mentoring too because it's those same kinds of techniques of, 'How do you really get the person to really question and think about it?' "[12]

By reflecting back to her what has happened, Ellen frequently helps Annie to see contradictions in her own thinking or to see things differently. Annie described it like this:

I'll say, the kid said this, and she'll say, "Well, look what I have in my notes." And we'll look at it, and I'll say, "Oh, you're right, . . . It's in the notes. I didn't even hear her pick up on it."

In a way, Annie seems to see Ellen as another pair of eyes and ears that can help her see things she might have missed and, by reflecting back to her, can help her see things from another perspective. Annie concluded her comments about Ellen by saying that, "It has really helped me change." She said that it made her make a more conscious effort to think about what she is doing and to think about and watch what the kids are doing. She noted again that when Ellen is not there, she thinks about it so she can tell her—either call her up or tell Ellen when she sees her.

At the close of my interview with Annie, I was left to ponder the following questions: What is the "it" here that Annie concluded had helped her change? Is it Ellen, the person, or Ellen, the "researcher"? Is it Ellen in the role of provider of externalized dialogue that then becomes an internalized dialogue that Annie carries on with herself? Is it Ellen in the form of someone who gives "Annie" the teacher reason? Is it Ellen in the

role of provider of another perspective—another pair of eyes and ears in the classroom? Is it another supportive human adult who will share the ups and downs, the joys and the tears, the discouragement and the frustrations and the challenge of being a teacher of diverse children who is trying to teach in new ways?

A RESEARCHER LEARNING FROM CASE RESEARCH IN A TEACHER'S CLASSROOM

Ellen sees her role as "to see how children's knowledge of place value in particular progresses in relation to what they do in the classroom including how the classroom is organized, what kinds of problems they are working on, the social structure, and how Annie creates the classroom that she creates." Ellen tries to gain this research-based knowledge by observing and by querying students and Annie about their understandings and why they do what they do. Ellen said that she sits and takes notes. She spends the most time following Annie around, and she also follows around six "target" students whom they are studying longitudinally to see how the students learn to solve problems. Ellen interviews students in Annie's class, but doesn't share this information with Annie, because this is a decision made among researchers on the CGI project.

Ellen has said she frequently asks Annie questions about what she did. If Ellen sees something interesting during mathematics class, she asks Annie about it and asks if it surprised her. Sometime she asks Annie about what she is planning. Ellen has found that if she asks general questions of Annie, she doesn't get much. So Ellen often asks questions that are about specific, contextualized, and situated examples that arise during mathematics class that day, because it gives Annie and her a specific referent to ground their conversation. If something piques Ellen's interest, she has found that it is really worth trying to pursue.

One of the things that Annie has talked to Ellen about a lot is that children have explicit control of their learning and their learning environment. Annie talks a lot about children structuring their environment, choosing problems, and creating their mathematics. These are all aspects of children "being mathematicians" in Annie's classroom. The children create mathematical situations and then justify their own problem solving; they generate the problems, and they generate what becomes the mathematics in their classroom. Ellen has observed that whatever problems the children are solving in Annie's classroom, the children make the problems challenging. The children really control and challenge themselves. The children are constantly reevaluating their perceptions of their own abilities.

ANNIE'S LEARNING FROM TEACHERS: COLLEAGUES AS KNOWLEDGEABLE OTHERS

Annie also sees the teachers that she works with as having contributed significantly to her learning and change. Although Annie herself is designated as the "mentor" teacher for CGI in Muir School, Annie herself talked about each of her teacher colleagues on her first-grade team as her "mentors"—teachers from whom she has learned and is still learning. As Annie put it:

> The neat thing about mentoring is being able to have some time to go out and to work with teachers and go into their classrooms—to sit and talk with these teachers. Because as they're learning—it's interesting—because sometimes I see them going through the same things that I went through. It's awesome . . . I remember doing that, and I remember what I thought about it.

Annie then went on to say that when she sees teachers going through the same thing she is going through, she "bites her tongue" because she believes that they have to go through it. She says that often she will give the teacher "suggestions but not the answer." If a teacher asks her a question, Annie said she will pose it back as a question. When I asked, "Why do you pose it back

as a question?" Annie replied that it was like what I was doing as an interviewer. By asking "Why?" questions, I was getting her to "go deeper" and "dig deeper into thinking" about why she did things and why she thought things. As a mentor teacher, Annie wants the teachers to do the same—go deeper into their own thinking about why they did or thought something.

Then Annie described how so many of the teachers on this staff were also her mentors. She called it "a real special staff" and adjured as how she wasn't sure how many staffs were quite like this one at Muir School. She said that the teachers do a lot of reading of journals, and they share information. They read the different newspapers, and "there's always something in somebody's mailbox or up in the bathroom or there's a new article or a new something." Annie called the staff "professional." Further, she said that the teachers "really care about these kids. They think that all kids can learn."

Annie views her team as "a strong team," and she sees each of her team members as a "mentor." She acknowledges that they are all really different, but says that it wouldn't be such a strong team if they didn't have what each of them brought to the team. Annie pointed out here that respect was an important thing—that all four of them really respected each other. A second important thing was that all the team members were willing to share ideas. And a third important thing was that they were open to new ideas and to changing and shifting their own agendas.

Of the other three members on the team, Annie sees herself as most like Sue Berthoux. Annie sees them as similar in their planning styles. Sue B. was the first person that Annie really teamed with and worked with when she was a first-year teacher. Annie described Sue as follows:

> Sue knows so much about her kids, and she has such a way with them. She's so honest with her kids about things. She really incorporated the whole-language approach into her teaching and into the school. She really gets her kids involved in reading and writing. And

she's got us all going in that direction. So I look at her as a real mentor in that aspect—not only for how to teach and how to get kids interested, but also in terms of professional growth as a teacher.

SUE B: A TEACHER COLLEAGUE'S LEARNING FROM ANNIE

When the two of them have come together this year to talk about mathematics, Sue B. says that Annie always talks about what her kids thought about this or what they thought about that. Sue has been struck by Annie's "delight in some of the things that the kids have said." Annie would say that she really hadn't expected them to think about this the way they did. Sue described Annie's mathematics class by saying:

> I think a lot of the ideas come from the students, and then she takes their ideas, and she sort of does the planning of them. . . . She's just gotten so excited about that, and I suspect that her kids will get more and more and more and more into the planning. And if I don't do that, I'm going to lose my buddy. Not that we won't be friends and do things together, but they'll just be done in a different way. . . . But I think there's a little piece of the action in there for me too. (laugh) And so, I don't want to miss it.

Sue B. sees this year as "one of those quantum leap years for her (Annie)." Sue described it as the difference between having workbooks and moving into CGI; teachers begin paying attention to what children are doing and thinking, and they become interested in children's mathematical thinking: This is "another big step because it just deepens their investment in it." She views Annie as really valuing what students are thinking. During the interview with me, Sue B. said she thinks that she is ready to make some of the major changes in her own mathematics teaching that she has seen Annie making. By the end of the interview, Sue B. realized that she was "probably ready to make this move" because if she didn't, Annie would leave her "in the dust." What Sue said she meant was that their joint planning wouldn't be the same, because they would be "on such different levels." For Sue B., the kind of understanding and conversations that she shares with Annie seem particularly important for her own learning, and she wants them to continue.

TOWARD NEW RELATIONS: LEARNING, TEACHING, RESEARCH, AND PRACTICE

This chapter is about the learning of a first-grade teacher, Annie Keith. This chapter is about how Annie has learned through conversations with researchers, including one in her classroom who has been doing a yearlong case study of her; through conversations with her colleagues; through conversations with her first-grade students; and through reflective conversations that she has with herself. In all these conversations about her learning and teaching, Annie sees herself as both the learner and the teacher, and she is.

The way that Annie Keith teaches first-grade mathematics and the assumptions that she holds about mathematics learning and teaching are remarkably different than those she held six years ago. Similarly, over the last decade scholars have considerably revised their assumptions about mathematics learning from a behavioral view of learning toward more constructivist views.

Four key assumptions about learning are coming to be shared by many members of the education community. (See, Greeno, 1989; Schoenfeld, 1992; and Peterson, in press, for discussions of these assumptions, particularly as related to mathematical sciences education.) These revised assumptions are:

- Learners are knowledgeable "sense makers."

- Learning involves the negotiation of shared meaning, and the role of discourse is important in this negotiation.

- Knowing is contextualized or situated.

- Assumptions about knowing (personal and social epistemologies) influence learning.

Interestingly, unlike most experienced practicing teachers Annie Keith has not only revised her assumptions about mathematics learning and teaching, but her revised assumptions are remarkably like those of researchers and the scholarly community. Why might this be the case?

A simple answer to this question is that Annie is a learner and she sees herself as one. But the answer is more complex and multifaceted than that.

One facet concerns Annie's perspective on knowledge. For her, knowledge is dynamic, fluid, changing, and growing, not fixed, static or inert. This is the way she sees her own knowledge—she is learning from everyone around her. But it is also the way she sees her first graders' knowledge and the knowledge of her teacher colleagues. Annie is engaged in her own exploration and analysis to figure out the knowledge that her first graders construct while participating in a learning community where they talk about, debate, and create mathematics. On this exploration, she is venturing into new domains of mathematical knowledge for first graders, as well as for herself, and into new domains of students' knowledge and understanding that are yet to be charted and perhaps even yet to be created in their process of exploration.

Another facet reflects Annie Keith's learning through participation as an active member of multiple learning communities or multiple communities of discourse. She is and has been a teacher for six years. In this role she participates as a member of professional communities and associations in reading and mathematics to which teachers belong. She also reads the journals and magazines that elementary teachers read. But she has also created a smaller discourse community

of teachers, or a community of teacher learners, at Muir School, and within it Annie participates in an even smaller community defined by the first-grade teachers in her team. A second major discourse community within which Annie now participates is the community of researchers and university professors. On her days off, Annie feels free to go to the CGI offices at the university and to spend the afternoon talking about her teaching with CGI project leaders Elizabeth Fennema, Tom Carpenter, and Megan Loef Franke and with the graduate students there. By doing so, she has access to the on-line thinking, knowledge, and understandings of leading-edge scholars that most teachers would not have access to except through reading research articles or through attending a national conference and hearing a researcher give an invited address. Through these conversations with Annie Keith, the researchers also have on-line access to the knowledge, thinking, and understandings of a first-grade teacher, fresh from the challenges of learning and teaching a new mathematics in new ways to a diverse group of wriggling, laughing, boisterous young learners.

A third important facet is that Annie Keith is considered to be a knowledgeable participant by the members of the multiple communities of learning and discourse in which she participates. These include her teacher colleagues at Muir School on her primary team, who respect her knowledge and thinking and with whom Annie engages in joint planning and sharing of ideas for mathematics teaching. But it also includes the CGI researchers and teacher educators with whom she works. Carpenter, Fennema, and Franke assert explicitly their assumption of treating teachers as active constructors of knowledge just as they assume that teachers will treat the students in their classrooms.

A fourth facet concerns the patterns of discourse and negotiation of meaning that seem to be going on in Annie Keith's mathematics teaching and that are reflected in the classroom conversation about negative zero. These discourse patterns and ways of negotiating meaning seem to be reflections of experiences that Keith herself has had this past year as she has interacted on an ongoing basis with a graduate student, Ellen Ansell, who has been doing a case study of students' mathematics learning in her classroom. Both Ellen and Annie report on the power of this kind of reflective dialogue for learning, and their reports are remarkably similar to those of other researchers who have engaged in such dialogues with practitioners (Schon, 1983; Berkey, Curtis, Minnick, Zietlow, Campbell, & Kirschner, 1989; Wasley, 1991).

Ellen said she frequently asks Annie questions about what she did and why. These kinds of questions and conversations occur around nearly every observation that Ellen makes and occur at least once a week, and often more frequently. If Ellen sees something interesting during math class, she asks Annie about it and asks if it surprised her. Annie says that Ellen helps her see things—by pointing out "inconsistencies" in what Annie is seeing or saying about what a child has done or said in mathematics and leading her through or back to work that the child did earlier that showed something different. In turn, Ellen has noticed that one way that Annie works with her children is through questioning, by leading them to see inconsistencies in their own reasoning, solutions, or in what they have said or done, both individually and as a group. This kind of questioning then seems to get reflected further in the way the children then talk with each other. Ellen has noted that Annie's students then use this same way of questioning or thinking when they are on their own or with other children.

The case of Annie Keith stands as proof of the power of Annie's experiences as a learner being reflected in own assumptions about her students' learning and then enacted in her mathematics teaching. Although this is only one case, substantial evidence exists for the need for educators to work from the same shared assumptions about learning and to apply these same assumptions in their teaching at all levels. One implication that might be drawn from Annie Keith's case is that if teacher educators want teachers to act on revised assumptions about students' mathematics learning in their own teaching, then teacher edu-

cators must apply these same assumptions to teachers as learners. Cooney (in press) discusses research and theory to support this position in the case of teacher education in mathematics.

From the perspective of the larger educational system and need for systemic change, Cohen and Barnes (1993) have argued that the same model of learning be applied at all levels of the educational system. In this case the learning assumptions described above might be used to frame the work not only of teachers and learners in the classroom, but also of teacher educators and teachers as learners, and also the work of policymakers and researchers as learners. The optimum outcome would be an educational system that is truly a learning system in which participants at all levels are engaged in their own learning and development as well as in the creation of new educational knowledge. Such a system would be one which would encourage more teachers to be learners like Annie Keith, but would also encourage more first graders to be like Erica and Daniel, who query their teacher and classmates about infinity, negative numbers, and negative zero.

MY PERSPECTIVE: RESEARCHERS, RESEARCH, AND LEARNING

▼

In the final analysis, this chapter is about *my learning,* and *it reflects my knowledge and understanding* at this point in time from my perspective.[13] What have I learned from Annie Keith and from my own involvement with CGI? A great deal. I venture to say that my own learning and the transformations in my own knowledge, thinking, and understandings have been as great as those that Annie Keith has experienced over the last six years. Indeed, my own friends have described me in ways that sound remarkably like the ways that friends of Annie's (such as Sue B.) have described her, and I see many similarities between Annie and me. A lot of our learning is interwoven with the story of CGI and the CGI project, because both Annie and I began with the CGI project when it started six years ago—

myself as one of the researchers and three coprincipal investigators of the project, and Annie as one of the first-grade teachers in the experimental group in the study.

Several things that Annie and I have learned are directly the result of our participation in the CGI research—Annie as a teacher being "studied" and myself as a researcher studying her. As a researcher, I learned from our empirical results from the first year of study that CGI teachers who were best at facilitating problem solving were those who listen carefully to the ways that students solve problems. Annie was one of those teachers. Annie and I both listen very carefully, and we have been doing so intensely for the past six years. I think that both of us listen with an attempt to understand rather than decide whether the person is "right" or "wrong" or whether the person "knows" or "doesn't know." This focus on understanding or negotiating meaning rather than on "right" answers was a second thing that we learned from CGI. But for both of us, CGI was only a beginning point because we found that in listening and trying to understand, *we learned* things that we hadn't "known."

In trying to understand the perspectives of our students, Annie and I came to understand things that we hadn't understood before, and in hearing and seeing others' perspectives, we expanded our knowledge and understandings. But in doing so, our knowledge was no longer constrained or confined by the research-based knowledge of the CGI problem types or strategies or by the knowledge of what "effective" teachers did in the original CGI process-product experiment. So, Annie learned with her first graders as they developed their "number sense" and constructed their knowledge of numbers including odd and even numbers, negative numbers, and zero. Similarly, during the past several years I have learned with my own graduate students as I have taught educational psychology and students have queried me about the "empirical research findings" and the relationship of these to the knowledge, understandings, and practices of the CGI teachers. I began to transform, change, and expand upon the "research-based knowledge and empirical find-

ings" of CGI just as Annie began to transform and change the research-based CGI knowledge of children's problem types and strategies.

But Annie and I have each also learned from participating in conversations and sharing knowledge in written and spoken forms with those in the multiple learning communities within which we reside. We both share a common stance of being open with the knowledge that we share with others. Sue B. described Annie as being open and willing to share any and all of her materials, activities, and curriculum with others on her team. She noted that others have now developed an openness and willingness to share in response. We are both fortunate to reside and participate in communities where many around us see themselves as learners and are willing to share their knowledge and understandings with each others. Many of our colleagues are willing to acknowledge and understand where we differ in what we "know," to debate openly where differences in understandings exist, and to attempt to develop understandings that we share.

Over the past six years, I have learned much from the teachers who have participated in my research. For example, three years ago I conducted a case study of Alyjah Byrd, a third-grade teacher in East Lansing, MI, who had learned by observing and conversing with her colleague, Deborah Ball, who teaches in the same elementary school. I took a similar stance and asked questions in ways similar to those of Ellen Ansell. Interestingly, I see striking similarities in the puzzling that Ellen is doing now and the puzzling that I did then. Also, Alyjah has told me that my questioning influenced her to think harder, dig deeper, and be more reflective in the same ways that Annie reports Ellen's questioning has influenced her. I have also learned much from other teachers I have observed as well as from teaching my own students at Michigan State. I have also learned from the colleagues in a research community with whom I have been conducting an ongoing study of reforms in mathematics classrooms over the past five years. These colleagues include David Cohen, Deborah Ball, Suzanne Wilson, Ralph Putnam, Dick Prawat, Dan Chazan, and about

10 graduate students. With these colleagues I participate in weekly discussions and daily E-MAIL conversations in which we share understandings of our fieldnotes of classrooms, and debate what we have seen as well as what we think, what we know, and what we understand.

What has happened to me is that I have changed my views of research and my stance as a researcher in the last six years. *One important learning is this—in the end, "research" individual scholars, and communities of scholars offer only some of the multiple perspectives on knowledge and understanding.*[14] Our task as researchers is first to understand this and then, having done so, to reconsider seriously our own scholarly knowledge and work.

Perhaps I can help you understand best what I mean by ending where I began—with the perspective of a literary figure from another part of the world. But this time the point of view is of a playwright turned politician who represents the perspective of scholars and adults in this modern world, rather than the perspective of children and teachers in the world of Swedish children's author Astrid Lindgren. This text was published in *The New York Times* on March 1, 1992. And as typical of the kind of daily, ongoing knowledge sharing that goes on in the College of Education at Michigan State, the article was given to my husband by one of our colleagues, Susan Florio-Ruane, who found the article thought provoking and had a conversation with my husband, Patrick Dickson, in the hallway about it. Interestingly, Susan had received the article from another MSU colleague, Chris Clark. Patrick shared the article with me in a conversation over the breakfast table, as a natural part of the intensified, ongoing, stimulating conversation that he and I now carry on continuously about learning, teaching, knowledge, and technology. The article, "The End of the Modern Era," is by Vaclav Havel, then president of Czechoslovakia, and is excerpted from an address he gave to the World Economic Forum in Davos, Switzerland, on Feb. 4. For me, the important part of Havel's message is this:[15]

The modern era has been dominated by the culminating belief, expressed in different forms, that the world—and Being as such—is a wholly knowable system governed by a finite number of universal laws that man can wholly grasp and rationally direct for his own benefit. . . . This, in turn, gave rise to the proud belief that man, as the pinnacle of everything that exists, was capable of objectively describing, explaining, and controlling everything that exists, and of possessing the one and only truth about the world. . . . We are looking for new scientific recipes, new ideologies, new control systems, new institutions, new instruments to eliminate the dreadful consequences of our previous recipes, ideologies, control systems, and instruments. We are looking for an objective way out of the crisis of objectivity. . . . What is needed is something different, something larger. Man's attitude toward the world must be radically changed. . . .

We must try harder to understand than to explain. The way forward is not in the mere construction of universal systemic solutions to be applied to reality from outside, it is also in seeking to get to the heart of reality through personal experience.

APPENDIX 3-1: METHODOLOGY

My analysis of Annie Keith's current thinking and practice is based on interviews and observations that were conducted during two one-week site visits—the first in May 1991, and the second in March 1992. During this fieldwork, I used interview and observation procedures that were constructed jointly by Cathy Brown and me. Post-observation interview questions and observation procedures were adapted from those developed by the National Center for Research on Teacher Learning (Ball, Kennedy, McDiarmid, & Schmidt, 1991), as well as from those used in a recent study of policy and practice by Cohen, Peterson, Ball, Wilson, and colleagues (1990). The teacher interview consisted of two parts: (a) a post-observation interview about the mathematics teaching just observed; and (b) a structured interview that centered specifically on CGI, what CGI meant to the participants, and the support and constraints teachers saw themselves facing in attempting to implement CGI. The post-observation interview focused on what teachers were trying to teach, why the teacher was trying to teach it, the materials used, and what the students gained from the lesson. Specific questions emerged within the particular context of the lessons I observed. I wanted to understand the teacher's rationale for the content she taught and her perspective on the way she taught within the particular context of her classroom.

I also interviewed all first- and second-grade teachers at Muir School and observed each of them teach mathematics for one period during each of the two site visits. Using a structured interview about CGI similar to the teacher interview, either Brown or Peterson also interviewed the science-math specialist, two English as a Second Language (ESL) teachers, one fifth-grade teacher, and the school principal. In June–July, 1991, the researchers conducted lengthy telephone interviews with the three project directors (Fennema, Carpenter, and Franke), the graduate student assigned to collect data at Muir School (Ellen Ansell), and a second CGI mentor teacher, Mazie Jenkins, who works with Muir teachers as part of the CGI project, but who was actually teaching at Lincoln School. In March,

1992, I conducted telephone interviews with Ellen Ansell and with Tom Carpenter. All interviews and observations were audiotaped; then interviews and observations were transcribed. Narrative records of classroom events and discourse were constructed with the aid of extensive field notes taken during on-site fieldwork and supplemented with the audiotaped transcriptions.

In this chapter, I also used my own knowledge of Annie Keith and the CGI project that I had gained as an ongoing participant in the project in its first two years. In addition, I used a transcript of an hour-long telephone interview conducted by Nancy Knapp, a graduate student who worked with me on an interview study that we did of 20 CGI teachers in Spring 1990. (See Knapp & Peterson, 1991.)

In writing this chapter, I drew extensively on and used the exact words of participants as I described their perspectives and ideas. Because of this, in some sense I am not the sole author of this chapter, and I am certainly not the sole "owner" of these ideas. Those that have contributed to this chapter and the ideas herein are many, but most particularly, they include: Annie Keith, Tom Carpenter, Ellen Ansell, Elizabeth Fennema, and the first-grade students in Annie's class.

FOOTNOTES

1. Lindgren, A. (1950). *Pippi Longstocking*. New York: Scholastic, Inc., pp. 34–35.

2. Deborah Tannen (1990) provides other poignant examples of failures to understand and the role of discourse in the breakdown of understanding.

3. See, for example, Cazden, D. (1986). Classroom discourse. In M. Wittrock, *Handbook of research on teaching* (3rd ed., pp. 432–464). New York: Macmillan.

4. See, for example, Romberg, T., & Carpenter T. (1986) Research on teaching and learning mathematics. In M. Wittrock, *Handbook of research on teaching* (3rd ed., pp. 850–873). New York: Macmillan.

5. Two teachers were not included in this part of the analysis because we were unable to judge from the teachers' description of their practice whether they were using it "mainly" or "supplementally" in their mathematics teaching. Because this was a key distinction between Groups 1 and 2, we judged that these two teachers fell somewhere between Groups 1 and 2. In the report of this particular study, we use pseudonyms for teachers' names.

6. I use this metaphor because Magdalene Lampert has used it to describe her mathematics teaching, and this metaphor seems apropos to Annie's teaching as well. See, for example, Lampert (1990).

7. I was doing fieldwork at Muir School this week, but I observed Annie's class on the day previous to this one. This transcription comes from my analysis of a videotape of Annie's class that was done by Susan Baker, a CGI project staff person and sent to me by Tom Carpenter. This videotape constitutes data being collected by the CGI researchers as part of their NSF-funded project. My analysis is in no way intended to substitute for or supplant their own analysis of these data.

8. In reading an earlier draft of this paper, noted psychometrician and educational psychology professor Lee J. Cronbach was intrigued by these six-year-olds' discussion of the possible existence of negative zero. Cronbach recalled an instance in which he actually got "−0" on a computer printout due to the procedure that the computer used to round numbers. Another university professor, Susan Luks, read this episode and recalled a recent instance in which her adult computer science students vigorously debated the existence of negative zero as they were learning about computer architecture. In some machine representations one of the "bits" indicated whether the number is positive or negative. Luks' adult students puzzled about how then to represent zero in computer language. They proposed the idea of "negative zero" and "positive zero" to try to solve their problem of how to represent zero in the computer.

9. It is important to note here that these qualities were *not* derived from any direct knowledge of

specific or actual communities of mathematicians. Rather, they represent Annie's and her students' ideas of how *they* want to function as a community investigating mathematical ideas.

10. Tom came to know Deborah Ball's work and teaching in her classroom because she participated in a conference that he and Elizabeth Fennema organized as part of the work of the Mathematical Sciences Education Research Center at the University of Wisconsin. Out of that conference came a paper that Ball has published in their edited book, *Rational numbers: An integration of research.* In another paper, "With an eye to the mathematical horizon," (in press, *Elementary School Journal*), Ball gives specific examples of mathematics tasks and discourse from her elementary teaching and also talks about her third-grade students' discussions of odd and even numbers and negative numbers and the representations that she and the students construct to understand these kinds of numbers.

11. Anne and Ellen seem to be engaged jointly in what Eleanor Duckworth (1987) has called "giv-ing students reason." Through her questioning of Annie about her thinking, Ellen seems to be engaged in what Duckworth has called "giving teachers reason."

12. Mentoring is the word that Annie uses to describe her work with her teacher colleagues.

13. Ann Brown (1992) describes a similar perspective on her learning as a researcher creating complex interventions in classroom settings.

14. For a similar perspective and the implications of this view for researchers on teaching and teacher educators, see M. Lampert and Christopher Clark (1990). Expert knowledge and expert thinking in teaching: A response to Floden and Klinzing. *Educational Researcher, 19*(5), 21–29.

15. Havel's message reminds me of the message of someone whom I have regarded as my teacher since my graduate school days at Stanford and whom I have continued to regard as my mentor over the past two decades, Dr. Lee J. Cronbach. (See, for example, Lee J. Cronbach's article "Social Science for Earthlings.")

REFERENCES

Ball, D. L. (in press). With an eye on the mathematical horizon: Dilemmas of teaching elementary school mathematics, *Elementary School Journal.*

Ball, D. L. (in press). Halves, pieces, and twoths: Constructing representational contexts in teaching fractions. In T. Carpenter, E. Fennema, & T. Romberg (Eds.), *Rational numbers: An integration of research.* Hillsdale, N.J.: Erlbaum.

Berkey, R., Curtis, T., Minnick, F., Zietlow, K., Campbell, D., & Kirschner, B. (1989). Collaborating for reflective practice: Voices of teachers, administrators and researchers. *Education and Urban Society, 22*(2), 204–232.

Brown, A. (1992). Design experiments: Theoretical and methodological challenges in creating complex interventions in classroom settings. *The Journal of Learning Sciences, 2*(2), 141–178.

Carnegie Forum on Education and the Economy. (1986, May). *A nation prepared: Teachers for the 21st century: The report of the task force on teaching as a profession.* New York: Carnegie Corporation.

Carpenter, T. C., Fennema, E., Peterson, P. L., Chiang, C. P., & Loef, M. (1989). Using knowledge of children's mathematical thinking in classroom teaching: An experimental study. *American Educational Research Journal, 26,* 499–531.

Carpenter, T. P., Fennema, E., & Franke, M. L. (1992, April). Cognitively guided instruction: Building the primary mathematics curriculum on children's informal mathematical knowledge. Paper presented at the annual meeting of the American Educational Research Association, San Francisco, CA.

Carpenter, T. C., Moser, J., & Romberg, T. (1982). *Addition and subtraction: A cognitive perspective.* Hillsdale, N.J. Erlbaum.

Cazden, C. (1986) Classroom discourse. In M. Wittrock, *Handbook of research on teaching* (3rd ed., pp. 432–464). New York: Macmillan.

Cohen, D. K., & Barnes, C. A. (1993). Conclusion: A new pedagogy for policy? In D. K. Cohen, M. W. McLaughlin, & J. E. Talbert (Eds.), *Teaching for understanding: Challenges for practice, research, and policy* (pp.240–275). San Francisco, CA: Jossey-Bass, Inc.

Cooney, T. (in press). Inservice models in teacher education in the mathematical sciences. In S. Fitzsimmons (Ed.), *Pre-college teacher enhancement in science and mathematics: Status, issues and problems.* Washington, DC: National Science Foundation.

Duckworth, E. (1987). *"The having of wonderful ideas" and other essays on teaching and learning.* New York: Teachers College press.

Florio-Ruane, S. & Lensmire, T. J. (1990). Transforming future teachers' ideas about writing instruction. *Journal of Curriculum Studies, 22*(3), 277–289.

Greeno, J. G. (1989). A perspective on thinking. *American Psychologist, 44,* 134–141.

Havel, V. (1992, March 1). The end of the modern era. *The New York Times,* 13F.

Holmes Group. (1986). *Tomorrow's teachers: A report of the Holmes Group.* East Lansing, MI: Author.

Knapp, N., & Peterson, P. L. (1991, August). *What does CGI mean to you: Teachers' ideas of a research-based intervention four years later.* (Elementary Subjects Center Series No. 48). East Lansing, MI: Center for the Learning and Teaching of Elementary Subjects, Michigan State University, 44 pages.

Lampert, M. (1990). When the problem is not the question and the solution is not the answer: Mathematical knowing and teaching. *American Educational Research Journal, 27,* 29–64.

Lampert, M., & Clark, C. (1990). Expert knowledge and expert thinking in teaching: A response to Floden and Klinzing. *Educational Researcher, 19*(5), 21–29.

Lindgren, A. (1950). *Pippi Longstocking.* New York: Scholastic, Inc.

National Council of Teachers of Mathematics (NCTM). (1989). *Curriculum and evaluation standards for school mathematics.* Reston, VA: Author.

National Council of Teachers of Mathematics (NCTM). (1991). *Professional standards for teaching mathematics.* Reston, VA: Author.

Peterson, P. L. (in press). Learning and Teaching Mathematical Sciences: Implications for Inservice Programs. In S. Fitzsimmons (Ed.), *Pre-college teacher enhancement in science and mathematics: Status, issues and problems.* Washington, DC: National Science Foundation.

Peterson, P. L., Carpenter, T. P., & Fennema, E. L. (1989). Teachers' knowledge of students' knowledge and cognitions in mathematics problem solving: Correlational and case analyses. *Journal of Educational Psychology, 81*(4), 558–569.

Peterson, P. L., Fennema, E., and Carpenter, T. (1991). Using children's mathematical knowledge. In B. Means, C. Chelemer, & M. S. Knapp (Eds.), *Teaching advanced skills to at-risk children* (pp. 68–111). San Francisco: Jossey-Bass.

Riley, M. S., Greeno, J. G., & Heller, J. I. (1983). Development of children's problem solving ability in arithmetic. In H. Ginsburg (Ed.), *The development of mathematical thinking* (pp. 153–200). New York: Academic Press.

Romberg, T., & Carpenter, T. (1986). Research on teaching and learning mathematics. In M. Wittrock, *Handbook of research on teaching* (3rd ed., pp. 850–873). New York: Macmillan.

Schoenfeld, A. (1992). Learning to think mathematically: Problem solving, metacognition, and sense making in mathematics. In D. A. Grouws (Ed.), *Handbook of research on mathematics teaching and learning* (pp. 334–370). New York: Macmillan.

Schon, D. A. (1983). *The reflective practitioner.* New York: Basic Books.

Tannen, D. (1990). *You just don't understand: Women and men in conversation.* New York: Ballentine Books.

Wasley, P. (1991, October). Reflective dialogue. Presentation at a conference on Critical Issues in Educational Restructuring, Center on Organization and Restructuring of Schools, University of Wisconsin, Madison, WI.

The following study was funded by the U.S. Department of Education, Office of Educational Research and Improvement, Field Initiated Studies Program Grant No. R117E0051. However, the findings and opinions expressed here do not necessarily reflect those of the funding agency. Carla Confer, Barbara Risalvato, Doralyn Roberts, Eija Rougle, and Mary Sawyer each made critical contributions throughout the project, while Carla Confer and Mary Sawyer also contributed to the preparation of the paper. The author gratefully acknowledges their contributions.

CHAPTER FOUR

TEACHING DISCIPLINARY THINKING IN ACADEMIC COURSEWORK

JUDITH A. LANGER

▼

NATIONAL RESEARCH CENTER ON LITERATURE TEACHING AND LEARNING,
STATE UNIVERSITY OF NEW YORK AT ALBANY

Dr. Judith A. Langer is professor of education at the State University of New York at Albany, and codirector of the National Research Center on Literature Teaching and Learning funded by the U.S. Department of Education, Office of Educational Research and Improvement. She specializes in issues of literacy and learning. Her research focuses on how people become skilled readers and writers, on how they use reading and writing to reason and learn, and on what this means for instruction. Langer has published extensively in a wide variety of journals and collections and has authored several books. She is currently writing a new book, *Literary Understanding and Literature Instruction.*

In a series of studies, I have been addressing the hypothesis that a variety of current problems in American education stem from an unrealistically narrow conceptualization of the nature of academic learning—one that fails to take the uniquely discipline-specific ways of reasoning into account. These studies grow from the assumption that there are two components of academic learning in each discipline, one having to do with particular content knowledge, the other having to do with ways of knowing and reasoning that are accepted as appropriate and necessary for learning and understanding within the particular field. In the context of reasoned thought, for example, this means that in addition to deriving a surface understanding of information, students must learn to understand the ways in which evidence is presented and arguments are developed in the texts they read and write for particular subjects. Comprehending subject-area reading material goes beyond understanding the content and includes the ability to construe and critique the information in appropriate ways. So, too, writing about the content requires a reasoned understanding of the material and also a knowledge of ways to present the information that are appropriate to that particular discipline. That the content differs from discipline to discipline is obvious and trivial; our understanding of the ways of knowing embedded within each discipline is less clear.

There is a long tradition in American education of granting equivalent "mental discipline" to all academic subjects, as well as of teaching generic modes of argument and exposition as part of the curriculum in English. At the same time, the philosophy of each school subject has usually stressed its unique value to culture and society— the value of "historical perspective," "scientific objectivity," or "literary sensitivity," for example.

One study (Langer & Applebee, 1988; Langer, 1992a) traced these conflicting views in the history and philosophy of several disciplines, testing the argument that the lack of a clear conception of what is unique and what is generic has led to an overemphasis on particular content (where the uniqueness of each discipline is clear and easily assessed), and a paucity of attention to ways of thinking and knowing (which we have failed to articulate clearly or to implement well in any subject). It then looked at the conceptions of academic learning held by specialists in particular disciplines, including a spectrum of university and high-school teachers. The focus was on their general view of what counts as important in their subjects, as well as on the ways in which they were able to articulate the features of that knowledge. To provide a manageable universe of study, the project team focused on four subject areas: American literature, American history, physics, and biology. This allowed examination of the extent to which teachers in different disciplines emphasize different rules of evidence and procedure—that is, the extent to which they reflect discipline-specific ways of knowing and reasoning in their teaching. Findings from this study suggest the following:

1. Each of the disciplines has increasingly focused on the tentative nature of "truth," leading to an emphasis on the need for more active *questioning* and *interpreting* rather than on simple accumulation of facts.

2. The shift from stable "truths" to conditional knowledge found in the disciplinary literature is often paralleled in educational

theory, but has not necessarily made its way into the teaching journals.

3. All teachers in the study wanted their students to think. However, they more often talked about such issues when discussing abstract goals and more likely focused on specific content when talking about the day to day details of teaching and learning.

Findings also suggested that although ways of thinking are a central concern to each community, there seems to be a gradual shift in priorities. The "pure" disciplines' belief in the instability of knowledge and the need for inquiry are replaced in the schools with a focus on stable content and less inquiry. Further, teachers do not seem to have a "codified" language to talk about ways of knowing, even when they want to. The closer to the daily activities of the student, the more the focus seems to turn to facts, to the exclusion of ways to think about them.

However, this study was limited to teacher interview data, which needed to be augmented with classroom observation. The follow-up study discussed in this chapter took the next step, by observing cross-disciplinary conversations among teachers concerned with explaining what they value to one another, and by "living in" classrooms in order to examine the relationships between teachers' expressions of the knowledge and reasoning they value and their ways of teaching—the pedagogical strategies the teachers adopt as they shape the ways their students read, write, and discuss. The study sought to contribute to (a) a rethinking of instruction in terms of ways of knowing and doing within particular content domains; (b) a reinterpretation of the goals of particular courses of study in terms of that rethinking; and (c) a grounding of the general argument in the detail and complexity of the language and communication of the classroom. It grows from the position that although notions of discipline-specific thinking need not be considered at odds with more general theories about reasoning (but rather as providing specifications for contextualized actualizations), in pedagogical research and practice they are polarized, with little attempt to understand the different approaches to reasoning that underlie the differing academic contexts that students encounter.

RELATED STUDIES

In the past few years, a number of studies have reported that American children are not learning to think deeply enough or to deal with issues broadly enough across a wide range of academic subjects (e.g., Applebee, Langer, & Mullis, 1989; Applebee et al., 1990; Boyer, 1983; Langer et al., 1990; Mullis and Jenkins, 1988, 1990; National Commission on Excellence in Education, 1983). We find these results troubling. Further, I have explored the relationship between the teaching of academic subjects and students' ability to reason about what they read and write in a series of studies with Arthur Applebee (Applebee, Langer, et al., 1984; Langer, 1984; Langer & Applebee, 1987). These studies have examined writing across a variety of academic disciplines and traced the relationships between that writing, the teachers' values, and the types of learning fostered in their classrooms. Though the focus in these studies was on the teaching of writing, the typical writing assignment was in fact a response to assigned reading in the class textbooks. Thus these studies of writing skills were also studies of students' opportunity to reason about what they had read in their various subject classes. Results indicated that students were rarely challenged to explain their interpretations or encouraged to examine the evidence on which they had based their conclusions. More typically, in all areas of the curriculum, they were asked to summarize information and points of view that had been presented to them by the teacher or the textbook.

The initial studies attributed such findings to a lack of effective models of alternative approaches to instruction—in particular, they noted the lack of instructional models that stressed the process of thinking about what students had read or learned (even though recent trends in the teaching of both reading and writing have placed great value on such approaches). In response to the need for such models, a series of studies of teachers who used writing after reading in interesting and effective ways, in a variety of academic disciplines, was initiated. Though these studies were planned as a way to develop a series of models of effective instruction, the major outcome was to suggest new ways to conceptualize academic learning.

From these studies, it was learned that if new activities stress one kind of knowledge but teachers have been trained to look for other types of performance as evidence of learning, the new approaches make little difference. Results were consistent across these subject areas (science, history, and English). Most teachers focused upon relatively factual knowledge about a subject and were relatively successful in ensuring that students developed an understanding of their subject at that level; they trained students to comprehend and remember particular facts. At the same time, their students failed to reason about those facts, whether in science, history, or English. Some of the causes are institutional, tied to evaluation systems, public expectations, and conditions of instruction. Others are more directly related to the *content* of instruction—to what students are asked to learn and what teachers have learned to look for as evidence of that learning. One central problem is that while teachers can easily recognize (and reward) surface understanding and "correct" information, they have more trouble articulating the rules of effective reasoning that govern ways of knowing and doing within their particular disciplines. As a result, their definitions of progress, and of success, are inevitably based on those aspects of learning that they can articulate—the facts or information out of which textbook arguments are presented, rather than the reasoning skills that students need in order to analyze such arguments or to construct new arguments themselves.

A recent series of studies (Langer, 1990, 1991, 1992b), has involved collaboration with a group of English teachers, with the goal of developing more thought provoking activities in the teaching of literature. These studies have shown that these activities occur on a sustained basis only in those situations where the teacher has been able to conceptualize a notion of learning that has at its core the ways in which students think about the course content. However, because this way of viewing the goals of instruction runs counter to most of the traditional materials, tests, and objectives that dominate the school curriculum, it is very difficult for teachers with strong intentions for change to develop a consistent and stable way of viewing, teaching, and talking about ways to think in their subjects. Thus, if teachers are to help students reason when they read, write, and talk about their coursework, then university-based and teacher researchers must begin by engaging in collaborative studies to articulate the ways of knowing and reasoning—of how to know and talk about "what counts" as central to their courses. Only then can we begin to help teachers develop new and consistent ways to evaluate student learning in terms of higher-level reasoning rather than in terms of surface understanding of particular content. (For a discussion of these distinctions see, for example, Vygotsky's notion of pseudoconcepts, Vygotsky, 1962; Rieber & Carton, 1987; Wertsch & Stone, 1985.)

It is worth contrasting this point of view with traditional notions of content area reading and writing (see Langer & Allington, 1992). For example, in the past, content area reading and writing have been treated as consisting of a variety of generic strategies that teachers should be aware of so that they can help their students understand the content and learn to deal with difficult text. They have been seen as part of "skills" instruction, either within the domain of reading teachers or English teachers who taught generic reading, writing, and study skills, or transferred to the content area classroom. And, as taught by the subject area teacher, such instruction was seen as part of the teaching of reading and writing skills, not as a central part of the subject area curriculum.

In contrast, the rationale motivating this work is that a focus on reading, writing, and reasoning in the content classroom is (or should be) central to the contemplation of the subject area itself. This notion of socially based academic learning is at the root of a sociocognitive view of learning (see Langer, 1987; Scribner & Cole, 1980; Vygotsky, 1962), which holds that cognitive behaviors are influenced by context and affect the approaches toward knowing as well as the meanings that learners produce. It is these approaches toward knowing, rather than generic reading and writing strategies, that are seen as central to academic learning and reasoning.

The validity of this argument depends, in part, on the level of analysis that one adopts. Previous studies have made it clear that there are broad strategies of argument or uses of language that are common to the various high-school subjects (Applebee, 1984; Britton et al., 1975; Calfee & Curley, 1984; Langer & Applebee, 1987). Students of literature, of history, and of science write reports about specific events, for example, and also read and write analyses of such events. These strategies capture consistencies across varied contexts of language use. At the same time, however, the similarity in underlying purpose may be masking very important differences in the ways in which these purposes are achieved. These differences are likely to involve very fundamental concepts—notions of causality and proof, of evidence or warrants for claims, of assumptions that can be taken for granted, and of premises that must be made explicit and defended. Such concepts may lie at the heart of successful understanding of a new discipline, as well as at the heart of the development of the reasoning abilities that so few students seem to achieve.

My studies of effective teachers of English, science, and history have highlighted the extent to which schools and textbooks treat reading and writing as a way to present particular content (often codified in elaborate scope and sequence charts) rather than as an introduction to new ways of knowing and doing. It is this content that drives their curriculum and that is reflected in the class, school, and district examinations that students face.

There is another way to view the classroom, however, that transforms the nature of the reading and writing activities that occur. This is to view the classroom as a community of scholars (or scholars and apprentices) with its own public forums with associated rules of evidence and procedures for carrying the discussion forward. (See, for example, Anderson et al., 1990; Bazerman, 1981; Bizzell, 1982; Faigley & Hansen, 1985; Herrington, 1985; McCarthy, 1987.) Students must learn, then, not only the "basic facts" around which texts are structured, but the legal and illegal ways in which these facts can be mustered in the forum defined by that classroom. The forum will be partly oral, in the presentations and discussions that make up the dialogue of instruction, and partly written, in the materials that students read and papers they write. The quality of the reading material and the nature of the teacher's questions, assignments, and interactions are important, since these will provide the most extensive models of what counts as effective discourse and reasoning. Reading, writing, and discussion become vehicles for learning the ways of organizing and presenting ideas that are most appropriate to a particular discipline. In such a view, the development of literate thought (see Langer, 1987) becomes a major agenda of instruction in all of the academic disciplines.

This is a sociocognitive view of both literacy and instruction. What evidence is there for it? A variety of scholars have put forth related arguments, developing them in the context of an examination of the conceptual, intellectual, or social traditions of a given disciplinary community (Bazerman 1981, 1982; Bizzell, 1982; Kuhn, 1962; Odell, 1980; Roland, 1982; Toulmin, 1958, 1972). Herrington (1985) complements this theoretical work by studying the nature of such disciplinary communities (or forums) at the college level. Basing her conclusions on lengthy ethnographies of two chemical engineering classes, she found that even within the specialized context represented by this subject matter, the characteristics of the "forums" in the two classes were very different. Students were learning not only the specific content of chemical engineering, but also the specific types of claims and warrants that were construed as appropriate in particular contexts. Success in these classes, then, depended in part upon learning highly specific strategies and routines for evaluating and judging what they read, routines that were inextricably linked with the particular content under study. McCarthy (1987), in related work, studied the various writing and thinking experiences of undergraduate students as they moved from course to course, describing the different ways of communicating and concerns for knowing that characterized the courses. In yet another study, Berkenkotter et al. (1988) traced the socialization of a first year graduate student into the particular rhetorical and intellectual traditions represented by a doctoral program in rhetoric and composition. All three of these studies highlight the discipline-specific as well as the community- or classroom-specific nature of the particular reasoning strategies which students must develop. In a very different tradition, Applebee, Durst, and Newell (1984) analyzed the structure of published texts, as well as of student writing, in high-school science and social studies. Using a variety of text-analytic procedures, this study found not only that the texts produced by students and published writers differed in consistent ways, but also that the patterns of these differences were different in the two subject areas. These differences between subjects were particularly clear in the patterns of linguistic features marking causality, time sequence, logical sequence, and the like—the features most likely to reflect differing types of evidence as well as different ways of organizing that evidence to sustain an extended discourse.

Yet, characteristics such as those described in these various studies are rarely articulated by the teachers involved, though there may be an intuitive recognition that such differences exist. If we are to create powerful student-thinkers we must better understand (and come to articulate) the features of argument and analysis that characterize good thinking in particular disciplines. This will create a focus on ways of knowing and doing, as well as on particular content. To do this will require studies, such as the one reported in this chapter, that seek to describe ways in which teachers' implicit values of discipline-appropriate reasoning are evidenced in subject-matter coursework.

THE STUDY

This study was designed to examine the language and interactions that occurred in classes where teachers felt they were providing an environment that fosters reasoning about their coursework. It focused on the ways in which teachers' conceptions about knowing and concerns for content affected the day to day goals, activities, and interactions in their classes—their students' academic environment for learning. We examined the discourse within the diverse classrooms of eight high-school teachers (two each in American literature, American history, biology, and physics). All of the teachers had taught from 7 to 31 years and were considered to be excellent teachers by their department supervisors and colleagues. In each discipline, the teachers' instructional styles differed, with one placing more emphasis on the content and the other on the students' ways of thinking about that content. A brief description, by subject area, follows:

BIOLOGY

Marge Rhodes teaches biology in an upper-middle-class suburban community. To her, biology is an important course for students to take because, "Students need to know science as adults, especially biology to understand illnesses, disease, reproduction. . . ." She encourages her students to participate in discussions. Marge moves around the room, in front to introduce a lesson, then to help in groups. Of the two biology teachers we

studied, her classroom provided more frequent opportunity for students to express and examine their own ideas.

Gabe Rose is a biology teacher in a middle-class suburban community. As to his course goals, he says, "I would like to polish scientific reasoning skills—the uses of control, the formulating of hypotheses, the observational skill. . . ." He provides his students with an extensive outline at the beginning of a unit that lists the teacher's plans, labs due, work sheets, exams, and so forth. He relies on the outline to keep track of what he has covered and the students' progress.

PHYSICS

Stan Canfield is a physics teacher in a high school in a small city. In discussing his views of physics instruction, Stan says, "Students remember what they control and what they do. . . ." He always provides shared experiences (lab demonstrations) as a way to bring the group together to discuss what they've seen. From this, Stan guides them to make links. Of the two physics teachers we studied, Stan invites students to work through their own ideas more often.

Ken Rivers teaches physics in the same high school as Marge. He says, "Physics . . . [relates] so easily to things within one's own experiences." He carries this out in class, giving his students many examples from everyday life. Ken's lab work interactions are informal, with students working in self-chosen groups and Ken available for questions. His lecture class is more traditional, with straight rows of desks, and the time is more formal and fast paced than his labs. Ken admits to being teacher-centered ("I'm always uncomfortable when I'm not in charge").

AMERICAN HISTORY

Kenny Craft teaches American history and government in an inner-city school, with approximately half the students belonging to ethnic and racial minority groups. He says,"It is important to develop a love of your country . . . and an understanding of your fellow man and his behaviors. . . . History can also be a medium for teaching thinking skills. . . ." Although he lectures a good portion of the time, his students are listened to and engaged. He has them discuss, debate, and work on joint projects—communicate.

Laura Barnes teaches American history and government at a suburban high school. She thinks it is critical for all students to study history. "It's part of our cultural literacy. It leads to understanding of current events. . . . [and] . . . an appreciation of their past." She uses cooperative learning activities in her class with small group discussions and collaborative projects. Yet, of the two history teachers, Laura more often directs the instructional interactions.

AMERICAN LITERATURE

Terry Andrews teaches American literature at the same high school as Laura. He sees himself as ". . . striving to help [students] make the connections between what they are reading in class and the values of today. . . ." Terry's class is characterized by student-centered activities and student-to-student cooperation; the development of students' ideas and interpretations are the focus of instruction.

Linda Reed teaches American literature in an urban high school. She feels it is important for students to study literature because, "They need it to function effectively in the world, to be informed citizens. . . ." The students keep logs where they write about their own ideas and responses. However, these are at the periphery of class concerns. Linda is often after a particular interpretation, and she uses the literature lessons

as a time to retrace the piece with her students, from beginning to end.

During the yearlong project, the teachers, research assistants, and Langer met as a collaborative project team to focus on the similarities and differences within and across classes in goals, activities, and issues that surround students' reasoning; and they focused on ways to identify and talk about that thinking in each subject. Each research assistant worked closely with two teachers, observing classes, and meeting and interviewing the teachers before and after the lessons to understand better their goals when planning, as well as when reflecting back on the lessons. Interviews with teachers focused on their general goals for the course, as well as on their planning of particular lessons.

The research assistants and Langer met weekly for case study sessions. In these meetings we jointly discussed the whole-group meetings, class observations, and interviews, identifying and finding evidence for patterns of concerns as well as communication between and across disciplines.

FINDINGS

▼

Through recursive analyses of the data, we searched for patterns in what the teachers in each field valued as knowing, based upon what they said and wrote about their teaching goals and practices, as well as in the assignments they gave, the discussions and activities they encouraged, and what they acknowledged as thoughtful in their responses to student papers.

The findings will be discussed in two parts,

| TABLE 4-1 | COLLABORATING TEACHERS | |
Subject	Less Traditional	More Traditional
Biology	Marge Rhodes	Gabe Rose
Physics	Stan Canfield	Ken Rivers
American History	Kenny Craft	Laura Barnes
American Literature	Terry Andrews	Linda Reed

each focusing on a different aspect of the ways of thinking emphasized and rewarded in the eight classrooms. The first section will examine how the teachers' common ways of talking about reasoning—in particular their shared valuing of making connections and asking good questions—play themselves out in the different subject areas. In general, these analyses will conclude that the shared vocabulary masks real differences in what counts as knowing and reasoning in different subjects. The second section will examine the pedagogical strategies that teachers use to shape their interactions with students, and through which they model and scaffold appropriate ways of thinking in their disciplines. In this section, one set of interactive strategies (finding common ground in discussing new concepts, clarifying what students know, and focusing on significant detail) are used in very similar ways across the subject areas studied. A second set of concerns are reflected in different lesson segments (orienting students' attention, refining their understanding, and helping students select appropriate evidence) and play themselves out in ways that are discipline specific. This section will conclude that teachers' tacit knowledge of their discipline leads them to guide students toward ways of thinking appropriate to each discipline. While their teaching styles affected the amount of access the students had to thinking through their own understandings, the discipline-specific nature of the various kinds of thinking was reflected in each of their classrooms.

DISCIPLINE-SPECIFIC WAYS THAT TEACHERS VALUE STUDENTS' THINKING: WHAT THEY SAY, WRITE, AND TEACH

All of the teachers voiced similar concerns about how students come to know, and they often used similar words to voice those concerns. Making connections and questioning appeared as two significant themes in the teachers' conceptions of knowing their disciplines; they said and wrote

that they wanted their students to learn to make connections and to ask good questions. They also said they wanted their students to analyze, to interpret, to provide evidence, and to predict. But these reasoning behaviors were implicitly treated as necessary components or subsidiaries of connecting and questioning, rather than as serving different purposes. Across disciplines, when they explained what they meant, their language was similar, for example, about connections: "You know, making links, connecting knowledge with new material"; and about questions: "Using what they know to learn more." But when they provided examples, when they discussed student work, and when we observed what they valued in their actual teaching contexts, we soon realized that these terms had very different meanings across subject areas. Their general language let them talk with us and with one another about the importance of reasoning abilities, but at the same time it masked real but unarticulated differences in the ways of thinking modeled and rewarded in their classes. This was evidenced in the subtle but consistent ways in which they supported certain types of sense making on the part of their students—ways that were not in conflict with, but rather were discipline-appropriate actualizations of the generalized vocabulary. Their knowledge of discipline-specific ways of knowing was tacit, based in previous experiences within their disciplines rather than in their general educational training.

Across subjects, all teachers said they wanted their students to make connections and ask good questions. But what they meant by this was quite different based on their subject area.

BIOLOGY

Connections

When the biology teachers spoke of wanting students to make connections, they were concerned with moving from smaller to larger units of understanding, as well as linking terminology to taxonomies. Because biological functions and systems are not readily visible, they felt it was important for their students to learn about the parts of systems and their properties and to make connections among them, as they operate in organisms or function within systems. For example, Gabe focused on physical properties of cells as a way to build toward an understanding of cell division. He said:

> Students need to make connections among the different parts of plant and animal cells. One is rectangular and the other is square. There needs to be a connection of properties [in this case shape]. Then the student needs to connect knowledge of the properties in a way to understand and approach new material [e.g., cell division].

The biology teachers also placed a great emphasis on their students' acquisition of subject-specific vocabulary, stressing conceptual connections between new vocabulary and its meaning within the system being studied. For example, Marge wanted her students to be able to connect their new words with those the students already knew in order to help them understand their meaning (and function) within the reproductive system, their topic of study. She said:

> Like telophase chromosomes are far apart. What's the Greek word for far? Think about telephone and television.

This focus on connecting word meanings results from their conviction that the acquisition of the technical vocabulary is an integral part of concept learning. Almost every lesson introduced new words.

Questions

In talking about the role of questions, the biology teachers focused on the students' lack of knowledge due to the fact that biological systems are not visible. They did not feel their students had useful prior knowledge to call upon and, therefore, considered student questions as requests for direct information. Thus, they provided factual responses to student questions and did not help them ponder and find answers for themselves. We see this being enacted in Marge's lesson on reproduction, which looks closely at cell division and chromosomes.

> **Jim:** . . . I have a question. If you get 23 chromosomes from each parent, why do you look like one parent sometimes?
> **Teacher:** Ahh, you use dominance. Sometimes it masks another trait.

And later in the same lesson:

> **Stacy:** When women go through menopause, they don't produce eggs. Do men have the same thing where they don't produce sperm?
> **Teacher:** Actually, men, I think, always continue to produce sperm. That's why you have someone like Cary Grant, a 70-year-old father . . . .

Gabe responds to student questions in much the same way in the following lesson on reproduction.

> **Teacher:** A cell will have a nucleus with 12 chromosomes in the nucleus. So this is the mother cell with 12 chromosomes . . . From this mother cell, how many daughter cells are produced and how many chromosomes in each daughter cell? . . . Tobi . . . how many daughter cells will exist?
> **Tobi:** Two.

It is then established that each daughter cell will contain 12 chromosomes. Shelby then raises a question.

> **Shelby:** Since there are two daughter cells, wouldn't you think the 12 chromosomes would split up between them?
> **Teacher:** But it doesn't. . . . One mother cell equals 12 chromosomes; two daughter cells equals 24 chromosomes total . . . .

Both teachers interpret their students' questions as an indication of their desire to have an answer to their questions, rather than an opportunity to explore the ideas that led to them in the first place, or as an opportunity to allow the students to formulate their own possible answers based on what they had already learned. The questions the teachers ask leave little room for students to formulate their own possible answers.

Thus, in the biology classes studied, students' ability to make connections and ask good questions seems to be related to the centrality of taxonomies in the structure of the course and to their notions that the taxonomies need to be learned in a part-to-whole manner, with new vocabulary assisting an understanding of how the system works. The taxonomies seem to be as much a system for reasoning as for labeling; the two seem intertwined. Therefore, students' ability to make connections and ask good questions is defined in terms of their ability to manipulate the particular concepts under study and to fit them into a larger classificatory system. However, underlying this is the teachers' sense the functions and systems being studied were generally new to the students (primarily invisible in daily life); they felt the students had few underlying concepts on which to build, and their major goal was to supply this base.

PHYSICS

Teachers' concerns in physics were somewhat different, focusing primarily on students' ability to make observations about phenomena in nature, and using these observations to understand underlying principles of physics. Although physical principles are not observable, they underlie the ways in which things operate in the natural world, and thus natural phenomena become a central part of the lessons.

Connections

The physics teachers in the study felt that the understanding of patterns and relationships in nature is the goal of physics, and that making these sorts of connections is an integral part of learning to understand the principles of physics. Through observation of natural phenomena, they hoped their students would be able to make connections between and among the phenomena being observed and their concepts and properties. However, because the teachers often felt that the concepts were complex (e.g., "Friction is messy"), they treated them in a simplified manner, with smaller facts and observations connected to a generalized concept of the whole.

For instance, in Stan's unit on refraction, the class had firsthand experiences with the ways in which light passes through various objects. First they established that the light ray bends when it hits the flat surface of the prism at an angle, but not when it hits it straight on. He began by making connections the next day:

> **Teacher:** Actually, we are going to take a look at this refraction business again, but today what I am going to do is address the concern I sensed all of you had, the question. I want to actually put together one of the continuing themes of the course, looking for patterns in numerical data. Which means we're going to have to get some numerical data and we're going to have to understand what the phenomenon is—refraction, this business of light-bending. And I want to address the concern that I sense you all have . . . that all that we have done with refraction has been qualitative. We've seen light bend when it passes from one material to another, but we haven't measured how much it bends. . . . We'll start doing that today with this little device here [the spectroscope]. The first thing I would like you to do is just check again. There's something neat about this semicircular piece of glass when I aim light at it. And I would like us all to have a good idea of why I use a glass that shape. What's so great about it? Why does it allow us to see this refraction business more nicely?

And later said: [after measuring]

Teacher: OK, now we can look for some kind of pattern between these angles. . . .

Ken's course is set up to start with "big" things that can be easily observed, such as the motion of objects to the motion of electrons and other subatomic particles. He said he hopes his students will see that "all the stuff interrelates. . . . I tell them that the stuff you learned at the beginning comes back to haunt you later on."

Although Ken is more concerned than Stan about the naive misconceptions his students have about scientific concepts, both physics teachers feel that their students implicitly know about physics as a result of having spent their entire lifetimes observing natural phenomena in the world around them. Thus, their challenge is to help students connect and refine this everyday knowledge with theory in order to understand physical properties and phenomena—the nature of the outer world.

Questions

In a similar manner, the physics teachers in the study believed good student questions indicated a search for understanding of the principles in nature. The point Ken and Stan made over time was that they valued the accretion of a growing body of factual knowledge about physics, but that the students' ability to ask good questions about how things operate in nature and what their properties might be underlay such learning.

We can see Stan's attention to students' questions about the thickness of light beams during their unit on refraction. The students are engaged in measuring angles of refraction, and the following discussion is the result of a student's procedural question in which a property of light (the thickness of the beam) is being used to try to understand the angle of refraction.

Sam: How are we getting tenths if the light beam is like one unit thick?
Teacher: That's a good question. How are you estimating?

Conway: Looking at the middle of the light beam.
Teacher: [To Sam] You don't like that?
Sam: No, it's fine.
Teacher: OK. Yes, Skeets.
Skeets: Wouldn't it be easier to do it by the edge, because the middle is easier to make a mistake?
Teacher: Good point.
Conway: The edge isn't really, the middle is definitely better.
Teacher: Why would you say it's better to use the middle?
Conway: Well, like, you have a clock with a hand. The edge is on 12, but it's not straight up and down. At 12, it would be straight up and down and you would use the middle.
Teacher: So, if it's a pointer of some sort, you'd use the middle of the pointer. But Skeets is saying if you're inconsistent about using one edge . . .
Skeets: Well, see, the thing is, in *this* pointer, it would be a wedge of the light beam, because it can't be a pointer if it keeps on going. It stops and you see the very end of the point. It goes right to the edge of the scale. The point is the edge of the light.
Conway: I think it doesn't make that much difference really.
Skeets: Neither does 7.5. [Oooo's from students in response to Skeets' criticism of Conway.]
Teacher: Point well taken. Folks, let me tell you, I am impressed by this concern for accuracy. That's one of the things that comes very late for high-school students, typically. Often there's very little concern for accuracy when, in fact, that can often be the difference between someone getting a good lab and someone getting a bad lab. It's just this very kind of concern for accuracy. You can take it too far; you can take it beyond the accuracy that this can give you. In other words, the best thing we can get for this set-up is

the nearest tenth of a degree. If we are arguing over one-hundredths of a degree, that would be silly. I'm not sure it's silly to be arguing over a tenth of a degree. And I think you are making excellent points.

Stan could have immediately supplied the answer to Sam's initial question, "How are we getting tenths if the light beam is one unit thick?" Instead, he allows his students to make their own observations about the measuring procedure and to draw their own conclusions before commenting. In doing this he invites them to think like physicists and to probe issues related to degrees of accuracy. And he demonstrates that he values such thinking by complimenting them for pondering the issues.

Although Ken does not encourage students' questions in the way that Stan does, his students are free to ask them, and when they do, he treats them as attempts to understand some principles of physics. He says he wants "the kids to find out, or at least to question things." He explained that, for example, he wants his students to ask questions about the hole in the ozone.

"It's over Antarctica. Why is the hole over Antarctica? Is it because penguins use an awful lot of deodorants? That doesn't make sense. Why would there be a hole there?" Here, Ken implies that good questions grow from observations the students make in nature and are moves toward more refined understandings of underlying principles of how things operate.

Overall, the physics teachers in the study displayed a continuing focus on the understandings of physical properties their students were developing, always considering their students' connections and questions as evidence of their moves between what they have known or can see in the real world and the phenomena being studied.

AMERICAN HISTORY

The teachers' focus in American history was on the cultural experience, on students' abilities to gain an understanding of the issues underlying the situations they studied, and to use these to interpret past, present, and future events and eventualities.

Connections

The American history teachers in the study focused on their students' ability to see topical relationships between and among people, events, and ideas across time and place. Both teachers indicated that they valued their students' ability to connect historical topics—to see cause and effect relationships and generalize about them, to connect current life experiences to events of the past, and to relate one person, event, or idea to another. Thus, making connections, to the history teachers, involves searching for parallels and points of departure within and across cultures and eras. Similar to the physics teachers, they believed their students already had useful knowledge on which to draw in helping them understand the issues under study, and thus provided room for their students to make connections between the topics at hand and their own experiences.

Both teachers encouraged their students to work in groups and used this as an opportunity to help them try to find connections in underlying themes and issues across time and place. Laura provided prepared activity packets to guide her students to make such connections when they met in groups. Following is an example from a lesson on "Problems of the Cities in 1870–1900." In their group activity packet, the students were asked to find a connection between racism and ethnocentrism, and to link it to present-day concerns. Three students work together using the packet as a guide:

> **Tanya:** Racism, ethnocentrism?
> **Gary:** Is that . . . ?
> **Tanya:** That's when Americans, that's when a country thinks . . .
> **Gary:** . . . they are the best, yeah.
> **Tanya:** Like America, Iraq.
> **Rick:** Now, how would you solve racism in a city? It's still not solved in 1990.

Several students talk at one time.

Rick: Racial equality ... you can instigate laws of [inaudible] equality, but you
still have to worry about [inaudible] citizens and personal feelings of those.

In a later lesson, the students were also expected
to make connections—this time considering the
situation in the United States today in regard to
immigration and comparing it to other countries.
In the following discussion, the students are trying
to make those connections.

Rick: Still, the United States is the
number one place to immigrate.
Tanya: I agree.
Crystal: I disagree because of Japan.
Rick: I don't know, you got, Germany
is together. That's going to be economically and militarily a strong country. That
wouldn't be a bad place to immigrate
to. What else?

Later in the packet, they are asked to connect
the understandings they have gained from this
discussion to the era and locus of study: problems
of the cities, 1870 to 1900.

Both teachers also encouraged their students
to make connections between their own personal
experiences and the topic they were studying.
Here, Kenny's students introduce relevant personal experiences during their class discussion on
labor unions.

Teacher: Why are labor unions good
for the society? What do you think?
Matt: In some aspect good ... compen-
sation.
Joseph: I'm not sure. I'm a member of
a musicians union. It doesn't have so
much to offer.
Teacher: What do unions try to offer?

When the students called upon their personal
experiences, Kenny helped them connect the
appropriate issues to the particular topic under
discussion.

Teacher: In most states, public employees can go on strike. Under the Taylor law
there are very strong penalties in New York
State.
Matt: Work to rule. What happened
here in Midtown, when the teachers
here were marching outside the school.
Teacher: That's called picketing; some
workers do that when they go on strike.

In general, the focus in the American history
classes was on topical connections, making connections over time, place, and event in order to
better understand the topic of the lesson and its
broader implications.

Questions

The American history teachers felt that the ability to ask good questions was a critical feature of
learning in their classes, because "Students indicate their consideration and manipulation of the
content by asking questions." Following is an
example from Laura's class of ways in which students ponder historical topics across time. They
are studying about immigration, and a student's
question indicates his concern about governmen-
tal quotas on immigration.

Geoffrey: I just ... they used to not be
able to ... I'm just wondering ... they can't
... could the Chinese have the right, now?
Teacher: Could the Congress make the
laws now saying no Chinese could come
in?
Geoffrey: Yes, I think if they wanted
to.
Teacher: Yes, if they wanted to they
could. Do we have the right to decide
which people can emigrate to the United
States?
Geoffrey: More or less.

This student's question indicates that he is considering the issues beyond what has already been
read and discussed. He knows that earlier in the
century Congress passed a law restricting the
number of Chinese who could enter this country

and wonders if the same legislation could be enacted today. Laura accepts Geoffrey's question as evidence that he is pondering an appropriate issue, helps him to tighten his question, and then goes on to answer it. Kenny also takes his students' questions as evidence that they are working through their understandings of the content. In the following example, although Kenny is about to make a link to a new topic, Crystal's question about anarchy, the topic they had previously been discussing, leads him to help the students understand anarchism more fully.

> **Students:** Anarchists. [In response to the teacher's question.]
> **Teacher:** Popular 19th-century idea. Ultimate good. . . . Was man good rather than evil?
> **Crystal:** When you say anarchist, don't you think everyone will kill each other?
> **Teacher:** What's your question for me?
> **Crystal:** Isn't the idea of anarchism more idealistic?
> **Teacher:** Well, yes . . . .

Thus, like the other teachers in the study, the American history teachers expect their students to make connections and to ask questions to further their understanding of cultural/historical topics. They expect their students to use their previous knowledge of life situations to help them understand the new content they are studying and to make connections over time, place, and event. Because they expect to see growth in the students' understanding of the issues, they monitor students' responses and model ways of reasoning like historians.

AMERICAN LITERATURE

The American literature teachers were also concerned with their students' ability to make connections and ask good questions as ways to gain greater understanding of the human condition. Like the physics and American history teachers, they assumed that their students' cumulative lifetime experiences provide them with a good deal of relevant knowledge that can help them understand the coursework. However, the ultimate goal of the literature teachers seemed to be for their students to use life to understand texts as a way to then use texts to understand their own lives—and the human condition.

Connections

The American literature teachers valued their students' ability to make personal connections between what they read and their own lives. They also wanted their students to make connections between two or more works, with the expectation that their students would, in turn, use these connections to reflect on their own lives. For the American literature teachers we worked with, connection as a way of thinking expressed itself in two ways: (a) in students' ability to relate ideas, situations, issues, and feelings to their own lives, and (b) in their ability to arrive at interpretations of text and life based on those connections. Both literature teachers continually encouraged their students to make connections between their own experiences and those about which they were reading. For example in Linda's class after reading Melville's *Billy Budd*, a character who receives unfair treatment, the students were asked to write about an incident in their own lives when they felt they were treated unfairly. One student not only wrote about the personal incident, but also tried to relate her story to Billy's.

> Like Billy, I was accused of forming a group, which he did not do, and I got punished for missing my curfew like Billy did get punished for killing the master at arms which was a reaction to what he was saying. My staying out late was a reaction to what my Mom said. So, in many ways, my situation was similar to Billy's situation.

This student received an A for her paper, and Linda also praised the connection her student made by writing "Great!" in the margin of her paper.

The teachers saw the reading of literature as a personal and sometimes idiosyncratic experience, and tried to help their students make connections that were personally meaningful to them. For example, Terry tried to elicit his students' personal reactions to the assassination of JFK as described in *Born on the Fourth of July* by Ron Kovics, but soon became sensitive to the fact that his students were too young to personally recall the assassination. They were reminded instead about the explosion of the Challenger space shuttle.

> **Cameron:** It was like, I mean, I can relate it to how I felt when the space shuttle, the Challenger, blew up. I was in school when I watched it, and I felt pretty bad, but not that many people in the class were taking it that seriously.
> **Teacher:** How many of you saw the shuttle explode . . . ?

The next day he opened the discussion by returning to Cameron's connection.

> **Teacher:** Yesterday Cameron brought up the issue of the Challenger, and we used it for a couple of minutes. It was a good point, and I'd like to take it one step further.

He then asked the students to recall and jot down some of the emotions they felt when the space shuttle exploded. He also elicited some language from Kovics' piece that the students felt described the author's emotions. The students discussed some of the emotions they felt and compared them to the emotions Kovics had expressed. During the discussion, Terry was overt about the fact that their personal experiences can help them understand the text better—even if they haven't experienced the particular situation:

> **Teacher:** OK. What I'm trying to bring out here is that I kind of assumed that you understood Kovics' reaction, but what Cameron brought out is that you're much closer to the Challenger event. You can connect to this; you can relate to

it. That's the kind of response to literature that should happen to you. The literature makes you say, "Yeh, I can connect to that. I may not have been there, but I can understand this." What I want you to see is that you have a basis for understanding this.

Terry also shows his students that he values literary connections. The following comment was made after completing the Kovics book, by way of introducing *The Red Badge of Courage*.

> **Teacher:** Think about what Kovics' response might have been had he seen *Platoon* instead of John Wayne movies. Tomorrow, I'll give you *Red Badge of Courage*, and we'll read about four pages that are similar to what we read in Kovics' book, and we'll see what you make of it.

In doing this, Terry ends his unit on *Born on the Fourth of July* by not only giving the students something more to think about, but also by scaffolding their ways to make connections between literary works. That one is a modern piece and the other from an earlier period in history lends substance to Terry's claim in the follow-up interview that one of his responsibilities as a literature teacher is to "help students make the connections between the value systems of their forefathers and the value issues of today."

Questions

The American literature teachers regarded questions as an indication that students are trying to personally relate to what they are reading. Similar to their interest in connections, their primary concern was with the use of questions to refine their students' understandings of human experience, theirs and others'. For example, Terry responds to Robin's question in the following manner, and Etta joins the discussion to open it up for further scrutiny.

Heather: Is that really happiness, or is it just relief that you weren't the one who died.

Teacher: Happiness might not be the right word. We're trying to deal with Jim's reaction. It's a wonderful, honest reaction . . .

Etta: I was confused when I saw it. I didn't understand it.

Overall, the literature teachers assumed that essential meaning was *in* their students, based on the life experiences they had engaged in or witnessed, and that the literature lesson involved using these in relation to the text and other texts in order to gain more complex understandings not only of the piece being read, but of life in general.

MAKING CONNECTIONS AND ASKING QUESTIONS: A LOOK ACROSS DISCIPLINES

▼

Connections: General Comments

In the preceding section, we have discussed ways in which the biology, physics, American history, and American literature teachers in this study value the ability of their students to make connections. However, there are differences in the kinds of connections they value. The biology teachers value the students' ability to build taxonomies in order to understand how biological systems work, which are not openly visible for students to inspect; the physics teachers value the ability to see physics in action and to use these experiences to understand physical patterns and properties in nature; the history teachers value the ability to see connections within and across situations, people, and time; and the teachers of literature value the personal connection, leading to enhanced understanding of the piece being read and of the self, as well as the connections across texts.

Although the notions of connections in history and literature seem similar at first glance, we have seen that they are enacted in different ways

in the classroom, with greater focus on objective content in history and on subjective responses to text and life in literature. For example, the history teachers we studied want their students to be able to draw parallels between past and present events, believing such connections can help guide present understandings and actions. Although such connections focus on human situations and therefore seem to involve personal links such as those valued by the literature teachers, they are quite different. In history, the focus is on connecting personal experience and the topic at hand in order to better understand the present content of study; the focus of the personal experience is on the content—the information to be linked. In literature, the students' connections of their general understanding of feelings, motives, or behaviors are the focus, leading to a better understanding of human elements in text or in life. In one, the main focus of the connection is about general human feeling and behavior; in the other, it is about a specific subject-matter content.

Questions: General Comments

Although all the teachers valued student questions, considering them an important part of the process of learning, their notions of the particular role the questions play in students' thinking seemed to be affected at least as much by the particular discipline as by their approaches to teaching. More so, the ways in which the students' questions were treated seemed to be implicitly related to the kinds of knowledge teachers think students have (and need) in order to be able to approach an answer themselves. The biology teachers seemed most certain that their students had little prior knowledge about the topics being studied. To them, familiarity with the technical labels identifying aspects of the organism or system being studied, and the role of those parts within the larger taxonomy, are essential to understanding. This is certainly related to the fact that the high-school course of study in biology contains some 500 vocabulary terms the teachers feel compelled to "cover." However, they (and as far as we can surmise, their field in general) believe students won't be able to understand more until they have learned the basic language and concepts. Because these are unknown to the student, the purpose of questions is to gain the needed information, and the ability to answer the questions lies with the teacher who knows these basics. In contrast, the physics teachers expected that the students have had some experiences with natural phenomena and assumed this knowledge would be useful for answering questions in class. Thus, even when the students' questions seemed highly technical, the teachers assumed the students would find some way to explore the problem. Though students in both physics and biology often asked questions about the unknown (What's a proton made of? What does a prostate gland do?), they were treated in different ways. In biology, the focus was on learning the label or definition; while in physics it was on reasoning about the problem.

The similarity between the valued questions in biology and physics was that both sought information—whether supplied by the teacher or reasoned about by the students. So, too, in history, where there was particular content to be questioned and considered across people, places, eras, and situations.

However, the literature teachers' notions of good questions were qualitatively different from the other teachers'. Good questions in literature class were more exploratory musings than information-seeking in intent, both on the part of the student and, often, on the part of the teacher. They were closer to what Langer (1990, 1991) calls exploring horizons of possibilities, where the shape of the piece and the students' notions of what it is about are fluid—flexing and shifting as possibilities are pondered and their implications imagined.

These analyses suggested to us that it may be simplistic to assume that students in these classes are not learning to reason in their academic coursework. From our in-depth study of the eight teachers (see final report for additional analyses and discussion), we came away feeling that some reasoning seems to be taught. There appear to be sensible and purposeful subject-specific ways of reasoning embedded in the intentions underlying the activities and learning goals of the coursework, but never identified or singled out as essential evidence of good thinking. Because they are implicit, the teachers were unable to "flag" them at will and mark them for their students as important elements of disciplinary learning.

HOW TEACHERS SUPPORT STUDENT THINKING: EXAMINING DISCIPLINE-SPECIFIC PEDAGOGICAL ROUTINES

All the teachers we studied had a generalized knowledge about reasoning reflected in a common vocabulary, which enabled them to discuss their professional goals and instructional activities in broad terms. But, as we have already seen, this general understanding did not capture the differing kinds of thinking they actually valued and supported in their classrooms. The teachers imbued these general concepts with more particular meanings, meanings that were shaped by their sense of modes of thought appropriate to their particular disciplines. These notions of discipline-specific ways of knowing were tacit, systematically recurring within the classrooms, but unmarked as principles or guides the teachers were following. It is at this level of reinterpretation of general pedagogical concepts in discipline-specific ways that we need to seek evidence for reasoning within each discipline.

Commonalities Across the Disciplines

Across disciplines, there were some commonalities in the ways teachers tried to shape students' thinking as the lessons developed. These commonalities included finding common ground before discussion of new concepts, clarifying students' understanding, and focusing attention on significant details.

For example, at the beginning of almost all lessons, there was a "search for common ground," similar to what Stubbs (1980) calls "keeping in touch." This search sometimes also occurred at other points in the lesson, marking a change in topic or the attempt to help the students make links with a difficult concept introduced during the lesson. Although at one level this seemed to call on factual recall, in the social context of the class, it always served as a way to provide the students with an opportunity to become aware of their own ideas, hear what others had to say, and relate them to the topic at hand—in preparation for dealing with more complex issues. It served an interactive surveying, stock-taking, and pooling function, inviting the students to develop initial envisionments (Langer 1990, 1992) from which to build new learnings. For example, Gabe (biology) called for common ground in this way: When a student asked a question, he thought the other students might not understand.

> **Carol:** Do hydras have stinging tentacles?
> **Teacher:** Yes, however, *were any of you viciously stung a couple of months ago by the hydras?*
> **Eric:** No, how come?

Stan began a physics lesson at the beginning of a new unit with a search for common ground, in an attempt to help his students collectively brainstorm about force. He explained to his students that the key idea they were going to focus on in the new lesson was force, and opened the discussion by asking them what the idea of force meant to them. And, when Terry wanted his students to make some difficult comparisons between two works his students had just read, he too called for common ground.

> **Teacher:** On the board is what we want to think about ["The Emerson piece leads to images, implications, and outcomes that are different from 'Thanatopsis' "]. *Do you agree or disagree? What do you think?*

In each case, the teachers used a public forum to invite the students' immediate responses, as a way for them to become aware of, and begin to select and refine, related prior knowledge.

At other points in their lessons, all of the teachers were concerned with helping students clarify their understandings. For example, in Kenny's American history class, he tried to help his students clarify their understandings of carpetbaggers and how people felt about them in the past in comparison to today.

> **Teacher:** OK. These negative people, carpetbagger is a negative word today, were they nasty people?
> **Linda:** Some might have good intentions—businessmen.
> **Teacher:** *What do you mean?*
> **Linda:** [not audible]
> **Teacher:** *Do you see that positively or negatively?*

Stan (physics) encouraged a student to clarify his thoughts in the following:

> **Teacher:** . . . How do the amounts compare, Ben?
> **Ben:** They're equal.
> **Teacher:** Equal. *Why do you say that?*

In these exchanges, the teachers were helping students move beyond their initial thoughts and responses, to become aware of and clarify more specific understandings.

Another set of techniques used at least some of the time by all of the teachers focused students' attention on details of the subject matter, asking them to recall or locate information. These moves generally focused on particular facts and terminology, rather than broader understandings, and were sometimes used simply as a check on whether students had done their reading or were paying attention in class. Following are brief examples from Linda's (American literature), Ken's (physics), Marge's (biology), and Kenny's (American history) classes.

American Literature:

> **Teacher:** *Pearl associates Chillingsworth with who?*

Gail: The devil.
Teacher: *What does he say?*

Physics:

Teacher: *Now, what causes this? [pointing at diagram]*
Students: Mirror reflection.
Teacher: Yes, that's reflection, believe it or not. Yes it is.

Biology:

Teacher: *Go from what to what?*
Joe: The testes to the urethra
Teacher: The testes to the urethra— and that is the tube the sperm gets shot through. *In females what's the tube?*

American History:

Teacher: *What did they call those white Southerners?*
Mark: Scalawags.
Teacher: OK. *What's the pejorative word?*
Kim: Carpetbaggers.

In each of these cases, the teacher was monitoring students' recall of significant details and focusing students' attention on them. Thus certain instructional moves were orchestrated by the teachers in ways that guided students toward one or another type of thinking about the material. These moves functioned as a kind of instructional scaffolding that was independent of teachers' disciplinary frames of reference, being guided primarily by the teachers' general pedagogical approach.

DISCIPLINARY PATTERNS OF LANGUAGE AND THOUGHT

Although the teachers' awareness of specific ways of thinking appropriate to their discipline was tacit, there were patterns of thought that were systematically modeled and sought within each discipline. Across the disciplines we studied, embedded in the teachers' lessons were three different concerns that dominated different lesson segments, and which took different shapes in each discipline: orienting students' attention, refining their understanding, and helping them select appropriate evidence. These concerns guided the teachers in scaffolding disciplinary ways of thinking. (For a discussion of scaffolding ways to discuss and ways to think, see Langer, 1991.) As they focused on these three concerns, the teachers guided students' understanding of the particular nature of the discipline-specific content and of the appropriate ways to think about it.

BIOLOGY

Orienting Attention in Biology

Reflecting their overarching sense of what matters most in the study of biology, the biology teachers in this study used guiding questions to help their students focus on the features of biology they considered critical: in this case, to focus on biological functions, their labels, and their place within a larger system. We see this in Marge's unit on sexual reproduction.

Teacher: They (the tubes) go from what to what?
Joe: The testes to the urethra.
Teacher: The testes to the urethra. And that is the tube the sperm gets shot through. In females, what's the tube?
Jim: Fallopian.
Teacher: And what's the common name?
Jim: Oviducts.
Teacher: And we have how many?
Jim: Two.
Teacher: One from each _____?
Jim: Ovary.

Through this close modeling, the teachers helped their students determine what to attend to—what counts as knowing—in their classes.

Refining Understanding in Biology

Also reflecting their overall emphases, the biology teachers helped the students to refine their understandings of biological terms and functions, as well as their place within the larger system of which they were a part, by encouraging them to review and repeat the terms and patterns. In Gabe's class, it looked like this.

> **Teacher:** Do you understand what he said?
>
> **Jo-Jo:** Yes.
>
> **Teacher:** So, what are you going to draw next to the arrow?
>
> **Jo-Jo:** [inaudible, struggling to get out answer]
>
> **Teacher:** Who regenerates the most?
>
> **Jo-Jo:** Complex.
>
> **Teacher:** No, you're not looking at trends. Kevin, who is going to regenerate the most?
>
> **Kevin:** The first one.
>
> **Teacher:** Number one, next to number one, which is the tip of the arrow, the greatest regeneration. Number one is the greatest regeneration. Number five is _____?
>
> **Kevin:** Least.

Thus, refinement, in the biology classes we studied, frequently took the form of explicit review, often using unmarked diagrams to be filled in or charts to be developed by the students.

Selecting Evidence in Biology

Because the focus in biology was strongly on systems, the teachers asked the students to provide evidence of this knowledge by using proper labels for the parts and relating them to the system. In discussion, they often were asked how the parts functioned; but when working alone, they were more often expected to place the parts within the system. Thus, giving evidence of learning in biology involved the ability to generate the appropriate label for a particular function within the system being studied, and sometimes the ability to discuss the ways in which the systems functioned.

Following is an example from Marge's class. She helps them find evidence that erection can occur in males without the ejaculation of sperm. Notice that she reviews the meanings of terms as well as providing an example.

> **Gerry:** Can you have an erection without ejaculation?
>
> **Teacher:** Yeah, didn't we talk about little kids going in the water all the time?
>
> **Leslie:** Yeah, I've seen them [get an erection].
>
> **Teacher:** Erection is the penis becoming firm, straight. Ejaculation is the release of sperm.
>
> **Teacher:** [later in discussion] If you have little brothers or if you babysit, it is real common if they go into cold water they get an erection.
>
> **Jim:** They can't control it.
>
> **Teacher:** The nervous system, it's a real sensitive area and the cold causes an erection. It has nothing to do with sex. If you have an infant and you put something cold, water, on him when you are changing a diaper, oops, it happens.
>
> **Class:** [laughter]
>
> **Teacher:** The kid is not having sexual fantasies. This will happen. You have brothers, you will have kids someday. It's real common. It's just something that happens to a little boy. OK, have we covered everything? Oh, why does the penis have to do this?

Thus, we see that in the biology class we observed, the pattern of instruction oriented students' attention, refined their understandings, and asked them to select evidence in ways that would systematically lead them toward the kinds of knowledge that their teachers valued as important in biology.

PHYSICS

Orienting Attention in Physics

The physics teachers apprenticed students in ways to think by guiding them to carefully observe and investigate the natural phenomena they were studying. The teachers oriented students' attention primarily through close guidance about what to think about. Ken guides Sam in what to attend to in the following:

> **Teacher:** Lean [the water-filled beaker] so your coin is on the edge now. Take a look at all those images that are in there now. You've got a really nice big one, nice reflection on the bottom . . . Notice that your coin looks "bended" in the back. Yes? OK? Also, take a look at it through the side surface, so you're looking straight through the thing. Very easy to see a nice reflection on the bottom now.
>
> **Sam:** I see six coins.
>
> **Teacher:** Oh, yeah, you can see a lot of things this way.

While Ken helped Sam orient his attention to real-world phenomena during a class activity in the previous example, the physics teachers also carefully guided students' attention during class interaction as well. Stan's lesson is an example.

> **Joe:** Is there any difference between individual atoms, like neutrons?
>
> **Teacher:** One neutron and the next are totally indistinguishable.
>
> **Joe:** What about the stuff like neutrons and protons in the same atom? Any difference in areas inside?
>
> **Teacher:** Oh, ahhh, you've got me. I know that neutrons and protons have lots of characteristics that make them different. Are they made up of the same stuff, just different sizes? No. But there are some similarities. In other words, if you break protons apart and neutrons apart, you'd find some similarities in their components, some of the same constituents.

Thus, in both experiments and discussions, the physics teachers helped the students learn to closely observe and investigate—modeling appropriate ways of thinking in physics.

Refining Understandings in Physics

The undergirding goal of the physics teachers was to help their students integrate the physicist's ways of describing physical phenomena with their own. Thus, the teachers served as mediators between students' understandings and accepted understandings, trying to refine students' understandings toward general scientific interpretations of reality. Sometimes the teachers actively shaped the students' thoughts to match physicists' constructions; at other times the teachers would explain how a physicist would depict the phenomenon they were discussing. In the following example, during a unit on electrostatics, Stan shapes his students' observations, guiding them to link their observations to explanations of phenomena they had already studied.

> **Teacher:** It would become negative. If there's a transfer of negative charge from the comb to the ball, the ball would become negative. And if that happened, what would the ball do to the comb?
>
> **Joelle:** Repel.
>
> **Teacher:** Repel. And then see, it's still attracted [he has not allowed the comb to touch the ball]. But let me show you what happens when they touch. [Allows the comb and ball to touch and then they immediately repel each other.] OK, now what do they do?
>
> **Jacob:** Repel.
>
> **Teacher:** Repel pretty well. So, what happens when they touch?
>
> **Jacob:** Transfer of electrons.
>
> **Teacher:** Transfer of electrons from the comb to the ball. Now they are *both* negative, and they repel quite nicely. So that happens when they can touch, but not when they don't. Let me show you [draws on chalkboard].

Thus, the physics teachers helped their students refine their interpretations in discipline-appropriate ways.

Selecting Evidence in Physics

The physics teachers made it quite clear to their students that the provision of evidence in their classes required them to make direct links between the phenomena they had observed (or discussed) and the principles of physics they had learned (or were learning). Acceptance of a principle or reaching such an understanding was supposed to be based on the ability to replicate the evidence a number of times. We see this in Stan's class, later in the unit on electrostatics. He was helping his students group materials by the common ways they reacted to other materials.

Teacher: Repel, but there was contact. We did it without touching yesterday. We found that white plastic rubbed with felt repelled clear plastic rubbed with denim. . . . These are two kinds of things we can learn in class. We're learning this today, on a specific day, so there's number one, specific things. Secondly, there are things that carry over through the whole course. I'm interested in looking for patterns, and trying to figure out how something works. So, what I want to do today is to try to figure out how something works. And the way that you know that you've done that is that you're able to make good predictions. . . . So, let's try this out. Let's try to build some theories, look for patterns, build a hypothesis and the way to do that is to muck around with this stuff. [Reviews the data they have already discovered concerning how the three piles of things attract, repel, and so forth.] Can you build a, do you see a pattern here? Can you make a general statement that says, "Whenever blah, blah, blah, blah, then blah, blah, blah? Conway, what would it be?

Conway: Like objects repel. Does that fit our data so far?

Students: Yes.

Teacher: Three for three. [Reviews the three different ideas again.] Can you build a conclusion?

Students: Opposites attract.

Teacher: Now start testing our hypotheses, and do so by making predictions. How compare?

Skeets: It's different.

Teacher: How do you think it's, do you think this is going to behave with these two materials?

Some students: Attract.

Teacher: Agree?

Skeets: Attract the clear plastic and repel the white vinyl.

Teacher: Attract the clear and repel the white, but some are saying attract both, which is fine. Folks, I don't have a problem with dissention. We don't all have to think the same thing yet, [whispering] but we will. Teri, why did you say it was going to attract both of them?

Teri: Well, because based on our conclusions, they're different objects and we said they would attract and they're different.

Teacher: So, now I put it to Skeets and Irving. Didn't you say attract one and repel the other?

Irving: I think it will repel the white and attract the clear.

Teacher: Can you tell me why?

Irving: [No response, shrugs]

Teacher: So far we have three competing models. So far I've heard three things: like things repel, opposites attract, and things aren't really that different. Any other thoughts? Sam?

Sam: Does it have something to do with, like light goes through it?

Teacher: Jacob?

Jacob: I don't think the cloth makes that much difference.

Teacher: OK, we can test that. [This leads to a search for evidence during a series of experiments with a variety of materials.]

Thus, in physics, the teachers in this study asked their students to select evidence for their explanations for physical phenomena by making relevant connections between aspects of the specific occurrences they had witnessed and scientific principles that could account for them.

AMERICAN HISTORY

Orienting Attention in American History

In comparison, the American history teachers in this study oriented their students toward contextualizing the historical information they were studying. First they narrowed the content they were focusing on, highlighted it, and then helped the students consider it from a human/cultural perspective. Thus, the teachers oriented their students' attention not only to the specific material being studied, but toward forming their own contextualized understandings and explanations. Both history teachers guided their students to explore and consider the implications or outcomes of cultural and social aspects of the material they were studying, as Laura does in the following segment:

Teacher: What was missing? In what way was his [reasoning] faulty? If poverty was the effect, what was the cause?
Molly: Immigrants.

Refining Understandings in American History

Since the focus in the history classes was on contextualizing the content the students were studying, the teachers sought to refine students' understandings by asking questions that invited them to view the event or situation in more complex ways. For example, the teachers would ask their students to determine motivations and biases, or to consider an explanatory argument

from the vantage point of specific historical contexts (e.g., a particular era or culture) or perspectives (e.g., their own, an author's, or a particular political, economic, or gender-related view). We see this as Laura's class discussion continues.

Daniel: If we get rid of immigrants, we get rid of poverty.
Teacher: Anything else? Any other way you thought that his reasoning might not be correct?
Rosa: You can change numbers.
Teacher: I . . . I wouldn't say he was specifically lying about the numbers, but, often when numbers are used they can be manipulated.
Mike: Audience . . .
Teacher: All right, what do we know about the audience? What do we know about the audience who is going to receive this speech?

Selecting Evidence in American History

Because the goal in the history classes was to help the students gain the ability to understand and explain historical events and situations from the perspective of cultures and contexts, learning to select evidence involved explaining and defending particular interpretations. To this end, the teachers guided their students in ways to provide the facts, as well as the students' explanations and interpretations—through similarities and contrasts, and by explaining connections across time, cultures, and situations. For example, in Laura's unit on immigration, the class is guided to gain evidence for their disagreement with an author's view, based on some reports, that immigrants caused unemployment.

Teacher: OK, the reports [the students have already agreed] are reinforcing a bias. Prejudices . . . . And so, if you say that 39.4% of, look at that, you may view that as a very high number or you. . . . Any other faults you can find in his reasoning?
Gary: In "Relevant Information," he

says that most of the crimes are committed by adult males, and in his statistics he includes men, families, and children.

Teacher: All right, when in any of these numbers, remember it says in "Relevant Information" that mostly males, and he is talking mostly male population carrying it into total population. . . . Also, lacking in his argument are the reasons for the poverty. What's the reason that the immigrants are poor?

Rick: Low wages,

Teacher: Yes, they make low wages when they come here. Well, why do they make such low wages?

Tanya: They don't really know any better. . . .

Teacher: . . . So he makes this, when you read that you think just because they are immigrants from Southern and Eastern Europe they are poor, they must be poor without taking even into consideration any of the things that might be happening in America. OK, so when you read that, you automatically think, well, they are causing poverty . . . pretty far out assumptions.

Gary: It's not true, there are no facts in his argument.

Teacher: All right, there is absolutely nothing in his argument to suggest that the crime rate in those countries is high. OK?

[Later, Laura helps them think about other evidence she thinks is relevant.]

Teacher: Once again, what we are lacking is the reasons for the crimes. Maybe they didn't have enough food to eat. Questions?

Teacher: Did the immigrants cause higher employment?

Similarly, during the lessons in his class, Kenny frequently asks his students to look for evidence and at the same time weigh that evidence. When they make assertions, he requests evidence by saying, "You can back it up with what kind of evidence?"

LITERATURE

Orienting Attention in Literature

The literature teachers in the study invited their students to become literary thinkers by orienting them toward examining, sharing, and expanding their personal interpretations. This was often accomplished by asking open-ended questions that tapped the students' responses. For example, Terry asked his students such questions as:

> What do you think?
> What do you mean?
> Do you mean . . . ?
> What are we to do with this?

Linda's questions looked like this:

> Why don't you think Hawthorne says this?
> Why does Hawthorne leave it out?
> How many people thought the same as Raymond?

In Terry's class, the students' responses were often treated as more important than the text.

Refining Understanding in Literature

Refining understandings in the literature classes involved having students share their interpretations with class members, exploring and elaborating them, and considering possible implications. By asking questions, Terry guides his students to refine their understandings.

> **Teacher:** Do you agree or disagree [with the statement "The Emerson piece leads to images, implications, and outcomes that are different from 'Thanatopsis' "]?
> What do you think? . . . What about the images?
> **Marie:** The earth is a tomb. That's how you see it when it's dead.
> **Teacher:** What do you mean?
> **Marie:** Nature is death.
> **Teacher:** Anyone agree?

By inviting other students to counter with their own perspectives, Linda also helped class members refine and develop their own interpretations (e.g., "How many people thought the same as Raymond?" "Anyone want to add to that?" "Anyone agree?"). Both literature teachers systematically help their students learn to refine their understandings by sharing ideas with the class, elaborating on them, and drawing implications.

Selecting Evidence in Literature

By use of questions, the literature teachers frequently guided their students to use their texts, their previous class discussions, their personal knowledge and experiences, and other literature as sources of evidence for their responses. In Linda's class, the students were led to locate evidence for accepted interpretations; while in Terry's class, they were led to think through the reasonableness of the evidence in interaction with their own developing understandings.

Terry asks his students to provide their own evidence, but guides them in doing so, providing them room to question and seek evidence for various lines of thought:

> **Sal:** He can see what's going on but he's transparent, so no one can see him, so he can't affect what happens.
> **Teacher:** Where does that come from in your thinking?
> **Jen:** He's just . . .
> **Teacher:** It comes back to what we were talking about—the unity.
> **Eddie:** I don't understand what you just did, the connection you made, Mr. Andrews [referring to the teacher].
> **Jen:** It's the reason for the unity, that he is able to see it.
> **Helen:** It doesn't mean that he sees all. It just means his vision is clear.

Linda, on the other hand, guides her students back to the text to find evidence, moving them from the text toward the interpretation she wants them to understand. She also expects her students to provide information from the text as evidence

for their interpretations. For example, in a unit that included Thoreau, Stanton, Truth, Douglas, and Harper pieces, Linda asked her students to write an essay on the authors' beliefs, with evidence as stated in the texts. Sheri offers these examples in support of Elizabeth Cady Stanton and Sojourner Truth's beliefs that women should be treated equally to men:

> . . . women should be able to have a say in the laws that they must follow and women should get the children after a divorce.

And she offers the following examples from the Sojourner Truth piece as evidence for her claim:

> Some of these men say that a woman should be treated delicately for they are fragile, but Truth says that she is a woman and has never really been treated that way. [The men] also say that since Christ was a man it is only natural that men have more rights than women. Truth's reply to this is that Christ had to have a mother and she was a woman.

What Linda was looking for, and what she got, was evidence that her students were able to use the text to support their understandings.

Thus, the literature teachers guided their students in how to select evidence to back up their assertions by using the text and their previous discussions, as well as other related knowledge from life and other literature. In both teachers' classrooms, all these sources of knowledge were sanctioned some of the time; but Linda sought far more textual evidence, and Terry, far more student-based evidence.

DISCIPLINARY FOCI

Thus, as depicted in Table 4-2, the biology teachers helped their students examine the invisible world of living systems and functions; the physics teachers helped their students examine the outer world (their observations of physical phenomena); the history teachers helped their students examine the social world (contextual information); and the literature teachers helped their students examine their inner worlds (their responses to and interpretations of literature).

What labels and taxonomies were to biology, observations were to physics, social contextualiza-

tion was to history, and personal interpretations were to literature in the particular courses and teachers we studied. In helping their students learn how the various biological systems worked, the teachers guided their students to remember the parts of systems, how they functioned, and the technical terminology they felt was prerequisite to

---

TABLE 4-2   **DISCIPLINARY FOCI**

Biology: Examining Invisible Worlds

Orienting Attention

isolating critical features of system to be studied and focusing on their labels and functions

Refining Understandings

connecting names and explaining functions within the larger system of which they are a part

Selecting Evidence

replicating labels and functions in accordance with accepted systems of classification and description

Physics: Examining Outer Worlds

Orienting Attention

flagging and observing aspects of natural phenomena under investigation

Refining Understandings

examining possible explanations based on related scientific knowledge

Selecting Evidence

making direct links between observed phenomena and accepted principles of physics

American History: Examining Social Worlds

Orienting Attention

identifying and contextualizing particular historical content

Refining Understandings

exploring content from multiple social and cultural perspectives

Selecting Evidence

explaining interpretations by example, through similarities and contrasts

American Literature: Examining Inner Worlds

Orienting Attention

identifying personal response or interpretation to be explored

Refining Understandings

developing interpretations by exploring multiple perspectives and considering possible implications

Selecting Evidence

using text, previous discussions, personal knowledge and experiences to explain interpretation

---

talking and thinking about them. In helping their students understand their observations, the physics teachers guided their students to link particular observations to accepted principles. In helping their students learn to interpret and gain insights from historical events and situations, the American history teachers guided their students to explore the content from a variety of social perspectives. And in helping their students understand and interpret literature, the English teachers helped their students share, elaborate on, and reflect on the personal and the possible. While all teachers in all the classes we studied were concerned with orienting students' attention, refining their understandings, and helping them select appropriate evidence, in conveying their subject-specific ways of reasoning to their students, they guided their students to think in ways that were particular to their discipline.

DISCUSSION

⬩

The purpose of this study was to examine ways of knowing and reasoning in academic coursework, and of the ways in which teachers' general goals are realized in their subject-specific pedagogical strategies. In an earlier study, we found that although teachers talked about the discipline-specific goals they saw for their field, the closer to the daily activities of the student, the more the focus seemed to turn to facts, to the exclusion of ways to think about them. However, the earlier study was limited to review of the scholarly and pedagogical literature and to teacher interview data that needed to be augmented by classroom observation. The present study provides the next step, linking the initial studies of teacher knowledge to studies of teachers talking with teachers, as well as in-depth observations of classroom practices.

The findings of this study suggest that our earlier findings were not wrong, but limited; it is insufficient to conclude that students are not learning about ways to think about the facts that are part of their coursework simply because teach-

ers lack the vocabulary to talk about those goals. Instead, this study suggests the following:

1) Reasoning is being taught and learned in academic classes similar to those in this study.

2) Such reasoning is subject-specific and embedded in the pragmatic routines of subject-driven lessons.

3) The specifications of such reasoning are implicit—not a recognized part of a teacher's knowledge or language base, and therefore unavailable for overt use in lesson planning or as strategic knowledge that can be shared with or taught to students.

4) The kind of discipline-specific reasoning described in these findings may or may not be sufficient for successful participation in disciplinary learning or in meeting the literate thinking goals of our society.

5) Certain types of pedagogical approaches or styles may inhibit or support such discipline-appropriate thinking.

6) Additional studies involving more teachers are needed before we can comfortably make explicit suggestions for the recasting of instruction along discipline-specific lines.

7) The categories identified in this report, representing disciplinary ways of thinking in each of the four disciplines studied, may provide a useful place to start an investigation leading toward productive instructional reform.

In addition, findings suggest that there is a general pedagogical vocabulary that teachers use to indicate their concerns about student thinking. By their very nature, these general terms mask underlying differences in the kinds of thinking they are meant to represent. What counts as thinking seems to be deeply related to the particular discipline and to the underlying ways of thinking embedded in it. However, these disciplinary concerns seem to compete with the more general pedagogical notions of reasoning that are part of the field of education. Thus, curriculum goals, assessment instruments, and instructional approaches that focus on general reasoning abilities across the disciplines may fail to teach or test the particular skills that are most useful in the thinking activities of the actual disciplines. And this may, in part, be a shortcoming of the recent critical thinking reform movement in American education.

Additional research is needed. The teachers in this study were a select group who were interested in professional change and in providing rich reasoning contexts for their students. Even they, however, were relying on tacit knowledge. Thus, teachers not overtly trying to create such think-ing-rich classrooms might look much different in the reasoning behaviors they provoke in their students. In any case, the discipline-specific descriptions and categories reported here have the potential to provide the various fields with ways to reflect on the kinds of language and thought that are valued and on the pedagogical routines that support rich and thoughtful reasoning in particular academic subjects. Such reflection contributes to a growing but still under-conceptualized movement that wishes to place students' thinking and reasoning at the center of educational reform, and it reinforces the underlying goals of strengthening our understanding of, and commitment to, a rigorous, academic, and, above all, more thoughtful education for all.

REFERENCES

Anderson, W., Best, C., Black, A., Hurst, J., Miller, B., & Miller, S. (1990). Cross-curricular underlife: A collaborative report on ways with academic words. *College Composition and Communication, 41*(1), 11–36.

Applebee, A. N., Durst, R., and Newell, G. (1984). The demands of school writing. In A. Applebee (Ed.), *Contexts for learning to write.* Norwood, NJ: Ablex.

Applebee, A. N., Langer, J. A. (1984). *Contexts for learning to write: Studies of secondary school instruction.* Norwood, NJ: Ablex.

Applebee, A. N., Langer, J. A., and Mullis, I. (1989). *Crossroads in American education.* Princeton, NJ: National Assessment of Educational Progress, Educational Testing Service.

Applebee, A. N., Langer, J. A., Mullis, I., Jenkins, L., and Foertsch, M. (1990). *Learning to write in our nation's schools.* Princeton, NJ: National Assessment of Educational Progress, Educational Testing Service.

Bazerman, C. (1981). What written knowledge does: Three examples of academic prose. *Philosophy of Social Science, 11,* 361–87.

Bazerman, C. (1982, March). *Discourse paths of different disciplines.* Paper presented at annual meeting of the Modern Language Association, Chicago, IL.

Berkenkotter, C., Huckin, T., and Ackerman, J. (1988).

Conventions, conversations, and the writer. *Research in the Teaching of English, 22*(1), 9–44.

Bizzell, P. (1982). Cognition, convention, and certainty: What we need to know about writing. *PRE-TEXT, 31,* 213–243.

Boyer, E. L. (1983). *High school: A report on secondary education in America.* NY: Harper & Row.

Britton, J. (1975). *The development of writing abilities.* London: Macmillan Educational.

Calfee, R. C., & Curley, R. (1984). Structures of prose in content areas. In J. Flood (Ed.), *Understanding reading comprehension.* Newark, DE: International Reading Association.

Faigly, L., & Hansen, K. (1985). Learning to write in the social sciences. *College Composition and Communication, 36*(2), 140–149.

Herrington, A. (1985). Writing in academic settings: A study of the contexts for writing in two college chemical engineering courses. *Research in the Teaching of English, 19*(4), 331–361.

Kuhn, T. (1962). *The structure of scientific revolutions.* Chicago: University of Chicago Press.

Langer, J. A. (1984). Literacy instruction in American schools: Problems and perspectives. *American Journal of Education, 93,* 107–132.

Langer, J. A. (1987). A sociocognitive perspective on literacy learning. In J. Langer (Ed.), *Language, Liter-*

acy, and culture: Issues of society and schooling. Norwood, NJ: Ablex.

Langer, J. A. (1990). The process of understanding: Reading for literary and informative purposes. *Research in the Teaching of English, 24*(3), 229–260.

Langer, J. A. (1991). *Literary understanding and literature instruction.* (Report 2.11). Albany, NY: Center for the Learning and Teaching of Literature, State University of New York at Albany.

Langer, J. A. (1992a). Speaking of knowing: Conceptions of understanding in academic disciplines. In A. Herrington & C. Moran. (Eds.), *Research and scholarship in writing across the disciplines.* NY: Modern Language Association.

Langer, J. A. (1992b). Discussion as exploration: Literature and the horizon of possibilities. In G. Newell & R. Durst (Eds.), *Exploring texts: The role of discussion and writing in the teaching and learning of literature.* Norwood, MA: Christopher-Gordon Publishers.

Langer, J. A., & Allington, R. L. (1992). Curriculum research in writing and reading. In P. Jackson (Ed.), *Handbook of research on curriculum.* NY: Macmillan.

Langer, J. A., & Applebee, A. (1987). *How writing shapes thinking: Studies in teaching and learning.* Urbana, IL: National Council of Teachers of English.

Langer, J. A., & Applebee, A. N. (1988). *Speaking of knowing: Conceptions of learning in academic areas.* Final report to U.S. Department of Education, Office of Educational Research and Improvement, Grant No. G008610967. (ERIC Document No. ED 297 336).

Langer, J. A., Applebee, A., Mullis, I., & Foertsch, M. (1990). *Learning to read in our nation's schools.* Princeton, NJ: National Assessment of Educational Progress, Educational Testing Service.

McCarthy, L. (1987). Stranger in a strange land. *Research in the Teaching of English, 21*(3), 233–265.

Mullis, I. V. S., & Jenkins, L. B. (1988). *The science report card.* Princeton, NJ: Educational Testing Service.

Mullis, I. V. S., & Jenkins, L. B. (1990). *The reading report card.* Princeton, NJ: Educational Testing Service.

National Commission on Excellence in Education (1983). *A nation at risk.* Washington, DC: Department of Education.

Odell, L. (1980). The process of writing and the process of learning. *College Composition and Communication, 31,* 42–50.

Rieber, R. W., & Carton, A. S. (Eds.). (1987). *The collected works of L. S. Vygotsky.* NY: Plenum Press.

Roland, R. (1982). The influence of purpose on the field of argument. *Journal of the American Forensic Association, 18,* 228–244.

Scribner, S., & Cole, M. (1981). *The psychology of literacy.* Cambridge, MA: Harvard University Press.

Toulman, S. (1958). *The uses of argument.* Cambridge: Cambridge University Press.

Toulmin, S. (1972). *Human understanding.* Princeton, NJ: Princeton University Press.

Vygotsky, L. S. (1962). *Thought and language.* Cambridge: Harvard University Press.

Wertsch, J. V., & Stone, C. A. (1985). The concept of internalization in Vygotsky's account of the genesis of higher mental functions. In J. V. Wertsch (Ed.), *Culture, communication, and cognition.* Norwood, NJ: Lawrence Erlbaum.

2

STRATEGIES FOR IMPROVING LEARNING AND THINKING IN OUR SCHOOLS

Writing of this chapter was supported in part by a grant from the U.S. Department of Education, Office of Educational Research and Improvement to the National Center for the Study of Reading at the University of Maryland and the University of Georgia. The program of research summarized in the chapter was supported partially by the center and at various times in part by grants and awards from the General Research Board and the Graduate School of the University of Maryland and by a grant from the McDonnell Foundation to Benchmark School. The author gratefully acknowledges the contributions of Pamela El-Dinary, Rachel Brown, Ted L. Schuder, Maryrose Pioli, Kathy Green, and Irene Gaskins.

CHAPTER FIVE

TRANSACTIONAL INSTRUCTION OF READING COMPREHENSION STRATEGIES

MICHAEL PRESSLEY

STATE UNIVERSITY OF NEW YORK AT ALBANY

Dr. Michael Pressley is currently professor of educational psychology and statistics at the State University of New York at Albany. He complements his research on cognition and instruction with basic research on memory and cognitive development.

INTRODUCTION

For two decades I have been interested in children's use of strategies—which are the processes they use when performing demanding tasks—and what is required to teach students to use effective strategies, especially cognitive strategies, that they do not use autonomously. Because of the importance of learning from text, much of my work in the past half dozen years has been concerned with strategies that can increase children's comprehension and memory of what they read. Thus, the focus of this chapter is the teaching of comprehension strategies. I have never contended, however, that strategies instruction alone could produce skilled reading, thinking, or memory (see Pressley, Borkowski, & Schneider, 1987, 1989; Schneider & Pressley, 1989). Rather, my perspective is that students must be taught strate-

gies in conjunction with other knowledge possessed by students. For strategies to be coordinated with factual and conceptual knowledge, the learner must possess metacognitive knowledge, especially understanding when, where, and how to use the strategies the student knows. In addition, the active use of strategies and other knowledge is very much dependent on student motivation to learn (e.g., motivation to read the text now being considered during a social studies lesson). Because of my interest in instructional issues, much of my theoretical thinking about the nature of effective thinking has been posed as theories of instruction (e.g., Harris & Pressley, 1991; Pressley, Borkowski, & Schneider, 1989; Pressley, Goodchild, Fleet, Zajchowski, & Evans, 1989; Pressley, Harris, & Marks, 1992).

In brief, the theory I have proposed is that effective strategies instruction must be long-term and aimed at developing coordinated use of strategies in conjunction with knowledge of other sorts. Such instruction must be metacognitively rich, including information about where and when to use the strategies taught. Extensive practice is necessary to promote efficiency and automaticity of execution. Such practice also permits additional opportunities to discover how, when, and where to use the thinking strategies one knows. Effective instruction develops in students the sense that they can be effective thinkers—that is, effective strategies instruction motivates students to learn and use strategies with other information.

My perspective on thinking shares components with other popular theories of intelligent cognition. All such models include procedural knowledge (e.g., strategies), declarative knowledge (i.e., nonstrategic factual knowledge), and metacognition (e.g., Baron, 1985; Brown, Bransford, Campione, & Ferrara, 1983; Chipman, Segal, & Glaser, 1985; Nickerson, Perkins, & Smith, 1985; Segal, Chipman, & Glaser, 1985). The great emphasis on motivation in my own model reflects in part increasing scholarly interest in the late 1980s about the role of motivation in determining academic cognition (see Borkowski, Carr, Rellinger, & Pressley, 1990; Pressley, El-Dinary, Stein, Marks, & Brown, 1992). It then follows that effective instruction should enhance understanding of strategies, nonstrategic knowledge, metacognition, and academic motivation.

I originally developed my theories of instruction like many psychologists do, by reflecting on research; on theories of thinking, learning, and development; on professional interactions with schools; and on personal experiences as a student. I have abandoned that approach, convinced that psychology provides only part of what must be known in order to propose realistic and complete instructional theories. More positively, effective educators have been able to take the many instructional prescriptions provided by psychologists and transform these bare-bones and inadequate ideas about teaching thinking into pedagogy that fits into school and transforms the thinking of students. My view is that teacher ingenuity is an important part of instruction.

Compelling theories of instruction and convincing research on instruction must capture educator insights. The understandings of skilled teachers are exceptionally well-grounded in experiences with students and classrooms. The experiments and quantifiable observations so preferred by the educational psychology community in the past are not sufficient to the task of generating instructional theory that is fully consistent with what goes on in real schools that succeed in using psychologically inspired interventions, such as the cognitive strategy instruction so dear to me.

In contrast to traditional quantitative approaches, the research tactic taken by my colleagues and me in the past three years has been to identify educational settings where effective strategies instruction was being carried out, in particular effective teaching of reading comprehension strategies. Then, a variety of qualitative methods (e.g., Lincoln & Guba, 1985; Strauss & Corbin, 1990) were used to document the nature of the strategies instruction occurring in these settings (see Pressley, El-Dinary, Gaskins et al., 1992). These qualitative investigations succeeded in producing detailed understanding of the many components comprising strategies instruction in two strategies instructional programs that seemed to be successful. The first was Benchmark School, which serves high-ability elementary students who experience difficulties learning to read; most Benchmark students learn to read and return to succeed in regular education. The second was a comprehension program developed in and used by the Montgomery County, MD, public schools. This program was targeted originally at Chapter 1 students; it produced much better reading comprehension in at-risk students than did other instructional programs deployed in the county.

The purpose of this chapter is to discuss briefly these studies and to detail the instructional conclusions emanating from them. The instruction will then be analyzed in terms of its transactional qualities, constructivist theories of learning, and theories of intelligent assistance. To be certain, however, the instruction that has been analyzed is far from perfected, with the teachers in these programs in a unique position to provide insights about possible ways to improve their programs. Thus, the chapter concludes with insights from teachers about how comprehension strategies instruction might be made more effective.

REVIEW OF BACKGROUND LITERATURE: RESEARCH ON READING COMPREHENSION STRATEGIES INSTRUCTION IN THE 1970s AND 1980s

Most research on comprehension strategies instruction has been of the following form: A researcher believes that if students would construct particular types of text representations (e.g., mental images representing the story told in a narrative, summaries) or react to texts in a particular way (e.g., relating them to prior knowledge, explicitly seeking clarifications when unsure of meaning), comprehension and long-term memories of text would improve. These experimenters usually had reasons to believe that students were not already engaging in such thinking when reading, or they were doing so less systematically and completely than they could. Thus, the experimenter created instruction to stimulate the desired thinking processes. The reading comprehension of students receiving such instruction, measured by some type of objective test of understanding (e.g., multiple-choice items over literal and inferred messages in text), was compared to the reading comprehension of students not receiving such instruction (e.g., control subjects permitted to read as they normally would in preparation for an objective test). When strategy-trained students outperformed control students, the experimenter concluded that (a) students probably were not using the trained strategy(-ies) on their own or were not using it (them) systematically, but more positively, and (b) students could be taught to do so. That is, students were production deficient, to use Flavell's (1970) term, in that they were capable of producing the strategies but did not unless they were instructed to do so.

There were many such experiments in the 1970s and 1980s, producing evidence that students could benefit from instructions to use a number of thinking strategies aimed at improving learning from text (see Pearson & Dole, 1987; Pressley, Johnson, Symons, McGoldrick, & Kurita, 1989):

- Summarization: Construction of summaries of text content as reading proceeds.

- Representational imagery: Construction of internal images representing the meaning of text.

- Mnemonic imagery: Construction of images that transform text meaning in some way in order to make it more memorable (e.g., when reading a biography of Charles Dickens, imagining each of the events occurring to a "Mr. Magoo" Scrooge in order to remember these were events in Dickens' life, rather than events from some other biography).

- Story grammar analysis: Explicitly identifying and attending to the setting, characters, problems, and resolutions in a story, since these are common elements of stories which, if remembered, permit recall of the most critical parts of the story.

- Question generation: Thinking of questions about the meaning of text as reading proceeds.

- Prior knowledge activation: Relating what one already knows to related information contained in text. If this activation occurs before reading, it can be the basis of expectations about and predictions of the content of text.

What resulted from these studies was a collection of strategies that could be applied before (e.g., making predictions based on prior knowledge), during (e.g., imagery generation), and after (e.g., summarization) reading (Levin & Pressley, 1981). Even so, this research was not aimed at coordinated uses of strategies before, during, and after reading, but rather was aimed at the validation of a specific individual strategy. More complicated studies of cognitive strategy instruction were required, for many sophisticated models of thinking emerged specifying that multiple strategies were needed to make sense of the world, including worlds created in texts (e.g., Baron, 1985; Brown et al., 1983; Levin & Pressley, 1981; Nickerson et al., 1985). A few prominent investigations of this type were conducted in the 1980s.

For example, Scott Paris and his associates (e.g., Paris & Oka, 1986) developed a set of lessons that could be used across a year of elementary reading instruction. "Informed Strategies for Learning" included instruction of many of the individual strategies that had been validated in research, as well as some attention to metacognitive and motivational components in strategy use. Although approximately 20 weekly lessons resulted in improved performance on some of the specific tasks practiced in the curriculum, more general changes, such as those documented by standardized reading comprehension assessments, did not occur.

More positively, Duffy et al. (1987) reported success with a year of instruction in which third-grade teachers recast the skills taught during third grade reading as strategies, with the teachers providing many direct explanations about how to attack text and comprehend it. Collins (1991) produced improved comprehension in fifth- and sixth-grade students by providing a semester (three days a week) of lessons on reasoning skills. Her students were taught to seek clarification when uncertain, look for patterns and principles, analyze decision making that occurs during text processing, problem solve (including the use of backward reasoning and visualization), summarize, predict, adapt ideas in text (including rearranging parts of ideas in text), and negotiate interpretations of texts in groups. Although the trained students did not differ from controls before the intervention with respect to standardized comprehension performance, there was a 3 standard deviation difference between treated and control conditions on the post-test. Bereiter and Bird (1985) demonstrated that students in seventh and eighth grade benefit from instruc-

tions to use a few comprehension strategies used by older, more sophisticated readers (i.e., restate difficult text, backtrack as necessary, watch for pertinent information in text, and resolve apparently anomalous information in text). These data could be combined with Duffy et al.'s (1987) and Collins' (1991) outcomes to produce optimism that instruction of multiple strategies is an intervention that is potentially effective to develop students' thinking during most of the elementary- and middle-school years.

Notably, Duffy et al. (1987), Collins (1991), and Bereiter and Bird (1985) all involved extensive direct explanations of cognitive strategies by teachers to students. In all three cases the teachers made visible otherwise invisible mental processes by thinking aloud (i.e., mental modeling; Duffy, Roehler, & Herrmann, 1988). In all three cases, students were provided with extensive practice opportunities and with teacher assistance provided during practice, as required by students. In all three cases, there was opportunity for gradual acquisition of the repertoire of strategies and long-term instruction about the coordination of the strategic competencies acquired.

The best known multiple-strategies intervention developed during the 1980s was reciprocal teaching of comprehension strategies, perhaps because it was the first report of a classroom-deployed multiple-strategies intervention that seemed to promote reading comprehension (Palincsar & Brown, 1984). This intervention produced consistent increases in lower-ability students' use of the processes taught (i.e., prediction, seeking clarification, question-generation during reading, and summarization); often, this type of instruction also produced at least modest gains on more general measures (e.g., standardized reading comprehension; for a review, see Rosenshine & Meister, 1992).

Reciprocal teaching of the four comprehension strategies occurs in reading groups. There is an adult teacher who provides input to the group as necessary and who initially introduces the prediction, clarification, questioning, and summarization strategies to the group using explanations and modeling. The role of the adult teacher is downplayed in group functioning, however. For any lesson sequence, one of the students is designated "teacher" of the group, with this student leading a discussion of the content. The leader typically begins discussion of a segment of text by asking a question and then concludes commentary on the section by offering a summary, a summary that leads to a prediction about subsequent text content. The adult teacher, outside of the discussion orchestrated by the student leader, provides prompting and feedback to members of the group on an as-needed basis. Palincsar and Brown (e.g., 1984) believed that this instructional arrangement is extremely motivating, for example, since the availability of as-needed feedback should reduce frustration and increase task persistence. Long-term participation in such groups is presumed to lead to student internalization of the cognitive processes practiced in the group. This expectation is consistent with the Vygotskian (e.g., Vygotsky, 1978) notion that interpersonal processes can be internalized by individuals and become the basis for intrapersonal cognitive processes, which Kozulin explains in Chapter 12.

In summary, by the end of the 1980s, there had been substantial success in demonstrating that instruction of some individual cognitive processes improves comprehension of text. In addition, a few investigators succeeded in teaching multiple strategies in ways that improved reading comprehension, at least as measured by standardized comprehension instruments. What was missing, however, was information about how real educators were translating strategies instruction into effective educational practice. As I reflected on this latter issue in particular, near the end of the 1980s (see Pressley, El-Dinary, Brown, et al., in press, for extensive commentary on these reflections), I found myself filled with questions. I knew of educational researchers who were attempting to deploy cognitive strategies instruction of various sorts in school, investigators who seemed to be having some success doing so (e.g., Deshler & Schumaker, 1988; Englert, Raphael, Anderson, Anthony, & Stevens, 1991; Gaskins & Elliot, 1991). The strategies instruction they were offering to students was very long-term, provided over

years. Why did such instruction take so long? In addition, strategies instruction was clearly taking place in the context of an ongoing curriculum: How was it meshed with other parts of the school day? As I read the experimental studies (including the ones detailing multiple-strategies interventions), I felt that little attention was paid to the instructional dynamics of lessons—the interweaving of teacher and student behaviors that is instruction. What did complete strategies instruction lessons look like? What do years of such lessons look like? These concerns were disturbing for dissemination of effective strategies instruction might be facilitated substantially if educators in general were informed about how successful strategies teachers adapt the strategies instructional recommendations of theoreticians and researchers to real schools. It was high time to produce such information.

STUDIES OF EFFECTIVE STRATEGIES INSTRUCTION PROGRAMS

In this section of the chapter, I want to report specific classroom practices that increase students' higher-order thinking. Before attempting systematic study of effective school-based strategies instruction, I became as personally familiar with it as I could. I did so by traveling to sites where such instruction was reputed to be occurring, talking directly with the curriculum developers and educators responsible for such programs, and observing strategies instruction in school whenever I had the opportunity to do so. I made a trip to the University of Kansas to learn about the Kansas Strategies Instruction Model, a curriculum that had been disseminated nationally by the University of Kansas Learning Disabilities Institute (see Deshler & Schumaker, 1988, for a summary of the evidence validating the Kansas model); there were sorties to Michigan State for visits with Gerry Duffy, Laura Roehler, Annemarie Palincsar, Carol Sue Englert, and Taffy Raphael; Tom Scruggs and Margo Mastropieri welcomed me to their program at Purdue University and provided substantial instruction about how some of my basic research on elaboration and mnemonics was being translated into long-term special education curricula (see Mastropieri & Scruggs, 1991); Karen Harris and Steve Graham detailed their instructional programs with learning disabled students, especially informing me about how writing strategies instruction can be shaped so that it is effective with mildly handicapped students; and Irene Gaskins hosted a visit to Benchmark School so I could observe and discuss the reading strategies instruction offered there with her and the Benchmark teachers. These trips to research sites were complemented by visits to classrooms where individual teachers struggled to implement what seemed like a good idea to them based on some exposure to the cognitive strategies instruction literature. These teachers had "war stories" about the challenges of understanding strategies instructions and adapting the approach to the needs of their students using only the resources available to a classroom teacher.

An especially illuminating opportunity occurred when three counselors from the University of Western Ontario studies skills center enrolled in one of my graduate seminars: Fiona Goodchild, Joan Fleet, and Richard Zajchowski provided me with many hours of conversation about the challenges associated with teaching cognitive strategies to bright and motivated students, such as the ones attending a relatively selective university like Western Ontario.

Pressley, Goodchild et al. (1989) summarized the informal knowledge I had accumulated from my many visits and conversations with strategies instruction practitioners between 1987 and 1989. The main theme developed in that article was that effective strategies instruction was anything but easy, requiring demanding forms of teaching (e.g., direct explanation and mental modeling tailored to student needs involves sensitive and continuous diagnosis of how learners are reacting to explanations). Pressley, Goodchild et al. (1989) made the case that such teaching must be long-term if students are to understand fully

when and where the strategies they are learning can be adapted to new situations. They argued that challenges to strategies teaching are aggravated when teachers are committed previously to approaches inconsistent with good strategies instruction; sometimes teachers have been exposed to misinformation about cognitive strategies interventions (e.g., from published strategies instruction kits produced by authors who are not well informed about the challenges of cognitive strategies instruction, kits in which many, many strategies are offered in a very short period of time). Pressley, Goodchild et al. (1989) also acknowledged that much of the best information about strategies instruction simply was not available to educators because it was published in archival, scholarly journals that are inaccessible to teachers. In addition, they concluded that much of the know-how built up by educators as they attempted to implement strategies teaching as part of their curricula was not codified at all! By 1989, my colleagues and I were ready to document this know-how and report it in ways that would make sense to the education communities—and to scientists as well!

BENCHMARK SCHOOL STUDIES

The first studies in this program of research were conducted at Benchmark School in Media, PA, which is dedicated to the education of high-ability students who experience difficulties learning to read in the first two years of schooling. Even though these students are at great risk for long-term school failure, most emerge after four to seven years at Benchmark well prepared to return to regular education. Virtually all Benchmark graduates complete high school, and many attend college. Because much of the Benchmark approach involves teaching higher-level thinking strategies to accomplish reading and other literacy tasks, the school seemed like a perfect place to do an initial investigation of effective strategies instruction.

Irene Gaskins, the founder and director of the school, and I worked on several research projects during the course of my year at Benchmark

(1989–90). One was an interview study, with the questions posed during the interview largely inspired by the instructional possibilities I had observed informally when visiting the strategies instruction sites that informed Pressley, Goodchild et al. (1989). The 31 academic teachers at Benchmark were asked 150 questions, with each requiring not only an objective answer (e.g., a response on a Likert scale) but also permitting any additional input the responding teacher might wish to provide. Up to five hours of face-to-face interviews permitted ample opportunity for teachers to provide detailed explanations of what they believed about strategies instruction based on their extensive experience, as well as why they believed it. A common perspective was evident in the interview responses. The 31 teachers generally agreed on many points, including the following:

- The Benchmark teachers strongly endorsed direct explanation and modeling as essential components of effective strategies instruction. Many observations at Benchmark confirmed that such explanations occur during both small and large group instruction and as part of one-to-one tutoring and reinstruction. Teachers reported that their initial explanations and modeling are more complete than later explanations and modeling, although the faculty members, especially the more experienced ones, were emphatic that explanations and modeling should continue for a long time after introduction of strategies.

- Extensive practice in use of strategies was endorsed by the teachers, as was extensive guidance and feedback in response to students' needs during such practice. Even so, the teachers admitted that it is often difficult to diagnose the specific problems experienced by students and challenging to devise remediation. The teachers were aware that students did not learn cognitive strategies quickly, with facile use of strategies across a wide range

of tasks and materials occurring after extensive practice, which included struggling to adapt strategies to a wide range of academic problems.

- Strategies teaching and applications of strategies were reported to occur across the curriculum.

- The teachers considered it essential to provide extensive information to students about when and where to apply the strategies they were learning, as well as information about the learning benefits produced by use of strategies.

- The teachers recognized that transfer of the strategies learned to new academic tasks and contents was anything but automatic, but rather required extensive teaching about when strategies might be applied, as well as practice applying strategies across a number of situations.

- The teachers were emphatic that only a few strategies could be introduced at a time, with in-depth instruction of strategies over months and years the preferred approach to teaching at Benchmark. Their view was that students developed strategic thinking repertoires over the course of their years in the school—cognitive strategies instruction was definitely not seen as a quick fix.

- Although cognitive in their orientation, the teachers also recognized the need for explicit reinforcement of student efforts and successes in applying strategies and accomplishing difficult academic tasks. Feedback to students was considered essential, with positive feedback following success critical if students were to be motivated in the school. The teachers were well aware that their students had already experienced several years of school failure and believed that their Benchmark successes needed to be rewarded in order to offset the damage produced by the previous failures.

- The Benchmark teachers believed they should develop students who are habitually reflective and 'planful'. Cognitive strategies instruction was seen as a way of accomplishing this higher-order goal.

I was struck by how easy it was to discern broad-based agreement in these interview data. One possibility was that the agreement represented an institutional consensus produced by selective hiring and retention, perhaps combined with common in-service training at the school. More optimistically, an alternative was that the consensus represented the collective "horse sense" that emerges when dealing with the challenges of strategies instruction given the constraints of a real school, especially one serving students who have academic difficulties. Fortunately, Pressley, Gaskins, Cunicelli et al. (1991) also produced data that permitted the inference that the consensus reflected the latter rather than the former possibility.

Pressley, Gaskins, Cunicelli et al. (1991) presented the same questions that had been given to the Benchmark teachers to a sample of nine nationally known researchers in strategies instructions. These distinguished investigators all had had extensive hands-on experience in implementing long-term strategies instruction at their home institutions. What was striking was the congruence in the response of the Benchmark teachers and this researcher sample, with correlations from .65 to 1.00 between teachers and researchers (depending on the subscale). My conclusion was that extensive experience with strategies instruction produced perceptions of strategies instruction consistent with the perceptions of the Benchmark teachers.

Two additional studies at the school provided even more detailed understanding of how Benchmark teachers do what they do. One was a case study of the instruction occurring in one Benchmark classroom during spring semester 1990 (Pressley, Gaskins, Wile, Cunicelli, & Sheridan, 1991). The focal strategy taught during this semester was generation of semantic maps to understand text, including analyses of text to determine relationships such as cause and effect, temporal sequence, compare and contrast, and simple description. Teaching of these strategies was thoroughly integrated with the teaching of content, with focal strategies instruction occurring during reading, writing, and social studies as teachers and students interacted to create semantic maps. For example, semantic maps were generated by students as they planned writing assignments as part of social studies. Also, social studies homework often required students to make semantic maps.

Consistent with the teacher claims in the large interview study, explanations and modeling of the semantic mapping strategy was more extensive and explicit early in the instruction. After several months, students often began to map the meaning of a text given a simple, one-line direction from the teacher to do so (e.g., "Make a map of what's in this text"). At this point, the teachers only provided assistance to students on an as-needed basis, often giving gentle hints about how specific relationships in a text might be represented in a semantic map.

Instruction of other strategies did not stop when semantic mapping was introduced. Rather, teachers modeled and explained use of semantic mapping in conjunction with other strategies. For example, the cognitive strategies of activating prior knowledge, predicting, seeking clarification, and summarizing were all prompted frequently during lessons intended primarily to provide new information about semantic mapping as a strategy.

An important insight I had at Benchmark was that cognitive strategies were being taught as methods to encourage individual interpretations (i.e., constructing personally significant understandings). For example, teachers in the Pressley, Gaskins, Wile et al. (1991) case study taught their students that no two semantic maps should be alike and that each student's map should reflect individual reactions to the content of the text.

Interpretive activities were especially apparent

in the analyses of Benchmark classroom dialogues produced by Gaskins, Anderson, Pressley, Cunicelli, and Satlow (1993), who studied the strategy instruction lessons of six teachers at Benchmark. The discourse in these classrooms was much different than the discourse in conventional classrooms: Cazden (1988) and Mehan (1979) observed that typical classroom discourse includes many cycles of a teacher asking a question, a student responding, and the teacher evaluating the response (i.e., IRE cycles involving teacher initiation, student response, and teacher evaluation as Peterson described in Chapter 3). IRE cycles were not found in the Benchmark data, however. Instead, the teachers engaged in interactive dialogues with their students 88% of the time in what Gaskins et al. (1993) referred to as process-content cycles: The teacher used content as a vehicle to stimulate application and discussion of strategies. When students make comments in discussions, Benchmark teachers do not attempt to evaluate their responses, but rather encourage the students to elaborate on them— encouraging students to process the content additionally using strategies. The goal is to encourage student understanding of content through strategic processing. Thus, a teacher might request that a student summarize a passage. Once the summary is offered, the teacher might ask the student to describe any images that came to mind while reading the text or encourage the student to liven up the summary by relating the text content to prior knowledge (e.g., When you visualize how a third-class level works, where do you see the fulcrum? How is that picture different from what you visualized when the author described first- and second-class levers? Can you tell about an occasion when you have used a third-class lever? How did this simple machine benefit you?).

An extremely important finding in the Gaskins et al. (1993) investigation was the identification of events that occur often in lessons that increase students' higher-level thinking:

- Students are provided instruction about how to carry out the strategies.

- Teachers model the focal strategies (and sometimes use of other strategies as well).

- Students practice strategies, with teacher guidance and assistance provided on an as-needed basis.

- The focal strategy for a lesson and the focal curriculum content for the day are identified for students early in the lesson.

- Information is presented about why the focal strategy (and sometimes nonfocal strategies as well) is important. Often teachers provide anecdotal information about how strategies have helped them.

- Information about when and where strategies apply is conveyed to students.

In retrospect, the Benchmark studies were extremely satisfying as a package. When teachers were interviewed, when they were observed, and when their discourse was analyzed thoroughly, direct explanations about, and modelings of strategies used in, student practice were apparent. The practice was guided and assisted by teachers who monitored carefully student attempts to use cognitive strategies, offering help when needed. Elementary content coverage was not displaced in favor of strategies instruction, but rather strategies were applied as students learned elementary content. The coherent outcomes from the Benchmark investigations complement well the coherent outcomes of the studies conducted in the Montgomery County, MD, schools.

MONTGOMERY COUNTY, MD, STRATEGIES INSTRUCTION PROGRAMS

Ted Schuder, Jan Bergman, and Marcia York, all working as curriculum developers for the Montgomery County schools, developed and deployed several strategies-based programs aimed principally at encouraging reading comprehension. My colleagues and I focused on two of these programs, one dubbed SAIL (i.e., Students Achieving Independent Learning), which was designed for implementation across the elementary years beginning with primary reading. The second program, SIA (i.e., Summer Institute for Achievement), was a summer-school program emphasizing similar strategic processes and methods of teaching. The strategies highlighted in SAIL are ones validated in the research of the 1970s and 1980s: prediction of content based on picture, title, and text cues; evaluation of predictions and updating of expectations as reading of text proceeds; question generation in response to text; esthetic responses to text, including personal evaluations and interpretations; summarization; seeking clarification; visualization; and selective attention to important and interesting parts of text.

SAIL and SIA instruction occurs around high-quality texts, often in reading groups small enough to encourage exchanges between all students about interpretations of text, imaginal reactions to content, and summaries. When strategies are introduced initially (i.e., in grades one or two), lessons often focus on individual strategies. For example, there may be several weeks of students making prediction after prediction, followed by weeks of students practicing visualization. Once students are familiar with the strategies, the lessons emphasize coordinated use of strategies, with a great deal of teacher prompting required for this to happen and with substantial prompting continuing for months and perhaps years. Eventually (e.g., in the third year of SAIL instruction), students meet in groups and carry out strategic processes in a self-directed fashion—that is, teacher prompting and cuing is much less pronounced than it had been in previous years. El-Dinary, Pressley, and Schuder (in press) and Pressley, El-Dinary, Gaskins et al. (1993) have observed a number of common activities in SAIL and SIA lessons:

- Students are provided with instruction about how to carry out the strategies emphasized in curriculum. Usually this is re-explanation of strategic processes

somewhat familiar to the students, amounting to a recasting of the strategies in new terms.

- Teachers model use of the SAIL/SIA strategies.

- Students practice strategies, with teacher guidance and assistance provided on an as-needed basis. Often prompts are in the form of questions suggesting additional strategic processing or possible ways to extend or expand an interpretation.

- Information is presented about why the focal strategies (and sometimes nonfocal strategies as well) are important. Often teachers provide anecdotal information about how strategies have helped them.

- Students are often required to model and explain use of the SAIL/SIA strategies.

- Information about when and where strategies apply is conveyed to students. The positive effects of strategies are continuously pointed out to students.

- Sophisticated processing vocabulary (e.g., terms like "predictions," "clarifications," "validation of predictions," and "summaries") are used frequently.

- Flexibility in strategy use is apparent, with teachers emphasizing how different students might apply strategies in different ways to the same content.

- Teachers send the message that student thought processes matter.

Of course, these behaviors were apparent at Benchmark as well. Both settings had developed strategies instruction involving a great deal of direct explanation and modeling, consistent with the claims in Pressley, Goodchild et al. (1989) about the nature of effective strategies instruction. At both Benchmark and in Montgomery County, students and teachers talked aloud about their thinking processes (i.e., did mental modeling). They shared their interpretations of texts in an open and generally relaxed group context.

Coordination of strategies was emphasized in both programs, with years of practice in such coordination.

What had happened in these two settings was that educators with years of field experience were aware of the comprehension strategies research literature. They selected from that literature the strategies and methods that made the most sense to them in light of their years of experience as educators. They were particularly impressed with the work of Gerald Duffy and his associates (e.g., Duffy et al., 1987, 1988) on direct explanation of strategic processes. Indeed, I would go so far as to claim from my reading of the strategies instructional literature and the many programs I have visited that Duffy's perspective on direct explanation—including mental modeling and subsequent guided practice of students—is the most influential perspective to date about how to teach strategic processes in classrooms. It is also consistent with the method of strategies teaching in some of the most influential basic research studies relating to strategies (see Pressley, Snyder, & Cariglia-Bull, 1987, for an analysis).

Explaining strategies to students, showing them how to use strategies, and helping them as they attempt to apply strategies as part of in-school practice seems sensible to many teachers. Although explanation of strategies, modeling, and guided practice of strategies were all studied in the basic research literature, transactional strategies instruction goes well beyond anything presented in the basic literature. The transactional strategies instruction described here evolved as teachers worked with it. Credit more the educators for this intervention than the researchers, although basic research provided great impetus and guidance for initial efforts, including information about which strategies might be worth teaching.

Often applications are not theoretically interesting. In the next three sections of this chapter, I make the case that this is not so with respect to transactional strategies instruction. The studies reported here have provided many new theoretical insights about the nature of cognitive strat-egies instruction at its best—including its transactional nature, relation to effective instruction in general, and constructivist features.

THEORETICAL INTERPRETATION I: TRANSACTIONAL NATURE OF COGNITIVE STRATEGIES INSTRUCTION

What an instructional approach is called is absolutely critical, with well-known educational interventions almost always having memorable names that capture succinctly an important characteristic of the intervention (e.g., reciprocal teaching, cooperative learning, criterion-referenced instruction)! Thus, I knew I had to come up with some memorably succinct name for the type of strategies instruction I was watching. One candidate, of course, was simply to use Duffy's preferred term of "direct explanation." I elected not to do that for two reasons: First, the term direct explanation sometimes evokes the behavioristic conception of effective teaching known as "direct instruction" (e.g., Rosenshine, 1979). Given that even hints of behaviorism are not received well in the cognitive and constructivist circles which I frequent, direct explanation did not seem right. Second, the term direct explanation focuses on the teaching behaviors rather than on what happens between teachers and students and in the minds of the teachers and students. I really wanted a summary term that reflected better the dynamic give-and-take between teachers and students that is typical of the effective strategies instruction I had witnessed.

The descriptive label "transactional strategies instruction" seemed appropriate at first because of Louise Rosenblatt's (e.g., 1978) classical analyses of text interpretations as products of reader-text transactions. Rosenblatt's position was that meaning is not in text alone or in the reader's head alone but is constructed by readers as they consider text content in light of their previous knowledge and experiences. Such meaning construction was certainly emphasized in the instruction I was watching, with students encouraged to use strategies such as prediction, visualization, and summarization to create personalized interpretations and understandings of text.

The term transactional is appropriate for other reasons as well, however. In the developmental psychology literature (e.g., Bell, 1968), the term transaction is used to refer to child-adult interactions in which the child in part determines the behaviors of others in the child's world. Thus, a child who is sanctioned by a parent can control the parent's next behavior by his or her reaction to the sanction, with immediate deference to the parent likely to result in a cessation of punishment, and immediate defiance likely to result in additional and more severe reactions from the parent. Analogously, teachers' reactions are determined largely by the reactions of the students at Benchmark and in the SAIL and SIA programs. Teachers react to student interpretations and student difficulties. If a student offers a good summary, the teacher may prompt elaboration of the summary; if the student's summary is off the wall, the teacher may prompt rereading or reconsideration of the text. What happens in transactional strategies instructional groups is determined largely by the reactions of students to teachers and to other students.

The strategies instruction I have been studying is transactional in yet a third sense. Organizational psychologists (e.g., Hutchins, 1991) in particular have been concerned with the types of solutions produced during group problem solving compared to individual problem solving. Groups invariably produce solutions that no one individual in the group would have produced. Groups also produce memories that would have never occurred to individuals unless they had participated in the group (e.g., Wegner, 1987). There is a transactive mind when individuals get together to think about things. So it is with the strategies instructional groups we have been studying, with ideas about text emerging as one student's elaboration of content stimulates another child's elaboration of the same text.

Thus, there are three senses in which the classroom strategies instruction I have documented is

transactional: (a) Meaning is determined by minds applying strategies to text content, (b) How one person reacts is largely determined by what other participants in the group are doing, thinking, and saying, (c) The meaning that emerges is the product of all of the heads in the group. Such instruction is transactional in all of these senses largely because what is going on during strategies instruction is extremely intelligent assistance by teachers of students.

THEORETICAL INTERPRETATION II: INTELLIGENT ASSISTANCE THEORY

The term "intelligent assistant systems" has been coined in the cognitive science literature with respect to machine systems that can assist people to perform complicated tasks (e.g., Boy, 1991). The goal of workers in this area of artificial intelligence is to produce something like C3PO and R2D2, although the technology is far from the point of producing machines with the intellectual sensitivities of the *Star Wars* droids. Nonetheless, this movement in artificial intelligence has produced sophisticated models about what occurs when any intelligent entity gives assistance to another entity. A brief consideration of four of the most important ideas in intelligent assistance will make clear that strategies teaching by human teachers to human students is simply one instance of intelligent assistance. These analyses will also shed more light on the complicated nature of such assistance.

AUTOMATIC, SITUATED KNOWLEDGE OF STRATEGIES POSSESSED BY INTELLIGENT ASSISTANTS VERSUS THE KNOWLEDGE OF COGNITIVE STRATEGIES THAT MUST BE CONVEYED TO NOVICES

Comprehension strategies instruction teachers are often very good readers. They know a variety of strategies (i.e., in cognitive science terms, procedural knowledge) and are facile at coordinated use of these strategies in conjunction with factual knowledge (i.e., declarative knowledge; e.g., Anderson 1983). They can use comprehension procedures automatically, recognizing immediately situations that call for the strategies they are using. There is no need for reflection about what to do when they are reading; they simply do it (see Flower et al., 1992, for discussion of highly skilled reading and writing in these terms). Such automaticity and situational knowledge is built up through years of practice and experience.

Paradoxically, such facility in strategies use can make strategies teaching difficult. To use a computer programming analogy, such strategy experts must "decompile" their knowledge of comprehension processing in order to teach beginning readers—modeling the execution of strategies in a step-by-step fashion rather than as a rapid continuous sequence of events. In the strategies instruction programs I have studied, teachers are provided with decompiled information by the program curriculum developers about what young readers can do to understand better. Thus, the automatic comprehension processes of good readers are broken down into simple descriptions of processes such as prediction, relating to prior knowledge, clarification, question generation, problem solving, and summarization. At first, teachers encourage execution of these strategies one at a time, with students carrying them out slowly. The assumption is that with a great deal of teacher-cued practice of the strategies in the context of reading, automatic execution of the cognitive processes will develop in students as will the situational knowledge permitting recognition of points during reading that call for each of the strategic processes. With the development of automaticity and situational knowledge, strategy use becomes more flexible (e.g., the situational knowledge that develops is not a rigid set of rules, but rather fuzzy, general notions about when to be active during reading and in what ways to be active). The irony here is that the initial teaching must be directed at reflective, deliberate use of strategic procedures (i.e., in computer science terminology, procedures not yet compiled), even though the long-term goal is automatic, nonreflective comprehension processing—processing that resembles in many ways the processes specified by the strategy formulae but is much faster and varied (i.e., compiled knowledge) than the strategy attempts of novices.

INTELLIGENT ASSISTANT DIAGNOSIS OF DIFFICULTIES EXPERIENCED BY PERSONS BEING ASSISTED

Workers in machine intelligent assistance are painfully aware of the problem of diagnosing the needs of those receiving assistance. For example, intelligent assistance devices in cockpits must be able to recognize pilot errors and their significance and provide information about how to correct such problems. Although there are some systems in place that can recognize a limited number of problems (e.g., when a plane is headed straight for a mountain) and can provide a limited repertoire of directives (e.g., a voice command to "pull up" as the mountain approaches), artificial intelligence is a long way from producing a robotic copilot that approaches the competence of an experienced human copilot.

An especially great challenge for computer scientists is to figure out how to build machines that can accumulate knowledge of the types of errors made by those being assisted and the responses from the machines that produce improved performance. The development of such knowledge is especially challenging because it is "fuzzy" knowledge: The error committed by a person receiving assistance today can at a deep level be the same error committed by another person tomorrow, although the two errors may "look" very different because of different surface features. Thus, the system must be able to recognize the deep structural similarities between present difficulties experienced by those being assisted and difficulties "witnessed" and corrected previously.

Analogous problems of diagnosis and the development of expertise in correcting errors exist with respect to strategies instruction. Strategies teachers must be able to size up student needs, something that can be very challenging and require a great deal of knowledge beyond knowledge of the strategies. Only through years of experience with students can teachers build up a sophisticated understanding of student problems and appropriate reactions to those problems. A great challenge for educational scientists is to determine how best to develop such knowledge in teachers, although it seems almost certain that years of teaching experience is going to be required for really expert diagnostic teaching to develop (see Chi, Glaser, & Farr, 1988).

COMMUNICATION BREAKDOWNS AND MISCOMMUNICATIONS DURING INTELLIGENTLY ASSISTED INSTRUCTION

The cognitive science analyses of intelligent assistance are especially illuminating about why the information provided by teachers often seems to miss the mark—why many redundant explanations are sometimes required in order to get across important ideas about strategies and their use (e.g., Ellis, 1989). Suppose that a child hears some piece of information in a reading group about how to apply summarization to a particular type of text. What can go wrong? (See Chapter 9 of Boy, 1991.) The instruction might not be complete enough for the child to understand it. There may be ambiguities because of a mismatch in the knowledge of the teacher and the child. Unfortunately, some teacher explanations offered in the middle of a story and "on-line" are simply incoherent. Sometimes the explanation of the strategy is fine, but it really does not apply very well in the current situation—at least not given what this student knows about the topic (e.g., suggesting a student relate the content to what he or she already knows about a topic when in fact the child really knows very little about the topic).

Sometimes the student is not paying attention and does not receive the message. What analyses of intelligent assistance have made clear is that the assistance message only sometimes is helpful. Having witnessed many teacher explanations that just did not do anything for the student, I am aware that this problem in the world of machine-human interactions is every bit as keen with respect to instructional encounters of the strictly human kind.

PERCEPTION OF QUESTIONS BY THE INTELLIGENT ASSISTANT

In order to understand questions posed by those needing assistance, intelligent assistance devices must have "beliefs" about the people they are helping (Maida & Deng, 1989). So must human teachers (Bowers & Flinders, 1990). The question "Why?" following a teacher's explanation of a strategy can be construed to mean, "Why use this strategy—what immediate goal does it fulfill?" or "Why use this strategy—what long-term goal does it fulfill?" or "Why would you do it that way rather than another way? and so on (e.g., Cooke, 1989, p. 117; Hayes-Roth, Waterman, & Lenat, 1983). These beliefs also affect what is said in response (e.g., an answer requiring high prior knowledge or low prior knowledge to comprehend), how to say it (e.g., with advanced vocabulary or simple vocabulary), and how much to say about it (e.g., at the level of detail of a technical manual or an owner's manual) (Weiner, 1989). The intelligent assistant must size up whether a short answer is sufficient given the intelligent assistant's perception of the importance of the question, or whether a longer answer is critical because the person being helped seems to have fundamental misunderstandings. Determining how to build machines that can do this is a critical part of research on machine intelligence. It is also critical to the development of excellent teachers, in part because answers to questions cannot exceed learners' total mental resources—including their attention span (short-term memory), which is discussed next.

SENSITIVITY TO CAPACITY LIMITATIONS OF THOSE BEING ASSISTED

Any help that comes from an intelligent assistant cannot be too complicated. Human beings have limited short-term memory capacity. When humans need help with something, their capacity often already is stretched to the limit. Consider a situation in which a first-grade teacher is the intelligent assistant. When Robbie is having difficulty sounding out a word, for example "frog," a great deal of Robbie's limited attention is devoted to the task (LaBerge & Samuels, 1974). That is, humans can only attend to a few things at once, and if they are attending to something very difficult, there is little attentional capacity (sometimes known as short-term memory capacity, sometimes known as consciousness) left over to attend to other things. Thus, assistance such as, "Remember 'f' sounds like f-f-f and 'r' sounds like r-r-r and when they are blended, they sound like _____" probably would not be effective because Robbie would not be able to attend to it and work away at the word at the same time. Less short-term, capacity-demanding prompts would work better; so a hint like "What would you already know that has the same vowel sound—that has 'o-g' in it?" might be much more helpful. Experts in intelligent assistance are always attempting to devise simple cues that prompt desired actions. Thus, some rapid transit systems have developed computer-controlled oral directions that are automatically broadcast over speaker systems when there is trouble on a train. These messages are simple and low capacity demanding (necessary because the anxiety and confusion of a train emergency consume cognitive capacity). One such message is, "Get out of the train!"

SUMMARY

Helping a person perform a cognitive task or learn a cognitive skill is challenging, whether the helper is a computer or a human teacher. What the analysis in this section suggests is that it is not nearly enough for the intelligent assistant to know how to do something—the intelligent assistant must also know how to communicate the process in question to novices. This involves being able to slow down the processing in question and discussing it in a step-by-step fashion. These explanations must be formulated to accommodate learner limitations—for example, it should not be so long or complicated that the message demands more short-term capacity than the student has. The intelligent assistant can also

re-explain processing so that students who do not get it the first time might be able to get it with additional explanation. Part of the ability to re-explain is the ability to discern the specific difficulties experienced by a student, including the meanings of questions that the student might pose.

This analysis complements well the discussion in the previous section. Identifying that effective strategies instruction involves processes such as direct explanation, modeling, and guided practice is not nearly enough to understand the sophistication of effective strategies instruction. During the last two years, El-Dinary et al. (in press) studied teachers who were using strategies instruction for the first time. It was rough going. Even those teachers who quickly understood that they had to model and explain and guide practice often experienced difficulties doing it. They were not able to rephrase strategies explanations fluidly; they were not able to understand why some students might be faltering. Intelligent assistance theory provides a framework for understanding such difficulties.

One paradox is that theoretical analyses emerging from models of machine learning do not lead to a mechanistic conception of strategies instruction. What the analysis presented in this section makes clear is that strategies instruction is not a "pouring" of information from the teacher to the student but rather involves an intelligent "other" assisting students to construct an understanding of strategies and their applications. Thus, the theoretical analyses presented in this section set the stage for an expanded discussion in the next section of the constructivist nature of strategies instruction.

THEORETICAL INTERPRETATION III: THE CONSTRUCTIVISTIC NATURE OF STRATEGIES INSTRUCTION

▼

One knock on strategies instruction by some critics (e.g., Poplin, 1988a, 1988b) is that it is mechanical and encourages rote responding by students. Students are portrayed as being taught to execute strategies in a rigid fashion. Karen Harris, Marilyn Marks, and I (Harris & Pressley, 1991; Pressley, Harris, & Marks, 1992) recently confronted these claims, making the case that good strategies instruction does anything but encourage rote passivity. Good strategies instruction invites creative and flexible construction and use of strategies by students. It is definitely constructivist!

Analyses of strategies teaching according to Moshman's (1982) classification of three different types of constructivism is helpful in understanding how strategies instruction of various types is constructivist: (a) *Endogeous constructivist* teaching, based largely on Piagetian theory, mostly involves child-determined exploration and discovery rather than direct instruction; (b) *Exogenous constructivist teaching* emphasizes explicit teaching much more than does endogeous constructivism. For example, the modeling and explanation that is teaching according to social learning models (e.g., Bandura, 1986; Zimmerman & Schunk, 1989) certainly involves exogenous constructivism. The learning that occurs is not rote, however, but rather involves personalized understandings and interpretations of content. Students discover a great deal as they grapple to understand the explanations provided to them and to act as the models they have observed. Such students come to very different understandings of the content they are learning than is possessed by their teachers; (c) *Dialectical constructivist teaching* is especially favored by those who identify themselves as constructivists. This form of teaching lies in between endogenous and exogenous constructivist teaching. It is recognized that students left to discover on their own will learn inefficiently at best. Even so, dialectical constructivists are uncomfortable with teaching as explicit as that favored by exogenous constructivists. Dialectical constructivists like to provide hints and prompts to students rather than large doses of direct explanation and modeling (although some explanations and modeling are provided using this approach). That is, dialectical constructivists

favor providing just enough support so that students can proceed with a task or learn a new skill but no more than the minimum required for students to make progress. The idea is that by interacting with an adult who gently prompts and guides efficient processing, the child will eventually internalize such processing operations, an idea consistent with Vygotsky's (1978; also Wood, Bruner, & Ross, 1976) theory of the socially mediated development of cognitive competence. Pressley, Snyder, and Cariglia-Bull (1987, p. 102) characterized dialectically constructivist instructional interactions that presumably produce long-term commitment to and use of approaches to processing that children are taught:

> . . . mature thought develops in social contexts. Children first experience sophisticated processing in interpersonal situations, with more mature thinkers modeling good thinking and guiding young children's problem solving, often by providing cues to assist the children when they cannot manage on their own. The adults provide what has been referred to as proleptic instruction (i.e., instruction that typifies the child's needs). Adults direct children's attention appropriately; they provide strategies to children; in general, they serve a supervisory role, making their own good processing as visible as possible. They also try to guide the child to process in the same efficient fashion (e.g., Brown & Ferrara, 1985; Childs & Greenfield, 1980; Day, 1983; Greenfield, 1984; Palincsar & Brown, 1984; Vygotsky, 1978; Wertsch, 1985; Wood et al., 1976). Eventually children adopt as their own the thought processes that adults have externalized for them and encouraged them to use. They *internalize* the mature processing they have witnessed and participated in, although the internalized version is not an exact copy of the external processing. The explicit, heavily verbal processing that characterizes the adult-child interactions becomes abbreviated and highly efficient as it becomes intrapsychological functioning. (Vygotsky, 1962)

I take up here three specific characteristics of effective strategies instruction that make clear that such instruction is constructivist (see Pressley, Harris, & Marks, 1992, for a longer list, however). Each of these characteristics contrasts with claims about strategies instruction made by some critics of strategies instruction.

STRATEGIES TEACHING ACCOMPLISHES WHOLE TASKS

Some critics believe that strategies instruction decomposes tasks into parts rather than dealing with wholes and that it resembles skill teaching rather than education to accomplish whole tasks. That is certainly not true for the type of cognitive strategies instruction considered in this chapter, which involves teaching children how to tackle whole texts. Similarly, contemporary writing strategies instruction is aimed at creation of whole texts. Good problem-solving strategies instruction is aimed at teaching students to resolve challenging problems.

Complex tasks involve a number of processes used in a coordinated fashion—for example, reading comprehension involves generation of expectations, relating text meaning to prior knowledge, seeking clarification when confused, visualizing, and summarizing. What effective strategies instruction does is to encourage use of the many processes required to complete tasks that are ambitious in scope. I have not been watching years of lessons in which students do text prediction drills out of the context of real reading, or visualization drills, or any other type of drills. The instruction I have been watching occurs while students are reading entire stories and entire books. Students are encouraged to apply a developing repertoire of procedures as part of constructing rich and personalized understanding of stories and expositions they hear and read.

ERRORS ARE IMPORTANT DURING STRATEGIES INSTRUCTION

Some behavioristic models of teaching focus only on correct performance and view the making of errors as something to be extinguished. In contrast, constructivists view errors as revelations about student understanding and opportunities for cognitive growth. So it is with effective strategies instruction. Errors during strategies learning permit diagnosis of difficulties as students struggle to understand and apply strategies; the errors committed by a student can be revealing about student understanding of the strategies being taught. The teacher can then craft instruction intended to clarify the strategic processing the teacher is trying to encourage.

Errors during strategies learning can also serve as an indicator to the student of the value of strategies learning. Good strategies instruction includes reflection on how performance is improving as a function of learning strategies, with students often asked to explain why their strategies-mediated performances are getting better. See Schank and Leake (1989) for a discussion of the power of creating such explanations in promoting the construction of powerful thinking competencies.

WHAT IS LEARNED FROM STRATEGIES INSTRUCTION DEPENDS IN PART ON WHAT THE STUDENT ALREADY KNOWS

Constructivists believe that developmental level, interest, and prior knowledge are determinants of what students learn during any instructional interaction. An extreme example is the traditional Piagetian (e.g., see Flavell, 1963) perspective that developmental stages determine when a concept can be acquired; a second example is schema theory (e.g., Anderson & Pearson, 1984), with its assumption that material is easier to learn if it is consistent with knowledge already possessed by the learner (e.g., it is easier for a four-year-old to understand what to do at Pizza Hut if the child has previous knowledge of the routines in other sit-down restaurants).

Strategies instructors are also very much aware of student characteristics, with this awareness translated into consistent monitoring of whether students are learning from instruction. When instruction is not successful, strategies instructors try to discern how instruction might be restructured and represented so that learners' needs are accommodated.

SUMMARY

Pressley, Harris, and Marks (1992) summarized the nature of constructivist instruction, based on a review of programs that are identified by many as constructivist instruction (e.g., Pontecorvo & Zucchermaglio's [1990] literacy learning curriculum; instruction at Kamehameha School [Tharpe & Gallimore, 1988]; Pettito's [1985] mathematics instruction). Constructivist instruction has the following characteristics:

- Modeling and explanations are provided that are aimed at promoting greater competence in students, not by simple student copying of the skills that are modeled and explained, but by creative adaptation and personalization of the skills taught.

- There are some occasions when instruction is more explicit than other occasions, with the explicitness of prompting determined in part by whether students react successfully to the instruction provided to them (i.e., less prompting, instruction, and reinstruction when things are going well).

- The student constructs knowledge in interaction with a more competent adult, with much of this knowledge construction occurring as the student practices applying the skills modeled and explained, assisted by an adult who intervenes when the student needs assistance but not otherwise.

- Dialogues between teachers and students are not scripted. Adult reactions to students are somewhat opportunistic, providing feedback and instruction matched to need as students attempt to write, read, speak, or problem solve.

- Sometimes these interactions go smoothly; other times there are difficulties, with the nature of the difficulties used to adjust subsequent instruction.

- There is an emphasis on learning through understanding.

- Instruction occurs in groups, with students providing input and feedback to their peers.

- The adult continuously assesses the child's competence, assuming that current competence determines what the child will be able to learn.

- Constructivist teachers encourage their students to apply what they are learning to new tasks.

- There are individual differences in rates of progress.

Of course, all these characteristics of constructivist instruction are also characteristics of effective thinking strategies instruction. The difference between the instruction preferred by those who prefer the label "constructivist educator" and those who embrace the term "strategies instructor" is in the explicitness of the statement, modeling, and explanation of strategies. Good cognitive strategies instruction is probably more explicit in detailing for students the procedures and process being taught than is instruction identified as constructivist. The more the instruction is endogenously constructivist, the less it resembles good strategies instruction. Both exogenous and dialectical constructivist positions share many characteristics with good strategies instruction. No good strategies instructor can ever completely specify a strategy or strategies for students. Students are expected to fill in gaps in information provided about strategies, adapt the strategies they are learning, and use the strategies on new tasks. What the good strategies instructor does is to provide beginning information about strategies. Good strategies instruction is a specific instance of providing students with " . . . the 'material' upon which constructive mental processes will work" (Resnick, 1987, p. 47).

FUTURE RESEARCH ON TRANSACTIONAL STRATEGIES INSTRUCTION

My colleagues and I are continuing work on transactional strategies instruction. Three prominent directions for future research, all informed by our ongoing qualitative research, will be discussed in this section.

BETTER INSTRUCTION AT THE PRIMARY LEVEL

As part of Pressley, Schuder, SAIL Faculty and Administration, Bergman, and El-Dinary (1992), I held focus-group discussions with SAIL teachers to identify benefits and problems with the program. Then, I watched hours of such strategies instruction, followed by informal interviews with particular teachers about the strengths of the program and the potential weaknesses. Finally, I prepared a formal questionnaire, which was administered to 14 teachers in the SAIL program, who first answered in written form. Then there was a face-to-face interview to permit the teachers to expand on their answers and offer insights that might not come through in written responses to the printed questions.

The SAIL teachers perceived many more strengths than weaknesses with the program: The teachers believed that many aspects of literacy have been improved by SAIL, including oral reading, comprehension, student understanding that comprehension is under student control, writing, higher-order thinking, use of background knowledge to interpret texts, attention to meaning of texts, intertextual comparisons by students, involvement in reading group, and student excitement about reading. The teacher also perceived that academic self-concepts and self-esteem were improved since SAIL began and that social interactions during reading were better.

The teachers also believed that SAIL was compatible with whole language, which is critical because the whole language approach is the curricular umbrella philosophy for Montgomery County schools.

Even so, there were also some great concerns about the comprehension strategies instruction that defines the SAIL program, especially at the primary level. Teachers of nonreaders felt that the intervention made no provision for teaching of decoding and that hard thinking needed to be done in order to determine how SAIL could be meshed with decoding instruction. Primary teachers also felt that it was difficult to identify first-grade stories that were complicated enough to justify the SAIL strategies. These insights from the enthnographic interview study provided the impetus for change of the program during 1991–92.

Pamela Beard El-Dinary and I set out to study what might happen if SAIL primary teachers tried to integrate SAIL and conventional decoding instruction and if they were assured that it was all right to use the method more flexibly than had been suggested in previous years. One tangible form of support was the provision of a decoding-oriented basal program to the teachers (Open Court Reading and Writing) which teachers were free to use as part of their reading instruction. (Primary teachers in the 1990–91 SAIL program had reviewed this program and believed it could be meshed with SAIL.) Four of the five first-grade teachers who were studied in 1991–92 used Open Court materials; the fifth teacher adapted materials from various reading series in order to provide phonics instruction to her students. Weaker readers in particular received a great deal of additional phonics instruction during 1991–92 SAIL than in previous years of the program.

As in previous years, the first-grade SAIL lessons were designed largely to familiarize the students with the strategic processes encouraged in SAIL, with students provided with repeated explanations of the SAIL strategies and many lessons involving a great deal of emphasis on one or two of SAIL's cognitive processes. In previous years, SAIL was used almost exclusively in the context of actual reading. In 1991–92, Pam and I were struck by its predominant use as part of listening comprehension. First-grade students can listen to and comprehend much more complicated stories than they can read, so that teaching of SAIL as part of listening comprehension in first grade seems sensible and circumvents somewhat the difficulty of identifying first-grade stories appropriate for SAIL processes.

Two primary-grade SAIL teachers, one a first-grade teacher, Maryrose Pioli, and the other a second-grade teacher, Kathy Green, who taught a class involving many second-grade students with decoding difficulties, provide some insights into the importance of meshing decoding and SAIL comprehension instruction:

> **Pioli:** Decoding skills help the grade-1 students become independent readers in the sense they can at least read the text without stumbling over individual words. By combining high quality decoding instruction with SAIL comprehension instruction, the grade-1 students experience a lot of success in reading quickly. What is especially important is that the two approaches together permit them to read more on their own with confidence.
>
> **Green:** Decoding instruction at first goes a little slowly, with not as much time with real literature as might be ideal. But when the goal is independently decoding stories, explicit decoding instruction cannot be beat. I used a motivating approach to decoding, which was not at all aversive for the students. Once they were decoding well, it was natural and easy to get started with the SAIL comprehension strategies.

These same teachers also perceived advantages of introducing SAIL strategies gradually, with listening comprehension playing an important role in primary-grade strategies instruction:

> **Pioli:** When I read orally and modeled use of strategies, my grade-1 students

could begin to identify the strategies I was using as I read. That is a good introduction to strategies.

> **Green:** My oral reading of stories gets the students to listen to each other—I ask them to help me, with suggestions for strategic processing of the story. Students help come up with predictions, suggest vivid images, and assist in construction of story summaries. From hearing each others' predictions, images, and summaries, the students come to realize that there is not one right prediction or visualization or summarization but many, depending on their background knowledge. The students acquire a good understanding of these strategic processes before having to apply them to actual reading.

In summary, progress was made this last year in understanding how to improve one transactional strategies program, SAIL, at the primary level. The teachers themselves received very little outside help in revising this cognitive strategies curriculum. The progress made this year in understanding how to conduct comprehension strategies instruction at the primary level increases my optimism that comprehension instruction can be devised that really makes sense at the primary level. Much more research and development at the primary level are required and justified for three reasons: (a) There is little guidance in the basic research literature with respect to teaching of comprehension strategies to students at the first-and second-grade levels; (b) The whole language philosophy that now predominates in early reading instruction emphasizes comprehension; (c) My colleagues and I have observed that primary children do seem able to predict, seek clarifications, summarize, and visualize as they listen to stories in groups, and they seem to like doing it. Instruction rich in such comprehension processes is likely to be much more engaging for students than the skills-oriented instruction that has predominated during the primary years. The development of reading instruction promoting student engagement in literacy is and should be a high priority (Guthrie, Alvermann et al., 1992).

TEACHER DEVELOPMENT

In the first interview study of transactional strategies instruction conducted at Benchmark School (Pressley, Gaskins, Cunicelli et al., 1991), the teachers told us tales about how difficult strategies teaching had been during their first year. Similar sentiments were conveyed by SAIL teachers when they were probed about their experiences in learning how to be strategies teachers (Pressley, Schuder et al., 1992). No transactional strategies instruction teacher has ever told me that the first year was easy!

Pam El-Dinary and I (El-Dinary et al., in press) have studied first-year SAIL teachers during the last two years, watching and talking with them as they have attempted to teach their students the SAIL processes. During both years, the teachers were introduced to SAIL through professional development in-service meetings supplemented by some observations of teaching. The teachers received limited feedback themselves as they taught reading groups according to the SAIL model. Three teachers were studied in 1990–91 and four in 1991–92. In the first year, one of the three teachers made a clear commitment to SAIL and made great progress; in the second year, two of the teachers did. That is, less than half of the teachers were committed to SAIL after a year and were teaching in a fashion generally consistent with the model. The other teachers either did not "buy into SAIL" or if they did buy into it, they were not able to implement SAIL effectively on a regular basis in their curriculum. None of the teachers felt totally comfortable with SAIL after their first year; all felt that there was quite a bit to learn that was new.

All of the war tales I have heard about learning how to be a strategies instruction teacher and the struggles my students and I have witnessed make clear to me that research needs to be done about how best to prepare teachers so they can teach strategies. There is much for teachers to learn before they can teach strategies and not nearly

enough information conveyed in the faculty development workshops (although see Anderson & Roit, in press, for some data on effective workshops they have been studying). Enormous effort is required for teachers to become good at modeling and explaining strategies as they cope with many other demands in their curricula.

I am optimistic that it is possible to develop large numbers of strategies instruction teachers, for there are already successful efforts. For example, Deshler, Schumaker, and their colleagues at Kansas (e.g., Deshler & Schumaker, 1988) have trained thousands of teachers in the implementation of the Kansas strategies instruction curriculum. Gerald Duffy has educated a number of young teachers at Michigan State to be strategy instructors. Irene Gaskins has developed an entire faculty at Benchmark School. In each of these cases, however, teacher training was long-term and involved extensive practice and feedback. Indeed, a likely hypothesis is that like many complex skills, transactional strategies instruction teachers will continue to improve their teaching of strategies for many years following introduction to the approach (see Brown & Coy-Ogan, in press). Teacher development must be a priority area of research during the next few years for those of us interested in strategies instruction if effective strategies instruction is to be widely disseminated.

STRATEGIES ACROSS THE CURRICULA AND SCHOOL DAY

Any particular transactional strategies instructional intervention that is now being invented will operate as part of an overall curriculum. For example, reading strategies instruction at Benchmark School and in Montgomery County, MD, both occur in conjunction with writing strategies instruction and process-oriented mathematics instruction. The reading and language arts curricula also reflect whole language influences. There is no single cognitive process instruction predominating here, no single strategy that is a magic bullet. Rather, there is a repertoire of strategies, many of which can be applied in different ways throughout the school day. It is really exciting when such integration occurs, such as when expository text analysis strategies are turned around by students and used to plan for the writing of essays, such as happened during my semester case study at Benchmark (Pressley, Gaskins, Wile et al., 1991). SAIL students sometimes transfer visualization strategies from reading to mathematics. I have spent many mornings in Montgomery County and Benchmark classrooms when strategies were applied throughout the morning.

One of the saddest realizations I have had with respect to strategies instruction, however, is that integration is rare. Many teachers teach strategies like separate skills. There is faith by many who offer strategies instruction "in-services" and strategies instructions in basal manuals that if the separate strategies are practiced and mastered, somehow the kids will get it all together. (Gerald Duffy offered this insight to me about how many educator and publisher groups view strategies instruction as a bundle of skills.) I have no such faith, believing that strategic cognitive activity as a typical way of writing, reading, or problem solving will be most likely to develop for the largest number of children if schooling environments foster and expect students to be intelligently active throughout the day. The refined understandings that have emerged about how to teach writing, reading, and problem solving strategically (see Pressley & Associates, 1990) must be meshed in real school settings.

Educators, rather than researchers, are going to take the lead in creating whole schools that foster strategic competence. Researchers' talents are better matched to documenting what occurs in such environments, developing summaries of such instruction that can be comprehended by other educators and researchers. That is what my colleagues and I did with respect to the transactional strategies instruction summarized here.

SUMMARY AND CONCLUDING REMARKS

Experimental investigations of reading comprehension strategies provided a great deal of valuable information. Particularly relevant here, the experimental and basic research literatures informed the Benchmark and Montgomery County SAIL curriculum developers about cognitive strategies that might be taught to elementary students. These educators combined what they learned from the research-based literature with their well-grounded understandings of classrooms to design thinking strategies–based interventions that were tried by teachers. In attempting to implement these interventions, teachers discovered what worked and what did not work and how to teach thinking strategies so that students would "get it." There probably is not an end point to such discovery—I am struck that the good strategies instruction teachers I met several years ago seem better today. I expect there are many refinements to come as educators gain greater experience with strategies instruction and intermix it with everchanging curricular demands. For example, there is now tremendous impetus to expand the SAIL program into all content areas because of the emphasis on strategies and strategic thinking in the new state assessment.

What my colleagues and I have done is to document how strategies instruction is carried out in two settings that seem to be doing it well. The heart of the instruction we have observed is modeling and direct explanation of cognitive strategies, followed by teacher guidance and assistance as students attempt to apply the thinking strategies they are learning to realistic academic tasks. Effective strategies instruction is a multiple-year enterprise (see especially Pressley, Faculty and Administration of Summit Hall School et al., in press), and there are many "wrinkles" to it, one of the most significant of which is that such instruction encourages students to be interpreters of text.

One criticism of instructional research that I have endured in my career is that even if it is pragmatically important, it is theoretically vacuous. In general, I disagree with such analyses. In the case of transactional strategies instruction, there are multiple linkages to important theoretical perspectives. For example, transactional strategies discussions are simultaneously examples of applied schema theory and applied reader response theory: Meaning is definitely jointly determined by what is in the text and what is in the heads of readers. As our understanding of comprehension in such groups improves, new models of classroom communications should develop: How communications between diverse students and miscommunications between reading group participants shape the development of meaning are only two of the issues that need to be addressed as development of meaning in reading groups is studied. The implications of limited short-term capacity for classroom functioning is another example of an important theoretical direction that should be pursued as work on cognitive process instruction in classrooms continues. Transactional strategies instruction settings also provide a fantastic laboratory for studying the dynamics of constructivist instruction, because transactional strategies instruction is both exogenously and dialectically constructivist.

If theory is not your interest, but classroom application is, plenty of work on implementation remains to be done. How transactional strategies instruction can be useful across all of the grade levels remains to be spelled out. That is, as my colleagues and I make progress in tailoring strategies instruction for the primary grades, we are haunted by an awareness of the need for much more comprehension instruction at the secondary level and perhaps beyond that (see Pressley, El-Dinary, & Brown, 1992). As we congratulate ourselves for coming to terms with what happens in reading groups, we know that our understanding of comprehension instruction during the remainder of the school day is much less complete. Even though a lot has been learned about how cognitive strategies can be taught, little is understood about how to develop teachers who are effective strategy instructors.

I made so much progress in the last four years in understanding effective strategies instruction because I changed methodological tactics. Qualitative methods seemed better suited to the task of developing an understanding of large-scale instruction than the experimental methods I relied on exclusively in the past. As I write this, Rachel Brown and I are completing data collec-

tion on a quasi-experimental evaluation of the efficacy of SAIL instruction, with preliminary results suggesting that a year of SAIL affects both standardized and nontraditional measures of comprehension. Tommie DePinto and I are planning another quasi-experimental study of the effectiveness of an alternative version of transactional strategies instruction, one that had Palincsar and Brown's (1984) reciprocal teaching as its starting point (Marks, Pressley, Coley, Craig, Rose, & Gardner, in press). I never gave up an experimentation (quasi-experimentation when random assignment is not possible), with that reflected in the work in progress and in the planning stages. Nonetheless, many of the dependent variables in these new quantitative studies are much more qualitative than experiments I conducted five or more years ago. In addition, I continue to believe that individual strategies often can (and should) be nurtured in the laboratory before they are transported to a real world that is very complex, as exemplified by my ongoing research on elaborative interrogation (Pressley, Wood et al., 1992). It is exciting to have one research foot in the laboratory and the other in the real world of schooling; it is also much more fully informative about cognitive strategies instruction than if both feet were planted in only one of the two worlds.

There is no doubt that I will be looking to effective teachers to inform me about the nature of high-quality instruction. With luck, I will continue to be able to say some things to them in return that they can take and use to improve their practice some more. Participating in never-ending cycles of researcher and teacher contact is an exciting and attractive career prospect for me. I suspect this career will benefit schoolchildren more certainly than if I had continued as an aloof psychologist who prescribed instruction on the basis of only carefully controlled experiments, observations, and theories far removed from the classroom world of teachers. A quote that seems appropriate for closing this chapter, which is directed principally at graduate students, is the title of Robert Frost's compilation for young readers: *You Come, Too* (Frost, 1959).

REFERENCES

Anderson, R. C. (1983). *The architecture of cognition.* Cambridge, MA: Harvard University Press.

Anderson, R. C., & Pearson, P. D. (1984). A schema-theoretic view of basic processes in reading comprehension. In P. D. Pearson (Ed.), *Handbook of reading research* (pp. 255–291). New York: Longman.

Anderson, V., & Roit, M. (in press). Collaborative strategy instruction: The meeting of minds. *Elementary School Journal.*

Bandura, A. (1986). *Social foundations of thought and action: A social cognitive theory.* Englewood Cliffs, NJ: Prentice-Hall.

Baron, J. (1985). *Rationality and intelligence.* London & New York: Cambridge University Press.

Bell, R. Q. (1968). A reinterpretation of the direction of effects in studies of socialization. *Psychological Review, 75,* 81–95.

Bereiter, C., & Bird, M. (1985). Use of thinking aloud in identification and teaching of reading comprehension strategies. *Cognition and Instruction, 2,* 91–130.

Borkowski, J. G., Carr, M., Rellinger, E. A., & Pressley, M. (1990). Self-regulated strategy use: Interdependencies of metacognition, attributions, and self-esteem. In B. F. Jones & L. Idol (Eds.), *Dimensions of thinking: Review of research* (pp. 53–92). Hillsdale, NJ: Erlbaum & Associates.

Bowers, C. A., & Flinders, D. J. (1990). *Responsive teaching: An ecological approach to classroom patterns of language, culture, and thought.* New York: Teachers College Press.

Boy, G. (1991). *Intelligent assistant systems.* London & San Diego: Academic Press.

Brown, A. L., Bransford, J. P., Ferrara, R. A., & Campione, J. C. (1983). Learning, remembering, and understanding. In J. H. Flavell & E. M. Markman (Eds.), *Handbook of child psychology: Vol. 3. Cognitive development* (pp. 177–206). New York: Wiley.

Brown, A. L., & Ferrara, R. A. (1985). Diagnosing zones of proximal development. In J. V. Wertsch (Ed.), *Culture, communication, and cognition: Vygotskian perspectives* (pp. 273–305). London & New York: Cambridge University Press.

Brown, R., & Ogan, L. C. (in press). The evolution of transactional strategies instruction in one teacher's classroom. *Elementary School Journal.*

Cazden, C. B. (1988). *Classroom discourse.* Portsmouth, NH: Heinemann Books.

Chi, M. T. H., Glaser, R., & Farr, M. J. (Eds.). (1988). *The nature of expertise.* Hillsdale, NJ: Erlbaum & Associates.

Childs, C. P., & Greenfield, P. M. (1980). Informal modes of learning and teaching: The case of Zinacanteco weaving. In N. Warren (Ed.), *Studies in cross-cultural psychology* (Vol. 2, pp. 169–216). London: Academic Press.

Chipman, S. F., Segal, J. W., & Glaser, R. (1985). *Thinking and learning skills: Vol. 2. Research and open questions.* Hillsdale, NJ: Erlbaum & Associates.

Collins, C. (1991). Reading instruction that increases thinking abilities. *Journal of Reading, 34,* 510–516.

Cooke, N. J. (1989). The elicitation of domain-related ideas: Stage one of the knowledge acquisition process. In C. Ellis (Ed.), *Expert knowledge and explanation: The knowledge-language interface* (pp. 58–75). New York: John Wiley & Sons, Halsted Press.

Day, J. D. (1983). The zone of proximal development. In M. Pressley & J. R. Levin (Eds.), *Cognitive strategy research: Psychological foundations* (pp. 155–175). Berlin & New York: Springer-Verlag.

Deshler, D. D., & Schumaker, J. R. (1988). An instructional model for teaching students how to learn. In J. L. Graden, J. E. Zins, & M. J. Curtis (Eds.), *Alternative educational delivery systems: Enhancing instructional outcomes for all students* (pp. 391–411). Washington, DC: National Association of School Psychologists.

Duffy, G., Roehler, L., & Herrmann, B. (1988). Modeling mental processes helps poor readers become strategic readers. *Reader Teacher, 41,* 762–767.

Duffy, G. G., Roehler, L. R., Sivan, E., Rackliffe, G., Book C., Meloth, M., Vavrus, L. G., Wesselman, R., Putnam, J., & Bassiri, D. (1987). Effects of explaining the reasoning associated with using reading strategies. *Reading Research Quarterly, 22,* 347–368.

El-Dinary, P. B., Pressley, M., & Schuder, T. (1992). Becoming a strategies teacher: An observational and interview study of three teachers learning transactional strategies instruction. In C. Kinzer & D. Leu (Eds.), *Forty-first Yearbook of the National Reading Conference.* Chicago, IL: National Reading Conference.

El-Dinary, P. B., Pressley, M., & Schuder, T. (in preparation). *The first year of grade-1 comprehension strategies instruction.* College Park, MD: National Center for the Study of Reading at the University of Maryland.

Ellis, C. (1989). Explanation in intelligent systems. In C. Ellis (Ed.), *Expert knowledge and explanation: The knowledge-language interface* (pp. 108–126). New York: John Wiley & Sons, Halsted Press.

Englert, C. S., Raphael, T. E., Anderson, L. M., Anthony, H. M., & Stevens, D. D. (1991). Making strategies and self-talk visible: Writing instruction in regular and special education classrooms. *American Educational Research Journal, 28,* 337–372.

Flavell, J. H. (1963). *Developmental psychology of Jean Piaget.* New York: van Nostrand.

Flavell, J. H. (1970). Developmental studies of mediated memory. In H. W. Reese & L. P. Lipsitt (Eds.), *Advances in child development and behavior* (Vol. 5). New York: Academic Press.

Flower, L., Stein, V., Ackerman, J., Kantz, M. J., McCormick, K., & Peck, W. C. (1990). *Reading to write: Exploring a cognitive and social process.* New York & Oxford, England: Oxford University Press.

Frost, R. (1959). *You come too: Favorite poems for young readers.* New York: Henry Holt.

Gaskins, I. W., Anderson, R. C., Pressley, M., Cunicelli, E. A., & Satlow, E. (1993). The moves strategy instruction teachers make. *Elementary School Journal, 93*(4), 323–350.

Gaskins, I. W., & Elliot, T. T. (1991). *The Benchmark model for teaching thinking strategies: A manual for teachers.* Cambridge, MA: Brookline Books.

Greenfield, P. M. (1984). A theory of the teacher in the learning activities of everyday life. In B. Rogoff & J. Lave (Eds.), *Everyday cognition: Its development in social context* (pp. 117–138). Cambridge, MA: Harvard University Press.

Guthrie, J. T., Alvermann, D. E. (1992). *National Center for the Study of Reading Proposal* (funded). College Park, MD & Athens, GA: University of Maryland & University of Georgia.

Harris, K. R., & Pressley, M. (1991). The nature of cognitive strategy instruction: Interactive strategy construction. *Exceptional Children 57,* 392–404.

Hayes-Roth, F., Waterman, D. A., & Lenat, D. (1983). *Building expert systems.* Reading, MA: Addison-Wesley.

Hutchins, E. (1991). The social organization of distributed cognition. In L. Resnick, J. M. Levine, & S. D. Teasley (Eds.), *Perspectives on socially shared cognition* (pp. 283–307). Washington, DC: American Psychological Association.

James, W. (1958). *Talks to teachers.* New York: Norton. (Original work published 1899).

LaBerge, D., & Samuels, S. J. (1974). Toward a theory of automatic information processing in reading. *Cognitive Psychology, 6,* 293–323.

Levin, J. R., & Pressley, M. (1981). Improving children's prose comprehension: Selected strategies that seem to succeed. In C. M. Santa & B. L. Hayes (Eds.), *Children's prose comprehension: Research and practice* (pp. 44–71). Newark, DE: International Reading Association.

Lincoln, Y. S., & Guba, E. G. (1985). *Naturalistic inquiry.* Beverly Hills: Sage.

Maida, A. S., & Deng, M. (1989). A language to allow expert systems to have beliefs about their users. In C. Ellis (Ed.), *Expert knowledge and explanation: The knowledge-language interface* (pp. 127–143). New York: John Wiley & Sons, Halsted Press.

Marks. M. B., Pressley, M. in collaboration with Coley, J. D., Craig, S., Rose, W., & Gardner, R. (in press). Teachers' adaptations of reciprocal teaching: Process toward a classroom-compatible version of reciprocal teaching. *Elementary School Journal.*

Mastropieri, M. A., & Scruggs, T. E. (1991). *Teaching students ways to remember: Strategies for learning mnemonically.* Cambridge, MA: Brookline Books.

Mehan, H. (1979). *Learning lessons: Social organization in the classroom.* Cambridge, MA: Harvard University Press.

Moshman, D. (1982). Exogenous, endogenous, and dialectical constructivism. *Developmental Review, 2,* 371–384.

Nickerson, R. S., Perkins, D. N., & Smith, E. E. (1985). *The teaching of thinking.* Hillsdale, NJ: Erlbaum & Associates.

Palincsar, A. S., & Brown, A. L. (1984). Reciprocal teaching of comprehension-fostering and comprehension-monitoring activities. *Cognition and Instruction, 1,* 117–175.

Paris, S. G., & Oka, E. R. (1986). Children's reading strategies, metacognition, and motivation. *Developmental Review, 6,* 25–56.

Pearson, P. D., & Dole, J. A. (1987). Explicit comprehension instruction: A review of research and a new conceptualization of instruction. *Elementary School Journal, 88,* 151–165.

Petitto, A. L. (1985). Division of labor: Procedural learning in teacher-led small groups. *Cognition & Instruction, 2,* 233–270.

Pontecorvo, C., & Zuccermaglio, C. (1990). A passage to literacy: Learning in social context. In Y. M. Goodman (Ed.), *How children construct literacy: Piagetian perspectives* (pp. 59–98). Newark, DE: International Reading Association.

Poplin, M. S. (1988a). Holistic/constructivist principles

of the teaching/learning process: Implications for the field of learning disabilities. *Journal of Learning Disabilities, 21,* 401–416.

Poplin, M. S. (1988b). The reductionistic fallacy in learning disabilities: Replicating the past by reducing the present. *Journal of Learning Disabilities, 21,* 389–400.

Pressley, M., & Associates. (1990). *Cognitive strategy instruction that really improves children's academic performance.* Cambridge, MA: Brookline Books.

Pressley, M., Borkowski, J. G., & Schneider, W. (1987). Cognitive strategies: Good strategy users coordinate metacognition and knowledge. In R. Vasta & G. Whitehurst (Eds.), *Annals of child development* (Vol. 4, pp. 89–129). Greenwich, CT: JAI Press.

Pressley, M., Borkowski, J. G., & Schneider, W. (1989). Good information processing: What it is and what education can do to promote it. *International Journal of Educational Research, 13,* 857–867.

Pressley, M., El-Dinary, P. B., & Brown, R. (1992). Is good reading comprehension possible? In M. Pressley, K. R. Harris, & J. T. Guthrie (Eds.), *Promoting academic competence and literacy: Cognitive research and instructional innovation* (pp. 91–127). San Diego: Academic Press.

Pressley, M., El-Dinary, P. B., Brown, R., Schuder, T., Bergman, J. L., York, M., Gaskins, I. W., & faculties and administration of Benchmark School and the Montgomery County, MD SAIL/SIA programs. (in press), A transactional strategies instruction Christmas carol. In A. McKeogh & J. Lupart (Eds.), (volume in preparation). Hillsdale, NJ: Erlbaum & Associates.

Pressley, M., El-Dinary, P. B., Gaskins, I. W., Schuder, T., Bergman, J. L., Almasi, J., & Brown, R. (1992). Beyond direct explanation: Transactional instruction of reading comprehension strategies. *Elementary School Journal, 92*(1), 32–50.

Pressley, M., El-Dinary, P. B., Stein, S., Marks, M. B., & Brown, R. (1992). Good strategy instruction is motivating and interesting. In A. Renninger, S. Hidi, & A. Krapp (Eds.), *The role of interest in learning and development* (pp. 333–358). Hillsdale, NJ: Erlbaum.

Pressley, M., faculty and administration of Summit Hall School, Almasi, J., Schuder, T., Bergman, J., Hite, S., El-Dinary, P. B., and Brown, R. (in press). Transactional instruction of comprehension strategies: The Montgomery County MD SAIL program. *Reading and Writing Quarterly.*

Pressley, M., Gaskins, I. W., Cunicelli, E. A., Burdick, N. J., Schaub-Matt, M., Lee, D. S., & Powell, N. (1991). Strategy instruction at Benchmark School: A faculty interview study. *Learning Disability Quarterly, 14,* 19–48.

Pressley, M., Gaskins, I. W., Wile, D., Cunicelli, E.

A., & Sheridan, J. (1991). Teaching literacy strategies across the curriculum: A case study at Benchmark School. In J. Zutell & S. McCormick (Eds.), *Learner factors/teacher factors: Issues in literacy research and instruction* (pp. 219–228). Chicago: National Reading Conference.

Pressley, M., Goodchild, F., Fleet, J., Zajchowski, R., & Evans, E. D. (1989). The challenges of classroom strategy instruction. *Elementary School Journal, 89,* 301–342.

Pressley, M., Harris, K. R., & Marks, M. B. (1992). But good strategy instructors are constructivists! *Educational Psychology Review, 4,* 3–31.

Pressley, M., Johnson, C. J., Symons, S., McGoldrick, J. A., & Kurita, J. (1990). Strategies that improve memory and comprehension of what is read. *Elementary School Journal, 90,* 3–32.

Pressley, M., Schuder, T., SAIL faculty and administration, Bergman, J. L., El-Dinary, P. B. (1992). A researcher-educator collaborative interview study of transactional comprehension strategies instruction. *Journal of Educational Psychology, 49*(6), 337–344.

Pressley, M., Snyder, B. L., & Cariglia-Bull, T. (1987). How can good strategy use be taught to children. In S. M. Cormier & J. D. Hagman (Eds.), *Transfer of learning: Contemporary approaches and applications* (pp. 81–120). Orlando, FL: Academic Press.

Pressley, M., Wood, E., Woloshyn, V. E., Martin, V., King, A., & Menke, D. (1992). Encouraging mindful use of prior knowledge: Attempting to construct explanatory answers facilitates learning. *Educational Psychologist, 27,* 91–110.

Resnick, L. B. (1987). Constructing knowledge in school. In L. S. Liben (Ed.), *Development and learning: Conflict or congruence?* (pp. 19–50). Hillsdale, NJ: Erlbaum & Associates.

Rosenblatt, L. M. (1978). *The reader, the text, the poem: The transactional theory of the literary work.* Carbondale, IL: Southern Illinois University Press.

Rosenshine, B. V. (1979). Content, time, and direct instruction. In P. L. Peterson & H. J. Walberg (Eds.), *Research on teaching: Concepts, findings, and implications* (pp. 28–55). Berkeley, CA: McCutchan.

Rosenshine, B. V., & Meisner, C. (1992). *Nineteen experimental studies which used reciprocal teaching: A review of research.* Manuscript submitted for publication.

Schank, R. C., & Leake, D. B. (1989). Creativity and learning in a case-based explainer. *Artificial Intelligence International Journal, 40,* 353–385.

Schneider, W., & Pressley, M. (1989). *Memory devel-*

opment between 2 and 20. New York: Springer-Verlag.

Segal, J. W., Chipman, S. F., & Glaser, R. (1985). *Thinking and learning skills: Vol. 1. Relating instruction to research.* Hillsdale, NJ: Erlbaum & Associates.

Strauss, A., & Corbin, J. (1990). *Basics of qualitative research.* Newbury Park, CA: Sage.

Tharpe, R. G., & Gallimore, R. (1988). *Rousing minds to life: Teaching, learning, and schooling in social context.* London & New York: Cambridge University Press.

Vygotsky, L. S. (1962). *Thought and speech.* Cambridge, MA: MIT Press.

Vygotsky, L. S. (1978). *Mind in society.* Cambridge, MA: Harvard University Press.

Wegner, D. M. (1987). Transactive memory: A contemporary analysis of the group mind. In B. Mullen & G. Goethals (Eds.), *Theories of group behavior* (pp. 185–208). New York: Springer-Verlag.

Weiner, J. L. (1989). The effect of user models on the production of explanations. In C. Ellis (Ed.), *Expert knowledge and explanation: The knowledge-language interface* (pp. 144–156). New York: John Wiley & Sons, Halsted Press.

Wertsch, J. (1985). *Vygotsky and the social formation of mind.* Cambridge, MA: Harvard University Press.

Wood, P., Bruner, J., & Ross, G. (1976). The role of tutoring in problem solving. *Journal of Child Psychology and Psychiatry, 17,* 89–100.

Zimmerman, B. J., & Schunk, D. H. (Eds.). *Self-regulated learning and academic achievement.* New York: Springer-Verlag.

CHAPTER SIX

DEVELOPING PROBLEM-SOLVING ABILITIES

CATHY COLLINS BLOCK

▼

TEXAS CHRISTIAN UNIVERSITY

Dr. Cathy Collins Block is professor of education at Texas Christian University. She has directed several research studies concerning thinking development. She is the director of the Texas Network of Thinking Schools and codirector of the Texas Education Agency Project charged with identifying the most successful instructional practices in Texas's highest achieving schools. She has written numerous articles in professional journals and several books, is coauthor of the *Stanford Early School Achievement Test,* and has served as consultant for numerous school districts in the United States, Russia, and Hungary. She holds offices in several professional associations and served as a research assistant at the Wisconsin Research and Development Center for Cognitive Development.

Throughout time philosophers have tried to define man. Aristotle stated that "man is the rational animal" and in jest added, "All my life I have been searching for evidence to support this definition!" (*Ethics: I*, p. 13). The Hebrew Talmud defines man as "the creatures that pray"; Adam Smith distinguishes humans as "the only animals that bargain. Dogs do not exchange bones." More recently, Polya proposed that problem solving is the most characteristically human activity.

In this chapter I will examine problem-solving abilities, and explore ways in which we can strengthen students' problem-solving capabilities through elementary- and middle-school curriculum.

I would like to begin with an experiment to enhance our awareness of strategies employed in problematic situations. In a moment I will ask you to read three sets of questions. Your mind will engage several operations for each query. Because these cognitive operations are executed in milliseconds, attend closely to your mind's activity, how you feel, and the strategies you expend to construct answers.

Read the following sets of sentences, pausing after each question to note your cognitions and emotions before you read on.

You have a problem that you cannot solve. What are you feeling and thinking as you reflect upon this problem?

How did you answer? How did you feel? Most

successful problem solvers use both emotional and cognitive energy in problematic situations. Did you have an emotional surge, as well as a cognitive response, as you reflected upon your problem? Successful problem solvers are aware that their emotions are more closely tied to problem solving thinking than any other type of cognition they experience (Goldman, Vye, Williams, Reivey, & Pellegrino, 1991).

Read the next question and create your answer.

Think of the last successful solution you reached. Why was this solution successful?

Did you judge yourself to play an important role in solving the problem you recalled? Successful problem solvers identify facets of their efforts that contributed to creating a successful solution; less successful problem solvers more heavily credit luck or the good will of others. In addition, more successful problem solvers have a more positive level of self-worth than less successful problem solvers. They judge themselves to be proactive and effective thinkers (Doise & Hanselmann, 1991).

Now, read the next word and answer the question related to it.

Failure. Think of your last failure. What caused this failure to attain a goal?

To maintain a personal homeostasis of self-efficacy in light of failures, less successful problem solvers blame setbacks on forces beyond their control. More successful problem solvers, however, operate from an internal locus of control, viewing failures as resulting from inattention to conditions that *they can change* (Bandura, 1992).

Through this experiment, you may have realized that problem-solving abilities are interwoven with an individual's emotional health, level of positive self-esteem, belief in an internal locus of control, and need to maintain a positive psychological self-image. Because of these interconnections, if our schools are to improve the problem-solving abilities of our youth, special additions to the curriculum are required.

The purpose of this chapter is to describe such additions and to present methods of improving students' problem-solving processes. The chapter is divided into four sections: (1) an overview of the research that supports instruction designed to improve students' problem-solving abilities; (2) a description of aspects within the problem-solving process that such lessons should address; (3) an outline of the basic lesson plan followed in my studies of elementary- and middle-school students' abilities to solve problems; and (4) a report of research data concerning problem-solving instruction.

REVIEW OF LITERATURE

Problem solving may be defined as a starting condition where one begins to obtain a goal state. It includes the information, manipulations, and strategies used to change a beginning benchmark reference point into a goal state. The process may also include intermediate states.

In a review of research concerning problem solving, several questions emerged: Does problem solving involve different processes for variant tasks, or is "problem-solving skill" a generalized ability? Does the abstractness or complexity of a problem change the thinking processes involved in its solution, or do the mental problem-solving interactions remain the same regardless of the sophistication of the solution needed? Does solving one problem enhance the ability to solve subsequent problems? Does the mind store problem-solving experiences differently than non-problem-related situations? Can educators create better problem solvers through instruction? What is the difference between the interactions "expert problem solvers" have, which assist their winning attitude, and those "novice problem solvers" experience, which tend to lower their self-esteem, risk-taking tendencies, and creativity?

In the earliest research concerning problem solving, physical characteristics such as brain weight, head circumference, stature, and limb length were used as measures of an individual's problem-solving capacity. For example, in the 1900s, archeologists judged cavemen with larger skulls to be better problem solvers than smaller-headed peers. Their augmented cranials were believed to have resulted from their increased sensitivity to the physical environment. This alliance between physical endowments and problem-solving ability remained until Terman and Thorndike's work in the 1930s and 1940s.

By the 1950s, through the use of intelligence tests, calipers and scales were dethroned as measures of problem-solving ability. Researchers discovered that problem-solving abilities involve more than recall capabilities and speed of learning. Distinct mental and emotional elements enable people to move from positions of no change, or merely responding to change, to creating it. Understanding what these elements are has become the life work of many psychologists and educators, as we will see. What are the components of successful problem-solving ability?

Research suggests that problem-solving ability is not a single capability. It comprises many interactive components, some of which are evasive, illusionary, and emotionally governed sensors (Zellermay, Salomon, Globerson, & Givon, 1991; Poincare, 1955; Wolf, Bixby, Glenn, & Gardner, 1991). As Poincare (1955) reports:

The incidents of travel made me forget my [problem]. Having reached Coutances, we entered an omnibus to go someplace or other. At the moment when I put my foot on the step, the [solution] came to me, without anything in my former thoughts seeming to have paved the way for it. . . . I did not verify the idea; I should not have had time, as, upon taking my seat in the omnibus, I went on with a conversation already commenced, but I felt a perfect certainty [that I had solved my problem correctly]. (p. 37)

Einstein also recognized the emotive component in problem solving:

Solving this problem [relativity] involved a six-year struggle to locate and define the prob-

lem. This struggle was primarily a groping feeling, and encompassed a definite, and important, yet indescribable stage in my problem solving strategies. My dazed uncertainty was marked by recurring "feelings" of being right; of moving in the right direction. This was the creative, imaginative stage in which occurred a succession of intuitive flashes of insight; some minor, others major and rare. These followed exploratory episodes of feeling and emerged only as new dimensions of the whole structure and I felt them via feedback transformations. Verbal, logical analysis was never resorted to until after the flash of illumination and then only for verification, never for discovery. (Einstein & Infield, 1938, pp. 290–1)

DOES SOLVING ONE PROBLEM ENHANCE ONE'S ABILITY TO SOLVE SUBSEQUENT PROBLEMS?

It seems that problem-solving ability can be increased with practice. Improvements, however, do not arise as much from the strength practice provides to cognitive components of problem solving as from the strength it generates for the emotional components. For example, when people enact a successful solution, they increase their confidence in their ability to solve problems and in their belief in an internal locus of control. For cognitive strategies to strengthen, problem solvers must be familiar with the perplexities and complexities of the specific problem to be solved (Anderson, 1991). Thus, optimal growth in problem-solving ability occurs when individuals acquire specific knowledge about a subject and have the opportunity to practice solving similar problems so there exists the confidence to reason about the application and consequences of their knowledge. Therefore, it seems that the complexity of a task is not as important in determining the success one will experience in problem solving as is one's level of expertise in the domain in which the problem appears.

Research also suggests that problem solving, from novice to expert, progresses along a continuum. The continuum ranges from reasoning by recognition of physical descriptors, to identification of functional operators, and, finally, to making predictions about integrated relationships (Schultz & Lockhead, 1991). For example, people who have had few problem-solving experiences appear capable of viewing problematic events solely at the *classification level*. They attach labels and match problematic features as their major cognitive strategies. Conversely, intermediate-level problem solvers address difficult situations at the *understanding level*. They associate meanings and link concepts or events to phenomena. They add personal beliefs and needs to their reasoning strategies. Further along the continuum, expert problem solvers *anticipate problematic situations*. They apply relationships and phenomena to varied problematic elements by discerning and predicting the connections between elements (Anderson, 1991).

Other differences exist between expert and intermediate/novice problem solvers. First, expert problem solvers base solutions on interactions between contextual, social, economic, physical, political, and cultural criteria and do not impose their own standards for success upon problems, as intermediate-level problem solvers do. Instead, they validate goals through consequence testing. They use principle-based hypotheses, which lead to reasoning about, and making judgments from, a holistic approach. For example, less skilled problem-solvers will judge themselves to be successful if their solution satisfies a personal need. More skilled peers, however, must have evidence that a wider sphere of contingencies were strengthened before they judge a goal to be achieved.

Second, when compared to less able peers, expert problem solvers use more of their memory and have faster recall of prior successful problem-solving situations. They interrelate semantic attributes from these past experiences to present difficulties, focus less upon non-meaningful dimensions of stimuli, and spend less time disengaging with tasks (Anderson, 1991). They more reasonably estimate the accessibility of known facts, because they have fewer misconceptions, and know which facts cannot be known and which can be deduced on the basis of what they already know. Further, they know what is needed to perform optimally and will settle for nothing less. They allocate more effort and ingenuity to the more difficult aspects of tasks. They predict which method "feels" as if it will be most effective, and if it doesn't perform optimally, they shift.

Expert problem solvers also are distinguishable in their abilities to: (a) organize quantitative calculations through an understanding of qualitative relations; (b) represent a problem via diagrams or drawings; and (c) use problem-solving tools. For example, in Mackey's study of business personnel (J. Mackey, personal communication), expert problem solvers were the only group to rank and weigh attributes and to use note taking as a memory aid.

DOES THE MIND STORE PROBLEM-SOLVING EXPERIENCES DIFFERENTLY THAN NONPROBLEM-RELATED SITUATIONS?

Problem-solving experiences are stored differently than nonproblematic events. They are stored in two ways. First, problem-solving experiences enter the brain as distinct but ill-formed cognitive entries that attach to several separate schemata. Second, they enter as "spill-over entries," profoundly influencing a wide range of previously stored facts. In storage, problem-solving experiences become interconnected mental webs (Chi, Feltovich, & Glaser, 1981). These networks expand as new problematic situations begin. Networked emotions and cognitions from prior schema, as well as recall of past problematic situations, engage as each new problem enters the mind. When a new problem occurs, "electricity" soars through the networked circuits. The strength of the entire system increases, and all connecting parts are rejuvenated. As new problems "drizzle" over the brain, they coat previous problem-solving knowledge with a "thicker insulation" (rubber coating), which in turn protects the dendrites (electrical circuits) from singes of overload during subsequent problematic situations.

Moreover, because the mind stores problem-solving experiences differently than nonproblem-related events, we tend to forget exactly how a problem was solved. When we are distressed, sections in our mental network of prior problematic situations are charged electrically and cause components to repel each other, leaving us bewildered. To illustrate, picture sections of the brain as two half magnets shaped like half shells of a peanut. When a solution is reached, the negative charges between these circuits are neutralized and the repelling half shells unite, creating a fully formed peanut. In the process, the problem solution becomes an entirely new entity. When problems pull new sections together, how they united is no longer visible. (The higher level cognitive strategies used to solve a problem is embedded in the new creation and often cannot be retrieved as an entity unto itself.)

In summary, expert problem solvers are defined as "knowing how" to solve problems. But what exactly is it that they know? Can we teach it? Can we help students avoid years of failure in trial-and-error problem-solving processes? In this chapter I will demonstrate that we are beginning to understand how expert problem solvers think and that we can teach these processes to students. We must teach students how to evoke a set of higher-level cognitive processes, emotional responses, self-efficacy, and positive self-images in problematic situations. Through instruction, we must also sensitize students to the psychological resistances that automatically engage during problem solving: (a) mental equilibrium is disrupted by new or discrepant information; (b) the dual processes of assimilation and accommodation emerge to resolve repelling mental forces; and (c) equilibrium is reinstated when either a higher level of efficacy results (the solution is successful) or learned helplessness occurs (the solution does not prove effective). Disequilibrium is a more permanent state for unsuccessful problem solvers than for their more successful peers.

DEVELOPING LESSONS THAT ASSIST STUDENTS TO BECOME BETTER PROBLEM SOLVERS

In this section, I will describe the psychological, emotional, cognitive, efficacy, and self-esteem factors that we must address, through instruction, if our students are to improve their problem-solving capabilities. I will also present an instructional program for second graders and middle-school students that increased problem-solving abilities. Lessons in this program (a) built students' commitment, (b) increased their engagement in difficult thinking processes, (c) developed their self-efficacy, (d) decreased their tendencies toward learned helplessness, (e) resolved their cognitive dissonance, and (f) increased their personal problem-space.

BUILDING STUDENTS' COMMITMENT

To solve problems, students need to commit effort to define problems (Moore, 1991; and Perry, 1970). Currently, this type of commitment is not taught in schools. We must begin to teach students *how to state an objective so as to identify and then solve problems*. Students can learn to do so when they (a) are allowed to identify problems they want to solve (Part 2 of the Lesson Plan, see page 149), and (b) are taught how to state three-part objectives (Part 1 of the Lesson Plan, see page 148). When these two components are available, students are more likely to commit to sustaining problem-solving thinking because they choose activities (a) in the face of legitimate alternatives, (b) after experiencing doubt about whether they want to exert the mental and physical energy needed to solve a problem, and (c) affirming their positive self-worth through their ability to solve problems. In most curriculum today, these components are not in lessons. Instead, students are told when to solve a problem, prescribed which method to use, and graded on their ability to solve the problem quickly using rote recall.

In my research, we began lessons by telling students that successful problem solvers make a commitment to solving a problem, and this commitment enables them to cope with disequilibrium until they create a solution. Students were also told that sometimes in life there will not be "correct or perfect answers"; but, that it is important to be willing to think and struggle with the problem-solving process until better states and conditions result.

TEACHING STUDENTS ABOUT THE HUMAN TENDENCY TO AVOID COMPLETIONS

In the first lessons in my research, students were taught that some unsuccessful problem solvers do not complete the final steps for success because anxiety interferes. It seems that such people fear they will become the object of criticism if they are successful, or they will be unable to live up to higher expectations that could be a by-product of success. It appears that when success becomes imminent, anxiety manifests itself so strongly that unsuccessful problem solvers' desires for success are replaced with a self-imposed mandate to avoid it. In such cases, unsuccessful problem solvers abandon long-cherished goals and substitute easier alternatives.

Students were also taught that anxieties of this type can be exhibited early in the problem-solving process as well, for example, a student who misses the deadline for the graduate entrance exam or experiences a "choke" response in clutch situations. Because causes for such anxieties are subconscious, explanations by teachers during problem-solving tasks that credit cognition only are inadequate. Instead, students in our studies were taught to use "thinking guides" so that small, measured steps could be implemented in the final stage of a problem-solving process, to suppress their negative anxiety.

INCREASING STUDENTS' SENSE OF EFFICACY

To develop students' efficacy, we taught that the ability to solve problems was an *incremental skill,* which is a perspective that successful problem solvers maintain. We realized that students who obtained an incremental skill perspective were more likely to regard their errors as natural, instructive parts of the problem-solving process. Similarly, because of this perspective, the need for a successful solution to every task weighed less heavily upon their estimates of self-worth. Such students came to believe that they could control many problematic matters. Small-step successes, in turn, provided behavioral validation of students' personal efficacy and the worth of the problem-solving strategies they used. This resulting self-belief system became resilient, enabling students to override repeated, early failures in their problem-solving process (Collins Block, 1993).

Lessons in the next section of this chapter enabled students to develop this strong sense of efficacy and to deploy their cognitive resources twice (in Parts 1 and 2). In so doing, they learned to remain task-oriented in the face of repeated difficulties. In Part 2 of the lessons, students ferreted out relevant information, constructed options, and tested the knowledge they used in Part 1. Such reconstructions reinforced the incremental skills perspective.

On the other hand, students not taught the incremental skills perspective tended to judge the number of successes they attained as a reflection of their general intellectual capacity. Errors and deficient performances posed high personal evaluative threats. As a result, many untrained students selected tasks beneath their potential because they held less chance for errors, and permitted an easy display of their intellectual proficiency (Collins, 1991a).

TEACHING STUDENTS TO AVOID LEARNED HELPLESSNESS

As stated previously, unsuccessful problem solvers experience learned helplessness, a *belief that they are incompetent.* When students equate present problems with past inabilities to control difficulties, they feel "helpless" when facing future problems. When students were taught to guard against the tendency to group failures together, they overcame feelings of "being defeated before the problem-solving process began."

In my studies, students were taught not to group failures together in two ways. First, they received predictable rewards from their teachers. Students received rewards for each successful small step they took in using their thinking guides. They received immediate feedback at the end of Part 1 of each lesson as well. Also, students could consistently expect that they would be able to follow through with the recommendations from this feedback during the second part of each lesson (Collins, 1992).

Second, illusions of incompetence were dispelled because students became mindfully engaged in the problem-solving task. Students engaged their attention and energy toward attainable aspects of the problem, first, which raised their self-judgment of capabilities (Collins, 1991a; Harter, 1985). Moreover, we found that because our problem-solving lessons were sustained for two to five days, the length of time they had to solve problems increased students' positive self-efficacy beliefs. The longer students persevered in the face of repeated failures, the more they increased their faith that they would reach successful solutions.

TEACHING STUDENTS TO OVERCOME COGNITIVE DISSONANCE

Cognitive dissonance is using behaviors, explanations, and excuses to maintain a positive self-image in problematic situations (Festinger, 1957). According to this theory, the need to maintain a positive self-image is a powerful motivator. In problem-solving situations, however, difficult conflicts challenge students' positive self-image. In such situations, unsuccessful problem solvers engage considerable energy rationalizing the difficulty of the task in order to maintain a positive self-image. For example, in an episode of "Candid Camera," sugar packets that could not be opened were placed in a coffee shop. The hidden, candid camera recorded customers trying to open the packets and the irrational solutions they created to keep others from staring at them as they wrestled to open different packets. One customer, after an extraordinary, unsuccessful effort to open a sugar packet, looked around and quickly dropped

the entire, unopened packet of sugar into his coffee! When a member of the "Candid Camera" crew asked why he had dropped an unopened sugar packet into his coffee, the man replied that he always did it that way, that he really liked the flavor it gave his coffee! This man exhibited cognitive dissonance by responding to an embarrassing situation by rationalizing his strange behavior, hoping that the rationale would be acceptable to others so he could maintain a positive image in others' eyes (and thereby keep his own self-image positive).

In our lessons, students were taught 14 problem-solving strategies, so they would have tools to employ in challenging situations. With these tools in hand, they could make fewer mistakes and would be less likely to lower their positive self-images. Because their self-expectations were not lowered, their motivation did not decrease. Because their motivation was not diminished, they, in turn, did not establish smaller, less desirable goals for themselves. Thus, because their large goal enabled their full potentials to be engaged, their work resulted in higher levels of performance. In turn, because their teachers accepted these higher levels of performance as true indications of their students' cognitive abilities, their expectations for the students elevated. Because of the interactions between these conditions in our lessons, cognitive dissonance was unable to interfere with the development of successful problem-solving abilities for our subjects.

DESIGNING LESSONS WHERE STUDENTS CREATE PERSONAL PROBLEM SPACE

Successful problem solvers create an internal "problem space" (Lewis, 1990; Yekovich, Thompson, & Walker, 1991). This space enables time for the individual to "think about his or her own thinking;" to review and analyze the process of problem solving; and identify, modify, and adopt successful problem-solving patterns. In our lessons, we gave students choices as to the objectives and thinking guides they wanted to use. These choices taught students that thinking (creating problem space) was a necessary part of the lessons and the problem-solving process they were learning.

OUTLINE OF THE BASIC LESSON PLAN

▼

In my research studies, 14 problem-solving lessons were developed. Each lesson followed the same lesson plan format, as described below.

PART 1: INTRODUCTION TO A PROBLEM-SOLVING STRATEGY

In Part 1, students were taught 1 of the 14 thinking strategies presented on pages 149–153. They were told about (a) the strategy, (b) reasons why they were learning it, (c) history about the development of the strategy, and (d) real-world settings in which the strategy is being used today. These introductory remarks were followed by the statement of a three-part objective. This objective contained the goal for the day's work, provided the rationale for it, and describe methods of instruction that would be used to learn the problem-solving strategy. The three-part objective ended with descriptions of how students could recognize that they had learned the problem-solving strategy.

By stating the objective in this way, students learned how to *commit* to solving a problem and how to *overcome the tendency of human nature to not complete a difficult thinking process*. They knew what they were going to do and why, the methods they could use to accomplish the task, and how they would know they had been successful. This direct explanation and prompting of high level thinking processes, strategies, and products substantially increases learning (Duffy & Roehler, 1986; Pressley, Goodchild, Fleet, Zajchowski, & Evans, 1989; Pressley, El-Dinary, & Brown, 1992).

Immediately following the prompting of reading/thinking strategies, students *dispelled their misconceptions* (Beck & Dole, 1991; Eichinger & Roth, 1990; Glaser, 1986). As discussed previously, in the face of a problem situation, students' strong sense of efficacy and internal locus of control is challenged. When students are allowed to discuss their fears and self-doubts at this point in the problem-solving lesson, their sense of efficacy is strengthened and their internal locus of control is engaged.

Students learned six methods to dispel misconceptions. Each was used four or five times in the study. These methods were:

(a) Students gave testimonials as to the benefits they expected to receive from learning a problem-solving strategy. Testimonials came from students in the class who used the strategy under study prior to the lesson, or from older schoolmates and representatives from the community invited to class to give a testimonial.

(b) Teachers and students performed pre-lesson "think alouds" to describe a problem-solving strategy and what it would be like when students were engaged in using it. A "think aloud" is when someone describes the steps he or she followed to reach a solution.

(c) Students shared their concerns about learning a particular strategy. Members of the class empathized with their peers and encouraged them to commit to taking the first step outlined on the thinking guide.

(d) Students discussed past failures in attempting to solve a problem and differentiated these from the problem to be attempted in the lesson.

(e) Students discussed their ideas about the strategy they were about to learn and ways in which they wanted to use it in their lives outside the classroom.

(f) Students stated their strongest negative beliefs about a strategy in a positive way (e.g., "I believe that I'm too stupid to learn to select only relevant information as a problem-solving strategy" was restated as "Today I want to discover one way I can select relevant information when I face a problem").

Thinking/Reading Strategy Charts

The third section of the lesson taught a *thinking guide*. Each thinking guide was a one-page chart that depicted the steps in a problem-solving strategy. Each guide named and differentiated the strategy so students could discuss it in the course of their work. Many thinking guides contained graphics, so students could imagine problem-solving strategies with less effort. The 14 problem-solving strategies, presented on distinct thinking guides, are described on pages 149–153.

Students' Selection of Goals, Objectives, and Assessments

After the thinking guide was introduced, students read three or four examples of how to use the problem-solving strategy in real-life situations. Examples came from people who had used the strategy effectively. These examples engaged student desires to think deeply about their problem and initiated their motivation to set their own purposes for thinking, as they will have to do in real life.

By selecting or creating their own objectives for a problem-solving strategy, students also took a risk and invested themselves before they began. The selection placed students in charge of their depth of thinking, what they would think during their work, and how they would use the problem-solving strategy to reach their objective. Students used the thinking guide to solve a problem they chose. What they learned in the process was evaluated through unplanned and planned assessments. Unplanned assessments were incidents where students used the problem-solving strategy without being asked to do so. When students initiated a strategy's use, it was noted and dated on the Unplanned Assessment Classroom Monitor, recorded once a week throughout the study. In this way, students had many weeks to demonstrate their self-initiated use of problem-solving strategies. Planned assessments were criterion-based, norm-referenced, and administered at the end of Part 1 of each lesson and at the end of the study.

PART 2: RETHINK, REREAD, AND REFORMULATE COMPREHENSION

Part 2 of each lesson placed students in a state of disequilibrium, so they practiced turning to a problem-solving tool to overcome cognitive dissonance. In this part of the lesson, students selected their own reading materials and planned their own self-assessments. As reported on page 155, evidence suggests that activities in this part of the lesson increased students' abilities to generate alternatives and reconsider opinions. Students also answered the question, "What have I learned from this lesson that I will use later in life?"

Self-assessments students made included:

(a) generating back-up strategies to rely upon when the problem-solving strategy did not work;

(b) characterizing an unplanned insight gained through the lesson;

(c) planning ways to explain what they learned to the class;

(d) reporting pleasurable/effective experiences outside of the classroom where they used the strategy successfully;

(e) reporting specific aspects of the lesson that taught them the most about problem-solving abilities;

(f) completing exercises in applied citizenship, using a thinking guide to project solutions to problems in the world today;

(g) making tests or diagrams for themselves and others concerning lesson objectives.

PROBLEM-SOLVING STRATEGIES TAUGHT IN OUR LESSONS

The following problem-solving strategies were presented to the experimental subjects on individual thinking guides on separate days of the research study.

1. Storytelling

Throughout history, people have turned to "storytelling" to explain complex problems, and storytelling has been used by successful problem solvers as a productive problem-solving strategy (Langer, 1991). Students learned that hearing and recalling events similar to the difficulty at hand assists in problem solving. They learned that in life, solutions often emerge in the flow of an ongoing event. By recalling or retelling "real-life stories" to present dilemmas, solutions can be triggered by event sequences, plot scenarios, and the past intentions and achievements of others (Smith, 1990). For example, Bateman (1990) studied ways in which technicians repair highly complex machines by telling and remembering stories told to them.

In our studies, students were told the stories from *50 Inventions* (Scholastic, Inc., 1990); they interviewed successful "living heros" they admired; and they applied thinking guides to the problems faced by characters in their favorite selections of children's and adolescent literature.

2. "What if _____ were not _____"

Brown and Walter (1990) and Kuhn (1970) suggested that we teach students to use "What if _____ were not _____" as a problem-solving strategy. Such thinking helps students deviate from standard and well-trodden knowledge, illuminating an interesting irony about problem solving: that we often understand things best in the context of changing them. The "What if _____ were not _____" strategy also assisted students to see that things can be varied, and this understanding is not as easy as we might expect. Without this or a similar strategy, even the most perceptive problem solvers cannot see more than a limited variety of options due to the limitations of their cultural experiences and individual needs. In my studies, elementary- and middle-school students read separate poems by Judy Viorst in *If I Ruled the World*. They created their own "What if _____ were not _____" about conditions in their lives, and through poems and prose they implemented a realistic solution to those conditions.

3. Learning How to Make Repeated Minor Corrections

Students were taught that their first step in problem solving is not necessarily to aim for a full-blown solution. They were shown how skilled performances can result from repeated corrective adjustments in conceptual and behavioral actions. In my studies, two thinking guides were used for this strategy: attribute listing and highlighting contrasts and similarities. Through attribute listing and contrasting, students overcame the tendency to view problems categorically.

In attribute listing, students identified as many attributes of a problem situation as they could. Through the listing, students more clearly saw "the givens" and tended to look at problematic conditions as variable rather then stable, which contributed to their problem-solving success. In our study, students then picked one attribute, examined it carefully, and listed as many options as they could that this attribute made possible. Then they selected new attributes and combined attribute options to create new problem solutions.

The second thinking guide, creating contrasts that highlight similarities, was based on the work of Bransford and his colleagues (1992). They use videotapes to highlight the similarities and differences between concepts, which encourages students to view problems from multiple perspectives. In our lessons, we offered three choices (scenes, examples, and non-examples) on a thinking guide. Students combined these elements to create solutions of a scenario that could occur.

4. Visualizations in Problematic Situations

Highly self-efficacious problem solvers visualize successful solution scenarios before beginning their performances. Alternatively, those who judge themselves as inefficacious are more inclined to visualize failure scenarios which undermine their future performances (Bandura, 1992). Numerous studies have shown that cognitive reiteration of scenarios in which individuals visualize themselves executing activities skillfully enhances subsequent performances (Carey, 1990; Mayer, 1989; & Smith, 1990).

In our study, students visualized what the solution to a complex, current events problem would be "if we lived in a perfect world." Then they depicted the dimensions of that solution on a thinking guide. Visualizations were also taught in group work settings where apprenticeship was discussed. Doise and Hanselmann (1991), Lord (1989), and Lord, Lepper, & Preston (1985) have evidence that to change attitudes and stereotypical behavior, one should place people in close working relationships with others involved in a problem situation.

A third way in which the visualization strategy was developed was through teaching students to verbalize to a partner. Lewis (1990) showed that poor problem solvers improved their skills by systematically analyzing problems aloud while working in pairs. In my studies, students turned to their partners and discussed their ideas about the problem-solving strategy under study before they shared the strategy as a class. Journals and portfolios were also used as "quiet thinking partners." Fourth, students taught problem solving to younger students to develop their visualization processes.

5. Learning to Select Only Relevant Information

Students learned to decide which information is relevant, how to avoid being misled by misinformation, and how to be clear about the goal state. Students were asked to use their thinking guide to rewrite problems in their textbooks so they would apply to a real-world setting. For example, "How fast will a 100-foot pole be moving when it hits the ground?" was changed to a real-world encounter: "Suppose you want to produce a television commercial for a certain kind of pickup truck. You want to show how tough it is. Before you drop a 100-foot telephone pole on top of it, you may want to estimate the likely damage in order to see whether you need to fake the sequence. So you need to know how fast the pole is falling when it hits the truck" (Schultz & Lockhead, 1991). Students were also taught how to summarize, as simplification often assists in separating relevant from irrelevant givens.

6. "I'm not sure, but I think it's like . . . ."

Because we are aware that the human reflex reaction to confusing, complex, or strange situations

is to ignore, reject, or shrink from them, students were taught to reduce the complexity in problem-solving tasks. Students were asked to refrain from thinking "I can't" and "I don't know" and to replace these phrases with "I'm not sure, but it's like. . . ." Teachers modeled this by using the phrases themselves and challenging students' thinking with responses such as "Show me an example so I can see it clearly" or "First look at _____." Dole, Valencia, Greer, and Wardrop (1991) found that when students were given carefully structured information about concepts important to understanding a problem, they comprehended the problem better than when they were engaged in activities to activate, discuss, and integrate their prior knowledge about those same concepts. Adhering to this research, we taught problem-solving strategies before students read the new content that would be included in the problematic situation.

7. Give a Person a Reason for a Request and Tell People Both Sides of an Issue

"Don't give [a person] two sides of a question to worry him. Give him one; better yet, give him none!" (Ray Bradbury, *Farenheit 451*)

Students were taught to give reasons for engaging in an action. Because people want to have a reason for engaging in actions, they will more likely agree to meet requests if the reason for doing so is made clear. It also appears that telling people both sides of the issue helps them feel more confident about difficult problems and decisions that could arise (Sternberg & Kolligan, 1990). Moreover, it seems that once a decision is made, because of their desire to avoid cognitive dissonance, people tend to believe that the decisions they made were positive, even if they do not prove to be as successful as they had hoped. In this lesson, students developed thinking guides which gave reasons for requests they wanted to make and told both sides of an issue. They shared their creations with classmates.

8. Use Hints

Another way to reduce the difficulty in problem solving is to give hints. Hints can be *very general* in nature. Even when students have a minimum amount of prompting, they can apply knowledge that had previously appeared to be absent. As an example, in one study all the experimenter said was "What do you need to do?" and "What now?"; and armed with only this general hint, experimental students solved problems more rapidly than controls (Yekovich, Thompson, & Walker, 1991). Hints create general self-clues for students to seek a purpose and test for a certain condition. The ability for hints to stimulate the brain may explain why so many people discuss problems with significant others. In our study, students were taught a list of questions they could use as problem-solving hints for themselves and other problem solvers.

9. Analogies

Students were taught to solve problems by drawing analogies to personal experiences, to make direct comparisons to nature and natural phenomena, to use symbolic comparisons, and to make analogies to ideal solutions that are fanciful. We followed the work of Mayer (1989) in creating analogies. Mayer stated that good analogy problem strategies have the following characteristics; they are:

- complete—contain all of the essential actions of the system and the essential relations among them;

- concise—the level of detail is summarized in about five parts;

- coherent—make intuitive sense to the learner;

- concrete—presented at a level of familiarity that is appropriate for the learner;

- conceptual—material is potentially meaningful;

- correct—correspond at some level to the actual events of objects they represent;

- considerate—use learner-appropriate vocabulary and organization.

10. The Creative Problem-Solving Process

Students were taught the creative problem-solving process, CPS, which was created by Alex Osborn and Sidney Parnes and includes the following steps:

1. MESS-FINDING: considering goals, concerns, and personal orientation to determine the most important or immediate starting point for problem solving. Students found facts, wrote, said, and thought about the fuzzy statements that needed to be explored before they could find the true problem.

2. FACT-FINDING: turning facts into a problem-finding statement. Students stated as many problems and subproblems as possible for each problematic situation.

3. PROBLEM-FINDING: selecting the best problem statement.

4. IDEA-FINDING: brainstorming alternative solutions and ideas. Students applied all the relevant problem-solving strategies described previously to novel situations.

5. SOLUTION-FINDING: selecting criteria to demonstrate that a problem has been solved, while not yet thinking about possible solutions. Solution-finding is to write feelings, values, and alternative criteria relative to a problem's solution in advance of selecting a solution.

6. ACCEPTANCE-FINDING: using the above criteria to accept a best solution. Students considered all things which would or wouldn't work to stretch beyond the first ideas for solving problems.

7. PLAN-OF-ACTION: checking progress while implementing the solution. Students applied CPS to a main character's problem in children's literature. Before this book was read to the students, they

were taught these seven steps in CPS. Then, as they read the book, students completed Steps 1–7 as they would recommend them to the main character.

11. Setting Three-Part Objectives

Setting three-part objectives involves writing a desired goal with three parts. Students stated their goal in one or two sentences. Then they outlined the action plan they would follow to reach it. Students then projected what they would see, feel, and experience when they had reached their goal. This projection also included a predicted date when the goal was expected to be reached.

12. Bargaining and Stating Intermediate Goals

Bargaining and intermediate goals are temporary steps toward reaching larger, far-reaching goals. Students were taught procedures to follow in bargaining and establishing intermediate goals.

13. Backward Reasoning

Students were taught to use backward reasoning when their end result was easy to visualize, but their paths to reach that goal were not easy to discern. Because the end goal was clearer than the first step they could take, students thought about the action that would immediately precede the end goal state. For example, if their goal was to become members of the school's relay team, they would use the backward reasoning strategy to picture how fast they would have had to run on the day the coach announced that they had qualified. Then, they listed the step that would occur right before that step, that is, ask the coach how fast that would be. They continued to reason backward until they could develop a day-by-day practice routine of timing themselves as they ran.

14. Forward Inferencing

Forward Inferencing is the problem-solving strategy of drawing logical conclusions from given, verified information and premises. "Creating a Language Sandwich" was the activity students were taught to develop forward inferencing. In this activity, students turned to the middle of an unfamiliar book and read a passage. When finished, they used backward reasoning and forward inferencing to write paragraph(s) that described what could have happened before and after the passage they read. They compared their inference to the events in the book. Then students explained the thinking processes they used to inference and reason backward.

In the next section of this chapter, data concerning the effects of incorporating these lessons into the curriculum at the second-grade and middle-school levels is reported.

REPORT OF RESEARCH

The need to explore the distinguishing characteristics of the problem-solving process arose from a study conducted in 1990 (Collins, 1991). This study was designed to increase eight types of thinking abilities in middle-school students (i.e., the abilities to execute basic thinking skills, cognitive processes, decision-making tools, metacognitive strategies, problem-solving strategies, thinking more effectively in groups, thinking creatively, and thinking effectively when working alone). In this study the 104 experimental subjects significantly outperformed control subjects in all types of thinking abilities except problem solving and decision making (see Figure 6-1).

The fact that problem solving did not significantly improve, when other types of thinking did, suggested that problem solving is distinct from other types of cognition. Perhaps the problem-solving process was more complex, and lessons in that study had not included specific instructional strategies that enhanced these processes for middle-school students.

The review of literature reported in this chapter was then undertaken and the basic lesson plan created. Subsequently, the strategies cited previously were taught to middle-school subjects and second-grade students in one and one-half hour blocks over the course of one-half school

FIGURE 6.1

DIMENSIONS OF THINKING REFLECTED IN FREE RECALL

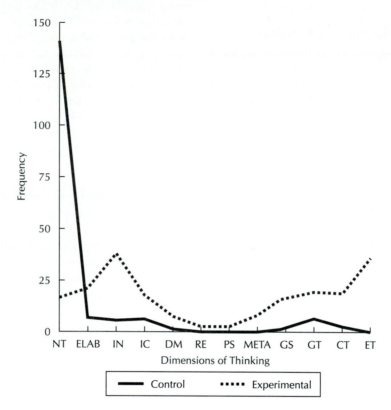

NT, notetaking (Level 1—recall); ELAB, elaboration (Level 1—clarifying); IN, producing inferences (Level 2—processing and producing new interpretations); IC, interpreting content (Level 2—making comparisons and analyzing concepts); DM, decision making (Level 3—selecting information to use in life); RE, research (Level 4—establishing criteria and solving problems); PS, problem solving (Level 4—judging credibility of sources); META, metacognitive thinking (Level 5—assessing one's own knowledge relative to tasks); GS, goal setting and establishing redirection when alone (Level 8—ability to think productively when alone); GT, thinking effectively in groups (Level 7—using talents interactively); CT, creative and innovative thinking (Level 6—specific actions for improving); ET, evaluating one's own thinking ability (Level 5—metacognitive thinking).

year. Specifically, 433 middle-school students and 168 second-grade students were randomly assigned to experimental and control groups. Students in experimental groups received lessons that included the strategies described in this chapter two days a week, until all strategies had been taught twice.

Looking at the effect of this instruction on middle-school subjects first, we assessed their abilities to solve problems, think critically, and generate alternatives as a result of their instruction through a problem-solving transfer test, designed by Irving Segil of Educational Testing Service, shown in Figure 6-2.

Middle-school students' problem-solving abilities were analyzed by two criteria: the number of problem-solving strategies cited in the essays as well as the number of alternative solutions they stated. A significant effect was found between mean performance scores of experimental and control groups concerning the number of thinking strategies used to solve a problem (t = −11.15, $p < .0001$). Similarly, a significant effect was found between the mean scores of experimental and control groups concerning the number of alternative solutions experimental and control subjects cited, shown in Figure 6-3 (t = −7.69, $p < .0001$).

The second assessment concerned middle-school students' abilities to select the best reason for a problem's proposed solution. The assessment was two questions taken from the California State Department of Education Statewide Assessment Test, as shown in Figure 6-4. A significant relationship was found between experimental and control groups relative to their selection of the

FIGURE 6.3

MEAN THINKING STRATEGIES AND ALTERNATIVE SOLUTIONS GENERATED ON ESSAY TEST

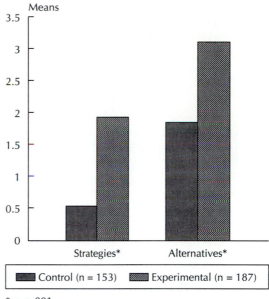

* p < .001

FIGURE 6.2

ESSAY TEST TO ASSESS STUDENTS' SELF-INITIATED USE OF PROBLEM-SOLVING STRATEGIES

NAME _____
TEACHER _____

PLEASE COMPLETE THE FOLLOWING ESSAY:

A FRIEND COMES TO YOU WITH A PROBLEM ABOUT SCHOOL. YOUR FRIEND DOES NOT KNOW HOW TO SOLVE IT. YOU DO NOT KNOW HOW TO SOLVE IT EITHER. DESCRIBE IN ESSAY FORM WHAT YOU AND YOUR FRIEND DO TOGETHER TO TRY TO SOLVE THIS PROBLEM.

most valid reason for a stated judgment (x^2 = 361.98, df = 4, $p < .0001$).

Looking at data for second-grade students, experimental subjects were taught the same 14 strategies in the same number of days as middle-school subjects. In this study, controls for the second-grade sample were third- and fourth-grade students, enrolled in the same school as the experimental subjects. The purpose of this study was to determine if young students benefitted from problem-solving instruction.

At the end of the treatment period, second-grade experimental subjects and their third- and fourth-grade controls took Level A, Form 1 of the Creative Reasoning Test written by John H. Doolittle (Midwest Publications Critical Thinking Press, 1990). This test is designed to test students' ability to solve problems through use of critical and creative problem-solving processes. I

FIGURE 6.4

Test of Students' Ability to Select Most Valid Reasons for Their Judgments

NAME _____ DATE _____

TEACHER _____ PERIOD _____

In the following questions, rank the answers to each statement as to which is the smartest and most logical. By the smartest we mean the one that is most defensible. For example read this sample:

__5__ 1. PETS TEACH CHILDREN RESPONSIBILITY.
__3__ 2. CHILDREN WILL SPEND MORE TIME OUTSIDE WITH PETS.
__4__ 3. CHILDREN UNDER TWELVE CAN DECIDE IF A CAT OR DOG IS A BETTER PET.
__2__ 4. CHILDREN WILL GET TIRED OF PETS ONCE THEY BECOME ADULTS.
__1__ 5. CHILDREN HAVE AN INSTINCT TO BE CRUEL.

AS YOU CAN SEE, THE SMARTEST REASON THAT CHILDREN UNDER THE AGE OF TWELVE SHOULD HAVE PETS IS THAT PETS TEACH CHILDREN RESPONSIBILITY, SO IT IS RANKED 5. THE WEAKEST REASON IS THE LAST STATEMENT AND IT IS RANKED 1. NOW COMPLETE THE NEXT FEW QUESTIONS.

CHILDREN UNDER THE AGE OF TWELVE SHOULD HAVE ALL OF THEIR IMPORTANT DECISIONS MADE FOR THEM BY THEIR PARENTS AND OTHER APPROPRIATE ADULTS BECAUSE:

_____ 1. ALLOWING THEM TO MAKE ALL IMPORTANT DECISIONS FOR THEMSELVES WILL UNDERMINE PARENTAL RESPECT AND AUTHORITY.
_____ 2. ALLOWING THEM TO MAKE ALL IMPORTANT DECISIONS FOR THEMSELVES WILL ENCOURAGE FALSE PRIDE AND STUBBORNNESS.
_____ 3. CHILDREN ARE NOT MATURE ENOUGH TO MAKE ALL IMPORTANT DECISIONS FOR THEMSELVES.
_____ 4. CHILDREN CAN BE EXPECTED TO MAKE GRAVE MISTAKES, SOME OF WHICH COULD HARM THEM FOR LIFE.
_____ 5. CHILDREN SHOULD NOT BE EXPECTED TO TAKE LIFE'S PROBLEMS SO SERIOUSLY UNTIL THEY GROW UP.

CHILDREN UNDER THE AGE OF TWELVE SHOULD MAKE SOME IMPORTANT DECISIONS FOR THEMSELVES BECAUSE:

_____ 1. CHILDREN ARE LESS PREJUDICED THAN ADULTS AND MORE OPEN TO THE TRUTH.
_____ 2. CHILDREN SPEND A LOT OF TIME WATCHING T.V. SO THEY KNOW A LOT ABOUT WHAT IS GOING ON IN THE WORLD.
_____ 3. CHILDREN ARE LIKELY TO MAKE MANY REASONABLE DECISIONS AFFECTING THEMSELVES.
_____ 4. CHILDREN WILL BE MORE APT TO BECOME RESPONSIBLE ADULTS IF THEY ARE ALLOWED TO MAKE SOME IMPORTANT DECISIONS FOR THEMSELVES AS THEY ARE GROWING UP.
_____ 5. CHILDREN WILL BECOME DEPRESSED IF THEY ARE NOT ALLOWED TO MAKE SOME IMPORTANT DECISIONS.

used third- and fourth-grade students as controls to estimate the relative strength of thinking that second-grade experimental subjects obtained. That is, I wished to assess if their growth in problem-solving skills would surpass untrained subjects who had experienced 12% and 22% more life experiences than they. As shown in Figure 6-5, second-grade students were able to give significantly more correct answers on the Creative Reasoning Test than their third- and fourth-grade control subjects (F = 60.346, df = 2, p < .0001).

At the same time these elementary- and middle-school subjects were taught problem-solving strategies, 53 preservice and in-service teachers were learning how to teach such strategies. Each experimental teacher wrote and taught three lessons. One purpose of this instruction was to identify if teaching such strategies would be a powerful

FIGURE 6.5

MEAN RAW SCORES ON THE
CREATIVE REASONING TEST

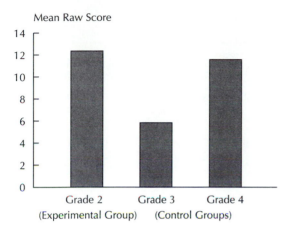

Mean Raw Score

Grade 2   Grade 3   Grade 4
(Experimental Group)   (Control Groups)

enough instructional intervention to increase adult problem-solving behaviors.

To assess this question, 25 control subjects and 53 experimental adults answered the following question three weeks after the instructional program for experimental subjects ceased: Describe the last professional or personal problem you solved. What did you do? Did you solve the problem, in your opinion?

When subjects' answers were analyzed, experimental subjects not only named significantly more strategies that they used in personal problem-solving activities, but stated that they used more than one strategy per problem. For example, one experimental teacher wrote: "I had a homework problem to solve. I had too many papers to grade each night. I solved it by looking for alternative ways to finish. I did direct, fantasy, and personal analogies, attribute listing, and CPS to solve it. I did solve it!"

No control subject used more than one strategy. If that strategy was unsuccessful, control teachers did not take any further action (e.g., "I had a problem feeling that I had to use consumable books. I wrote a letter to my principal requesting that I should not have to use the ones

bought by the district. My principal has still not answered my request. I still have the problem").

SUMMARY AND CONCLUDING REMARKS

It appears that problem solving is a complex ability that involves many cognitive, emotional, and efficacy elements. Based on these data, students can be taught strategies that increase their problem-solving abilities. According to our data, untrained subjects were particularly prone to attempt only one-step solutions and, without instruction, did not improve their abilities to solve problems. In the past, our educational system has been successful in helping students learn how to "pick out and to correct errors" and to use memorized procedures to solve prescribed textbook problems. Future curriculum must move beyond these approaches. Students must develop tools that increase their problem-solving abilities in situations they face in, as well as outside of, school. Instead of organizing and memorizing facts, future students must create their own solutions and ideas.

Through instruction, students can learn to generate more than one solution. Such instruction can begin by incorporating strategies described in this chapter and seeking real-world applications for them. Tasks must be holistically authentic, inviting, perceptually clear, and appealing so they challenge and inspire students to develop their problem-solving abilities. Curriculum must relate to what students already realize to be problematic.

Based on these data, our schools can build students' abilities to solve complex problems in their lives. We must give them strategies they can initiate independently when difficulties arise. Lessons in this chapter provide such instruction and strategies. As teachers we can also engage in challenging problem-solving activities ourselves and share these with our students, as instructive stories. We do not need to wait for prepackaged, instructional programs that will ultimately be available. We must begin to design daily class-room experiences that develop students' problem-solving ability. It was my intent that you could use the information in this chapter to assist your students to become more successful problem solvers.

REFERENCES

Anderson, L. K. (1991, March). *Phases of reasoning along a developmental continuum: Implications for instruction of housing programs.* Paper presented at the annual meeting of the American Educational Research Association, Chicago, IL.

Bandura, A. (1992, April). *Self-efficacy.* Paper presented at the annual meeting of the American Educational Research Association, San Francisco, CA.

Bateman, W. L. (1990). *Open to question: The art of teaching and learning by inquiry.* San Francisco, CA: Jossey-Bass Publishers.

Beck, I., & Dole, J. (1991). Reading and thinking with history and science text. In C. Collins & J. Mangieri (Eds.), *Thinking development: An agenda for the twenty-first century.* Hillsdale, NJ: Lawrence Erlbaum.

Bransford, J. (1992, April). *New methods of developing cognition.* Paper presented at the annual meeting of the American Educational Research Association, San Francisco, CA.

Brown, S. I., & Walter, M. I. (1990). *The art of problem posing* (2nd ed.). Hillsdale, NJ: Lawrence Erlbaum Associates.

Carey, S. (1990). Cognitive science and science education. In C. Hedley, J. Houtz, & A. Baratta (Eds.), Cognition, curriculum and literacy. Norwood, NJ: Ablex.

Chi, M. T. H., Feltovich, P. J., & Glaser, R. (1981). Categorization and representation of physics problems by experts and novices, *Cognitive Science, 5,* 121–152.

Collins, C. (1991). Thinking development through intervention: Middle school students come of age. In C. Collins & J. Mangieri (Eds.), *Teaching Thinking: An Agenda for the Twenty-First Century.* (pp. 67–83). Hillsdale, NJ: Lawrence Erlbaum.

Collins, C. (1991a). Reading instruction that increases thinking abilities. *Journal of Reading, 34*(7), 510–516.

Collins, C. (1991b, December). *Problem solving with text.* Paper presented at the annual meeting of the National Reading Conference, Palm Springs, CA.

Collins Block, C. (in press). *Teaching the language arts: Expanding thinking through student-centered instruction.* Boston, MA: Allyn and Bacon.

Collins, C., & Mangieri, J. (Eds.). (1991). *Thinking development: An agenda for the twenty-first century.* Hillsdale, NJ: Lawrence Erlbaum.

Doise, W., & Hanselmann, C. (1991). Conflict and social marking in the acquisition of operational thinking. *Learning and Instruction, 1,* 119–127.

Dole, J. A., Valencia, S. W., Greer, E. A., & Wardrop, J. L. (1991). Effects of two types of prereading instruction on the comprehension of narrative and expository text. *Reading Research Quarterly, 26*(2), 142–159.

Duffy, G. G., & Roehler, L. (1986). *Improving classroom reading instruction: A decision-making approach.* New York: Random House.

Eichhorn, D. (1966). *The middle school.* New York: The Center for Applied Research in Education.

Eichinger, D., & Roth, K. J. (1990, April). *Critical analysis of an elementary science curriculum.* Paper presented at the annual meeting of the American Educational Research Association. Boston, MA.

Einstein, A., & Infeld, L. (1938). *The evolution of physics.* NY: Simon and Schuster, Inc.

Festinger, L. (1957). *A theory of cognitive dissonance.* Evanston, IL: Row and Peterson.

Glaser, W. (1986). *Control theory in the classroom.* New York: Harper & Row.

Goldman, S. R., Vye, N. J., Williams, S., Reivey, K., Pellegrina, J. W., & the Cognition and Technology Group at Vanderbilt. (1991). Solution space analyses of the jasper problems and students' attempts to solve them. Paper presented at the annual meeting of the American Educational Research Association, Chicago, IL.

Greeno, J. G. (1991, April). *A view of mathematical problem solving in school.* Paper presented at the annual meeting of the American Educational Research Association, Chicago, IL.

Harter, D. (1985). *Harter self-perception profile for children.* Boulder, CO: University of Colorado.

Kuhn, T. J. (1970). *The structure of scientific revolutions.* Chicago, IL: University of Chicago Press.

Langer, J. A. (1991). *Literary understanding and literature instruction.* (Report Series 2.11). Albany, NY: Center for the Learning and Teaching of Literature.

Lewis, H. (1990). *A question of values: Six ways we make the personal choices that shape our lives.* San Francisco, CA: Harper & Row.

Lord, C. G. (1989). The "disappearance" of dissonance in an age of relativism. *Personality and Social Psychology Bulletin, 15,* 513–518.

Lord, C. G., Leeper, M. R., & Preston, E. (1985). Considering the opposite: A corrective strategy for social judgment. *Journal of Personality and Social Psychology, 47,* 1231–1243.

Mayer, R. E. (1989). Models for understanding. *Review of Educational Research, 59,* 43–64.

Moore, S. W. (1991, April). *The Perry scheme of intellectual development: An introduction to the model and major assessment approaches.* Paper presented at the annual meeting of the American Educational Research Association, Chicago, IL.

Perry, W. G. (1970). *Forms of intellectual and ethical development in college years: A scheme.* New York: Holt, Rinehart, and Winston.

Poincare, H. (1955). Mathematical creation. In B. Gheslin (Ed.), *The creative process.* Berkeley, CA: University of California Press.

Pressley, M., Goodchild, F., Fleet, J., Zajchowski, R., & Evans, E. D. (1989). The challenges of classroom strategy instruction. *Elementary School Journal, 89,* 301–342.

Pressley, M., El-Dinary, P. B., & Brown, R. (1992). Is good reading comprehension possible? In M. Pressley, K.R. Harris, & J. T. Guthrie (Eds.), *Promoting academic competence and literacy: Cognitive research and instructional innovation.* San Diego, CA: Academic Press.

Schultz, K., & Lockhead, J. (1991, March). A view from physics. Paper presented at the annual meeting of the American Educational Research Association, Chicago, IL.

Smith, F. (1990). *To think.* New York: Teachers College Press.

Sternberg, R. J., & Kolligian, J. (1990). *Competence considered.* New Haven, CT: Yale University Press.

Wolf, D., Bixby, J., Glenn, J., & Gardner, H. (1991). To use their minds well: Investigating new forms of student assessment. In G. Grant (Ed.), *Review of Research in Education, 17,* 31–74.

Yekovich, F. R., Thompson, M. A., & Walker, C. H. (1991). Generation and verification of inferences by experts and trained nonexperts. *American Educational Research Journal, 28,* 189–209.

Zellermayer, M., Salomon, G., Gloverson, T., & Givon, H. (1991). Enhancing writing-related metacognitions through a computerized writing partner. *American Educational Research Journal, 28,* 373–391.

CHAPTER SEVEN

EXPERTISE

THE WONDER OF EXEMPLARY PERFORMANCES

DAVID C. BERLINER

ARIZONA STATE UNIVERSITY

Dr. David C. Berliner is professor of curriculum and instruction and of psychology in the College of Education at Arizona State University. He is a former president of the American Educational Research Association and a fellow of the Center for Advanced Study in the Behavioral Sciences. He has published numerous books, textbooks, and research studies in the fields of educational psychology, teacher education, and curriculum and instruction. He has served on the board of directors of several professional associations and as editor for numerous research journals, including his most recent work as editor of *Educational Researcher*.

The work to understand how one develops competency or expertise or how we can assist students to develop these skills began many years ago. Originally, the root word for experience and expertise was the same. At one time the two terms apparently signified the same thing. An experienced person—a brewer, a tanner, a jewelry maker—had a form of knowledge that was beyond that possessed by ordinary individuals. Guilds and unions, through their apprenticeship systems, portrayed the senior members of their associations as experts. It was obvious, however, that some of those experienced individuals were superior to others, and therefore not everyone who was experienced deserved to be called an expert in his work. Thus, the notion of expertise eventually became independent from the notion of experience, though the meanings of the terms are thoroughly entangled, and the latter is probably the most important prerequisite for the building of the former.

Experts attain their admirable status through experience of a special kind. In the domains in which they are acquiring their abilities, developing experts learn more from experience than do the rest of us. It is highly motivated learning in which they are engaged, whether it is the acquisition of baseball knowledge, chess moves, or computer programming. Their learning probably is also reflected upon more than is the learning in which others engage. What is learned in the domain in which they have their talent is better coded and remembered by the expert than that which is learned in other domains or that which is learned by others who are not as motivated to learn in a particular domain as the expert. What is learned by the expert appears to be linked better to other knowledge that the expert possesses. It also appears that such knowledge is more easily retrievable in appropriate situations and more transferable to new situations than is most other kinds of knowledge that they acquire or that is possessed by other individuals without the commitment that the expert has to excel in a particular domain. In the domain in which they have acquired their unique skills, experts usually perform appropriately and effortlessly, hallmarks of an exemplary performance, whether it be in chess, radiology, physics problem solving, taxi driving, or teaching.

Although expertise is universally admired, it was not systematically studied by psychologists and others until recently. Certain areas in psychology were related to contemporary scholarship on expertise, however, such as research on idiot savants; training studies on the acquisition of complex skills, such as diagnosis in medicine or in electronic systems repair; and research on the acquisition of psychomotor skills. The training of telegraphers at the turn of the century by William Bryan and his student, Noble Harter (1899), was a remarkable example of the latter, revealing the importance of practice, organization, and automaticity in the development of expertise:

> The learner must come to do with one stroke of attention what now requires half a dozen, and presently in one still more inclusive stroke, what now requires 36. He must systematize the work to be done and must acquire a system of habits corresponding to the system of tasks. When he has done this he is master of the situation in his [professional field]. . . . Automatization is not genius, but it is the hands and feet of genius. (p. 375)

Insight into exceptional individuals was also obtained through biographies of people like Einstein, Curie, and Toscanini. In the best of such works we learn about the ways that people of distinction prepared for their achievements, how their attitudes and habits of mind related to accomplishment, and how they went about organizing their knowledge and practicing their skills. But, the scientific study of those who were exemplary in some specific domain was not undertaken in any systematic way by psychologists, and others, until a decades-old masterpiece by the Dutch psychologist Anton deGroot was published in English translation under the title *Thought and Choice in Chess* (deGroot, 1965). Two scientific events of great importance occurred at about that same time, helping to make this one of the most influential books ever to appear in the field of psychology.

Psychology had been preparing to change when deGroot's book was published in English. The domination of the field by behaviorists was quickly coming to an end, in part because they had no methods to study intrinsically interesting cognitive phenomena. DeGroot presented an interesting inquiry as he examined the differences between chess masters who win tournaments and those who are less able. He showed, for example, that the chess masters had spent thousands of hours staring at chess boards studying chess, that they had stored in memory the moves from thousands of games, and that they had remarkably fast and accurate pattern recognition abilities. These domain-specific abilities were not possessed by those who were less able at the game of chess. With further studies of chess experts by Newell and Simon (1972) and Chase and Simon (1973), we gain a perspective on the commitment it takes to become an expert in a particular field:

> [A] student who spends 40 hours a week for 33 weeks spent 320 hours studying. Imagine spending more than ten years in college studying one subject, chess, and you get some appreciation of the time commitment of master level players. . . . It is reasonable to assume a chess master can recognize 50,000 different configurations of chess, not too far different

from the number of different words an English reader may be able to recognize. (Posner, 1988, p. xxxi)

Designing research to understand the experts' motivation to learn, their memory and organization of domain-specific knowledge, and their pattern recognition abilities was not easy from a behaviorist perspective. So the new work on expertise was quickly adopted by the emerging cognitivists in psychology as work of significance and interest that could never be adequately explored by behavioral psychologists.

A second issue affecting the zeitgeist at this time was the recognition of the computer as a tool of singular importance. Computer scientists of that time period were beginning to develop expert systems and became aware of the deGroot studies, immediately recognizing their relevance for that work. An expert system for diagnosing infectious diseases or playing chess is nothing more or less than a computer program that can match the expert physicians or expert chess players (e.g., Duda & Shortliffe, 1983). To program a computer to perform as an expert requires studying human experts in a particular domain to learn how they solve problems, organize information in memory, perceive patterns, and so forth. Advances in artificial intelligence then, in part, are dependent upon some understanding of human intelligences. So the cognitive scientists from the fields of computer science and psychology both became enamored with expert-novice studies, and scores of such studies were carried out in just a few years (Chi, Glaser, & Farr, 1988). The deGroot studies, therefore, achieved instantaneous recognition and launched a wave of investigations about expert performance because psychology was changing paradigms and computer science was emerging as a powerful new field of inquiry.

What was learned from studies of expertise? Glaser (1987, 1990) has reviewed the literature on expertise and believes that about two dozen propositions about the development of expertise are defensible. Paraphrased and abbreviated, some of these propositions are:

1. Expertise is specific to a domain, developed over hundreds and thousands of hours, and it continues to develop.

2. Development of expertise is not linear. Non-monotonicities and plateaus occur, indicating shifts in understanding and stabilization of automaticity.

3. Expert knowledge is structured better for use in performances than is novice knowledge.

4. Experts represent problems in qualitatively different ways than do novices. Their representations are deeper and richer.

5. Experts recognize meaningful patterns faster than novices.

6. Experts are more flexible, are more opportunistic planners, and can change representations faster when it is appropriate to do so. Novices are more rigid in their conceptions.

7. Experts impose meaning on ambiguous stimuli. They are much more "top down processors." Novices are misled by ambiguity and are more likely to be "bottom up" processors.

8. Experts may start to solve a problem slower than a novice, but overall they are faster problem solvers.

9. Experts are usually more constrained by the task requirements and the social constraints of the situation than are novices.

10. Experts develop automaticity in their behavior to allow conscious processing of ongoing information.

11. Experts develop self-regulatory processes as they engage in their activities.

These propositions are derived from scores of studies of expertise in different fields of endeavor, from chess and taxi driving to radiology and physics problem solving. The propositions are reasonably robust across the different fields, though experts in each field do demonstrate some unique characteristics. One field, and therefore one group of experts, was noticeably missing from the initial set of studies that comprised the corpus of work in this domain of cognitive science. That field was teaching, where my experience as a researcher on classroom processes led me to believe there were some expert pedagogues.

It is no surprise that in the initial rush to conduct studies of expertise none of the investigators thought to study teachers, even though many of those scientists have close ties to educational psychology. Pedagogical knowledge has always been devalued. It is erroneously believed by many legislators and parents that teaching is like child care, an occupation that seems to require no special abilities. Furthermore, teaching is seen as primarily women's work and, therefore, surely not as complex as, say, physics problem solving, a male domain. Finally, teaching is seen as an ill-structured domain of endeavor, without any inherent "proper" and "elegant" solutions such as occur in chess or physics. I would submit, however, that because teaching is ill-structured and takes place in a public setting that requires mastery of a complex social and political environment, it is inherently *more* difficult than many other professions. I believe it is a far tougher job in which to excel than is radiological analysis, computer programming, or tournament bridge play. It is for these reasons that my work focused on the development of pedagogical abilities. I wanted to study in more depth the wondrous performance of a small number of teachers that had enthralled me as I visited public school classrooms.

THE DEVELOPMENT OF EXEMPLARY PERFORMANCE

▼

As experience is gained in teaching and other areas, such as computer programming, nursing, piloting an airplane, or playing chess, some individuals get better at what they do. Psychological theories of performance acquisition, corresponding to both common sense and empirical data, usually specify three levels or stages of development: (a) a novice stage, where errors are frequent; (b) an intermediate stage, where some consolidation of learning takes place and automaticity is developed; and (c) for some who work hard at acquisition of their skills, there is a stage where high levels of performance occur (Shuell, 1990, reviews some of these models). The developmental model of Dreyfus and Dreyfus (1986) is a bit more complex, but with adaptations, it fits the data we collected on the acquisition of pedagogical expertise. This heuristic model specifies five stages as an individual moves from novice to expert. It is described next, using examples from many fields, but primarily illustrating the model with examples appropriate to learning to teach.

Stage 1: Novice Level

We begin with the greenhorn, the raw recruit, the novice. At this stage the commonplaces of an environment must be discriminated, the elements of the tasks to be performed need to be labeled and learned, and the novice must be given a set of context-free rules. In learning to drive an automobile, for example, one is taught the meaning of yellow blinking lights, double-yellow lines, the "yield" sign, and other commonplaces of driving. When teaching a novice to drive a standard shift automobile, we might tell them to shift from first gear at 12 miles an hour, despite the fact that such a rule is terribly inadequate for driving on hills, slippery roads, or for certain engine/gear ratios. An expert driver shifts when it is appropriate to do so or when the sound of the engine reveals to that experienced individual that it is time to shift. Such "know-how" is virtually impossible to communicate to a novice. So to start them off, we often provide an inadequate, context-free rule, and it suffices until more experience is gained. There are similarities to these situations in learning to teach. The novice teacher is taught the meaning of terms like higher-order questions, reinforcement, and learning disabled. Novices are taught context-free rules such as "give praise for right answers," "wait three seconds after asking a higher-order question," and "never criticize a student." Understanding of the commonplaces and some context-free rules are what is needed to begin to teach. The behavior of the novice, whether automobile driver, chess player, or teacher is usually rational, relatively inflexible, and tends to conform to whatever rules and procedures they were told to follow. Only minimal skill at the tasks of driving, chess playing, or teaching should really be expected of a novice. This is a stage for learning the objective facts and features of situations. It is a stage for the gaining of experience and the one at which real-world experience appears to the learner to be far more important than verbal information, as attested to by generations of drivers, chess players, and student teachers. Student teachers and many first-year teachers may be considered novices.

Stage 2: Advanced Beginner Level

As experience is gained, the novice becomes an advanced beginner (see Bullough, 1989, for a case study of a teacher in the transition from a novice to an advanced beginner). Many second- and third-year teachers are likely to be in this developmental stage. This is when experience can become melded with verbal knowledge and where episodic and case knowledge is accumulated. Similarities across contexts are recognized. Without meaningful past episodes and cases to which to relate the experience of the present, individuals are unsure of themselves, they do not know what to do or what not to do. This is true of learning to drive a car, when the advanced beginner is suddenly confronted with fog, ice, or a traffic jam. In education we see advanced beginners having difficulty knowing what to do when a child challenges the teacher's authority, neurotically seeks the teacher's attention, or boasts of an "A" performance. Such incidents in driving or teaching are understood better after the second and third time they happen. Strategic knowledge—when to ignore or break rules and when to follow them— is also developed in this stage as context begins to guide behavior. For example, in learning to teach, you learn that praise doesn't always have the desired effect, as when a low ability child interprets it as communicating low expectations. You also learn that criticism after a bad performance by a usually good student can be quite motivating. Experience affects behavior but the advanced beginner may still have no sense of

what is important. Benner (1986, pp. 23–24) makes this point in describing the difference between novices and advanced beginners on the one hand, and competent nurses on the other:

I give instructions to the new graduate, very detailed and explicit instructions: When you come in and first see the baby, you take the baby's vital signs and make the physical examination, and you check the IV sites, and the ventilator and make sure that it works, and you check the monitors and alarms. When I would say this to them, they would do exactly what I told them to do, no matter what else was going on . . . They couldn't choose one to leave out. They couldn't choose which was the most important. . . . They couldn't do for one baby the things that were most important and then go on to the other baby and do the things that were most important, and leave the things that weren't as important until later on. . . . If I said, you have to do these eight things . . . they did those things, and they didn't care if their other kid was screaming its head off. When they did realize, they would be like a mule between two piles of hay.

The novice and the advanced beginner, though intensely involved in the learning process, often fail to take full responsibility for their actions. This occurs because, although they are labeling and describing events, following rules, and recognizing and classifying contexts, they are not yet actively determining through personal agency what is happening. The acceptance of full personal responsibility for classroom instruction occurs when one develops a sense of personal agency, willfully choosing what to do. This occurs in the next stage of development.

Stage 3: Competent Level

With further experience, and some motivation to succeed, most of the advanced beginners become competent performers of the skills needed in their domain of interest: nursing, piloting a plane, driving a car, or teaching. Not all advanced beginners, however, are likely to reach this level. Evidence shows that some teachers remain "fixed" at a less than competent level of performance (Borko, 1992; Eisenhart & Jones, 1992). This is consistent with other facets of life; we all have muttered at drivers who, though experienced, are not in our judgment competent. Nevertheless it is believed that many third- and fourth-year teachers, as well as more experienced teachers, reach a level of performance that we consider to be competent. There are two distinguishing characteristics of the competent performer of a skill. First, they make conscious choices about what they are going to do. They set priorities and decide on plans. They have rational goals and choose sensible means for reaching the ends they have in mind. Secondly, while enacting their skill, they can determine what is and what is not important. From their experience they know what to attend to and what to ignore. This is the stage in which teachers learn not to make timing and targeting errors, because one has learned through experience what to attend to and what to ignore in the classroom. This is also when teachers learn to make curriculum and instruction decisions, such as when to stay with a topic and when to move on, based on a unique teaching context and a particular group of students.

Because they are more personally in control of the events around them, following their own plans and responding only to the information that they choose to, teachers at the competent stage tend to feel more responsibility for what happens. They are not detached. Thus they often feel emotional about success and failure in their area in a way that is different and more intense than it is for novices or advanced beginners, and they have more vivid memories of their successes and failures as well. Competent performers still are not very fast, fluid, or flexible in their behavior. These are characteristics of the last two stages in the development of expertise.

Stage 4: Proficient Level

Perhaps about the fifth year, a modest number of teachers may move into the proficient stage of development. This is the stage at which intuition or know-how becomes prominent. Nothing mys-

terious is meant by these terms. Consider the micro-adjustments made in riding a bicycle or learning a dance step. At some point in learning to ride a bicycle or performing the mambo, individuals no longer think about the kinds of adjustments needed. They no longer worry about balance and stop counting their steps to keep time to the music. In both cases they simply develop a more "intuitive" sense of the situation. Furthermore, out of the wealth of experience that the proficient individual has accumulated comes a holistic way of viewing the situations they encounter. They recognize similarities among events that the novice fails to see. That is the residue of experience. For example, the proficient teacher may notice, without conscious effort, that today's mathematics lesson is bogging down for the same reason that last week's spelling lesson failed. At some higher level of pattern categorization, the similarities between disparate events are understood. This holistic recognition of patterns as similar allows the proficient individual to predict events more precisely, because they see more things as alike and therefore as having been experienced before. Their rich case knowledge can be brought to bear on the problem. Chess masters, bridge masters, expert air traffic controllers, and expert radiologists rely heavily upon this ability. The proficient performer, however, while intuitive in pattern recognition and in ways of knowing, is still likely to be analytic and deliberative in deciding what to do. While the proficient stage is that of most tournament chess and bridge players, the grand masters are those few who move a stage higher, to the expert level.

Stage 5: Expert Level

If the novice is deliberate, the advanced beginner insightful, the competent performer rational, and the proficient performer intuitive, we might categorize the expert as often being arational. Experts have both an intuitive grasp of the situation and seem to sense in nonanalytic and nondeliberative ways the appropriate response to be made. They show fluid performance, as we all do when we no longer have to choose our words when speaking or think about where to place our feet when walking.

We simply talk and walk in an apparently effortless manner. The expert safety in football, the expert martial artist in combat, the expert chess master, and the expert teacher in classroom recitations all seem to know where to be or what to do at the right time. The great hockey player Wayne Gretsky, when asked by an interviewer for the secret of his remarkable success, answered modestly, "I don't know; I just go to where the puck is going to be." If the rest of us were that prescient, we would all be experts in our chosen fields.

As mentioned earlier, experts engage in performances in a qualitatively different way than do the novice or the competent performer. They are more like the race car driver or fighter pilot who talk of becoming one with their machine, or the science teacher who reports that her lesson just moved along so beautifully today that she never really had to teach. The experts are not consciously choosing what to attend to and what to do. They are acting effortlessly, fluidly, and in a sense, that is arational because it is not easily described as deductive or analytic behavior. Though beyond the usual meaning of rational, since neither calculation nor deliberative thought are involved, the behavior of the expert is certainly not irrational. Insight into the behavior of the expert can be obtained from the writings of Schon (1983), as he discusses knowledge in action, and from the work of Polya (1954), in his discussion of the role played by tacit knowledge in problem solving.

Experts do things that usually work, and thus, when things are proceeding without a hitch, experts are not solving problems or making decisions in the usual sense of those terms. They "go with the flow," as it is sometimes described. When anomalies occur, when things do not work out as planned or something atypical is noted, deliberate analytic processes are brought to bear upon the situation. Conversely, when things are going smoothly, experts rarely appear to be reflective about their performances.

This theory of development has heuristic value for thinking about the education and evaluation of teachers. It is also reasonably well supported by data my colleagues and I have collected over the last few years, although we did not know about the theory when we started our work. Bents and Bents (1990) also studied the transitions that occur between novice, advanced beginner, and expert teachers and verified the sensibility of these stages. They characterized the transition as moving from a teacher-centered, or self-centered, novice, to a more student-centered advanced beginner, to a stage in which the expert teacher was a much more integrated individual.

Our data and that of other researchers in this field, are more compatible than might be expected from such a small set of qualitative studies. Some of the findings in this area will be reported in the form of descriptive propositions.

DESCRIPTIVE PROPOSITIONS ABOUT PEDAGOGICAL EXPERTISE

Almost all studies of pedagogical expertise have been small-scale and nonexperimental. Remarkably, however, there is some consistency across these studies, and a number of propositions about expertise in pedagogy seem to be robust. Some of these overlap with the general characteristics of experts, described above. Some are specific to the domain of teaching.

PROPOSITION ONE: Experts excel mainly in their own domain and in particular contexts.

Chi, Glaser, and Farr (1988) and Glaser (1987) note that experts excel primarily in a single domain. The reason for this is because experts have a great deal more experience in some domains than in others. In studies by Lesgold and his colleagues (1988), expert radiologists were estimated to be looking at their 100,000th X-ray. Chess experts have spent 10,000 to 20,000 hours staring at chess positions (deGroot, 1965; Newell & Simon, 1972; Chase & Simon, 1973). Considering the lengthy time commitments that are necessary to become expert in complex areas of human functioning, it is no wonder that individuals generally excel in only a single domain.

Time and experience play a similar role in the development of pedagogical expertise. Similarly, anecdotal reports lead us to estimate that teachers will not hit their peak performance until at least five years of on-the-job experience have been obtained. The expert teacher, say with ten years' experience, will have spent a minimum of 10,000 hours in classrooms as a teacher, preceded by at least 15,000 hours in classrooms as a student, though it is unknown if the latter experience is of any value. Experience alone certainly will not make a teacher an expert, but it is likely that almost every expert pedagogue has had extensive classroom experience.

In further support of the single-domain quality of expertise, we have found that this domain-specific knowledge is acquired through lengthy experience that is quite contextualized. For example, in one of our research studies, experts, advanced beginners, and novices were asked to teach a 30-minute lesson on probability to a group of high-school students (Berliner, Stein, Sabers, Clarridge, Cushing, & Pinnegar, 1988). The teachers were given 30 minutes to plan the lesson. While they taught the lesson, they were video-taped. After the lesson, during stimulated recall, teachers were asked to tell us about and to justify their actions during teaching. Despite the fact that, as a group, the experts were judged to be better teachers on a number of dimensions (Clarridge, 1988), the task triggered a good deal of anger among this group of teachers. One of them quit the study, another broke down and cried in the middle of the study, and all were unhappy. They all stated their fears about performing well when we moved them from their own classroom contexts to the laboratory situation that we had created for them to teach in. We had allocated 30 minutes for planning, enough for the advanced beginners and the novices to feel comfortable. But the experts said they needed more time. One suggested three hours, another claimed to need three weeks to prepare that material. Our interviews revealed that experts rarely entered their classrooms without having taken all the time they needed to (a) thoroughly understand the content they would teach, and (b) plan one or more activities to teach that content. In addition, the experts noted that they did not know the students in this situation and that their expertise depends, in part, on knowing their students in three different ways:

1. Experts know the cognitive abilities of the students they teach regularly, giving them insight for determining the level at which to teach.

2. They know their regular students personally; in their classrooms they did not need to rely on bureaucratic and formal mechanisms of control while teaching, as they did in the experiment.

3. They did not have a history with the students in this study. In their own schools, students knew about them and had certain expectations about what their teaching would be like. These teachers always had students who expected to be well taught and to learn a great deal, even though they knew they would likely be pushed to their intellectual limits.

When facing a group of strangers, as in our teaching laboratory, none of these three aspects of "knowing the students" was present, and the teachers felt they suffered from that. In addition, all the experts commented on the problems created by their inability to use routines. Routines are a basic part of any expert's performance (Bloom, 1985, 1986; Leinhardt & Greeno, 1986; Berliner, 1987), a point addressed in Proposition Two.

By taking these experts out of their classrooms, we had taken away the particular context in which these pedagogues had learned to excel. Thus, we conclude that we should regard expert knowledge as, for the most part, contextually bound. Their cognitions are usually situated; they are not usually adrift in the brain, unconnected to actions and situations (e.g., Brown, Collins, & Duguid, 1989). And this raises problems for transfer. Transfer across contexts and domains of knowledge appears to be very difficult and does not often appear spontaneously. It seems to require cognitive work, some form of mental effort (Perkins & Solomon, 1989). Thus we can anticipate that expert pedagogues, like experts in many other fields, will excel mainly in their own domain and in particular contexts within that domain. Their expertise will not automatically transfer across domains.

For teachers, such a conclusion has policy implications. One is that a K–12 certificate, a license to teach at any level of schooling, is probably inappropriate. Furthermore, exemplary performance by a teacher at the 10th grade does not automatically mean one will see exemplary performance at the 4th grade, if that teacher were to change grades. Pedagogical knowledge is contextualized, it is not easily generalized. These interpretations of the data suggest also that too many false negatives will occur in the simulations and assessment-center exercises that are being created for the certification and licensure of teachers by national and state boards. Such tests may identify too many teachers as less than exemplary because those teachers were assessed outside of the context in which they excel. It may only be possible to obtain valid judgments about the degree of expertise a teacher possesses from observing them in their own classrooms, an expensive form of assessment.

PROPOSITION TWO. Experts often develop automaticity for the repetitive operations that are needed to accomplish their goals.

Glaser (1987) notes the efficient decoding skill of the expert comprehender in reading as an example of the way automaticity frees working memory to allow other more complex characteristics of a situation to be realized. Examples of the automaticity or routinization of some teaching functions among expert teachers serve the same purpose. For example, Leinhardt and Greeno (1986), in studying elementary-school mathematics lessons, compared an expert's opening homework review with that of a novice. The expert teacher was found to be quite brief, taking about

one-third less time than the novice. This expert was able to pick up information about attendance, about who did or did not do the homework, and about who was going to need help later in the lesson. She elicited mostly correct answers throughout the activity and managed also to get all the homework corrected. Moreover, she did so at a brisk pace and never lost control of the lesson. She also had routines for recording attendance, handling oral responding during the homework checks, and hand-raising to get attention. This expert also used clear signals to start and finish the lesson segments. In contrast, when the novice was enacting an opening homework review as part of a mathematics lesson, she was not able to get a fix on who did and did not do the homework, she had problems with taking attendance, and she asked ambiguous questions that led to her misunderstanding the difficulty of the homework. At one point the novice lost control of the pace. She never did learn which students were going to have more difficulty later in the lesson. Of importance is that the novice showed a lack of familiarity with well-practiced routines. She seemed not to have habitual ways to act. Students, therefore, were unsure of their roles in the class.

The routines of novice and well-regarded experienced teachers were studied in a study by Krabbe and Tullgren (1989). English and language arts lessons at the junior high school level were analyzed. The experts took an average of 14 minutes to introduce a literature lesson, while the novices took 2 minutes to do so. The experts needed that time to follow a routine for the set inducement or introductory phase of the daily lesson. First, they briefly stated the immediate objective of the activity (e.g., "We will discuss several ways that we can learn about the qualities of people"). Then, they gave clear and explicit directions about what they wanted students to be doing (e.g., "Put everything away. Here are three situations for you to think about answering"). Next, they created a positive environment for the phase of the lesson that would follow. The experts found ways to increase student involvement, often arousing curiosity through use of analogies that had something to do with the central concept and theme of the lesson. The goal of the lesson was apparent throughout its introduction. This three-step routine was also accompanied by a mood shift among the expert teachers, from humorous and playful at the beginning of the introduction to serious and businesslike as the presentation, discussion, or oral reading phases of the lesson drew closer (Krabbe, McAdams, & Tullgren, 1988). This regularly occurring pattern of teaching, this routine, was not evident when the videotapes of the novice teachers were analyzed. Krabbe and Tullgren (1989) also identified a routine in the way that the presentation phase of the lesson was conducted by the experts. The expert teachers introduced material gradually and in hierarchical order, illustrated their points by using student background and daily experiences, and provided practice opportunities as they went along. Novice teachers during this phase of the lesson tended to ask text-specific, factual questions until the lesson was over. No sense of a routine was noted in the way the novices taught either a literature or language arts lesson.

In one of our studies, we had experts, advanced beginners, and novices teach a short lesson on probability to about 15 high-school students. As previously noted, the experts were very unhappy about their participation in this task, in part, because the students they had to teach were not trained in routines to make the classroom run smoothly (Berliner, 1988). One expert, reflecting on what was wrong with the task, said:

My expectations when a kid comes into my classroom for math is that he has pencil and paper ready at all times, because I make them take notes, just as you do in social studies. They have practice problems. And this is kind of tough 'cause I don't know what was the routine these kids were used to, you know? . . . You know, with the kids that are used to your routine, you can stand up and talk for 15 or 20 minutes, and by your questioning techniques, and by having them work with guided practice at their desks [you keep them working]. But these kids didn't know me, and

they didn't know the way that I operate, that all are supposed to participate, and why, and that they're all supposed to be on task [constantly].

Brooks and Hawke (1985) provide similar data about the differences in routinization of procedures when they compared an expert and a novice teacher opening a lesson. Hawkins and Sharpe (in press) did very precise micro-analyses of the videotapes of the teaching behavior of an expert and a novice physical education teacher. They found that the expert more frequently used repetitive chains of behavior than did the novice, and that certain behaviors were conditional on other behavior occurring. For example, the computation of conditional probabilities of one behavior following another revealed that if behavior 18 followed behavior 12, routine A was usually used; but, if behavior 16 followed behavior 12, routine B was usually used. These apparently complex behavioral chains resembling the branches of a tree are really automated, routinized behaviors. Novices showed no such patterning.

In another of our studies (Carter, Sabers, Cushing, Pinnegar, & Berliner, 1987), experts, advanced beginners, and novices talked about what they would do first if they had to take over a class that had been running for five weeks. The experts all made mention of the need for routines. One put it this way:

I have to be organized before I can be comfortable. It can't be chaotic. I can't run a class when I don't know what's going on. I've got to be with it, what's going on, and have a routine set up for the kids to respond to, when they know what's expected. . . . It's like training a two-year-old. They have to know what's expected. So I put a lot of emphasis at the start of the year training the students.

Another said:

Okay, the first day I had in mind that I'm going into a brand-new class. They possibly don't know me at all. I would quickly go over what

[I] would expect for rules and expectations: raising their hands before talking, courtesy to teachers and students. . . . I'd give them some rules to follow to get us started.

In this situation the experts, more than the novices, recognized the need to impose their own routines on the classroom and to automate procedures so there would be order, enabling them to teach in the manner to which they were accustomed.

The well-practiced routines of expert telegraphers, surgeons, ice-skaters, tennis players, and concert pianists (Bloom, 1986), no less than expert teachers, are what give the appearance of fluidity and effortlessness to the performance of experts. What looks to be so easy for the expert and seems so clumsy for the novice is the result of thousands of hours of reflective practice, experience from which learning derives.

Again, some policy issues are suggested by the findings that support Proposition Two. First, because some of the problems of the novice teacher occur due to their lack of automaticity and routinization, novice teachers might be better off if their training included practice in automating the opening homework review; taking attendance; assigning, collecting, and giving back homework; testing; introducing a new topic; closing a lesson; and so forth. Second, while a good deal of learning to teach is cognitive, some of it is skill-like in its nature. These skill-like parts of teaching should be mastered and routinized during preservice education. That might also increase both the confidence and the efficiency of the novice teacher.

PROPOSITION THREE. Experts are more sensitive to the task demands and social situation when solving problems.

Glaser (1987) noted that the mental models that experts develop to guide their behavior are constrained by the requirements of the situation in which they must work. Housner and Griffey (1985), in a study of experienced and novice physical education teachers, provide evidence of the sensitivity of experienced teachers to those issues. They found that the number of requests for information made by experienced and novice teachers during the time they were planning instruction was about the same. Each group made reasonable requests for information about the number of students they would be teaching, their gender, their age, and so forth. However, in two areas, the experienced teachers made many more requests than did the novice teachers. They needed to know about the ability, experience, and background of the students they were to teach as well as about the facility in which they would be teaching. In fact, five of the eight experienced teachers in this study of planning and instruction demanded to see the facility in which they would teach before they could develop their plan! Novices made no such requests. The experienced teachers were sensitive to the social and physical environment in which instruction was to take place. Furthermore, when actually performing in the teaching role, the experienced teachers implemented changes in their instruction more often than did novices, using social cues to guide their interactive instructional decision making. The experienced teachers used their judgment about student performance as a cue to change instruction 24% more frequently than did novices. Similarly, they used their judgments about student involvement as a cue 41% more often. They also used student enjoyment of the activities as a cue 79% more frequently and their interpretation of mood and student feelings 82% more often as a cue to change the way they were conducting instruction. On the other hand, the novices were using student verbal statements about the activity as their primary cue for instituting a change in their instructional activity. They responded to these cues 31% more often than did the experienced teachers. Clearly, the novice teachers changed what they were doing, primarily, when asked to; they seemed unable to decode the social cues emitted by students about the ways in which instruction was proceeding. The experienced teachers, however, were far more sensitive to the social cues emitted in the situation, and they used these social cues for adjusting their instruction.

Other examples of this sensitivity to the task demands and social setting abound. In one study we conducted, we asked experts, advanced beginners, and novices to look at a series of slides depicting a class from start to finish and talk about any of the slides that caught their interest. The remarks of one of our expert science teachers about certain slides follows (Cushing, Sabers, & Berliner, 1989):

Slide 6: I would remind people that if they have long hair . . . it can be a real hazard and it needs to be tied back or somehow held back.

Slide 9: I would monitor situations where you've got water on high [boiling water above a bunsen burner] . . . [these are] not real stable situations, [ones] that you could get burns from.

Slide 21: [Here I would] probably go around [the classroom] and just monitor, making sure that they are reading the right kinds of observations.

Slide 25: [Here] if the water is not being used it ought to be taken off the tripod . . . it's a potential accident waiting to happen. . . . This is just sort of a classroom management type of thing. . . . Kids tend to forget about thinking of those kinds of things. Being a teacher, generally you tend to be able to tell where accidents are more likely to happen.

Slide 28: At this part, if they're having to make any calculations [I'd] probably go around and check their calculations, making sure not necessarily that the answer is right, but that their procedures are.

Slide 36: I think [here] I would encourage comparisons . . . just go around and kind of spot check. How do other people's [observations] compare to what your doing?

Clearly, in this expert's mind, the laboratory situation had safety problems that called for extensive monitoring of the task demands and the social situation. Student behavior was also closely monitored to ensure that the instructional task demands were interpreted correctly. Other expert teachers showed this same kind of concern for close monitoring of the situation, while novice teachers did not.

In another study of instruction by an expert and a novice physical education teacher (Hawkins & Sharpe, in press), the novice teacher seemed unable to maintain central proximity to the students in the classroom, while the expert was found to almost always move within the center of the gymnasium. This allowed the expert to talk more easily and frequently to the students at many different activity stations at which instruction was occurring. The centrality of the teacher's location allowed for more effective monitoring, resulting in less bureaucratic and more informal control of the class. The expert also showed a markedly higher rate of change in teaching behavior throughout the lesson, responding to perceived student needs as instruction occurred, needs he was in a position to interpret through his close monitoring of instructional progress.

The rich episodic and case knowledge of an expert and the lack of that same kind of knowledge by a novice is vividly contrasted in protocols from a study by Karen Nelson (1988). The expert's comments include sensitivity to the task demands and the social setting, which display her richer knowledge base. Both teachers are commenting on a slide of a physical education class in which a student on the slide is not in gym clothes.

Novice: What I'm assuming is that this is an on-looker. Somebody [who's] just walked in. Maybe someone that's late to class or someone who's hesitant about doing gymnastics, a little scared so they're off in another area just watching.

Expert: Here is one girl I noticed earlier who is not dressed out. She could have a doctor's excuse or something, but she's far away from the remainder of the class and she should be involved, maybe with spotting, or at least in a closer proximity to the rest of the students. She needs to learn just like everyone else in the class. The teacher [then wouldn't] need to be worried about what she is doing, either. If something is missing from the teacher's desk or any of the students' belongings, [that girl] may have to take the responsibility. [Also], the doors are so close by, if she wants to leave, there's always a possibility, and the teacher is responsible for her. She's just not involved in the class in any way.

Compared to the novice, the expert perceived much more than the girl's lack of gym clothing. The instructional demands and the social setting were part of her concerns as well. A policy implication is also derived from these data. We should not expect the novice teacher to be able to perform like an experienced teacher. The ability to validly read the task-related and social cues of the classroom and, in addition, to know how to change teaching techniques to accommodate those conditions, constitute a skill that is built up slowly over time, if ever. Our data suggest that we should not believe that universities turn out competent teachers. They can do no more than turn out educable novices and advanced beginners. Thus, the university supervisors and the local school districts should conceive of the first few years of teaching as more apprentice-like than is now the case, requiring more direct supervision than is now afforded most new teachers. Mentoring and other forms of assistance in the first few years on the job might enable the developing teacher to learn more and appreciate the complexity of teaching more, than does the usual "sink or swim" educational induction program.

PROPOSITION FOUR. Experts are more opportunistic and flexible in their teaching than are novices.

Glaser (1987) reports that experts are opportunistic in their planning and their actions. They take advantage of new information, quickly bringing new interpretations and representations of the problem to light. Novices are seen as less flexible. Borko and Livingston (1988) discuss these same behaviors among novice and expert teachers. The term these researchers use to char-

acterize the opportunistic quality of the lessons of expert teachers is that of the "improvisational performer." They see expert teachers as having a well-thought-out general script to follow, but being very flexible in following it in order to be responsive to what students do. One expert, discussing his planning, made clear the improvisational aspect of teaching:

A lot of times I just put the objective in my book, and I play off the kids.

This expert also described his interactive teaching as similar to a tennis match:

I sort of do a little and then they do a little. And then I do a little and they do a little. But my reaction is just that, it's a re-action. And it depends upon their action what my reaction's going to be.

Borko and Livingston (p. 20) concluded that:

The success of the expert teachers' improvisation seemed to depend upon their ability to quickly generate or provide examples and to draw connections between students' comments or questions and the lesson's objectives.

This was not the case when the novices were teaching. All three of the novices in this study ran into problems when students made comments or asked questions that required explanations that had not been planned for in advance. Novice teachers were sometimes unable to maintain the direction of the lesson when they had to respond to student comments or questions. This was true even when the issues brought up by the students were relevant to the topic of the lesson. Experiences like this led two of the novices to stop students from asking questions and making comments while they presented their lesson. Although he valued student responsiveness, Jim, one of the novices, reasoned this way (p. 26):

I think . . . because I'm not that proficient yet in handling questions, it's better to cut off the questions, just go through the material, because it'll be much clearer to them if they just let me go through it . . . I don't want to discourage questions, but there are times I'd rather get through my presentation and then get to the questions.

Hawkins and Sharpe (in press) note that the expert they studied was quite predictable (had more automated routines than a novice), but at the same time, compared to a novice, was also more flexible as he taught (displayed both many more distinct behavioral elements and many more orders of those elements). Novices apparently do not have the ability to shift and be flexible as they enact their lesson plans and get into their routines. The novices and advanced beginners in nursing, described by Benner, previously illustrated this point quite dramatically. Westerman (1990) also has reported on a novice elementary teacher whose students were restless after having been at the same task too long. The novice failed to do anything about the problem because: "I had my lesson plan and I just wanted to get to every part of it and get it finished." An alternative response did not occur to her.

Professor Richard E. Snow of Stanford University once described teaching using the metaphor of "the teacher as a Baysian sheep dog." The image this brings to mind is that of the teacher or sheep dog letting the flock or students wander this way and that, but nipping at their heels if they get too far afield. The teacher can be flexible, opportunistic, catch the teachable moments, and ad lib chunks of the lesson, but based on remembrances of past experiences (the Baysian calculation of prior probabilities), the teacher also keeps the students on a course that has them end up at an appropriate place. The novice has neither the confidence to let the flock wander to see where it goes, nor the experience to know how to pull it back on course. Thus, opportunistic teaching is possible for the expert, but much more difficult for the novice. For novices, the pedagogical schemata necessary for improvisation or

opportunism seem to be less elaborate, less interconnected, and clearly less accessible than are those of the experts.

Concerns about some teacher education programs may be derived from these conclusions. The exhortations to beginning teachers to be creative and spontaneous, to abandon teacher manuals and create their own lessons, may be impossible to follow until later in their careers. Beginners may need more structured classrooms; they may need the directions of the manuals, even though many are notoriously bad guides for instruction. The manuals may provide the structure that enables a novice to start teaching, even if they are inappropriate to use later in their careers (see description of the novice, previously in this chapter, about the need for rules, even inadequate rules, from which to begin learning). Similarly, while colleges of education may eschew frontal teaching methods, most novices may be unable to experiment with alternatives. Perhaps cooperative learning techniques, peer tutoring systems, and project methods of instruction, all of which call for a different teaching role, are nearly impossible instructional techniques to ask a novice to use. We seem to forget the notion of developmental stages in teaching, though we all accept the homily that children must learn to crawl before they can walk. Perhaps teachers must learn to be structured before they can be unstructured, perhaps they must control before they can improvise. Opportunistic teaching may be the mark of the experienced teacher and not possible for the novice.

PROPOSITION FIVE. Experts represent problems in qualitatively different ways than do novices.

Chi, Glaser, and Farr (1988) note that experts seem to understand problems at a deeper level than do novices. Experts apply concepts and principles that are more relevant to the problem to be solved. The understanding of novices seems to be at a more superficial level, with fewer instances shown of principled reasoning. We have found support for that general statement from studies of expertise in the pedagogical domain. In one small study of ours, Hanninen (1985) created realistic scenarios about educational problems associated with gifted children. One scenario, for example, described Mark, an 8-year-old Asian boy with severe hearing deficits who likes mathematics and science and who has a strong interest in computers. Scenarios describing educational problems of this type were administered to 15 subjects. Five of the subjects were experts, experienced teachers of the gifted; another five were equally experienced teachers but without any background in gifted education; and five more were novice teachers of the gifted, still working on their certification. Just the opening sentence of some of the protocols revealed much about the thinking of experts and novices. The opening sentence from one novice reads: "Mark seems like a very talented individual with many diverse interests." Another novice comments: "Mark should be encouraged by his teacher to continue his science experiments and work on the computer." An experienced teacher who was a novice in the area of gifted education says: "He should be able to pursue his interests in greater depth." In contrast to these banal, unsophisticated beginnings to essays that attempted to address Mark's needs, in which only superficial characteristics of the problem were noted, one expert began right off with: "Mark's needs can be broken into three broad areas: academic enrichment, emotional adjustment, and training to cope with his handicap." The essay followed this form and was a more organized and sophisticated representation of the problems than was obtained from the novices. The experts also concentrated more on the affective characteristics of Mark's life than did the other teachers. This is a common occurrence among experts and will be noted again, below.

If one views pedagogical knowledge as a complex multidimensional domain of knowledge requiring sophisticated thinking, then it could be argued that the classification of a problem as solvable by using Newton's second law, or by considering it a conservation of energy problem, is no different than classifying Mark's educational needs as falling into three categories and describing action relevant to each of those categories.

This was an appropriate representation of a problem in the pedagogical domain. Experts in every domain must form a cognitive representation of the problems they face in the world. Whether it is to troubleshoot a faulty generator (Johnson, 1988) or develop a program for a special education child, the task of the problem solver is the same, to construct a mental representation of the problem and determine the parameters of the problem space. Experts, compared to novices, usually have better, more functional problem representations. Without these rich models of the situations, they cannot fix generators, debug computer programs, or develop educational programs that are likely to be successful.

The scenario methodology employed previously to learn about teachers' thinking was used in a better designed study by Nelson (1988), in which expert and novice physical education teachers were the subjects. She concluded that experts "displayed a greater variety of application of sound principles of teaching" than did novices. The experts were also more creative and thorough in descriptions of ways to address teaching problems, and provided more solutions to each problem that they addressed. In a different study, Peterson and Cameaux (1987) used videotapes to elicit comments from experienced and novice teachers. They found that the comments of experienced teachers "reflected an underlying knowledge structure in which they relied heavily on procedural knowledge of classroom events as well as on higher-order principles of effective classroom teaching." Similarities in these two studies are quite apparent. An expert in Nelson's study said of a problem concerning an exercise program designed for an overweight child:

> I'd find something positive about his workout.
> . . . If I don't give him some positive reinforcement, I may lose his dedication to the task.
> (p. 25)

An experienced teacher in Peterson and Comeaux's study said about a teacher returning an essay test:

I guess before he handed them back, it might have been a good idea if there was an excellent paper there to have read it with no name, or excerpts from it, or at least on the board, outline what a good answer would have been—that type of thing. He might have made some comments on errors that were made, again with no names, that were misconceptions, and clear those up with students right away. You can use the test as a learning experience rather than just hand it back, to put away, or throw away probably. (p. 328)

In the comments of both the expert and the experienced teacher, we see evidence of principled thought, the former enunciating a principle about reinforcement and motivation, the latter conveying a pedagogical principle about the usefulness of tests as learning experiences separate from their function in evaluation. Such pedagogically sound reasoning was not typical of the responses of novices.

Another study (Stein, Clarridge, & Berliner, under review) examined the ways that expert teachers predict how students would respond to mathematics and science items used in the National Assessment of Educational Progress. From the protocols obtained while the subjects "thought aloud," we learned that experts named or labeled items in a much more detailed and specific way than did novices or advanced beginners. The experts also engaged in a task analysis of the problem in a way that was quite sophisticated. They analyzed the demands of the task represented in the items, apparently to look deeper into the nature of the problems that students might experience. Task analysis was coded in their think-alouds when the subjects verbalized something about the reasons for an item's difficulty or when they traced out the various steps or competencies that a student would need to answer an item correctly. Eighty percent of the experts analyzed the task demands of the items, and they did this for between one and four of the five items for which they had to think aloud. This may be compared to the novices and the advanced

beginners, where only 50% of each group engaged in task analysis of the items, and when they did so, it was for only one of the five items they analyzed. The task analyses of the experts were also more embellished or more clearly formed than those of others.

The experts also differed in their inferences about the student cognitions used in answering an item. Experts seemed to have a fund of knowledge about the way students thought and how those thoughts interacted with the content of the specific mathematics or science items. In addition, the experts seemed able to think through the *mis*algorithms that students might apply. The experts had more experience dealing with student errors and therefore knew what types of errors students might make. Novices rarely discussed the issue of misalgorithms that students might apply to solve a problem. It was concluded from this study that experts in teaching mathematics and science, in comparison to novices and advanced beginners, were more likely to represent the test items that students would address in a more sophisticated way, through their better labeling of problem types. Furthermore, they gained insight into the nature of a particular problem type by more frequently doing a task analysis of it from the students' perspective. From the labeling and task analysis, the experts could more often predict the kinds of errors that students would make when attempting to answer those test items. Because their predictions were more accurate, they appeared to be better explainers than novices or advanced beginners and had a better understanding of their students' ways of thinking.

The implications that follow from acceptance of this proposition about differences between experts and novices are similar to ones already discussed. Novices will be unable to provide the principled kind of reasoning we might expect of experts. They will be unable to do a high quality cognitive task analysis of new curricula and will have trouble sequencing instruction and estimating what will be difficult and what will be easy for their students to learn. Experience will teach those who choose to learn from it. Those individuals will gain the "wisdom of practice" that is so characteristic of expert teachers; but there may be few short-cuts. Thus, our expectations about what a novice can do and think deeply about may need to be quite modest.

PROPOSITION SIX: *Experts have fast and accurate pattern recognition capabilities. Novices cannot always make sense of what they experience.*

The accurate interpretation of cues and the recognition of patterns reduce the cognitive processing load for a person. Sense is instantaneously made of a field, such as a chess board. Quick pattern recognition allows an expert chess player to spot areas of the board where difficulties might occur. Novices are not as good at recognizing such patterns, and when they do note them, they are less likely to make proper inferences about the situation.

One task in the study used slides as the stimulus materials and called for an updating of information by a subject, as a slide was viewed briefly three different times. One expert in science, after the second viewing of a slide, said:

> It's not necessarily a lab class. There just seemed to be more writing activity. There were people filling out forms. It could have been the end of a lab class after they started putting the equipment away. . . .

After the third viewing of the slide, the expert said:

> Yeah, there was . . . very little equipment out and it almost appeared to be towards the end of the hour. The books appeared to be closed. Almost looked like it was a clean-up type of situation.

Novices did not usually perceive the same cues in the classroom and could not, therefore, make the inferences which guided the expert's understanding of the classroom. The expert, by the way, was absolutely correct. It was a clean-up kind of activity. In another study where novice, advanced beginner, and expert teachers viewed three television screens simultaneously, each depicting a different group working in the same class, the same phenomena was at work (Sabers, Cushing, & Berliner, 1991). During a think-aloud viewing of the videotape, one expert commented:

> Left monitor again, I haven't heard a bell, but the students are already at their desks and seem to be doing purposeful activity, and this is about the time that I decided they must be an accelerated group because they came into the room and started something rather than just sitting down or socializing.

In fact, the students in the left monitor did begin working as soon as they entered the classroom and continued working throughout the entire instructional period. To the expert as well as the researchers, this group of students seemed to exhibit a lot of internal motivation. Further, just as this expert noted, this was an accelerated group. It was a science classroom for students identified as GATE (Gifted and Talented Education) students.

We may regard the reading of a classroom, like the reading of a chessboard, to be, in part, a pattern recognition phenomena based on hundreds and thousands of hours of experience. The ability of novices or other relatively inexperienced teachers to interpret classroom information in some reliable way is limited precisely because of their lack of experience. The information related to pedagogical events may be so rich and complex that novices and advanced beginners simply cannot agree on what is seen. In the study where three television screens had to be monitored simultaneously, novices and advanced beginners seemed to experience difficulty in making sense of their classroom observations and in providing plausible explanations about what was occurring within the classroom. For example, these two comments were made by advanced beginners who were asked to describe the learning environment in the classroom they were observing. According to one:

> It looked . . . I wouldn't call it terribly motivating. It was, well, not bored, but not enthusiastic.

The other made this observation:

> Very positive as well as relaxed. Very positive . . . it's good to be able to focus [student] energy into a group situation, yet at the same time, accomplishing the work that they need to do for the class and also lending to the relaxed feeling of the classroom.

Such contradictions were common. Even more discrepancy was noted when these subjects were asked to describe the students' attitudes toward this class. For example, one said:

> It didn't look like it was a favorite class for most of them. One boy looked kind of like, "Oh no, it's not this class again." They didn't look overwhelmingly enthusiastic to be there.

But the other saw the class differently:

> They seemed pretty excited about the class, excited to learn and a lot of times it's hard to get students excited about science, but this teacher seems to have them so that they are excited about it. They're willing to work and they want to learn.

As a group, these advanced beginners in their first year of teaching seemed unable to make sense of what they saw. They experienced difficulty monitoring all three video screens at once. Thus, they often reported contradictory observations and appeared confused about what they were observing and about the meaning of their observations. Novices are much less familiar with classroom events than are advanced beginners, and they often appeared even more overwhelmed than the advanced beginners. Many of them expressed difficulty or an inability to monitor all

three video screens at once. Generally, novices appeared able to focus on, and make sense of, only one video screen. Since this limited their observations, they also made errors and contradictions when they were asked about specific events. They were unable to see the overall patterns in the information presented to them.

Another study also showed this difference in interpretive competency between experts and novices (Carter, Cushing, Sabers, Stein, & Berliner, 1988). In this study subjects went through a series of slides depicting science or mathematics instruction over a class period in a high school. The subjects held a remote control and were told to move through the 50 or so slides at their own pace, stopping to comment on any slides that they found interesting. Novices and advanced beginners seemed to show no particular pattern in what they stopped and commented upon, and they showed the same kinds of contradictions in their interpretations that were found in the study using videotapes. That is, one novice might say "everything looks fine; they're all paying attention," and another novice might say "it looks like they're starting to go off task; they're starting to drift." A pattern was noted among the experts that was quite different. The experts, more often than the subjects in the other groups, found the *same* slides worth commenting on and had the *same* kinds of comments to make. For example, on slides of a science class, three different experts made these comments about one slide (Cushing, Sabers, & Berliner, 1989):

> It's a good shot of both people being involved and something happening.

> Everybody seems to be interested in what they're doing at their lab stations.

> Everybody working. A positive environment.

And, on the eighth slide from a mathematics class, four experts made these observations (Cushing, Sabers & Berliner, 1989):

[It] appears that only a few students are actually working on the problem.

The girl that was working has her hand on the side of her face like she might be thinking, or miserable, or something . . . and the boy with a pencil in his hand appears to be looking at his pencil.

Some students seem to be doing the assignment and some students have their books closed and are not doing it . . . some are turned around talking . . . I know there is a lot more [of class] to go, so I don't understand why some people are doing nothing.

We have those same groups of boys that still haven't regained focus. A couple of other students are fading out of the program.

This reduction in variance by the experts is particularly noteworthy. It means they have learned to pay attention to some of the same things and to interpret visual stimuli in the same way. This similarity in *what* is attended to and *how* it is interpreted is what we hope for when we visit an expert ophthalmologist or automobile mechanic. Novices, advanced beginners—anyone in the early stages of skill acquisition—simply will not have acquired enough experience for that.

It is interesting to note that the hiring of new teachers, immediately out of school, is seen by some principals, parents, and personnel directors as a good thing to do. They are said to possess both energy and commitment. Our data, however, inform us that they also cannot make a lot of sense out of what they experience. They have not accumulated the experience to do that. It is part of the continuing devaluation of pedagogical knowledge that leads some individuals to think that new teachers are more likely to be better at their jobs than experienced teachers. Would those individuals choose a surgeon in that way? I have never heard of criteria such as "enthusiastic," "bouncy," and "fresh" used to choose a surgeon, but such terms are used frequently to describe new teachers, indicating a deep underestimation of the complexity of teaching and the role of experience in the development of expertise.

PROPOSITION SEVEN: Experts perceive meaningful patterns in the domain in which they are experienced.

The superior perceptual skills of experts is readily apparent, but there is no reason to believe it is due to any innate, superior perceptual abilities (Chi, Glaser, & Farr, 1988). Rather, their superiority is due to the way that experience affects perception. After 100,000 X-rays or the 10,000th hour of observing students, *what* is attended to and *how* that information is interpreted are likely to have changed for anyone motivated to learn from their experience. In one study (Carter, Cushing, Sabers, Stein, & Berliner, 1988), we asked expert, novice, and advanced beginners to view some slides of classrooms and tell us what they saw. The slides were flashed on the screen for only a very brief time. The responses of the novices and advanced beginners to the slides were clearly descriptive and usually quite accurate. A novice saw this:

A blond-haired boy at the table, looking at papers. Girl to his left reaching in front of him for something.

Two advanced beginners made these comments:

[It's] a classroom. Student with back to camera working at a table.

A room full of students sitting at tables.

In contrast to these literal descriptions, typical of novices and advanced beginners, some of our expert teachers often responded with inferences about what they saw. Two made these observations:

It's a hands-on activity of some type. Group work with a male and female of maybe late junior high school age.

It's a group of students maybe doing small group discussion on a project, as the seats are not in rows.

For experts, the information that was often deemed important was information that had instructional significance, such as the age of the students or the teaching/learning activity in which they were engaged. They perceived more meaningful patterns than do novices. This was evident also in the protocols of the expert and novice physical education teachers studied by Nelson (1988), and presented previously as an instance of the richness of thought and sensitivity to the instructional and social demands of a setting that is possessed by experts. Similarly, when expert and novice physical education coaches watched a videotape of instruction, Pinheiro (1989) found that the experts acquired more cues than did novices, they missed fewer errors made in the video, and they needed fewer additional trials to pick out other errors. In short, they derived more meaning from the tape, in part, because of their superior pattern recognition skills and because they organize information better.

In any field, the information that experts extract from the phenomenon with which they are confronted stems, in part, from the concepts and principles that they use to impose meaning on phenomena in their domain of expertise. That is, experts in all domains appear to be top-down processors. They impose meaning on the stimuli in their domain of expertise. In studying the interpretation of slides, a focus of the experts was on the notion of work: "students *working* at the blackboard," "students *working* independently," "teacher looking over a person *working* in lab," and so forth. This work orientation, of course, is part of what promotes high rates of achievement among the students of experts. But some other characteristics of the experts that are less clearly tied to effectiveness (though contributing to it) have also been found. In two studies (Clarridge,

1988; Rottenberg, under review), it was found that expert teachers take student responsibility into account in a lesson, expecting students to somehow be involved in the creation of their own knowledge, perhaps through discussion, cooperative learning, questions, or projects. Somehow the experts seem to communicate this sense of responsibility and are sensitive to this when discussing their views of classes. In Clarridge's study (1988), videotapes of experts, novices, and advanced beginners were rated by a specialist in nonverbal communication. The specialist found the expert teachers to be high in incorporative behavior, behavior that invites the students to work jointly with them. The specialist also found that novice and advanced beginners set up barriers to keep authority in their own hands. The tapes, of course, were rated without knowledge of the experience level of the teachers that were viewed. Furthermore, the expert teachers seem to be unusually sensitive to the affective concerns of the students they teach and to individual differences among their students (Nelson, 1988; Bents & Bents, 1990; Rottenberg & Berliner, under review).

To place these data in context, a physicist may bring to bear Newtonian laws to make meaning of a problem in physics. A biologist may bring to bear concepts of homeostasis or ecological niche to make meaning of a problem in biology. A chemist, auto mechanic, or engineer will also bring to bear on the problems they face the most salient and useful concepts that they possess. Among the salient and useful pedagogical concepts with which teachers make meaning from phenomena that they encounter in their work are "attention," "work," "responsibility," "affect," and "individual differences." These concepts appear to have saliency among the experts and are not yet as important for novice teachers.

The implications of these ideas are relevant to the recent trend in many states to allow for alternative certification. Individuals who enter teaching in this way lack both pedagogical concepts and pedagogical experience. This leads us to predict that novice teachers from alternative certification programs will be ignorant about a good deal of what occurs in classrooms. They cannot help but to misinterpret events or interpret what goes on around them at a shallow level, and given the propositions stated above, we can expect such individuals to develop automaticity later, be slower to develop sensitivity to the task and social demands of the situation, be less opportunistic in their teaching, have more impoverished representations of pedagogical problems, and have slower pattern recognition. This does not bode well for the students of first-year teachers from alternative certification programs.

Our data do *not* suggest that the advanced beginner is markedly superior to the novice. On the contrary, we found it more difficult to separate these two groups than we had hypothesized. Although there were occasional hints in our studies that the advanced beginners were superior to the raw novices, both were usually clearly and markedly inferior in their performance to the experts. We do think, however, that there is a modicum of evidence to suggest that those who enter teaching from a teacher preparation program are likely to acquire the skills of a competent teacher sooner than those who do not.

PROPOSITION EIGHT. Experts may begin to solve problems slower, but they bring richer and more personal sources of information to bear on the problem that they are trying to solve.

In the study by Hanninen (1985) of expert and less expert teachers of the gifted, the mean time for a novice to read through a scenario and begin writing about ways to help solve the problems of a particular child was 2.6 minutes. The experienced teachers who had no background in gifted education took 3.0 minutes. The mean time for experienced/expert teachers of the gifted was 9.8 minutes. That is, from the start of reading their problem through the start of presenting their solutions, it took the experts three or four times as long as the other two groups. When scenarios were used in the same way with physical education teachers in Nelson's (1988) study, the experts also took more time to begin responding. Although the absolute differences between the

groups were less dramatic than in our study, the experts still took 40% longer to begin responding to the scenarios. Thus, when one knows a good deal more about teaching, or some other domain, more time seems to be needed to represent the problem and to access the relevant knowledge needed to address the problem. If you do not have much information in storage, you need not look too long for information relevant to the task at hand.

Experts, however, unlike novices, can bring to bear rich personal stores of knowledge when they begin to address the problems they face. Peterson and Comeaux (1987) found that their experienced teachers "often gave more elaborated answers to the questions and gave more justifications for their decisions or comments." Nelson (1988) found that experts:

> provide longer and more detailed analyses of situational data; were more creative and thorough in descriptions of ways to handle various teaching concerns; provided more solutions to problems; were more thoughtful to needs of individual students; [and] displayed a greater variety of application of sound principles of teaching.

This is consistent with the conclusion from our studies that, on a number of dimensions, the protocols obtained from experts were richer than were those of novices. The richness, in part, stems from the personal case knowledge, or procedural knowledge, that is brought to bear on the pedagogical problems that they face. The experts might report that "I had a kid like that once and what I did was . . . " Or they say, "I never do it that way, what I do is . . . " Or they point out, "That technique only works when everyone is well prepared; if the students have been away for a few days, like over a holiday, then. . . . " Memory of cases—for the internist and radiologist in medicine, the player of chess or bridge, or the classroom teacher—contributes to their expert performance. Problems can be classified and solution strategies proposed on the basis of previous experience. When confronted with a new problem, experts go through their case knowledge and search for what Herb Simon has called "an old friend," a case like the one now before them. When that "old friend" is found, a good start has been made in solving the problem.

The implications of these data support previous comments made about new teachers and teachers that enter the profession through alternative certification. They are likely to be less adequate than are those who have some reflective experience under their belt.

Additional Propositions

As the data base grows, additional propositions about the differences between expert and less expert pedagogues are being revealed. For example, we are beginning to have evidence to suggest a ninth proposition, namely, that experts make substantially more inferences from and assumptions about the information presented to them than do novices. Their inferences, assumptions, and predictions allow them, like hockey pro Gretsky, to "go where the puck is going to be." Their experience lets them take a less literal and more inferential view of teaching. They can intuit what shall be coming and can therefore ignore or influence the flow of events. Novices cannot engage in such thought and action.

If evidence continues to mount, I will support a tenth proposition as well: Experts are more evaluative than are novices. When viewing the videos of other teachers or reading scenarios, the experts are likely to say things like "he shouldn't be wasting time taking attendance that way; there are better ways to do that," or "I think that's a poor way to find out if they know the concept because . . . ." Novices have neither the confidence nor the successful past experience to be so evaluative.

For proposition eleven we might propose that experts, compared to novices, attend more to the atypical or unique events than to the typical or ordinary events in the domain in which they have expertise. Experts seem to ignore some things that go on. They seem to pick out anomalies to focus on, perhaps because they understand that not every bit of information is important to process.

Expertise, apparently, lets us process less, rather than more, of the information available from the environment, thus allowing more efficient use of the very limited working memory system that all of us possess. When Kounin (1970) noted that one of the characteristics of effective classroom managers was their ability to handle simultaneous events, he was probably studying experienced teachers. Novices cannot do that as well because their information processing system is apparently cluttered with information that is unimportant, though they do not yet know that.

A candidate for proposition twelve is that experts appear to be more confident about their abilities to succeed at instructional tasks than are novices. This is not surprising, because the experts have succeeded regularly over the years. However, this proposition suggests that only expert, proficient, or experienced competent teachers have the affective characteristics as well as the wisdom to take on the piloting of a new management structure. Trying to deal effectively with an ungraded class or a multidimensional teaching environment, both of which require the simultaneous occurrence of many different educational activities, would tax a novice enormously. New programs such as these should be tried first by those with the confidence and skill to implement them well. Such individuals are likely to be experienced teachers.

Additional Policy Considerations

Policy implications have been noted as each proposition was stated, but some additional considerations should be noted. For example, we noted how a K–12 certificate or other broad-span certification and licensure is challenged by the data suggesting that knowledge is contextualized, and that expert knowledge is probably highly contextualized. Thus, we should also note that grade levels and subject matters should not be seen as interchangeable for teachers. Principals and superintendents often move teachers around without thinking about the importance of domain-specific knowledge and the lack of immediate transfer to new contexts. They often act as if a good first-grade teacher can teach at middle school and a good earth science teacher in the suburbs can teach computers in the barrio. Our evidence questions their actions. Furthermore, because knowledge is so contextualized, tests and simulations to judge teachers will usually yield many false negatives—candidates that are expert in their classes, but not in the testing situation. Many of the experts in our studies were not very articulate. They could not describe what they did very well. Nevertheless, they did those things in their classrooms quite well. On the other hand, test situations often favor articulate individuals, so there may also be too many false positives—candidates who are quite articulate about teaching, but who are not exemplary in their classroom performance. It appears that all assessment of expert teachers outside of their classrooms is subject to validity problems that may not be possible to overcome.

Routinization of some procedures was also seen as a missing component of some teacher preparation programs. We need to note also that routinization is not just needed for management procedures, such as handing in homework, to make the class more efficient. Routinization can occur, as well for cognitive aspects of teaching the learning of the rule-example-rule principle of instruction, the use of explaining links in chains of complex assertions that are to be learned, or the procedures that tie material to be learned to some knowledge that students already know, and so forth (see Gage & Berliner, 1992, for additional cognitive instructional behaviors that can be routinized). In most teacher education programs, novices never are provided practice in such routines, and that is not sensible because routinization "is the hands and feet of genius."

We now recognize that many pedagogical skills are gained slowly, through experience only, and so we have come to understand the inability of teacher education programs to develop competent teachers. Such programs produce only beginners, albeit beginners who have been primed to learn from experience. For this reason it is appropriate to ask why a new teacher is given the same responsibility as that of an experienced teacher? For example, given what we now know about the limited abilities of novices, why do they get the same number of children to teach or the same number of courses to prepare for as someone with ten years of experience? The first year might result in more learning about teaching if the demands on the novice were not so great. They should have fewer children to teach and fewer classes for which to prepare. Of course, if the craft knowledge of teaching is devalued, then it doesn't matter. Novices can be expected to do as well as ten-year veterans. All that is needed to succeed as a teacher is enthusiasm and motivation!

That same misunderstanding of a novice's ability results in schools of education throughout the nation teaching things that are inappropriate for the level of development of the novice teacher. They often teach about techniques that require complex managerial structures, such as those required when running a whole-language reading program, a cooperative learning program, or a peer tutoring program. Teacher educators often do not provide any practice opportunities in these techniques. Rather, they tell novice teachers about them and then expect the novice teacher to immediately implement such activities. This is not sensible, particularly when we know that novices are terrified about losing control of their classes.

To compound the issue, many of the novices and advanced beginners are assigned to schools that have the most difficult children to teach, and within that setting, they are often assigned the most difficult classes with the most difficult students to teach. This policy occurs frequently throughout the nation, is patently unfair to children and novice teachers, and is one reason for the high attrition rate among new teachers during their first few years of teaching.

CONCLUSION

The research on expertise reveals the wonders of exemplary performance in many areas of human endeavor, including teaching. At least two-and-one-half million teachers toil in the public schools at jobs that are inherently difficult, emotionally draining, and require public performances. Those teachers must also accept lower social status and lower remuneration than others with the same abilities and investment in education. Society is indeed fortunate that many talented individuals stay in the profession long enough to acquire sufficient craft knowledge to be competent at their jobs, and the nation is blessed that some small number of those teachers also become expert at what they do. Their display of virtuosity in the classroom is no different than that shown by the concert violinist in a concerto or the chess master in a tournament. When compared to the performance of the novice or even the competent pedagogue, it is exemplary performance with which the expert provides us. Society just seems to value it so much less than exemplary performances in other areas.

Capturing the uniqueness of classroom performance in teaching is difficult to do with our research. All the studies to date have been small, generally qualitative, and highly interpretive. They have tended to be descriptive rather than experimental. In addition, unlike chess, we have no "winners" of tournaments by which to evaluate exemplary performance. The equivalent of a Pillsbury teach-off would be helpful, if that were possible in education; but it is not. So we have continuing problems in adequately identifying expert, proficient, and competent teachers, and this leads to problems with theory development in this area.

On the other hand, we do not have an insurmountable problem for those in search of a heuristic rather than a scientifically adequate theory about the development of expertise. Theory, it should be remembered, is not to be judged on its truthfulness, but on its usefulness. The five-stage theory presented earlier fits data well enough to

allow us to think sensibly about the development of knowledge and skill in teaching.

Generalizing from studies in this domain should be difficult, but remarkably, that has not been the case. The propositions offered by Glaser from studies of expertise across disparate fields were provided at the start of this chapter. As has been made clear in this review, those propositions are highly compatible with the ones we derived from studies of teaching. We, therefore, have an interesting case in which many imperfect studies, across many different fields, have yielded a coherent body of knowledge and a heuristic theory with which to think about the acquisition of expertise in teaching and in other domains.

The study of expertise is inherently interesting. Individuals that excel at a task whether it be physics, medical diagnosis, chess, or teaching fascinate us and also provide psychology with subjects that have unique perceptual, conceptual, and psychomotor skills. As we learn from them about how information can be organized and used efficiently, they remind us, as well, that motivated learning over extensive periods of time can lead to extraordinary levels of performance. The lesson for us all is that when people have reasons to learn some domain and the opportunity to pursue that learning, they can reach levels of competency, proficiency, and expertise not ordinarily achieved by others. Perhaps there is a lesson here for those who teach poor children in America. Without a reason for learning the subjects we teach in schools, the level of competency in those subjects that the nation can expect of such children will remain low. The causes of their generally poor performances may be in the economic systems of the nation and not in the schools themselves. Motivation, therefore, would seem to be a factor that needs greater attention. The expenditure of time to learn something well depends on it.

REFERENCES

Benner, P. (1984). *From novice to expert*. Reading, MA: Addison-Wesley.

Bents, M., & Bents, R. (1990, April). Perceptions of good teaching among novice, advanced beginner and expert teachers. Paper presented at meetings of the American Educational Research Association, Boston, MA.

Berliner, D. C. (1987). In pursuit of the expert pedagogue. *Educational Researcher, 15*, 5–13.

Berliner, D. C. (1988, April). Memory for teaching as a function of expertise. Paper presented at meetings of the American Educational Research Association, New Orleans, LA.

Berliner, D. C., Stein, P., Sabers, D., Clarridge, P. B., Cushing, K., & Pinnegar, S. (1988). Implications of research on pedagogical expertise and experience for mathematics teaching. In D. A. Grouws, & T. J. Cooney (Eds.), *Perspectives on research on effective mathematics teaching*. Reston, VI; National Council of Teachers of Mathematics.

Bloom, B. S. (Ed.). (1985). *Developing talent in young people*. New York: Ballentine.

Bloom, B. S. (1986, February). Automaticity. *Educational Leadership, 70*–77.

Borko, H., & Livingston, C. (1988, April). Expert and novice teachers' mathematics instruction: Planning, teaching and post-lesson reflections. Paper presented at meetings of the American Educational Research Association, New Orleans, LA.

Borko, H. (1992, April). Patterns across the profiles: A critical look at theories of learning to teach. Paper presented at meetings of the American Educational Research Association, San Francisco, CA.

Brooks, D. M., & Hawke, G. (1985, April). Effective and ineffective session opening teacher activity and task structures. Paper presented at the meetings of the American Educational Research Association, Chicago, IL.

Brown, J. S., Collins, A., & Duguid, P. (1989). Situated cognition and the culture of learning. *Educational Researcher, 18*, 32–42.

Bryan, W. L., & Harter, N. (1899). Studies of the telegraphic language: The acquisition of a hierarchy of habits. *Psychological Review, 6*, 345–375.

Bullough, (1989). *First year teacher: A case study*. New York: Teachers College Press.

Carter, K., Cushing, K., Sabers, D., Stein, P., & Berliner, D. C. (1988). Expert-novice differences in perceiving and processing visual information. *Journal of Teacher Education, 39*(3), 25–31.

Carter, K., Sabers, D., Cushing, K., Pinnegar, P., & Berliner, D. C. (1987). Processing and using information about students: A study of expert, novice and postulant teachers. *Teaching and Teacher Education, 3*, 147–157.

Chase, W. G., & Simon, H. A. (1973). Perception in chess. *Cognitive Psychology, 4*, 55–81.

Chi, M. T.H., Glaser, R., & Farr, M. (1988). *The nature of expertise*. Hillsdale, NJ: Erlbaum.

Clarridge, P. B. (1988). Alternative perspectives for analyzing expert, novice, and postulant teaching. Unpublished dissertation, University of Arizona, Tucson, AZ.

Cushing, K. S., Sabers, D., & Berliner, D. C. (1989, January). Expert-novice research studies: Implications for teacher empowerment. In J. A. Kerrins (Ed.), *Empowering the teaching learning process*, proceedings of the sixth annual conference on issues and trends in educational leadership, Colorado Springs, CO.

deGroot, A. D. (1965). *Thought and choice in chess*. The Hague: Mouton.

Dreyfus, H. L., & Dreyfus, S. E. (1986). *Mind over machine*. New York: Free Press.

Duda, R. O., & Shortliffe, E. H. (1983). Expert systems research. *Science, 220*, 261–268.

Eisenhart, M., & Jones, D. (1992, April). Developing teacher expertise: Two theories and a study. Paper presented at meetings of the American Educational Research Association, San Francisco, CA.

Gage, N. L., & Berliner, D. C. (1992). *Educational psychology* (5th ed.). Boston, MA: Houghton Mifflin.

Glaser, R. (1987). Thoughts on expertise. In C. Schooler & W. Schaie (Eds.), *Cognitive functioning and social structure over the life course*. Norwood, NJ: Ablex.

Glaser, R. (1990). Expertise. In M. W. Eysenk, A. N. Ellis, E. Hunt, & P. Johnson-Laird (Eds.), *The Blackwell dictionary of cognitive psychology*. Oxford, England: Blackwell Reference.

Hanninen, G. (1985). Do experts exist in gifted education? Unpublished manuscript, University of Arizona, College of Education, Tucson, AZ.

Hawkins, A., & Sharpe, T. (in press). Field system analysis: In search of the expert pedagogue. *The Journal of Teaching in Physical Education*.

Housner, L. D., & Griffey, D. C. (1985). Teacher cognition: Differences in planning and interactive decision making between experienced and inexperienced teachers. *Research Quarterly for Exercise and Sport, 56,* 44–53.

Johnson, S. D. (1988). Cognitive analysis of expert and novice troubleshooting performance. *Performance Improvement Quarterly, 1*(3), 38–54.

Krabbe, M. A., McAdams, A. G., & Tullgren, R. (1988, April). Comparisons of experienced and novice verbal and nonverbal expressions during preview and directing instructional activity segments. Paper presented at meetings of the American Educational Research Association, New Orleans, LA.

Krabbe, M. A., & Tullgren, R. (1989, March). A comparison of experienced and novice teachers' routines and procedures during set and discussion instructional activity segments. Paper presented at meetings of the American Educational Research Association, San Francisco, CA.

Kounin, J. S. (1970). *Discipline and group management in classrooms.* New York: Holt, Rinehart & Winston.

Leinhardt, G., & Greeno, J. (1986). The cognitive skill of teaching. *Journal of Educational Psychology, 78,* 75–95.

Lesgold, A., Rubinson, H., Feltovitch, P., Glaser, R., Klopfer, D., & Wang, Y. (1988). Expertise in a complex skill: Diagnosing x-ray pictures. In M. T. H. Chi, R. Glaser, & M. Farr (Eds.), *The nature of expertise.* Hillsdale, NJ: Erlbaum.

Nelson, K. R. (1988). Thinking processes, management routines and student perceptions of expert and novice physical education teachers. Unpublished dissertation, Louisiana State University, Baton Rouge, LA.

Newell, A., & Simon, H. A. (1972). *Human problem solving.* Englewood Cliffs, NJ: Prentice-Hall.

Perkins, D. N., & Salomon, G. (1989). Are cognitive skills contextually-bound? *Educational Researcher, 18,* 16–25.

Peterson, P. L., & Comeaux, M. A. (1987). Teachers' schemata for classroom events: The mental scaffolding of teachers' thinking during classroom instruction. *Teaching and Teacher Education, 3,* 319–331.

Pinheiro, V. (1989). Motor skill diagnosis: Diagnostic processes of expert and novice coaches. Unpublished doctoral dissertation, University of Pittsburgh.

Polya, G. (1954). *How to solve it.* Princeton, NJ: Princeton University Press.

Posner, M. I. (1988). Introduction: What is it to be an expert? In M. T. H. Chi, R. Glaser, & M. Farr (Eds.), *The nature of expertise.* Hillsdale, NJ: Erlbaum.

Rottenberg, C. V., & Berliner, D. C. (under review). Expert and novice conceptions of everyday classroom activities, unpublished manuscript.

Sabers, D., Cushing, K., & Berliner, D. C. (1991). Differences among teachers in a task characterized by simultaneity, multidimensionality and immediacy. *American Educational Research Journal, 28,* 63–88.

Schon, D. (1983). *The reflective practitioner.* New York: Basic Books.

Shuell, T. (1990). Phases of meaningful learning. *Review of Research in Education, 60,* 531–548.

Stein, P., Clarridge, P. B., & Berliner, D. C. (under review). Teacher estimation of student knowledge: Accuracy, content and process.

Westerman, D. (1990, April). A study of expert and novice teacher decision making: An integrated approach. Paper presented at meetings of the American Educational Research Association, Boston, MA.

CHAPTER EIGHT

SCHOLARLY WORK

New Definitions and Directions

ERNEST L. BOYER

▼

The Carnegie Foundation for the Advancement of Teaching

Ernest L. Boyer is president of The Carnegie Foundation for the Advancement of Teaching in Princeton, NJ, where he helps to shape the debate in precollegiate and higher education both in this country and abroad. His recent books include *High School, College, Campus Life, Scholarship Reconsidered,* and *Ready to Learn.* Mr. Boyer is also a senior fellow at the Woodrow Wilson School at Princeton University. He served as U.S. Commissioner of Education under President Jimmy Carter. Prior to his current position, he served as chancellor of the State University of New York, taught at Loyola University, was academic dean at Upland College, and directed The Center for Coordinated Education at the University of California, Santa Barbara. Mr. Boyer has been named to presidential commissions by three U.S. presidents and in recent years has chaired the National Education Goals Panel Advisory Group for the nation's first education goal, "ready to learn."

As we move toward a new century, profound changes are stirring the nation and the world. The contours of a new world order, and the dimensions of new challenges, loom large on the horizon. It is a moment for boldness in higher education. Many are now asking: How can the role of the scholar be defined in ways that not only affirm the past but also reflect the present and adequately anticipate the future?

In a recent report from The Carnegie Foundation entitled *Scholarship Reconsidered*, I presented a new typology of scholarship—one that includes not only the scholarship of discovery, or research, but also the scholarship of integration, the schol-

arship of application, and the scholarship of teaching. In the following pages, I explore these dimensions of scholarly activity, tracing their development through the history of American higher education and considering their implications for faculty and students as we look to the new century.

THE HISTORY OF SCHOLARSHIP

▼

When little Harvard College was founded in 1636, the focus was on the student. Teaching was a central, even sacred, function, and in that day, the highest accolade a professor could receive was the famous one that Chaucer extended to the clerk at Oxford: "Gladly would he learn and gladly teach."[1]

For a century and a half, that's what scholarship in America was all about. Indeed, as late as 1869, Charles Eliot declared in his inaugural address that "the prime business of American professors . . . must be regular and assiduous class teaching."[2]

Change was in the wind, however, as the focus of higher learning slowly shifted from the shaping of young lives to the building of a nation. In 1824, Rensselaer Polytechnic Institute was founded in Troy, NY, and according to historian Frederick Rudolph, RPI was "a constant reminder that the United States needed railroad-builders, bridge-builders, builders of all kinds."[3]

Then came the famous Land Grant Act, which linked higher learning with the nation's agricultural revolution. The act was signed by President Abraham Lincoln in the midst of the Civil War with the intent of making the free states more accessible. But it also had a powerful and enduring influence on the priorities of the professoriat in higher education.

In 1867, Ezra Cornell in Ithaca, NY, said he would found an institution "where any person can find instruction in any study."[4] At the turn of the century, Stanford President David Starr Jordan declared that the entire university movement in this country was toward "reality and practicality."[5] And when social critic Lincoln Steffens visited Madison a few years later, he remarked, "In Wisconsin the university is as close to the intelligent farmer as his pig-pen or his tool-house."[6] Meanwhile, on the Eastern seaboard, Charles Eliot of Harvard declared, "Most of the American institutions of higher education are filled with the modern democratic spirit of serviceableness."[7]

I find it fascinating that, at the conclusion of the nineteenth century, the words "reality," "practicality," and "serviceableness" were being used to define the academic world. The scholar-

ship of teaching had been joined by the scholarship of building and the scholarship of service.

Meanwhile, another tradition was beginning to emerge, signaled in 1861 when Yale University granted the first Ph.D. ever awarded here in the United States. American academics who were studying abroad at the distinguished German universities were profoundly influenced by the emerging scholarship of science. Men like Daniel Coit Gilman became convinced that a new kind of university was required in the United States—one that focused on graduate education and research. That, of course, was the European model, and the notion of general education was unfamiliar within that tradition.

Gilman became president of the University of California in 1872, but he left three years later, under criticism for wanting to emphasize literature, language, and history and to diminish agriculture, which was heresy at that land grant institution. He then moved east to launch Johns Hopkins University in 1876, and upon his retirement two decades later, Woodrow Wilson described him as the first president to create a true university in America, "one in which the discovery of new truth was judged superior to mere teaching." "It is interesting to note that when the first blueprint for Johns Hopkins was developed, no undergraduates were included. They were added later, presumably because the university needed the money they would bring—a tradition that lingers to this day.

For the first time in the history of American higher education, two great traditions were on a collision course. On the one hand, there was the Colonial college tradition with its emphasis on the student, on general education, on loyalty to the campus, and on teaching. On the other hand, there was the European university tradition with its emphasis not on the student, but on the professoriat; not on general, but on specialized knowledge; not on loyalty to the campus, but on loyalty to the guild; and not on teaching, but on research.

It is true that well into the twentieth century, most colleges and universities in this country continued to give priority to teaching and service.

Following World War II, however, the priorities of higher education in this country shifted profoundly. Sparked by the "G.I. Bill," higher education enrollments expanded exponentially, and new colleges were built at the rate of nearly one a week for several years.

At the same time, the pool of research funds began to deepen. Vannevar Bush, former president of Massachusetts Institute of Technology, argued persuasively to President Franklin D. Roosevelt that the universities had helped win the war and could also help win the peace. Soon federal funds began to flow into research as never before.

To put it briefly, two major shifts were occurring simultaneously. On the one hand, we had rising expectations and rising student enrollments. On the other, we had a growing research capacity, as a new generation of faculty who had been trained at research universities fanned out to campuses across the country, determined to re-create their own experiences.

At the very time the mission of American higher education was expanding, the reward system for the professoriat was being narrowed. Academics spoke in glowing terms about the great diversity among institutions, but on a growing number of campuses, research—not teaching—became the yardstick of success. The harsh truth is that American higher education was becoming a hugely imitative system, with two models, Berkeley and Amherst, representing the icons of excellence. Rather than take pride in their own distinctive missions, many campuses sought to copy the institutions just above them. And the impact of these changes continues to be felt today.

The irony is that neither faculty nor students are happy with the situation. In a recent Carnegie Foundation survey of the American professoriat, more than 60% of the faculty said they'd rather teach than do research. And when asked whether we need better ways to evaluate their performance, beyond research and publication, 70% of the faculty at all kinds of institutions, from the research universities to the community colleges, say "yes."

Further, when students come to campus, they find that institutional priorities are not what they had been led to believe. Most higher education institutions like to think of themselves as collegiate, and they play this up when they are recruiting. But students, especially freshmen and sophomores, quickly discover that faculty and students live in two separate worlds.

NEW DEFINITIONS OF SCHOLARSHIP

What are we to do about all of this? In *Scholarship Reconsidered,* I proposed that the time has come to move beyond the tired old "teaching versus research" debate and begin to ask the more compelling question: What does it mean to be a scholar? I believe that there are, in fact, four interlocking dimensions of scholarship, all of which should be recognized and rewarded.

First, we must continue to celebrate research— what I call *the scholarship of discovery.* Research is and must remain at the very heart of academic life, and the pursuit of new knowledge must be continuously defended. Robert Oppenheimer put it this way: "Discovery follows discovery, each both raising and answering questions, each ending a long search, and each providing the new instruments for new search."[8]

Not every institution can or should focus on this essential mission. Still, in the century ahead, the world will urgently need scholars who focus on discovery. I firmly believe that federal research funds should be significantly expanded and that basic research should stay within the academy to ensure that freedom and integrity are safeguarded.

In addition to the scholarship of discovery, we must affirm the *scholarship of integration.* In our fragmented academic world, there is an urgent need for scholars who go beyond the isolated facts, who make connections across the disciplines, and who can help students reach a more coherent view of knowledge and a more integrated, more authentic view of life.

I'm suggesting that while scholarship surely means specialized research, it also means moving beyond traditional academic boundaries and putting our discourse in historical, social, and ethical perspective. The writings of Stephen Jay Gould, the essays of Lewis Thomas, and Stephen Hawking's brilliant book on the history of time illustrate the kind of integrative scholarship I have in mind.

Frank Press, president of the National Academy of Sciences, once suggested that the scientist is, in some respects, like the artist. To illustrate his point, he observed that "the magnificent double helix which broke the genetic code is not only rational, but beautiful, as well."[9]

As I considered Frank's words, I thought of the days when I used to watch the liftoffs at Cape Kennedy. As the final countdown went from nine to eight, seven, six, five, I observed the tension on the faces of the scientists and engineers as they stared at the monitors above. But when the countdown got to three, two, one, liftoff, and the space shuttle went rocketing successfully into orbit, suddenly there was a great burst of satisfaction. If I read their lips correctly, the engineers didn't say, "Well, our formulas worked again." Almost without exception, they said, in unison, "Beautiful!" It always intrigued me that they chose an esthetics term to describe a technological achievement.

I also found it fascinating that when the world renowned physicist Victor Weisskopf was asked what gave him hope in troubled times, he replied, "Mozart and quantum mechanics."[10] He was suggesting that there is an esthetics satisfaction at the core of science as well as art. Scientists and artists are engaged in the same quest: the search for relationships and patterns.

But where in today's fragmented academic world can students or faculty discover connections such as these? We have broken up the disciplines into smaller and smaller units. We have organized academic life in a way that causes fragmentation and blurs shared interests. There are academic departments on the campus that are administratively and politically convenient but not intellectually compelling or coherent. We make it difficult for faculty to reach into other disciplines. Instead, they remain trapped within the intellectual boxes that we have created.

Still, there is cause for hope. Some departments are beginning to reexamine themselves because the new intellectual questions don't fit our old academic categories. In fact, some of the most exciting work going on in the academy today is in what might be called the "hyphenated disciplines"—in psycho-linguistics, bio-engineering and the like—in what philosopher-physicist Michael Polanyi calls "overlapping [academic] neighborhoods."[11]

Over 50 years ago, Mark Van Doren wrote that the connectedness of things "is what the educator contemplates to the limit of his capacity." He concludes by saying, "Those who begin early in life to see things as connected have begun a life of learning."[12] And it seems to me that this is what scholarship, at its best, is all about.

Beyond the scholarship of discovery and the scholarship of integration, we also need what we call the *scholarship of application,* to relate theories and research to the realities of life. This idea is rooted in the land grant colleges, the polytechnic institutes, the normal schools, and the conservatories—institutions that were in the nation's service in the nineteenth century.

In recent years, however, the term "service" has fallen into disfavor, because no sharp distinction has been drawn between doing scholarship and doing good. For service to be considered scholarly, it must flow directly out of one's work within a field.

I have been intrigued by the writings of Donald Schön at MIT, who writes about what he calls "the reflective practitioner"—the professional who moves not just from theory to practice, but also from practice back to theory. Certainly those in the fields of medicine, law, education, business, and even science understand the reciprocity between theory and practice. They know that as you engage in your work, you begin to reconsider and redefine the theories you have learned.

Today, the universities are increasingly viewed as being more for the individual's private benefit than for the public good—as places where young people get their credentials and where faculty get their tenure, but where there is no concern about the urgent social problems of our times. We must change this perception by giving new dignity and new status to the scholarship of application.

As we look to the twenty-first century, I think it will be increasingly important for our colleges and universities to confront some of our most pressing and most urgent social problems. I can imagine the twenty-first-century university as one in which faculty are brought out of the various departments and organized in different ways as they seek to apply their specialized knowledge and their insights to problems of health and ecology and public education, among others.

This brings me, then, to the final dimension of scholarship. We say in the Carnegie report that scholarship means not only the ability to discover, to integrate, and to apply knowledge, but also to inspire future teachers in the classroom—a process we call the *scholarship of teaching*.

Over the last 20 or 30 years, teaching has been profoundly undervalued. Professors get more credit for presenting a paper at a convention than they do for inspiring future generations on the campus at home. This is, I believe, profoundly inappropriate and cannot be defended either educationally or ethically.

To achieve quality in the undergraduate experience, teaching simply must be a top priority on the campus. Faculty who teach core undergraduate courses must be adequately rewarded for that work. It is unjust for us to recruit students aggressively, take their time and money, and then put them in huge sections taught by untrained teaching assistants, sending the message that they are second-class citizens on the campus. To put it simply, good teaching is essential to the quality and vitality of our higher education system.

Robert Oppenheimer, at the 200th anniversary of Columbia University, put it this way: "It is proper to the role of the scientist that he not merely find new truth and communicate it to his fellows, but that he teach, that he try to bring the most honest and most intelligible account of new knowledge to all who will try to learn." Surely this means inspiring future scholars in the classroom.[13]

Helping students move from competence to commitment is, I believe, an essential part of the scholarship of teaching. In other words, questions of values must be thoughtfully examined in the classroom. Thinking back on the outstanding teachers of my life, I realize what it was that made them truly great. Every one of them was well-informed. Each one could pace the subject material according to students' needs. Each one created a climate of active learning in the classroom. And finally, every single one of my great teachers was an open, authentic human being.

In sum, the teachers I have had helped me to understand that all of learning is value-laden and that we live by values every moment of our lives. They didn't dictate answers, but they made the quest for answers honorable.

Teaching values does not mean requiring a course in morality or ethics. It means having classrooms where life's most probing questions can be thoughtfully examined and where faculty serve as mentors. The greatest crisis we confront in our schools today is not a lack of knowledge, but a lack of wisdom. If we are to resolve this crisis, the classroom must become a place where ethical choices are candidly confronted. Students in the twenty-first century must, I believe, be guided not just by competence, but by conscience.

To summarize, we must continue to reaffirm the importance of research and celebrate the scholarship of discovery. But to avoid pedantry, let us also reaffirm the scholarship of integration. To avoid irrelevance, let us affirm the scholarship of application. And to avoid discontinuity, let us strengthen and celebrate the scholarship of teaching. The time has come to celebrate the array of faculty talent on the campus, to breathe new life into a suffocating system, and above all, to inspire the coming generation.

NEW DIRECTIONS IN SCHOLARSHIP

An expanded view of scholarship is, I believe, absolutely necessary in order for the academy to remain vital. In recent years, faculty have expressed serious and growing reservations about the enterprise to which they have committed their professional lives. This deeply rooted concern reflects, I believe, a recognition that teaching is crucial, that integrative studies are increasingly consequential, and that, in addition to research, the work of the academy must relate to the world beyond the campus.

Higher education leaders are acknowledging that diversity brings with it important new obligations. Colleges and universities are being called upon to respond to the needs of a large and increasingly varied community of students, many of whom have special needs as well as special talents. In response, greater attention to students, to teaching, to the curriculum, are being demanded. There is a recognition that faculty obligations must extend beyond the classroom and that both the academic and civic dimensions of collegiate life must be carefully balanced to serve the new constituencies.

Beyond the campus, colleges and universities are being asked to account for what they do and to rethink their relevance in today's world. Many believe that higher education must play a far greater role in responding to contemporary social problems.

Derek Bok, former president of Harvard, warns of the dangers of detachment when he writes: "Armed with the security of tenure and the time to study the world with care, professors would appear to have a unique opportunity to act as society's scouts to signal impending problems long before they are visible to others. Yet rarely have members of the academy succeeded in discovering the emerging issues and bringing them vividly to the attention of the public."[14]

Mr. Bok further observes that "what Rachel Carson did for risks to the environment, Ralph Nader for consumer protection, Michael Harrington for problems of poverty, Betty Friedan for women's rights, they did as independent critics, not as members of a faculty. Even the seminal work on the plight of blacks in America was written by a Swedish social scientist, not by a member of an American university. After a major social problem has been recognized," Bok concludes, "universities will usually continue to respond weakly unless outside support is available and the subjects involved command prestige in academic circles. These limitations have hampered efforts to address many of the most critical challenges to the nation."[15]

Clearly, higher education and the rest of society have never been more interdependent than they are today, and embedded in Bok's pointed observations is a call for campuses to be more energetically engaged in the pressing issues of our time. Our world has undergone immense transformations. It has become a more crowded, less stable place. The human community is increasingly interdependent, and higher education must focus with special urgency on questions that affect profoundly the destiny of all: How can the quality of the environment be sustained? Should the use of nuclear energy be expanded or cut back? Can an adequate supply of food and water be assured? How can our limited natural resources be allocated to meet our vast social needs? What new structures of world order can be devised to cope with the challenges of the post–cold war era?

The nation's schools, its health-care delivery system, and its banking system, for instance, all cry out for the application of knowledge that faculty can provide. New discoveries, rooted in research, can produce cures for dreaded diseases and improve the quality of life. Other problems that relate, for example, to the environment, to ethical and social issues, to crime and poverty also require more careful study and, indeed, solutions that rely on new knowledge and on integration, as well. And surely the scholarship of teaching will be necessary to produce an informed citizenry capable of the critical thinking that is so needed in America today.

The conclusion is clear. We need scholars who not only skillfully explore the frontiers of knowledge, but also integrate ideas, connect thought to action, and inspire students. The very complexity of modern life requires more, not less, information: more, not less, participation. If the nation's colleges and universities cannot help students see beyond themselves and better understand the interdependent nature of our world, each new generation's capacity to live responsibly will be dangerously diminished.

We must continuously remind ourselves that the aim of education is not only to prepare students for productive careers, but also to enable them to lead lives of dignity and purpose; not only to generate new knowledge, but to channel that knowledge to humane ends; not merely to study government, but to help shape a citizenry that can promote the public good. Thus, higher education's vision must be widened if the nation is to be rescued from problems that threaten to deteriorate the quality of life.

If the potential of American higher education is to be fully realized, then campuses should be encouraged to pursue their own distinctive missions, and innovation should be rewarded. Would it be possible, for example, for visiting teams to ask graduate schools to report on how doctoral students are being prepared for teaching? Could a college be asked to demonstrate how its institutional mission relates to criteria for faculty tenure or promotion? Would it be possible for accreditation teams to ask campuses how procedures for faculty assessment have been developed—and whether they encourage the full range of scholarship?

One last point. Faculty, to be fully effective, cannot work continuously in isolation. It is toward a *shared* vision of intellectual and social possibilities—a community of scholars—that the four dimensions of academic endeavor should lead. In the end, scholarship at its best brings faculty together.

A campuswide, collaborative effort around teaching would be mutually enriching. A similar case can be made for cooperative research, as investigators talk increasingly about "networks of knowledge," even as individual creativity is recognized and affirmed. Integrative work, by its very definition, cuts across the disciplines. And in the application of knowledge, the complex social, economic, and political problems of our time increasingly require a *team* approach.

The team approach applies not only to individuals, but to institutions, as well. Looking to the future, I envision a national network of colleges and universities with great diversity—a vast system in which the full range of human talent is celebrated and recorded. In such a system, the discovery of knowledge, the integration of knowledge, the application of knowledge, and great teaching would be fully honored and would powerfully reinforce one another. If the vision of scholarship can be so enlarged on *every* campus, it seems reasonable to expect that across the entire country a true community of scholars will emerge—one that is not only more collaborative, but more creative, too.

American higher education has never been static. For more than 350 years, it has shaped its programs in response to the changing social context. And as we look at today's world, with its disturbingly complicated problems, it is clear that higher learning must, once again, adapt. It would be foolhardy not to reaffirm the accomplishments of the past. Yet, even the best of our institutions must continuously evolve. To sustain the vitality of higher education in *our* time, then, a new vision of scholarship is required—one dedicated not only to the renewal of the academy but, ultimately, to the renewal of society itself.

FOOTNOTES

1. Geoffrey Chaucer, *The Canterbury Tales,* line 308.

2. Charles Eliot (1898). *Educational Reform: Essays and Addresses* (p. 27). New York: Century. In Walter P. Metzger (1987), The Academic Profession in the United States, *The Academic Profession: National, Disciplinary, and Institutional Settings,* Burton R. Clark (Ed.) (p. 135). Berkeley: University of California Press.

3. Frederick Rudolph. (1962). *The American College and University: A History* (pp. 48–49). New York: Alfred A. Knopf.

4. Ezra Cornell. (1965). Address. In Laurence R. Veysey, *The Emergence of the American University* (p. 163). Chicago: University of Chicago Press.

5. David Starr Jordan. (1903). *The Voice of the Scholar* (p. 46). San Francisco: P. Elder and Co.; (p. 61) in Veysey.

6. Ibid.; (p. 61) in Veysey.

7. Ibid.; (p. 61) in Veysey.

8. Robert Oppenheimer. (1954, December 27). *The New York Times,* p. D27.

9. Frank Press. (1984, May 30). Science and its Connections. Address at Case Western Reserve University, School of General Studies, Cleveland, OH.

10. Victor Weisskopf, quoted by Frank Press. (1986, October 25). Address to Phi Beta Kappa Associates annual meeting.

11. Michael Polanyi. (1967). *The Tacit Dimension* (p. 72). Garden City, NY: Doubleday. In Ernest L. Boyer. (1987) *College: The Undergraduate Experience in America* (p. 91). New York: Harper & Row.

12. Mark Van Doren. (1959). *Liberal Education* (p. 115). Boston: Beacon Press.

13. Robert Oppenheimer. (1954, December 27). *The New York Times,* p. D27.

14. Derek Bok (1990). *Universities and the Future of America* (p. 105). Durham, N.C.: Duke University Press.

15. Ibid.

CHAPTER NINE

IMPLICATIONS OF COGNITIVE SCIENCE FOR TEACHER EDUCATION

MARY M. KENNEDY

MICHIGAN STATE UNIVERSITY

HENRIETTA BARNES

MICHIGAN STATE UNIVERSITY

Mary M. Kennedy is codirector of the National Center for Research on Teacher Learning and director of the Institute for Research on Teaching and Learning across the Lifespan, both at Michigan State University. Her scholarship has focused on the nature of knowledge used in practice, on how research is used in both policy and practice, and on problems of research method. She has won four awards for her publications. Prior to joining the faculty at MSU, she worked primarily on policy research and program evaluation.

Henrietta Barnes is chair of the Department of Teacher Education at Michigan State University and director of MSU's Professional Development School partnerships. Her most recent work has focused on the design of teacher education programs that can influence teacher learning. In 1975 she received the MSU Teacher-Scholar award, and in 1992, she received the MSU Alumni Association's Distinguished Faculty award. Much of her writing is devoted to describing reform efforts in which she has personally been involved.

The literature on teacher education is replete with evidence that teachers have either not learned the things that teacher educators wanted them to learn or that they learned new ideas while in college but then abandoned those ideas when they began practicing on their own. The hypothesized reasons for these apparent failures of teacher education are numerous: programs are underfunded, too brief, too fragmented, too theoretical, or too practical. The problem addressed in this paper, therefore, is not *what* should be taught to prospective teachers but rather *how* it should be taught.

All professional educators face two interrelated problems: the need to define professional expertise and the need to promote it in their students. In the case of teacher education in particular, the field has always suffered from competing views of what a teacher is, what a teacher needs to know, and how teachers can learn the things they need to know. But recent literature in these areas differs from earlier literature in that much more of it is empirically based than was true in the past. The field of teacher education is moving from visionary rhetoric toward grounded argument.

This paper combines literature on the nature of expertise that is uniquely needed for teaching with the broader literature on learning and on expertise more generally, in an effort to illustrate their implications for the formation of teacher education programs. The paper has four main sections. In the first, we offer a tentative definition of teaching expertise. In the second, we examine some of the reasons why this kind of expertise is particularly difficult to foster. In the third, we describe a series of challenges to teacher education that follows from the findings of these two bodies of literature. Finally, in the fourth, we describe a teacher education program currently being developed at Michigan State that is designed to respond to these challenges.[1]

EXPERTISE IN TEACHING

In nearly all professions, ideas about the nature of professional expertise have evolved in similar ways. In the days when expertise was transmitted through apprenticeships, there was an assumption that expertise consisted largely of a set of techniques. As professions became more sophisticated, and their formal preparation moved from the master craftsman to the university, expertise came to be redefined as a body of knowledge—general principles that should guide practice. Aspiring physicians, teachers, or engineers gained this body of knowledge in the university and were expected later on to apply their knowledge in practical situations. More recently, as researchers have begun to examine professionals at work, the definitions of professional expertise have become both more complex and more subtle. We now recognize that professional expertise consists of far more than a body of skills or a body of facts and far more than the simple sum of these. Moreover, the relationship between knowledge and skill—or between idea and action—is more complicated than earlier models of acquisition and application had supposed. Expert practitioners are engaged in a continual process of reinventing their practices—of using their experiences both to devise their practices *and to revise their theories of practice*. Moreover, contemporary views of professional expertise are more cognizant of the important role of judgment in *interpreting* situations before action is taken.

Professional expertise is a combination of several things, not all of which are knowledge per se, and the way in which these several aspects of expertise interact is not at all clear. Before discussing the way in which professional expertise is organized or drawn on in practice, let us first review some of the things that have been nominated as part of it. For want of a better term, let us call these aspects of expertise *personal resources*.

One resource, of course, is declarative knowledge—the body of facts, principles, theories, or concepts that, when taken together, form the professional curriculum in a given field. Virtually everyone agrees that professionals within a field hold some body of knowledge that is uniquely relevant to their practice. This body may include basic disciplinary knowledge (anatomy or physiology in the case of medicine, political science in the case of law) or knowledge formed specifically for the profession, such as a set of rules for how to handle certain ethical situations. While members of every profession agree that there is a body of knowledge all members should share, each profession has experienced serious arguments among its members about what should be included in that body of knowledge. Teaching is no exception: It has been plagued not only by difficulties in defining its professional knowledge base but with problems of defining the relative importance of professional knowledge (the part that is usually taught by the education department) versus subject matter knowledge (the part usually taught by disciplinary departments) (e.g., McDiarmid, Ball, & Anderson, 1989). The most recent example of an effort to define the knowledge base for teaching is the *Knowledge Base for Beginning Teachers* by the American Association of Colleges of Teacher Education (Reynolds, 1989).

A second important personal resource, also recognized as important in virtually every profession, is a set of skills: the procedures and techniques one uses in practice. These may include such diverse skills as stitching wounds, calculating stress on a girder, or subduing a violent patient. Teachers, like members of other professions, are presumed to be able to do certain things—explain fractions, recognize handicapping conditions, assess student understanding of what has been taught. In fact, in one period of its history, teacher education attempted to define teaching expertise exclusively through lists of such discrete skills and then to organize teacher education programs around these skills (e.g., Orlosky, 1980).

Though there may have been a time when these two personal resources—knowledge and skills—were thought to encompass all of professional expertise, numerous other resources have since been recognized as important. For instance, many observers want to see evidence of certain *beliefs, values, or commitments* in professional practitioners. In the case of teaching, the evidence for the importance of beliefs is growing, and there now are several examples in which teachers' beliefs have been shown to significantly influence both their own classroom practices and what stu-

dents learn in those classes (e.g. Peterson, Fennema, Carpenter, & Loef, 1989; Anderson, Raphael Englert, & Stevens, 1991).

Even after including knowledge, skills, beliefs and values in a definition of professional expertise, other personal resources have been recognized as important. Every profession, for instance, expects its practitioners to subscribe to an *ethical code*—not merely to espouse a set of principles, but to be aware of ethical issues associated with different features of practice and to recognize instances where ethical issues may come into play. In the case of teachers, for instance, we hope that they would be aware of the subtle ways in which they may differentially treat different students and, thereby, further reinforce differences among them (e.g., Rist, 1970). Equally invisible but important to professional expertise is the professional *persona* one adopts; each profession subscribes to one or more ideals of what a member of the profession should be like as a person. The professional persona could be defined as a particular set of skills, but it is actually more than that: It includes an attitude toward one's work and a belief about one's role that is expressed through one's behavior. Adopting a professional code requires conscious thought and judgment and may entail some alteration of one's self-concept as well. A persona is particularly important in teaching, because teachers' work entails a lot of social interaction. A teacher may adopt the persona of a counselor, a strict taskmaster, a friend, or an intellectual, for instance. The choice may have significant implications for students.

Still another important personal resource that contributes to professional expertise is a set of *dispositions* to pursue certain kinds of practices over other kinds of practices. In the case of teaching, numerous writers have suggested that teachers need to be more reflective about their work—to be motivated to improve their practices, to study and be critical of their own behaviors and strategies, and to continue to seek improvements. Zeichner, for instance, has argued that it is important for teachers to define their criteria for good teaching in a way that includes not merely technical accomplishment of curriculum goals but, in addition, the extent to which the class-room processes meet a variety of social and moral criteria as well (Kennedy, 1989).

Most professions also expect their practitioners to have a sense of *purpose* in their work—to see their task as more than merely filling up a 40-hour work week. In the case of teachers, we would hope that teachers see their purpose not merely as one of maintaining order or silence in the classroom but also of trying to help students gain deeper and more substantial understanding of subject matter.

Finally, professional expertise requires an ability to *reason* about practice: to interpret and assess particular situations, to monitor and adjust one's own actions, to formulate and test hypotheses, to weigh the relative importance of general principles and unique circumstances, to draw on a variety of ideas from one's field, and to justify one's decisions with arguments grounded both in principles of practice and in the specific circumstances of practice (e.g. Schon, 1983; Kennedy, 1987).

While each of these personal resources is individually important to professional expertise, each is also important as it interacts with others, for it is the *package* of all these resources, forged into a way of thinking, seeing, and responding to the world, that constitutes professional expertise. Together, these resources provide experts with a *mode of operation*, or MO, that provides them with goals, strategies, knowledge, skills, reasoning, beliefs, ethical guidelines, and even a persona with which to function.

Carl Bereiter (1990) calls these packages *modules*, and he ascribes certain properties to modules. For instance, Bereiter says that the various personal resources that comprise modules are compatible and that they support and reinforce one another. That is, the persona one adopts is compatible with the beliefs, knowledge, and purposes one subscribes to, and the reasoning strategies one uses are compatible with one's disposition, values, and ethical code, for instance.

In addition, Bereiter argues that a given individual may hold more than one module that is relevant to a particular kind of activity. To illustrate this point, Bereiter argues that students in

school may have two completely different learning modules: a schoolwork module and an independent-learning module. Both modules enable the student to learn. Both include the full set of personal resources: propositional knowledge, skills, beliefs, a sense of purpose, ways of reasoning, dispositions, and so forth. But these resources take on a different character in each module. That is, depending on which module, or mode of operation, is in use, the student has different goals, draws on different knowledge and skills, subscribes to different values and beliefs, and enacts a different persona and different problem-solving strategies. Applying this notion to teaching, we might imagine that teachers, too, could hold multiple modes of operation for teaching, each consistent with a particular view of teaching, and each of which is called upon in different circumstances. Teachers may envision one mode of operation in their idealized image of themselves as teachers, but actually practice another MO in their daily practice as teachers. They may use different MOs when teaching mathematics versus language arts, when teaching in first-grade versus third-grade classrooms, or when teaching gifted students as opposed to difficult-to-teach students. To the extent multiple MOs exist, teachers may adopt different goals and different personas in different settings, reason differently in different settings, and draw on different knowledge and different skills to carry out their tasks.

Bereiter's analysis is useful for understanding both the variety of resources that contribute to expertise and for understanding how it is that we may see different behavior patterns, justified with different arguments, in the same person on different occasions. But the notion that these modes of operation contain so many different kinds of resources also poses problems for the development of professional expertise. Professional educators know how to influence only two of these resources: knowledge and skills. In addition, these various resources do not add up to expertise unless they are woven together into coherent modes of operation, yet professional educators traditionally impart each resource separately, as if each had nothing to do with the others. Physicians, for instance, study anatomy separately from neurology, and they study these bodies of knowledge separately from clinical skills. Finally, if individuals can sustain different and even conflicting modes of operation, how can professional educators assure that their students, even if they have developed the MOs they need, will in fact call upon these MOs on the right occasions. In the section below, we address these problems with regard to fostering expertise specifically in teaching.

WHY EXPERTISE IN TEACHING IS HARD TO FOSTER

The development of expertise in teaching presents its own special dilemmas. One of these, for instance, derives from the fact that virtually every teacher or teacher candidate enters this professional field with a package of ideas about teaching already formed. Because prospective teachers have observed teachers for some 13 to 17 years, while they themselves were students, they approach their own teaching with highly elaborated ideas about what the practice consists of, what its goals are, what strategies they would use to accomplish their goals, what their own teaching persona is, and so forth. In fact, not only do teacher candidates already have knowledge, skills, and beliefs about teaching, but most ordinary adults hold similar teaching MOs, based on their observations of their own teachers. We can, then, refer to these as *naive* teaching MOs. They are *visions* of teaching—imagined roles played by the individual, along with scripts for students to play as well.

These naive MOs can impede learning to teach in several ways. For instance, because student observers never see their teachers thinking, they may not realize that thought is an important part of the work. Their images of teaching, then, assume that teaching strategies comes naturally, that they are automatic responses to situations. In the Teacher Education and Learning to Teach (TELT) study, a multisite study of changes in

teacher candidates' beliefs about teaching, we found many instances of this assumption. When asking teachers and teacher candidates to describe how they would handle certain teaching situations (Kennedy, 1991), we often found them saying that they did not know what they would do but that when the time came, *they would know what to do*. For instance, one problem we pose is this:

> Students often make remarks such as, "This is boring. Why do we have to do this?" If a student in your class made such a remark when you were working on organization in writing, how would you react and why?

"Lori's" response indicates the view that the appropriate response will come naturally from the situation:

> It is easy to sit here and say I would, uh, very casually try to impress him that it is boring stuff that leads to better stuff. I don't know, I don't know how I would react to that. . . . When I get into the classroom I would know.

Similarly, Grace's response illustrates this view when she says:

> If the teacher takes a little bit of extra time maybe before they do the lesson or whatever you can always come up with some valid reason to relate to them, to the students, always. And I know I would have done that to begin with. I don't know exactly how I would have done it.

The teaching MOs that teacher candidates bring with them may also include beliefs about their role as a teacher and about their relationship with students. Some teachers who responded to this question, for instance, perceived the question not as one of justifying the content to be learned but, instead, of defending their authority against a hostile student. For them, the student's question challenged their persona as an expert. Jade's response indicates such a view when she says:

I'm one to say, "OK, fine, don't do this, sit there and don't do anything. Do nothing. You can't talk, you can't move. Just sit there and watch everybody else write. We'll see which one is more boring."

To the extent that candidates bring this belief to college with them, as part of their teaching MOs, they will not expect to learn anything of value in their teacher education courses and, consequently, are likely not to learn anything of value.

A second way in which naive teaching MOs might interfere with learning occurs when teacher candidates hold beliefs about the nature of school subjects or the purposes for learning school subjects that differ remarkably from those held by members of the academic disciplines. The "tool" subjects of reading, arithmetic, and writing are prime candidates for such disparities; even though most higher educators envision school subjects as intellectually engaging enterprises, most teacher candidates were taught these subjects as lists of discrete skills. Thus, they are now likely to perceive "writing" as a collection of correct procedures for spelling and punctuating sentences, while contemporaries in this field would argue that writing should be taught as an iterative process of developing ideas and communicating them to real audiences (Hillocks, 1990). Similarly, they may perceive "arithmetic" as a collection of addition and subtraction facts to be memorized and recited on worksheets (Ball, 1988b, 1990), whereas contemporaries in this field would argue that students need to learn to reason about numbers and to connect mathematical ideas to a variety of concrete and everyday situations (NCTM, 1988).

Finally, the teaching MOs that teacher candidates have devised assume that learning occurs in all children as it did for themselves. Since they enjoyed school, they expect that all children enjoy school. Since they learned by passively listening and by filling out repetitive worksheets, they expect all students to learn through these processes. Yet cognitive research, much of which is described elsewhere in this book, suggests that students learn by actively thinking about ideas and constructing their own knowledge of the material.

These teaching MOs derive from what Lortie (1975) called the "apprenticeship of observation": the lengthy period of time during which teachers observed other teachers from the perspective of student. Moreover, consistent with Bereiter's argument, the many ideas and values that contribute to these MOs are internally consistent and mutually reinforcing. If subject matter consists of discrete facts and skills, then the teacher's task is to assure that students acquire as many of these as possible, and the most efficient way to do this is to force-feed these bits of knowledge to students and to use examinations and worksheets to assure that students get it all.

Standing in sharp contrast to this naive teaching MO is one held by many contemporary researchers and teacher educators. In their teaching MO, the goal of teaching is to enable students to reason about school subjects and to use school subjects for their own purposes. Subject matter does not consist of lists of facts and skills to be memorized but, instead, of ideas that need to be weighed and analyzed. A student question about why the class has to learn this material is interpreted not as a challenge to the teacher's authority but as a signal that something is amiss and needs to be investigated. Teaching strategies consist more of methods of engaging students in reasoning than of allocating work sheets for students to fill out.

One inescapable conclusion from the contrast between these two modes of operation is that if contemporary research about how students learn is to make any impact on teaching practice, then teachers' MOs must be changed. The task of professional education, at least for the teaching profession, is one of getting novices to give up the MO they arrive with in favor of another one. This cannot happen merely by giving teachers new knowledge about academic subjects, or about how students learn those subjects or by giving novices different pedagogies. These alternative teaching MOs also require different goals, different values and dispositions, different ethical codes, and different personas. Moreover, because all of these personal resources must be consistent with one another, we are not likely to succeed if we try to change them one at a time, for each alternative resource can be rejected if it is not consistent with the remaining resources in the novice's existing MO. That is, teacher candidates are likely to reject a teaching strategy that entails group discussions about problem-solving strategies if they believe subject matter consists of discrete facts and skills that need to be memorized through repetition. The challenge for teacher educators, then, is to find a way to change the whole MO rather than to change the individual resources one at a time.

THE CHALLENGE TO TEACHER EDUCATORS

If we define teacher education as a systematic effort to replace candidates' naive teaching MOs with new teaching MOs, then teacher educators face six major challenges. Next, we examine each of these challenges.

The first challenge is finding time to foster this kind of change. Candidates need time to rethink their prior assumptions, to reconceptualize the task of teaching, and to reconstruct their whole packages of teaching. By the word *time,* we do not necessarily mean more course credits but rather an arrangement of course credits that is extended over time so that candidates have ample opportunities to reconsider their naive ideas. Conventional teacher education programs often happen within only a one-and-one-half-year time span, from the beginning of the junior year through the middle of the senior year. Students are presumed to be ready to enter student teaching at the end of their senior year, with all of their new professional knowledge in place and ready to use.

The second challenge facing teacher educators is how to address candidates' naive assumptions. The literature offers two promising but competing ideas for how to do this. On one hand is the notion that new ideas need to be tied in some way to existing ideas so that they can be understood and rendered meaningful to the learner

(e.g., essays in Resnick, 1989). On the other hand is the notion that the prior ideas must be challenged and shown to be wanting before learners will be willing to abandon them. The literature on conceptual change (e.g., Posner, Strike, Hewson, & Gertzog, 1982) suggests this approach. Both of these bodies of literature, however, address mainly changes in conceptual understanding, not changes in whole modes of operation.

The third challenge facing teacher educators comes from the fact that the personal resources that contribute to professional expertise are interrelated and mutually supportive. The combinations of knowledge, skills, beliefs, persona, and so forth, that comprise the teaching modes of operations are bundled together and have to be learned as *systems of thought and ways of being and behaving.* Altering one or two resources without influencing the rest may not yield the kind of change that is desired. Any given teaching act entails, at a minimum, a consideration of both the subject matter and the students, and these two considerations alone bring in not only teachers' knowledge about each of these but also their assumptions about how learning occurs in general, their notion of what is most important for students to learn, their sense of persona, and their ability to reason about all of these together (Kennedy, 1991). Yet, although the literature on learning and problem solving offers several clues about enhancing individual resources, it offers very little about changing whole systems of thought.

The fourth challenge facing teacher educators is that of situating important ideas in practical contexts that give them meaning. That is, teacher educators must do more than simply change the frame of reference that teachers use when they approach their work. They must also situate knowledge about teaching and learning and situate strategies for handling teaching dilemmas. For, as Brown, Collins, and Duguid (1989) have argued, even simple, presumably stipulative, concepts do not take on the rich and varied meanings practitioners need unless they are learned in the situations to which they apply. Concepts take on increasingly elaborate meanings as they are encountered in more and diverse situations. Professional expertise cannot be meaningfully attained apart from practice. Bear in mind that all the ideas in candidates' naive MOs are situated, for they were all devised in the context of real classrooms. If new ideas are not situated, the old ideas, those that are part of the naive MO, will remain operative when teachers finally reenter classrooms.

The fifth challenge is that teacher educators must find ways to guide novices in their early practical experiences so that they learn to invoke their new MOs rather than falling back on their naive MOs. That teachers can rarely make this transition to practice is apparent in a substantial body of literature on student teaching and first-year teaching practices. Teachers, like practitioners in law and several other professions, often complain that they learned nothing relevant from their professional education but, instead, learned to teach from their own experiences (Smylie, 1989). Yet, what they learn from their own practice often reinforces their *naive* MOs, because they haven't become sufficiently facile with their new MOs to use them to interpret their experiences. This is one of the reasons teachers so often learn bad practices rather than good ones from experience (Feiman-Nemser & Buchmann, 1983). Strategies must be devised for assuring that candidates are not overwhelmed by the details and that important concepts are infused into their ruminations about their work. Assuring that practical situations reinforce a new teaching MO, rather than reinforcing the naive teaching MO, is no simple task (Kennedy, 1992).

The sixth challenge for those who want to alter candidates' teaching modes of operation is that teachers can hold strong emotional commitments to their naive MOs. These MOs are, after all, part of their character, part of their identities. They include personas, professional values, dispositions, and ethical codes that are at least as important, perhaps more important, than knowledge and skills. If teacher educators try to alter these personal resources, they are tampering with the very identities of their students and may also be undermining the very reasons why these candidates chose to enter the profession in the first place. It should be no surprise that candidates will resist such efforts. Moreover, teaching is, by its very nature, an anxiety-provoking activity, because it is a public performance, because it involves interpersonal relations with children, and because these children will be making their own interpersonal demands on the teacher. The nature of this performance is such as to engender self-consciousness, fear, and a concomitant resistance to new ideas.

Thus, research on cognition, particularly as it applies to teachers as learners, suggests that the task of creating new modes of operation for teachers presents six important challenges for teacher educators:

- how to *extend the learning process* over a longer period of time;

- how to *confront the naive modes of operation* that teacher candidates bring with them;

- how to *develop new modes of operation* rather than simply adding individual personal resources;

- how to *situate new ideas* in practical contexts;

- how to *guide novice practitioners* so that they don't fall back on their naive MOs;

- how to *manage candidates' emotional resistance* to new modes of operation.

In the next section, we describe a teacher education program under development at Michigan State University that is trying to respond to these six challenges.

AN ILLUSTRATIVE EFFORT TO IMPROVE TEACHER EDUCATION

Faculty at Michigan State University are currently trying to develop a new program that builds on this emerging body of cognitive research, as well as on successful features of our earlier programs (e.g., Roth, Rosaen, & Lanier, 1988), and on our research on teacher education and teacher learning (Ball, 1988a; McDiarmid, 1990; Wilson & Wineburg, 1988). The ideas we present in this chapter still represent gleams in our collective eyes more than a finished program, but they also represent our best predictions about the conditions that will enable candidates to develop new modes of operation—MOs that are more consistent with literature on student learning and more consistent with education reform agendas. Next, we describe the ways in which the program responds to the six challenges just discussed.

EXTENDING TIME FOR LEARNING

We have argued that if teacher education is to enable candidates to "unlearn" their prior teaching MOs as well as learn a new one, the program will have to be extended over a longer period of time than are most contemporary teacher education programs. We address the problem of time in three ways. First, students who anticipate enrolling in teacher education can enroll in two required *preadmission* courses that explore learning, learner diversity, and schools. Our hope is that in these courses we can heighten students' awareness of the assumptions they bring with them and raise questions about teaching and learning that they will continue to ponder over time, using their experiences in other university courses as material for considering these questions. Second, once they enroll in the program, the program itself spans a three-year period extending from the junior year through a fifth year. During the first two of these three years, both elementary and secondary teacher candidates are engaged in professional studies while concomitantly pursuing their subject matter preparation. That is, the actual course credits they take *within the teacher education curriculum* through the fourth year are not increased. Third, the program is a five-year program. Upon completion of the baccalaureate degree, students will enter a full-time, year-long internship in schools that is accompanied by graduate-level coursework. The intent of this design is to provide students with more time to rethink ideas and to change their MOs without having to take significantly more education courses.

CONFRONTING NAIVE MODES OF OPERATION

Getting teacher education students to become students of education is not easy. The MOs that candidates bring with them are naively optimistic about their own potential as teachers and often are self-serving. They tend to believe, for instance, that the characteristics of an ideal teacher are the characteristics they already have and that they will not have the difficulties other novice teachers have (Pajares, 1992). These beliefs make them impatient with teacher education courses that raise questions about the goals of education or about *why* teachers might do what they do. If they expect anything from their teacher education courses, it is a bag of clever tricks that can help them solve occasional logistical problems in their classrooms.

These naive beliefs add to the challenge of teacher education, for teacher educators cannot simply work on the MOs they think teachers need; they have to attend to the assumptions and MOs that candidates bring with them. One task, for instance is to get candidates to suspend their eagerness to acquire the behaviors that will make them *look* like teachers long enough to help them learn how to *think* like teachers. A critical part of their new MOs, after all, consists of strategic reasoning. Candidates need to learn how to weigh the relative merits of alternative actions in practical situations.

One way to get students to begin thinking strategically about teaching is to ask them to analyze videotaped instances of atypical teaching. Bird (1991) has presented such examples to candidates and asked them to assume that the actions make sense to the teacher and to figure out why it makes sense to that person rather than judging whether the teacher did the "right" thing or not. By granting the most forgiving interpretation to the episode, students are forced to take alternative points of view in their attempts to understand the dynamics of the situation. Bird argues that by beginning with the actions of real teachers in real situations and then extending the conversation to focus on the "whys" of those actions, teacher educators might be able to overcome some of the candidates' resistance to serious examination of teaching practices.

Bird (1992) also proposes starting with questions that students have when they come into the program. For example, the most pressing question for students might be "how should teachers manage classrooms?" Faculty might prefer to delay consideration of this important question until a theoretical foundation has been laid for thinking about it. But by addressing the students' questions first, teacher educators might be able to assure students that the content of the course is actually going to be helpful to them as future teachers. And if students are persuaded, they, in turn, might open themselves up to deeper consideration of the issues of teaching and learning, which is our primary agenda. Bird has found that it does not take long for the conversation to turn from what teachers should *do* to broader issues of teaching, learning, and subject matter.

Based on our faculty's experience with a course designed in this way, we now plan to precede our new program with two courses that will be offered prior to admission into the formal teacher education program. The goal of these courses will be to challenge students' naive beliefs about teaching, learning, learners, and schools. The first of these courses, *Reflections on Learning,* will introduce students to some of the central questions in education: What is learning? Who is capable of learning what? Where and how does learning happen? What can teachers do to enable learning? The declarative knowledge in this course will be similar to that often taught in educational psychology courses, but the pedagogy will be designed to try to engage many personal resources other than knowledge per se. We hope to get students to use their own experience as learners as the context for considering both the learning experiences of others and a variety of theories of learning and

development as well. Not only would such a course encourage students to reconsider some of their naive assumptions, it might also help them apply new insights to their current university experiences. If we can accomplish this latter goal, we also contribute to our goal of extending the learning process over a longer period of time without necessarily increasing the number of course credits students take in education.

The second preeducation course, *Human Diversity, Power, and Opportunity in Schools,* engages students in similar ways around another critical issue about which they hold many naive beliefs: the nature and consequences of student diversity. Again, in this course, we hope to help students recognize their own deeply embedded attitudes and assumptions about different learner characteristics. Course content will include ways in which teacher attitudes and assumptions might exacerbate student differences and curtail student opportunities to learn. We hope the course will influence the dispositions, ethical codes, and commitments of future teachers as well as their knowledge and beliefs about diverse learners.

DEVELOPING NEW MODES OF OPERATION

We argued above that teacher education programs must find ways of altering integrated systems of thought and action rather than working separately on individual personal resources such as knowledge or skills. One way to do this, of course, is to provide role models for students by becoming the kind of teachers we hope they will become. It is no small matter to teach as we want our students to teach—by questioning, probing, encouraging students to speculate about possibilities, without squelching ideas with which we disagree.

Another approach to this problem is to assure that students have numerous opportunities to make connections among the various ideas they learn of in their courses. The more connections are made, the more likely students are to integrate these ideas into the kind of coherent systems of thought that are needed to form a new mode of operation. Courses such as those described above are intended to help candidates build new systems of thought about all aspects of teaching—subject matter, learners, learning, context, community, and pedagogy. We hope candidates will also begin to tie these new ideas to nascent observation skills as they analyze videotaped and written cases of teaching and learning. And, through journals, class discussion, conferences with both faculty and practicing teachers, and modeling, we hope to develop habits of strategic reasoning.

In addition to altering the strategies we use in individual courses, we hope to design the course sequence to help novices make connections among the numerous ideas they are learning. We are abandoning the traditional teacher education curriculum, which is organized by content areas, such as educational psychology, reading methods, math methods, classroom management, and so forth. Instead, we are trying to develop a spiraling curriculum that is structured around central questions and problems of practice. While the program will still provide roughly the same knowledge base as before (after all, the faculty have not changed and these are the content areas our faculty value), the goal is to rearrange that content so that it can better help candidates connect ideas to one another and to practical teaching situations.

Connecting the Various Educational Foundations

Although the university recognizes courses as the building blocks of degree programs, we are trying to change the *function* of courses from one of parceling knowledge into discrete pieces and transmitting them chunk by chunk into one of weaving ideas together to address larger issues. We do this by creating larger credit blocks that allow for the integration of content around six major questions. Two of these questions have been mentioned above: What do students learn in school? and What should and could students learn in school? The other questions are: Who are the diverse students who come to school?

What is worth knowing and learning in school? How does one teach that which is worth knowing? and What does it mean to be a professional who is capable of teaching worthwhile knowledge?

The use of these questions to organize course content enables traditional domains of knowledge to be connected to each other and to the goals of teaching. For example, each question can be considered in light of specific subject matter; such as, what do students typically know about photosynthesis or light, and what should they know? Each question can also be answered by thinking about a particular foundational discipline. What, for instance, does cognitive research suggest about how students' naive conceptions contribute or detract from their learning about photosynthesis or light? Similarly, what do anthropologists' findings about culture have to say about enabling diverse learners to comprehend scientific theories?

The courses allow candidates to revisit these questions over time as they become better informed about teaching practices and more able to invoke different modes of operation for teaching.

Connecting Disciplinary Knowledge and Professional Knowledge

We also want to help candidates see the connections between disciplinary knowledge and teaching school subjects. To that end, we are trying to form collaborations that include arts and sciences faculty, education faculty, and K–12 teachers—three populations of teacher educators that have traditionally operated almost independently of one another. This is not a simple task. On one hand, we want future teachers, especially elementary candidates who are typically denied access to upper division courses, to have the same disciplinary knowledge as other students who major in these subjects. On the other hand, we are concerned about the substance and the pedagogy that may be provided in college and university courses. Students often do not learn much about why a discipline is organized as it is, what kinds of questions are considered important and why, what the central debates are in the field, or how evidence and argument are used in these debates. Yet it is often these most fundamental questions that arise in K–12 classrooms, so that even elementary teachers often must grapple with these questions (Kennedy, 1990). And the teaching they observe in these courses may do more to reinforce their naive modes of operation than to stimulate the formation of a new mode of operation for teaching.

Though we are only beginning to understand what the content of a disciplinary major for teachers ought to be, we do have some ideas about how to help teachers transform their own subject matter knowledge into subject matter that is both substantively important and engaging for students. For instance, by focusing candidates' attention on what their students know and believe about a discipline, we might be able to help candidates see the gaps in their own knowledge. The instructional task for faculty is one of helping candidates construct both their own understanding of the subject matter and their understanding of how to help children understand it. The traditional separation between disciplinary knowledge and pedagogical knowledge is one of the most difficult barriers to overcome in any effort to provide teachers with integrated knowledge that can contribute to a coherent mode of operation for teaching.

Connecting Special Education and Regular Education

Another important aspect of integration involves preparation to work with special needs students in the least restrictive environment. Typically, the preparation of special educators is separate from the preparation of regular classroom teachers, but this practice has not served special needs students well (Pugach & Leake, 1991). Many educators and policymakers have therefore supported a move toward more inclusive teacher education. Yet neither regular classroom teachers nor special educators are accustomed to working together. Moreover, though most of our faculty are committed to integrating these content areas, not all are.

Our current thinking is that we should intro-duce issues related to special students and to the ways schools respond to them early in the curriculum, and we should revisit these issues later on through the use of cases that illustrate dilemmas associated with mainstreaming. Finally, during the internship year, we hope to enable interns to work with both regular and special educators, so that they continue to see the tensions between different perspectives on learning offered by these professionals.

Connecting Courses and Field Experiences

By the term "field experiences," we mean not only time in schools, either observing or actually teaching, but also time spent examining videotapes and written cases of teaching. All of these provide opportunities to connect theoretical ideas to practical situations. We hope to include in our field experiences not only classroom observations but also some form of involvement with families and community members. We envision a sequence of field experiences tied to the course work, so that the bulk of the content we teach can be "situated" (Brown, Collins, & Duguid, 1989). These experiences will culminate in a fifth-year internship.

The Question of Program Coherence

All of these arguments for promoting connections among new ideas and other personal resources suggest that there must be a great deal of substantive coherence among program components. This is necessary, we suspect, in part because of the need to create teaching modes of operation rather than simply bodies of knowledge, and in part because candidates' naive modes of operation are highly resistant to change (Feiman-Nemser & Featherstone, 1992; McDiarmid, 1992; Bird, 1991; Holt-Reynolds, 1991). The tacit hypothesis behind all of our efforts at drawing connections is that candidates are more likely to build coherent systems of thought and action when their preparation program is also coherent (Barnes, 1987). Long criticized for fragmentation and redundancy, teacher education programs comprised of the usual collection of courses and practicum experiences are not seen as powerful enough to overcome candidates' naive modes of operation (Bird, 1991; McDiarmid, 1990). A coherent curriculum, on the other hand, might be able to produce a cumulative impact and foster the integration of a wide range of personal resources.

But strong arguments can also be made for not forcing coherence into programs. Procedurally, such a goal entails numerous time-consuming meetings among faculty who are not necessarily like-minded. Intellectually, we face the possibility, as Buchmann and Floden (1990) point out, of indoctrinating students into a "party line" approach to teaching rather than helping them learn to think for themselves. This potential is a serious one, and our faculty are divided on the merits and demerits of curricular coherence. Over the next several years, as these new programs evolve, this issue will be returned to again and again as faculty seeks ways to develop connections across ideas, situations, and other personal resources, while at the same time encouraging candidates to think hard about both what they believe about teaching and learning and what is yet unknown about these fundamental questions. We are trying to define program coherence not in terms of a rigid set of student outcomes but as an organized study of a set of teaching problems that can direct both faculty and student energies.

SITUATING IMPORTANT IDEAS IN PRACTICAL CONTEXTS

The fourth challenge facing teacher educators is finding ways to situate the ideas they believe are important, so that students learn to interpret these situations using new, rather than naive, modes of operation. Without situating our messages, candidates are likely to interpret the language we use in terms of their naive modes of operation. A discussion about mathematical problem solving, for instance, can be interpreted as referring to computational problems, when the faculty mean it to refer to problems that require reasoning about mathematical concepts. Or discussions of the writing process are interpreted by candidates as referring to a linear sequence of

outlining, developing note cards, and then writing the text. These new concepts will not be correctly understood unless candidates also learn the concrete situations to which they apply.

The need to situate new concepts means that, in addition to changing our curriculum, our pedagogy must also change to accommodate these problems. An important reason for focusing on central questions of teaching is so that students can connect ideas from educational psychology, sociology, and pedagogy to the purposes of teaching, to real classroom situations, and to real classroom decisions. An important reason for exposing students to, and asking them to examine closely, videotaped and written cases of teaching is so that they situate the ideas they are discussing. Instead of the traditional "methods" course that is taught with little or no connection to classroom teaching, we hope to tie issues of method to field experiences that enable candidates to examine what real students know about particular content and how they respond to various representations of new ideas in the discipline. Among the many issues that must be dealt with if we take situated knowledge seriously is that experienced teachers may not be able to articulate their highly situated knowledge so that novices can learn from them (Heaton & Lampert, in press).

GUIDING INTELLECTUAL DEVELOPMENT

Although formal field experiences are universally recognized as an essential component in teacher education, they are also widely recognized for their potential to be more *miseducative* than educative (Buchmann & Floden, 1990). Most novices enter their first teaching experiences with two different modes of operation. One MO is new, still tentative, fragile, and vague; the other has been developed and elaborated upon since childhood. It is sturdy and is highly situated. Without some forceful assistance in implementing their new modes of operation, candidates are likely to set them aside in favor of their original MOs to get through the difficult early days of teaching.

The internship will be a yearlong, full-time, intensive experience that will include both classroom teaching and systematic study of teaching. On the teaching side, we hope to arrange a variety of experiences that include not only the traditional student-teaching format, with a single intern and a single mentor teacher, but also membership in instructional teams that include experienced classroom teachers and university faculty. Experienced teachers and university faculty will try to emphasize the strategic nature of teaching practice by discussing alternative strategies and by tying these alternatives to theoretical ideas that novices learned about earlier. They will try to model the mode of operation they are trying to foster in novices.

The internship provides an opportunity to develop those personal resources that are hard to influence in a university setting. For instance, it is important not only that students adopt appropriate values and ideals for teaching, but that they also develop the capacity to *be* the sort of teacher they envision. Thus, prospective teachers must not only *want* to teach in ways that are productive for student learning, they must also develop the skills to do so (Fullan, 1985). Working with teams can provide a more varied set of opportunities for such development.

One way we hope to encourage better interpretation of field experiences is by providing prospective teachers with experience in a variety of settings and with a range of students. If candidates are to understand students who come from communities different from those the candidates come from, they will need to have field experiences in different kinds of communities (e.g., urban and rural, or urban and suburban). Our current thinking is that we will require experiences in at least two communities and will require candidates to work with a wide range of learners—learners who differ in language, race, gender, and mental and physical abilities. We will ask novices within these settings to cast a critical eye on the way these schools and communities respond to diverse learners. Our hope is that such experiences might further enable candidates to develop alternative modes of operation that are based in a recognition

of the potentially negative effect of teacher responses to these learners. Because urban settings offer significantly more difficult contexts for learning, we hope to assure that each teacher candidate can spend a significant portion of time in such a setting.

Since the community surrounding the professional development school provides an important resource for improving student learning, these locations can also offer opportunities for novices to extend their understandings. For example, in one junior high school, Centers for Opportunity have been created so that students can pursue their talents in particular areas. In an elementary school, novices might have a chance to work in Head Start, Smart Start, and other preschool readiness programs. Participation in such an environment would offer novices a model of teaching and student advocacy that is unavailable in typical field experiences, and it would enable them to develop those personal resources that are difficult to address in a university classroom—resources such as the disposition to seek support from others who can meet different aspects of a student's needs rather than despairing that the problems go beyond their own capacity to respond.

These teaching experiences will be accompanied by two yearlong graduate seminars. One, entitled "Reflection and Inquiry in Teaching Practice," is being designed to move novices from informal methods of inquiry to more formal strategies for testing ideas in the context of practice. The other, "Professional Role and Community," is being designed to help novices study the community surrounding the school and to learn to view the school in this larger context.

MANAGING EMOTIONAL RESISTANCE

Just as teaching is both intellectual and practical, it is also highly personal. Teacher candidates enter teacher education with modes of operation that include not only ideas about teaching and learning, but values, ethical codes, personas, dispositions, and other attitudes toward teaching. These MOs not only constitute their personal resources, but also are an important part of their personal identities. These values and beliefs often define their reasons for choosing teaching as a career in the first place, and challenges to these values can be highly threatening.

Certainly, changes in dispositions and attitudes are more likely to occur in contexts that are supportive and where personal risks are minimized. But it is easier to define than to create the sort of environment we seek. Such environments should foster respect for alternative perspectives, honest exchange of views, openness to critical feedback, willingness to explore feelings as well as ideas, and responsibility for the well-being of others as well as for oneself. We have two strategies for creating such an environment. One is to group students into cohorts, so that they form collegial groups while moving through the program; the other is to create a supportive learning environment for these cohorts.

Cohorts

We plan to organize students into cohorts that stay together throughout the three-year program. We hope that if students proceed through all seminars together and are assigned to the same schools and classrooms, they will develop close relationships with their colleagues so that they have opportunities to vent their feelings and share their confusions as they gradually begin to entertain different ideas about teaching and learning. To promote collegiality among candidates, we will try to place students in groups to carry out focused field assignments. We hope that peer observation and feedback on teaching episodes will become familiar modes for their learning, as will sharing journals and lesson plans. Social occasions are also important opportunities for building trust and personal regard for colleagues. Studying with a group of peers can help candidates develop a persona that integrates their ethical codes, goals, and conceptions of themselves as teachers and as members of the teaching profession.

Cohorts have other advantages as well. Students learn that others depend on them for critical commentary on their thinking and actions. They are, in a very real sense, accountable to each other for the learning and success of all members. The feedback we have received from students who have participated in student cohorts over the past 10 years suggests that they continue to interact with colleagues and are often instigators of cooperative ventures. The habit of seeking feedback and critical discourse, then, can become ingrained to an extent not possible in programs where students take courses according to their own individual schedules.

But there can be a serious downside to cohorts. Unless faculty spend time developing collegial norms of respect, responsibility, and openness to critical feedback and dialogue, cohort members can form cliques that are destructive to personal and professional growth and that reinforce the already strong naive modes of operation. Just having students proceed through a series of courses together is no guarantee that students will overcome the stereotypes and competitive behavior they may have developed as students. Students who perceive themselves to be outstanding students may, in fact, resist cooperative strategies if they perceive that their academic records may suffer because of poor group performance. The ways in which we treat cohorts, then, must be designed to help individuals take responsibility for the learning of other members of the cohort.

A Context That Encourages Self-Examination

We would like to make both university classes and field experiences into environments that develop prospective teachers' dispositions and their capacity to inquire about teaching dilemmas (Wildox, et al., 1991). The program is being designed so that a core of faculty will work with a given cohort of students for the entire three-year duration of their program. The idea is that perhaps faculty cohorts can help candidates make connections between disciplinary and pedagogical studies, and between theory and practice. If they know individual students better, faculty may be in a better position to monitor candidates' thinking as well as their own interpretations of the learning situation.

In addition, we want to place candidates in school environments that provide support and encourage risk taking. Professional development schools can provide such environments if teachers in these schools are themselves engaged in self-examination and risk taking. We hope, therefore, to locate interns in professional development schools as much as possible so that novices can observe teachers who are comfortable with different modes of operation and with raising questions about their practice.

SUMMARY

Research on learning, and on teacher learning in particular, suggests that the task of teacher education is not merely to give candidates new knowledge about teaching strategies but is, in addition, to help them change their entire way of thinking about teaching: their beliefs about how students learn, about what is important to learn, and about how teachers can facilitate student learning; their knowledge of students, of subject matter, and of teaching; their professional values; their skills; and the persona they adopt as teachers. Given that teacher candidates already hold internally consistent modes of operation that include all of these personal resources, the challenge for teacher educators is to find ways to reveal those MOs to the teacher candidates who possess them, raise questions about their merit, and offer candidates alternative teaching ideas, beliefs, values, and personas with which to develop their roles as teachers.

In an effort to indicate how this view of teacher education and learning to teach might influence the design of teacher education programs, we have described one particular program that is intended to respond to what we now believe about teacher learning and about teacher expertise. The program is still in its formative stages, and no doubt there are other ways in which these findings might be accommodated in teacher education. The most important lesson we draw from this research is that teacher education must respond to new research findings not only by altering the content of its programs, so that candidates learn what researchers have learned, but also by altering their character as well, so that they reflect the learning principles that they espouse to their students.

FOOTNOTE

1. We are indebted to numerous faculty at Michigan State University who were involved in developing this new program. The program is still highly formative and will no doubt change in the forthcoming years.

REFERENCES

Anderson, L. M., Raphael, T., Englert, C. S., & Stevens, D. (1991). Teaching writing with a new instructional model: Variations in teachers' beliefs, instructional practice, and their students' performance (Research Report No. 91-7). East Lansing, MI: The National Center for Research on Teacher Education.

Ball, D. L. (1988a). Research on teaching mathematics: Making subject matter knowledge part of the equation (Research Report No. 88-2). East Lansing, MI: The National Center for Research on Teacher Education.

Ball, D. L. (1988b). The subject matter preparation of prospective teachers: Challenging the myths (Research Report No. 88-3). East Lansing, MI: The National Center for Research on Teacher Education.

Ball, D. L. (1990). The mathematical understandings that prospective teachers bring to teacher education. The Elementary School Journal, 90(4), 450–466.

Barnes, H. L. (1987). The conceptual basis for thematic

teacher education programs. *Journal of Teacher Education, 38*(4), 13–18.

Bereiter, C. (1990). Aspects of an educational learning theory, Review of Educational Research, 60(4), 603–624.

Bird, T. (1991, August). Making conversations about teaching and learning in an introductory education course (Craft Paper No. 91-2). East Lansing, MI: The National Center for Research on Teacher Education.

Brown, J. S., Collins, A., & Duguid, P. (1989). Situated cognition and the culture of learning. *Educational Researcher, 18*(1), 32–34.

Buchmann, M., & Floden, R. E. (1990, June). Program coherence in teacher education: A view from the United States (Issue Paper No. 90-6). East Lansing, MI: The National Center for Research on Teacher Education.

Calderhead, A. (1991). The nature and growth of knowledge in student teaching. *Teaching and Teacher Education, 7*(5/6), 531–535.

Cohen, D. K. (1988). Teaching practice: Plus change . . . (Issue Paper No. 88-3). East Lansing, MI: The National Center for Research on Teacher Education.

Feiman-Nemser, S., & Buchmann, M. (1983). Pitfalls of experience in teacher education (Occasional paper No. 65). East Lansing, MI: Michigan State University Institute for Research on Teaching.

Feiman-Nemser, S., & Featherstone, H. (Eds.). (1992). *Exploring teaching: Reinventing an introductory course.* New York and London: Teachers College Press, Columbia University.

Fullan, M. (1985). Integrating theory and practice. In D. Hopkins and K. Reid (Eds.), *Rethinking teacher education* (pp. 195–212). Kent, England: Croom Helm Ltd.

Heaton, R., & Lampert, M. (in press). Learning to hear voices: Inventing a new pedagogy of teacher education. In M. McLaughlin, J. Talbert, & D. K. Cohen (Eds.), *Teaching for understanding: Challenges for practice, research, and policy.* San Francisco: Jossey Bass.

Hillocks, G., Jr. (1991). The knowledge necessary to teach writing effectively. In M. M. Kennedy (Ed.), *Teaching academic subjects to diverse learners* (pp. 142–162). New York: Teachers College Press.

Holt-Reynolds, D. (1991). *The dialogues of teacher education: Entering and influencing preservice teachers' internal conversations.* East Lansing, MI: National Center for Research on Teacher Learning.

Kennedy, M. M. (1987). Inexact sciences: Professional education and the development of expertise. In E. Z. Rothkopf (Ed.), *Review of research in education* (Vol. 14, pp. 133–167). Washington, DC: American Educational Research Association.

Kennedy, M. M. (1989). Ken Zeichner reflecting on reflection: An interview with Ken Zeichner. *NCRTE Colloquy, 2*(2), 15–21.

Kennedy, M. M. (1990). *Trends and issues in: Teachers' subject matter knowledge.* Washington, DC: AACTE ERIC Clearinghouse on Teacher Education.

Kennedy, M. M. (1991). Merging subjects and students into teaching knowledge. In M. M. Kennedy (Ed.), *Teaching academic subjects to diverse learners* (pp. 273–284). New York: Teachers College Press.

Kennedy, M. M. (1992). Developing a professional development school. In M. Levine (Ed.), *Professional practice schools.* New York: Teachers College Press.

Lampert, M. (1990). When the problem is not the question and the solution is not the answer: Mathematical knowing and teaching. *American Educational Research Journal, 27*(1), 29–64.

McDiarmid, G. W. (1990). Challenging prospective teacher's beliefs during early field experience: A quixotic undertaking. *Journal of Teacher Education, 41,* 12–20.

McDiarmid, G. W. (1992). Tilting at webs of belief: Field experiences as a means of breaking with experience. In S. Feiman-Nemser & H. Featherstone (Eds.), *Exploring teaching: Reinventing an introductory course* (pp. 34–58). Elmsford, NY: Pergamon.

McDiarmid, G. W., Ball, D. L., & Anderson, C. W. (1989). Why staying ahead one chapter doesn't really work: Subject-specific pedagogy. In M. Reynolds (Ed.), *The knowledge base for beginning teachers* (pp. 193–206). Elmsford, NY: Pergamon.

NCTM (1988). *Curriculum and evaluation standards for school mathematics.* Reston, VA: National Council of Teachers of Mathematics.

Orlosky, D. (1980). Skill training for teachers. In E. Hoyle and J. Megarry (Eds.), *World yearbook of education, 1980: Professional development of teachers* (pp. 270–279). New York: Kogan Page.

Peterson, P. L., Fennema, E., Carpenter, T. P., & Loef, M. (1989). Teachers' pedagogical content beliefs in mathematics. *Cognition and Instruction, 6*(1), 1–40.

Posner, G. J., Strike, K. A., Hewson, P. W., & Gertzog, W. A. (1982). Accommodation of a scientific concept: Toward a theory of conceptual change. *Science Education, 66,* 211–227.

Pugach, J. & Leake, H. (1991). The KBBT and the preparation of teachers for contemporary society: An unmatched set? In M. Pugach, H. Barnes, & L. Beckum (Eds.), *Changing the practice of teacher education.* Washington, DC: American Association of Teacher Educators.

Resnick, L. B. (1987). The 1987 presidential address:

Learning in school and out. *Educational Researcher, 16*(9), 13–20.

Resnick, L. B. (Ed.). (1989). *Knowing, learning and instruction: Essays in honor of Robert Glaser.* Hillsdale, NJ: Erlbaum.

Reynolds, M. (Ed.). (1989). *The knowledge base for beginning teachers.* Elmsford, NY: Pergamon.

Rist, R. (1970). Student social class and teacher expectations: The self-fulfilling prophesy in Ghetto education. *Harvard Educational Review, 40*(3), 411–451.

Roth, K. J., Rosaen, C. L., & Lanier, P. E. (1988). *Mentor teacher project program assessment report.* East Lansing, MI: Michigan State University College of Education.

Schon, D. A. (1983). *The reflective practitioner: How professionals think in action.* New York: Basic Books.

Smylie, M. A. (1989). Teachers' views of the effectiveness of sources of learning to teach. *The Elementary School Journal, 89*(5), 543–558.

Wilcox, S. K., Schram, P., Lappan, G., & Lanier, P. (1991). The role of a learning community in changing preservice teachers' knowledge and beliefs about mathematics education (Research Report No. 91-1). East Lansing, MI: The National Center for Research on Teacher Education.

Wilson, S. M. (1990). The secret garden of teacher education. *Phi Delta Kappan, 72*(3), 204–209.

Wilson, S. M., & Wineburg, S. S. (1988). Peering at history from different lenses: The role of disciplinary perspectives in teaching American history. *Teachers College Record, 89,* 525–539.

3

STRATEGIES FOR IMPROVING INSTRUCTION FOR AT-RISK CHILDREN

CHAPTER TEN

PLAY FOR IDENTITY

WHERE THE MIND IS EVERYDAY FOR INNER-CITY YOUTH

SHIRLEY BRICE HEATH

▼

STANFORD UNIVERSITY

Dr. Shirley Brice Heath is professor of English and linguistics, with courtesy appointments in anthropology and education, at Stanford University. Her primary self-identification is as an anthropological linguist who studies oral and written language in learning contexts of different populations and settings. She has done fieldwork in inner cities and rural working-class communities of diverse ethnic and linguistic backgrounds in the United States. She has also studied language policies of educational and bureaucratic institutions in Mexico and Guatemala. For two decades, she has found ways to work with students and teachers in cooperative research teams studying how different forms and uses of language work in the display, retention, and transfer of learning.

The centre of transformations that
Transform for transformation's self,
In a glitter that is a life, a gold
That is a being, a will, a fate.
  "Human Arrangement"
  Wallace Stevens

When the early 20th-century American poet Wallace Stevens wrote of transformations we undergo in life, he captured the central core of everyday learning in human experience across the life span. This chapter looks at effective inner-city youth organizations to see how we might capture some of the ways of learning there as part of the everyday thinking of formal education.

In cultures around the world, the mind constantly adjusts to take in what is happening as we move through transitions as individuals and as groups, and as we undergo transformations—often sudden and shocking. Some transformations are those of biological maturations—the rapid gains in height and change of voice of adolescent males, for example. Others come through self-assessment in response to external forces for change.

Some settings, such as inner-city streets, offer far more unexpected transitions and transformations than others, and learning to adjust to change for those who live there seems to be constant. In these environments, the young have *to learn to learn* in order to survive. They are rarely afforded the relatively slow and gradual transitions of aging, job changes, and seasonal reversals; instead, they suffer shocking jogs of transformations—often accompanied by unplanned physical displacements, violence, disability, or death to loved ones. Such changes may come from distant and seemingly anonymous forces (such as war, ecological disasters, global economic shifts), as well as local agents (such as employers, family members, and neighbors). But nevertheless, they come, and the young who are likely to emerge from these changes with new skills and strategies are most often those who have found their way into inner-city organizations that use the realities of everyday transitions and transformations to build optimal learning environments for them.

These organizations have acknowledged that the power of such transformations derives not only from their immediate influence, but from their unexpectedness and defiance of ideal trajectories of how relationships and the environment are supposed to work. They recognize that the generally held images of life and learning that come through family ideals, communal myths, and public portrayals rarely include the unpredictability and violence of the many transformations through which inner-city youth must learn. The leaders of these organizations, therefore, work to create safe environments in which learning as a group member, being part of a disciplined structure, and engaging in a performance outcome comes to be everyday thinking. These institutions encompass numerous roles usually assumed by families—building a sense of identity and providing a flow of activity and experience that sustains continuity in relationships. Much of what these organizations do has relevance for formal educational institutions. First we consider just how inner-city young people learn as they participate in the learning environments of their youth-based

organizations. Then we consider how features of such organizations and the everyday problem solving and creative thinking of activities they illustrate can be incorporated into formal educational systems.

HOW YOUTH-BASED ORGANIZATIONS APPROACH LEARNING

▼

In this chapter, we step into the lives of some inner-city youngsters as they participate in the learning environments of youth-based organizations. These include baseball teams, community centers, and clubs (such as, Boys' and Girls' Clubs, Girl Scouts, Boy Scouts, etc.), as well as community theaters that offer teen drama, Ballet Folklorico, and youth choirs for community youth. Young people who belong to these groups find that they lack the dangers of gangs, but they offer many similar attractions: a sense of security, strong collective membership, socialization across ages, and meaningful everyday learning in work and play. These are organizations that allow youngsters to explore in play the "real world" while being buffered from the consequences of the harsh judgments of the street, school, and society. Their primary activities and events are either athletic or artistic.

The materials of this chapter come from five years of fieldwork in youth organizations located in three major metropolitan areas of the United States. Each of these urban areas had a vision of promise in their approaches to youth. In each, a team of "junior ethnographers" from the community worked with the trained ethnographers of the research group. Together they documented, through field notes, audiotapes, and videotapes, the talk, activities, and reflections on life of the young people participating in the events of practice, performance, and evaluation at the youth centers. The following common threads of being mindful ran through these documentations.

The central unit of reference within these groups is usually "the team," through which young people develop a consciousness of an experiential reality composed of associates who share common activities both within the group and in the rarely talked about world beyond the youth organization—family, school, the street, or neighborhood gangs. Furthermore, leaders of such organizations come up through the organizations, move into youth "reform" after earlier difficult experiences in street life, migrate from public school teaching, or represent groups that are external to the local site of the organization but are eager to invest in the community's youth. The leaders talk repeatedly about the need to "keep these kids' heads together, you know, give their minds something to work with, so they'll learn to think, know where they can go and what they can do."

But what else marks those youth organizations that inner-city young people judge "effective" or "successful"? How do these organizations compete with gangs to keep young people committed to practice, work, and performance together?

All the organizations that were studied, reflected the following characteristics. They:

1. *Make it clear that youngsters are not "problems" but "resources."* Every institution has a shortage of money, time, space, and equipment, so the message goes out that everybody is needed to help keep the organization going.

2. *Ensure that young people can be busy learning all the time, and not just between certain hours or during only some weeks of the year.* Everybody has to keep the life of the organization in mind: cleanup, security, equipment protection, and accounting for the whereabouts of other members means staying alert. Youngsters join in tasks that just keep the institution operating and sustain its central activities, as well as the specialized activities of their age group—such as playing ball or planning dramatic performances.

3. *Engage youngsters in specific seasonal activities to work toward peak performance(s).* Playing ball, performing tumbling team

routines, perfecting dance or choir numbers, or tutoring younger children ensure occasions in which youngsters perform at a level and on an occasion they consider their best effort or peak display.

4. *Offer spaces that give protection from the street with limited access and entry, so that youngsters will feel safe, out of view of their peers who choose other kinds of activities.* To avoid peer ridicule or attack, youngsters who choose alternatives to street attractions must have a safe place.

5. *Make travel out of the community possible, so that youngsters can see how what they learn in their own community organizations pays off and has relevance elsewhere.* Learning by observing, seeing a range of models, and experiencing choices expands horizons of hope and stabilizes the motivation to learn, to improve, and to help others in these efforts.

6. *Make it clear that efforts must "go beyond" merely pleasing teachers, coaches, and leaders on the inside of the organization.* The performance must hold up to the evaluations—often harsh and unfriendly—of disengaged audiences, referees, and other coaches and leaders.

7. *Keep the rules few, simple, and meaningful; enforce them.* A consistent ethos or philosophy, usually stated in a few "ground rules" that carry maximal impact, pervades the institution; "nobody's supposed to get hurt here" summarizes the core meaning of any rules of operation for the organization. Such guides, though minimal in number, carry maximal impact because they encompass almost any action or word that may come up for possible negotiation of their meaning.

All these features of the youth organizations pervade the language and thinking of the youth leaders as well as the youngsters themselves. Such language and perspectives stand in sharp contrast to the customary language of classrooms. Youth organization leaders think, act, and talk constantly about the value of the structure and ethics of their groups or teams, for these elements give these groups their identity. Moreover, they stress learning by demonstration, trial and error, teaching others, and self-assessing.

HOW YOUTH LEADERS USE LANGUAGE TO HELP THE YOUNG MAKE SUCCESSFUL LIFE TRANSITIONS

It is commonplace to acknowledge that when we talk about meaning, we have to depend on language for our evidence of the ways that people understand their world and communicate about it with one another. In this study, we will look at how the content of messages and the ways in which youth organization leaders use language with activities and within social structures assists young people in creating a collective identity within their youth-based organizations. Their activities assign symbolic value to objects, activities, and verbal, as well as nonverbal, routines. Ritual processes—repeated language, events, and relationships—work together to build and sustain young people's collective representation of themselves (Turner, 1967).

Such identity-building for individuals and the group takes place within a system of relations and structures that make much of transformations, acknowledging repeatedly that sharp changes, "tough breaks," unexpected outcomes, and unfair consequences are natural occurences in a life span. However, the organizations both prepare young people and shield them from these shocks; they do so by ensuring that within the activities of the groups, there are marked transitions, from season to season, from level to level, from position to position, and from practice among intimates to performance before strangers. Such identity building can occur in our schools if teachers note what youth leaders do and adopt some of their own techniques to the following strategies.

First, youth leaders help make the experience of each individual verbally and visually available to other learners. They do so by oral scripting of activities, narrative replays of practices and performances or games, and *eventcasts*—verbal future scenarios—of what will come in the next practice session. For example:

(1) OK, Wednesday, we'll practice
      tomorrow again, with the way
      we're doing now, and then Wednes-
      day we'll practice with the stuff,
      (unintelligible)
         furniture right on the stage.

Leaders provide a running commentary on events as they are forecast and acted, and also summary narratives of performances after they have occurred.

Second, team members are led to focus their attention on such talk, because they are frequently and rapidly called by name, as in (2), below; assigned roles in sociodramatic enactments, (3); or narrativized in replays of events and projections of future possibilities, (4).

(2) All right, let's go everybody, Kao.
      [whistles] All right, let's everybody
      over here.

      Willie, come over here. Rob. See
      where that thing goes up, Rob?
      That little one?

      No, no. Hey Dude. Hey Dude, don't
      worry about him now. I want all
      the Blues over here.

(3) I want you behind these screens, just
      like in a game . . .

(4) **Sam:** I thought he was gonna throw
      it [leader fakes a throw to third].

      Ion: That's why they usually got
      [unintelligible]

      Ed: WOW, you like . . .

      Dino: . . . man, you know where that
      dude slid, he just out, man (unintelligi-
      ble)

Rich: . . . I know, he caught his foot. He caught right here. And then . . .

Ed: . . . that was a good play you did back there.

Third, as in (4), team members and leaders jointly reenact key events and retell experiences shared by all during practices and games; the extent of repetitions, successful interruptions, overlaps, and sentence continuations across speakers indicate the fine tuning of the listening and attending stances of the speakers. When speakers overlap their talk, finishing each other's sentences acceptably, and saying just ahead of another speaker what is to come, they are "finely tuned" (Tannen, 1989).

Fourth, the gestures, voice modulations, dramatic reenactments, and telegraphic speech of leaders (5) consistently offer positive reinforcement and project current actions and attention to the team goal:

(5) OK, big Mike, let's go now.

OK Mike, let's see you hit.

A man on third, let's strike him in, don't leave him there.

Ball one.

Let's go, dude.

That's it, strike one.

Let's go, dude.

Last, failure to listen, or even to try to participate, amounts to a refusal to accept one's necessary identification as a member of the action team. Shifts in action come rapidly and are cued by both voice and gesture, so that team members need to be both looking and listening to know when they are to shift their perspective from present practice to future game, from one role to another, or from spectator to key player. "Hold your mind to it" is the frequent cry of athletic or drama coaches.

For learners to stay focuses on learning and thinking, they must keep their eyes and ears open and be alert to the need to rethink a strategy or tactic quickly. Often only a nod of the head, or a cast of the hand, directs a player to move, realign, take up a new task, get out of the way of another, or look in a particular direction. These reminders to take the local context of action into account come in the company of numerous mental state verbs from leaders: "think," "remember," "know," etc. Time is compressed, action fast paced, and the call to think ahead, reflect, and hypothesize frequent.

HOW LEADERS USE RITUAL TO BUILD HYPOTHESIS THINKING

What enables youth from inner-city high-rise projects filled with crime, violence, and unpredictability to enter the rule-governed, strictly disciplined, and task-oriented world of youth-based organizations? Since 1969, when his work *The Ritual Process: Structure and Anti-structure* was published, anthropologist Victor W. Turner has repeatedly written of the role of rituals in transformations. Unlike much of the work that has focused on rituals in rites of passage, Turner's work and that of those who followed his lead emphasize not a completed or final cultural performance as the ritual of focus, but the processes of ritual that over time form structures and link various symbolic systems (from gesture, song, narrative, and drama, to painting and dance). Turner reminded us as early as 1969: "Rituals reveal values at their deepest level . . . [members] express in ritual what moves them most, and since the form of expression is conventionalized and obligatory, it is the values of the group that are revealed" (p. 241).

These rituals often surround rites of passage or transitions marking changes of place, state, social position, and age. Such transitions are marked by separation, margin, and aggregation. The first includes symbolic behavior that signifies the detachment of the individual from an earlier fixed point in the social structure or set of cultural conditions. Marginal periods are those of transition through which homogeneity and colleague-ship begin to create "communitas"—or a sense of social relationship that is relatively undifferentiated and in which individuals coalesce with the help of ritual leaders. The final phase moves the individual or group into a new, steady state. These changes come in large part through the appropriation by the youngsters of a "multivoicedness"—a series of speech genres or forms that mediate their actions (Wertsch, 1991).

Within many youth organizations, there is a waiting, or trial period; for others, the marginal time is that of the early part of the season when individuals congregate to be chosen for the team, the performance, or the musical or dance group. Early practices extend this marginal time, until the group coalesces into an aggregate team of performers at play for a season. Central to eventual integration within the group is one's ability during this period to act *as if* he or she were a member without overstepping the boundaries appropriate for a newcomer. Judgment of acceptability within the group swirls around "keeping your eyes open," "holding your head up," "keeping your mouth shut, but your ears on." *Such multiple attentiveness signals the extent to which the newcomer is likely to handle the transition successfully both into the group and across the plateaus and stages of the group.*

Turner and those following him have stressed the similarities between the ritual process as theater or play and the resulting workshop-rehearsal process well known in Euro-American dance and theater. In such a workshop atmosphere, the goal is to "deconstruct the ready-mades of individual behavior, texts, and cultural artifacts into strips of malleable behavior material; the work of the rehearsal is to reconstruct these into a new, integral system: a 'performance' " (Schechner, 1986, p. 345; see also Schechner, 1985). Preparation for such performances centers in the strict rules that lie at the heart of ritual; these rules of *play* designate "this *is* play" and announce the signal that a special process of interpretation is called for and the players carry a double consciousness: *The play is both about itself and about the world*

transformed by the play (Bateson, 1972; Schwartzman, 1978, pp. 232–247).

Knowledge of this world transformed in play is fundamental to the game or play that remains in the heads of players. Taking roles and elaborating in metalinguistic ways what those roles mean to other roles in the game or drama reminds individuals of their interdependence and the need for negotiations in which players must shift identities, positions, and roles for the benefit of the performance. Turner has suggested that in many cases, the presence of conflict situations leads to a high frequency of ritual performances, and decisions to perform rituals are especially connected with crises in the social life of the group.

Because all of the youth in these organizations carry a keen awareness of crises, turbulence, violence, and pain in the streets, their reasons for entering the "safe place" of the organizations and accepting the heavily ritualized behaviors there often lie in their sense of being out of control elsewhere or living in places and with people whose loss of control continually threatens. Thus, for the youth within the inner-city neighborhood organizations, the crises and conflict situations lie in the known but rarely named features of the environment beyond the walls of the "safe place" of the youth organizations. Among team members within these organizations, rituals first re-costume and rename individuals to mark them as part of the collectivity. Some organizations insist that certain items of clothing not be worn within the institution (hats, bandannas, belts, street shoes, etc.); other groups insist that young people put on club T-shirts at the door. Within the neighborhood-based organizations, members acquire nicknames or special pronunciations of their street names, and joking with such names provides much of the casual banter of the group. Through change of costume, shift of language, and focus on constitutive rules (those that create the game or play), group members structure themselves around other rituals that mark numerous aspects of daily experience within the organization.

Unspoken rules apply as well. Almost no talk of life on the street or beyond the walls of the youth organization takes place; the work of the group organizes the talk as well as the flow of activity. Consistently, the *we* of the group members' talk is the *we* of the group or the activity. When each group convenes, it brings forth similar frames for the organization of time and the focus on task; performances, such as games, recitals, or dramas, do not compose the essential ritual, but are merely part of the process of ritual membership over a particular season or time of preparation for the peak performance before outsiders. Members work themselves into a frenzy of top performance for the culminating events, but their rituals remain stable throughout the season until such occasions. Practices begin in certain ways: leader eventcast of the day (sometimes called "run-downs"), exercises, regrouping, enactment of some version of the ultimate performance (practice game, run-through of act one, etc.), and summation with projection to the next practice's events and goals.

Leaders tell young people: "Play it like the pros. You know how the pros do it; you can do it." By playing and performing through the narrative of such identities, new actualities come into existence; young learners come to accept that their play is not fiction, "only unrealized actuality" (Schechner, 1986, p. 363). Practice sessions, walks, moves, attitudes, costume, and attitude are self-consciously imitated, replayed, and recaptured in narrative and one-liner reminders. Each individual is called upon to "play like a pro" while at the same time recognizing that over the season, the progress and pattern of each individual's activities will be shaped as part of the larger picture—the group's record of success or failure. The choice of any individual as pitcher, catcher, or shortstop; forward or guard; or lead-player or dancer rather than chorus member emerges over the first weeks of practice, with numerous assignments of possible "fill-ins" or "backups." Moving up depends on readiness; moving down depends on activities that indicate lack of adherence to groups norms of collective identity.

Leaders and players value diversity within the group. To have everyone of the same level of ability in the same set of skills could be disastrous to the group's goals. Being short works well for some dramatic parts of positions on the baseball or softball field; having a husky voice fits a character in a particular play. Having several abilities of moderate level benefits the group far more than having special talent in only one area. Team members are frequently asked by leaders: "What can you do? Show me." Leaders do not set particular levels of performance arbitrarily and assess individuals by their ability to meet these predetermined levels. Often leaders tell the group that in a particular game or performance, they exceeded anything he or she might have expected of them: "You outdid yourselves"; "You sure fooled me— I never thought you could pull it off."

The narratives the young people tell of their experiences within the group work as "rituals of intensification" of their membership—much the same as family reunions or class reunions do. In addition, these narratives give an opportunity for the young to replay events in which they have taken part; as they retell stories of their own actions and events, they learn as well as teach those who listen. Both leaders and team members tell such stories at regular intervals. These narratives, over time, become those of individuals' portrayals of themselves beyond the organization's walls. Leaders elaborate on their hope that these narratives will come to contradict and replace those in which youths often hear themselves characterized as products of "broken" families, "criminals waiting to happen," "street kids," "school dropouts," and "societal problems." The new narratives of self rest in direct and shared experiences *and* repeated practice of not only actions but also team narratives jointly constructed as in (5), above. These narratives order, mold, and shape a motif of progress, of getting better and smarter, of learning more, and of taking up new strategies, but transformations or exceptionality mark these autobiographical (of self) and biographical (of group) accounts.

When told by leaders as bits of embedding in practice overviews or team warm-up, the progress motif and the relationship of the here and now to life "out there" stand out clearly.

(6) There's rules to be followed. You
     gotta follow 'em in life, you're
     gonna have to follow 'em in baseball.
     You don't do what you wanna do.
     And the next one that talks, I'm
     gonna pull out of the line [pause].
     It's one thing you learn, you have to
     listen. In any phase of life, you
     have to listen, and follow rules and
     follow orders. I do. There's people
     tell me what to do and I listen. That's
     part of life. Now next week. I see
     a lot of progress in a lot of you. A
     lot of you are doing very good. By
     the time we get out on that field
     you'll be very good ball players,
     because I'm seeing a lot of progress.

Such direct connections between the course of
the team and the demands of life beyond the
game come early in the season and help make
clear the ethos of the group to newcomers.

HOW LEADERS
USE STORYTELLING TO
CHALLENGE THINKING

▼

Leaders in youth organizations use stories to
build thinking skills in young people. Because
most of the narrative that leaders and team members tell during the season have been lived by
group members, they are fully comprehended
before the telling, as well as often reenacted and
reinterpreted, and even reshaped, through their
joint hearing and retelling. Having been a part
of such tales makes these stories more pleasurable
in the hearing, analogous to the pleasure that
young children have of being told stories of themselves as infants or of last week's antics. These
retellings build myths through remaking practices
and performance, always encouraging the reflex-
ive potential of the youths and pulling them forward to improved performance. Yet such
narratives are also describing problem solving,
seeking to explain or to interpret, and therefore

filled with the language of logical inference
(because, so, not). They also include qualifications
of knowledge states (probably, maybe, and other
hedges or modals, such as might, could). As Collins
Block (in Chapter 6) and Feldman (1989) report,
problem-solving talk for the self that comes in
rich storylike frames is one of the best ways to
practice identifying and solving problems. If we
view the full play of the dramatic group, choir,
softball or basketball team as such a story—complete with beginning, middle, and end, as well as
a projected happy ending—then the pragmatic
activities of youth-based organizations, along
with the narratives that extend their events, may
be seen as exemplary sites of "everyday reasoning"
or "practical intelligence" (Stern & Wagner,
1986).

The openness of such stories for reapplication
appears in the fact that one-liners from the most
dramatic stories often emerge as reminders long
after the players and events of the original narrative have been forgotten. Thus, retellings actually
become foretellings, active ways of constituting
the future through a process of both experience
and expectation. Moreover, young people in
youth organizations work and play in groups that
vary in age, sometimes by only a few years, and
at other times by as much as 10 years. The expectation is that no one learns anything just for the
self as individual; all are teachers, role models, as
well as explainers and evaluators. Young dancers,
ballplayers, or tumblers apprentice themselves to
older youngsters, often working out routines or
plays together and practicing these again and
again. Learning is to be multiplied; this is perhaps
the central ethos of youth-based organizations.

For those groups involved in creating works of
art—dramatic performances, story-based dances
(such as Ballet Folklorico), creative shows of tumbling feats—there is an intensity of continuity
between these occasions of refined and practiced
experiences and their own everyday experiences
of suffering, struggling against poverty and unpredictable behaviors from family and friends, as well
as dealing with authorities ranging from school
personnel to police. Thus, though the young are
told again and again that they are "pros" and

"special" through their organizational group membership, they also use their art experiences in particular to reconstitute themselves by drawing from what they have experienced beyond the walls of the organization. For example, dramatic scripts or murals fashioned by the youths frequently center around the tragedies of drugs, violence, crime, and thwarted expectations of love. In creating these scripts or scenes, as well as their performances, the believability of both text and performance lies in the youngsters' abilities to build from, and agree jointly to, the transactional power of what they know outside to be a "safe place."

Filtered through the activities that lead toward performance in youth-based organizations is the central frame of "as if." The talk of leaders swirls with hypotheticals—"if . . . , then . . . " constructions, as in (7), or sociodramatic bids ("It's opening night, Jamie's sprained an ankle, and Susie, you're coming on in her place . . . ")—as well as invokes the imagination or the playful thinking of the youth, as in (8).

(7) If somebody, if somebody else goes in your place . . .

If we don't run and stop playin' . . .

If it is a charge and [if] the referee calls a . . .

If you don't take a charge . . .

If he wants you right there . . .

If you just let him run right across . . .

(8) Think, it's gonna be a good game.

Think, we can take these guys.

Think to yourself, Taurus, you and Tubb, and Pierre . . .

Youths check out what they are to do by asking or making "if . . . , then . . ." questions or statements.

(9) If it hit off the plate, it is, if it hits off the . . .

If you going so fast, how do you swing the . . .

If he pitch one of them low balls, then . . .

If the ball is comin' to you, . . .

During actual practice sessions (as opposed to opening or recapping narratives), approximately 80% of the utterances of more than five words ask "what if" questions. Of the "if . . . , then . . ." constructions of the youths themselves, about 95% are not counterfactual; they carry low conjecture and future time reference (as opposed to high conjecture with no time reference, e.g., "if only we had a thousand bucks, then we could all wear gold uniforms"). Thus, though the full frame for their activities within the youth organizations is that of *play*, they keep the realities of the current scene clearly in mind, and their hypotheticals work to give them direction and allow them assertions or knowledge displays.

(10) Then they can take it in bounds . . .

Then you'll get to play that position, and eventually you'll . . .

Then, then it was up there and you ran up . . .

Such statements have a place in our classrooms. In youth organizations, each young person's actions play a role in the daily discourse of the organization, and the conditional constructions and sociodramatic bids allow the leaders and players to make inferences that try out on a "small-scale" model the external reality that individuals carry around in their heads (Heath & Langman, in press).

PROJECTIONS BEYOND AND TO THE FUTURE FOR SCHOOLS

Individual experience, along with a stable frame for action, are illusions created by myths of stability and developmental progress through life. Formal educational teaching and learning reinforce these myths, as do models of socialization. In addition, both these myths and models ignore the realities of everyday learning and most especially the conditions of inner-city families and communities. There, young people are not adolescents becoming adults, but often young bodies and minds with an erratic array of adult experiences and responsibilities. Many of these young people learn very early through abrupt and traumatic transformational experiences that school and public media portrayals of happy families, steady development, and secure life paths do not match their experiences.

Within youth-based organizations, transformations are muted through a framework of transitions and transferrals and narrated by continuous talk about changes, ranging from transferrals of positions on the field or on the stage to sharp reversals in the fortunes of the team's luck. It is in the enacting of play and the telling and retelling of play's stories that young people reflect, analyze, and reinvent themselves and their contexts. Problem solving and play—through entry into a hypothetical world and numerous conditional scenarios—enable young people to see themselves as part of an interdependent collective.

What can be made of what we learn about learning in youth-based organizations for schools or other formal learning environments? Several key contrasts stand between these organizations and formal learning environments.

1. Effective youth organizations have open frames for learning and make learning and mindfulness possible primarily through demonstration, apprenticeship, extensive practice, and peer evaluation. These four learning approaches need to become a part of our school curriculum.

2. Youth organizations place the control of knowledge within the group as team members committed to a central goal. Knowledge and skills blend together: the facts of a myth for a Ballet Folklorico dance go along with skill in specific dance routines. Placing knowledge within

a context of a group-established goal is a valuable learning tool.

3. Learning is cumulative, multidirectional, and displayed through a variety of different kinds of symbols—verbal, kinesthetic, musical, and visual. Individual learners who want to practice on their own usually have access to the youth organization's space or to other team members outside regular times of meeting or scheduled practices and events. Reallocations of time, space, and resources in schools can accomplish similar ends.

4. Learning and thinking of the self as a learner for a set of purposes and goals of joint identification become synonymous with one's life, just as knowing oneself as a member of a family unconsciously merges with an individual sense of identity. When such merging occurs through schooling, our educational system will have achieved its goal.

Formal learning situations in school reverberate with verbal symbols—often primarily from the expert designated as "teacher" within a group of novices at the same age and stage of learning. Displays of knowledge on the part of novices must usually come through written forms and only sometimes through oral explanation and demonstration. Few are the opportunities to practice extensively in a team atmosphere bristling with motivation to succeed in an upcoming performance. Authentic audiences and evaluators rarely enter formal classrooms to assess the accomplishments of either the group as a whole or of small groups working on special projects within the class. Formal learning and teaching usually fit in proscribed times and adhere to prescribed routines, criteria of expertise, and judgments of individual knowledge through a narrow band of assessment tools and criteria for judging success.

What might schooling be like if some of its formal educational and structural features could be replaced by those of effective youth organizations? At the heart of such change would be the centrality of fostering thinking and of being a member of a learning, performing group. Let's imagine a kindergarten through secondary-school experience of this sort.

Spaces and Times of Learning

Schools would become clearing houses for learning and thinking activities that would take place in a variety of other places as well: museums, playgrounds, city halls, libraries, and business places. Schools would be available 50 weeks of the year, and open from early morning until early evening.

Agents for Learning and Teaching

Youngsters across ages would know that their learning was to flow back into their social relations with their peers and younger learners. Trained teachers in specific subject matter (such as mathematics, language, science, and social studies) would be complemented by leaders from community-based organizations with special talents in sports, arts, environmental studies, etc. Teachers would work eight hours a day, but only six hours with students and two hours in planning and coordination with community and business leaders also involved in "public education." Adults from a wide range of businesses and from public service agencies would have responsibilities for extending the domains and the places of learning of students.

Content and Methods of Learning

Science, mathematics, social sciences, and language would range from direct research to lecture. Students would need to display their knowledge and skills through written *and* oral language, as well as in various other forms of representations: graphs and diagrams, demonstrations and reenactments, and, for older students, through photography and videotape. Work would be developed both through solo individual effort *and* through cooperative enterprises, involving students of different ages in projects and design experiments.

Assessment

Each team of youngsters staying together over four years (K–grade 4, grades 5–9, and grades 10–12) would have a team of evaluators and counselors made up of subject matter teachers, youth leaders, and representatives from the businesses and public service agencies with whom the students would work. Forms of assessment would be multiple, as would be the agents. All students from kindergarten up would prepare every 9 to 12 weeks, a piece of writing summarizing their sense of where they currently stood as a learner, where they would like to move, and how they planned to do so. These materials, as well as a range of types of evaluations from others, would be included in the personnel binder that would accompany each child throughout his or her academic career—and into initial entry into the workplace.

Children of the ages we now associate with kindergarten through fourth grade would stay together as intact groups of 15 with the same core teacher. Each of these groups would be paired with a group of the same number and of the ages we now associate with grades five through eight. For a portion of several days each week, these paired groups would work in small groups on projects related to science, mathematics, or social sciences, with these projects reaching culmination and performance or public display every 9 to 12 weeks. Older students would stay together as a group, with the same core teacher for three-year terms. Places for carrying out these projects would include the school as well as local community settings: senior citizen centers, libraries, hospitals, and airports. All projects would require display through a variety of means of representations, ranging from written materials to photography, painting, and model-building.

INTEGRATION OF CONTENT INFORMATION AND LEARNING STRATEGIES

Everyday learning in sports and music, in particular, would be closely integrated with mathematics and science and would be handled by leaders from youth-based organizations. For example, during certain seasons of the year, as older youth took part in sports events or preparation for recitals or audition tapes, these young people would work solely on practice and preparation for their sport or art each morning, with afternoons given over to science and mathematics projects related to their particular music or sport. For example, if during morning weight training for soccer players, certain students were monitored for change in heart rate, body temperature, etc., these changes would be analyzed in comparison with similar records of other students of different weight, sex, and level of training. Similar projects on the physics of sound, the mathematics of music, and the chemistry of particular metals in combination would occupy young people during their afternoons of study. Late afternoons could be times for the study of various types of writing related to sports and music: biography, fiction, poetry, and history.

LEARNING AND THE TRANSITION TO WORK

All students 14 and older would take part in two, six-week work-study programs—one each in some kind of public service job and the other in any of a range of types of commercial or business enterprise. For four to six hours each day, students would intern or apprentice in teams of two, while several hours each day would be given over to reports on the work that would analyze three key features: decision-making and experimenting strategies, uses of language and mathematics, and features of person-to-person activities and events. Once each week, one or more members of the public service or business establishment would debrief with the students to go over write-ups of these features.

Every business taking part in this truly *public education* would receive tax benefits from the state; the eventual goal would be that all businesses would commit 1% of their time, staff, and resources to some form of public education. Initially, those businesses for which the presence of young people would pose a hazard or security risk could obtain similar tax benefits by providing four hours of paid volunteer time for 1% of their employees to participate within the school sites, demonstrating with students examples of the uses of language and mathematics on the job. Other businesses with large land holdings could receive similar tax benefits by making portions of their holdings open for environmental fieldtrips and locations of biology field stations with accompanying campsites in which teams of young people would study for several weeks of the school year. A proportion of all former military bases would be reconfigured as environmental science centers, with barracks available for housing year-round in rotation for students in six-week terms of study in field experiments that include lectures and demonstrations by resident employees.

This futuristic vision of learning—all day, all year in many places, with multiple teachers and learners, and with numerous ways of displaying knowledge—creates a seamless life of thinking development and learning. Students learn how science, language, and mathematics slip into and out of all types of work, bureaucracy, sport, and esthetic activity. Expertise is something that many people have about a whole host of subjects, skills, and institutions. The 50-week, 10-hours-a-day-of-learning plan coincides with the realities of the work patterns of most working adults, relieving the need for latchkey programs or after-school sports and music programs available only for those who can afford to pay and have transportation available. The plan here for year-round schooling provides for a series of different types of activities and places of learning throughout the year, so that the school and the classroom become only one site for learning. These are joined by community resources (such as museums and libraries), businesses, natural parks, sports and music camps of all types, and youth organizations. Play and work can, in this full round of learning, come to be seen as intensely related; every sports person, as well as every musician, must know something of the science, history, and mathematics of specific athletic endeavors and types of music, dance, or theater.

In the poet Wallace Stevens' words, much of what goes on in youth-based organizations or in these imagined learning times and places of the future does "glitter." It is staggering within our current frames of thinking about schooling to imagine environments of learning in which leaders bind with youngsters to lead them through jointly planned projects and performances—seasons of commitment. These leaders and the youngsters hold each other to high standards *for the group and the project outcome*. Verbal and non-verbal positive reinforcements, as well as strict discipline and intense practice, mediate the activities of the learners and build an everyday ecology of learning and belonging—a total sense of mindfulness.

But why should lessons or models be drawn for the learning of all youth from close-up, long-term studies of inner-city youth organizations? The youngsters who sustain some relationship with these organizations emerge as capable, responsible adults in work and family relations. Young people followed over five years after their entry into these groups held to a center of self-respect that moved them into jobs and further training, as well as into stable relationships in their social lives. They repeatedly reported that they had "learned about learning" and "about what life is all about" from their institutional membership in activities that embraced them as planners, performers, and assessors. These patterns echo those of others who have studied the effects of the arts on academic performance, problem solving, and persistence (Hanna, 1992).

Aside from the imminent proximity of violence and the pervasiveness of poverty, the lives of inner-city youngsters do not differ greatly from those of other young people at the end of the 20th century. All either have or will face drastic transformations in personal and work relations. All find themselves in families and schools that increasingly cannot meet their needs. All will face work environments that demand competent decision-making, problem-solving, and communication skills that must be demonstrated in cooperative work teams, moving through transitions created by new technologies, changes in the global economy, and new demands for quality and efficiency.

The close look available in this chapter at the life of youth-based organizations offers an inside view from which to begin thinking about what the "everyday mind" at work and play could be. The descriptions here of youth organizations give more than a hint of the nitty-gritty, the nuts and bolts, of what it takes to create an optimal learning context that motivates and inspires young people, as well as prepares them for the transitions and transformations ahead. The soul of learning is not in textbooks, curricula, buildings, technology, or in fads and fashions. It is instead in another place—in small encounters, tiny favors, and diversity and continuity of experiences. It is in the firm, steady direction of teachers as leaders, facilitators, learners, and experts—all wrapped together. It is in long-term projects that are cyclical; each season brings improvement and higher demands as well as new technology. It is, as we have seen in youth organizations, in a consistent call to use the mind, to think and plan ahead, to tie rules and practice together. It is perhaps most embedded in multiple opportunities to help others learn and to move the group along in accomplishing performances that will hold up to the scrutiny of judgment by a range of evaluators.

These fundamentals of identification shape *will* and *fate*, but they also transform young people through fate by cushioning them through transitions and offering them safe passage through a collective identity and memory. Theirs is a community of belief, a belief that turns inward to the group itself—to its purposes, potential, and power as a collective that prizes its individual members as learners. This community is one of belief that builds strong identity in and through learning, and it enables youngsters to turn outward—through work institutions and the bureaucracy of adult life—to sustain a sense of integrity, centeredness, and continuity.

REFERENCES

Bateson, G. (1972). *Steps to an ecology of mind*. New York: Ballantine.

Feldman, C. F. (1989). Monologue as problem-solving narrative. In K. Nelson (Ed.), *Narratives from the crib*. Cambridge, MA: Harvard University Press.

Hanna, J. L. (1992). Connections: Arts, academics, and productive citizens. *Phi Delta Kappan, 73*(8), 601–607.

Heath, S.B., & Langman, J. (in press). Shared thinking and the register of coaching. In D. Biber & E. Finnegan (EDs.), *Perspectives on register*. New York: Oxford University Press.

Heath, S. B., & McLaughlin, M. W. (in press). *Possible selves: Achievement, ethnicity, and gender for inner-city youth*. New York: Teachers College Press.

Irby, M. A. (1991). Black with an eager mind: The design of diversity in a neighborhood-based organization. *Future Choices, 3*, 55–64.

Irby, M. A., & McLaughlin, M. W. (1990). *Future Choices, 2*, 31–40.

Schechner, R. (1985). *Between theater and anthropology*. Philadelphia: University of Pennsylvania Press.

Schechner, R. (1986). Victor Turner's last adventure. In V. Turner (Ed.), *The Anthropology of performance*. New York: Performing Arts Journal Press.

Schwartzman, H. B. (1978). *Transformations: The anthropology of children's play*. New York: Plenum Press.

Sternberg, R. J., & Wagner, R. K. (1986). *Practical intelligence: Nature and origins of competence in the everyday world*. Cambridge, MA: Harvard University Press.

Tannen, D. (1989). *Talking voices: Repetition, dialogue, and imagery in conversational discourse*. New York: Cambridge University Press.

Turner, V. (1969). *The ritual process*. Chicago: Aldine.

Wertsch, J. V. (1991). *Voices of the mind: A sociocultural approach to mediated action*. Cambridge, MA: Harvard University Press.

The work upon which the following chapter is based was funded in part by the Office of Educational Research and Improvement (OERI), U.S. Department of Education. The opinions expressed in this publication do not necessarily reflect the position or policy of OERI, and no official endorsement by OERI should be inferred.

CHAPTER ELEVEN

COGNITIVE DEVELOPMENT THROUGH RADICAL CHANGE

RESTRUCTURING CLASSROOM ENVIRONMENTS FOR STUDENTS AT RISK

BARBARA Z. PRESSEISEN

RESEARCH FOR BETTER SCHOOLS, INC.

BARBARA SMEY-RICHMAN

RESEARCH FOR BETTER SCHOOLS, INC.

FRANCINE S. BEYER

RESEARCH FOR BETTER SCHOOLS, INC.

Dr. Barbara Z. Presseisen is director of national networking at Research for Better Schools (RBS) in Philadelphia. Her primary responsibilities involve coordinating RBS's role in the cross-laboratory collaboration projects with the 10 regional laboratories and national organizations, and taking essential leadership within RBS in the preparation of instructional improvement materials and staff development efforts related to cognitive development, curriculum integration, and thinking skills improvement. Dr. Presseisen works with several large city school districts and serves as consultant to numerous educational organizations. She has published several books and many articles both in the United States and abroad.

Dr. Barbara Smey-Richman is a Research for Better Schools (RBS) liaison with state departments of education within the mid-Atlantic region. She has written extensively on the topic of low-achieving students and has presented a variety of workshops for teachers and administrators on how to reorganize schools and classrooms to address the needs of students who perform poorly. For more than two decades, Dr. Smey-Richman has participated in a wide range of school reform efforts as a classroom teacher, ESEA Title IV-C project director, and external educational consultant.

Dr. Francine S. Beyer is a senior research associate at Research for Better Schools (RBS), where her eight years of experience have included designing and conducting program evaluations for educators at the school, district, and state levels and the development of a number of assessment instruments. Dr. Beyer is also editor of the *Teaching Thinking and Problem Solving* newsletter, recently recognized by EDPRESS for the high quality of its editorial and design elements. Dr. Beyer's previous positions have been with the Institute of Educational Research, the District of Columbia Public Schools, and Bell Laboratories.

For nearly a decade, American education has been engaged in a major examination of how to reform itself. Report upon report have detailed the need, if not the alternative paradigms, for extensive revamping of the goals, means, and outcomes of preparing graduates for a new world and a new century (Adler, 1982; Goodlad, 1984; Sizer, 1984). What was previously "school reform" or "educational improvement" has become a demand to "restructure" the entire system—not merely tinker with but radically redesign current, less-than-viable models.

At the same time, government officials, business leaders, and various educational researchers have contributed views of the specific problems they believe need to be addressed in this extraordinary effort (Carnevale, 1991; Conley, 1991; McDonnell, 1989; Schlechty, 1990). They are eager to suggest solutions they believe show promise for needed school change. In terms of educational activity, a great deal of this energy has been expended since the publication of *A Nation at Risk* (National Commission, 1983). Now the time is ripe to see how well focused this era of educational reform has become. Does it make a difference to teachers and students in the classroom? Does it serve the neediest as well as the most accomplished students in America's schools? Is there a national consensus as to how the nation's schools should change, and *why*?

THE PROBLEM OF RADICAL CHANGE

▼

Although restructuring education means different things according to different perspectives, the larger dimensions of current demands for change are fairly well agreed upon. "Dynamic and unanticipated global changes of a profound sort are shaping the world," says one report (Council of Chief State School Officers, 1991, p. 1), and with these changes come necessary shifts in political, economic, and social structures. The first aspect of restructuring suggests education must keep up with the global workplace and help American institutions prepare *all* employees for the higher-level skills required in an increasingly technological, computerized world (Secretary's Commission, 1991). Over the long haul, and into the 21st century, some say America must attend to the many complex transitions in its postindustrial economy or its workers may be forced to accept the alternative of lower wages and lesser work (Commission on the Skills of the American Workforce, 1990). On the heels of Russia's disintegration and with the realities of Japanese competition, America's reform educators seek a new paradigm for the nation's schools that will enable the nation to retain, or regain, its worldwide competitiveness.

A different understanding of learning is a second aspect that marks the vision of a restructured school, and with it a keener insight into the development of human potential (Dickinson, 1991; Feuerstein, 1990). The more traditional outcomes of America's school in the 20th century—academic success for some and marginal failure for many—are now held in grave doubt and are considered inherently unequal (Darling-Hammond, 1990). Many reformers maintain that workers at all levels must develop the abilities to learn more easily and adapt flexibly to new circumstances. Whether college bound or workplace directed, every citizen will need to be able to read complex materials, understand them, and apply multiple skills of literacy and numeracy to tasks associated with such materials (Brown, 1991a; Zuboff, 1988). Today, the "one-literacy schoolhouse," where knowledge is merely collected in a narrow, cumulative framework and then tested by traditional psychometric means, is as outmoded as a communication system dominated by print or a government insensitive to the influence of mass media.

Underlying this new appreciation for learning is an assumption regarding the importance of the learner's *active participation* in restructured schooling, as though the end of the century has somehow returned to John Dewey's (1964) initial vision of education and democracy (Glickman, 1991; Presseisen, 1991). The role of individual development and the significance of authentic student achievement in building intellectual competence are restructuring issues underscored in this context (Newmann, 1991). Being educated today requires that what is studied at school must mean something to the learner and change his or her perspective about the topic under examination; it calls for a particular knowledge base that is intellectually dealt with and, ultimately, reconceived. The relatively short time spent at school—compared to other activities in which students are engaged, such as television viewing—must reach far beyond:

> . . . the basic decoding and encoding, even beyond basic factual knowledge, to encompass understanding how different people know what they know, communicate, think, and attack problems. Always implicit—and explicit—is the assumption that one cannot acquire such an understanding without *practicing* [emphasis added] the requisite kinds of thinking, communicating, and problem solving. (Brown, 1991b, p. 142)

In one sense, restructured schooling means that the very definition of school is being reformulated. In terms of learning experience, school occupies a unique juncture between initial rearing in the home and community and ultimate performance in the world of work. In the dynamic framework of change and the growing sophistication of the global marketplace, schools are emerging as special locales for creating and refining learner competencies. To be effective, educational institutions are now also required to become human resource development centers, not mere sorters of ability. In particular, schools must address the learning needs of every student, even those historically most poorly served.

In this new view of education, there is an assumption that schooling must be involved in the enhancement of every student's learning potential. The primary focus of this chapter addresses the concerns of both Hodgkinson (1985, 1991) and Hilliard (1991); that is, how can school environments be restructured to address the key requisites of the *cognitive development* of every youngster in America, including those most at risk of school failure? As the recent riots in Los Angeles indicate—in terms of the changing demographics and severe deprivations affecting the school populations of America's major cities—if we have the will to educate all our children, then we must address this question. The historic concerns related to changing American schooling and the research underlying them are the focus of the following section, after which the essential elements of a restructured classroom environment are examined in depth. The chapter then presents implications of this examination for at-risk students and their learning. The final section summarizes the findings of the study and projects needed future research and development.

HISTORIC CONCERNS AND RESTRUCTURING

Ideas about reforming America's schools are rooted in various historic issues that influence changes in many social institutions. Four areas of concern are relevant to the focus of this study: an understanding of the roots of the cognitive revolution, the impetus of the current teaching thinking movement, the nature of restructured classroom environments for learning, and the needs of a burgeoning, at-risk student population in our nation's public schools. It is proposed that research and analyses of these topics form a basis for understanding the needed alterations in American schooling.

THE ROOTS OF THE COGNITIVE REVOLUTION

To understand the various viewpoints of restructured schooling, one needs to appreciate the impact of the so-called "cognitive revolution" that occurred during the second half of the 20th century, as will be described in Chapter 12 (Baars, 1986; Gardner, 1985). Cognition is a branch of psychology that gradually has become a discrete science on its own. As an interdisciplinary approach, it offers new ways of examining mind and mental processes in humans, other animals, and even machines. Studies of intelligence (natural and artificial), memory, brain research, and creativity in many contexts are only a part of the emergent literature on cognition (Diamond, 1988; Gardner, 1985; Penrose, 1989). "The word 'cognitive' may suggest that this field deals not with the whole mind but only with knowledge, including perception, reasoning, language, and even learning," says Boden (1990, p. 9). But cognitive scientists also seek to explain purpose, emotion, and even consciousness. In cognitive neuroscience, the special connections between mind and brain are pursued as related parts of an integrated, intelligent system (Miller, 1989). It is not surprising that schools—as generators of thoughtful learners—would find much to explore in the field of cognitive science. But such a relationship has not always been in fashion and, currently, many schools remain unaware of this content and its implications for curriculum, instruction, and assessment.

For a long time, developmental psychologists were the lone voices interested in the importance of cognition for schooling. With them, some early childhood specialists and special educators stood opposed to an educational psychology—particularly as practiced in the United States—marked by static behaviorism and mechanistic theory (Baars, 1986; Elkind, 1979). The focus on the developing learner, the explicit instruction of thinking and metacognition, and the critical importance of learners' dispositions and attitudes, as well as the emphasis on the social context of intellectual change, have all been outcomes of the new hegemony of cognition in the world of teaching and learning (Collins, Brown, & Holum, 1991). At the same time, however, teacher preparation and program evaluation research resisted these new modes (Beyer, 1988; Detterman & Sternberg, 1982; Dillon & Sternberg, 1986; Resnick & Klopfer, 1989; Sternberg, 1982). Today, educational research is rediscovering the works of Vygotsky (Kozulin, 1990; Lipman, 1991; Moll, 1992; Wertsch, 1985) and Feuerstein (Jones & Pierce, 1992; Lidz, 1987; Presseisen & Kozulin, 1992; Sharron, 1987). It is confronted by a rich literature on cognition which maintains that thinking and comprehension actually can be taught to all children (Bransford & Vye, 1989; Haller, Child, & Walberg, 1988). Thus, says Costa (1991), if restructured schools are inherently places of cognitive development, they must—by definition—also be organized as institutions that are "homes for the mind."

Restructured schools, in this view, are places in which teachers strive to be cognitively creative in their instruction, where, as lifelong learners themselves, they seek to refine their professional ability to enhance every student's autonomy and ability to think, and where they constantly seek to create conditions for optimal student achievement. This is the heart of the new cognitive paradigm in education. It is a model that stresses the explicit need to teach students thinking—albeit in particular contents—and to focus on intellectual concerns as the central purpose of schooling.

THE TEACHING THINKING MOVEMENT

The teaching of "thinking" to all students in school is a relatively new concept in education, although the general goal of thoughtfulness has long been a hallmark in liberal education (Paul, 1987; Resnick, 1987a). Essentially, the current movement developed to counter the "back to basics" view as an inadequate goal for youngsters who will work most of their adult lives in the 21st century. Teaching thinking first and foremost involves cognitive outcomes; it seeks to make learners more successful in their academic achievement by helping *all* students to improve their intellectual ability. The movement also seeks student autonomy and independence of thought as an ultimate aim (Kamii, 1984).

Advocates of teaching thinking have proposed the instruction of various specific cognitive operations or skills (Beyer, 1988; Marzano et al., 1988) and the advancement of subjective dispositions (Ennis, 1991). Comprehensive listings of these processes vary according to specific objectives, such as a goal for critical thinking expertise, creative design outcomes, or problem-solving strategies. Whatever the specific objective, several key assumptions are usually operative in all teaching thinking efforts: (a) the student needs to be actively involved in *using* the particular skills, so that his or her adaptation and control over the processes increase; (b) intervention or instruction planned for the learner should be tailored to meet his or her distinctive needs, should involve social interaction as well as personal reflection (especially as facilitated by a more knowledgeable mediator), and should aim to develop the mental potential of the learner as far as possible (Feuerstein, 1990); and (c) knowledge areas

within the curriculum should be integrated with the thinking operations as quickly as possible and be applied in varying contexts and settings (Collins, Brown, & Holum, 1991; Nickerson, 1986).

Teaching thinking is associated with multiple literacies and generally focuses on higher-level content, even for young children (Brown, 1991b; Eisner, 1982). The mere coverage of subject matter, the heart of the old paradigm of schooling, has been replaced as a goal for all learners by deeper understanding of disciplinary constructs, more sophisticated problem-solving strategies, and an awareness of alternate approaches to characterizing particular subject matters. The current thinking movement seeks to make students adept at building connections among similar constructs and, ultimately, aims at operational, if not systematic, transfer among similarly patterned knowledge areas (Perkins & Salomon, 1988; Sternberg, 1990a). Domain-specific knowledge combined with higher ability in science, for example, is projected to help students develop both a conceptual and a practical understanding of scientific reasoning and inquiry that goes far beyond the memorization of discrete facts or even carefully assembled, but rote-learned, "experiments" (Adey, 1990).

There are a variety of approaches to implementing teaching thinking in the school's curriculum (Presseisen, 1992). In one sense, every academic area has sought to make its subject more thoughtful and students more strategic. These applications have benefitted a great deal from specific thinking programs that have been developed by researchers seeking particular objectives, such as teaching philosophy and reasoning (Lipman, Sharp, & Oscanyan, 1980), remediating particular cognitive dysfunctions (Feuerstein, 1980), and developing critical thinking ability (Pogrow, 1992; Winocur, 1986). The impact of these programs has been the subject of various research-based examinations (Chance, 1986; Sternberg & Bhana, 1986). Although these efforts have been found to be generally effective, more objective and extensive research is still needed. Training for these programs and various support efforts to aid their implementation are currently being conducted across the United States, as well as around the world (Presseisen, 1992).

It must be remembered that teaching thinking is a revolution in process. Although keenly intertwined with the movement to reform educational practice, and talked about extensively in educational research literature, there is no guarantee that it is a revolution that will succeed. Much depends on whether schools are successfully restructured and what is focused upon in that transformation.

RESTRUCTURED ENVIRONMENTS FOR LEARNING

Although there is no concise, commonly held definition of restructuring, nor a single model that can be universally applied, there is general agreement on what counts as school restructuring and what does not (Harvey & Crandall, 1988; Smey-Richman, 1991). Since restructuring advocates believe that schools in their current form are performing about as well as possible, restructuring is not aimed at adding more of the same or making significant improvements to the current structure (Goodlad, 1984; Schlechty, 1989). Rather, restructuring involves altering a school's pattern of rules, roles, and relationships—both within one building and among the several schools in a district—in order to produce substantially different results from those currently obtained (Corbett, 1990; Schlechty, 1989; Sparks, 1991; Wilson, 1971). The shared belief that the current system must be dramatically rethought and redesigned to be more effective underlies all discussions about school restructuring. Herein lie the ties to both the cognitive revolution and the goal to teach intellectual skills.

The attractiveness of restructuring as a theme for educational reform may stem from its ability to "accommodate a variety of conceptions of what is problematical about American education, as well as a variety of solutions" (Elmore, 1991, p. 4). Since opinions vary, a number of schemes for categorizing restructuring activities have been proposed (Council of Chief State School Officers,

1989; David, 1987; Elmore, 1988; McDonnell, 1989). These schemes usually include three main themes: (1) focusing on teaching academic subject matter in ways that promote understanding and problem solving; (2) shifting power toward individual schools and the people who work in them; and (3) ensuring the accountability of educators to their clients and to the broader public (Elmore, 1991). Thus, reformers have focused on four broad dimensions of restructuring: curriculum and instruction, authority and decision making, new professional roles for teachers; and accountability systems (David, 1987). A fifth dimension, collaboration with others, is also often added (Smey-Richman, 1991).

While for analytic purposes it is useful to treat each restructuring dimension separately, in practice reform proposals frequently address more than one dimension simultaneously. Also, regarding practice, the overarching criteria for judging the potential effectiveness of a reform effort lies in its link to student achievement and other desirable student outcomes. Choosing a single dimension as a point of departure for school restructuring has serious implications for both the process of reform and anticipated results (Elmore, 1991; McDonnell, 1989). Furthermore, changes in one dimension are not always consistent with changes in the others.

In several restructuring schemes, curriculum, instruction, and assessment are the three central school variables examined because they focus most directly on student learning (Conley, 1991). They are also the key concerns of a teacher's behavior and understanding in creating a seminal environment for intellectual change. If one were to restructure the classroom environment as the major point of teacher-student-learning interaction, what would such an experience look like? Presseisen (1992) suggests:

> The construct of a "learning environment" is an important concept on the road to intervention. Environment is more than mere surroundings or the "climate" of a classroom. A learning environment amply provides social opportunities for instruction, and when mutual and reciprocal, for learning. Such an

environment includes provocative information, but also feelings, dispositions, and lively models of cognitive strategizing. It is a qualitative locale, a nurturing, mediating, and mind-expanding exploratorium. (p. 11)

Advocacy for restructured schools must deal initially with the three variables of curriculum, instruction, and assessment, and how these variables go together in an environmental whole. How they influence the diverse students in a given classroom then becomes the essence of education's radical change. In the new paradigm for schooling, how these variables are addressed by the teacher, both in everyday and long-term planning for learning, is the key to student intellectual development. Nowhere is this more significant than in understanding students at risk of school failure.

THE NEEDS OF AT-RISK STUDENTS

Just as there is no one, commonly held definition of restructuring, there is no one, commonly held definition of our nation's "at-risk student" population. Although Comer (1988) states that in this complicated age all students are potentially at risk, for purposes of this study the at-risk student is the low-achieving learner plagued by academic failure and, unfortunately, tempted to drop out of public school. These are the children with underdeveloped talents who, through no fault of their own, are ill-prepared for schooling, for academic endeavors, and for later life and work success. Sadly, the number of youngsters for whom schools are such unhappy and unthoughtful places is steadily increasing. Hodgkinson (1991) maintains that at least one third of the nation's children are at risk of school failure *even before they enter kindergarten!* In both urban and rural areas, many students are leaving school without diplomas, and still more find little meaning in their schooling (Beyer & Smey-Richman, 1988; Mirman, Swartz & Barell, 1988; Report on Education Research, 1992). These problems have serious implications for the individual learner, for beleaguered educational systems, and for American society as a whole.

In many cases, at-risk students have not been presented with the same opportunities to become successful, thoughtful learners as have their higher achieving peers (Passow, 1991). Minimally challenging school programs have been compounded by discrimination—racial, cultural, class, sex, and handicap—and lowered expectations. Lowered expectations, in turn, lead to an overemphasis on drill, remediation, and discipline—practices which perpetuate low self-esteem, a lack of motivation, and student alienation. More important, cognitive research has challenged the assumption of a sequence of activities from lower level "basic" skills to higher order "thinking" skills in a reductionist manner (Kozulin, 1990; Means & Knapp, 1991). Indeed, research shows just the opposite. Processes such as making inferences, constructing meaning, and problem solving are all part of a constructivist approach to learning (Fosnot, 1989; Resnick, 1987a). It is these complex cognitive abilities that are the "new basics" of the 21st century, the very outcomes which the National Assessment of Educational Progress data indicate are not currently well developed in the majority of the nation's students and, particularly, not in at-risk student populations (Educational Testing Service, 1990).

The timely reform issue is not so much to raise educational standards for at-risk students, but to create a kind of schooling in which *all* students receive support in striving to achieve higher standards and greater expectations (National Coalition of Advocates for Students, 1991). That is the real challenge of restructuring education for the coming millennium. The new educational paradigm must be grounded in both a commitment and a researched knowledge base which demonstrates that all students have the potential to be successful, thoughtful learners (Costa, 1991; Feuerstein, 1990). America's at-risk students are no exception.

The major problem that school restructuring needs to examine is the creation of a new learning environment for all students, including student populations considered at risk of failure in elementary and secondary education. In particular, this examination must answer three key questions.

1. How can the vision of restructured schooling be interrelated with the cognitive paradigm—the movement to make schooling an intellectually developing experience?

2. How can every child, even those at risk of academic failure, be prepared fully as thinking persons?

3. What kind of learning experiences need to be developed to serve diverse students, many of whom have been poorly served by traditional educational practices?

These are the significant queries that guide the presentation of the remainder of this chapter.

BUILDING A RESTRUCTURED CLASSROOM ENVIRONMENT

The most important task of this study is to determine, as completely as possible, the essential elements of a restructured classroom environment, for what goes on in the classroom is most influential on what students are enabled to do (Pauly, 1991). By examining pertinent literature, by seeking relevant research—especially as related to the historic concerns noted earlier—and by considering what is empowering to a youngster's cognitive development, eight elements appear to be the major characteristics of such an environment.[1] It is the authors' position that the radical change needed in a learner's experience at school involves transforming the classroom in such a way that all eight elements can operate fully and strongly influence the child's advancement.

THE ESSENTIAL ELEMENTS OF RESTRUCTURED CLASSROOM ENVIRONMENTS

1. The purpose of the classroom is to develop every student's mind and to enhance every learner's potential; the primary goal of a classroom restructured for learning is to increase—for every student—understanding and higher-level comprehension of the several subject matters that generally constitute elementary and secondary schooling.

2. The long-term goals of this environment are the autonomy of the learner, the development of self-regulation, and the independence of lifelong learning. Everyday activities are to be consistently planned to reflect these objectives.

3. The learning processes emphasized in this environment involve cognition, metacognition, and conative dimensions within content epistemologies that seek both individual and group gain.

4. In this environment, all students, even those of differing abilities and diverse backgrounds, are viewed as naturally active and curious constructors of meaning who, over time, modify or seek to create conceptions of information and experience at their unique rates and in their preferred styles.

5. The teacher encourages and provides for important social interactions in this environment, thereby assuring each student a personalized, respectful, and meaningful experience in learning and cognitive development.

6. The teacher in this environment acts as a facilitator of student learning, a mediator, a coach, a mentor, and a collaborator with students and other teachers in the larger school setting.

7. The classroom is linked to life beyond its boundaries, that is, to the school as a whole, to other educators and staff, and to the entire community, including parents and other agents.

8. The restructured classroom environment for learning integrates curriculum, instruction, and assessment in such a way as to maximize the achievement of these

"essential elements" in the dynamic and practical aspects of everyday schooling.

The educational literature supporting these elements is extensive and varied. Much of the research on teaching higher-order thinking strives to realize the first element, increased thoughtfulness, as does much of the current discussion on literacy and numeracy development (Baron & Sternberg, 1987; Brown, 1991a; Hiebert, 1991). While it is acknowledged that particular contents are the appropriate domains of an education, knowing these contents and connecting them through meaningful understanding are central to the processes of learning and interpretation. The long-term goals of autonomy and life-long learning in the second element are the outcomes for which restructured schooling must strive, countering the reductionist view of "basic skills training" and the "quick fix" mentality of programs that are trendy and superficial (Wittrock, 1987). A rich store of research information on learning and teaching within the cognitive framework is available and needs to be used by classroom practitioners in the restructured school.

Elements three and four present learning as a constructive process with building blocks that are fairly well understood and defined. In schooling, it is not sufficient to concentrate on cognitive operations alone. How metacognitive and conative dimensions interact with content knowledge are also important relationships (Presseisen, 1990). One must keep in mind that reasoning and intelligence are an individual's *developed* abilities, and that it is children's conceptual growth and mental modification *over time* that are the fundamental outcomes of schooling (Brown & Campione, 1986; Feuerstein, 1980). Beyond these outcomes, an awareness that culture and consciousness are developed through socially interactive learning may be one of the most important aspects of restructured education (Kozulin, 1990).

The responsibility of the classroom teacher is underlined in elements five and six. Schooling is a very human enterprise and teachers play the key roles of diagnostician, interpreter, creator, and communicator in their mediational task

(Feuerstein, 1990). Although materials and methods are significant in the restructured classroom, the ultimate goals are the experience and meaning their use has for the engaged learner (Kamii, 1984; Shulman, 1987; Wittrock, 1987). Similarly, the teacher helps link the classroom to other environments that impinge on students' lives, notably the rest of the school community and the children's experiences outside school (Comer, 1980; Wehlage, Rutter, Smith, Lesko, & Fernandez, 1989). This connecting aspect is the underlying emphasis of the seventh element.

Finally, the eighth element calls for an integration of curriculum, instruction, and assessment in the restructured classroom, in order to maximize the other seven dimensions. Traditionally in education, these are rather loosely coupled concepts. Curriculum developers and instructional specialists sometimes integrate their efforts; however, neither of them talk frequently with assessment personnel (Valencia, 1990). The current thrusts for meaningful instruction and "authentic" assessments have heightened understanding of the need for such collaboration (Nickerson, 1989; Stiggins, Rubel, & Quellmalz, 1988; Wiggins, 1989b, 1992). The following sections examine at greater length the need to integrate curriculum, instruction, and assessment in the restructured classroom environment.

CURRICULUM IN THE RESTRUCTURED CLASSROOM ENVIRONMENT

By tradition, curriculum is the content-oriented part of a school's program, the substantive aspect of what needs to be studied and learned (Eisner, 1982). Until recently, discrete subject matters—heavily influenced and conceived by university specialists—was the preferred curricular approach of American schooling (Tanner, 1989). But cognitive concerns in education challenge that perspective. A more dynamic conception, one in which teachers and students interact in the construction of ideas and richer meanings, has become the focus of the supportive learning environment sought for all students. The essential elements presented in this study form the underpinnings of such a curricular conception.

The curriculum of a restructured classroom needs to be organized mainly to help students develop and use ideas to understand formal knowledge systems, but, at the same time, to assist learners to formulate conceptions that are transferable to problem solving in their everyday lives (Beyer, 1988; Presseisen, 1987; Sternberg, Okagaki, & Jackson, 1990). The content of such a curriculum needs to include the skills and higher processes of cognitive functioning, but also the dispositions and awarenesses of more conative striving (Ennis, 1986; McCombs & Marzano, 1989). Affect and emotion can be key to the creative dimensions of such a cognitive-based education, and intrinsic interest and curiosity may be as motivating to meaningful learning as a teacher's absolute authority or the competitive framework of the more traditional classroom. Thus, the epistemologies of classic school subjects need to be related to both cognitive and conative aspects of the curriculum, because the concepts of a particular discipline are the "holding bins" of students' experience in subject learning and the points of departure for learners' interests and thinking.

The curriculum of a restructured classroom is chiefly centered on the student as a constructor of meaning and a manager of learning. There are at least four major concerns that such a curriculum needs to address:

- *Managing information*—Many bits of knowledge or information are constantly present in the classroom environment; the student needs to develop skills and processes to organize these bits and to gradually develop mental constructs that make handling these data meaningful and connected to other things that need to be known and used.

- *Managing tasks*—Learning in the classroom involves activities or problems that require certain routines to complete successfully; the student needs to develop strategies for working on these tasks at school and for understanding a variety of procedures that may have differing influences over ultimate task completion.

- *Managing self*—Successful learning involves awarenesses about intelligent performance by oneself and others; the student needs to develop and apply these awarenesses in a user-friendly setting to improve learning and performance.

- *Cooperation in learning*—Successful learning is based on social collaboration and exchange and on the ability to communicate one's ideas; the student needs to have experience with such dynamic exchange and time to reflect on the consequences that are derived from such interaction.

Many of the ideas in current literature on restructured schooling address one or more of these concerns. A focused, practical question to ask is: What do teachers need to do with curriculum in order to help students be successful in terms of these four concerns?

Managing Information

There is a great deal of information to be mastered at school. An emphasis on the cognitive development of learners highlights the point that thinking operations need to be consciously developed in relation to regular subject matters, particularly relative to the "key concepts and strategies that students must acquire to function effectively in a particular domain" (Bransford & Vye, 1989, p. 182). A curriculum needs to expose students to exemplary thinking in history, language, or science that shows both how ideas are formulated and how they are represented in that particular domain (Bruner, 1960; Oliver, 1990). But mere exposure is not sufficient. To present a list of higher-order thinking skills or to display key ideas of a particular subject is merely the first curricular act, a starting place for planning a course of study.

At a second level of curricular understanding, knowledge needs to be integrated in various ways in the instructional program (Martinello & Cook, 1992). Expert teachers understand the challenge of such a problem. Leinhardt (1990) suggests these teachers use their "craft expertise" within a content domain to help them know which parts of the rich information pool available are significant for teaching and which parts are irrelevant. She agrees with Newmann (1987) in emphasizing the need for *in-depth* experiences in a content area, so that students come to understand not only the apparent subject matter but also the kinds of mental processes and operations that constitute a complex domain (Shulman, 1987). Material in such a curriculum needs to be selected to be influential on the learner, because it transfers and transforms, leads to "grounded knowing," and captivates and inspires (Oliver, 1990; Perkins & Salomon, 1988; Schama, 1991).

The problem of data in an information-rich age raises another issue of curriculum integration. Exactly how should a classroom teacher blend the thinking processes of cognition and the concepts of a knowledge domain in a student's course of study? Some researchers, and many textbook publishers, maintain that these two information bases need only be commonly presented or mutually infused into subject matter (Ennis, 1989; Swartz, 1987). Others call for interdisciplinary or multidisciplinary reconceptualizations (Fogarty, 1991; Jacobs, 1991). Obviously, articulation among subject teachers and a debated scope and sequence of appropriate topics, agreed to across grade levels, follow from this position. But what is most essential, according to either position, is that mastering thinking operations and not mere content coverage lies at the heart of understanding content disciplines. These operations are also basic to generating student meaning (Ammon & Hutcheson, 1989). This challenge leads to the concern for teachability and student response in learning (Bereiter & Scardamalia, 1992).

Managing Tasks

In the limited hours students attend school, a finite number of activities or specific lessons can be included in the curriculum. How can teachers assure that these activities lead to the meaningful outcomes a cognitive experience requires? Shulman (1987) suggests that one of the most important aspects of pedagogical expertise involves knowing what problems to present in a course, when to present them, and how to relate them to student activity in a lesson design that challenges student thinking and motivates student interest and activity. Vygotsky's (1978) cognitive theory emphasizes the concept of "tools" in human learning, concentrating on the connections between material and psychological instruments that influence conception, on one hand, and lively social interaction, on the other. The problems of content presentation focused on "toolness" lie at the center of task management in a curriculum, addressing issues of cognition and content representation, as well as providing mechanisms for conveying meaning in the teaching-learning act (Kozulin, 1990).

What are the major material tools of a given discipline? What problems and problem formations do students need to be prepared to solve? What documents or key products represent the best display of expertise or beauty in a particular domain? These are questions that form the foundation of curriculum decision making. They are the heart of what a teacher needs to determine before the specific tasks of classroom work can be prepared. In short, concrete tasks need to be designed consistent with the standards of excellence implied or explicated in a content domain. At the same time, educators must consider what is most elemental for learning a particular content, as well as the skills, attitudes, and knowledge that make that subject intellectually come alive (Presseisen, 1988b).

The current task concerns of curriculum focus on student activity and appropriate designs to accommodate various developmental levels of conceptualization. Science teaching in the middle grades, for example, is very involved with "hands-on" experimentation and authentic activity presentation (North Central Regional Educational Laboratory, 1991). Mathematical reasoning, under the new professional guidelines of the National Council of Teachers of Mathematics, seeks real world applications of theorems and axioms and still recognizes that not all of the variables in a given problem can be responded to by every student in any one lesson (Black, 1989; Lockwood, 1991). Language arts programs emphasize more "holistic" experiences across the various genres of expression, leading to greater comprehension and more creative understanding of complex ideas (Palincsar & Brown, 1989; Scardamalia & Bereiter, 1985; Shanahan, 1991). Such classroom tasks need to be carefully positioned for any given population of students.

An underlying problem of the curricular task is the question of "bridging the gap," that is, to help students move from their initial conception of what is in the curriculum to something further along the increasing sophisticated sequence of ideas in the subject matter (Rogoff, 1990). How do students internalize what is presented in class? How do they come to understand the qualities of curricular content spontaneously and with a commitment to resolve discrepancies? The restructured classroom conceives of this problem as one of *strategic* learning (Belmont, 1989). For Collins, Brown, and Holum (1991), this constitutes the central issue of cognitive apprenticeship. Based on Vygotsky's (1978) notion of the "zone of proximal development" (ZPD), apprenticeship requires that classroom tasks not only present information to the student but also provide experience by which he or she is able to go beyond what is presented. The student becomes intellectually engaged in learning by relating what is already known to what might be. Every student's potential for learning becomes mutually involved in the real experience of a specific lesson. The curriculum must account for this learner awareness of both a student's own role in the instructional process and the influence of others in the classroom. This conative dimension of the essential elements suggests a third major concern of curriculum.

Managing Self

In order to achieve optimal student experience, the curriculum in a restructured classroom environment must actively engage every student in his or her own learning and knowledge building.

Self-regulation and metacognitive skill acquisition are two vital aspects of student involvement in learning. The development of self-regulation is a cornerstone of learner autonomy and lifelong learning. It involves the students' "awareness of the variables that are important to learning and their ability to take control of their learning environment" (Palincsar & Brown, 1989, p. 19). Metacognitive skill development relates to strategies for learning particular content and heightened awareness of the cognitive demands of specified classroom tasks.

McCombs and Marzano (1989) conceptualize *self-as-agent* as a central phenomenon that brings together both a student's "skill" and "will" in the development of thoughtful behavior. They theorize that such integration makes possible the development of personal expertise in a particular task or subject, driven initially by the will or motivation of the learner and subsequently by instructional intervention that assists in the delineation of task and the self-regulated development of competencies. The meshing of the learner and the learning is central to a restructured classroom. To be educated is to be *personally* involved, as well as cognitively engaged, in the community of thinking that is fundamental to a learning environment.

Given these requisites for the restructured classroom, how can a curriculum contribute to developing a student's self-regulatory behavior and metacognitive awareness? Teachers need to focus on materials and activities that arouse student curiosity and engage their interest. Providing roles for student choice and voluntary association at the outset of a classroom assignment are important initial concerns. Casting problems and activities in novel and challenging ways are additional considerations. After students are involved in an assignment, relating the curricular materials to strategic skill development becomes a major concern of pedagogy. For example, Palincsar and Brown (1989) identify six strategies that are central to the student's ability to monitor and foster reading comprehension. These strategies then become the scaffold, or lattice, upon which particular reading activities are made meaningful.

In addition to developing strategic abilities within the specific content, students must learn self-regulatory procedures that enable them to efficiently accomplish specific tasks embedded in a particular curriculum. Sternberg (1990a) cites executive monitoring skills, assessed through an individual student's development of personal style, as important for knowledge development. He and his associates (Sternberg, Okagaki, & Jackson, 1990) maintain that the student, while simultaneously learning content controls, needs to consciously improve his/her own learning techniques. The use of prior knowledge, visualizing contents, recognizing a point of view, looking for effective learning strategies, listening for meaning, and learning by doing are examples of such techniques. The curricular problem for student advancement is to create classroom activities and a learning environment in which these dual improvements can take place.

McCombs and Marzano's (1989) concept of the self-system in cognitive development also raises the issue of what is unconscious in the student's awareness. They see the emerging self in holistic terms, a "consciousness that directs more unconscious processes" (McCombs & Marzano, 1989, p. 3). This highlights the question of how a curriculum can foster a student's *in-depth* perspective of subject matter—mindful of the time constraints on instruction and learning. Perkins (1991a) sees this concern as part of the problem of developing insight about a particular subject; he ties this to goals of teaching for transfer and building an integrated curriculum. Suhor (1992) suggests that a whole range of semiotic functions are introduced with this problem. How can the classroom teacher help students "go beyond the information given" (Bruner, 1964) and make creative connections to other knowledge? The curriculum must be used to help students trust their own minds, to build connections to what they know and do beyond the classroom, and to consider their own and their classmates' ways of thinking. Through such elaborative experience, the learner-as-self becomes defined, cognitive competence becomes owned, and commitment to learning is enjoined. Thus, Anne

Frank and Romeo and Juliet will emerge from the pages of literature and extend a student's understanding to his or her own consciousness.

Cooperation in Learning

The interactive, social nature of the restructured classroom puts a high premium on cooperative activity as a curricular requisite of learning. Students need to work on mutually challenging tasks that build complementary roles and perspectives, and which engender respect for diversity and variation. Cooperative learning methods assume that students can learn *from* as well as *with* their peers, that work can be pursued by collaborative teams, and that, with some well-thought-out, group-based assignments prepared by sensitive teachers, different youngsters with varying abilities can meaningfully contribute to a unified assignment (Slavin, Klarweit, & Wasik, 1991). In such cooperative learning, the talent of every youngster can be bolstered and the meaning of the shared task internalized (Presseisen, 1992).

The social context of the classroom is also important to Vygotsky (1978), who viewed learning as embedded in experiences bound by communication and exchange. Vygotsky maintained that the student becomes aware of his or her own cognitive operations only *after* they are practiced and endorsed by others. Further, he proposed that scientific concepts in that exchange need to be both built into the formal context of a body of knowledge or subject matter and systematized through *everyday use* by the learner and his or her peers (Kozulin, 1990).

The role of the teacher as mediator in the learning exchange is a critical link between the student and the curriculum. Good teachers serve as both interpreters and questioners who assist students' construction of knowledge and finely tune classroom exchange for maximum meaning and student benefit (Feuerstein, 1990). Such teaching establishes where a student is in the ZPD and determines the most productive activity for both the individual learner and for groups of learners in a classroom (Brown & Ferrara, 1985; Bruner, 1984). Similarly, Feuerstein's "mediated learning experience" (MLE) relates the learner's needs to the concepts that ought to be known by the student in the interactive exchange. The teacher is both a tool of instruction and a creator of additional classroom tools. Through such a mediational approach, social interaction is the essence of the environmental exchange. The teacher provides the "bridge" to student transfer and the actual subject learning.

Cooperating with others, then, raises the need for building a social presence in the course of schooling (Brophy & Alleman, 1991). Making choices, building on social networks, figuring out and applying rules, and extending various relationships among people and ideas are as much a part of a particular curriculum as the technical components (Sternberg, Okagaki, & Jackson, 1990). How individual students master such social requisites of group learning must be a significant concern of both curricular focus and teacher attention. Such a social dimension is part of the full interpretation of a learner's construction of meaning at school. It remains to be seen how such a curriculum blends with instruction in the classroom.

INSTRUCTION IN THE RESTRUCTURED CLASSROOM ENVIRONMENT

While curriculum is the subject matter taught in the classroom, instruction is the interaction of the teacher and students with the subject matter (Erickson & Shultz, 1992). Unfortunately, teaching in schools today is mainly recitation, consisting of unrelated teacher questions chiefly aimed at having students deliver a correct answer (Kamii, 1984; Tharp & Gallimore, 1988). Because traditionally learning is seen as linear and sequential, students are required to master surface-level information and discrete, decontextualized skills—often using drill and practice—before moving on to more advanced or complex tasks (Gagné, 1970; Popham, 1987). As proposed in the eight essential elements, the cognitive agenda is profoundly at odds with these premises and begins with different assumptions about student learning.

The aim of instruction in a restructured class-

room environment is to change the teacher's instructional role from information provider to assistor or facilitator of student performance (Brown, 1991b; Tharp & Gallimore, 1988). When students respond to open-ended questions and are encouraged to develop multiple solutions to a single problem, the teacher acts as a coach or co-learner, a pedagogue who selects and develops meaningful learning activities (Wood, Cobb, & Yackel, 1991). When more in-depth explanations are required, the teacher becomes a mediator who provides students with additional guidance, supportive modeling and practice, and interactions with others (Haywood, 1990). Key to all these roles is the teacher's ability to ask more provocative questions and to know the exemplary steps of a youngster's cognitive development (Case, 1992).

As with curriculum, teachers in a restructured classroom must design instruction in concert with the four learner-centered concerns of managing information, managing tasks, managing self, and cooperation in learning. Therefore, another important question of this study asks: What types of instructional experiences should teachers select to enable students successfully to process the school's curriculum?

Managing Information

Since learners continuously interact and interpret the world, the process of information acquisition in the restructured classroom is viewed as the learner's successive development of structures which are assessed, revised, or replaced in ways that facilitate learning and accommodate the learner's background and purposes (Case, 1992; Hiebert, 1991). When students lack an efficient way of organizing and storing information, teachers should directly supply a beginning knowledge structure to support the development of specific content domains (Beyer, 1987). Information organizers and concept attainment are two examples of instructional approaches that assist students' understanding and recall of information.

Advanced organizers are generally introduced prior to new learning tasks to provide relevant anchoring ideas for more differentiated and detailed material to follow (Ausubel, 1977; Mayer, 1989). While the exact design of the organizer depends upon the characteristics of the learner and material to be mastered, advanced organizers are generally short sets of verbal or visual information that provide a means for generating logical relationships. Beyer (1987) has extended this strategy to his program for teaching critical thinking. Furthermore, post-organizers also appear to be effective in facilitating learning and retention of information, even after it is introduced (Alexander, Frankiewicz, & Williams, 1979).

By tradition, teachers have taught linear outlining as the primary verbal representation of information. But today, graphic organizers or conceptual models—matrices, webs, cycles, and sequences—are used to reflect better the structure of ideas and, hence, make information more meaningful and memorable (Jones, Pierce, & Hunter, 1988–89; Mayer, 1989). Such visual cues become the "tools" of instruction in Vygotsky's sense and are thus transformational instruments of thinking (McTighe & Lyman, 1988). Further, student learning is more positively affected when students construct their own graphic organizers, preferably in collaboration with other students, or complete those begun by the teacher (Alvermann, 1988; Moore & Readance, 1984).

Similarly, in a restructured classroom environment, learners should be assisted to construct and refine concepts, preferably with metacognitive awareness of goals and strategies (Schroeder & Lester, 1989; Wood, Cobb, & Yackel, 1991). In an effort to solve a problem or make a decision, students' concept understanding is enhanced when they engage in "instructional conversation" (Tharp & Gallimore, 1988) or "substantive conversation" (Newmann, 1991). An instructional conversation is characterized by authentic, open-ended teacher questions—teacher questions that build on previous student answers, or "uptake" (Collins, 1982), and sustained discussions in which student engagement is substantive, not just procedural (Nystrand, 1992). Also, as part of this substantive discussion, conceptual change is facilitated when learners are encouraged to differenti-

ate relevant from irrelevant concept attributes, distinguish examples from nonexamples, hypothesize the hierarchical relationships among concept clusters and create their own representative exemplars (Barth, 1991). By participating in such experiences, students begin to expand their understanding of a concept and gain more flexibility in their own thinking (Nickerson, 1989).

Overcoming resistance to conceptual change can be a difficult cognitive struggle (Bransford & Vye, 1989; Gardner, 1990). Researchers have found that misconceptions are so powerful and entrenched that they survive years of formal education (Resnick, 1985). If these inaccurate ideas are allowed to go undetected or unchallenged, the misconceptions can continue to interfere with the students' understanding of important subject matter. Thus, Sternberg (1990a) cites the need to use information to create doubt, whet the learner's curiosity, and challenge the constructs that exist. Similarly, Vygotsky's theory cites the useful contrast between scientific ideas (concepts) and "everyday thinking" (Presseisen & Kozulin, 1992).

Managing Tasks

The central element of teaching is the way a teacher translates curriculum into student tasks or assignments. The teacher's choice of task influences student learning by directing the learner's attention to particular aspects of content (e.g., facts, concepts, principles, solutions) and by specifying ways for processing information (e.g., memorizing, classifying, inferring, analyzing) (Knapp & Shields, 1990). These effects on learning are clearly apparent in the contrast between the outmoded behavioral emphasis on accumulating isolated facts and the constructivist's goal of meaning construction.

In the restructured classroom environment, the student is expected to assume more responsibility for task-management. While such a goal is laudable, Perkins (1991b) cautions that throwing unprepared students suddenly into complex cognitive problem-solving situations may actually be a prescription for student failure. Obviously, coping strategies need to be carefully interrelated with the classroom content and the assigned tasks closely aligned to what students already know. Several intervention models of instruction exist that purport to do this.

A mediational teaching style is one promising approach for assisting unskilled learners to adapt to their expanded task-manager role. In MLE, Feuerstein and his colleagues (1980, 1985) refer to the unique interactions by which adults intentionally interpose themselves between the student and an external stimulus to alter the stimulus prior to the learner's perception. As part of this process, the mediator selects, frames, and filters the lesson presented, interpreting it for the learner. In addition, mediators interpose themselves between the student and the student's response to the stimulus, thus helping learners be aware of their own metacognitive functioning and their ability to self-regulate (McCombs & Marzano, 1989). No longer do students interpret stimuli as accidental occurrences, but rather as contextually bound problems, about which an array of reactions are potentially effective (Brown, Collins, & Duguid, 1989).

According to Feuerstein's theory, intentionality (and reciprocity), transcendence, and meaning are the three essential characteristics of every mediated interaction (Feuerstein, 1990; Presseisen & Kozulin, 1992). The intentionality of the mediator, which is shared by the learner, produces a sense of vigilance that is evidenced by greater attentiveness, focus, and acuity of perception. The transcendence of the mediation interaction refers to going beyond the specific situation or need and reaching out or "bridging" to goals that may be only slightly, or not apparently, related to the original situation. Finally, MLE is characterized by an affective, motivational, or value-oriented event or experience that leads the student to become meaningfully involved in the learning. According to Feuerstein (1990) and his associates (Haywood, 1990; Link, 1985), these three mediational characteristics—intentionality, transcendence, and meaning—interact and form the universal, necessary conditions for every successful teaching-learning experience.

The cognitive apprenticeship approach to instruction—aimed at making thinking explicit and visible—is another innovative intervention to help students deal with cognitively complex problems (Collins, Brown, & Holum, 1991; Means & Knapp, 1991). Built on a Vygotskian basis, and similar to Feuerstein's MLE, apprenticeship is designed to assist students in acquiring an integrated set of skills through the processes of observation and guided practice (Rogoff, 1990). The apprenticeship approach seeks to promote the development of expertise through the three core instructional methods of modeling, scaffolding, and coaching. Modeling requires the teacher to externalize the usually internal processes and activities, specifically heuristics and control processes, by which the teacher applies conceptual knowledge. Scaffolding seeks to aid the learner in the ZPD, providing just enough support or guidance for student cognitive advancement (Brown & Ferrara, 1985). In this context, the teacher's relationship with students involves the accurate diagnosis of each student's current skill or ability level and the implementation of intermediate steps of instruction at an appropriate level of difficulty (Rosenshine & Meister, 1992). Finally, coaching—the general process of overseeing student learning—involves observing students as they carry out a learning task and facilitating the enhancement of their cognitive activity (Collins, Brown, & Holum, 1991).

Palincsar and Brown's (1984) reciprocal teaching method offers a third instructional model for developing better thinkers and learners. While similar to both Feuerstein's MLE and the cognitive apprenticeship approach, the Palincsar and Brown intervention centers on modeling, scaffolding, and coaching students in four strategic reading skills: formulating questions, summarizing, predicting, and clarifying. Briefly, the procedure begins when the teacher models these four strategies in the context of understanding written passages. After silently reading the text, the students each take turns playing the role of instructor and leading the other students through the four strategies. Initially, the teacher provides sufficient support to allow students to take on whatever portion of the task they are able to do. Gradually, however, the prompts fade until the students can perform independently (Brown, Palincsar, & Purcell, 1986; Palincsar, 1992; Palincsar & Brown, 1984).

In all of these models of mediational instruction, the key to a reflective classroom dialogue is how the teacher talks, listens to students, and encourages student-to-student discourse (Englert, Raphael, Anderson, Anthony, & Stephens, 1991). In the traditional classroom, student talk and shared understanding occur minimally (Pogrow, 1991; Tharp & Gallimore, 1988). But in the restructured classroom environment, the teacher acts extensively and responsively to aid student comprehension through a dialogue, or "instructional conversation" (Goldenberg, 1991). A clear focus on the task is the initial step in such a conversation; elaborating that task is the next pedagogical link in the instructional exchange (Stigler & Stevenson, 1991). Charged with the task of assisting students to construct their own context, the teacher listens carefully and adjusts the immediate response to meet the learner's emergent understanding (Brown & Campione, 1986; Englert et al., 1991; Tharp & Gallimore, 1988, 1991). Teacher questioning also leads students through appropriate post-activity reflection, sharing insights about what they have learned through the task (Brophy & Alleman, 1991).

Managing Self

Not only is teaching the process of truly conversing, it is also the act of facilitating the students' capability to assume full responsibility for their own learning. Nearly two decades ago, Maxine Green (1973) wrote that teaching "happens" when students can do certain things on their own—for example, when learners extend themselves to find answers to questions they have posed, when students give reasons and see connections within their experiences, and when they recognize their own or someone else's errors and propose appropriate corrections. Thus, teaching is ultimately assisting students to self-manage and to actualize the concept of self-as-agent.

Using the mediational teaching style based on Feuerstein's theory of cognitive modifiability, the teacher can promote student awareness of feelings of competence using a dual process: first, structuring tasks for student success; and, second, interpreting even minimal signs of student success as an indication of increased competence (Clark & Peterson, 1990; Feuerstein & Hoffman, 1990; Haywood, 1990). Moreover, mediational dialogues can enhance the student's conception of himself or herself as a thinker by providing immediate feedback, especially on process-oriented responses, and by making the student aware of the precise aspect of thoughts and behaviors that led to success. Thus, rather than saying "Good job!" the teacher might reply, "Good! You developed a plan and now you know how to proceed." Mediation of a sense of competence enhances a student's motivation to persevere on increasingly difficult tasks and is necessary to secure the development of autonomous functioning (Feuerstein, 1990; Markus & Wurf, 1987; McCombs & Marzano, 1989; McTighe & Clemson, 1991).

Just as mediational teachers reinforce the student's self-concept as a successful performer, teachers must also assist students—especially younger and low-achieving students (Palincsar & Brown, 1989; Smey-Richman, 1988; Zimmerman & Martinez-Pons, 1990)—to self-evaluate, and to control their own cognition and behavior (Feuerstein, 1990; Smith & Nelson, 1992). Sometimes, self-regulation means the students seek to improve their ability to attend, become more precise and accurate, or inhibit their impulsivity (Feuerstein, 1980; Wittrock, 1990); at other times, self-regulation for academic tasks means setting goals, self-reinforcement, and self-instruction (Smith & Nelson, 1992; Zimmerman & Martinez-Pons, 1990). Critical to the success of student self-regulation is the teacher's ability to maintain a nonthreatening classroom environment conducive to good thinking—one in which challenge and risk taking are promoted and where originality, independent thought, and differences of opinions are welcome (Barell, Liebmann, & Sigel, 1988; Caine & Caine, 1991; Marzano et al., 1988).

Metacognition—a component of self-regulated learning (Pintrich & de Groot, 1990)—occurs when students become more strategic in planning, monitoring, and evaluating their mental performance (Barell, Liebmann, & Sigel, 1988; Costa, 1991; Flavell, 1976; Palincsar & Brown, 1989). Students experience metacognition when they use their inner voice or self-talk—"language turned inward" which has its origins in social dialogue (Vygotsky, 1978)—to monologue with themselves about their own writing (Englert et al., 1991). In composition classes, scaffolding tools—for example, cue cards, think sheets, or self-checking lists—can be designed to reduce the burden of information processing and to support student attempts to plan, elaborate, and revise their drafts (Englert, Raphael, & Anderson, 1992; Rosenshine & Meister, 1992; Scardamalia & Bereiter, 1983). Similarly, thinking aloud and concrete prompts aimed at metacognitive functioning are used as a part of the cognitive apprenticeship model (Palincsar & Brown, 1984; Schoenfeld, 1985; Singer & Donlan, 1982). As students accept more responsibility for cognitive and metacognitive thinking, the use of scaffolding tools gradually is diminished.

Cooperation in Learning

In a restructured classroom environment, students working cooperatively to accomplish shared goals is the context within which managing information, tasks, and self best occurs. Unfortunately, contemporary learning processes in American schools tend to focus on the individual and, too often, remove students from interpersonal contexts which support and provide meaning to learning (Tharp & Gallimore, 1988). Unlike learning in society at large, classroom instruction seldom involves sufficient group efforts to achieve understanding or to solve problems (Resnick, 1987b; Tharp & Gallimore, 1988).

In practice, providing for social construction of knowledge means moving from strictly whole-class instruction, sometimes followed by individual seatwork, to a greater reliance on interactive, small-group activities. Theoretically, pair and small-group collaboration can sharply increase the rate of social dialogue and improve the quality of assisted performance by teachers and peers (Englert et al., 1991; Rosenshine & Meister, 1992; Tharp & Gallimore, 1991). During small-group activities, the learner can benefit from peers who model complex cognitive processes and from classmates at different levels of understanding (Collins, Brown, & Holum, 1991; Schroeder & Lester, 1989). Practically, small-group activities can help eliminate students' requests for immediate help and can provide teachers with opportunities to observe students' thinking and to make interventions when appropriate (Good, Reys, Grouws, & Mulryan, 1989–90; Wood, Cobb, & Yackel, 1991).

Collaborative peer editing or peer response groups is another strategy based on the understanding that writing involves an interaction between readers and writers in a literate community (Englert et al., 1991; Freedman, 1987; Rosenshine & Meister, 1992; Sealey, 1986). Peer editing groups—usually organized in pairs or small groups of three or four students—confer at various stages of the writing process, that is, prewriting, drafting, revising, editing, and publishing (Sealey, 1986), and provide opportunities for students to dialogue about the content, form, and creation of their texts (Barrett, 1989; Beyer, 1992; Englert et al., 1991). Asking advice and peer feedback, especially at the initial stages of writing (Olson, 1990), helps students develop a sense of audience beyond that of the teacher-examiner and an awareness of how revision through collaboration extends and elaborates one's ideas (Barrett, 1989; Brown, 1989; Brown & Campione, 1986).

Peer and cross-age tutoring are additional strategies for students to share not only the "answer," but the processes used to solve a problem. Those tutored generally benefit because they identify easily with peer models and they receive more immediate feedback or clarification (Ashley, Jones, Zahniser, & Inks, 1986). Furthermore, peer tutors learn through the act of teaching: they reinforce their own knowledge and skills, and gain in social maturity factors including self-confidence, sense of responsibility, and self-esteem (Ashley et al., 1986; Jenkins & Jenkins, 1987; Reisman, 1988).

The emergence of "real" conversation about academic matters is an important feature of cooperative learning (Davidson & Worsham, 1992). In this approach to instruction, heterogeneous groups of four or five students work "together to maximize their own and each other's learning" (Johnson & Johnson, 1991, p. 298). Slavin (1983, 1991) suggests that group goals, often in the form of group rewards or recognition, and individual accountability must be present for cooperative learning tasks to promote academic learning. Moreover, interactions within groups must have certain qualities—helping, ensuring all do a fair share, giving constructive feedback, challenging others' reasoning without engaging in personal criticism, sharing resources, being openminded, and promoting safety so members feel free to share their thoughts (Johnson & Johnson, 1989; Presseisen, 1992). Thus, to promote cognitive change, teachers must facilitate cooperation in learning as well as attend to instructional concern for curriculum, task, and student self-development.

ASSESSMENT IN THE RESTRUCTURED CLASSROOM ENVIRONMENT

Just as our understanding of how children develop and learn challenges our curriculum and teaching practices, it forces us to reexamine how we assess student learning, as well. Conventional tests of educational progress are designed to quantify indirectly, in a single setting, whether or not the student possesses or recalls factual knowledge or discrete skills, irrespective of the context. Students work individually within a specified time frame to select the one "right" or "best" answer for each test item. These traditional tests are based on the empiricist approach to cognitive development, which first views learning as sequential and linear, and then sees complex learning as composed of smaller prerequisite elements (Shepard, 1991). Resnick and Resnick (1992) use the terms "decomposability" and "decontextualization" to refer to the underlying assumptions of such a theory, where higher-order skills occur only after component skills are independently mastered. Shepard (1991) further describes the

relationship between assessment and instruction as a "teach-test-teach" mode in which, at each learning juncture, tests are used for the purpose of measuring specific behavioral outcomes of instruction.

The limitations of conventional testing are frequently cited in school reform literature (Linn, Baker, & Dunbar, 1991). Chief among them is that paper-and-pencil tests are proxies rather than examples of the actual performances we want students to master (Wiggins, 1989a). Moreover, evidence suggests that standardized achievement tests foster segregating students by ability, lower expectations for some students, lead to student disengagement in learning and thinking, and neglect the application of learning in the real world (Paris, Lawton, & Turner, 1992). Further, these tests provide little diagnostic information on the quality of student understanding (Fleming & Chambers, 1983). Conventional testing can also negatively impact instruction, when teachers focus on limited content and simplistic format (Brown, 1989; Nolen, Haladyna, & Haas, 1990). As a result, these tests are not only poorly serving students, teachers, and parents, but their validity is diminished (Frederiksen & Collins, 1989). Test scores themselves become meaningless, a concept which Messick (1984) refers to as "test score pollution."

If the primary goal of the restructured classroom environment is to foster *authentic* student achievement—the demonstrated performance of an accomplished mind—then the assessment goal is to develop high quality measures of this valued achievement. The alternative or direct assessments being proposed are performance-based measures that require students to demonstrate specific performances or abilities that are valued as educational outcomes (Archbald & Newmann, 1988). Emphasis is placed on students demonstrating thoughtfulness, making judgments, applying new understandings, and making connections in a variety of ways. Moreover, these alternative assessments are referred to as authentic when performance is assessed in "real," life-relevant rather than contrived, conditions (Newmann, 1991). Although basic skills and knowledge are obviously important to a thinking person, in the new assessments the mere reproduction of subject matter is not valued as authentic achievement. Rather, thinking is considered an ongoing process, not something concluded after the acquisition of facts (Shepard, 1991). Examples of these "rediscovered modes of assessment" (Wolf, Bixbey, Glenn, & Gardner, 1991) include portfolios of work products and performance-based tasks, such as extended projects and presentations, and what Sizer (1992) refers to as "exhibitions," which thoughtfully demonstrate accumulated knowledge.

The alignment and integration of curriculum, instruction, and assessment are critical in the restructured classroom environment. But how should this alignment come about and what is the appropriate role for assessment? To some, assessment can be a vehicle to redirect instruction toward the conscious pursuit of authentic achievement (Shephard, 1991; Wiggins, 1989a). When assessment shapes instruction, "teaching to the test" is an educationally effective strategy (Resnick & Resnick, 1992). It allows student and teacher to focus on higher-order, cognitive functioning and other valued standards of performance. It provides a bridge for students to understand the bases of instruction from a perspective of assessing their own performance, a major metacognitive and self-regulating goal (Garcia & Montes, 1992). To others, assessment and instruction need to be well integrated and dynamic (Feuerstein, 1980) and, in Vygotskian terms, allow for continual movement between the two processes and constant regrouping to reach goals. For example, Feuerstein (1979) and others look at a child in the process of learning to determine his or her potential for change. Such an assessment of cognitive potential reflects two types of measures, an existing level of competence and a measure of "responsivity to instruction" (Short, Cuddy, Friebert, & Schatschneider, 1990) which provides qualitative information regarding cognitive change. However, regardless of the proposed degree of integration of assessment and instruction, there is general agreement that the static results and outcome-orientation of tradi-

tional tests provide insufficient measures of competence or ability, particularly for low-achieving or at-risk students, where *qualitative* information concerning processing strategies is critical.

Will a teacher's use of alternative or performance-based assessments facilitate a better learning environment for students at risk? The following discussion describes how use of such assessments can, when combined with meaningful classroom activities and carefully selected curricula, transform the classroom to allow the eight essential elements of a restructured classroom environment to operate and support learning and development. The discussion is organized in two sections: first, the major rules that guide assessment in a restructured classroom environment are described; and second, the role changes required of teachers in developing and implementing these rules are presented.

Rules Guiding Assessment in a Restructured Classroom

Educational restructuring, as with any genuine reform effort, implies altering existing rules to facilitate adaptation to major change. A central theme of the current reform movement is that these alterations will achieve "a different order of results" (Corbett, 1990). How should progress toward these newly defined outcomes of high performance be measured? There are at least three basic rules, or principles, which must guide the development and implementation of authentic classroom assessment. These rules concern the development of standards, the construction of knowledge, and the role of collaboration in fostering autonomy.

Central to authentic assessments in the restructured classroom environment is the development of a set of standards of excellence for *all* students, that is, clear, explicit definitions of the particular performances and understandings that must be mastered by all students as outcomes of instruction (Wiggins, 1992). Such standards include tangible goal statements for both the academic content areas and the higher-level cognitive operations. Implied here is a view of thinking as a type of performance to be sampled and assessed, just as in auditions, athletic competitions, and driving tests (Wiggins, 1989b). Thinking as a performance shares a number of characteristics with other performances, including a balance of humility or quality and risk, a nonlinear developmental progression over time, and interpretation of information and beliefs (Wolf et al., 1991).

High expectations for all students are based on the premise that intelligence is not a fixed trait—all children have the ability to learn at their own rate and style. Also, with this paradigm, the goal of schooling is to maximize each individual student's achievement and mastery of standards. Evidence suggests there are negative effects of ability grouping and other special placements for lower-achieving students (Oakes, 1992; Slavin, 1987). Providing these students with a watered-down curriculum denies them the opportunity to master complex performance and reinforces their placements through the provision of boring, static tasks. Having high expectations for all students implies that teachers need not assess student readiness to participate in a thoughtful task by assessing whether they possess the independent skills involved in task performance. In a restructured classroom, the preferred approach is to have all children focus on the task, thus permitting students who need to develop specific skills to see their relevance, in context, and providing all students an opportunity to engage in understanding and thinking. Moreover, providing all students with high quality assessment tasks communicates a shared understanding of high expectations. In this way, assessment provides an opportunity for students to learn valuable skills, rather than to merely produce "right" answers.

Related to this view of intelligence is a new understanding of cognitive development. This understanding reflects a change from an early Piagetian view of cognitive development, that is, the development of basic processes which apply to all contexts, to a view of development as gradual advances in skills and domain-specific knowledge (Rogoff, 1990). The implication here for assessment, as well as for curriculum and instruction, is that children will display different abilities and

skills depending on the specific purpose and context of the task (Beyer & Nodine, 1985; Fischer, 1980; Siegler, 1989). Rogoff (1990) emphasizes the significance of microgenetic development when she includes in her definition of development "transformations in thinking that occur with successive attempts to handle a problem, even in time spans of minutes" (p. 11). Authentic assessment recognizes the significance of context and task demands by proposing tasks that are longitudinal, that involve students and teachers working together, and that allow students to use resources, such as books and calculators. In short, these are tasks that model serious adult work and reflect the mediational quality of the classroom.

Recently, based on the dynamic view of intelligence, a number of clinical programs have been developed that have implications for classroom instruction and student assessment (Budoff, 1987; Feuerstein, 1980). Although educators have known for some time that children who do not spontaneously exhibit certain abilities may, in fact, respond with cues, suggestions, or prompts (e.g., Flavell, 1976; Freeman, 1980), it is only recently that researchers have begun to examine the educational implications of these findings (Lidz, 1987). In contrast to the traditional diagnostic use of tests to determine a child's "readiness," or instructional level, the *Learning Potential Assessment Device* (Feuerstein, 1979), for example, assesses the child's performance by identifying a range of skills, as in the ZPD, bound at one end by an existing level of competence and at the other end by a *potential*, developmental level. This potential level can be reached by gradually developing learner responsibility through mediation, metacognition, and self-regulating activities, as described in mediational pedagogical strategies (Brown & Campione, 1986; Brown & Ferrera, 1985; Campione, Brown, Ferrara, & Bryant, 1984). In the restructured classroom, assessment becomes a central dimension of cognitive transfer with both curriculum and instruction.

Unlike conventional assessments, alternative assessments inform students and involve them in meaningful discussion about what is valued and intended. This in itself can be a learning process for both students and teachers. Some even go so far as to define a goal of assessment to be to "promote intense discussion of standards and evidence among all of the parties who are affected" (Wolf et al., 1991, p. 59). Examplars of levels of performance that set the standards must also be communicated to students, so it is clear as to how their performance is to be judged; students can monitor their own performance (Wiggins, 1989a). The dramatic change is from conventional testing, where students are passive and the teacher has all the answers, to empowering students to actively "assess their own performance reliably and thus develop clear goals to strive for in their learning" (Frederiksen & Collins, 1989, p. 30). Ultimately, such assessments foster student autonomy and self-regulation. Rather than just receiving a score on a test, students can measure their own achievement against a standard of excellence.

Assessment, then, is a means for monitoring a student's performance in comparison to some agreed-upon standards. The purpose is not to compare or rank students based on some quantitative score (e.g., Wiggins' "gatekeeping") by requiring students to provide answers from which it is impossible to determine underlying strategies, but rather to provide the student and teacher with qualitative information, over time and across situations, about student cognitive functioning. This does not mean that quantitative information, such as the use of grammatical rules in producing a composition, are irrelevant. It does mean, however, that what is valued is the application of basic information in authentic ways to facilitate the development and enhance the quality of student thinking. If high standards and expectations are not developed, and student performance in relation to these standards are not monitored and assessed over time, many students, particularly those at risk, will not be challenged to become self-regulated learners.

The second and third rules guiding assessment in the restructured classroom environment follow from what we know about the nature of knowledge and understanding. First, that teachers need to provide all students with experiences that

require the active construction of knowledge; the goal is for students to demonstrate their thinking and learning *potential* by actually "doing" (as opposed to transmitting or acquiring) science, for example. This doing, according to Greeno (1989), is the student's elaboration and reorganization of his or her knowledge and understanding. Implied here is the significance of context, which is known to profoundly influence children's cognitive functioning (Bronfenbrenner, 1991; Ceci, Ramey, & Ramey, 1990) and test performance. Interestingly, although research focusing on the use of such assessment practices in the classroom is scarce (Nickerson, 1989; Stiggins, 1985, 1991), and more general issues of quality remain unaddressed (Linn, Baker, & Dunbar, 1991), subjective reports of their powerful motivating and engaging qualities are abundant in educational literature and the current popular press (Mezzacappa, 1992b; Wiggins, 1992). Further, it appears that new, inviting assessment activities can be powerful and meaningful learning experiences for both students and teachers (Wolf, LeMahieu, & Eresh, 1992).

Viewing knowledge as socially constructed gives rise to the third rule guiding assessment in the restructured classroom environment, which is that teachers in such a classroom must construct social environments for both learning and assessment. This follows from the new understanding of the social nature of cognition. Thinking, according to Vygotsky (1978), is an activity which is dependent on speech and which is developed and maintained through interpersonal experience. In terms of classroom assessment, this interpersonal experience is twofold: First, it stresses the importance of the teacher-student relationship to provide experience necessary for advancing skills and understanding. Teachers need to guide students to internalize their "tools" for thinking and thus transform to higher levels of competence (Brown & Ferrara, 1985). The second interpersonal context of assessment refers to collaboration and interaction among peers and others. Included here are group projects and presentations, which provide occasions for modeling thinking strategies and scaffolding complex performances in order to share and learn from others (Resnick & Klopfer, 1989). In addition, there are ways for presenting assessment tasks to individuals and groups of students, parents, school staff, and community members.

Alternative Assessment and Teacher Role Changes

What is required of teachers in developing and implementing the rules guiding assessment in the restructured classroom environment? Are teachers well prepared for and receptive of this new evaluative role? The answers to these questions involve building an environment that supports at least three types of teacher change. First, teachers need a new belief system based on the current research, referenced throughout this chapter, on cognitive development and how students learn. Understanding this new paradigm means providing *all* students with equal opportunities to use new information, through meaningful problem-solving situations, and to achieve meaningful goals; it means understanding that there are many ways to solve problems rather than one simple, correct solution; it means being sensitive to each student's context and mindful that "the way we tend to construct our world is only one construction among many" (Brown & Langer, 1990, p. 332). It also means understanding the range of strategies that students may use to solve particular problems and the circumstances and advantages of each (Siegler, 1989). For example, does a particular solution to a mathematical problem reflect a mechanical computation or a conceptual understanding? Also critical is that teachers develop an open and collaborative atmosphere where beliefs such as reconceptualized understandings about learning and testing, along with goals and standards, are clearly communicated to students. Obviously, what and how a teacher chooses to assess learning in the classroom send important messages to students (Wolf, et al., 1992).

A second understanding required of teachers concerns the purpose and characteristics of "good" classroom assessments. Assessments in the restructured classroom are designed to directly inform both teacher and student on the skills and understandings of the individual student. Thus, they support both teachers in their instructional planning and students in the development of their cognitive capacity. As authentic measures, they have value beyond evaluation and are relevant, foster disciplined inquiry, and require the integration of knowledge (Archbald & Newmann, 1988). To develop these assessments means, after establishing standards, that teachers must identify a range of performance levels within these standards to monitor and facilitate student progress. If teachers do not select good tasks and measures and establish criteria for what to value, the reliability and validity of these new assessments will be in serious doubt. Teachers must also be open to students having a more active and responsive role in classroom assessments, through participating in the development of tasks and standards, through self- and peer-evaluation, and through collaborative work with others.

Third, teachers need practical knowledge and experience in designing and scoring these new measures and in using the findings. In order to determine initially what they want students to know and be able to do at the end of the academic year, teachers need a new understanding of "literacy" within their content areas of expertise, the fluidity of knowledge, and connections among disciplines, as opposed to the traditional use of text-as-curriculum (Brown, 1991b; Eisner, 1982). Teachers need opportunities to develop, use, and score the three basic types of assessments—paper-and-pencil assessments (e.g., teacher and text tests, quizzes, homework), performance assessments (e.g., observations of student behaviors, judgments of student products), and direct personal communication with students (e.g., student interviews and conversations, teacher intuitions and feelings about students) (Stiggins, 1991). Teachers must learn to be cautious in developing and using these new measures. Before jumping on the portfolio "bandwagon," they need to understand that a portfolio is more than just a file crammed full of student products. Rather, a portfolio is a purposeful collection of student work with criteria established for both selecting and judging the merit of the pieces included (Camp, 1990). It is a metacognitive tool of learning. Finally, teachers need support and encouragement in the development and use of these new measures.

Following from this new belief system is the proposition that knowledge about how students learn must similarly guide a teacher's curricular, instructional, and assessment practices. Thus, the teacher's challenge is to adopt a mindful, flexible perspective (Brown & Langer, 1990)—to create appropriate, meaningful apprenticeship experiences for students—by modeling tasks, scaffolding or supporting the student, coaching through the student's entire learning process (Collins, Brown, & Holum, 1991), and being a "reflective practitioner" (Zessoules & Gardner, 1991). What needs to be addressed is much more than just "assessment literacy." Although currently this knowledge seems to be available to only a select group of educational researchers and scholars (Stiggins, 1991), it is the implications that a coordinated effort has for all school decision making that is so important for the restructured classroom. Indeed, it is these interrelationships of curriculum, instruction, and assessment which ought to be the center of teacher education in general, as well as the focus of preparation of all those involved in changing schools. These interrelationships should also be the bases of conversations and collaboration within grade levels, school buildings, districts, and even states. Without the support of school values and regulations in the context of these interrelationships, the new vision of learning and assessment in the restructured classroom environment is not likely to be fulfilled. It must be pointed out once again that it is in the classroom itself—Pauly's (1991) crucible of education—where the new paradigm for schooling in the 21st century begins.

IMPLICATIONS FOR AT-RISK STUDENTS

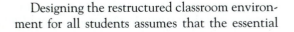

Designing the restructured classroom environment for all students assumes that the essential elements are functional for students at risk of school failure as well as for those for whom success seems relatively assured. In fact, the movement to radically transform American education calls for a redefinition of education in this country in which "normed thinking"—where students are seen as either successes or failures—is no longer a viable option (Jones & Pierce, 1992).

But what does a restructured learning environment seek to accomplish in terms of the cognitive capacity of youngsters who have historically been poorly served by schooling and who are "locked-in" to educational communities in crisis? There appear to be at least four major implications of restructured schooling for students at risk: (1) the need for inclusion in the classroom and the larger school community; (2) the emphasis on the development of student potential; (3) the focus on thinking as key to intelligent performance; and (4) the search for more explicit intercultural relationships. These implications are herein discussed relative to the eight essential elements.

NEED FOR INCLUSION IN THE SCHOOL COMMUNITY

At-risk youngsters have all too often been viewed as learners outside the regular classroom. Often forged into groups labeled by handicap or deficit, these students rarely escape such categorical treatment and generally fail to see the higher-order thinking they so badly need. Although tracking students is a complex and dynamic process, research shows that after more than 70 years of study, homogeneous sorting in elementary schools fails to foster the desired achievement outcomes (Oakes, 1992). In terms of social placement, Oakes proposes, negative effects result from the influences of tracking, especially for African-American and Latino youngsters who are disproportionately represented in low-track academic classes.

The restructured classroom needs to be a user-friendly workplace in which all students are warmly welcomed to full-right membership and feel they are significant contributors to the learning exchange (Jones & Hixson, 1991). Cushman (1992) calls for heterogeneous grouping in secondary schools, too, modeling the larger, democratic society and challenging educators to initiate de-tracking procedures. Alternative grouping, special projects and apprenticeships, and cooperative learning assignments are only a handful of the activities that teachers can design on a continuous progress path to challenge differing student abilities and to stretch each learner's mental accomplishments. While more collaborative work is called for among teachers to create these growth opportunities, the expectation of success makes the additional effort worthwhile.

Inclusion in the regular educational community enables at-risk students to join in the exchange of academic problem resolution. Sometimes the give-and-take is with a "wiser" adult; sometimes it is with classmates. What is underlined in such instructional conversations, so important to every learner's development—and even more so to youngsters with limited experience—are the differing means by which the teacher can both appreciate and intervene in a student's thought processing (e.g., modeling, feeding back, contingency managing, directing, questioning, explaining, task structuring) (Ballenger, 1992; Tharp & Gallimore, 1991). By contrast, to be sorted out, to be given a watered-down curriculum, and to be expected to perform according to less stringent standards are aspects of built-in-failure. For America's at-risk students, this is not legitimate membership in a learning community.

Inclusion needs to be extended to at-risk students' lives beyond school. Parents and caregivers, potential mentors and assisters in the community, all need to be apprised of the at-risk student's higher-level experience in learning. As these students begin to formulate real meanings concerning their work in classrooms, they can share these meanings with friends, family, and others. While there may be tensions between academic experience and the actual lives of urban youngsters, such tensions need to be surfaced and dealt with to ensure valid instructional success (Palincsar, 1992).

EMPHASIS ON THE DEVELOPMENT OF STUDENT POTENTIAL

The developmental nature of the learner, which underlies many of the essential elements, is primarily a dynamic view of learning. At-risk students need to be viewed the same as their more able peers. They should not be measured by *how much* of a given ability they possess, but seen as potentially moving along a similar sequence of thought development—only at a differing *rate* (Elkind, 1989). Kaniel and Feuerstein (1989) call for students with learning difficulties to become candidates for "cognitive modifiability," conscious educational efforts to change their ways of thinking, to challenge them with new learning, to be creative, and to build their own innovative conceptions of reality.

For at-risk students to share in the restructured learning environment, their circumstances and diverse cultural backgrounds need to be carefully considered and appreciated by the classroom instructor (Means, Chelemer, & Knapp, 1991; Moll, 1992). Moreover, such characteristics do not mean that these students formulate fundamental knowledge in ways inferior to other learners; Gardner's (1983) multiple intelligences are equally attainable across cultures and subcultures (Elkind, 1989). What is apparently different is their inability to focus on understanding and its generalizability (Pogrow, 1992). Paris and Winograd (1990) maintain that a heightened appreciation of metacognition is what is called for in the instruction of at-risk students. They propose that metacognition helps these students in at least three ways: (1) to understand their own thinking and learning, (2) to become aware of and to begin to deal with "bugs" or difficulties in a particular problem solution, and (3) to relate to instructional situations with better comprehension and more positive affect. Thus, these researchers see potential for both cognitive and conative change in students whose learning once was considered marginal.

The message of student modifiability needs to be carried beyond the classroom and school, as well. Strategic learning that is concomitant with metacognitive behavior must be recognized in the larger community in which at-risk students reside (Jones & Pierce, 1992). Feuerstein (1990) calls this the need to mediate for an optimistic alternative. Other researchers see the possibility that through such transfer, student resilience can be enhanced (Benard, 1991). Ultimately, to carry the learning of the restructured classroom to the real world experienced by at-risk students means to see their lives, their problems, and the constraints they face on a daily basis in a different perspective.

FOCUS ON THINKING AS KEY TO INTELLIGENT PERFORMANCE

The restructured classroom casts cognitive development as central to teaching and learning, and key to the assessment of performance. Such expectations should be no different for at-risk learners. Some researchers see these relationships as closely aligned with principles for creating powerful apprenticeship opportunities in the classroom: content, method, sequencing, and sociology (Collins, Hawkins, & Carver, 1991). Content must aim for student expertise development; method focuses on ways to develop that expertise; sequencing prepares orderly advancement to better and more complex performance; and sociology demands positive situations which can interrelate the individual with the group. But the most telling aspect of such learning for at-risk students lies in their ability to *internalize* the cognitive aspects of instruction, to *self-regulate*, to build on personal strengths, and to become spontaneous thinkers. By contrast, this is exactly what Kaniel and Feuerstein (1989) suggest is the missing ingredient of the outmoded "passive-acceptance approach" to teaching students with learning difficulties. Without restructured education, these youngsters are kept busy with minimal, rote tasks and alienated from serious, cognitive learning.

Self-regulation as an authentic educational goal is particularly important for long-range development of low-achieving and disadvantaged students (Au, 1980; Brown & Ferrara, 1985). Unfortunately, this goal is ignored in some of the major educational platforms set for America's schools. Uphoff (1991) notes the national misreading of the concept of "readiness" in early childhood, highlighting the current expectation that it is the child who must bend to meet the institution. Is that authentic? Where in the national program are the evaluation strategies that facilitate the gradual development of metacognitive abilities, including self-regulation, in children who may not be members of the mainstream population nor fluently speak standard English?

Assessments are available to diagnose at-risk students' learning potential and to identify their appropriate levels of instruction, but they are rarely found in actual practice. Consider the "think aloud technique" used in studies of problem-solving strategies (Newall & Simon, 1972), in diagnosing learning disabilities (Short et al., 1990), and in remediating problem-solving deficiencies (Bereiter & Bird, 1985). Few are the schools that are aware of dynamic assessment programs, such as those developed by Feuerstein (1979) and others (Lidz, 1987). A similar testing strategy has been noted as highly successful in the reciprocal teaching approach (Palincsar & Brown, 1984), but rare are the school systems in which such implementations are being conducted and researched (Campione, 1992). In terms of innovative evaluation of at-risk learners in the current reform period, unless assessment policies and procedures are adjusted to match new curricula and instructional goals in the classroom, Oakes' negative conclusion on tracking is likely to be repeated.

SEARCH FOR MORE EXPLICIT INTERCULTURAL RELATIONSHIPS

The need for education to respect the learner and the learning process are important implications of the restructured classroom's influence on at-risk populations. Good teachers are rare. Those instructors who hold the belief that poor and minority youngsters have little knowledge to contribute to a classroom's dialogue should not be teachers at all (Brown & Langer, 1990; Jones & Hixson, 1991). Considering the cultural diversity evident in America's changing demographics, the demand for effective teachers who can relate to students of many backgrounds and varied personal histories will only increase in the coming decade (Moll, 1990; Vobejda, 1992). These are the instructors with the positive belief systems called for in restructured classrooms.

A salient finding of the cognitive revolution is the acknowledgment that to understand how something works, it is necessary to experience it directly (Goldenberg & Gallimore, 1991). Such experience creates local knowledge-building: it is that which is proximal in the ZPD (Goldenberg, 1991). Feuerstein (1990) maintains that it is teachers who can mediate the various needs youngsters bring to the classroom who really engage students in their learning space. Mediated learning, then, must be an objective with regard to intercultural relationships in the classroom of present-day America (Presseisen & Kozulin, 1992). Teachers need to maximize such mediation for all students, but especially for those who are not members of the mainstream culture. Tharp (1989) proposes that such instruction delivers the significant, universalistic teaching/learning strategies that are embedded in the foundation of current educational reform: "varied activity settings, language development activities, varied sensory modalities in instruction, responsive instructional conversations, increased cooperative and group responsive instructional conversations, increased cooperative and group activities, and a respectful and accommodating sensitivity to students' knowledge, experiences, values, and tastes" (p. 356). In contrast to majority students, if these students do not have the opportunity for such training at school, learning very well may never occur.

Fundamental to education in a restructured classroom, then, is the opportunity to examine simultaneously one's own culture and that of one's neighbors, as well. With the new literacies of the cognitive revolution, every at-risk student's curriculum must seek intercultural exchanges,

reflected in every subject area and constantly revised with use (Hiebert, 1991). Constructing new meanings at school, in cooperation with teachers and classmates, will enable autonomous learners to brave the vexing problems they face beyond the school's confines.

CONCLUSION

The overall goal of this chapter has been to address the problem of creating a learning environment for all students that makes possible the achievement of restructured purpose in American education. In terms of the three questions that guided this examination (see p. 236), what has been learned and what still needs to be pursued?

RESTRUCTURED SCHOOLING AND THE COGNITIVE PARADIGM

Perhaps the clearest finding of this study is the importance of cognition to the restructuring goals of the current reform effort. Whether conscious or not, the major redesign of American education hinges on making real the higher-order processes involved in the development of competent students. This factor emphasizes that the thinking required for work and study in the world today is neither simplistic nor easy. Educators need to understand the complexity of developing minds; they need to review and know the research of nearly a century of theorizing and experimentation. They need to become active learners themselves in applying the principles of cognition to the practice of education.

Cognitive matters relate to the global marketplace as well as to the nation's schools. Teaching for thinking or inquiry should not be glibly presented as a "silver bullet" for American policymakers (Eisner, 1992). Rather the country needs to understand that success in both education and work, ultimately, is characterized by the ability to analyze and manipulate symbolic images—words, numbers, visual representations—in dynamic problem solving (Reich, 1991). Schools need to ask themselves what this type of performance requires of the learning process, not just when exit examinations are given but throughout a student's academic career from early childhood to graduation. As Tharp and Gallimore (1989) apply their research, the issue is not only one of "rousing minds to life," but rousing entire schools, as well, and connecting these institutions to the larger community and workplace.

An emphasis on cognition is not to focus on logic or reasoning as the sole definition of thinking, but to see the broader dimensions of a new, interdisciplinary science. Conation and metacognition, creativity as well as critical analysis, are called for in education's new understandings of the development of multiple thinking abilities. The importance of teacher education is underscored here, as well as the need to reevaluate how schooling defines "intelligences" and how it assesses the existence and performance of intelligent behaviors (Gardner, 1990). Further, the integration of curriculum, instruction, and assessment calls for a serious reorganization of traditional teacher roles (Cuban, 1992; Schlechty & Cole, 1991).

AT-RISK STUDENTS AND THINKING

We believe that developing the thinking ability of all students is a challenge to be confronted. For too long, American schools have not advanced the cognitive development of students considered at risk of failure and dropping out. Considering the recent census report on dropout rates (Mezzacappa, 1992b), the need to include these populations in a restructured approach to education is critical and immediate. Unfortunately, to date, it has not been an issue energetically addressed in either local or national political platforms.

The eight essential elements of a restructured classroom environment that form the basis of this study must underlie the learning experience of all students, while recognizing and respecting differences in background, ability, and perspective of each learner. Some of these differences reflect developmental concerns; educators must work on what is appropriate for the experience of each youngster to spark learning and understanding. Some reflect individual circumstances; educators must be cognizant of the diverse personal backgrounds of students, more varied now than classrooms have been since the beginning of this century. While other differences reflect group dimensions, educators must analyze the particular circumstances of populations isolated by history and cultural experience. Today, the importance of fulfilling all of the essential elements may be one way of seeking a kind of "standard" for student learning in an era when standardization does not so readily fit reality (Eisner, 1992).

To bring about the integration of curriculum, introduction, and assessment within the restructured classroom environment is not an easy task. For at-risk students, the question of appropriate tools for learning is matched by the need to understand the workings of a student's ZPD. Exploring the potential role of technology as a "tool" may also facilitate learning for these students. While some researchers reviewed in this study stress the primary importance of human interaction and mediation (Feuerstein, 1990; Kozulin, 1990), there are others who maintain that a parallel use of computers and electronic media can embrace learners' understanding and elaborate on meaningful classroom contexts (Collins, 1991; Polin, 1991; Salomon, Perkins, & Globerson, 1991; Scott, Cole, & Engel, 1992). These applications need to be researched further and their effects carefully documented. Also, impact of cognition depends on how technology is used by teachers and students (Shavelson & Salomon, 1985). It should not be forgotten that the most important aspect of restructuring American education is to bring at-risk students into a meaningful exchange of ideas as full members of a learning community (Thurow, 1991). The role of higher thought development versus remediation in efforts, such as Chapter 1 programming, is a particular case in point that deserves serious examination (Jones & Pierce, 1992; Lewis, 1992).

DIVERSITY AND LEARNING

The social context of learning is a condition that has been shown to be unique in the formation of reflective thought (Hiebert, 1991; Moll, 1992). The dynamism of a restructured classroom environment rests on the liveliness of classroom dialogue and the teacher's ability to create innovative curricular experiences, tied to cognitive development, which students can share and extend. An important aspect of restructured education yet to be examined is the balance between the purview of the individual and the collective vision required by knowledge in a particular domain. Experiments in current curriculum development and alternative assessment techniques have begun, yet they need to be monitored and assessed. It must not be forgotten that the goal of the current reform effort is to give every generation and every student a chance to become mindful.

Finally, the role of constructivism in the restructured classroom environment suggests that every student builds knowledge and understanding in his or her own way. The single "uniformity" to be pursued, within the cultural pluralism evidenced in America's classrooms today, is the need for each learner to become self-regulatively inventive and, simultaneously, able to analyze carefully. As Piaget (1964) suggested nearly three decades ago:

> The accent must be on auto-regulation, on active assimilation—the accent must be on the activity of the subject. Failing this there is no possible didactic or pedagogy which significantly transforms the subject. (p. i)

In short, there is no substitute for thinking something through on your own. In the current reform era, providing all students with an environment in which this can happen is the essence of radical change in America's schools.

FOOTNOTE

1. Various published descriptions of restructured learning environments were reviewed in conjunction with determining the model of the eight essential elements. In particular, *The Nine Common Principles of Essential Schools* (Coalition of Essential Schools, 1991) and the *Learner-Centered Psychological Principles: Guidelines for School Redesign and Reform* (APA Task Force, 1992) were drawn upon for this study.

REFERENCES

APA Task Force on Psychology in Education. (1992). *Learner-centered psychological principles: Guidelines for school redesign and reform* (rev. ed.) Washington, DC: American Psychological Association.

Adey, P. (1990). Thinking science. *Teaching Thinking and Problem Solving, 12*(3), 1–5.

Adler, M. J. (1982). *The Paideia proposal: An educational manifesto.* New York: Macmillan.

Alexander, L., Frankiewicz, R. G., & Williams, R. E. (1979). Facilitation of learning and retention of oral instruction using advance and post-organizers. *Journal of Educational Psychology, 71,* 701–707.

Alvermann, D. E. (1988). Effects of spontaneous and induced lookbacks on self perceived high- and low-ability comprehenders. *Journal of Educational Research, 81,* 325–331.

Ammon, P., & Hutcheson, B. P. (1989). Promoting the development of teachers' pedagogical conceptions. *Genetic Epistemologist, 17*(4), 25–29.

Archbald, D. A., & Nwmann, F. M. (1988). *Beyond standardized testing: Assessing authentic academic achievement in the secondary school.* Reston, VA: National Association of Secondary School Principals.

Ashley, W., Jones, J., Zahniser, G., & Inks, L. (1986). *Peer tutoring: A guide to program design* (Research and Development Series No. 260). Columbus, OH: Ohio State University, Center for Research in Vocational Education. (ERIC Document Reproduction Service No. ED 268 372).

Au, K. H. (1980). Participation structures in a reading lesson with Hawaiian children: Analysis of a culturally appropriate instructional event. *Anthropology and Education Quarterly, 11*(2), 91–115.

Ausubel, D. (1977). The facilitation of meaningful verbal learning in the classroom. *Educational Psychologist, 12,* 162–178.

Baars, B. J. (1986). *The cognitive revolution in psychology.* New York: Guilford Press.

Ballenger, C. (1992). Because you like us: The language of control. *Harvard Educational Review, 62*(2), 199–207.

Barell, J., Liebmann, R., & Sigel, J. (1988). Fostering thoughtful self-direction in students. *Educational Leadership, 45*(7), 14–17.

Baron, J. B., & Sternberg, R. J. (Eds.). (1987). *Teaching thinking skills: Theory and practice.* New York: W. H. Freeman.

Barrett, P. A. (1989). Finding their own voices: Children learning together. *Doubts and certainties (The Mastery in Learning Project), 4*(4), 1–5.

Barth, R. S. (1991). Restructuring schools: Some questions for teachers and principals. *Phi Delta Kappan, 73*(2), 123–128.

Belmont, J. M. (1989). Cognitive strategies and strategic learning: The socio-instructional approach. *American Psychologist, 44*(2), 142–148.

Benard, B. (1991). *Fostering resilience in kids: Protective factors in the family, school, and community.* Portland, OR: Northwest Regional Educational Laboratory.

Bereiter, C., & Bird, M. (1985). Use of thinking aloud in identification and teaching of reading comprehension strategies. *Cognition and Instruction, 2,* 131–156.

Bereiter, C., & Scardamalia, M. (1992). Cognition and curriculum. In P. W. Jackson (Ed.), *Handbook of research on curriculum* (pp. 517–542). New York: Macmillan.

Beyer, B. K. (1987). *Practical strategies for the teaching of thinking.* Boston: Allyn & Bacon.

Beyer, B. K. (1988). *Developing a thinking skills program.* Boston: Allyn & Bacon.

Beyer, F. S. (1992, April). Impact of computers on middle-level student writing skills. Paper presented at the annual meeting of the American Educational Research Association, San Francisco, CA.

Beyer, F. S., & Nodine, C. F. (1985). Familiarity influences how children draw what they see. *Visual Arts Research, 11*(2), 60–68.

Beyer, F. S., & Smey-Richman, B. (1988, April). Addressing the "at-risk" challenge in the nonurban setting. Paper presented at the annual meeting of the American Educational Research Association, New Orleans, LA.

Black, A. (1989). Developmental teacher education: Preparing teachers to apply developmental principles across the curriculum. *Genetic Epistemologist, 17*(4), 5–14.

Boden, M. A. (1990). Cognitive science. *Radcliffe Quarterly, 76*(2), 8–9.

Brandt, R. S. (1986). On improving achievement of minority children: A conversation with James Comer. *Educational Leadership, 43*(5), 13–17.

Bransford, J. D., & Vye, N. J. (1989). A perspective on cognitive research and its implications for instruction. In L. B. Resnick & L. E. Klopfer (Eds.), *Toward the thinking curriculum: Current cognitive research (1989 Yearbook)* (pp. 173–205). Alexandria, VA: Association for Supervision and Curriculum Development.

Bronfenbrenner, U. (1991). What do families do? *Family Affairs, 4*(1–2), 1–6.

Brophy, J., & Alleman, J. (1991). A caveat: Curriculum integration isn't always a good idea. *Educational Leadership, 49*(2), 66.

Brown, A. L., & Campione, J. C. (1986). Psychological theory and the study of learning disabilities. *American Psychologist, 14*(10), 1059–1068.

Brown, A. L., & Ferrera, R. A. (1985). Diagnosing zones of proximal development. In J. V. Wertsch (Ed.), *Culture, communication and cognition: Vygotskian perspectives* (pp. 273–305). New York: Cambridge University Press.

Brown, A. L., Palincsar, A. S., & Purcell, L. (1986). Poor readers: Teach, don't label. In U. Neisser (Ed.), *The school achievement of minority children: New perspectives* (pp. 105–143). Hillsdale, NJ: Lawrence Erlbaum.

Brown, J., & Langer, E. (1990). Mindfulness and intelligence: A comparison. *Educational Psychologist, 25*(3–4), 305–335.

Brown, J. S., Collins, A., & Duguid, P. (1980). Situated

cognition and the culture of learning. *Educational Researcher, 18*(1), 32–42.

Brown, R. G. (1991a). *Schools of thought.* San Francisco: Jossey-Bass.

Brown, R. G. (1991b). The one-literacy schoolhouse in the age of multiple literacies. *Educational Horizons, 69*(3), 141–145.

Brown, R. G. (1989). Testing and thoughtfulness. *Educational Leadership, 46*(7), 31–33.

Bruner, J. S. (1960). *The process of education.* New York: Vintage Books.

Bruner, J. S. (1964). On going beyond the information given. In R. J. C. Harper, C. C. Anderson, C. M. Christenson, & S. M. Hunka (Eds.), *The cognitive processes: Readings* (pp. 293–311). Englewood Cliffs, NJ: Prentice Hall.

Bruner, J. S. (1984). Vygotsky's zone of proximal development: The hidden agenda. In B. Rogoff & J. V. Wertsch (Eds.), *Children's learning in the "zone of proximal development"* (pp. 93–97). San Francisco: Jossey-Bass.

Budoff, M. (1987). Measures for assessing learning potential. In C. S. Lidz (Ed.), *Dynamic assessment: An interactional approach to evaluating learning potential* (pp. 173–195). New York: Guilford Press.

Caine, R. N., & Caine, G. (1991). *Making connections: Teaching and the human brain.* Alexandria, VA: Association for Supervision and Curriculum Development.

Camp, R. (1990, October). *Portfolio approaches to instruction and assessment in writing.* Workshop presented at Research for Better Schools, Philadelphia, PA (photocopy).

Campione, J. (1992, February). Assessment and cognition. Paper presented at the Third International Conference on Cognitive Education, University of California, Riverside, CA.

Campione, J. C., Brown, A. L., Ferrara, R. A., & Bryant, N. R. (1984). The zone of proximal development: Implications for individual differences and learning. In B. Rogoff & J. V. Wertsch (Eds.), *Children's learning in the "zone of proximal development"* (pp. 77–91). San Francisco: Jossey-Bass.

Carnevale, A. P. (1991). *America and the new economy.* Washington, DC: U.S. Department of Labor, Employment and Training Administration.

Case, R. (1992). *The mind's staircase: Exploring the conceptual underpinnings of children's thought and knowledge.* Hillsdale, NJ: Lawrence Erlbaum.

Ceci, S. J., Ramey, S. L., & Ramey, C. T. (1990). Framing intellectual assessment in terms of a person-process-context model. *Educational Psychologist, 25* (3–4), 269–291.

Chance, P. (1986). *Thinking in the classroom: A survey of programs.* New York: Teachers College Press, Columbia University.

Clark, C. M., & Peterson, P. L. (1990). *Research in teaching and learning: Vol. 3. Teachers' thought processes.* New York: Macmillan.

Coalition of Essential Schools. (1991). The nine common principles of essential schools. *Horace, 8*(2), 8.

Collins, A. (1991). The role of computer technology in restructuring schools. *Phi Delta Kappan, 73*(1), 28–36.

Collins, A., Brown, J. S., & Holum, A. (1991). Cognitive apprenticeship: Making thinking visible. *American Educator, 15*(3), 6–11, 38–46.

Collins, A., Hawkins, J., & Carver, S. M. (1991). *A cognitive apprenticeship for disadvantaged students* (Technical Report No. 10). New York: Center for Technology in Education, Bank Street College of Education.

Collins, J. (1982). Discourse style, classroom interaction and differential treatment. *Journal of Reading Behavior, 14,* 429–437.

Comer, J. P. (1980). *School power: Implications of an intervention project.* New York: Free Press.

Comer, J. P. (1988). Educating poor minority children. *Scientific American, 259*(5), 42–48.

Commission on the Skills of the American Workforce. (1990). *America's choice: High skills or low wages.* Rochester, NY: National Center on Education and the Economy.

Conley, D. T. (1991, February). Restructuring schools: Educators adapt to a changing world. *Trends & Issues.* Eugene, OR: ERIC Clearinghouse on Educational Management.

Corbett, H. D. (1990). *On the meaning of restructuring.* Philadelphia, PA: Research for Better Schools.

Costa, A. L. (1991). *The school as a home for the mind.* Palatine, IL: Skylight Publishing.

Council of Chief State School Officers. (1989). *Success for all in a new century: A report of the Council of Chief State School Officers on restructuring education.* Washington, DC: Author.

Council of Chief State School Officers. (1991). Restructuring learning to improve the teaching of thinking and reasoning for all students. *Concerns, 32,* 1–8.

Cuban, L. (1992, March 11). Please, no more facts; just better teaching. *Education Week, 11*(25), 30, 40.

Cushman, K. (1992). Essential schools' "universal goals": How can heterogeneous grouping help? *Horace, 8*(5), 1–8.

Darling-Hammond, L. (1990). Achieving our goals: Superficial or structural reforms? *Phi Delta Kappan, 72*(4), 286–295.

David, J. L., with Purkey, S., & White, P. (1987). *Restructuring in progress: Lessons from pioneering districts* (Results in Education Series). Washington, DC: National Governors' Association, Center for Policy Research.

Davidson, N., & Worsham, T. (Eds.). (1992). *Enhancing thinking through cooperative learning.* New York: Teachers College Press.

Detterman, D. K., & Sternberg, R. J. (Eds.). (1982). *How and how much can intelligence be increased,* Norwood, NJ: Ablex.

Dewey, J. (1964). *Democracy and education* (4th printing). New York: Macmillan.

Diamond, M. C. (1988). *Enriching heredity: The impact of the environment on the anatomy of the brain.* New York: Free Press.

Dickinson, D. (1991). *Positive trends in learning: Meeting the needs of a rapidly changing world.* Atlanta, GA: IBM Educational Systems.

Dillon, R. F., & Sternberg, R. J. (Eds.). (1986). *Cognition and instruction.* Orlando, FL: Academic Press.

Educational Testing Service. (1990). *The education reform decade.* Princeton, NJ: Author, Policy Information Center.

Eisner, E. W. (1982). *Cognitive and curriculum: A basis for deciding what to teach.* New York: Longman.

Eisner, E. W. (1992). The federal reform of schools: Looking for the silver bullet. *Phi Delta Kappan, 73*(9), 722–723.

Elkind, D. (1979). *The child and society: Essays in applied child development.* New York: Oxford University Press.

Elkind, D. (1989). Developmentally appropriate practice: Philosophical and practical applications. *Phi Delta Kappan, 71*(2), 113–117.

Elmore, R. F. (1988). *Early experience in restructuring schools: Voices from the field.* (Results in Education Series). Washington, DC: National Governors Association, Center for Policy Research.

Elmore, R. F. (1991). *Restructuring schools: The next generation of educational reform.* San Francisco: Jossey-Bass.

Englert, C. S., Raphael, T. E., Anderson, L. M., Anthony, H. M., & Stevens, D. D. (1991). Making strategies and self-talk visible: Writing instruction in regular and special education classrooms. *American Educational Research Journal, 28*(2), 337–372.

Englert, C. S., Raphael, T. E., & Anderson, L. M. (1992). Socially mediated instruction: Improving students'

knowledge and talk about writing. *The Elementary School Journal, 92*(4), 411–449.

Ennis, R. H. (1986). A taxonomy of critical thinking dispositions and abilities. In J. B. Baron & R. J. Sternberg (Eds.), *Teaching thinking skills: Theory and practice* (pp. 9–26). New York: W. H. Freeman.

Ennis, R. H. (1989). Critical thinking and subject specificity: Clarification and needed research. *Educational Researcher, 18*(3), 4–10.

Ennis, R. H. (1991, April). Critical thinking: A streamlined conception. Paper presented at annual meeting of American Educational Research Association, Chicago, IL (photocopy).

Erickson, F., & Shultz, J. (1992). Students' experience of the curriculum. In P. W. Jackson (Ed.), *Handbook of research on curriculum: A project of the American Educational Research Association* (pp. 465–485). New York: Macmillan.

Feldman, S. (1992). Children in crisis: The tragedy of under-funded schools and the students they serve. *American Educator, 16*(1), 8–17, 46.

Feuerstein, R. (1990). The theory of structural cognitive modifiability. In B. Z. Presseisen, R. J. Sternberg, K. W. Fischer, C. C. Knight, & R. Feuerstein (Eds.), *Learning and thinking styles: Classroom interaction* (pp. 68–134). Washington, DC: National Education Association.

Feuerstein, R., with Rand, Y., & Hoffman, M. B. (1979). *The dynamic assessment of retarded performers: The learning potential assessment device, theory, instruments, and techniques.* Glenview, IL: Scott, Foresman.

Feuerstein, R., with Rand, Y., Hoffman, M. B., & Miller, R. (1980). *Instrumental enrichment: An intervention program for cognitive modifiability.* Baltimore, MD: University Park Press.

Feuerstein, R., Hoffman, M. B., Jensen, M. R., & Rand, Y. (1985). Instrumental enrichment, an intervention program for structural cognitive modifiability. In J. W. Segal, S. F. Chipman, & R. Glaser (Eds.), *Thinking and learning skills: Vol. 1: Relating instruction to research* (pp. 43–82). Hillsdale, NJ: Lawrence Erlbaum.

Feuerstein, R., & Hoffman, M. B. (1990). Mediating cognitive processes to the retarded performer: Rationale, goals, and nature of intervention. In M. Schwebel, C. A. Maher, & N. S. Fagley (Eds.), *Promoting cognitive growth over the life span* (pp. 115–136). Hillsdale, NJ: Lawrence Erlbaum.

Fischer, K. (1980). A theory of cognitive development: The control and construction of hierarchies of skills. *Psychological Review, 57,* 477–531.

Flavell, J. H. (1976). Metacognitive aspects of problem solving. In L. B. Resnick (Ed.), *The nature of intelli-*

gence (pp. 231–235). Hillsdale, NJ: Lawrence Erlbaum.

Fleming, M., & Chambers, B. (1983). Teacher-made tests: Windows to the classroom. In W. E. Hathaway (Ed.), *New directions for testing and measurement: Testing in the schools* (pp. 29–38), San Francisco: Jossey-Bass.

Fogarty, R. (1991). Ten ways to integrate curriculum. *Educational Leadership, 49*(2), 61–65.

Fosnot, C. T. (1989). *Enquiring teachers, enquiring learners: A constructivist approach for teaching.* New York: Teachers College Press.

Frederiksen, J. R., & Collins, A. (1989). A systems approach to educational testing. *Educational Researcher, 18*(9), 27–32.

Freedman, S. W. (1987). Peer response groups in two ninth grade classrooms (Technical Report No. 12). Berkeley, CA: University of California, Center for the Study of Writing.

Freeman, N. H. (1980). *Strategies of representation in young children.* New York: Academic Press.

Gagné, R. M. (1970). *The conditions of learning.* New York: Holt, Reinhart & Winston.

Garcia, Y., & Montes, F. (1992). Authentic assessments for limited English-proficient students. *Intercultural Development Research Association (IDRA) Newsletter, 19*(4), 9–11.

Gardner, H. (1983). *Frames of mind: The theory of multiple intelligences.* New York: Basic Books.

Gardner, H. (1985). *The mind's new science: A history of the cognitive revolution.* New York: Basic Books.

Gardner, H. (1990, December). The proper assessment of multiple intelligences. Paper presented at the Second National Conference on Assessing Thinking, Baltimore, MD (photocopy).

Gardner, H. (1991). *The unschooled mind: How children think and how schools should teach.* New York: Basic Books.

Glickman, C. (1991). Pretending not to know what we know. *Educational Leadership, 48*(8), 4–10.

Goldenberg, C. (1991). *Instructional conversations and their classroom application.* Washington, DC: National Center for Research on Cultural Diversity and Second Language Learning.

Goldenberg, C., & Gallimore, R. (1991). Local knowledge, research knowledge, and educational change: A case study of early Spanish reading improvement. *Educational Researcher, 20*(8), 2–14.

Good, T. L., Reys, B. J., Grouws, D. A., & Mulryan, C. M. (1989–90). Using work-groups in mathematics instruction. *Educational Leadership, 47*(4), 56–62.

Goodlad, J. I. (1984). *A place called school: Prospects for the future.* New York: McGraw Hill.

Green, M. (1973). *Teacher as stranger: Educational philosophy for the modern age.* Belmont, CA: Wadsworth Publishing.

Greeno, J. G. (1989). A perspective on thinking. *American Psychologist, 44*(2), 134–141.

Haller, E. P., Child, D. A., & Walberg, H. J. (1988). Can comprehension be taught? *Educational Researcher, 17*(9), 5–8.

Harvey, G., & Crandall, D. P. (1988). *A beginning look at the what and how of restructuring.* Andover, MA: The Regional Laboratory for Educational Improvement of the Northeast and Islands.

Haywood, H. C. (1990, July). A total cognitive approach in education: Enough bits and pieces. Presidential address presented at the Second International Conference of the International Association for Cognitive Education, Mons, Belgium.

Hiebert, E. H. (1991). *Literacy for a diverse society: Perspectives, practice, and policies.* New York: Teachers College Press, Columbia University.

Hilliard, A., III. (1991). Do we have the will to educate all the children? *Educational Leadership, 49*(1), 31–36.

Hodgkinson, H. L. (1985). *All one system: Demographics of education, kindergarten through graduate school.* Washington, DC: Institute for Educational Leadership.

Hodgkinson, H. (1991). Reform versus reality. *Phi Delta Kappan, 73*(1), 9–16.

Jacobs, H. H. (1991). Planning for curriculum integration. *Educational Leadership, 49*(2), 27–28.

Jenkins, J. R., & Jenkins, L. M. (1987). Making peer tutoring work. *Educational Leadership, 44*(6), 64–68.

Johnson, D. W., & Johnson, R. T. (1989). *Cooperation and competition: Theory and research.* Edina, MN: Interaction Book Company.

Johnson, D. W., & Johnson, R. T. (1991). Collaboration and cognition. In A. L. Costa (Ed.), *Developing Minds* (Vol. 1, pp. 298–301). Alexandria, VA: Association for Supervision and Curriculum Development.

Jones, B. F., & Hixson, J. (1991). Breaking out of boundaries into a learner-friendly world. *Educational Horizons, 69*(2), 97–103.

Jones, B. F., Pierce, J., & Hunter, B. (1988–1989). Teaching students to construct graphic organizers. *Educational Leadership, 46*(4), 20–25.

Jones, B. F., & Pierce, J. (1992). Restructuring educational reform for students at risk. In A. Costa, J.

Bellanca, & R. Fogarty (Eds.), *If minds matter: A forward to the future* (Vol. 1, pp. 63–82). Palatine, IL: Skylight Publishing.

Kamii, C. (1984). Autonomy: The aim of education envisioned by Piaget. *Phi Delta Kappan, 65*(6), 410–415.

Kaniel, S., & Feuerstein, R. (1989). Special needs of children with learning difficulties. *Oxford Review of Education, 15*(2), 165–179.

Knapp, S., & Shields, P. M. (1990). *Better schooling for the children of poverty: Alternatives to conventional wisdom* (Vol. 2). Menlo Park, CA: SRI International.

Kozulin, A. (1990). *Vygotsky's psychology: A biography of ideas.* Cambridge, MA: Harvard University Press.

Leinhardt, G. (1990). Capturing craft knowledge in teaching. *Educational Researcher, 19*(2), 18–25.

Lewis, A. C. (1992). Previews of chapter 1 changes? *Phi Delta Kappan, 73*(10), 740–741.

Lidz, C. S. (Ed.). (1987). *Dynamic assessment: An interactional approach to evaluating learning potential.* New York: Guilford Press.

Link, F. R. (1985). Instrumental enrichment: A strategy for cognitive and academic improvement. In F. R. Link (Ed.), *Essays on intellect* (pp. 89–106). Alexandria, VA: Association for Supervision and Curriculum Development.

Linn, R. L., Baker, E. L., & Dunbar, S. B. (1991). Complex, performance-based assessment: Expectations and validation criteria. *Educational Researcher, 20*(8), 15–21.

Lipman, M. (1991). Squaring Soviet theory with American practice. *Educational Leadership, 48*(8), 72–76.

Lipman, M., Sharp, A. M., & Oscanyan, F. S. (1980). *Philosophy in the classroom.* Philadelphia, PA: Temple University Press.

Lockwood, A. T. (1991). Mathematics for the information age. *Focus in Change, 5,* 3–7. Madison, WI: National Center for Effective Schools Research and Development.

Markus, H., & Worf, E. (1987). The dynamic self-concept: A social psychological perspective. *Annual Review of Psychology, 38,* 299–337.

Martinello, M. L., & Cook, G. E. (1992). Interweaving the threads of learning: Interdisciplinary curriculum and teaching. *Curriculum Report, 21*(3), 1–6.

Marzano, R. J., Brandt, R. S., Hughes, C. S., Jones, B. F., Presseisen, B. Z., Rankin, S. C., & Suhor, C. (1988). *Dimensions of thinking: A framework for curriculum and instruction.* Alexandria, VA: Association for Supervision and Curriculum Development.

Mayer, R. E. (1989). Models for understanding. *Review of Educational Research, 59*(1), 43–64.

McCombs, B., & Marzano, R. (1989). Integrating skill and will in self-regulation: Putting the self as agent in strategic training. *Teaching Thinking and Problem Solving, 11*(5), 1–4.

McDonnell, L. M. (1989). Restructuring American schools: The promise and the pitfall (Conference Paper No. 12). New York: Teachers College Press, Columbia University, Institute on Education and the Economy.

McTighe, J., & Clemson, R. (1991). Making connections: Toward a unifying instructional framework. In A. L. Costa (Ed.), *Developing minds* (Vol. 1, pp. 304–311). Alexandria, VA: Association for Supervision and Curriculum Development.

McTighe, J., & Lyman, F. T., Jr. (1988). Cueing thinking in the classroom: The promise of theory-embedded tools. *Educational Leadership, 45*(7), 18–24.

Means, B., Chelemer, C., & Knapp, M. S. (1991). *Teaching advanced skills to at-risk students: Views from research and practice.* San Francisco: Jossey-Bass.

Means, B., & Knapp, M. S. (1991). Cognitive approaches to teaching advanced skills to educationally disadvantaged students. *Phi Delta Kappan, 73*(4), 282–289.

Messick, S. (1984). Abilities and knowledge in educational achievement testing: An assessment of dynamic cognitive structures. In B. S. Plake (Ed.), *Social and technical issues in testing: Implications for test construction and usage* (pp. 152–172). Hillsdale, NJ: Lawrence Erlbaum.

Mezzacappa, D. (1992a, June 2). Crossroads: A new testing method is getting a tryout: What you know, how you use it. *Philadelphia Inquirer,* pp. A1, A5.

Mezzacappa, D. (1992b, June 5). Bleak report on dropout rates for minorities. *Philadelphia Inquirer,* p. A19.

Miller, G. (1989). Two foundations contribute $12 million for mind-brain research. *McConnell-Pew program in cognitive neuroscience* (news release). Princeton, NJ: Princeton University.

Mirman, J. A., Swartz, R. J., & Barell, J. (1988). Strategies to help teachers empower at-risk students. In B. Z. Presseisen (Ed.), *At-risk students and thinking: Perspectives from research* (pp. 138–156). Washington, DC: National Education Association.

Moll, L. C. (1990). Social and instructional issues in educating "disadvantaged" students. In M. S. Knapp & P. M. Shields (Eds.), *Better schooling for children of poverty: Alternatives to conventional wisdom* (Vol. 2, pp. III-3–III-22). Washington, DC: U.S. Department of Education.

Moll, L. C. (Ed.). (1992). *Vygotsky and education:*

Instructional Implications and applications of socio-historical psychology. New York: Cambridge University Press.

Moore, D. W., & Readance, J. E. (1984). A quantitative and qualitative review of graphic organizer research. *Journal of Educational Research, 78*(1), 11–17.

National Center for Education Statistics. (1991). *The nation's report card: The state of mathematics achievement in Pennsylvania* (Report 21-ST-02). Washington, DC: Office of Educational Research, U.S. Department of Education.

National Coalition of Advocates for Students. (1991). *The good common school: Making the vision work for all students.* Boston: Author.

National Commission on Excellence in Education. (1983). *A nation at risk: The imperative for educational reform.* Washington, DC: Government Printing Office.

Newall, A., & Simon, H. A. (1972). *Human problem solving.* Englewood Cliffs, NJ: Prentice-Hall.

Newmann, F. M. (1987). Higher order thinking in the high school curriculum. Paper presented at the annual meeting of the National Association of Secondary School Principals, San Antonio, TX. Madison, WI: National Center on Effective Secondary Schools, University of Wisconsin (photocopy).

Newmann, F. M. (1991). Linking restructuring to authentic student achievement. *Phi Delta Kappan, 72*(6), 458–463.

Nickerson, R. S. (1986). *Reflections on reasoning.* Hillsdale, NJ: Lawrence Erlbaum.

Nickerson, R. S. (1989). New directions in educational assessment. *Educational Researcher, 18*(9), 3–7.

Nolen, S. B., Haladyna, T. M., & Haas, N. S. (1990, April). A survey of actual and perceived users, test preparation activities, and effects of standardized achievement tests. Paper presented at the annual meeting of the American Educational Research Association, Boston, MA.

North Central Regional Educational Laboratory & PBS Elementary/Secondary Service. (1991). *Schools that work: The research advantage* (Guidebook 3: Children as explorers). Oak Brook, IL: Author.

Nystrand, M. (1992, April). Dialogic instruction and conceptual change. Paper presented at the annual meeting of the American Educational Research Association, San Francisco, CA (photocopy).

Oakes, J. (1992). Can tracking research inform practice? Technical, normative, and political considerations. *Educational Researcher, 21*(4), 12–21.

Oliver, D. (1990). Grounded knowing: A postmodern perspective on teaching and learning. *Educational Leadership, 48*(1), 64–69.

Olson, V. L. P. (1990). The revising process of sixth-grade writers with and without peer feedback. *Journal of Educational Research, 84*(1), 22–29.

Palincsar, A. S. (1992, April). Beyond reciprocal teaching: A retrospective and prospective view. Cattell Talk presented at the annual meeting of the American Educational Research Association, San Francisco, CA. (photocopy).

Palincsar, A. S., & Brown, A. L. (1984). Reciprocal teaching and comprehension-fostering and comprehension-monitoring activities. *Cognition and Instruction, 1*(2), 117–175.

Palincsar, A. S., & Brown, A. L. (1989). Instruction for self-regulated reading. In L. B. Resnick & L. D. Klopfer (Eds.), *Toward the thinking curriculum: Current cognitive research* (1989 Yearbook, pp. 19–39). Alexandria, VA: Association for Supervision and Curriculum Development.

Paris, S. G., Lawton, T. A., & Turner, J. C. (1992). Reforming achievement testing to promote student learning. In C. Collins & J. M. Mangieri (Eds.), *Teaching Thinking: An agenda for the 21st century* (pp. 223–241). Hillsdale, NJ: Lawrence Erlbaum.

Paris, S. G., & Winograd, P. (1990). Promoting metacognition and motivation of exceptional children. *Remedial and Special Education, 11*(6), 7–15.

Passow, A. H. (1991). Urban schools a second (?) or third (?) time around: Priorities for curricular and instructional reform. *Education and Urban Society, 23*(3), 243–255.

Paul, R. W. (1987). Dialogical thinking: Critical thought essential to the acquisition of rational knowledge and passions. In J. B. Baron & R. J. Sternberg (Eds.), *Teaching thinking skills: Theory and practice* (pp. 127–148). New York: W. H. Freeman.

Pauly, E. (1991). *The classroom crucible: What really works, what doesn't, and why.* New York: Basic Books.

Penrose, R. (1989). *The emperor's new mind: Concerning computers, minds, and the laws of physics.* New York: Oxford University Press.

Perkins, D. N. (1991a). Educating for insight. *Educational Leadership, 49*(2), 4–8.

Perkins, D. N. (1991b). What constructivism demands of the learner. *Educational Technology, 31*(9), 19–21.

Perkins, D. N., & Salomon, G. (1988). Teaching for transfer. *Educational Leadership, 46*(1), 22–32.

Perkins, D. N., & Salomon, G. (1989). Are cognitive skills content-bound? *Educational Researcher, 18*(1), 16–25.

Piaget, J. (1964). Dedication. In R. E. Ripple & V. N. Rockcastle (Eds.), *Piaget rediscovered: A report of the conference on cognitive studies and curriculum development* (p. i). Ithaca, NY: School of Education, Cornell University.

Pintrich, P. R., & de Groot, E. V. (1990) Motivational and self-regulated learning components of classroom academic performance. *Journal of Educational Psychology, 82*(1), 33–40.

Pogrow, S. (1992). Converting at-risk students into reflective learners. In A. L. Costa, J. Bellanca, & R. Fogarty (Eds.), *In minds matter: A forward to the future* (Vol. 2, 117–125). Palatine, IL: Skylight Publishing.

Polin, L. (1991). Vygotsky at the computer. A Soviet view of "tools for learning." *The Computing Teacher, 19*(1), 25–27.

Popham, W. J. (1987). The merits of measurement-driven instruction. *Phi Delta Kappan, 68*(9), 679–682.

Presseisen, B. Z. (1987). *Thinking skills throughout the curriculum: A conceptual design.* Bloomington, IN: Pi Lambda Theta.

Presseisen, B. Z. (1988a). *At-risk students and thinking: Perspectives from research.* Washington, DC: National Education Association.

Presseisen, B. Z. (1988b). Avoiding battle at curriculum gulch: Teaching thinking AND content. *Educational Leadership, 45*(7), 7–8.

Presseisen, B. Z. (1990). Important questions. In B. Z. Presseisen, R. J. Sternberg, K. W. Fischer, C. C. Knight, & R. Feuerstein, (eds.), *Learning and thinking styles: Classroom interaction.* Washington, DC: National Education Association.

Presseisen, B. Z. (1991). Thinking skills: Meanings and models revisited. In A. L. Costa (Ed.), *Developing minds: A resource book for teaching thinking* (Vol. 1, rev. ed., pp. 56–62). Alexandria, VA: Association for Supervision and Curriculum Development.

Presseisen, B. Z. (1992, February). Implementing thinking in the school's curriculum. Paper presented at the third annual meeting of the International Association for Cognitive Education, University of California, Riverside.

Presseisen, B. Z., & Kozulin, A. (1992, April). Mediated learning: The contributions of Vygotsky and Feuerstein in theory and practice. Paper presented at the annual meeting of the American Educational Research Association, San Francisco.

Reich, R. B. (1991, January 20). Secession of the successful. *New York Times Magazine,* pp. 16–17, 42–45.

Report on Education Research. (1992). *Rural children worse off than urban, suburban peers, 24*(1), 1–2. Washington, DC: Capitol Publications.

Resnick, L. B. (1985). *Cognitive science and instruction.* Pittsburgh, PA: Learning Research and Development Center, University of Pittsburgh (photocopy).

Resnick, L. B. (1987a). *Education and learning to think.* Washington, DC: National Academy Press.

Resnick, L. B. (1987b). Learning in school and out. *Educational Researcher, 16*(9), 13–20.

Resnick, L. B., & Klopfer, L. E. (Eds.). (1989). *Toward the thinking curriculum: Current cognitive research* (1989 Yearbook). Alexandria, VA: Association for Supervision and Curriculum Development.

Resnick, L. B., & Resnick, D. P. (1992). Assessing the thinking curriculum: New tools for educational reform. In B. R. Gifford & M. C. O'Connor (Eds.), *Changing assessments: Alternative views of aptitude, achievement and instruction* (pp. 37–75). Boston, MA: Kluwer.

Riessman, F. (1988). Transforming the schools: A new paradigm. *Social Policy, 19*(1), 2–4.

Rogoff, B. (1990). *Apprenticeship in thinking: Cognitive development in social context.* New York: Oxford University Press.

Rosenshine, B., & Meister, C. (1992). The use of scaffolding for teaching higher-level cognitive strategies. *Educational Leadership, 49*(7), 26–33.

Salomon, G., Perkins, D. N., & Globerson, T. (1991). Partners in cognition: Extending human intelligence with intelligent technologies. *Educational Researcher, 20*(3), 2–9.

Scardamalia, M., & Bereiter, C. (1983). The development of evaluative, diagnostic and remedial capabilities in children's composing. In M. Martlew (Ed.), *The psychology of written language: A developmental approach* (pp. 67–95). London: Wiley.

Scardamalia, M., & Bereiter, C. (1985). Fostering the development of self-regulation in children's knowledge. In S. F. Chipman, J. W. Segal, & R. Glaser (Eds.), *Thinking and learning skills: Research and open questions* (Vol. 2, pp. 563–577). Hillsdale, NJ: Lawrence Erlbaum.

Schama, S. (1991, September 8). Clio has a problem. *New York Times Magazine,* pp. 30–34.

Schlechty, P. (1989). *Creating the infrastructure for reform.* Washington, DC: Council of Chief State School Officers.

Schlechty, P. C. (1990). *Schools for the 21st century: Leadership imperatives for educational reform.* San Francisco: Jossey-Bass.

Schlechty, P., & Cole, B. (1991). Creating a system

that supports change. *Educational Horizons, 69*(2), 78–82.

Schoenfeld, A. H. (1985). *Mathematical problem solving.* New York: Academic Press.

Schroeder, T., & Lester, F. (1989). Developing understanding in mathematics via problem solving. In P. T. Trafton (Ed.), *1989 Yearbook of the National Council of Teachers of Mathematics* (pp. 31–42). Reston, VA: National Council of Teachers of Mathematics.

Scott, T., Cole, M., & Engel, M. (1992). Computers and education: A cultural constructivist perspective. In G. Grant (Ed.), *Review of research in education* (Vol. 18, pp. 191–251). Washington, DC: American Educational Research Association.

Sealey, J. (1986). *Peer edition groups.* R & D Interpretation Service Bulletin on Oral and Written Communication. Charleston, WV: Appalachia Educational Laboratory.

Secretary's Commission on Achieving Necessary Skills. (1991). *What work requires of schools: A Scans report for America 2000.* Washington, DC: U.S. Department of Labor.

Shanahan, T. (1991). New literacy goes to school: Whole language in the classroom. *Educational Horizons, 69*(3), 146–151.

Sharron, H. (1987). *Changing children's minds: Feuerstein's revolution in the teaching of intelligence.* London: Souvenir Press.

Shavelson, R. J., & Salomon, G. (1985). Information technology: Tool and teacher of the mind. *Educational Researcher, 14*(5), 4.

Shepard, L. (1991). Psychometricians' beliefs about learning. *Educational Researcher, 20*(6), 2–16.

Short, E. J., Cuddy, C. L., Friebert, S. E., & Schatschneider, C. W. (1990). The diagnostic and educational utility of thinking aloud during problem solving. In H. L. Swanson & B. Keogh (Eds.), *Learning disabilities: Theoretical and research issues* (pp. 93–109). Hillsdale, NJ: Lawrence Erlbaum.

Shulman, L. S. (1987). Knowledge and teaching: Foundations of the new reform. *Harvard Educational Review, 57*(1), 1–22.

Siegler, R. S. (1989). Strategy diversity and cognitive assessment. *Educational Researcher, 18*(9), 15–19.

Singer, H., & Donlan, D. (1982). Active comprehension: Problem-solving schema with question generation of complex, short stories. *Reading Research Quarterly, 17*(2), 166–186.

Sizer, T. R. (1984). *Horace's compromise: The dilemma of the American high school.* Boston: Houghton Mifflin.

Sizer, T. R. (1992). *Horace's school: Redesigning the American high school.* Boston: Houghton Mifflin.

Slavin, R. E. (1983). When does cooperative learning increase student achievement? *Psychological Bulletin, 94,* 429–445.

Slavin, R. E. (1987). Cooperative learning and the cooperative school. *Educational Leadership, 45*(3), 7–13.

Slavin, R. E. (1991). Synthesis of research on cooperative learning. *Educational Leadership, 48*(5), 71–82.

Slavin, R. E., Karweit, N. L., & Wasik, B. A. (1991). Preventing early school failure: What works (Report No. 26). Baltimore, MD: Center for Research on Effective Schools for Disadvantaged Students.

Smey-Richman, B. S. (1988). *Involvement in learning for low-achieving students.* Philadelphia, PA: Research for Better Schools.

Smey-Richman, B. S. (1991). *School climate and restructuring for low-achieving students.* Philadelphia, PA: Research for Better Schools.

Smith, D. J., & Nelson, J. R. (1992). The effect of a self-management procedure on the classroom and academic behavior of students with mild handicaps. *School Psychology Review, 21*(1), 59–72.

Sparks, D. (1991, September). Restructuring schools through staff development: An interview with Phil Schlechty. *The Developer,* pp. 1, 5–7.

Sternberg, R. J. (1982). Who's intelligent? *Psychology Today, 16*(4), 30–39.

Sternberg, R. J. (1990a). Intellectual styles: Theory and classroom applications. In B. Z. Presseisen, R. J. Sternberg, K. W. Fischer, C. C. Knight, & R. Feuerstein, (Eds.), *Learning and thinking styles: Classroom interaction* (pp. 18–42). Washington, DC: National Education Association.

Sternberg, R. J. (1990b). *Metaphors of mind: Conceptions of the nature of intelligence.* New York: Cambridge University Press.

Sternberg, R. J., & Bhana, K. (1986). Synthesis of research on the effectiveness of intellectual skills programs: Snake-oil remedies or miracle cures? *Educational Leadership, 44*(2) 60–67.

Sternberg, R. J., Okagaki, L., & Jackson, A. S. (1990). Practical intelligence for success in school. *Educational Leadership, 48*(1), 35–39.

Stiggins, R. J. (1985). Improving assessment where it means the most: In the classroom. *Educational Leadership, 43*(2), 69–74.

Stiggins, R. (1991). Assessment literacy. *Phi Delta Kappan, 72*(7), 534–539.

Stiggins, R. J., Rubel, E., & Quellmalz, E. (1988). *Mea-*

suring thinking skills in the classroom (rev. ed.). Washington, DC: National Education Association.

Stigler, J. W., & Stevenson, H. W. (1991). How Asian teachers polish each lesson to perfection. American Educator, 15(1), 12–20, 43–47.

Suhor, C. (1992). Semiotics and the teaching of thinking. Teaching Thinking and Problem Solving, 14(1), 1, 3–6.

Swartz, R. (1987, August). Structured teaching for critical thinking and reasoning in standard subject-area instruction. Paper presented at the Conference on Informal Reasoning, Learning Research and Development Center, University of Pittsburgh, Pittsburgh, PA.

Swartz, R. (1991). New ways to assess learning in science. Andover, MA: The NETWORK (photocopy).

Tanner, D. (1989). A brief historical perspective of the struggle for an integrative curriculum. Educational Horizons, 68(1), 7–11.

Tharp, R. G. (1989). Psychocultural variables and constants: Effects on teaching and learning in schools. American Psychologist, 44(2), 349–359.

Tharp, R. G., & Gallimore, R. (1988). Rousing minds to life. New York: Cambridge University Press.

Tharp, R. G., & Gallimore, R. (1989). Rousing schools to life. American Educator, 13(2), 20–25, 46–51.

Tharp, R. G., & Gallimore, R. (1991). The instructional conversation: Teaching and learning in social activity (Research Report No. 2). Washington, DC: National Center for Research on Cultural Diversity and Second Language Learning.

Thurow, L. (1991). The centennial essay. The American School Board Journal, 178(9), 41–43.

Uphoff, J. K. (1991). School readiness issues: Conflicting claims confuse and confound. Teaching Thinking and Problem Solving, 13(6), 1, 4–5.

Valencia, S. (1990). A portfolio approach to classroom reading assessment: The whys, whats, and how. The Reading Teacher, 43(4), 338–341.

Vobejda, B. (1992, June 1). A diverse U.S. seen in census. Philadelphia Inquirer, pp. A1, A7.

Vygotsky, L. S. (1978). Mind in society: The development of higher psychological processes. Edited by M. Cole, V. John-Steiner, S. Scribner, & E. Souberman, Cambridge, MA: Harvard University Press.

Wehlage, G. G., Rutter, R. A., Smith, G. A., Lesko, N., & Fernandez, R. R. (1989). Reducing the risk:

Schools as communities of support. London: Falmer Press.

Wertsch, J. V. (Ed.). (1985). Culture, communication, and cognition: Vygotskian perspectives. New York: Cambridge University Press.

Wiggins, G. (1989a). A true test: Toward more authentic and equitable assessment. Phi Delta Kappan, 70(9), 703–713.

Wiggins, G. (1989b). Teaching to the (authentic) test. Educational Leadership, 46(7), 41–47.

Wiggins, G. (1990). Reconsidering standards and assessment. Education Week, 9(18), 36, 25.

Wiggins, G. (1992). Creating tests worth taking. Educational Leadership, 49(8), 26–33.

Wilson, E. K. (1971). Sociology: Rules, roles and relationships. Homewood, IL: Dorsey.

Winocur, S. L. (1986). IMPACT: Improve minimal proficiencies by activating critical thinking. Bloomington, IN: Phi Delta Kappa.

Wittrock, M. C. (1987). Teaching and student learning. Journal of Teacher Education, 38(6), 30–33.

Wittrock, M. C. (Ed.). (1990). Students' thought process. In American Educational Research Association, Research on teaching and learning (Vol. 3, pp. 4–49). New York: Macmillan.

Wolf, D., Bixby, J., Glenn, J. III., & Gardner, H. (1991). To use their minds well: Investigating new forms of student assessment. In G. Grant (Ed.), Review of research in education (Vol. 17, pp. 31–74). Washington, DC: American Educational Research Association.

Wolf, D. B., LeMahieu, P. G., & Eresh, J. (1992). Good measure: Assessment as a tool for educational reform. Educational Leadership, 49(8), 8–13.

Wood, T., Cobb, P., & Yackel, E. (1991). Change in teaching mathematics: A case study. American Educational Research Journal, 28(3), 587–616.

Zessoules, R., & Gardner, H. (1991). Authentic assessment: Beyond the buzzword and into the classroom. In V. Perrone (Ed.), Expanding student assessment (pp. 47–71). Alexandria, VA: Association for Supervision and Curriculum Assessment.

Zimmerman, B. J., & Martinez-Pons, M. (1990). Student differences in self-regulated learning: Relating grade, sex, giftedness to self-efficacy and strategy use. Journal of Educational Psychology, 82(1), 51–59.

Zuboff, S. (1988). In the age of the smart machine: The future of work and power. New York: Basic Books.

4

STRATEGIES FOR IMPROVING INSTRUCTION IN EARLY CHILDHOOD

CHAPTER TWELVE

THE COGNITIVE REVOLUTION IN LEARNING

PIAGET AND VYGOTSKY

ALEX KOZULIN

HADASSAH-WIZO-CANADA RESEARCH INSTITUTE

Dr. Alex Kozulin is the head of research and director of the cross-cultural unit at the Hadassah-WIZO-Canada Research Institute, Jerusalem, and a visiting associate professor of psychology at Boston University. From 1984 through 1990 he taught psychology at Boston University. He has been a visiting scholar at Harvard University and a visiting lecturer at Ben-Gurion University and at Bar-Ilan University in Israel. Dr. Kozulin is one of the best-known students and interpreters of Vygotsky's psychological theory. He is the translator-editor of the revised edition of Vygotsky's *Thought and Language* (1986) and the author of the definitive monograph *Vygotsky's Psychology: A Biography of Ideas* (1990). He has taught and written in the areas of developmental theory, cross-cultural cognition, learning processes, and the history of Russian psychology. In Israel, his unit works with learning-disabled immigrant children and their parents.

INTRODUCTION

The current cognitive revolution in learning theory and educational psychology, as readily acknowledged by the majority of American psychologists (Horowitz, 1989), did not appear from nowhere but occurred as a culmination of a lengthy and arduous process. This process brought some figures to the fore, while others faded into the background. For quite some time behavioris-tic and psychoanalytic theories were in the limelight, while cognitive approaches remained in the shadows. By the same token, children's thinking was almost universally perceived as a reflection of each individual's abilities, while social and cultural characteristics of the learning process were either taken for granted or ignored. In both cases they remained beyond the scope of learning theory.

The reversal of fortune in this cognitive and sociocultural revolution is associated with the contributions of two great psychologists, Jean Piaget of Switzerland and Lev Vygotsky of Russia. Both made their first significant contributions to psychology in the 1920s, but in English-speaking countries, true renown came in the 1960s to Piaget and even later to Vygotsky, in the 1980s. This late recognition simply underscores the universal value of the contributions made by these psychologists: Their theories address the fundamental problems of child development and learning and do not aim at providing quick answers that follow current fashion in popular science or education.

In this chapter I will review the commonalities and differences between the basic premises of Piagetian and Vygotskian theories. Their common denominators include the child-centered approach, the emphasis on action in the formation of thought, and the systemic understanding of the psychological functioning. Differences in their position are reflected in the Piagetians' focus on the inner restructuring of child thought and the Vygotskians' emphasis on the formative influence of the sociocultural model upon this thought. I will endeavor to make differences between these theories more tangible through illustrations of actual applications of Piagetian and Vygotskian ideas in the classroom. Finally, I will discuss the issue of different mediating agents in learning, and in relation to them, I will present Feuerstein's (1990) theory of mediated learning, which seems to augment some of the problematic moments in both the Piagetian and the Vygotskian approaches.

COMMON GROUND IN VYGOTSKY'S AND PIAGET'S THEORIES

For a variety of reasons, Piaget and Vygotsky are most often presented as scientific antagonists, with their views negating each other. Although it is true that there are many differences in their understanding of psychological development and learning, it is advantageous to acknowledge that there are similarities in their positions and that

these elements have become the cornerstones of the cognitive revolution that we are now experiencing.

Child-Centered Psychology

Acknowledging Piaget's revolutionary impact on child psychology, Vygotsky (1986) wrote: "Like many another great discovery, Piaget's idea is simple to the point of seeming self-evident. It had already been expressed in the words of J. J. Rousseau, which Piaget himself quoted, that a child is not a miniature adult and his mind is not the mind of an adult on a small scale" (p. 13).

The idea appears simple, indeed, unless one realizes its theoretical consequences. First, the popular behavioristic search for the universal building blocks of behavior similar in children, adults, and animals becomes senseless in this perspective. J. B. Watson's (1970) thesis that "all complex behavior is a growth or development out of simple responses" (p. 137) loses its attractive simplicity. If a child's behavior is qualitatively different, then linear extrapolation from "simple responses" is misleading and it is erroneous to search for small-scale copies of adult behavior in children. The traditional notion of universal thought processes that are just underdeveloped in a child fares no better. As Edouard Claparede observed in his Preface to Piaget's first book: "After all, the error has been, if I am not mistaken, that in examining child thought we have applied to it the mould and pattern of the adult thought" (Claparede, 1959, pp. x–xi).

In retrospect, Piaget's insight into the unique and self-important character of child thought fit reasonably well into the more general pattern of structuralist ideas, which at that time were taking hold of social and behavioral sciences (Kozulin, 1978). In zoopsychology, ethologists promoted the idea of species-specific behavior that cannot be reduced to such universal elements as conditional reflexes or stimulus-response pairs. In anthropology, early attempts to portray so-called "primitive" cultures as qualitatively similar but developmentally inferior to the European culture were challenged by a relativistic approach that focused on self-important and unique characteristics of each culture. At about the same time, Werner (1965) acclaimed that in psychology itself, the demand to acknowledge the irreducible character of different cognitive and psychological structures in children, mental patients, and "primitive" people was important.

From Action to Thought

The second issue on which Piaget and Vygotsky were in agreement concerns the relationship between action and thought. Classical mentalistic psychology presumed the primacy of thought over action in such a way that action was perceived as only a realized thought. An individual was first supposed to have an idea of a certain solution and only then to realize it in a chosen act. Thought, in its turn, was considered primarily as only a representation of reality, rather than the means of acting upon it. In his theory of sensory-motor intelligence, Piaget (1969) effectively challenged this position. He demonstrated that thought itself has an operational structure derived from actual behavior performed by children. For example, by physically putting objects together or by separating them, a child, in a form of action, performs what later will be internalized as mental operations of addition and subtraction. Thus, the key to the child's thinking lies not in some *sui generis* ideas, but in the child's practical activity which in the course of development becomes internalized and transformed into cognitive operations.

While in agreement with Piaget concerning the formula "from action to thought," Vygotsky made an important amendment to it. In Piagetian theory, action appears first and foremost as a spontaneous physical interaction between the child and the physical objects. Later in life the child becomes capable of substituting words and of developing logical formulae for these physical interactions, and in this way arrives at symbolic operational thought. Vygotsky argued that such a picture does not correspond to the reality in which child development takes place. The child's interaction with objects is always only one element in a wider activity that is socially and historically specific (Vygotsky, 1978; Kozulin, 1986,

1990). This activity is organized and controlled by society and its representatives; that is, parents infuse even the earliest of a child's operations with meaning that has not only individual, but also sociocultural connotations. Therefore, the formula "from action to thought" should take into account the sociocultural nature of action and how actions develop and are internalized by children.

Systemic Organization of Child Thought

Both Piaget and Vygotsky argued against the popular attempt to present a child's mind as a sack filled with discrete cognitive skills and pieces of information. Both strived for a systemic explanation of cognitive functioning. In Piagetian theory, systemic explanation is based on two major notions: the notion of a group of operations and the notion of the developmental stage. Individual operations always appear as elements of the whole, and their nature is determined by the nature of this whole system. An isolated operation is an abstraction. "A single operation could not be an operation, because the peculiarity of operations is that they form systems. Here we may well protest vigorously against logical atomism, whose pattern has been a grievous hindrance to the psychology of thought" (Piaget, 1969, p. 35). Classical mentalistic psychology, like classical logic, speaks of concepts as elements of thought. It is clear, however, that any concept depends on other concepts, that is, on their system. This dependence, moreover, is expressed in terms of operation. A concept such as "class" cannot exist by itself; it necessarily requires the notion of "classification," and the former grows out of the latter, because only operations of classification can engender particular classes. Independently of such a system, "class" will remain an intuitive collection rather than a "class" in the true meaning of this concept. The same is true for other concepts, such as that of asymmetrical relations; for example, A < B is impossible in isolation from the system of serial relationships: A < B < C < D, and so forth. "In short, in any possible domain of constituted thought, psychological reality consists of complex operational systems and not isolated operations conceived as elements prior to these systems" (Piaget, 1969, p. 36).

This same idea of a system as a whole guided Piaget in this concept of the developmental stage. Piaget distinguished four major stages: sensory-motor, intuitive, concrete operational, and formal operational. At each of these stages, which, according to Piaget, appear in a strict developmental order, the child is acting in a way characteristic of the respective level of cognitive development. For example, different schemas of preoperational thought belong to one system that at this level endows a child's reasoning with a certain consistency and homogeneity.

Similarly, Vygotsky approached this same problem of the systemic organization of child thought from the point of view of the relationships between different psychological functions. He pointed out that, while such psychological functions such as perception, memory, or logical reasoning in themselves may change very little during childhood, their relationships do. For example, in younger children reasoning often plays a subordinate role to memory—a child reasons by remembering concrete instances or episodes. In adolescents this relationship is often reversed—the task of remembering some item comes first and is transported by an adolescent to the more important reasoning task. The adolescent can also reverse this process and logically reason a sequence of events that will ultimately lead him or her to the item to be recalled. Only at this late stage in development can memory, in its pure form, be called into service.

The same is true for the verbal function. According to Vygotsky, the development of both thinking and speech in childhood depends primarily on the changing relationships between these two functions, which enter into the different types of systemic relationships. "It was shown and proved experimentally that mental development does not coincide with the development of separate psychological functions, but rather depends on changing relations between them. The development of each function, in turn, depends upon the progress in the development of the interfunctional system" (Vygotsky, 1986, p. 167). Psychological development, therefore, is

envisaged by Vygotsky as a construction of ever more complex systems of different psychological functions that work in cooperation to mediate each other. The failure to form an interfunctional system manifests itself as a learning disability or even, in more severe forms, as cognitive retardation (Luria, 1960).

DIFFERENCES BETWEEN PIAGET AND VYGOTSKY: COGNITIVE INDIVIDUALISM VS. THE SOCIOCULTURAL APPROACH

Now that the common ground for what nowadays constitutes the cognitive revolution has been established, it is possible to distinguish between Piagetian and Vygotskian theoretical positions and to inquire into the consequences of these differences for educational practice. Probably the most essential difference lies in their respective understanding of the subject of psychological activity. For Piaget, this subject involves an individual child whose mind, through interaction with the physical and social world, arrives at the mature forms of reasoning associated with formal operations. For Vygotsky, psychological activity from the very beginning of development includes a sociocultural character; subjects, therefore, are not lone discoverers of logical rules, but children who master their own psychological processes do so through tools offered by a given culture. The following stories, one reported by Piaget and the other by Vygotsky, underscore the difference in their understanding of what constitutes a paradigmatic learning situation.

You may recall Piaget's account of a mathematician friend who inspired his studies in the conservation of number. This man told Piaget about an incident from childhood, where he counted a number of pebbles he had set out in a line. Having counted them from left to right and found there were 10, he decided to see how many there would be if he counted them from right to left. Intrigued to find that there were still 10, he put them in a different arrangement and counted them again. He kept rearranging and counting them until he decided that, no matter what the arrangement, he was always going to find that there were 10. Number is independent of the order of counting. . . . I think that it must be that the whole enterprise was [the child's] own wonderful idea. He raised the question for himself and figured out for himself how to try to answer it. (Duckworth, 1987, pp. 4–5).

Vygotsky (1978, pp. 33–35), in contrast, reports the following observations. He requested 4- and 5-year-old children to press one of five keys on a keyboard in response to picture stimuli. Because the task exceeded the children's natural capabilities, it caused serious difficulties for them. Moreover, the whole process of selection was carried out in a motor sphere—the children made a selection from possible movements instead of first arriving at a decision and then realizing it in a movement. This type of activity changed dramatically when an auxiliary system of signs attached to keys was introduced. Although on the surface the task became more complex, because in addition to stimuli and keys the children were supposed to pay attention to signs, the results were impressive. Children ceased to respond with a sequence of hesitant or impulsive movements, developing instead an internal decision-making procedure linked to a sign, with movements used to implement an already-made decision. The natural form of activity was replaced by the activity mediated by artificial signs that were introduced by adults and reflected their system of cultural tools.

These two vignettes are sufficient to pinpoint the major difference in Vygotsky's and Piaget's attitudes toward learning. For Piaget, learning occurs in an unassisted interaction between the child's mental schemas and the objects of the external world. As a result, the child is having "wonderful ideas" of his or her own. The only requirement for the learning milieu is to be sufficiently rich so that the child has enough objects and processes with which to practice his or her schemas. Alternatively, from Vygotsky's point of

view, learning occurs in the collaboration between the child and adults who introduce symbolic tools-mediators to the child and who teach him or her how to organize and control his or her natural psychological functions through these cultural tools. In the process, the natural psychological functions of the child change their nature becoming culturally and socially informed and organized.

The same difference in attitudes is reflected in the choice of an assessment situation. For Piaget, an ideal testing of a child's reasoning occurs when the child is confronted with an unfamiliar problem or task. Only when specific knowledge is absent may one hope to identify the "infantile" way of reasoning unaffected by the imitation of adult logic. Vygotsky, on the contrary, considered a collaborative situation as paradigmatic. For that reason he strongly criticized standard psychometric methods, which take into account only the manifest level of the child's performance. This manifest level is then interpreted as reflecting the intellectual development of the child. Vygotsky argued that two children whose manifest level corresponds, for example, to the mental age of eight, may have very different learning potentials, and that these learning potentials rather than actual performance levels, are indicative of the future success or failure of these children in school learning. To measure these learning potentials, children are given somewhat more difficult but similar tasks and are provided with assistance, such as orientation in the task or a leading question. If one child can perform with assistance at the level of the mental age of 12 and the other, at the mental age of 9, we may conclude that the *zone of proximal development* (ZPD) for the first child is 4 years, while for the second child it is just 1 year. Vygotsky concludes that it would be erroneous to claim that the level of intellectual development is similar in those two children. "Experience has shown that the child with the larger zone of proximal development will do much better in school. This measure gives a more helpful clue than mental age does to the dynamics of intellectual processes" (Vygotsky, 1986, p. 187).

In recent years the notion of dynamic assessment based on the principle of the ZPD has captured the attention of many American psychologists (Lidz, 1987). (Independent of Vygotskian tradition, a somewhat similar approach to dynamic assessment has been developed in Israel by Reuven Feuerstein, 1979.) Apart from these assessment techniques, ZPD helped to establish the notion of collaborative learning. In collaborative learning, the child is neither a passive recipient of knowledge offered by the teacher, nor an independent thinker who arrives at his or her own solutions, but rather a participant in learning activities shared by children and adults (Rogoff & Wertsch, 1984; Newman, Griffin, & Cole, 1989).

The Role of Language

Piaget's early recognition as a new force in child psychology owes much to his first books dedicated to the problem of child speech. There is a certain irony in such a beginning, since in his mature works Piaget avoided the issue of language. Some of his followers in the field of education even make attitude toward language into a litmus test separating Piagetians who emphasize thinking from "traditionalists" who focus on verbal development. "The general conclusion which I press on you," wrote Hans Furth in *Piaget for Teachers* (1970, p. 65), "is not to exaggerate the role of language in the development of thinking."

For Vygotsky, language in its different forms constitutes the central theme of cognitive development. For him, cognitive development can be imagined as a dynamic pattern of engagements and separations between intellectual and verbal functions. Rather than a merger of two "strings," the relationships between language and thought look more like a nodical line with some threads from one string being interwoven into the other after each node.

The dynamic character of the relationships between thought and language may sometimes give an impression of certain "regression" on the part of a child's language. For example, the child's first steps in written language are made when his or her oral speech is already quite well developed. As a result the child's writing appears as a "regression" when compared to its pure verbal quality. At the same time, writing involves advanced cog-

nitive elements that are still missing in the oral exchanges. For example, while much in oral exchanges is carried out unconsciously, writing necessitates closer attention to the formal properties of language, requires more careful planning, and puts additional emphasis on the self-conscious motivation of the writer's activity.

The same apparent "regression" is also demonstrated in transitions to new stages of verbal activity as is manifest in the phenomenon of so-called egocentric speech of younger children. Egocentric or private speech is not addressed or adapted to a listener and is carried on by the child with apparent satisfaction in the absence of any response from others. From Piaget's (1959) point of view, egocentric speech is but a mere verbal accompaniment to the child's egocentric thought that is insensitive to contradictions and does not take into account the point of view of others. The fate of a child's egocentric speech is that it will disappear as socialized speech emerges. The replacement occurs as a child becomes attuned to the expectations of the listener. Vygotsky (1986) challenged this point of view. He argued that although private speech looks immature when compared to the communicative speech of the same child, it nevertheless is cognitively superior to it. Through a series of simple but ingenious experiments Vygotsky showed that instead of being a mere accompaniment to immature thought, private speech serves as a precursor of the silent inner speech, which in turn serves as an important tool of a child's reasoning. When confronted with a difficult task, the child significantly increases the amount of his or her private speech utterances that help him or her in problem solving. These early findings of Vygotsky were confirmed in more recent studies (Zivin, 1979). Moreover, it was shown that with appropriate training of parents, the amount of a child's private speech can be increased and thus can lead to the enhancement of the child's propensity toward self-regulation.

The current research literature (Cromer, 1991) continues to register an ongoing debate between those who believe that cognitive structures come first and support the progress of language and those who insist that language has its own more or less independent course of development. The truth may still lie between these two extremes.

> Our cognitive abilities at different stages of development make certain meanings *available* for expression. But, in addition, we must also possess certain specifically linguistic capabilities in order to come to express these meanings in language. . . . Though language development depends on cognition, language has its own specific sources. . . . It appears that much of what is being discovered during the current vogue of psycholinguistic research supports Vygotsky's view. (Cromer, 1991, p. 54)

THE PIAGETIAN SYSTEM IN THE CLASSROOM

One of the important consequences of the Piagetian revolution in learning theory is the change in teachers' attitudes toward children's thinking. The following is an excerpt from Eleanor Duckworth's (1987, pp. 89–92) account of her work with primary school teachers.

> The problem was a classic one from *The Child's Conception of Geometry* (Piaget, Inhelder, & Szeminska, 1948/1981) known as "The Islands." In its classic form, the child is presented with a solid wooden block, 4" high and 3" × 3" cross-section [see Figure A]; a pile of small (1") wooden cubes; and a blue board (meant to be a lake) on which there are three patches of cardboard (meant to be islands)—one 4" × 3", one 3" × 2", and one 2" × 2". The child is told that the solid block is an apartment building; that everyone has to leave that building; and that with the small cubes the child is to build a new building to accommodate the occupants on one of the islands. The base of the new building is to cover the entire island, but it can't go off into

the water. *The new building has to have just as much room in it as the original one.*

FIGURE A

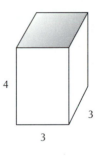

FIGURE B

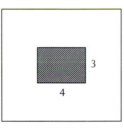 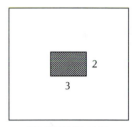

TIMMY'S ISLAND   SANDY'S ISLAND

> Piaget outlines, of course, three stages, each with two substages. It is not necessary here to repeat his outline. Consistent with our approach, I used the problem to explore the thinking of these two children, as far as possible. This entailed keeping in mind the basic question inherent in the task and a variety of possible responses, and—most important—engaging in an interesting intellectual discussion with the children.
>
> In our version, the model was oil-based clay. Each child had his own "lake" and one, "island," Timmy's being 4" × 3" and Sandy's 3" × 2" [Figure B].
>
> Sandy built his building one layer higher than the model—five layers on a 3" × 2" base [Figure C]—then moved the model over beside his building and took off a layer, so they would be the same height. He recognized that he now had less room in it, but couldn't imme-

FIGURE C

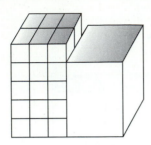

FIGURE D

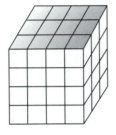

FIGURE E

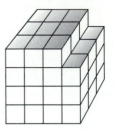

FIGURE F

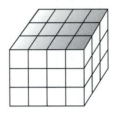

FIGURE G

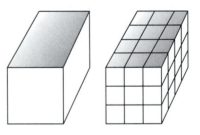

diately see what to do about that without building out into the water. Timmy suggested building it higher; Sandy thought it was a good idea, and added two layers.

Timmy also stopped when his building was the same height as the model [Figure D] and, while acknowledging that his had a little more room in it (note that it is on a larger base) neither of the boys could see what to do about it other than cutting out a patch of cardboard to make an island the same size base as the model, and starting again.

"What if you took off some like that?" I asked, removing just three cubes, that is, part of one layer [see Figure E]. "It would goof up the whole thing," said Timmy. "It's just a little smaller, that's all," said Sandy. I responded to Timmy's "goofing up" objection by removing the rest of the layer [see Figure F]. Neither of them found that an acceptable solution. After repeated suggestions from them—to cut a new base or to add more clay to the model—I said, "All you can do is take more blocks off or put

more blocks on." Timmy said, "You'd have to get thinner blocks."

I then made a suggestion—to see how the children reacted to it. I turned the *model* on its side so that it was on a base identical to Timmy's [see Figure G]. With surprise and pleasure, the boys responded that the two buildings were now "equal." "So that, you think, is equal, do you?" I asked. "Yeah," said Timmy. Sandy nodded. I turned the model upright again [see Figure H]. "Now what do you think?" Timmy answered, "Now you have to put more on." Timmy explained this for a

FIGURE H

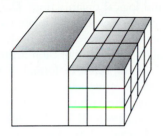

while, but did not in fact do it, and then I ask, "Has one of them got more room in it than the other?"

> **Timmy:** Yup.
> **Duckworth:** Which one?
> **Timmy:** This one right now. (*The model.*)
> **Duckworth:** Why do you say that?
> **Timmy:** No, I think they have the equal amount of . . . (*mumbles*)
> **Duckworth:** Pardon?
> **Timmy:** Because this one's bigger (*the model*) and this one's wider (*his*).

He then proceeded to measure (with his fingers, not with a block) to see by how much the one is "bigger" (higher), and by how much the other is wider.

> **Timmy:** The same width up and the side. (*That is, the model is taller by the same amount as his building is wider.*)
> **Duckworth:** The same width? Is it?
> **Timmy:** Yup, I just measured it, and they both came out the same way.

His procedure convinced Sandy, to whose building attention then turned.

After an initial tendency to want Sandy's building to be the same height as the model again, they settled on having one extra layer [Figure C]. This time Sandy measured with the blocks, to show that one layer was missing

in width, and thus one layer needed to be added on top.

Their solutions, then, were a three-layered building on Timmy's 4" × 3" base (correct), and a five-layered building on Sandy's 3" × 2" base (one layer too short). I probed some more, made some countersuggestions; they stayed with their solutions, and I stopped there.

My interpretation was that both boys were drawn to judge the overall amount of space by the most salient dimension, the height; that they were able to think how to remedy it in one case (Sandy's, when they had to build higher) but not in the other (Timmy's, when they had to take off a layer); that they then saw that a greater size in one dimension (height, say) could be compensated for by a smaller size in another (width, say); that in both cases they judged that it needed not only to be higher (or wider) but the *same amount* higher (or wider); that this worked in one case (Timmy's) but not the other (Sandy's)—indicating that "the same amount" applied to a single dimension, and not to a two-dimensional slice; that there was no tendency to think of the original solid block as composed of units whose number could be calculated.

Piaget's interest in this problem concerns the epistemology of the notion of volume. Of the kind of work Sandy and Timmy did, for example, he says:

> In all these trends, there is growth in the articulation of Euclidean intuitions of volume. It is through that increasing articulation that notions of volume lose their topological character and come to conform with Euclidean notions of length and area which are elaborated at this level. However, although these articulations pave the way for operational handling of the various relations together with their logical multiplication, they are insufficient to enable children to effect those reversible compositions which mark the operational level proper. Thus these responses are inter-

mediate in character, and this fact appears most clearly in the answers given to our questions about conservation. (Piaget, Inhelder, & Szeminska, 1981, p. 369)

Now this takes some effort to understand; moreover, it takes a far broader context—references are made to notions that have been studied and subsequently discussed through two entire volumes (Piaget & Inhelder, 1948/ 1967; Piaget et al., 1948/1981). It is not a criticism of Piaget to point out that the quoted discussion is not easy to grasp if one has not read the rest of the volume, and if one is not concerned with those epistemological issues. But the fortunate thing is that this kind of work with children has other values that are directly useful to teachers as *they* work with children. The main thing—common to Piaget's interests, as well—is the focus on how children are making sense of the situation in their own way. We can all appreciate, and even be awed by, watching this happen without putting our emphasis on Piaget's interpretation of what is meant by "in their own way."

Piaget's contributions here are, on the one hand, having located what are essentially crucial intellectual issues for children, and finding ways to put the issues in a form that catches their interest; and on the other hand, developing the "clinical interview" technique in which the adult role is to find out as much as possible about what the child believes about an issue. Both these aspects are what gave the session with Timmy and Sandy its significance.

THE VYGOTSKIAN SYSTEM IN THE CLASSROOM

▼

One of Vygotsky's most educationally potent notions is that of "spontaneous" vs. "scientific" concepts (1986). Spontaneous concepts emerge from a child's own reflections on immediate, everyday experiences; they are rich but unsystematic and highly contextual. Scientific concepts originate in the structured and specialized activity of classroom instruction and are characterized by systemic and logical organization. The concepts themselves do not necessarily relate to scientific issues—they may represent historical, linguistic, or practical knowledge—but their organization is "scientific" in the sense of formal, logical, and decontextualized structures.

Unlike Piagetians, who assume that only when a certain developmental level is achieved can conceptual learning start, Vygotskians propose that scientific learning itself promotes cognitive development. Of course, in order to start acquiring scientific concepts, the child should have some experience with generalizations, which usually take the form of spontaneous, everyday concepts. However, once the learning of scientific concepts gains momentum, it begins to exercise a reciprocal influence on everyday cognition. Scientific concepts move from the "top" downward—from verbal-logical formulae to concrete material. Spontaneous concepts move in the opposite direction, from the "bottom" upward—from contextual everyday experience to the formal structures of well-organized thought. "In working its slow way upwards, an everyday concept clears the path for a scientific concept in its downward development. It creates a series of structures necessary for the evolution of a concept's more primitive, elementary aspects, which gives it body and vitality. Scientific concepts, in turn, supply structures for the upward development of the child's spontaneous concepts toward consciousness and deliberate use" (Vygotsky, 1986, p. 194). The already mentioned zone of proximal development can be conceptualized as a zone in which scientific concepts introduced by teachers interact with spontaneous concepts preexistent in children.

From the educational point of view, the most interesting aspect in conceptual development is the dynamics of change in child thought under the influence of exposure to scientific concepts. Instead of simply studying how children's concepts change with age and at which point they become indistinguishable from those of adults, one may wish to undertake a dynamic analysis of what happens when scientific concepts introduced by teachers start to interact with spontaneous concepts held by children. Precisely this task was established by Panofsky, John-Steiner, and Blackwell (1990) in their study of biological reasoning in fifth-grade students.

The study took place in a small rural school in New Mexico. Ranching, farming, hunting, and fishing were common experiences for many children in the class. The ethnic composition of the school was 75% Hispanic and 25% Anglo. All the children in the fifth grade were native English speakers, though some of them understood Spanish. The study took place during two months late in the school year.

Before the study began, children received explicit instruction in the principles of biological classification. In particular, instruction focused on the distinctions between plants and animals, between vertebrates and invertebrates, and between such categories as mammal, reptile, amphibian, bird, and fish. Hierarchical relationships between these categories were also explained. The game Animal-Vegetable-Mineral played an important role in teaching the above mentioned categories. In order to succeed at this game, one must be able to use a hierarchical structure with nonoverlapping categories and to manipulate this structure in a logical and sequential way.

The study itself included two experimental activities: a set of concept-sorting tasks and a film-retelling task.

The children were asked to do three classification tasks, two in the initial session and one several weeks later. At the first session, the children were given a set of 20 pictures, 6 of plants and 14 of animals. They were asked to sort the pictures into two piles, to put each pile into an envelope, and to write on the envelope something that explained why these items "belonged together." During the second session, children were given the same pictures but with seven empty envelopes. Children were asked to sort the pictures into as many groups as they wanted, but no fewer than three. Several weeks later, the children were asked to sort 23 animal pictures into at least three groups. Pictures included 13 of the original group plus 10 new ones.

In the first task, 82% of the children separated the pictures taxonomically into plant and animal categories and labeled the envelopes accordingly. In the second and third tasks, which required a greater number of categories, the scientific grouping was much less pronounced; only 19% of children used an exclusively taxonomic approach in the second task, and 25% used it in the third task. Often children employed a combination of spontaneous and scientific principles in their sorting. For example, one of the students used the following grouping labels in the third task: *birds, water animals, insects, animals that hunt, animals that are hunted*. Everyday experience with hunting, plus some ecological knowledge, were combined here with taxonomic principles. In some children, the appropriate use of taxonomic categories was coexistent with the mixing of the levels of abstraction. One of the children sorted pictures into the following categories in the third task: *all birds, all fish, all insects, all reptiles, animals with backbones, animals without backbones, both amphibians*. Some taxonomic labels were used in a pseudoscientific way, for example, the label of reptiles was also applied to *frog* and *earthworm* because "They're all slimy." Obviously, the perceptual feature here overpowered other possible criteria for inclusion.

From the results of the sorting tasks it became clear that acquisition of scientific concepts by primary school children is indeed a complex, interactive process. It is not an "all or nothing" switch from everyday to scientific conceptualization, but an intricate process that contains a number of intermediate stages further diversified by the specific cultural experiences of the children. The following aspects of the acquisition of taxonomic principles can be tentatively identified: (a) learning the distinction among everyday, ecological, and taxonomic categorizations; (b) learning different hierarchies within the taxonomic categorization; and (c) learning the principle of consistency of categorization. The authors of the reviewed study suggested that one possibility for advancing children's understanding of these principles is to make classification systems an object of study.

> Questions for investigation might include the organization of objects in space—such as how items are arranged in kitchens or workshops—and comparative analysis of different findings by peers investigating similar domains. Such investigations should lead to the development of active strategies for sorting or categorizing, which can be effectively applied as a system of discourse rather than as a rote fashion. (Panofsky, John-Steiner, & Blackwell, 1990, pp. 265–266)

As you will see later in this chapter, precisely such an approach was realized by Feuerstein (1980) in his mediated learning program.

The second activity was the film-retelling task. The entire class viewed a 15-minute science film about different types of vision in animals. After the group discussed the film, a representative subgroup of children participated in the experimental retelling task. The analysis of individual retellings suggested a correlation between recall and conceptional organization. Children who utilized taxonomic sorting strategies produced the most extensive recall. They also recalled a greater portion of the taxonomic information contained in the film. The utterances of the children who used scientific concepts differed from others not only in quantity but also in quality. These speakers used strategies more characteristic of written language. They utilized a number of devices to achieve the greater coherence of their narratives: explicit marking of topics, elaboration, transitions, and connectives. The use of such strategies implies that a speaker is able to plan both the form and the content of his or her speech.

The findings of the film-retelling task confirm Vygotsky's belief that the acquisition of scientific concepts has a reciprocal relationship with the acquisition of the higher-order forms of verbal discourse (Wertsch, 1985). One may suggest that the same aspects of planning and awareness that are essential for conceptual activity are also realized in the child's discourse formation.

PIAGET AND THE SPIRIT OF PROGRESSIVE EDUCATION

Theoretical ideas usually undergo considerable change in the course of their transition from the laboratory to the classroom, and Piagetian ideas were no exception to this practice. One of the most characteristic features of the assimilation of Piagetian ideas into the American educational system was that this assimilation was carried out in a spirit of "progressive education" tradition (Silberman, 1970).

Indeed, some of the old principles associated with progressive education turned out to be highly compatible with the Piagetian system. The principle of "learning by doing" could be easily translated into the Piagetian principle "from action to thought." The suggestion that a child is a true agent of his or her own learning was also characteristic of both trends. Even the method of projects that was featured so prominently in the progressive education tradition found its safe place within the Piagetian-based learning programs (Wickens, 1973).

What is unmistakably Piagetian in such a hybrid system is the emphasis on the sequencing of curriculum material, depending on the level of a child's cognitive development as established through Piagetian assessment procedures. For example, it is argued that the teaching of material requiring formal logical operations should be delayed until the necessary operations spontaneously appear in a child's reasoning. "We should try where possible, to teach children new concepts in the same order that these concepts emerge during spontaneous cognitive development" (Brainerd, 1978).

Predictably, the infusion of Piagetian ideas into the American classroom produced mixed results. On the positive side, one can mention the increased awareness on the part of educators of the role of reasoning in children's learning (Duckworth, 1987). The emphasis on independent discovery helped a number of gifted students reveal their true potentials, which could have become stymied by rote learning. Finally, the Piagetian approach stimulated an interdisciplinary cooperation between cognitive psychologists and teachers. Teachers' attention was drawn to the fact that the methods for delivery of content material become effective only when the child's reasoning during the acquisition of this material is taken into account.

These positive aspects notwithstanding, there are serious doubts regarding the net effect of the popularity of Piagetian ideas, particularly where assimilated in a spirit of progressive education. One of the problematic points concerns the proliferation of thinking games at the expense of teaching verbal skills and content knowledge (Furth, 1970). Such thinking exercises are attractive for the child, but they often lack the systematization provided by coherently presented content material. Attempts at teaching nonverbal thinking as a substitute for teaching language result in the worst cases in such reading and writing backwardness that this forecloses any possibility for the higher forms of learning (Modgil et al., 1983).

Another point of concern is the notion that learning should follow the course of development. In practice this leads to delays in teaching science and certain sections of mathematics until much later in school. The problem is that even at the age of 14 only 75% of students consistently use concrete operations, and only 20% master the formal operations (Shayer & Adley, 1981). This often necessitates special cognitive enrichment programs to prepare students for learning science. One may argue that this can be done much more efficiently, and at an earlier age, if one accepts the Vygotskian position that education should lead development rather than follow it.

Piaget's equivocality regarding Vygotsky's distinction between "scientific" and "spontaneous" concepts translates into educational practices that do not prepare a child for genuine scientific

reasoning, as opposed to everyday cognition. An attempt to move school closer to life, which is another legacy of progressive education, often results in presenting the real-life phenomena on a scriptlike, preconceptual level. As a consequence, in the higher grades when students become confronted with problems requiring scientific, conceptual reasoning, they experience real shock, because nothing in their previous experience prepared them for such a change of perspective.

Finally, and probably most important, the Piagetian notion that a child is a true agent of his or her learning fits well into the American cultural belief that education is the primary way of revealing individual abilities and potentials. This belief leads to the overemphasis on individualized learning and the playing down of the issue of acquiring knowledge as a group activity oriented toward specific sociocultural goals. One example may help to clarify this distinction. In a comparative analysis of mathematics teaching in schools in America and Asia (Taiwan and Japan), it was shown that one of the apparently highly effective classroom activities employed by Asian educators is a group analysis of mistakes made by a specific student (Stigler & Perry, 1990). The student in question does not feel ashamed to be singled out, because his or her learning problem is not attributed to him or her as an individual, but rather it serves as an example of what can go wrong in the learning process as such. In this context, learning is understood as the process of acquiring knowledge, skills, and concepts existent in culture and not as a manifestation of individual abilities.

Of course, there is nothing wrong with an attempt to make education individualized. However, in the reality of the contemporary classroom, such an attitude often has negative consequences. The first of them is that only better and more highly motivated students benefit from being considered true agents of their own learning. The second problem lies in the fact that where learning is detached from sociocultural models, it becomes exceedingly difficult to agree on comprehensive educational requirements. The following section will focus on how these problems have been dealt with in the Vygotskian system.

VYGOTSKY AND THEORETICAL LEARNING

▼

For many years Vygotskian theory has been developing exclusively in Russia. This cannot fail to leave a specific imprint on its educational applications. The Russian educational system always presupposed a rather rigid set of comprehensive requirements including a strong emphasis on the study of science, mathematics, and a standard list of classical works of Russian literature. At the same time, and for obvious political reasons, creativity, pluralism, and a critical approach in social sciences were systematically discouraged. The highly centralized system of educational bureaucracy ensured that these requirements became truly comprehensive at least as a goal, if not as a reality. As a result, special cultural-historical conditions favorable for theoretical learning in ideologically neutral areas have been created.

As mentioned earlier, Vygotsky made an important distinction between scientific and spontaneous concepts. Spontaneous concepts originate in a child's everyday activity, while scientific concepts emerge from systematic school-based learning. Contemporary Vygotskians (Davydov, 1988; Hedegaard, 1990) further refined this distinction to include the difference between various types of school-based learning. They argued that in practice a considerable amount of school-based learning does not transcend to the limits of empirical concept formation. Concepts acquired in this way differ from everyday concepts only in the domain but not in the method of acquisition and generation. The line should be drawn, therefore, between empirical and theoretical concepts. Empirical concepts are acquired through the procedure of identifying similar features in a group of concrete objects or observable phenomena and then labeling this feature with a verbal notion. For example, the notion of the circle is traditionally introduced in primary schools by demonstrating a number of round objects, such as a wheel, the sun, a pancake, etc., and then explaining that a common feature of all these objects is their circular form. The principle of concept formation in this case is a simple abstraction that does not require any higher level of thinking and that can actually be achieved through habit formation.

Theoretical concepts have an essentially different nature. To understand an object or a process theoretically is to construct its ideal form and then to be able to experiment with it. A paradigm of such experimentation is provided by the mental experiments carried out in classical science by Galileo, Descartes, and others. A theoretical concept is "generative" in the sense that it should be possible to generate from it a number of empirical outcomes. In addition, it is universal so that all empirical data are explainable through it, and it should not require the prior knowledge of all the phenomena it is expected to explain. For example, the theoretical definition of a circle (suggested by Spinoza) says that it is a figure produced by the rotation of a segment of a line with one free and one fixed end. Such a definition is generative because it provides a procedure for the generation of circles, it is universal because all possible circles can be generated in such a way, and it is theoretical because it requires no previous knowledge of round objects.

One may argue that there is little difference in introducing the notion of a circle to a child through the comparison of a number of round objects or through the manipulation of the rotating line; in both cases, the child would most probably understand the meaning of a circle. The difference, however, is significant because in the first case the child would only learn how to distinguish round objects, while in the second case he or she would acquire a skill of theoretical comprehension. The first approach is product-oriented; the second one focuses on the process. This process helps the child construct the essence of the object and thus liberates him or her from the domination by the empirically given. The child starts to realize that essential characteristics of objects do not necessarily lie on the surface but should be uncovered. This is an important lesson for understanding scientific truth where the lack of coincidence between the empirical appearance and the theoretical essence is the norm and not an exception.

When designing a program based on the principles of theoretical learning, the teacher should start with the most general definition of the problem so that the relationships central to this problem are revealed. For example, in a traditional primary school, "nature" class students usually acquire interesting, but often disjointed, information about various physical and biological phenomena. In the framework of a theoretical learning program, the teacher always first formulates some central scientific problem. For the nature class, for example, the teacher may choose the problem of the contradictory relationships between organism and environment. The teacher then assists students in formulating the *model* that serves as a conceptual tool for exploring the learning material. Such a model includes three main elements: organism, population, and environment. In the next step, all possible relationships between the elements of the model are explored. New problems and tasks stemming from the model are generated. The learning process involves what Hedegaard (1990) calls a "double move": The teacher guarantees that the theoretical model is used by children as a conceptual tool, while children are encouraged to observe and to manipulate with concrete manifestations of the principles embodied in the model. Through trips to nature museums, films, and textbook material, students learn about the lifestyle of specific animals, their habitats, and the structure of their group life. Then, students "map" the empirical data into the model. The model itself becomes transformed to account for the new types of relationships. As a result, students learn about ways of survival, cohabitation of different species, variation, and selection, all within the scientific concept of biological evolution.

Another important aspect of learning explored by Vygotskians relates to the value attached by students to different types of activities. For example, Elkonin (1971) maintains that the failure to teach scientific concepts to young adolescents often stems from the incorrect premise that learning activities *per se* have a high value for this age group. He further argues that it is group activities and the establishment of these personal relationships that have the highest priority for young adolescents. In the traditional classroom, based on the teacher's narrative and students' individual work, the lack of recognition of this priority leads to serious problems. The teacher has a hard time keeping the students' attention, because in the classroom the students are engaged in a "parallel activity" focused on nonacademic problems of an interpersonal nature. Vygotskians suggest turning this "obstacle" into the motor of learning. This can be achieved through the organization of class work according to the principle of collectively distributed problem solving. The essence of this approach is in presenting the task not for individuals but for the whole class. The task is presented in such a way that several groups of students are responsible for different segments of problem solving. The final result can be achieved only when all partial solutions are integrated. The partial results become compatible, however, only when all students are using the same theoretical approach and the same model for the representation of essential relationships. Thus, the students' desire to engage in the interpersonal contacts becomes fully realized, but it is employed as a means for achieving the goals of learning.

The role of a teacher also changes in this context. Instead of appearing as an authoritarian figure who can change the course of the lesson at his or her will, the teacher becomes a senior member of the "scientific group." His or her role is that of advisor and participant. The character of the teacher's involvement is now dictated by the logic of problem solving itself. This change in the teacher's role not only leads to the relaxation in the teacher-student relationships, but it also serves as an important model of the distribution of functions within the group engaged in problem solving. This fits well into Vygotsky's (1978) understanding of the process of activity internalization. According to Vygotsky, many relations that first appear in a real group activity are later internalized by the student as the relations between his or her inner intellectual processes. Thus, the role of a teacher as an expert and advisor working within the group becomes internalized by the child as his own internal function of reference and control.

As mentioned at the beginning of this section, the emergence of theoretical learning programs in Russia was facilitated by the specific cultural-historical context. One should be aware of these contexts when planning the implementation of the theoretical learning programs in other countries.

Firstly, the Russian theoretical learning programs took for granted the existence of a wide social consensus regarding the ultimate goals of education. It was supposed that society as a whole expects its children to appreciate classical literature on the one hand and to prepare themselves for careers in modern science and technology on the other. In a society with many divergent and often antagonistic subcultures, this presumption may well be groundless. The task of an American educator, therefore, is more difficult. The educator must simultaneously demonstrate the value of verbal and scientific literacy in modern society while introducing students to the theoretical methods of acquiring this literacy.

Secondly, by focusing on physics, mathematics, and language, the advocates of theoretical learning largely neglected social and political sciences. It is not a secret that these subjects are difficult to present in a theoretically coherent form even for scholars. The task confronting psychologists and educators is twofold, that is, to develop the theoretical learning models for social sciences and to elaborate on the relationship between these models and the social knowledge that resists scientific conceptualization.

Thirdly, the model of different activities for different age groups (Elkonin, 1971) has been developed with a certain social-cultural framework in mind. At the same time, this model appears to contain certain universal features, since in some instances it closely resembles Erik-

son's (1963) psychosocial stages theory. Only further research and application of this model can determine the degree of its universality and those adjustments needed to be made so that it will work for the diverse populations of students.

All in all, the educational applications of Vygotskian ideas teach us that psychological theories can be neither value free nor culturally neutral. When proposing the explanation of a child's learning processes or suggesting methods for their enhancement, we cannot escape from the questions about the cultural and societal goals this learning strives to achieve.

MEDIATED LEARNING

The last issue to be discussed in this chapter is that of different agents mediating between a child and the world in the course of learning interaction. Since for Piaget the child's direct experimentation with the physical and social world is of primary importance, the role of a mediator is assigned to the inner mental schemas of the child. For Vygotsky, in contrast, a child's interaction with the world is mediated by symbolic tools provided by the given culture. Adults and more competent peers introduce symbolic tools to the child and teach him or her how to use them. Still, the role of the human mediator is not fully elaborated within this theoretical framework. This theoretical gap can be filled with the help of Feuerstein's (1990) theory of mediated learning, which assigns the major role to a human mediator.

According to Feuerstein, all learning interactions can be divided into direct learning and mediated learning. Learning mediated by another human being is indispensable for a child, because it helps to create in him or her those cognitive prerequisites that then make direct learning effective. There are many criteria of mediated learning, but three of them are the most important: intentionality, transcendence, and meaning. One of the major contributions of the human mediator is to turn the learning situation from incidental into intentional, so that material is experienced rather than simply registered by the child. This is achieved by constant affirmance of the adult's intention to present certain material to the child and to remain open for the child's response.

Transcendence is another of the major criteria of mediated learning. If in the case of direct learning one may only hope that a particular interaction will affect the child's cognition beyond the immediate task, in mediated learning, this "going beyond the present" situation constitutes the very essence of interaction. The human mediator indicates the general possibilities imbedded in the concrete problem solving and builds bridges from the task at hand to the other areas of experience. For example, a simple errand of going to a neighborhood drugstore can be turned by thoughtful parents into a cognitive exercise for the child involving action planning, orientation in space, appreciation of time, and other functions that have value beyond the task at hand.

Finally, each of the child's interactions with the world of objects and processes should be infused with meaning. The child should not be left in a position where he or she simply confronts material or where he or she is asked to perform certain acts without being informed about their meaning.

In optimal conditions children receive enough mediated learning through their parents and other caretakers. Unfortunately, the conditions of a child's upbringing are often less than optimal. Sometimes children are simply deprived by their parents of mediated learning experience. Such parents provide for the child's basic physical needs, but completely ignore the task of mediation in the child's learning. The lack of mediated learning may also be triggered by the specific organic or psychopathological conditions of the child. Feuerstein (1979, 1980) insists that it is not a primary defect of the child that leads to retarded cognitive performance, but the secondary lack of mediated learning. For example, an impulsive child may suffer not so much from original impulsivity as from the secondary lack of mediated learning. Parents, who would succeed as mediators if their child were not impulsive,

fail because they do not adjust their mediating behavior according to the child's special needs.

The most general syndrome observable in children deprived of mediated learning experience is an episodic grasp of reality (Feuerstein, 1979). For such children, every element of their experience remains detached spatially, temporally, and causally from each other. They may behave quite adequately in routine circumstances, but they lack the cognitive prerequisites necessary for prospective planning, hypothesis testing, and the integration of experience. Other deficient cognitive functions that can be observed in children deprived of mediated learning include lack of spontaneous comparative behavior, difficulties in projecting virtual relationships, and unsystematic exploratory behavior (Feuerstein, 1979).

If the above mentioned cognitive prerequisites are not established in children, there is no reason to expect them to succeed in cognitive operations which, according to Piaget, are characteristic of their age. Similarly, children could hardly benefit from the introduction of a new psychological tool if such an introduction is not appropriately mediated by an adult. Fortunately, Feuerstein did not stop at diagnosing the cases of deprivation but developed the whole system of remediation. This system is based on a combination of special cognitive exercises, including spatial, temporal, analytic, and classification tasks, with the technique of intensive mediation provided by the teacher or psychologist. The system, Instrumental Enrichment (Feuerstein, 1980), has been successfully used with diverse groups of children and adolescents with learning problems.

The importance of Feuerstein's findings extends far beyond the issue of learning disabilities or special education. He draws our attention to the fact that learning based on a solitary interaction of the child with the world is a theoretical mirage. The mediating participation of an adult or more competent peer is the necessary condition for the establishment of cognitive prerequisites indispensable for the child's further learning. Mediation through another human being cannot be replaced by any technical or symbolic devices. Actually, the child's success in using technical or symbolic mediating agents depends on his or her cognitive readiness, which in turn depends on the mediated learning experience requiring human mediation.

CONCLUSION

The survey of different approaches to a child's learning undertaken in this chapter allows us to distinguish in them some pivotal points. The first of them is the child-centered character of the contemporary learning theory. A child's cognition has its own specific features, which should be constantly kept in mind if we wish to meaning-fully improve the processes of teaching and learning. The second pivotal point is the recognition that learning is not an individual process but a cultural-historical one, both in respect to symbolic tools internalized by the child as his or her mental processes and in respect to the sociocultural goals of education established by society. The last pivotal point is the role of the human mediator in learning. Specific contributions of the human mediator should be distinguished both from the content of learning and from the symbolic tools offered by the given culture. It is only by providing each child with adequate mediated learning experience that we can ensure his or her normal cognitive development and an opportunity for further learning.

REFERENCES

Brainerd, C. (1978). *Piaget's theory of intelligence*. Englewood Cliffs, NJ: Prentice Hall.

Claparede, E. (1959). Preface. In Piaget, J., *The thought and language of the child*. London: Routledge & Kegan Paul.

Cromer, R. (1991). *Language and thought in normal and handicapped children*. Cambridge, MA: Basil Blackwell.

Davydov, V. (1988). The concept of theoretical generalization. *Studies in Soviet Thought, 36,* 169–202.

Duckworth, E. (1978). *The having of wonderful ideas and other essays on teaching and learning*. New York: Teachers College Press.

Elkonin, D. (1971). Toward the problem of stages in the mental development of the child. *Soviet Psychology, 10,* 538–653.

Erikson, E. (1963). *Childhood and society*. New York: Norton.

Feuerstein, R. (1979). *Dynamic assessment of retarded performer*. Baltimore, MD: University Park Press.

Feuerstein, R. (1980). *Instrumental enrichment*. Baltimore, MD: University Park Press.

Feuerstein, R. (1990). The theory of structural cognitive modifiability. In B. Presseisen (Ed.), *Learning and thinking styles: Classroom interaction* (pp. 68–134). Washington, DC: National Education Association.

Furth, H. (1970). *Piaget for teachers*. Englewood Cliffs, NJ: Prentice Hall.

Hedegaard, M. (1990). The zone of proximal development as basis for instruction. In L. Moll (Ed.), *Vygotsky and education* (pp. 349–371). New York: Cambridge University Press.

Horowitz, F. D. (Ed.). (1989). *Children and their development*. [Special issue]. *American Psychologist, 44,* 95–445.

Kozulin, A. (1978). Structural and developmental paradigms in theories of behavior and mind. Unpublished doctoral dissertation, Moscow Institute of Psychology.

Kozulin, A. (1986). The concept of activity in Soviet psychology. *American Psychologist, 41,* 264–274.

Kozulin, A. (1990). *Vygotsky's psychology: A biography of ideas*. Cambridge, MA: Harvard University Press.

Lidz, C. (Ed.). (1987). *Dynamic assessment*. New York: Guilford Press.

Luria, A. (1960). *The role of speech in regulation of normal and abnormal behavior*. New York: Pergamon.

Modgil, S., Modgil, M., & Brown, G. (Eds.). (1983). *Jean Piaget: An Interdisciplinary critique*. London: Routledge and Kegan Paul.

Panofsky, C. P., John-Steiner, V., & Blackwell, P. J.

(1990). The development of scientific concepts and discourse. In L. Moll (Ed.), *Vygotsky and education* (pp. 251–267). New York: Cambridge University Press.

Piaget, J. (1959). *The thought and language of the child.* London: Routledge & Kegan Paul.

Piaget, J. (1969). *Psychology of intelligence.* Totowa, NJ: Littlefield, Adams & Co.

Piaget, J., & Inhelder, B. (1967). *The child's conception of space.* New York: Norton.

Piaget, J., Inhelder, B., & Szeminska, A. (1981). *The child's conception of geometry.* New York: Basic Books.

Shayer, M., & Adley, P. S. (1981). *Toward a science of teaching.* London: Heinemann.

Silberman, C. (1970). *Crisis in the classroom.* New York: Random House.

Stigler, J. W., & Perry, M. (1990). Mathematics learning in Japanese, Chinese, and American classrooms. In J. W. Stigler, R. Schweder, and G. Herdt (Eds.), *Cultural psychology* (pp. 328–356). New York: Cambridge University Press.

Vygotsky, L. (1978). *Mind in society.* Cambridge, MA: Harvard University Press.

Vygotsky, L. (1986). *Thought and language* (rev. ed.). Cambridge, MA: MIT Press.

Werner, H. (1965). *Comparative psychology of mental development.* New York: Science Editions.

Wertsch, J. (1985). *L. S. Vygotsky and the social formation of mind.* Cambridge, MA: Harvard University Press.

Wickens, D. (1973). Piagetian theory as a model for open system education. In M. Schwebel and J. Raph (Eds.), *Piaget in the classroom* (pp. 179–198). New York: Basic Books.

Zivin, G. (Ed.). (1979). *The development of self-regulation through private speech.* New York: Wiley.

The research reported here was supported by grants from the Rockefeller Foundation, New York; the Lilly Endowment, Indianapolis; and the Center for Technology in Education, Bank Street College, New York. We would like to acknowledge two colleagues, Kim Powell and Jim Gray, who helped us with many of the ideas in this chapter. We are also grateful to the staff at Veterans Memorial Elementary School in Provincetown, MA, and Jerry Halpern of the Pittsburgh Public Schools for their collaborations with us.

CHAPTER THIRTEEN

CHILDREN AS REFLECTIVE PRACTITIONERS

BRINGING METACOGNITION TO THE CLASSROOM

JOSEPH WALTERS

PROJECT ZERO
HARVARD UNIVERSITY

STEVE SEIDEL

PROJECT ZERO
HARVARD UNIVERSITY

HOWARD GARDNER

PROJECT ZERO
HARVARD UNIVERSITY

Dr. Joseph Walters is research associate in education for Project Zero at the Harvard Graduate School of Education. Project Zero is a center for research on children's development in the arts.

Steve Seidel is research assistant at Project Zero at the Harvard Graduate School of Education.

Dr. Howard Gardner is codirector of Project Zero at the Harvard Graduate School of Education. For the past 25 years, Project Zero has been a center for research on children's development in the arts. In the past decade, researchers at Project Zero have focused attention on exploring the implications of Dr. Gardner's theory of multiple intelligences for school practice, the development and implementation of alternative forms of assessment, and issues related to learning in educational settings outside of schools.

INTRODUCTION

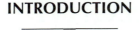

Andi is a third grader at Veterans Memorial Elementary School in Provincetown, MA. The school recently completed a monthlong study of African culture. One day Andi's teacher played a recording of African dance music for the class, and Andi spontaneously improvised several dance steps to go along with it. The teacher suggested that Andi create a dance to go with the music that the students would perform in the schoolwide assembly to mark the culmination of the Africa study. Andi agreed.

She worked for several weeks during free time, recess periods, and after school to choreograph a dance that involved a dozen students from two classes. Over the course of the project, Andi encountered a variety of problems, including making esthetic judgments, designing costumes, dealing with stage fright, organizing rehearsals, and simply managing a large group of 7- and 8-year-old children on a day-to-day basis.

After the final performance, Andi was interviewed by a visitor to the class, and she talked at length about these various elements of the project and how she worked through the many problems. During this interview she said:

[Tell me a bit about what was happening in the dance.]

The two (dancers with) black masks are a baboon and a chimpanzee; and then there are a lion and a cheetah that are chasing them. I am dancing around this circle, and when I shoot the first arrow, (everyone) goes halfway down; I shoot the second arrow and they go all the way down. Then I go down, they go up; I go up and they go down.

At the end, they come over me, and that was (to show) that I was trying to trap them and (instead) they trap me.

[I see! You know, you took on the role of choreographer in this project.]

Yeah. I've thought of that a lot . . . Because I have to set them up the right way. You have to put a third grader between a second grader, because if there are two masks together, it gets all messed up. If there are two or three or four or five in a row, then it is just "off."

If someone wants to go away (quit), don't let them go, because (later) they will want to come back. Unless they are doing horrible on stage. (In that case) you *do* have to let them go because they are going to mess up the whole thing. You break it to them *easily*, but . . . that's what happens.

[I noticed that you videotaped the rehearsal. What did you learn from the tape?]

Well, I found out that a lot of people when they walked around were pushing the person in front. And then someone kicked another person in the back of the leg, on purpose, and the other one kicked it back. And that messed the whole thing up. So by watching that I figured out, *separate* those two! . . . *Just separate them!* So it will work out on Friday.

Although Andi is remarkably poised and articulate for an 8-year-old, her ability to step back from her work and comment on it is not unusual. In our research at Project Zero, we have examined numerous accounts like this, in which students react to their work, either in writing or conversation. We believe that these student *reflections* give us an important vantage point on students' work, and we will show how this vantage point marks a unique moment of learning.

In this chapter we will discuss student reflections or commentaries on their work in terms of three attributes. First, in reflections students often reveal how they grapple with *complex problems;* this is especially true for long-term projects that engage many interrelated issues. In her dance project, Andi was faced with esthetic decisions, group dynamics, project management, and other complicated issues. Second, as students become engaged in projects, they often raise their own questions and problems; reflection can reveal this *pursuit of individually defined challenges.* Such questions and issues may be quite different from those assigned by the teacher, even when they are appropriate to the project. Finally, throughout this work students are constantly struggling to understand, articulate, and bring to bear the criteria by which they judge the quality of their efforts; reflections record these deliberations on *standards of quality.* For example, Andi has a clear image of what works in her dance and what doesn't: "If there are two or three or four or five in a row, then it is just 'off.'"

In the next section, we draw a connection between these student reflections and the research literature on metacognition. After that, we review the research at Project Zero that led us in this direction in the first place, and we decide in some detail three examples to illustrate the three aspects of reflection mentioned above. Finally, we put forth our contention that student reflection reveals important insights into learning but that designing a classroom that nurtures such reflections poses significant pedagogical and organizational challenges to the teacher.

THE CALL TO STUDY STUDENT REFLECTION

At Project Zero our interest in student reflection as a classroom activity grew out of our contin-uing consideration of working artists as a model for educational practice. We noticed that despite the immediacy of the act of painting or composing, these artists were often adept at stepping back from their work. Studies of biographies and notebooks show that artists constantly engage in various kinds of reflective activities alone and with their peers. In fact, an important element in creating art is the moment at which the artist steps back from his or her work, when all kinds of thoughts, appraisals, and decisions may occur: Have I accomplished what I set out to achieve in this or these works? What kinds of surprises have there been for me in the creation of these works? Where do these works stand in relation to other works of art that deal with similar issues, problems, or materials? Am I satisfied? What do I do next?

There is a lovely example of this kind of moment in *Seeing Is Forgetting the Name of the Thing One Sees,* Lawrence Weschler's biography of Robert Irwin, a contemporary West Coast painter and sculptor. In this account of his first important gallery opening, Irwin suggests the deep connection between making thoughtful appraisals of one's work and the subsequent steps in one's development.

I had broken my leg skiing, and I was there putting up this exhibition that I was getting ready to have. Landau was a very respectable gallery; it was a big exhibition for me. So there I was, hobbling around on these crutches, helping to finish hanging the show. And for the first time, I think, I really got a good hard look at what I was doing, and it was terrible. I mean, it was really bad. A very frightening kind of experience.

I spent that evening—it was really a very painful evening—with people telling me how terrific the things were, you know, my friends. But at that moment I just stopped being involved with Felix Landau (the gallery owner), and I stopped being involved with the things I had been doing.

My education, I think, started then. (Weschler, 1982, p. 42)

This moment is noteworthy because it reveals Irwin's understanding, for the first time, of the importance of stepping back from the process of creating. It is especially significant that this insight occurred when Irwin could see a body of his work displayed and at a time when he was preparing to share this with others. For students, reflective moments are often simply tied to performances and presentations in public. In some sense, then, it is the presence of these outside judges that forces an individual to step back and reflect.

Such stepping back is one form of metacognitive activity, the act of thinking about one's own thinking. Another is the self-regulatory thought that is rooted in the moment of solving the problem. An artist or an expert in any field exhibits both. Experts constantly ask themselves self-regulating questions, although these are rarely articulated explicitly (Schoenfeld, 1989; Schön, 1983). Experts also deploy this metacognitive activity long after the problem has been addressed, as in the example from Irwin at the Landau or in Andi's reminiscences on her dance. This is not the self-regulatory activity of the reflection in action. Rather it is reflection after the fact, the metacognitive stepping back from the problem solving.

The student reflections that we are studying focus on the moment of this stepping back. We have found that this type of activity fits comfortably into the life of the classroom. These written or spoken reflections do not interfere with classroom tasks, and they provide the teacher and the students themselves with extremely valuable information about the students' learning. Also, we think that this stepping back is an important exercise in that it slows down the problem solving and gives students room to contemplate their actions. Just as Irwin found time to step back (despite being hobbled with a broken leg), novices must be given the opportunity to take this reflective stance toward their work.

The student reflections in our study were written well after the project work itself had been completed. Students wrote or discussed their work every few weeks or at the conclusion of a project. However, reflection can be brought closer to reflection-in-action. For example, the teacher

might periodically halt the student's work and ask for reflections "on the fly"; or a group that is rehearsing for a performance can stop playing and record their thoughts (Davidson & Scripp, 1990). The goal is to help students become more accustomed to reflective activity so that they undertake it regularly and in different ways.

When students work on complex problems and think and talk explicitly about their experiences with these problems, the work of the classroom can replicate important aspects of the work of an expert. Of course, students cannot be simply turned loose with these tasks and told to begin acting like experts. The teacher must skillfully model, coach, and even scaffold the appropriate techniques, both in terms of solving the problem and in thinking about that solving process (Brown, Collins, & Duguid, 1989; Resnick, 1987). Indeed, this is often the procedure used in training the aspiring experts in advanced fields of inquiry, such as architectural design or counseling (Schön 1983, 1987).

Our research shows that students at any school age can reflect knowingly and that those reflections underscore the significant metacognitive effort that students can bring to complex tasks and long-term projects. These reflections make effort and accomplishment visible to the students. They also reveal the students' thinking and planning to their teachers, who can then respond appropriately to individual circumstances. Finally, student reflections can contribute to the design of generative classroom activities that produce truly independent learning.

EARLY RESEARCH ON REFLECTION IN STUDENTS

An investigation of student reflection at Project Zero began in 1985 with Arts Propel, a curriculum and assessment project involving researchers from Educational Testing Service and administrators and teachers in the Pittsburgh Public Schools (Wolf, 1987/1988). In this project, the research team worked with high-school teachers in music, visual arts, and writing to create materials that blended making art (production), looking at art (perception), and stepping back and talking about one's own work and the work of others (reflection). The team created more than a dozen curriculum units and established procedures for designing, creating, and assessing collections of student work, called portfolios.

In the course of this project, students in many middle- and high-school classes were introduced to the activity of reflection. In a variety of ways, these students were asked to step back from their work, to examine it carefully, and to share their thoughts with others. Of the many reflections collected by Arts Propel teachers was one short yet provocative piece by Tony, a ninth grader in Jerry Halpern's language arts class in Pittsburgh. Jerry's students had in the previous two weeks written at least five dramatic dialogues. All of these students were new to the activity of playwriting. Like his classmates, Tony wrote five short dialogues on successive days and collected all of them in his portfolio folder without examining them. The following week, Jerry told the class to review the dialogues they had written, taking as much time as they needed to read and to write a critique. Tony wrote the following:

Jerry Halpern reports that this was the first reflection assignment ever in Tony's class. Nevertheless, on his first effort, Tony reveals an uncanny ability to look over his work and rank his pieces on the basis of standards that he has established for himself. What are these standards and where did they come from? Why does Tony think the last dialogue was so terrible? What made the fourth dialogue the best? What work of other playwrights appeal to him?

Tony's reflection, strikingly original in its form, is like many others that teachers and researchers read on Arts Propel. This suggests the presence of a thoughtful artist in the ninth grade boy who has seen or read few plays, let alone written one. He is certainly not as sophisticated in skill or concept as Robert Irwin with his show at the Landau Gallery, and yet he is capable of casting a keen and rigorous eye on his own work. The realization that novices were bringing such a capability to class led the Arts Propel team to include reflection as a central and critical component of its work on curriculum and assessment.

Project Zero researchers working on another assessment project, called Assessing Projects and Portfolios for Learning, or APPLE for short, were impressed by the reflections of the Pittsburgh stu-

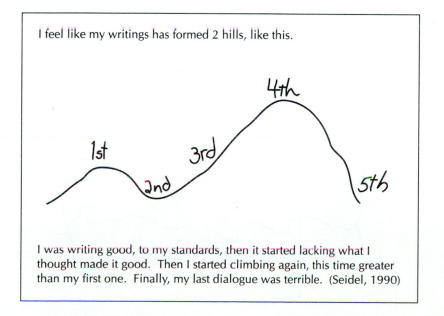

I feel like my writings has formed 2 hills, like this.

I was writing good, to my standards, then it started lacking what I thought made it good. Then I started climbing again, this time greater than my first one. Finally, my last dialogue was terrible. (Seidel, 1990)

dents. However, the APPLE project focused its attention on the elementary grades and was not restricted to classes in the arts. APPLE set about to develop methods of asserting the learning going on in any project-based classroom. The team was particularly eager to determine if younger children would reveal as much about the process of doing their work as the middle- and high-school students had in Pittsburgh. They wondered if reflection would prove an equally valuable source of information for elementary teachers about the learning of their students.

In brief, reflection became as central to the teaching and assessment activities of the APPLE researchers and teachers as it had been in Arts Propel. In reviewing the reflections of students in a score of classrooms in a half dozen schools, the team created a substantial collection. In studying these they determined that, indeed, children of any school age, even kindergarten, could participate sensibly in reflection activities.

Cathy Skowron's second-grade classroom is a case in point. Here, reflection is practiced in a variety of forms at regular intervals throughout the year. A selection of reflections from 7-year-old Alene reveals a student who is not only capable of insightful and revealing commentary about her work but who appears to grow in that capacity during the year.

In late September, Alene filled out a "work receipt," a simple form that all students fill out when they complete any specific activity through independent work. In this document, Alene not only names the activity but offers an evaluation of her performance and supplements this account with a small drawing of her work.

In January, Alene is interviewed by Cathy at the end of the unit on the American Revolution. In the first part of this assessment she names the many tasks she had engaged in, books she used as resources, and the things she had made. In her self-assessment, she said:

> I did great! I think weaving was the best because it took me a long time to do it. Also, pottery because I had to make it, bake it, let

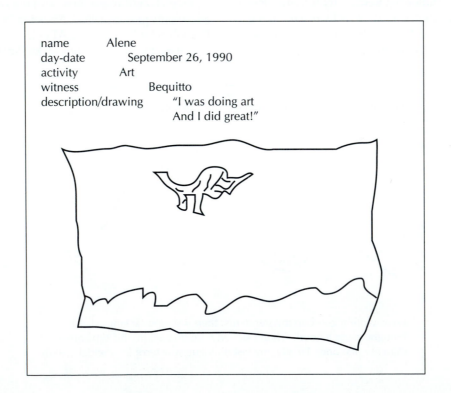

name   Alene
day-date   September 26, 1990
activity   Art
witness   Bequitto
description/drawing   "I was doing art
                        And I did great!"

it dry, glaze it, bake it again—it took a LONG time! I would have liked to do more pottery. Weaving was the hardest to do.

Clearly it is easier for Alene to get her many thoughts down in writing in this interview, and in this reflection on the unit, she combines assessment with explanations for her judgments, descriptions of the process involved in doing her complex tasks, and enthusiasm for things that take "a long time" to do.

In May, Alene offers a thoughtful insight into her sense of herself taken from the written comments she made after creating cardboard columns for a Greek building. This activity, Alene records, combined "social studies, art, and thinking." When asked what she learned, she wrote, "I'm really not a construction person but I did a good job on it. (And I learned) that team work is hard for me."

At the end of the year, Cathy interviewed each student and wrote down their answers to reflection questions. Just two of Alene's answers suggest the depth and complexity of her thought and insight about herself as a worker and learner in the classroom:

[How do you approach your work?]
If I can't figure something out I think before I do anything else because I might know it. If I don't, I look in a book. If nothing is there, I skip it and come back later. If I'm still stuck, I ask someone to give me a hint or help me.

[Describe how you do a project, from start to finish.]
Let's say someone said, "Draw a bear." If I don't know how to do it, I'd practice drawing the animal first to get the idea. I could also look in a book, get pencil and paper and draw it by looking without copying. I'd try my best. I'd start with the head, then the body, the legs, the feet. I'd look to see if I forgot something—like the tail. I'd think to myself—Is it done? Is it right? Is it good?

[How was your year? What was best? What needs improvement?]
I liked this year! It was good because we went on lots of field trips and we studied lots of science and social studies and art. [Where do I need to improve?] Nothing. I'm ready!

As clearly as reflection had become central to Arts Propel, it had also taken a special place in the portfolio assessment work of the APPLE project. This assessment of one's work, through regular occasions for stepping back together with the belief that all children are capable of this thoughtfulness, have become fundamental elements in many classrooms we have observed. The discovery that children as early as kindergarten are capable of making careful and appropriate decisions about the cataloging of their work in different categories and the selection of some pieces for a portfolio suggests that there are appropriate reflection activities for every grade in school. Surprisingly, many of the questions and forms for reflection appropriate for high-school students are, with only minor adjustment, also quite accessible and appropriate for children Alene's age.

EXAMINING STUDENT REFLECTION

Our examination of portfolio assessment for Arts Propel and APPLE has uncovered many examples of student reflections. Many of these are found in portfolio collections of work which in turn serve as the focal point of discussion and analysis, and from the careful consideration of their collected work, students can make judgments about how they might approach their work differently in the future. Through this research, collecting and reading student portfolios, interviewing many students, and consulting on a regular basis with their teachers, we have come to identify three component attributes: reflections in light of *complex problems or projects*; reflections that reveal *pursuit of an individually defined problem;* and reflections that record a student's deliberations on *standard of quality*. In this section, we describe the three attributes along with a case study of a student involved in reflection that illustrates each.

REFLECTION IN THE CONTEXT OF COMPLEX PROJECTS

Working through authentic problems and developing elaborate projects are fertile ground for reflections. This is partly because these complex problems or projects embody a number of distinct dimensions for consideration, and such variety can only be sorted out through careful reflection.

In contrast, simple problems or short-term projects usually do not generate the same kind of metacognitive activity. When students are asked about their performance on worksheets that contain sets of exercises designed to rehearse a specific skill, they generally refer to the accuracy of their work and the neatness of its presentation. Indeed, accuracy and neatness are the only two measures of quality on many worksheets; in multiple-choice examinations even neatness and handwriting have been eliminated. There is not a whole lot for students to "think" about here.

In tackling a complex task or a long-term project, in contrast, many different dimensions come into play and these prove to be fertile ground for meaningful reflections by students. Andi's African dance that we described in the Introduction is an excellent example.

She can remember that the project began with the teacher playing a record of African music in class:

> She turned on some music, one day. I just started . . . dancing! I just started doing the hands shaking thing from [music] class, like this. And she said that was good. So we got a big circle. And the teacher said, "Since you started the thing, Andi, you go in the middle."
>
> Then she said, "Do you want to do a performance?" and I said, "Yeah." But I

didn't know it would be in front of the whole school!

Andi had a specific design for the dance in mind and she refused to compromise on that design despite attendance problems at rehearsals. In this portion of the interview, she talks about this; she also reveals a tenacity and cleverness in handling her peers.

> We had a problem with people quitting. Just yesterday, someone wanted to quit; so I said, "Alice, just practice this part and [later] try it on the stage and if you don't like it on the stage, *then* you can quit." So, she tried that on stage yesterday and . . . she was *perfect!* And she said, "I'm glad I didn't quit."
>
> **[Is it upsetting when they quit?]**
>
> Yeah! Because I am all ready. I have to have that amount of kids, the amount that I need. So, if one goes away, then [often] a friend goes, and I have to find two new people.

Finally, in this particular performance, Andi faced many different aspects of choreography, including costuming and stage fright:

> I'm wearing that white necklace with my hair in a bun. But a lot of kids don't want to wear cloth. We tried white satin, so that it gives off a little bit of "shine," but they ripped it when they danced, "split!" So I am using stretchy material [instead].
>
> [The teacher] had [older] kids come all around [during the dress rehearsal]. And that made me start having butterflies, I was shaking like anything—I was nervous. . . . In the beginning I messed up a little bit, and my hands were shaking. . . . A lot of the [other] kids were really scared too.
>
> I had to try to remember [to think] that I was [back] in Ms. Smith's room.

In watching the videotape of the dance, one gets only a glimpse of the depth of this undertaking for Andi. The tape shows the children dancing in a circle with Andi in the middle, but many of their movements are imprecise and appear unplanned. Hearing Andi talk about the project, however, we come to understand something quite different about the project. Her remarks underscore the complexity of the undertaking, and indeed, it is partly this complexity that yields such a rich and reflective interview.

These excerpts also illustrate several symptoms of reflection—those characteristics that separate the thoughtful, metacognitive processes from "mere talk" about an event. For example, Andi's remarks reveal the effort that she has invested in this project. She describes the difficulties and setbacks as well as the successes with the insight and dedication of a true choreographer. Also, the interview substantiates the planning that went into the dance. In her remarks she shows that she can step back from the experience and draw conclusions—she has learned something about working with children from this experience. Finally, Andi lets us know that it is her passion for dance that guides her decisions and dealings with others; indeed, the ease with which she participates in this conversation suggests that she has been thinking about these issues throughout the project.

REFLECTION THAT REVEALS PURSUIT

In our conversations with students in Arts Propel classrooms in Pittsburgh and through careful readings of their reflections, we became aware of a sense of purposefulness in student work that seemed to be the motor driving many students to new levels of effort and accomplishment. While not evident in every student's work on every assignment, this quality of individual intent and purpose was certainly evident in any work that had sustained a student's interest and in works that were compelling and intriguing to others. In almost every case, the purpose that motivated the pursuit, while possibly related to the assignment made by the teacher, was also larger than or tangential to the assignment.

Some students managed to fulfill thoroughly the expectations embedded in the teacher's assignment while seriously pursuing their own purpose. Others, however, lost sight or interest in the teacher's assignment as they focused their attention on the issues that compelled them in the work. These students have essentially fashioned their own assignments out of the assignment made by the teacher. In most cases, of course, teachers only assessed whether the work handed them fulfilled the assignment they had given and demonstrated mastery of the conventions or ideas they were addressing at that moment. The consequences for students who lost sight of the teacher's plan are obvious. The seriousness and deeper purpose of their work was often hidden behind the success or failure of that work to meet the immediate demands of the teacher's assignment.

Last winter, Cathy Skowron's second-grade class was studying Greek mythology, the night sky and its constellations, and the work of Vincent Van Gogh. The morning after an evening trip to look at the stars, the class came across Van Gogh's famous painting "The Starry Night" in a book about the artist. After much discussion of the painting, Cathy asked the students to make as many paintings of a "starry night" as they could.

While all in the class made several paintings, Sonya made nine, more than anyone else. She recorded her reflections on her work in her daily work log and, taken together with the paintings themselves, these reflections constitute a fascinating document. They show how a compelling problem can emerge during the act of creating and how that problem can drive the work forward.

The nine paintings were all done with tempera paint on heavy 11-inch × 18-inch paper. Each painting contains a dark blue night sky that reaches down to the horizon or fills the page. In several paintings a tall rectangular structure juts prominently into the night sky; this shape represents the "monument," a tall building and landmark that stands within view of the school.

After completing each painting, Sonya immediately filled out a work receipt that included her reflections on her work. The teacher also talked to her and added notes from that conversation to the work receipt.

Painting #1

[What did you do?]
I pantid a picksher of the night sky.
[How did you do it?]
Paint brush and a paint nife.
[What did you learn?]
It was hard and easy.

[Dictated to the teacher] It was hard for Wayne because he didn't know what to draw. It was easy for me because I knew what I was going to do. He gave me the ideas—about the beach and the fence. He messed up. I didn't mess up. When I finished painting I look at it, if the color is what I want, it isn't messed up.

The next day, Sonya painted a similar picture. Her reflection shows that she is comparing her work although she does not describe the dimensions of her comparison.

Painting #2

[What did you do?]
I panted a picsher.
[How did you do it?]
A difrint way than my other one.
[What did you learn?]
That it is real fun.

Sonya's next painting is the first to feature the "Monument" at night. In Painting #4, she leaves the monument as a subject and paints the sky with stars and a large, yellow comet. In her work receipt, she describes the reemergence of her interest in color that she hinted at in her conversation with Cathy after painting the first picture.

Painting #4

[What did you do?]
I did my fourth starey night picksher.

[How did you do it?]
I painted with yellow and blue and some red and a little bit of whit.
[What did you learn?]
How to paint a comit.

As she continues to develop this series of paintings, Sonya remains concerned with colors and describes her troubles with color mixing. In one work receipt she says, "I looked at my first one a little, and I mickst (mixed) my colors. I leand how to make brown." After her seventh painting, she describes more experiments in mixing colors but reports, "I trid to make brown but it didn't come out the same way (as before)." In her eighth reflection, Sonya reports on another experiment in color mixing and, on looking over her paintings, notes that although she is continuing to do paintings of the monument and the night sky, "their difrint."

The project reaches a natural culmination when Sonya finally finds the solution to the color-mixing problem that has become so important to her.

Painting #9

[What did you do?]
I did my 9th painting.
[How did you do it?]
Looked at the monumint then I painted it.
[What did you learn?]
I got the brown I wantid.

Cathy interviewed Sonya when all of the paintings were completed and they could step back and survey the results of Sonya's efforts. This excerpt from Cathy's account of that interview suggests that mixing colors and getting the right colors were not the only compelling problems Sonya pursued in this work.

We looked quickly at the other paintings of the monument and then spread them out on the table. In one of them, Sonya told me she was trying to make something out of the stars.

I asked Sonya which painting she liked best, and she said the comet [Painting #4] was her favorite. Then I asked what she'd learned from doing this series, and she said she learned how to mix colors—brown and dark blue. Sonya told me, "The most fun part was I got to know how to make the things on my paintings and look at stuff to know how to feel how to draw it." Sonya said she looked at something to learn how to draw it [the landmark tower] and then she didn't have to look at it again.

Even though the fourth painting, with the "comit," was her favorite, Sonya did not stop her work at that point, because the serious and complicated problem of mixing colors to achieve a specific hue had become so important to her. She continued in her effort to get the "right brown," a pursuit that carried her through five more paintings. Sonya's daily log, her paintings, and her interview with Cathy suggest that there is an important link between her internal sense of standards and what she chose to pursue as problems and challenges in her "starry night" series. Given time, space, materials, and encouragement to paint as much as she wanted, Sonya had the opportunity to work until she had accomplished her objective.

This example reveals a student who has assigned herself a problem, that of mixing colors to achieve a desired effect, which she pursues vigorously over an extended period of several days. However, it is only through her reflections that we catch a glimpse of the importance of this issue for her—we can see the colors change in the paintings, but the purposeful experimentation is not evident. We might also speculate on the effect that writing the work receipts had on the work itself. Would she have painted so many paintings had she not been reflecting on the work, articulating her goals and her processes? Would the same challenges have emerged and been taken on? Would her teacher have been as able to support her in her efforts? Finally, we wonder how often students become involved with self-assigned problems that we don't know about, simply because we fail to ask.

REFLECTIONS ON STANDARDS OF QUALITY

As students work on projects and collect their efforts in portfolios, they can also be engaged in a continuing discussion of standards of quality. How does a student come to understand that one essay is more articulate than another? That this mathematical proof is more elegant? That this particular model ship is not properly built to scale? How do these judgments reach beyond the issues of simple accuracy in spelling, correctness of calculations, realism in representational design, and so on?

In their reflections on their work, students demonstrate these emerging principles, and they also let us understand the very nature of the enterprise from the point of view of the learner. Indeed, it is only through this reflective discussion that we can see how students grapple with this essential question.

Standards and quality are essential to education. Learning means changing, and changing implies some continuum of standards along which those changes can be marked. Learning also entails errors, and errors are most useful to learners when they are interpreted in terms of developing competence.

Of course, these standards are constantly changing for students. We don't expect the same products from 8-year-old children that we do from 18-year-olds. The standards must be set just beyond the abilities of the learner, and they must be adjusted to remain just beyond. Through reflection, we have found that students are quite capable of setting standards for themselves and that setting standards is an important element in continuing to learn outside of school. Schools must spend a greater portion of their time helping students set their own standards instead of *always* establishing those standards independently of the students and in advance of their experience.

As Tony, the ninth grader from Pittsburgh,

suggested in his reflection presented earlier, he brought, or had already evolved, a sense of what makes good playwriting to his assignment. "I was writing good, to my standards, then it started lacking what I thought made it good." Tony isn't articulating here what his standards are or how he came to them, but he is clear that he has them and that they guide his assessments of his work. Tony, like all writers, needs to be part of ongoing and open discussion with peers, teachers, and playwrights about the qualities of good playwriting. Those conversations must be specific and related to particular pieces, just as Tony's reflection is. In fact, his reflection and those of his peers are an excellent starting point for the kind of healthy, vigorous discussion that seems to be necessary in evolving standards that will be adopted by a group.

One of Tony's classmates, Scott, was similarly involved in writing short plays. A careful review of all of the reflections Scott wrote during the year reveals a fascinating picture of the early development of one person's ideas about drama, problems in writing comedy, the relationship of author and audience, and the struggle to understand what will work on stage when translated from the page. Even a quick look at Scott's final reflection on playwriting, written in May, highlights Scott's work in these varied areas and provides a good indication of some of the ways in which his standards and his sense of what makes good dramatic writing have evolved during the year.

It is important to note that Scott has pursued the challenge of writing comic scenes and is intent on entertaining his audience. This pursuit was entirely his own choice. Nothing about comedy or entertainment was part of the assignments made by his teacher. Like Sonya, it was the assignments he made for himself that sustained his interest in and invention through the work. Like Andi, it was his willingness to accept the complexity of his task that was key to his growth through the long process.

I see some changes in my writing. My approaches changed but my style always stayed the same. I've tried to be humorous the whole sequence. In the beginning, I thought of the most ridiculous scenes. I tried anything to be funny and now that I look back on it, it was weak. I always tried crazy voices. A lot of my scenes from the beginning were false, unrealistic.

At the time it [a particular scene] was written I really liked it but now that I read it again it doesn't do anything for me. As I read through my old scenes I found about 2 that I liked. They were the only ones written about real-life people. Now when I write scenes I always try to do them real-life, and be humorous at the same time.

Scenes that aren't realistic are weak. If I knew someone just starting to write plays my advice to them would be: Write about real-life experiences. Have solid characters, don't make their attitudes change line-by-line. Try to be funny. Have some conflict or tension. And most important is to have fun. Just relax and have a lot of fun doing the scenes. Also, keep the audience in mind. Write a scene to please yourself and also one that will please your audience.

Embedded in this statement are multiple indications that Scott has not only evolved a sense of what makes good dramatic writing but can also apply those criteria to his own work in an evaluative fashion. Would others agree with Scott's self-assessments? Are his standards rigorous and demanding? As important as these questions are, they cannot negate that Scott has engaged deeply and for nearly a year in the kind of careful and situated reflection that has led him to be able to speak with confidence and sophistication about the complex work of writing plays and how to become a better playwright.

REFLECTIONS IN CLASSROOMS

Student reflections offer an intriguing window on a child's view of his or her own efforts to make and do things and to achieve better results for those efforts. Each of the examples we've shared show children working on complex problems of their own design for which they have their own sets of standards. But these reflections are taken from the busy life of classrooms and reading them provokes thoughts about those classrooms.

For example, Scott's reflections raise questions about what his teacher might do to sustain Scott's engagement with playwriting and to ensure that he learns as much as possible from his study. If his teacher felt that students of playwriting must have good control of the elements of setting, time, and character before they take on the specialized problems of writing comedy, he might be inclined to discourage Scott from his pursuit. He might suggest instead that he hold off on trying to make his scenes funny and just work on establishing evocative settings and clear characters.

Indeed, by his own assessment Scott's early efforts showed a faltering grasp of how to create believable characters. And yet it seems that he is quite capable of working on those basic elements of playwriting while simultaneously tackling sophisticated problems of producing humor on stage. In fact, there is the suggestion in his reflections that he can *only* grapple with character in the context of his effort to write scenes that would "please" himself and his audience, scenes that were humorous.

In this way, Scott's case recalls the experiences Eleanor Duckworth (1991) describes in her essay "Twenty-three, Forty-two and I Love You: Keeping It Complex." Discussing her own efforts to explore and understand scientific concepts such as density and balance, Duckworth says:

I believe that it was because I started from my own ways into these parts of the world that my understanding of balances, "airs," and floating belonged so thoroughly to me. Notice the difference between what usually happens in formal education—presenting the simplest, neatest explanation of "density," "buoyancy," or whatever; and my experience of being enticed with the funny, frustrating, intriguing, unpredictable complexities of the world around me. Instead of disassociating myself from my own interests in my struggle to find out what whoever was supposed to "know" might have understood by the word "buoyancy," my learning was based on my own connections, within the idiosyncrasies of my own system of thoughts. The very complexities of the subject matters enabled me to connect with them, made them accessible, and the integrity of my own ideas enabled me to retrieve those connections when they could help me understand a new situation. (pp. 6–7)

The challenge of making assignments that are provocative and open enough to bring children into the arena of serious work without overwhelming them or limiting their sense of possibilities is a formidable one. The sensitivity to notice when a child has discovered a problem of deep interest is similarly challenging. Nurturing a child's ability to name and approach that problem is still another complex task for the teacher. And yet, such challenges are aided when students reveal the nature of their thinking in their reflections on their work.

At the same time, we must underscore the fact that reflection as portrayed here is not simply an "add-on" to regular classroom activity. One cannot simply halt instruction periodically and instruct students to "reflect" on their work. After all, reflection like anything else can easily become just another routine or drill that feels meaningless and fails to engage students in a genuine way.

To facilitate genuine reflection, the teacher must make time for it and then guide students' efforts until they become comfortable with the process and its benefits. Teachers must read these reflections and want to learn from them about the individual child and about the experiences children have in that classroom. What teachers learn from these reflections must transform and guide their specific actions in the classroom— from choices about when to move on and when to linger to the open negotiation of criteria for assessment.

Finally, the teacher must consider carefully those moments in the course of a day, week, or term that are most appropriate, even ripe, for reflection. Acknowledging the richness of those reflections, then, by having students share their work and their reflections also serves to make the practice of reflecting on one's work a valued one in the classroom community.

The reflections we've shared here, and many others we've reviewed with teachers in the course of our research, remind us of the integrity, depth, and rigor of children's efforts to learn and to make things. Andi's dance, Sonya's paintings, and Scott's comedies are indications that these young people are well on their way to becoming confident and serious participants in and contributors to their communities. Further, their reflections suggest that they have already developed some of the critical facilities for guiding their own learning. Our argument is that the regular opportunity to reflect on one's work (and the work of others) is an essential component in the development of the capacity to learn difficult concepts and master complex skills.

It is interesting to return to Robert Irwin, the artist whose "education" began the night he first stepped back and took a hard look at his finished paintings. Much later in his career Irwin began teaching, an activity he engaged in, on and off, for many years. Looking back on that experience, Irwin described his goals and guiding principles as a teacher.

All the time my ideal of teaching has been to argue with people on behalf of the idea that they are responsible for their own activities, that they are really, in a sense, the question, that ultimately they are what it is they have to contribute. The most critical part of that is for them to begin developing the ability to assign their own tasks and make their own criticism in direct relation to their own needs and not in light of some abstract criteria. Because once you learn how to make your own assignments instead of relying on someone else, then you have learned the only thing you really need to get out of school, that is you've learned how to learn. You've become your own teacher. After that you can stay on— for the facilities, the context, the dialogue, the colleagueship, the structure, and so forth— but you'll already be on your own. (Weschler, 1982, p. 120)

Irwin could be talking directly to Scott, Sonya, Andi, and to their teachers. These children have revealed through their reflections that they, indeed, have "the ability to assign their own tasks and make their own criticism in direct relation to their own needs." The will and capacity to learn is present and developing in these children. The challenge for their teachers is to make school a place in which students' efforts are not foiled but are nurtured and challenged in the most positive sense.

REFERENCES

Brown, J., Collins, A., & Duguid, P. (1989). Situation cognition and the culture of learning, *Educational Researcher, 18,* 32–41.

Davidson, L., & Scripp, L. (1990). Tracing reflective thinking in the performance ensemble, *The Quarterly, 1,* 49–61.

Duckworth, E. (1991). Twenty-three, forty-two and I love you: Keeping it complex, *Harvard Educational Review, 61,* 1–24.

Resnick, L. (1987). *Education and learning to think.* Washington, DC: National Academy Press.

Schoenfeld, A. (1989). Teaching mathematical thinking and problem solving. In Lauren Resnick and Leopold Klopfer (Eds.), *Toward the thinking curriculum: Current cognitive research.* Alexandria, Virginia: ASCD.

Schön, D. (1983). *The reflective practitioner: How professionals think in action.* New York: Basic Books.

Schön, D. (1987). *Educating the reflective practitioner: Toward a new design for teaching and learning in the professions.* San Francisco: Jossey-Bass.

Seidel, S. (1989). Even before portfolios: The activities and atmosphere of a portfolio classroom. *Portfolio, 1,* 6–9.

Weschler, L. (1982). *Seeing is forgetting the name of the thing one sees: A life of contemporary artist Robert Irwin.* Los Angeles: University of California Press.

Wolf, D. (1987–1988). Opening up assessment. *Educational Leadership, 46,* 35–39.

Research support for the studies discussed herein has been provided by the Spencer Foundation, the U.S. Department of Education (OERI/NIE), the Research Foundation of the National Council of Teachers of English, Northwestern University, and the Office of the Vice President of Research of the University of Michigan. Additional support has come from the North Central Regional Educational Laboratory, Apple Computer, Inc., International Business Machines, and Jostens Learning Corporation. I also thank the numerous children, teachers, administrators, school and school district personnel, undergraduates, graduate students, and faculty researchers who contributed to these projects. "We" in this chapter refers to the research teams who worked on various studies. I am, however, solely responsible for the statements in this chapter.

I THINKED IN MY MIND

KEEPING YOUNG CHILDREN'S POWERFUL THINKING ALIVE

ELIZABETH SULZBY

UNIVERSITY OF MICHIGAN

Elizabeth Sulzby is professor of education at the University of Michigan where she is on the faculties of the programs Reading and Literacy, Early Childhood Education, Instructional Technology, the Combined Program in Education and Psychology, and Linguistics. Her research area is emergent literacy. She particularly studies low-income and minority children and their teachers. Following on her studies of emergent storybook reading and emergent writing, she is now investigating children's use of the computer as an emergent literacy tool.

INTRODUCTION

Amazingly, preschool and kindergarten children of all ability levels and socioeconomic backgrounds often "write" letters, stories, poems, and other kinds of literature. Adults often miss seeing or hearing these pieces of literature because they cannot read children's ways of writing and they don't notice what children say about this writing. They may also pass over without notice children's "readings" from their favorite storybooks because the children are not yet reading print conventionally. They may not understand that these early forms are signs of children's thinking, their active engagement with literacy. For years, researchers were among these adults who missed the occurrence and significance of children's early literacy behaviors, or their emergent literacy. The few researchers such as Vygotsky and Luria who did write or lecture about this phenomenon tended to be ignored, although now they are being rediscovered and treated with the respect due prophetic voices (see reprints in Martlew, 1983; Vygotsky, 1978).

Researchers have helped us understand that these early writing and reading attempts are evidence that children are thoughtful about written language, just as they are thoughtful about oral language. Research can help uncover children's concepts and hypotheses about how language works that lead them to produce odd-appearing bits of language, such as inserting dialogue carriers ("he said," "she said," "John said to Mary," etc.) both before and after quoted speech in emergent storybook reading or spelling the cartoon character Fievel's name as the numerals 5-0. Research also helps us understand that children's thinking changes, or develops, over time and with experience. I have been using "read" and "write" in quotation marks thus far to alert the reader that I am talking about a special kind of reading and writing, *emergent reading* and *emergent writing*, that children produce prior to the time they become conventional readers and writers. I will drop the punctuation now as we go further in exploring children's thinking during early reading and writing.

A typical kind of question that I ask young children about these early forms of reading and writing is, "How did you figure that out?" or "How did you learn that?" A child's most typical response is, "I thinked in my mind." In my research, I have been tracking what children seem to mean by "I thinked in my mind" and how this thinking is manifested in their emergent reading and writing.

My research has both basic and applied goals. It primarily focuses on what occurs in the powerful "thinking in the mind" of young children as they become readers and writers. This is the basic research, or research about the thinking process, that underlies my applied research, or research in which findings from this basic research are used to help adults become better teachers and literacy models for young children and to set up rich environments for children's early literacy. My general area of research is called *emergent literacy*, and I have studied children's emerging concepts about and uses of writing, reading, and computers.

The purpose of this chapter is to acquaint you, the reader, with some of the kinds of thinking that have guided my own research, with the thinking that young children show us in their emergent reading and writing, and with some research questions for the future. In this chapter,

you will learn many of the related theories and studies that led to my work. Also, I mention some of the methodological and theoretical considerations underlying my program of longitudinal research. I summarize many of the things that I have learned about young children's emergent reading, writing, and computer usage—all before they become *conventionally literate*, or read and write using concepts such as those you and I use when we read or write. I describe children as they make the long, gradual transition to conventional literacy and suggest some ideas about how young children's emergent literacy is important for a theory that extends into adult literacy.

Our thinking about children's early or emergent literacy has changed radically over the past decade, or more. For about 30 years, people were beginning to realize that children's oral language development gave clear evidence that children possessed ideas about how language worked and that their knowledge could be detected through such data as children's "errors" or overgeneralizations of rules ("He tolded a story," etc.). Now theorists and researchers have turned their attention to children's hypotheses about written language. This area of research is, like most, not entirely new but the intensity and depth of research attention is new and has incorporated findings from other fields not available earlier.

In collaboration with colleagues, I have reviewed the history and current research in emergent literacy in other publications (Teale & Sulzby, 1986; Sulzby, 1991b, 1992; Sulzby & Edwards, in press; Sulzby & Teale, 1991; see also Mason & Allen, 1986; Teale, 1987). Research in emergent literacy can be divided many ways. In my own work, a three-part breakdown has been useful because it highlights divisions—somewhat arbitrarily—along lines of basic and applied research and theory.

The first is basic research into the child's concepts—what the child has internalized about literacy. Since this is an area of developmental psychology, change is an essential variable— change over time, with age, or with experience. Researchers attempt to identify the source of any change, even when the researcher does not instigate any intervention or change mechanism. Such change does not come easily and is resistent to instruction; children's concepts are abstracted from their interactions with the "objects" in their environment. These objects, including language, are not the same for everyone; children construct these objects through their manipulations and interactions with them. Children construct schemata for linguistic objects just as they do for physical objects, according to Ferreiro and Teberosky (1982). Here the theoretical underpinnings of Piaget (1959) are most applicable.

The second division is still also basic research, but its focus is the input from the environment, including other people, and the interactions between the child and environment. The epitome of such research focuses upon parent-child interaction. Researchers have identified parent-child interaction as a key factor in all of child language acquisition, literacy included. Vygotsky's (1962, 1978) theory of social-cultural interaction has helped us see that children not only construct schemata that they are not directly taught, but they also internalize patterns from the world around them, particularly the speech of significant adults. One goal in my own research has been to distinguish between the child's untutored constructions (e.g., scribble, decoding to nonsense syllables) and the child's internalizations of patterns adults use with them (as adults adapt their patterns to their theories of what children are like).

The third body of research is applied research into how knowledge from the child's concepts and their origins in parent-child interaction can be applied in instructional situations, such as day-care centers, preschools, and early schooling. Newer research in this area tends to be heavily influenced by ethnographic techniques, with thick or intensively and systematically documented descriptions of classroom or home interactions (i.e., Dahl & Freppon, 1991; Teale, 1986b). In the next sections, I review briefly the research trends that most directly influenced my own research agenda, both as I began and as my work has progressed.

RESEARCH BACKGROUND

CHANGING IDEAS ABOUT CHILDREN'S EARLY LITERACY

Depending upon your age, your family situation, and where you grew up, you may or may not have gone to kindergarten or preschool. You may or may not have had what is now often called "child care" outside of your own home. You may or may not have had parents or other adults who read to you and gave you books, pencils, and crayons to explore. If you experienced a variety of people and places in your early years, chances are that you also experienced a variety of adults with ideas about your thinking and your literacy. Children today are similar in their varieties of backgrounds, but increasing numbers of them receive long hours of care outside the home.

MEMORIES OF A RESEARCHER

You may have been one of the fortunate ones, as I was. From infancy, my mother read me books and said I asked for them to be read over and over. I still have fond memories of a book about a poodle that had flocking on its coat in the pictures. Our family has just inherited a dog walled Waldo (named after the "Where's Waldo?" books) and we learned that he has the nickname "Roofus." That brought back another memory: The dog in my favorite storybook was Rufus. My memories are tinged with warmth, with feelings of being loved and cared for. I also remember my mother bragging to people about how I loved for her to read to me and how I pretended to read my Rufus book.

Later, in school, learning to read was easy. My mining camp school in Alabama had no kindergarten, but we had a great first-grade teacher who spent the first semester with our class of 39 children reading lots of books to us, teaching us rhymes and fairy tales, letting us act out "Three Billy Goats Gruff" by climbing over a table to trip-trap over a bridge, and teaching us that the alphabet letters had sounds. We also had three recesses, morning, lunch, and afternoon, in which we did jump rope rhymes, handclaps, traditional group games ("Red Rover," "Slinging Statues," "London Bridge") and played "cowboys and Indians" and "house," with intricate social organizations (and much intrigue). It was not until the second semester that my teacher brought out the "reading books" and we began to read. I don't remember writing in first grade, but a few years ago I saw my old report cards from second grade and realized that handwriting had not come easily to me as most of the rest of my school lessons. It was then that I remembered that I had home writing and school writing. I composed my wild stories and gushy notes of love for my parents and teacher at home. My writing at school, except for Valentines, was handwriting exercises, workbook lessons, and copying my teacher's favorite proverbs from the board.

Memories such as mine are not unique. They fill pages in autobiographies of psychologists, philosophers, novelists, poets, and scientists. While memories are colored with interpretation from later life and often are quite faulty, nevertheless they furnish the clues of fruitful ground for research investigation.

VARIATIONS IN LITERACY BACKGROUNDS

Other children were not so fortunate as I, either in their homes or at school. I also remember having classmates in the "low group" that found reading to be a difficult task. For me, school and home fit together smoothly. When I visited friends in some of these homes, I could see that school was a very different kind of place with very different experiences.

Years of working as a classroom and remedial reading teacher gave a reality to the wide variation in children's experience that I later studied in books and articles on literacy and oral language research. Nevertheless, in spite of the deprivation and abuse that too many children experience, research is now showing that almost all, if not all, children who begin kindergarten in the United

States and many other countries (Bus & van IJzendoorn, 1988; Clay, 1966; Ferreiro & Teberosky, 1982) show evidence of already having internalized concepts about reading and writing and thinking powerfully about literacy. Research helps us move from anecdotes, such as my memories of childhood, to a systematic investigation of the literacy lives of young children. This research gives us broadly accurate stereotypes of groups of children to use as a backdrop for further research into group and individual differences and to use as the basis for changes in instructional practice.

PERSONAL HISTORIES MEET SCIENTIFIC KNOWLEDGE

As with most researchers, whether or not they admit it, my personal history has strongly affected the research questions that I find gripping—the ones that itch and itch over time and endure after momentary enthusiasms have faded. My personal history gives a continuity to the areas of research and theory that have caught my scholarly attention.

When I left classroom teaching to return to graduate study, I initially had the shock of losing status and of feeling that the researchers really were not writing about children as I knew them. However, a body of research began to stand out as having possibilities, as much as I begrudgingly gave my approval.

First was the work in oral language acquisition. I read that researchers were beginning to think that young children were active in their own learning and were not just imitating, poorly, the adults around them. I learned that children's "errors" in sentence or verb formations, for example, were often signs of internal hypotheses about how language worked that showed a generalization, or even *overgeneralization*, about an underlying rule in language. Second, I began to read a few researchers who were hinting that our theories of language were too limited to speech, that they needed to include *written language*, but most of this research flourished later. I learned that others such as King and Rentel (1981) were finding value in the idea that we must look at oral and written language relationships in child language acquisition.

Third, I began to read research that now fits in the category that Clay (1966) had called *emergent literacy*, although the term probably did not come into predominance until the publication of Teale and Sulzby (1986). Clay described early reading and writing *behaviors* of young children as being important parts of literacy. Read's (1975) research in invented spelling seemed to fit well with a growing picture of children as actively exploring literacy and developing highly sensible hypotheses about how letter-sound relationships work. In addition to nicely designed studies of children's ability to make similarity judgments about sound contrasts in English, Read reported data about spelling systems from naturalistically occurring compositions by preschoolers which their parents said they concocted without instruction.

Another line of research seemed to fit into this picture, although the picture it presented of young children seemed more pessimistic. Research in *metalinguistic awareness* (Papandropoulou & Sinclair, 1974; Downing & Oliver, 1974) emphasized children's confusions over linguistic terms that adults take for granted. Children showed confusions over the referents (what the terms referred to) of terms such as *story, letter, sound, word*, and so on. Downing (1986) developed a theory of cognitive confusion, arguing that young children's concepts are powerful but confused and that the role of development and task of schooling is to help children reach cognitive clarity. I objected to the assumption that children are confused. Their explanations about language in my informal observations and my growing body of research data indicated that children concoct internally coherent bodies of knowledge but that this coherence could be challenged by new knowledge. I found much more explanatory power in the theory of Piaget (e.g., 1959) and the work of researchers that he had influenced such as Papandropoulou and Sinclair (1974) and Ferreiro and Teberosky (1982).

The work of both Piaget and Vygotsky (1962, 1978) have been important in my research, both as sources of confirmation and positions against

which to strain. Piaget has contributed strong evidence and methodologies for detecting children's untutored constructions and for paying attention to their active thinking. Piaget constantly used children's explanations as evidence for their internalized concepts, and his colleagues (especially Ferreiro & Teberosky, 1982) have turned their focus upon written language. On the other hand, children build their concepts through interactions with the environment. Vygotsky (1962, 1978) suggested that much of what children learn about language, as well as other topics, comes from the social environment which is culturally situated. Children internalize speech which adults address to them. As Vygotsky's followers have developed his ideas posthumously, they have drawn our attention to this movement of language from the interpersonal (between child and another person) to the intrapersonal (within the child). While I seemed to see much evidence of children internalizing language from their social environment, I could see evidence of untutored or unmodeled constructions, so I have need of both theories and the tension between them to guide my own research.

METHODOLOGICAL OVERVIEW

Most researchers have favorite kinds of designs and research methodologies, including duration, settings, and subjects. In the sections that follow, I abstract from across different research studies, so here I alert the reader to the methodological frameworks used in my research.

The Need for Longitudinal Research

Since my research is developmental, I need to study children longitudinally, over periods of time. As a beginning researcher, I started using the school year as the time frame but soon found myself following children for longer periods of time. Some of my research uses a mixed design, studying longitudinal groups of children and making cross-sectional comparisons across groups. For example, I may make a cross-sectional comparison of kindergarten and first-grade children but follow each group longitudinally for a school year.

While much of my research appears to be primarily naturalistic—observing what takes place in a setting without intervention from the researchers or with a casual invitation to teachers to apply ideas from emergent literacy that they find useful—there is usually a framework to which a repeated-measures analysis of variance can be applied. For example, in one study (Sulzby, 1983), we did beginning-and end-of-year interviews with children about their knowledge of reading and writing; between those interviews, we collected repeated samples of children's writing and rereading from writing, did weekly observations of the children's kindergarten classes, and had ongoing discussion/interviews with the classroom teacher. Each kind of language sample was repeated more than once.

The Importance of Contexts

Increasingly, researchers are attending to the context of children's lives in research. Bronfenbrenner (1979) suggests that we must study development systemically, treating the child as embedded in multiple contexts, each of which must be studied in their multiple relationships with each other and the child. My first look at context was the classroom. I began much of my research focusing upon the knowledge that young children bring to public school, which typically begins at kindergarten.

In 1977, when my research began formally, kindergarten was a good setting for longitudinal research in children's literacy concepts because many kindergartens were not yet teaching reading and writing formally. Yet the research showed us that even teachers who were opposed to formal instruction with lessons and assigned tasks nevertheless taught reading and writing informally through their use of such devices as reading to children, allowing children free choice including pencils, markers, paper, and books, and even ritualized forms of language that are patterned after "book language." Thus I was drawn to younger and younger children, including research in private (Sulzby, 1988; Reuning, 1986; Reuning & Sulzby, 1985) and public (Sulzby & Teale, 1987)

preschools and day-care centers. In work I have done with Teale (Sulzby & Teale, 1987; Teale & Sulzby, 1987), we have studied parent-child interaction in storybook reading sessions with children as young as 18 months; this research was conducted, as was much of Teale's (1986a, 1986b) research, in the homes of children.

Research in classrooms entailed studying the concepts about children held by their teachers; yet, we found increasing evidence that teachers often felt great tension and stress from a conflict between their own beliefs and practices and beliefs that they felt were being passed down to them from higher levels, usually from the school district level. Beginning in 1984, I began to work with large suburban and urban districts for longitudinal periods of time with the three kinds of goals that I mentioned previously: the study of children's internalized concepts; the study of adult-child—in this case, teacher-child or teacher-children—interaction; and the study of the effects of interventions, planned to be gradual and developmental in nature. I worked in Palatine, IL, from 1984 to 1986, and my student Joyce Hieshima (Hieshima, 1990) continued that work through 1989. I am now in my fourth year of working intensively with the School District of Pontiac, MI. Work with the Ann Arbor, MI, public schools is now in its fifth year, but the research agenda has been less intensive. Again, in both Michigan settings, a number of graduate students (Kamberelis, 1992; Lee, 1992; Olson & Sulzby, 1991) have extended the work beyond the agendas I charted.

Research collaborations with large institutions such as school districts (e.g., Sulzby, Branz, & Buhle, in press) take much time and effort on all parts and involve risks on all sides, but I believe they are necessary for research to be translated into useful applications. Practitioners want to see the research work with "my children," "our children," "our teachers"—or "our patients," "our clients," "our customers."

Even beyond the crucial testing ground of practice, I believe research that is contextually based has theoretical implications. Change in the individual comes both from within and from without. I have claimed, along with many others, that literacy is a sociocultural phenomenon.

Who Are the Subjects?

Psychological (particularly developmental and cognitive psychology) and linguistic research traditionally have called the people who are discussed in research studies "subjects." Anthropological research has tended to refer to them as "informants." Some educational researchers have moved to terms such as "collaborators." These terminological differences tend to imply much about the researchers' stances toward the people about whom they write. I have tended to bypass these issues generally by using the article headings called for by the discipline but writing about the people by using role terms such as *children, teachers,* and *parents*. These terms also appear to be more friendly or people-oriented. I think of these people as being part of a culture, with linguistic repertoires that have developed differently depending upon characteristics of the given culture.

When one moves to study people who differ in various ways, one is still hit with the issue of perhaps being insensitive to groups of people. One is never an "insider" in all groups of people, and the role of being a researcher sets up particular kinds of boundaries. One way to deal with this issue is through doing longitudinal research in which much time and effort is spent in getting to know and become accepted into the context as a trusted person, to gain entree into the group or setting, as the anthropologists often put it.

This is the tactic I have taken, yet I still use "outsider" terminology to refer to groups of people, trying to be sensitive and explain my rationales for these terms. I have particularly compared poor and advantaged children and children across three main ethnic groups, Anglo-American, African-American, and Mexican-American. In my writing, I use socioeconomic status (SES) as a contrast, while acknowledging the variations within all such group distinctions. For shorthand, I often say that I study LSES and MSES white, black, and Hispanic children.

In my research, I had described the cognitive patterns of speech underlying a particular situation—the reading of favorite storybooks—and suspected that cultural differences might be found in these speech patterns. I had hypothesized that one reason a particular kind of emergent story-book reading language, called "oral monologue," was underrepresented in our data was because children reared in highly literate societies would tend not to recite a full story in an oral storytelling fashion, but would move from conversational reenactments to a mix of oral and written phrases and intonations. A colleague suggested that it was probably the differential emphasis given to oral storytelling versus storybook reading to children that differentiated such groups. This led to a study (Sulzby & Teale, 1987) of new immigrants into the industrial midwestern United States from the hill country outside Mexico City. These children indeed showed a much higher frequency of the oral monologue (Sulzby & Zecker, 1991) than had been found in other studies, and their oral monologues were very rich linguistically.

Whenever I describe group differences, I attempt to describe variation as well. Since my goal is the description of thinking development, it is important that I illustrate group differences with details of the development of individuals through case study methodology. Since I am studying conceptual change, it is important that I use these case studies to show that the conceptual change is indeed taking place and that it can be seen in various ways, particularly in situations where the child appears to work through conceptual conflict (Sulzby, Feldsberg, & Morrison, 1992).

Analytical Techniques

When I began this research, I was unsatisfied with most of the ways of "getting the data," often referred to as eliciting the data, data collection, or testing. I was less dissatisfied with ways of analyzing the data, but my decisions about data elicitation have affected data analysis decisions as well. My techniques can be summarized as being derived from a naturalistic stance. While it is difficult to distinguish the "natural" from the effects of "intervention," some situations are more "natural" to the thinking of informed researchers than others. My decision was that I would attempt to set up research situations (including classroom situations) where children were highly likely to show the same kinds of behaviors that they had used in highly literate home environments.

For analytic tools, I have tended to choose first those tools that can be seen and heard by classroom teachers, parents, and other people concerned with young children. Our studies of children's pauses and intonation curves (Sulzby, 1987; Reuning, 1986) are unusual, particularly because they involved such manipulations as masking children's speech with white noise, yet we clung to the naturalistic stance by using classroom teachers among the groups of people who were asked to make judgments about whether a given child was probably reading a book or telling a story (in fact, all were doing emergent readings that had previously been classified as either oral languagelike or written languagelike reading attempts).

Most of the data we use are verbatim transcriptions (often with nonverbal behavior coded from videotaping) of speech between participants, and, whenever space allows, we illustrate summarizations and category systems with examples of how children talk so that readers can judge whether or not children have powerful ideas about literacy. These transcripts also provide evidence for the modeling and ideas of adults that children either incorporate or reject from their thinking (see also Ferreiro, 1986).

CONTENTS OF THE RESEARCH

We will return to these issues. But now let's look at the details of my research. I have broken the research into four parts: emergent storybook reading, emergent writing, computers as emergent literacy tools, and the transition from emergent to conventional literacy. The reader should keep in mind that I view the child as the unit of thought, so I constantly reflect on the knowledge of a thinking child—knowledge that the child brings about writing to attempting to read storybooks, and vice versa, or knowledge that the child brings

from exploring letter-sound relationships on "Sesame Street," with a workbook, or from a computer program. I have summarized my research in a number of other articles; in this chapter, I focus on the evidence of children's powerful thinking that my research has uncovered.

Emergent Storybook Reading

For years, I had heard about the correlations between parents reading to their children and children's subsequent reading achievement that my colleague Bill Teale (1984, 1987) has reviewed so well. Just as I was finishing my dissertation, a study of LSES black children's concepts about words, I visited a friend with an 18-month-old girl. While we were talking, the toddler casually picked up a large picturebook, began leafing through it from front to back (using good "bookhandling" skills), and started to "read." Since I was studying child language acquisition, I was fascinated to hear her babble—using sounds but very few recognizable words—all the way through the book. Her intonation was that of a reader, even though she was babbling rather than talking.

This was a fruitful clue that I followed up on two years later when I began my research on storybook reading, as part of a larger study about the knowledges that kindergartners brought to school (Sulzby, 1983, 1985). In that research, a sign of children's thinking changed my research design. I had been interviewing children, asking questions about what they knew and could do in reading and writing and asking them how they knew what they knew and how they had learned it. Young children answered these direct "metacognitive questions" as being very sensible and gave me detailed answers, attributing their knowledge and learning to their parents and other family memories and to their own efforts: "I thinked in my mind," "I just figured it out." A final part of the interview was a bookhandling task based upon work by Goodman (1980) and Clay (1979). In this task, I wanted to see how well these children handled books and whether they recognized the form and function of various parts (cover, title page, pictures, print, etc.).

To bring the interview to a conclusion that would be satisfying both to the children and interviewer, I asked the children to "tell me about your book." This was a dramatic set of moments because children's responses were unexpected to me then; over half of the kindergartners began to read, emergently, from their books. The children showed me a way of looking at and listening to their emergent literacy. I had wanted to find a way to entice children in research situations to do the kinds of emergent reading and writing that they do in their homes, but I was surprised when they showed me how simple that would be—just ask and see how children respond!

When we analyzed their speech later, the readings seemed to fall into a possible developmental order that I have later tested in a series of studies with children from infancy through first grade, from various SES and ethnic backgrounds. We also tested our elicitations by comparing children's responses to requests to tell stories or to read books. Our general procedure in eliciting emergent storybook reading from young children (see Appendix 14-1) is the same. We either work with children whose parents or teachers have read books to them repeatedly (which varies by individuals) or we have teachers read common books to all the children repeatedly. Then we interview children individually, using the simple elicitation: "Read me your book."

Appendix 14-2 shows a diagram in a tree-structure form of the 11 levels of emergent storybook reading that we have found in this research. This analytic scheme appears to have developmental properties; the distribution of children's responses changes as children grow older or increase in experience. Another sign of developmental characteristics is that a number of the children's behaviors appear to be child constructions and not behaviors modeled or taught by adults. Other behaviors do appear to be modeled by adults as they scaffold, or attune their reading speech and behaviors to the child's age and level of attention. In all cases, the behaviors reflect children's thoughts and concepts about literacy.

The classification scheme for emergent reading of favorite storybooks (Sulzby, 1985, 1991a) looks as if it charts "stages" of development. My best judgment is that this is a misleading appearance, due in part to the scaffolding furnished by

parents in reading to young children. I think that it does reflect some general stagelike change, but children's performances and comments about their reading knowledge indicates much more fluctuation and exploration across levels than would be expected if the categories and subcategories were stages.

Also, we are dealing with the phenomenon of language. My view of language is highly sociolinguistic and influenced by speech act theory and pragmatics. I view language, both oral and written, as being a repertoire of linguistic registers which speakers, including children, choose among depending upon their purposes and audiences. This has influenced my insistence that we listen to children's speech for instances in which they use structures and intonation more suited to written contexts and examine their writing (and emergent readings) for instances in which they use structures and wording more suited to oral situations. Language choices, of course, reflect the ways that children are thinking about acting or responding with speech.

The research in emergent storybook reading has shown a number of findings worth restating. Children attempt to read long before they are attending to print, and their attention to print shows evidence of their active construction and hypothesis generation. They code-switch readily between "reading" speech and "talking" or conversing speech during these storybook reading sessions, with development in how clearly they signal the switches to a listener. They do appear to incorporate patterns from adults, but this incorporation is dependent upon how well adults adapt their reading to the child's ideas. They use patterns not modeled by adults as well as modeled or taught patterns. There are some detectable cultural differences in patterns of emergent storybook reading, but these do not seem, at this time, to be a strong determinant of how easily a child will make the transition to conventional reading. Finally, as we will see in the next sections, they use similar patterns of reading with their own composition in emergent writing, both on and off the computer, and explain how they are "thinking in my mind" about how writing should be done.

Emergent Writing

Samples of 24 kindergarten children typically included all or most of the categories of emergent storybook reading. This was not the case with writing, thus my studies (Kamberelis & Sulzby, 1990; Sulzby, 1989; Sulzby, Barnhart, & Hieshima, 1988) used multiple classrooms, usually following the children from kindergarten through first grade. With writing, one can see both the forms of the writing and all of the child's compositional behaviors, which include language about planning; language during writing, including on-the-spot and subsequent revisions; rereading; and judgments about the final product. In all cases, one must listen to how children explain their thinking about these writing acts.

The most prevalent forms of writing are scribble, drawing-as-writing, letterstrings (both random and patterned), invented spelling, and conventional orthography. The order of this list of the forms is misleading, as we will see below. It would have been economical if the forms and underlying concepts had gone hand in hand, such that scribble, for instance, was matched with low-level speech and conventional orthography was matched with conventional reading, but this is not the case. The research makes it extremely clear over and over that you cannot judge underlying concepts by the nature of the writing forms, yet it continues to be difficult to convince practitioners of this or, if convinced, that they can make sense of the more complex picture.

At the risk of oversimplifying children's writing, I will describe the forms of writing as I now think of them, but I know there is much yet to discover. One way of judging complexity of forms is to analyze the typical age of onset; another is to consider the evidence children give us about how they think about the forms. From the latter evidence of children's thinking, we have learned that children who have been showing one behavior that truly develops late—invented spelling—may revert to a form that he or she has seemed to drop out of the repertoire in order to create a more complex composition.

A toddler as young as 16–18 months may make repeated marks and call them writing or drawing. These scribbles are indistinguishable to the adult eye, yet children as young as 2 have shown different forms of scribble to stand for writing and to stand for drawing. In spite of this seeming ability to distinguish between writing and drawing, children will later call representational or recognizable drawing "writing." In fact, they begin this as young as age 2 and often continue it well into kindergarten or first grade. They both distinguish between writing and drawing and they use drawing as writing. In other words, they appear to be ambivalent about the status of drawing. Drawing shows a completely different development distribution from the forms that look more like letter-based writing (scribble, letterstrings, invented spelling). Scribble and letterstrings appear to be, for the most part, transformed into invented spelling and conventional spelling, but drawing appears to be treated as part of text that gradually becomes illustration or mutually supportive context with readable words.

Some 2-year-olds and many 3-year-olds write conventionally spelled words, such as MOM, DAD, NO, LOVE, and their own names. They may also write with letterstrings. They may later also "invent" the spellings of these words or they may hold them as what appear to be little-analyzed wholes. Our research and that of Ferreiro and Teberosky (1982) and their colleagues both document instances of children appearing to have conventional forms and of holding quite unconventional concepts for them. Some children have even denied that words they just wrote, such as "I LOVE YOU," are writing. One kindergarten girl stated, "I just draw pictures," and she later claimed that I LOVE YOU was both a picture (Valentine) and writing; she also declared that a picture of a flower was also writing.

Thus we have a picture of children prior to age 5 generally writing with four forms: scribble, drawing, letterstrings, and conventional strings. For most children, age 5 or 6 marks the beginning of a new phenomenon, although I have seen it as young as age 3; this is "invented spelling," or phonetically based writing. Children's compositional and reading behaviors with each of these forms may vary all the way from claiming that, "I didn't write," to labeling items in descriptive series of sentences, to oral-sounding stories, to written-sounding stories, to attempting to track the print, including scribble. They may make judgments about other children's writing that reflect an awareness of principles of writing slightly above their own productions (Shatz, Halle, Kamberelis, & Sulzby, 1991).

While children's thinking is evidenced in all these episodes, it is exciting to see children who have just begun to write phonetically. Often they do not attempt to reread phonetically from their written texts (Kamberelis & Sulzby, 1990). If they do attempt to read, they may lose their place easily. We have witnessed such children recursively add more and more text to try to make their reading match their print. The transition into reading conventionally from this print, as well as from conventional print, usually takes some time, is gradual, and may appear to have cognitive and emotional ups and downs for the child.

As with storybook reading and the rest of language, I conceive of children as acquiring and embellishing a repertoire of knowledges about writing as a compositional activity. Since children use forms at early ages that look conventional, it is easy for teachers (and even researchers) to misunderstand their underlying thinking. For teachers, this can lead to a misplaced stress upon didactic teaching. In our research, we have found that children reach points of conflict (Kamberelis & Sulzby, 1990; Sulzby, 1986; Sulzby, Feldsberg, & Morrison, 1992) in which they wrestle with their changing concepts. Examining groups of these kinds of episodes may help develop further our understandings of children thinking as they make the long transition into conventional literacy. There is another new literacy tool for young children—the computer—and we have begun to gather conflictive incidents from computer episodes as well.

Computers as Emergent Literacy Tools

I have been calling attention to the computer as an evolving literacy tool within our culture (Sulzby, 1990a, 1992; Sulzby, Olson, & Johnston, 1989; Sulzby & Spitulnik, 1992; Spitulnik & Sulzby, 1992). There are a number of ways of examining the computer. First, how does the computer allow or constrain children's uses of emergent forms of literacy that they use off the computer? Second, what forms of literacy does the computer bring to the child through new developments in software? As computers become capable of being multimedia machines, bringing together other machines and capabilities such as video, musical recordings, or animations as composition tools, we must expand the second question more and more seriously: What kind of literacy or literacies are children experiencing as they enter the 21st century? What kind of thinking underlies their experiences with computers as literacy tools?

For brevity, I collapse four years of research into a few generalizations and continue this discussion in the section on plans for the future. First, kindergarten and first-grade children from MSES and LSES settings can use a computer successfully as a writing tool. If the tools allow all of the emergent forms (which no one tool does easily), they will use emergent forms, although scribble has been continually underrepresented in our distributions, even though we have modeled it along with all forms of writing and have used drawing tools. (We have found that many teachers tend to discourage scribble in classrooms, even after they have agreed to honor all forms as part of our research designs.)

Second, children's composition behaviors on the computer seem to parallel those off the computer, but both can be depressed by the classroom context. As we have followed teachers and classroom settings longitudinally and have encouraged acceptance of emergent forms of writing, we have found children to show a greater wealth of compositional behaviors, including sitting and thinking or talking about their thinking, as the classroom context also encourages more freedom in writing.

Third, children show compositional behaviors including planning—some revision judgments and some actual revising—and they reread from computer writing. When software programs have synthetic speech feedback, children who are not writing with invented spelling tend to ignore the feature, and they show increasing sensitivity to it (giggling, replaying it, or attempting to respell) as their invented spelling increases in complexity and fluency.

Software designers are among the adults who have concepts about literacy and young children. These concepts are reflected in the software and provide contexts that must be analyzed along with children's behaviors. Similarly, composers in the popular media of television, movies, music video, arcade games, and books also have concepts about literacy, which they put into our culture for young children. Adults interact with children about these media, often not thinking about the relations to concepts about literacy. As we move into our continuing research agenda with computers, we are deliberately attempting to anticipate such changing concepts of literacy.

THE TRANSITION INTO CONVENTIONAL LITERACY

From all of this research, I have been attempting to trace children's cognitive transition into conventional literacy (Sulzby, 1989, 1991a). That has also required me to think what I and others mean by conventional literacy. One level of understanding of the term comes from common sense. The "person on the street" can detect when a child is reading from print or writing readable text—more or less. This kind of definition is useful but insufficient.

Another level of understanding has come from the data themselves. We have seen children making a gradual transition that follows some common patterns. In both storybook reading and writing, on and off the computer, we see children treating text as holistic until just before they begin to read and write conventionally. Then we see

them begin to explore the bits and pieces of language—reading books by sounding out to nonsense words, even books that they "know by heart," reading just random strings of words that appear on the page, or reciting the words of the text while pointing at print but not tracking it or using it to confirm or disconfirm the speech. This level of reading that I call *aspectual* is part of the evidence that I use to set aside questions of whether certain aspects precede others, such as whether phonemic awareness (Adams, 1990) precedes "reading" with comprehension or whether "meaning comes first." From viewing the child as a whole from infancy forward, one can see children working on all aspects of reading and writing. As Harste, Woodward, and Burke (1983) have suggested, we see children organizing and reorganizing their understandings of language over the long trajectory into conventional reading. My own work provides specific detail about the reorganization that just precedes children becoming able to move strategically and flexibly across all the aspects of reading, and this is the definition of conventional reading (Sulzby, 1989) that has emerged from my work.[1]

WHERE DOES THIS WORK FIT HISTORICALLY?

My research has had a set of related goals: (a) to describe and trace developmental patterns in emergent literacy and (b) to describe the transition into conventional literacy. As the work has progressed, a third goal has emerged—an analysis of changing concepts of literacy within the culture as well as the child.

Many other researchers have contributed to my thinking and to our understandings of young children's thoughts about literacy. The research that I find particularly challenging and useful is that of Emilia Ferreiro, the Piagetian scholar (Ferreiro & Teberosky, 1982; Ferreiro, 1986). My work parallels hers in that we are both attempting to understand children's underlying thinking or concepts. I have also seen most of the behaviors that she has described, although they come from different interviewing techniques. Her methodology forces children to deal with conventional models of literacy created by the adult or dictated by the adult, but allows the child to produce his or her own explanations or creations.

My work departs from Ferreiro's in that our theories of language differ. Her view of written language, as I understand it, differs from mine in two ways. She treats the written sentence or written word as representing a part-whole relationship. I treat all parts of language as evolving, culturally as well as within the individual child. Young children's thinking of the parts and whole are different from that of adults, but I think that adult concepts as well treat the parts of language as more fluid and synergistic. Ferreiro's work is primarily a stage theory, although it is very innovative and open, and mine is a model of language from the sociolinguistic vantage, as a repertoire of understandings and abilities about language.

I also find much value in the work of the neo-Vygotskians and especially Bruner. Bruner's (1978) emphasis upon scaffolding as a concept is far richer than most researchers of early development have yet discovered. We need to investigate further the model of the child and of child literacy that adults hold as they adapt their speech and actions to the young child. This is particularly important in the study of why some home environments and parents provide more supportive assistance than others.

THE FUTURE, PERSONAL AND GENERAL

Actually, the immediate future is fairly solid since my research is longitudinal. I have recently redesigned a five-year longitudinal study in Pontiac. Initially, the study was designed to contrast three instructional models (emergent literacy without computers, emergent literacy with computers, and "traditional instruction during basal reader adoption") in two longitudinal waves (1989–91 and 1992–93), with a year between the waves for analysis, dissemination, and refinements, particularly of the technology. The reason for the long name for the "traditional" condition was contex-

tual; across the United States, textbook publishers were responding to teachers' and researchers' recommendation to move to "whole language," or classroom situations that would encourage children to *use* reading and writing for their own purposes, rather than simply to *learn lessons about* reading and writing.

During year one, Pontiac piloted different programs in each of our five classrooms; during year two, Pontiac adopted a "literature-based" basal reading program that encouraged children to read and, to a lesser-degree, write emergently and encouraged teachers to set up whole language contexts in the classroom. The basal reader adoption grew from the district's restructuring efforts focusing on Kindergarten through second grade. The district adopted a philosophy that stressed children as being developmental and classroom instruction as needing to engage children with realistic tasks.

After the first longitudinal wave, I realized two things: (1) the large study was eating up precious resources that we did not have to supply without great sacrifice and (2) much of it was redundant with other research I had done and would yield little new knowledge. My enthusiasm was for the new information that we could gain through a more detailed focus on computers as emergent literacy tools. Following year two, we focused our research in one of the original five schools in which almost all of the children were LSES African-American children, the staff were dedicated to improving instruction both with and without the computer, and we had potential for increasing collaborative efforts with teachers and administration. For year three, we studied children's writing on and off the computer and children's collaborative writing on the computer.

We also increased our research from just Macintosh computers (in Pontiac) to include IBM computers (in Ann Arbor; see Juan, Thomas, & Sulzby, 1992). Most important for the decision to change focus, I realized that an emphasis upon the computer would advance my theoretical investigations of the nature of literacy within a given culture. For year four, we have begun a study of storybook reading on and off the computer screen, using local area networks (LANs) in both sites and using instructional programs designed by software developers that are supposed to be based upon emergent literacy principles. Our questions are fairly simple: Will children remain engaged with storybooks on a computer screen, and what kind of emergent reading behavior will we find with storybooks on the screen?

Our research sites are different; our hardware and software is different; our student and teacher populations are different. We are thus not proposing a direct comparison of these two sites but an in-depth description of each site. Additionally, we are conducting all of this research in the classrooms, alongside the teachers, attempting to help teachers see the emergent literacy behaviors and the thinking of their children in greater detail than we have been able to in the past.

To place our research in emergent writing into yet another functional context in the classroom, we are going to encourage children in both sites to write to each other about their storybooks. This writing will begin with the familiar—letters written on paper and mailed in envelopes. Then we will move to the new—sending letters by computer disk. In this latter phase, we want to explore multimedia capabilities of computers such as attaching speech to children's scribbling, invented spelling, or conventional orthography.

In the work with computers, a challenge is to keep focused on what we can learn theoretically about oral and written language and how children think about them, topics of basic research. There is a temptation to focus too much on the practical—how children use these tools—and not enough on what children's goals are, what their theories of language and communication are, and on what children's given uses of computers and software mean about their thinking. Focused basic research can help us decide whether modern cultures are changing so that children's conceptions of literacy are becoming different from those of their parents and teachers.

In the research off the computer, we need to put much more emphasis upon the child as a whole. One example is in the area of phonemic awareness. Research in emergent literacy in which children are asked to demonstrate knowledge through composition and comprehension has much to contribute to research in phonemic awareness, but methodological and theoretical issues may tend to separate groups of researchers from each other. Currently, I think I am optimistic that we are beginning to detect much more communication between the two research groups.

We must not, however, ignore applied research. All of our theories are oriented toward being of some use, and the development of young children as thinking readers and writers is of utmost value. I see at least two important challenges in this applied research. First, we need to demonstrate children's powerful thinking more effectively to teachers. My classroom-based research has alerted me to the strong resistance of many first-grade teachers to taking children's thinking about emergent literacy seriously. The temptation is simply to assimilate *emergent literacy* into *reading readiness* and interpret any sign that children are not yet conventional as meaning that they simply "aren't there yet" and either need to have much more skill instruction, such as practicing letters, copying from the board, phonics practice, and, now, storybook chanting, or that they need to "wait." These two interpretations, readiness as skills or readiness as maturation, are strongly embedded in the backgrounds of many teachers who feel a strong commitment to having children leave first grade as conventional readers. We need to unveil newer emergent ideas of "levels of literacy" that traditional tests and assessment instruments have masked, but this will be threatening to many teachers. On the other hand, we also need to unveil the children's emergent reading and writing as being signs of powerful thinking that has an upward trajectory.

This requires that teachers also engage in powerful thinking about children. The challenge to researchers and other educators is, in turn, to challenge and to help teachers in this shift in thinking. Research in teacher education is beginning to document the complexity of teachers' thinking and the tasks facing them and the time and conditions needed for teachers to change their concepts.

There is, however, a growing context of awareness for the general idea of emergence that may help our work with teachers. The ideas of emergent literacy appear to be part of a general emphasis upon acknowledging the developmental nature of human beings, from infancy through old age. When Teale and I (Teale & Sulzby, 1986) investigated the use of the term *emergent*, we found that it had a respected history in many disciplines, including developmental psychology and physical sciences. My subjective assessment is that it is appearing more frequently, even in the popular press, to refer to many different phenomena. I am often approached by researchers from other fields in literacy who point to similarities between these notions about young children and other people, such as older special education children, low-literate adults, adults learning new tasks, and even the elderly.

There are many aspects yet to be investigated. One that would have great practical application would be an in-depth study of the relationship between children's differing willingness to "do it my own way" or to follow adult models. Greater coordination between research in invented spelling and phonemic awareness is needed.

SUMMARY

I have provided a look at young children as powerful thinkers about reading, writing, and computers and have invited you to think about the ideas that you hold about children (including memories of yourself as a thinking child) and about literacy. These ideas have been posed both from the theoretical and practical considerations. I have raised ideas about the nature of literacy as we enter the 21st century and as newer technologies are entering our culture. I have also focused many of the descriptions on findings with LSES and minority children in institutions, such as urban public schools, as well as with advanced MSES children, so that you might begin to think about how these ideas apply in the multicultural societies of our changing world. In the appendices, I provide a simplified version of one of our research tools. You can try it out or modify it to gather your own samples of how children read, write, and think about literacy before they are conventionally literate.

FOOTNOTE

1. Conventional writing includes both the child and other people being able to read from the child's text conventionally.

APPENDIX 14-1

Sulzby's Methods for Eliciting Emergent Storybook Readings and Thoughts About Reading

The goal of this activity is for new researchers to experience the phenomenon of emergent storybook reading and to begin to think about ways to conduct more systematic research. For formal description of these methods, read the articles cited in the chapter or write to the author.

Preparation: Find a friendly parent with a 3- or 4-year-old child who loves to be read to and get acquainted with the child. Ask the parent for permission to spend time at a later date with the child, tape recording the child's "pretend" reading. Ask the parent to let you use two or three of the child's favorite storybooks and set up a quiet space for you to visit with the child. Be very careful to practice your *wording* and social behavior for meeting with the child.

Wording: Let the child hold the book and show you

the cover. Leaving the book in the child's hands, say, "Read me your book." Do not say, "Tell me about your book," for the child will probably interpret that as a different kind of request. If the child says, "I can't read," say, "Just do it your own way" or "Well, it doesn't have to be like grown-up reading—read it your own way." If the child is still resistant, say, "Let me read to you for a while and then you can read to me." After you have read a few pages, pause before ending some predictable sentences and see if the child chimes in. Then say, "Now it's your turn—you read."

Social behavior: Use a calm, matter-of-fact, but friendly tone. Do *not* use a sweety-sweet or overly solicitous tone. Try not to be overprotective, but ask confidently for the child to read. If the child continues to refuse, ask if he or she has another book that he or she would prefer

to read or discontinue by asking if you can come back another time for the child to read. Ask the child to think about a good choice of a book to share. Keep the social interaction calm and easygoing.

Eliciting talk about thinking: Ask the child, "Tell me how you learned so much about reading," and other questions that will elicit the child's thinking about literacy. Plan these questions ahead of time and keep track of those you used.

Finishing: Thank the child for sharing the book and talking with you. Follow the child and parent's lead in leave-taking or politely thank the parent and leave. Transcribe the event and analyze your data, then think hard about the data and write a description and explanation of what occurred.

APPENDIX 14-2

Sulzby tree structure from *Reading Research Quarterly*

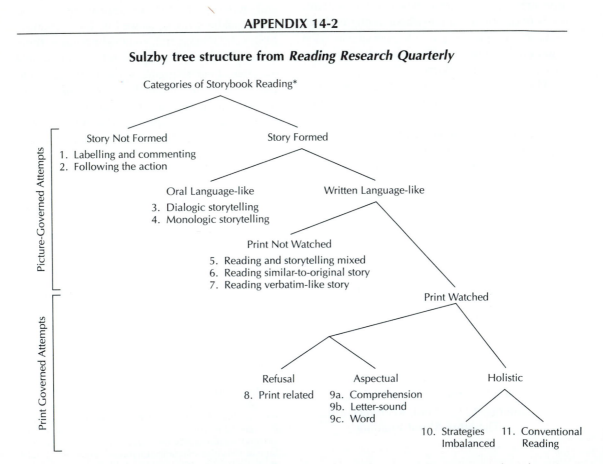

* This figure includes independent reading attempts only: the child is making the reading attempts without dependence upon turn-taking reading or interrogation by the adult.

REFERENCES

Adams, M. J. (1990). *Beginning to read: Thinking and learning about print.* Cambridge, MA: MIT Press.

Bronfenbrenner, U. (1979). *The ecology of human development: Experiments by nature and design.* Cambridge, MA: Harvard University Press.

Bruner, J. S. (1978). The role of dialogue in language acquisition. In A. Sinclair, R. J. Jarvella, & J. M. Levelt (Eds.), *The child's conception of language* (pp. 241–256). Berlin: Springer-Verlag.

Bus, A. G., & van IJzendoorn, M. H. (1988b). Mother-child interactions, attachment, and emergent literacy: A cross-sectional study. *Child Development, 59*(5), 1262–1272.

Clay, M. M. (1966). Emergent reading behaviour. Unpublished doctoral dissertation, University of Auckland, Auckland, New Zealand.

Clay, M. M. (1979). Theoretical research and instructional change: A case study. In L. B. Resnick & P. A. Weaver (Eds.), *Theory and practice of early reading* (Vol. 2, pp. 149–171). Hillsdale, NJ: Erlbaum.

Dahl, K., & Freppon, P. (1991). Literacy learning in whole-language classrooms: An analysis of low socioeconomic urban children learning to read and write in kindergarten. *National Reading Conference Yearbook, 40,* 149–158.

Downing, J. (1986). Cognitive clarity: A unifying and cross-cultural theory for language awareness phenomena in reading. In D. B. Yaden, Jr. & S. Templeton (Eds.), *Metalinguistic awareness and beginning literacy: Conceptualizing what it means to read and write* (pp. 13–29). Portsmouth, NH: Heinemann.

Downing, J., & Oliver, P. (1974). The child's conception of "a word." *Reading Research Quarterly, 9*(4), 568–582.

Ferreiro, E. (1986). The interplay between information and assimilation in beginning literacy. In W. H. Teale & E. Sulzby (Eds.), *Emergent literacy: Writing and reading* (pp. 15–49). Norwood, NJ: Ablex.

Ferreiro, E., & Teberosky, A. (1982). *Literacy before schooling.* Exeter, NH: Heinemann.

Goodman, Y. M. (1980). The roots of literacy. In M. P. Douglass (Ed.), *Claremont reading conference forty-fourth yearbook* (pp. 1–32). Claremont, CA: Claremont Graduate School.

Harste, J. E., Woodward, V. A., & Burke, C. L. (1984). *Language stories and literacy lessons.* Portsmouth, NH: Heinemann.

Hieshima, J. B. (1990). A garden where children and literacy should grow: A microethnographic study of the kindergarten. Unpublished doctoral dissertation, Northwestern University, Evanston, IL.

Juan, M., Thomas, L., & Sulzby, E. (1992, December). Teacher growth in integrating computers in multigrade emergent literacy classrooms. Paper presented at a symposium on computers and the transition from emergent to conventional literacy at the National Reading Conference, San Antonio, TX.

Kamberelis, G., & Sulzby, E. (1988). Transitional knowledge in emergent literacy. *National Reading Conference Yearbook, 37,* 95–106.

King, M., & Rentel, V. (1979). Toward a theory of early writing development. *Research in the Teaching of English, 13*(3), 243–253.

Lee, M. O. (1992). Young children's development of literacy and home literacy environments. Unpublished doctoral dissertation, University of Michigan, Ann Arbor, MI.

Luria, A. R. (1983). The development of writing in the child. In M. Martlew (Ed.), *The psychology of written language: Developmental and educational perspectives* (pp. 237–277). Chichester, EG: Wiley.

Martlew, M. (Ed.). (1983). *The psychology of written language: Developmental and educational perspectives* (pp. 295–333). Chichester, England: Wiley.

Mason, J. & Allen, J. B. (1986). A review of emergent literacy with implications for research and practice in reading. In E. Z. Rothkopf (Ed.), *Review of research in education, 13,* (pp. 3–47). Washington, DC: American Educational Research Association.

Olson, K., & Sulzby, E. (1991). The computer as a social/physical environment in emergent literacy. *National Reading Conference Yearbook, 40,* 111–118.

Papandropoulou, I., & Sinclair, H. (1974). What is a word? Experimental study of children's ideas on grammar. *Human Development, 17*(4), 241–258.

Piaget, J. (1952). *The origins of intelligence in children* (Margaret Cook, Trans.). New York: International Universities Press.

Piaget, J. (1959). *The language and thought of the child* (3rd ed.). (Marjorie Gabain, Trans.). London: Routledge & Kegan Paul.

Read, C. (1975). *Children's categorizations of speech sounds in English.* Urbana, IL: National Council of Teachers of English.

Reuning, C. (1986). Prosodic features of reading intonation: An exploratory study. Unpublished master's thesis in linguistics and language and cognition, Northwestern University, Evanston, IL.

Reuning, C., & Sulzby, E. (1985). Emergent storybook reading in high and low literacy background children. *National Reading Conference Yearbook, 34,* 310–319.

Shatz, M., Kamberelis, G., Halle, T., & Sulzby, E. (1991, April). Kindergartners' judgments of writing varying in conventionality. Presentation at the annual meeting of the Society for Research in Child Development, Seattle, WA.

Spitulnik, J., & Sulzby, E. (1992, December). Issues in human-computer interface: What young children show us. Paper presented at a symposium on computers and the transition from emergent to conventional literacy at the National Reading Conference, San Antonio, TX.

Sulzby, E. (1983, September). Beginning reader's developing knowledges about written language (Final Report to the National Institute of Education NIE-G-80-0176). Evanston, IL: Northwestern University.

Sulzby, E. (1985). Children's emergent reading of favorite storybooks: A developmental study. *Reading Research Quarterly, 20*(4), 458–481.

Sulzby, E. (1987). Children's development of prosodic distinctions in telling and dictating modes. In A. Matsuhashi (Ed.), *Writing in real time: Modeling production processes* (pp. 133–160). Norwood, NJ: Ablex.

Sulzby, E. (1988). A study of children's early reading development. In A. D. Pellegrini (Ed.), *Psychological bases for early education* (pp. 39–75). Chichester, England: Wiley.

Sulzby, E. (1989). Assessment of writing and of children's language while writing. In L. Morrow & J. Smith (Eds.), *The role of assessment and measurement in early literacy instruction* (pp. 83–109). Englewood Cliffs, NJ: Prentice Hall.

Sulzby, E. (1990). Roles of oral and written language in children approaching conventional literacy. In C. Pontecorvo (Ed.), *La costruzione dei primi testi scritti nel bambino*. Roma: La Nuova Italia.

Sulzby, E. (1991a). Assessment of emergent literacy: Storybook reading. *The Reading Teacher, 44,* 498–500.

Sulzby, E. (1991b). The development of prekindergarten children and the emergence of literacy. In J. Flood, J. Jensen, D. Lapp, & J. R. Squire (Eds.), *The handbook of research in the teaching of the English language arts* (pp. 273–285). New York: Macmillan.

Sulzby, E. (1992). Transitions from emergent to conventional writing [Research Directions column]. *Language Arts, 68,* 50–57.

Sulzby, E., Barnhart, J., & Hieshima, J. (1988). Forms of writing and rereading: A preliminary report (Technical Report No. 437). Champaign-Urbana: University of Illinois, Center for the Study of Reading; also (1989). (Technical Report No. 20). Berkeley: University of California, Center for the Study of Writing.

Sulzby, E., Branz, C. M., & Buhle, R. (in press). Repeated readings of literature and LSES black kindergartners and first graders. *Reading and Writing Quarterly.*

Sulzby, E., & Edwards, P. (in press). The role of parents in supporting literacy development of young children. In B. Spodek & O. N. Saracho (Eds.) *Yearbook in early childhood education: Vol. 4. Early childhood language and literacy*. New York: Teachers College Press.

Sulzby, E., Feldsberg, R., & Morrison, L. (1992, December). Writing on and off the computer: Will technology mask developmental conflicts? Paper presented at a symposium on computers and the transition from emergent to conventional literacy at the National Reading Conference, San Antonio, TX.

Sulzby, E., Olson, K. A., & Johnston, J. (1989). The computer and young children: An emergent literacy perspective (Working Paper No. 1, Computers in Early Literacy (CIEL) Research Project). Ann Arbor, MI: Institute for Social Research.

Sulzby, E., & Spitulnik, J. (1992, April). Emergent literacy and the computer. Invited presentation at the Research Roundtable for Basic Studies in Reading at the annual meeting of the American Educational Research Association, San Francisco, CA.

Sulzby, E., & Teale, W. H. (1987). Young children's storybook reading: Longitudinal study of parent-child interaction and children's independent functioning. Final report to the Spencer Foundation, Ann Arbor: University of Michigan.

Sulzby, E., & Teale, W. H. (1991). Emergent literacy. In R. Barr, M. L. Kamil, & P. Mosenthal, & P. D. Pearson (Eds.), *Handbook of reading research, Vol. II* (pp. 727–757). New York: Longman.

Sulzby, E., & Zecker, L. (1991). The oral monologue as a form of emergent reading. In A. McCabe & C. Peterson (Eds.), *Developing narrative structures* (pp. 175–213). Hillsdale, NJ: Erlbaum.

Teale, W. H. (1984). Reading to young children: Its significance for literacy development. In H. Goelman, A. Oberg, & F. Smith (Eds.), *Awakening to literacy* (pp. 110–121). Portsmouth, NH: Heinemann.

Teale, W. H. (1986a). The beginnings of reading and writing: Written language development during the preschool and kindergarten years. In M. R. Sampson (Ed.), *The pursuit of literacy: Early reading and writing* (pp. 1–29). Dubuque, IA: Kendall/Hunt.

Teale, W. H. (1986b). Home background and young

children's literacy development. In W. H. Teale & E. Sulzby (Eds.), *Emergent literacy: Writing and reading* (pp. 173–206). Norwood, NJ: Ablex.

Teale, W. H. (1987). Emergent literacy: Reading and writing development in early childhood. *National Reading Conference Yearbook, 36,* 45–74.

Teale, W. H., & Sulzby, E. (1986). Emergent literacy as a perspective for examining how children become writers and readers. In W. H. Teale & E. Sulzby (Eds.), *Emergent literacy: Writing and reading* (pp. vii–xxv). Norwood, NJ: Ablex.

Teale, W. H., & Sulzby, E. (1987). Literacy acquisition in early childhood: The roles of access and mediation in storybook reading. In D. Wagner (Ed.), *The future of literacy in a changing world* (pp. 111–130). New York: Pergamon Press.

Vygotsky, L. S. (1962). *Thought and language.* Cambridge, MA: MIT Press.

Vygotsky, L. S. (1978). *Mind in society: The development of higher psychological processes.* (M. Cole, V. John-Steiner, S. Scribner, & E. Souberman, Eds.). Cambridge, MA: Harvard University Press.

CHAPTER FIFTEEN

A POSTSCRIPT ON CREATING POWERFUL THINKERS

DAVID C. BERLINER

ARIZONA STATE UNIVERSITY

I have been awarded the privilege of making some final comments about the contexts of this book. Having the last word is a gift almost everybody enjoys, and I am no exception. But before making some comments relevant to sections and chapters, I think it is important to contextualize what some of this book is about—educational ideas that are simply revolutionary.

In the West, for centuries, we expected only small numbers of people to be highly literate. The nobles, ambassadors, clergy, historians, and a few merchants were the only people who actually needed high levels of literacy and numeracy. Most people were illiterate farmers or were engaged in simple mercantile work. And most women were thought not to need education at all. That state of affairs lasted until the invention of movable type and the occurrence of the Reformation, which facilitated production of books in large numbers and gave rise to the idea that even the common people should be able to read the Bible for themselves. Western nations believed that a low level of literacy was desirable for large numbers of people. For example, an education at approximately the fourth-grade level was thought to meet the needs of most colonial Americans, particularly men. Women were still not thought to need much education. The belief that a low level of literacy for the masses would suffice held into the twentieth century, changing slowly at first, and then more rapidly after the Second World War. From the launch of Sputnik until recent times, we have desired a high level of literacy, numeracy, and scientific knowledge for all of our students. This held true for all of those who had been excluded in previous decades and earlier centuries—women, African Americans, the physically disabled, and the mentally handicapped. America seems to have chosen a goal that no previous society has ever thought possible and that no contemporary society has pursued with such vigor, namely, high levels of literacy, numeracy, and scientific knowledge for all its citizens. I believe this goal is going to be impossible to achieve because of our cultural heterogeneity and the enormous disparities of income that characterize contemporary America. Nevertheless, many Americans use this goal as a standard for judging the performance of our schools. Perhaps that is why contemporary American schools are considered so deficient when they are really, in the aggregate, remarkably good (Berliner, 1993; Bracey, 1991, 1993).

It is important to note that even though I

think it is nearly impossible for our nation to achieve the goals we have set for education, I would not want to change these goals at all. We have all learned the power of high expectations. Perhaps our goals are out of our grasp, but they are so worthy that I think it proper to pursue them. To paraphrase Robert Browning, if our reach did not exceed our grasp, what need would we have of a heaven?

The most revolutionary thoughts imaginable were permeating society in general and education in particular during the decades following World War II; namely, that we should strive to achieve a very high level of literacy, numeracy, and scientific knowledge for all of our citizens. Something even more profound was happening in psychology and education. The influence of cognitive science led some daring individuals to question whether high levels of comprehension as we knew them were enough. They wrote that knowledge without mindfulness, critical thinking skills, or reflection was at best inert, at worst dangerous; knowledge that could not be transferred was poorly taught and learned; knowledge was situated, not decontextualized, and needed to be taught in some way that reflected its ties to real-world situations; and assessment had to be authentic to be more than ritual. These writers were right, but they have raised the ante. The United States is not only in the early stages of trying to do something never before achieved by another society, but it has also decided even that is not enough! Comprehension in mathematics, science, or history by all of our students is now the *minimum* acceptable level of achievement, for we also expect that students will think like mathematicians, scientists, or historians. They will reflect on what they know, use ideas, see relationships, transfer what they know to real-world situations, and solve authentic problems with their knowledge. Furthermore, we expect their teachers to be able to guide them in these endeavors, despite the fact that teachers today are generally from the working classes and the lower quartiles of the SAT distribution. Teachers are paid relatively low starting wages and have very few hours of preservice instruction for the complexity of their jobs. Noble motives

seem to be driving this movement, starting with the extraordinary belief that normal children of any social class can learn to be very thoughtful in and out of school. Some of the chapters in this book directly address our revolutionary thinking about the level of achievement that has now become the goal for a large number of our children. The creation of a generation of powerful thinkers is an enormous, exciting project for American educators to tackle. Although I am sure that we will have difficulty meeting our goal, it will be a fun and creative time for psychologists and educators.

Let me now turn to some of the themes in each section. I will also discuss some of the ideas in individual chapters that caught my attention and caused me to think, which is, after all, the goal of this book.

Section 1. What struck me as interesting about the first section of this book was that each author believed the power to influence teaching and learning was embedded in communities of one kind or another. Because of that, I think that Duffy, in Chapter 1, may have made a misstatement. He argued that we need to create a new psychology for preservice teachers, in order that they be transformed into powerful thinkers, mindful teachers, and teachers who reject compliant cognition and mere technical competence. But in fact, the mechanisms to achieve those lofty goals require more than a changed psychology. They require a changed social setting. It is through community, particularly an intellectual community, that the goals Duffy promotes may be reached. This requires more concern, therefore, for social psychology, anthropology, and sociology than it does general psychology, a discipline that almost always has the *individual* as its primary focus.

All of the authors in this section would take as a goal the one articulated by Duffy in the very first chapter, namely, the creation of mindful communities for teachers so that they can create mindful communities of students. I was amused, however, by the irony that one of the great social scientists, B.F. Skinner, who wrote about how a community of people can learn to act in certain ways, was someone that most authors of chapters in this book might reject. *Waldon Two* (Skinner, 1948), in fact, is precisely about the issues surrounding the creation and maintenance of a community that permeate this section. Although overly narrow and simply wrong in some of their views about learning, not all behavioral psychologists were associated with programs that led to mindless responding. It certainly would be too bad if, in the move toward a cognitive and social-constructivist theoretical view, we ignore all of the theorists and knowledge that came before.

Onosko and Newmann, followed by Peterson, describe for us what an intellectual or learning community might be like. These are communities characterized by having ordinary people—teachers and students—demonstrate an expanded use of their minds. This kind of higher-order or critical thinking occurs when one must interpret, analyze, or manipulate information, because a problem to be solved cannot be resolved through the routine application of previously learned knowledge. That is the norm for a community that promotes more than compliant cognition. This is why Duffy is passionate about ensuring that every teacher learn to be strategic, for problem solving in teaching is never routine. In fact, every teacher visited by every researcher informs the researcher that he/she should have been there yesterday, because today was not a typical day. It seems that no day of teaching is ever typical, thus teachers have to be strategic thinkers, creative problem-solvers, and very flexible people. This is the goal of the teacher education program that Duffy would build; one that is similar to that described in a later chapter by Kennedy and Barnes, former Duffy colleagues at the Michigan State University School of Education, which for many years had a reputation as an unusually thoughtful community.

Annie, the teacher that mastered the Cognitively Guided Instruction provided by Peterson and her colleagues, has developed communities of little scholars in her classes and demonstrates what Onosko and Newmann call the "disposition for thoughtfulness." It is wonderful to learn that she did not always have this disposition. She dem-

onstrates that dispositions of thoughtfulness can be induced; a position that many of the chapter authors would endorse. Such dispositions arise out of membership in the right kind of communities. A disposition to be thoughtful appears to be much harder to develop and maintain if working alone. Isolation, like censorship, apparently limits one's thoughts.

Onosko and Newmann inform us that three factors are necessary for critical thinking to occur: dispositions of thoughtfulness, intellectual skills or strategies, and in-depth knowledge of some content area. Contents of critical thinking for teachers include in-depth knowledge of pedagogy, subject matter, and children. The content in which students engage in critical thinking includes in-depth knowledge of content areas— mathematics, science, literature, history, and so forth. Put succinctly, critical thinking by teachers or students requires skill, will, and disciplinary knowledge.

Langer focuses on the teaching and learning of disciplinary knowledge. And this introduces another kind of community, that of the disciplines, with their attendant ways of knowing and, therefore, of teaching. Each of the disciplines she studied was a community with its own ways of orienting attention, refining understandings, and selecting evidence. Thus all of the authors in this section, in one form or another, remind us that we are very social creatures. Both our behavior and our most internal thoughts are conditioned in social contexts. If we do not like the behavior of individual teachers and individual students, we might choose to work with them on some form of individualized plan of remediation. But that is probably not nearly as fruitful as changing the social settings in which they teach and learn. It used to be said that it takes a whole village to educate a child. Now we finally see the truth in that, for it takes a whole community to foster teaching and learning in the ways we now think are desirable.

Section 2. The theme of community is repeated in some of the chapters in this section. Most important, however, is that in this section we see the emergence of the consensus that powerful students arise from powerful teachers. Acorns do not fall far from the tree. Since family is not as powerful in the lives of many Americans as it once was, the tree today is sometimes the classroom teacher. The powerful socializing force of the school, as represented by the teacher, assumes even greater strength in times when families may be stressed. If teachers and the intellectual communities that they are part of have the skill, the will, and something important to communicate, they can make a powerful difference in the lives of the children they teach.

Pressley gives us evidence, and therefore hope, that comprehension techniques can be taught and learned. The strategies he has studied for years provide teachers the kind of great confidence that accompanies having "good stuff to teach." And the communication of these strategies to students gives the students great confidence as well. The techniques described allow some students, even at a young age, to become independent strategic readers and writers. What could be more empowering in a democratic nation?

Block also provides evidence of the effectiveness of instruction in problem-solving, an area of the curriculum often thought to be unresponsive to direct instruction. She makes it clear that teachers can learn these techniques and teach them so that students can learn them as well. Students can then improve their performance on sophisticated outcome measures. What astounds me, and seems particularly noteworthy, is that in the chapters by Pressley and Block extraordinary findings are matter-of-factly presented. The authors write as if these are simply interesting research areas that show some pay-off. But what each has done is actually quite remarkable. Moreover, this is not a significant one-time event; their work has been replicable. They have each taught teachers and students things that were learned only by osmosis, if at all, a few years ago. Strategies for learning were mastered by some of our students, though we knew not how. Although some students were good problem-solvers, some were not, and we never understood how such ability was learned. We assumed cognitive learning strategies and problem-solving skills were in the genes,

carried along with social class, or learned through osmosis in particular settings. The skills underlying the use of strategies and the solution of problems were invisible. But Pressley, Block, and their colleagues have made visible and explicit some of the mental operations needed to accomplish complex cognitive tasks, communicating this knowledge to people who did not possess such skills. Those people became better learners and more powerful thinkers. If this were medical research, such findings of research would be hailed as miracles. Newspaper headlines would read: "Miracle Cure for Comprehension Deficits Found!" or "Students Learn to Solve Complex Problems: World Likely to Be a Better Place." The media and the public do not yet comprehend the strides that have been made in the last two decades by the educational research community.

In chapter 7, which I wrote, I present evidence that exemplary teachers exist and that they do extraordinary things with their students. Policy recommendations flow from the data, and it is clear that we might learn how to do preservice and inservice teacher education and teacher evaluation in a better way. Kennedy and Barnes inform us of the barriers to getting the kinds of teachers that we all admire, but they also elaborate on what a preservice teacher education program must be like to produce the kind of teachers that we want in classrooms. From their experience we might also learn how to do better teacher education. Boyer informs us that universities must change their way of doing business to produce the kinds of graduates that we want. He, too, has ideas that might help us better educate teachers and all other students in our colleges and universities. What is so exciting about these chapters is that they are all hopeful. From theory, data, experience, wisdom of practice, and reflection comes information on how to improve learning and thinking in our schools. Despite dreadfully underfunded research budgets, we have learned a lot about the processes of education and teacher education in the last few years.

Section 3. In Heath's chapter and the one by Presseisen, Smey-Richman, and Beyer, both dealing with improving instruction for at-risk youth, we see two of the themes in other sections of the book repeated. First, both chapters deal with the issue of community. Second, all the authors in this section believe that there is knowledge available for the design of teaching and learning environments that work. They write with some assurance that we know how to do things a lot better than we are doing them now. For example, Presseisen and colleagues describe eight elements of restructured classroom environments and then present ideas for teaching and learning in such classrooms that are congruent with the goals of this volume—building more powerful thinkers. Heath talks about learning for at-risk youngsters that takes place all day, every day, in many places, with multiple teachers, with different configurations of learners, and with various ways to display what is learned—"a seamless life of thinking, development, and learning." Such informed opinion and eloquence about what might be accomplished if we invested heavily in at-risk youth actually saddens me, because I know our society will not invest what is needed in such programs now. We seem happier to incarcerate and pay people for unemployment, activities that cost far more per year than would high quality schooling. We really do need to invest large amounts of time and money to design the environments where desirable teaching and learning can take place. Apparently, we have sound educational theory based on data, experience, and professional wisdom, but none of the capital to invest in the engineering part of the process. We do not seem to have many administrators that will take the ideas in these chapters and start to make them a reality. We desperately need existing proof that good ideas such as those offered in these pages can be brought to life in real learning communities.

The description by Heath of the safe and effective learning communities in the neighborhoods of at-risk children raises another issue. This has to do with the fragmentation of services in contemporary cities and counties. Heath makes it clear in a way that I have never thought about before, discussing the power of boys and girls clubs, the YMCA or YWCA, team sports, the drama club, and religious youth groups. These are powerful educative forces in the lives of at-risk children and offer alternatives to gangs in violent and impoverished neighborhoods. Such organizations ought to be part of the educational funding bills passed each year by states and local communities because they accomplish some very important educational functions. If a district is willing to spend a specified amount of dollars on regular and special education in the public schools, it ought to spend a piece of that, or preferably add a bit more to the budget, to support the work of community organizations that complement the work of traditional schools. When business people want to know how they can get the best bang for their educational buck, we can now respond to them. Put more money into community youth groups; they may pay off better in the long run than putting more police on the streets and building more jails.

Section 4. Discussions of the implications of theory for practice are provided in the chapters by Sulzby and by Kozulin. In the former, we learn about the ways in which emergent literacy is related to the development of conventional literacy and the incredibly powerful, but still pre-literate, ways of thinking that young children possess. We learn that the actions of adults in the literate communities in which children live provide the cues for the development of emergent literacy. So once again the sociocultural community is seen as an overwhelming force in the development of minds—which is precisely Kozulin's point as he relates the theories of Vygotsky and Feuerstein to the development of powerful minds among youth. Kozulin's chapter is about the power of the social community to shape the thinking of young people, the theme that runs throughout this book. The mediated learning environment, where an adult or other more competent individual helps a youngster to learn, is not just seen as desirable, but as a necessary event in the socialization of a thoughtful person. In contrast to Piagetian thought, where children can learn by doing for themselves, Feuerstein notes that the solitary interaction of the child with the world is a theoretical mirage.

In a similar vein, Vygotsky invites us to regard

the social concerns of youth as an ally in, not as an enemy of, instruction. By finding ways to socially distribute cognitive learning tasks and by making groups responsible for learning, we can use the need of youth for social interaction to foster learning, not to hinder it. This is an insight that is not often recognized in traditional educational communities. The research reported in this chapter reminds us that many high-school children go to school because that is where other young people congregate. We need not despair at that. We can design developmentally appropriate instruction for them (for example, group projects, cooperative learning activities, cross-age and peer tutoring, and so on) and not fight what seems to be an almost universal need for community and social interaction, a need that is magnified in adolescence. I believe that it is also worth noting that Kozulin's analysis of the work of Feuerstein and Vygotsky provides the theoretical background for the remarkably healthy, prosocial learning environments that develop in some community youth groups in difficult neighborhoods. These were described for us by Heath in an earlier chapter.

In this section, we have also the work by Walters, Seidel, and Gardner on reflection by students. It is exciting to read protocols in which students as young as second graders show evidence of reflective thought. These authors remind us that if we want young people in our schools to think reflectively, we need to provide them with time to do so, and we usually do not. They also inform us that time is not enough, that reflection has to be built into the life of the class, not be merely an appendage. Teachers need to guide students until they become comfortable with the process and its benefits, because many students have no models of reflective behavior in their home environment.

This chapter conveys that through reflective practices students can come to develop their own standards of quality. This is one of the most powerful motivational forces that I know. I have always believed that the ability to be partially free of external evaluation—the praise and criticism of friends, family, teachers, and others with whom

we interact—is the ultimate in personal agency. In this chapter we learn that there are ways to promote that kind of behavior. Powerful thinking is most likely to occur among people who have learned that they can judge things for themselves, and that others do not always set the standards for their behavior. It was this aspect of reflection that I found to be the most exciting, though reflection for learning to grapple with tough problems is also described, as is reflection for clarifying one's own problems. It seems obvious that the reflective activities described by these authors are one of the tools in the development of problem-solving, as described earlier by Block, and are also an intellectual strategy, as described earlier by Pressley.

Conclusion. This book presents diverse views about the creation of powerful thinkers. Even though the authors of this book were writing in isolation from one another, some common themes emerged. First, there is the issue of the power of the social community to influence behavior. For a psychologist like myself, who was taught that the focus of my discipline was the individual, this is a truly revolutionary insight. I think that the cognitive revolution in psychology that runs through this volume may be either eclipsed by or incorporated into the sociocultural or social-historical conceptions of the mind. It is simply not true that among humans cognition develops in a social world. That may be the most important insight of contemporary psychology, though no doubt John Dewey, who made this same point almost a century ago, is laughing in his grave about this "discovery." But there is a *zeitgeist*, and current times consider a socially constructed mind a better model for our thinking than was previously thought. This decidedly social conception of mind suggests that if we modify the social environments of our children, we may be able to change some of the problems that concern us in contemporary society.

This view, of course, fits into the second theme of the volume; that there is hope because we really do know a lot. What we need are the resources and the administrative daring to do some of the social engineering that we apparently now know how to do. Discussions of social engineering raise the red flag for some of our citizens, exactly as schools were designed to do, and we should keep that mission before us. Schools are not neutral. They reflect prevailing conceptions of childhood and the views of the general society, most of whom would applaud the ideas in this book. But some of what is put forth in this book about the development of powerful thinkers among youth and among their teachers is anathema to some of our citizens. Their views of childhood and the role of the teacher diverge from the ones suggested here. In their eyes this book may be a dangerous guide for educators. I can only say that I am pleased that I could be a part of something as dangerous as a volume of good ideas.

REFERENCES

Berliner, D.C. (1993). Mythology and the American system of education. *Phi Delta Kappan, 74,* 632–640.

Bracey, G.W. (1991, October). Why can't they be like we were? *Phi Delta Kappan, 73,* 104–117.

Bracey, G.W. (1993). The third Bracey report on the condition of public education. *Phi Delta Kappan, 75,* 104–117.

Skinner, B.F. (1948). *Waldon two.* New York: Macmillan

NAME INDEX